MANAGING:
Toward Accountability for Performance

ROBERT ALBANESE, Ph.D.
Texas A&M University

1978
Revised Edition

Richard D. Irwin, Inc. Homewood, Illinois 60430
Irwin-Dorsey Limited   Georgetown, Ontario L7G 4B3

The previous edition was published under the title
Management: Toward Accountability for Performance.

ISBN 0-256-02039-6
Library of Congress Catalog Card No. 77–085797
Printed in the United States of America

3 4 5 6 7 8 9 0 K 5 4 3 2 1 0

To
my wife, Jessica,
and our children,
Ruthann, Bob, Marianne, Gerry, and Diane

PREFACE

Focus of book

Managing: Toward Accountability for Performance is a comprehensive and student-oriented introduction to the academic discipline of management. It is intended for use in introductory courses in management and is designed to provide basic information about the work of managing to all students, regardless of their academic major. The book is primarily oriented toward a view of managing as a form of human behavior that occurs in an organizational setting.

A comprehensive introduction to managing

I view the book as *comprehensive* because it surveys a wide variety of topics relevant to effective managing. Topics that are new in this revised edition include personal goal setting, zero-based budgeting, delphi forecasting, problem-solving styles, the nominal group technique, conflict and stress, the organization-environment relationship, organizational climate, and organizational effectiveness. These topics, along with those retained from the first edition, provide a broad and contemporary foundation for further study of a discipline and type of work that are continually in a process of change.

A student-oriented introduction to managing

I feel that this book is *student-oriented* in two major ways. First, it respects the students' need for a challenging, current, and thorough examination of management. In my opinion, it is a disservice to students to present them with a simplistic, mechanistic, how-to-do-it view of the manager's job. Second, I view the book as student-oriented because of its generous use of several learning aids:

- Each chapter starts with a set of learning objectives and a chapter outline.
- Each paragraph has a marginal note that suggests the paragraph content.
- Two or three summary boxes per chapter provide concise summaries of chapter content.
- Each chapter ends with a list of key terms and a set of study questions.
- Selected chapters are followed by supplements that expand on chapter-related topics.

• All chapters end with one or two practical applications. This feature, new to the revised edition, provides a means for students to apply a chapter concept, to see how a real organization applies a concept, and/or to learn a practical technique related to the chapter content.

I am confident that, taken together, all of these learning aids will make this introduction to managing both readable for students and teachable for instructors.

Basic theme

I place major emphasis in the book on the manager's accountability for efficient and effective performance. This *basic theme* permeates the entire book. The primary justification for a managerial job is that the work performed by the person doing the job makes a contribution to the effectiveness of individual and organizational performance. Managers are accountable to a wide spectrum of people and forces for the effectiveness of their own job performance. The book takes the view that the manager's accountability for performance must be defined in broad terms, and that it ultimately includes a responsibility for making work organizations more fit for human habitation. It is this broad, professional view of the manager's accountability for performance that makes managing an exciting area of study and a type of work that offers potentially high intangible as well as tangible rewards.

Part One

The book's content is divided into four parts. Part One, General Management, begins with a chapter that defines managing, introduces the book's basic theme, and describes the overall approach of the book. Separate chapters follow on goals, planning, controlling, and decision making. Supplements to Part One deal with approaches to the study of managing, management history, profit and social responsibility, management by objectives (MBO), network analysis, linear programming, and quantitative decision criteria.

Part Two

Part Two, Behavior in Organizations: A Micro View, is an extensive coverage of several topics that are important to improving understanding of human behavior in organizations. These topics include job performance and the motivation process, perception, attitudes, values, behavioral consequences, interpersonal behavior, behavior in groups, leadership, communication, and conflict and stress. Part Two supplements deal with motives, job satisfaction, and assumptions about people.

Part Three

Part Three, Organizations: A Macro View, contains two chapters that highlight historically and currently important themes that influence thinking about organizations. Two additional chapters deal with the manager's task of designing organizations. They include discussions of designing jobs, grouping jobs, span of management, organizational levels, delegation, and line and staff. The final chapter in Part Two discusses organizational change and effectiveness and includes a discussion of organizational development (OD), an approach to changing organizations that draws heavily on knowledge from the behavioral sciences.

Part Four

Part Four, Recap and Epilogue, includes an integrative summary of the entire book, and an epilogue which presents a personal view of organizations as human communities.

The book is an approach

I have enjoyed the process of preparing both the first and this revised edition of this text. It has given me the chance to put into writing my own approach to an introduction to managing, an approach that reflects several years of teaching management to hundreds of students and managers. The feedback that I received from users of the first edition was very helpful in preparing this revised edition. I am delighted that I had the opportunity to prepare this revised edition and hope that I have responded to that opportunity in ways that will be beneficial to students and instructors.

Acknowledgments

It is important to me that I publicly acknowledge some of the help I have received during the process of writing this revised edition. I especially thank the following management professors who reviewed various portions of the manuscript and provided me with constructive suggestions: William C. Scott of Indiana State University, Timothy W. Scott of Mankato State University, Richard M. Steers of the University of Oregon, Frank Vandervegt of Wayne State University, Lawrence Foster of Michigan State University, and H. Kirk Downey of Oklahoma State University. I also received invaluable assistance from several colleagues at Texas A&M University and from four graduate students: David B. Spencer, Frank S. Hoy, Jack W. O'Grady, and Robert W. Rice. As with the first edition, Florance Kling did an excellent job of typing the manuscript and of meeting numerous deadlines. All of these people, and of course many others that are not mentioned here, made their own unique contributions to this book. I am grateful for their contributions while at the same time absolving them of any of the book's errors or omissions. I hope that you will forward to me any comments or suggestions you may have as a result of using *Managing: Toward Accountability for Performance.*

Robert Albanese

January 1978

CONTENTS

part two
BEHAVIOR IN ORGANIZATIONS: A MICRO VIEW

part three
ORGANIZATIONS: A MACRO VIEW

part four
MANAGING: RECAP AND EPILOGUE

part one
General Management

Chapter 1   Chapter 1 sets the stage for the rest of the book. A definition of managing is suggested and the idea of managing as a universal activity is discussed. We identify the book's basic theme and present an overview of the major parts of the book. In addition, we offer a view of what you can expect to learn about managing by studying this book. Supplements to Chapter 1 identify several approaches to studying managing and discuss two men who were early contributors to the development of managerial thought.

Chapter 2   Chapter 2 deals with the important topic of goals. Our view is that goals represent—or should represent—the beginning point of managerial thinking and action. We consider goals to be *the* strategic managing variable. Chapter 2 defines several goal-related terms, notes the uses and limits of goals, and identifies the criteria that goals should meet if they are to be useful to managers. We suggest a specific classification of goals that we will refer to throughout the book, and we discuss the process of goal setting. We outline a way of thinking about the potential conflict between the goals of individuals and of the organization in which they work. Supplements to Chapter 2 discuss profit, social responsibility, and management by objectives (MBO)

Chapter 3   Chapter 3 introduces the managerial function of planning—a function that, along with goal setting, provides the foundation for most other functions that managers perform. Characteristics and premises of plans are discussed, and several ways of organizing for planning are noted. Next, the idea of a formal planning process is explained and illustrated. In addition, the problem of finding time to plan is recognized, and a solution is suggested.

Chapter 4   Planning and controlling are two sides of the same coin; control is difficult to achieve in the absence of goals and plans. Chapter 4 raises several issues about the manager's control function: What can the manager control? What are some types of control systems? What are some of the human problems that can arise as a result of controls? A supplement to Chapter 4 deals with network analysis and PERT (Program Evaluation and Review Technique), a popular method of planning and controlling.

Chapter 5   Decision making is viewed by some as the manager's central task. All other tasks performed by managers are seen as contributing to the ultimate managerial act—decision making. Our view of decision making is somewhat more limited but, nevertheless, we consider it an important aspect of managing. Chapter 5 describes the decision-making process and a model for thinking about problem-solving styles. In addition, a framework for thinking about problems is presented along with viewpoints on the quality of decisions; group decision making; and on evaluating when decisions are "right." Supplements to Chapter 5 introduce the graphical method of linear programming and several quantitative decision criteria.

Objectives of Chapter 1

- To provide a definition of managing and to identify the distinguishing characteristic of managerial positions.
- To describe managing as a universal activity that occurs in all types, functions, levels, and sizes of organizations.
- To emphasize the basic theme of this book and to overview the major topics relevant to that theme.
- To present a viewpoint on what you can and cannot expect to learn about managing from this book.

Outline of Chapter 1

1

MANAGING:
AN INTRODUCTION

*The general principles of any study you may learn
by books . . . but the detail, the colour, the tone,
the air, the life which makes it live in us, you must
catch all these from those in whom it lives already.*

John Henry Cardinal Newman

*To my mind, there is a moral crisis in management.
. . . The danger is that we may focus on efficiency
and ignore the broader issues of man in society.*

William B. Wolf

*Survival
dilemma*

Recently three faculty members met before a student audience
to debate their individual claims for survival.[1] The situation: The
three professors—each representing a different branch of knowledge—are clinging to a raft. The raft has room and provisions for
only one of the three. Which one has the best claim for survival?

Social science professor: The social sciences and behavioral sciences are needed for what they teach about tolerance and the
appreciation of the variety of human experience.

Natural science professor: The natural sciences, especially chemistry and physics, are the basis for the technology that supports the amenities modern man finds important.

Management professor: If I survive you'll like it. People like to
manage things. . . . Another reason for my survival is that
if *I* don't survive, *you* won't—because an unmanaged system
goes to ruin.

Room for all

All of which goes to demonstrate, once again, that each branch
of knowledge has a reasonable claim for survival. In the final
analysis, they all complement each other. There is room on the raft
for all.

---

[1] Adapted from "Marginalia," *The Chronicle of Higher Education*, vol. 12,
no. 16 (December 20, 1976), p. 2. Reprinted with permission of *The Chronicle of Higher Education.* Copyright © 1976 by Editorial Projects for Education, Inc.

*Managing's
claim*

What is managing's claim for survival? Answering that question requires a personal judgment; there is no answer chiseled in stone somewhere in a hall of knowledge. Our judgment is that managing's claim for survival derives from two sources:

*Satisfying
activity*

1. It is, for some, an enjoyable and *satisfying activity*. As the management professor said, "People like to manage. . . ." They like the opportunity to use their skills, the challenge and frustration, the pace and the pressure, the power and the money, and the relative autonomy they have in doing their work. We are fortunate that some people can find joy in a managing career. Why are we fortunate? That question takes us to our second point.

*Essential
activity*

2. Managing is an *essential activity*. It is essential in the sense that it is necessary if we are to achieve our goals in an effective manner. Managing is an essential activity wherever resources—human, natural, financial—must be used efficiently, and that is true of almost every organized endeavor.

*Interesting,
understanding*

There are several reasons why you may want to study managing. First, the subject is intrinsically *interesting* because it is ultimately about people and their attempts to get along in the world of work. Second, knowledge of managing should *help you understand* and be more effective in a world increasingly characterized by life in organizations of all types.

Careers

Third, the odds are that you will eventually hold a managerial position. Even if you are majoring in another specialized field, the chances are that you will become a manager. For example, almost half of all engineers eventually become involved in managing. *Careers in management* are potentially lucrative, interesting, and challenging. They often provide opportunities for expressing creativity, for intellectual growth, and for developing personal skills. Since managing is so directly involved with people, it offers the opportunity to help others grow, develop, and satisfy their needs.

*Need for
managers*

Fourth, there is always a *need for good, experienced managerial talent*.[2] This need exists everywhere, from the highest level of the federal government to the corner grocery store. It is a need, not only for competent people with essential managerial skills, but also for people with vision and with ethical, moral, and professional values appropriate to contemporary society.

This chapter

In this chapter we define managing and identify a bias reflected throughout the book—managing occurs by and through people.

_____

[2] John B. Miner, *The Human Constraint: The Coming Shortage of Managerial Talent* (Washington, D.C.: Bureau of National Affairs, 1974). There is not necessarily a shortage of people who *want* to be managers. In fact, the potential young executive population is expanding very sharply in relation to the demand for its services. See Arch Patton, "The Coming Flood of Young Executives," *Harvard Business Review*, vol. 54, no. 5 (September–October 1976), pp. 20–22+.

Next we describe managing as a universal activity. Then we identify the basic theme of this book, the accountability of managers for performance, and we present a brief overview of the major topics discussed. The chapter ends with some remarks about what you can and cannot expect to learn about managing by studying this book.

MANAGING: SOME BASIC CONCEPTS

Opinions about managing

No Universal Definition. Almost everyone has opinions about what managing is. *Students* approach the study of managing with a variety of perceptions and attitudes about it and about managers. *Parents* manage their home and their budget. *Managers* have their own ideas about managing based partially on their experience— regardless of how limited that experience is. *Professors* of managing are likely to have a different orientation toward managing than either students or managers because of their interest in management theory. *Laymen* know something about managing because of their contacts with organizations and because of their exposure to managers. Even *children* have opinions about managers: "The manager is the head of the store. He keeps it clean but doesn't clean it himself." "Managers tell everybody what to do." "Management means running something and keeping it fixed up." "Managers take care of the problems of workers." What is managing? How will we use the term in this book?

A universally accepted definition not necessary

Before stating our definition of managing, we need to point out that there is no universally accepted definition. Managing can be and is defined in several ways, depending on the purposes of the definer. Differences of opinion exist about what should be included in the definition, and it is unlikely that this problem will ever be resolved permanently. If a universally accepted definition of managing were necessary before we could start our study of managing, we could never start! Fortunately, all we need is a definition that is (1) consistent with other widely used definitions and (2) useful for our purposes in this book. Such a definition follows.

Environments for goal achievement

Our Definition. Managing, or management, is used in this book to mean the work of creating and maintaining environments in which people can accomplish goals efficiently and effectively. These environments involve the integrated use of human, financial, and natural resources for the purpose of achieving goals. Although managing is work that can be performed by groups of people or by committees, we discuss it primarily as a type of work performed by individuals.

Job titles

The individuals that perform managerial duties in organizations have various job titles—president, executive vice president, production manager, general superintendent, foreman, and supervisor. Although the dividing line is arbitrary, an "executive" title usually connotes a higher-level manager than "foreman" or "supervisor." Most foremen would wonder who you were talking to if you called them "executives."

CEO

Top executives of large business firms often have different titles, such as president, chairman of the board, and executive vice president. Chief executive officer (CEO) is a descriptive title commonly used to identify top operating business executives regardless of the specific job title.

*Job titles
serve several
functions*

Since job titles serve various functions, you cannot always tell from one what work a person actually does. Of course, job titles often do provide an accurate description of duties. However, sometimes a title serves the primary function—at very little cost to the organization—of fulfilling the desire of an executive for status. In addition, a high-sounding title can be useful in dealing with customers. The idea that clients may like to "deal with a vice president, not just a flunky" may explain why one bank has over 300 vice presidents.[3] Finally, there are some unusual job titles that are not very informative of work duties. For example, a California amusement park has a vice president in charge of fun, and a fast-food chain has a position with the title vice president—people.

*Test of
managerial
positions*

The point we want to emphasize is that job titles cannot be relied on to differentiate managerial from nonmanagerial jobs. What is a test—a distinguishing characteristic—that we can use to identify a managerial position? The test we will use is whether the person holding the position is accountable, not only for personal job performance, but also for the job performance of those over whom the person has authority.

*Superiors,
subordinates*

In business firms, the terms "superior" and "subordinate" commonly refer to the relationship between persons. Thus, managers are accountable to a superior for their own job performance and for that of their subordinates—those over whom the manager has direct, formal authority. Since superior–subordinate relationships exist in any organizational setting, our view of managing is that it occurs in organizations.

*Administering,
supervising*

We use the terms "administering" and "supervising" to mean the same thing as "managing." In practice, administering is used more often in nonbusiness organizations such as hospitals, universities, and government agencies. The top managerial group in such organizations is usually called "the administration." Supervising refers to managing at the first or lower levels of an organization. Foremen in manufacturing plants and supervisors in department stores, for example, are part of "supervision." Although managing, administering, and supervising do have slightly different connota-

[3] Robert Levy, "The Executive Title Wave," *Dun's Review*, vol. 103, no. 3 (March 1975), pp. 70–72.

tions in practice, we do not distinguish among them. They all involve the work of creating and maintaining environments in which people can accomplish goals efficiently and effectively. Our concern in this book is with that type of work, wherever it is found.

People make the difference

Managers are accountable for the efficient and effective use of all the resources at their disposal. If one of those resources is a computer, then it must be used efficiently. If inventories or physical facilities are included among a manager's resources, then they must be used efficiently. The view we take is that these and all other non-human "performance factors" are efficiently utilized through the efforts of people. Such a view emphasizes the importance of *people* in creating and maintaining environments for goal accomplishment. People and their behavior are the overriding concern of managing. "Competent people are the dynamic force that determines the success of an organization. But ineffective managers, those who are unable to deal wisely with people, are the primary cause for inefficiency in present-day business."[4] That statement applies to all types of organizations. It is because of the crucial importance of people in managing that we choose to confine our use of the term to the management of people, rather than using it when referring to nonhuman performance factors.

Managing: A Universal Activity. Managing is often referred to as a universal activity because it is found in all types, functions, levels, and sizes of organizations.

Managing occurs in all types of organizations

Students often associate managing only with business organizations such as factories, retail stores, wholesale firms, banks, and hotels. Since academic courses in managing usually are offered as part of a business-administration degree program, the association of managing exclusively with business is not surprising. Indeed, several years ago a prominent author identified management as "the specific organ of the business enterprise."[5] However, as we, and most others, use the term, managing occurs in parks, ranches, hospitals, farms, universities, cities, labor unions, fraternities, police agencies, churches, airports, community organizations, and so on. The subject matter of this book applies to any situation in which people are attempting to achieve goals efficiently and effectively. Since that includes every organization, we say that managing occurs in all *types* of organizations.

Similarities and differences

Of course, the specifics of managing vary from one type of organization to another. We can say that all managers plan, and we can discuss planning as a general process. However, the approaches and techniques of planning used by, for example, hospital

---

[4] The staff of Rohrer, Hibler, & Replogle, *Managers for Tomorrow* (New York: New American Library, 1965), p. 25.

[5] Peter F. Drucker, *The Practice of Management* (New York: Harper & Row, Publishers, 1954), p. 7.

managers are different from those used by university administrators. Although a top business executive performs many of the same tasks as the head of a high-level government agency, the two executives could not easily change jobs. The general nature of their jobs is similar, but their specific skills, knowledge requirements, political abilities, and modes of operation are significantly different.

Successful transfers are the exception

The personal experiences of business executives who have accepted government administrative assignments suggest that the successful transfer of managerial talent requires considerable effort, skill, and luck. Although successful transfers from one type of organization to another do occur, they are the exception. One study of 270 CEOs in 26 diverse industrial groups concludes that those CEOs who transferred from another organization experienced lower levels of performance than those already inside. This was true even when the CEO transferred from a related, rather than a different, industry.[6]

Managing occurs at all levels of organization

In discussing organizations, it is common to refer to different levels. The first level consists of supervisors or foremen who have nonmanagerial personnel reporting to them. Managers at higher levels have other managers reporting to them. For example, supervisors may report to a general supervisor, general supervisors may report to a middle-level manager, middle-level managers may report to a vice president, and vice presidents report to the president. Managing occurs at all levels of an organization. Supervisors, middle managers, and presidents all manage.

Similarities among levels

The job of a president or CEO is both similar to and different from that of a middle manager or supervisor. All managers are accountable for the performance of other people; they plan, make decisions, implement controls, organize work, and so forth. Both presidents and supervisors must create and maintain environments in which goals can be accomplished efficiently and effectively. However, there are major differences between the jobs.

Differences

Supervisors focus primarily on the day-to-day direction and control of a small group of people within an organization. Higher-level executives, especially those at the very top of organizations, focus on long-term as well as short-term problems, and they interact with many people inside and outside of the organization. For example, in large business firms, top executives are increasingly concerned with external problems, such as dealing with consumer groups or government agencies. One management consultant estimates that "just a few years ago the CEO of a big company spent 10 percent of his time on external matters, today the figure is generally 40

---

[6] Y. K. Shetty and Newman S. Perry, Jr., "Are Top Executives Transferable across Companies?" *Business Horizons*, vol. 19, no. 3 (June 1976), pp. 23–28.

percent."[7] The point we are emphasizing here, however, is that managing occurs at all *levels* of organization. The ideas we discuss in this book are relevant to the work of presidents, supervisors, and all managers in-between.

Managing occurs in all functions of organizations

Many different functions are performed in organizations. Examples of functions in business firms are production, marketing, personnel, finance, accounting, engineering, and maintenance. Most colleges offer specialized courses in each of these functional areas. Examples of functions in universities are teaching, research, continuing education, public relations, extension services, and student health services. Examples of functions in hospitals are radiology, emergency, surgery, X-ray, and physical therapy. All of these *functions* require managing.

Similarities and differences

Our concern in this book is with what you can learn about managing that cuts across specific functions. Our interest is in general management, not production or marketing management, for example. Of course, every function has its own technical body of knowledge and different managerial problems. However, there is a significant body of knowledge potentially useful to managers, regardless of functional area. This is fortunate because it is impossible to predict what functional area of an organization you will find yourself working in after a few years. Rotation from one functional area to another is very common in the first five years of employment. It is even difficult to predict the type of organization in which you may work. Therefore, it is a good idea to complement your study of a functional area by studying the general managerial process.

Managing occurs in all sizes of organizations

Many students feel that much of what they learn in college and university business courses applies primarily to large, corporate-type organizations. It is true that such courses are often oriented to the large business firm. It is in such firms that the major functions of a business are highly specialized, and it is in such firms that many students seek employment. However, managing—the work of creating and maintaining environments in which people can accomplish goals efficiently and effectively—is essential in organizations of all sizes.

Similarities and differences

Most of the ideas we discuss in this book are applicable to managing people in small, as well as large, organizations. This is true because the managing problems have many similar characteristics. Of course, the context in which managing occurs influences how the managerial function will be performed. There are and must be size-related differences in the way business firms and other types of organizations are managed. Nevertheless, the basic work of managing occurs in all *sizes* of organizations.

---

[7] "The Chief Executive Officer," *Business Week*, May 4, 1974, p. 38.

Summary box

> There is no definition of managing on which everyone agrees. Our definition is (1) consistent with other widely used definitions, and (2) useful for our study purposes.
>
> *Managing* is the work of creating and maintaining environments in which people can accomplish goals efficiently and effectively. We use the terms "managing," "management," "administering," and "supervising" interchangeably.
>
> Job titles cannot always be used to differentiate managerial from nonmanagerial positions. The *test* of a managerial position is its accountability for the job performance of other people.
>
> Our view is that managing occurs by and through people. This means that only people manage, and only people are managed. Non-human performance factors are efficiently utilized through the efforts of people.
>
> Managing is often called a *universal activity* because it is found in all types, functions, levels, and sizes of organizations. There are both similarities and differences in the way managing is performed in different types and sizes of organizations and in different levels or functions of organizations.

BASIC THEME

Essence of manager's job

Throughout this book we continually emphasize a simple and yet important theme, the accountability of managers for the job performance of others. Accountability for performance is the essence of the manager's job. Improving the efficiency and effectiveness of the job performance of others is the reason managerial positions exist.

Narrow view of accountability

Accountability. In a narrow sense, almost everyone understands the nature of the manager's accountability. Managers are accountable to their immediate superiors for results in their area of responsibility. Managers know that their own careers are dependent on this accountability relationship. It is the most significant characteristic of managerial positions.

Broad view of accountability

The accountability of managers, however, involves more than accountability to their immediate superiors. Every manager is accountable to a variety of forces and people. First, managers are accountable to themselves. They have an obligation to use their managerial positions constructively and in ways that develop their capacity to help people accomplish goals efficiently and effectively. Second, all managers have people within their organization, other than their immediate superiors, to whom they are accountable, if not formally, then by informal agreement. Thus, managers are accountable to peers, to specialists who assist them in performing their job, and to the entire organization for competent performance.

Accountability outside the organization

Finally, managers are accountable to forces outside the organization of which they are an immediate part. Managers are accountable to a system of laws and generally accepted social norms and customs. They are accountable to their profession. They are accountable for their use of social power to assist in setting standards for the entire social good and for seeing that those standards are met. As a partner in one of the country's top accounting firms recently said, "The public is holding us to a higher degree of accountability."[8] That applies to all managers in all types of organizations.[9]

Central idea

Performance. Managers are accountable for performance. The urgency of this accountability is illustrated by the stark words of William T. Ylvisaker: "I say, 'Look, you've got to perform. And if you don't, then don't stick around here.' It's as simple as that."[10] The central idea for managers to keep in mind about performance is that it can always be more *efficient* and more *effective*.[11]

Efficiency

"Efficiency" commonly refers to a ratio of output to input. For example, managers are said to be efficient if they produce more and better output with less labor, fewer materials and machine time, and in a shorter period of time. Efficiency implies "more, better, faster, and cheaper." It means caring for more emergency room patients in a hospital at lower cost. It means doubling the number of students taught by a professor. Efficiency connotes the idea of doing well and without waste whatever is being done—whether it is worth doing or not. Efficiency focuses on *how* work is done; *what* should be done, in a world of options, is given less direct focus. We are all familiar with people who are extremely efficient in doing something that should not be done in the first place. Someone once said, "There is no point in doing well, something that should not be done at all."

Effectiveness

Effectiveness has a different connotation than efficiency. "Effectiveness" is concerned with the effect of work on people, with

---

[8] "Arthur Andersen Opens Its Books," *Business Week*, June 16, 1973, p. 82. Also see Marshall S. Armstrong, "Corporate Accountability: A Challenge to Business," *Conference Board Record*, vol. 8, no. 8 (August 1971), pp. 28–31.

[9] For a discussion of the view that power in the United States—whether in the form of government agencies, business, the professions, or the press —has not demonstrated a high degree of accountability, see Morton Mintz and Jerry S. Cohen, *Power, Inc.* (New York: Viking Press, 1976).

[10] "How Ylvisaker Makes 'Produce or Else' Work," *Business Week*, October 27, 1973, p. 112.

[11] For an interesting discussion of the evolution of the efficiency idea, see Dalton E. McFarland, "Whatever Happened to the Efficiency Movement?" *Conference Board Record*, vol. 13, no. 6 (June 1976), pp. 50–55.

the appropriateness of goals, with long-term results, and with humanistic and idealistic values. There is always a more effective way of performing work from the viewpoint of recognizing the desire of people to use their intelligence and imagination and to more fully develop their skill and talent. Jobs can always be improved so that they better meet human needs. Organizations can be designed to be more congruent with human personality and with the goals, norms, and values of society.

Importance of everyday performance

The importance of performance to business organizations was highlighted recently by the chairman and CEO of General Motors Corporation: "The hard fact is that a great deal of government regulation is a reaction to the mood of the large segment of the public that is disappointed, dissatisfied, and disenchanted with the everyday performance of American business, especially big business."[12] There is no simple or single explanation that accounts for the public's mood at any one time. Nevertheless, inadequate performance in terms of consumer goods and services undoubtedly accounts for much of the public's current low opinion of business.

The pursuit of excellence

Improving performance is a continuing concern of every manager. As you go through this book, consider the performance implications of each of the major topics.

> Standards! That is a word for every American to write on his bulletin board. . . . Free men must be competent men. In a society of free men, competence is an elementary duty. Men and women doing competently whatever job is theirs to do tone up the whole society. . . . But excellence requires more than competence. It implies a striving for the highest standards in every phase of American life.[13]

The ultimate accountability

This striving for high standards—for excellence—is the ultimate accountability of managers. High performance standards represent the first requirement of organizations. The "spirit of performance" is the "test of an organization."[14] A top-level business executive expresses the same idea in this way: "We can do that [demonstrate accountability] best, of course, through performance that leaves no room for skepticism about our commitment to providing full value to the public in terms of quality products and services, fairly priced and honestly delivered. No business has a higher priority than minding its own business just as well as it knows how."[15]

---

[12] Thomas A. Murphy, "Improving Public's Regard for Business by Doing a Better Job," *National Observer*, December 10, 1976, p. 10.

[13] John W. Gardner. *Excellence: Can We Be Equal and Excellent Too?* (New York: Harper and Row, Publishers, 1961), p. 136.

[14] Peter F. Drucker, *Management: Tasks, Responsibilities, Practices* (New York: Harper & Row, Publishers, 1973), pp. 455–56.

[15] John D. deButts, chairman of the board, AT&T, "Business—No Mean Calling," *The Arthur Andersen Chronicle*, vol. 37, No. 2 (September 1977), p. 102.

Summary box

> The *basic theme of this book is the accountability of managers for performance.* We view accountability as the essence of the manager's job. The unique aspect of managerial accountability is that managers are accountable for not only their own job results, but also for the job results of their employees. We define accountability broadly to include, not only the accountability of managers to their immediate superiors, but also to themselves and to their peers, their subordinates, their profession, and to the general public.
>
> *Performance* is the reason managerial positions exist. We often use the words "efficient" and "effective" when referring to performance. *Efficiency* connotes the idea of doing well and without waste whatever is being done. It is the "more, better, faster, and cheaper" side of performance. *Effectiveness* goes beyond efficiency and is concerned with the effect of work on people, with the appropriateness of goals, with long-term results, and with the norms and values implicit in goals and work.

OVERVIEW OF BOOK

Four parts

Our approach to discussing managing is to divide the subject into four parts, as shown in Figure 1–1.

FIGURE 1–1
Major Parts of This Book

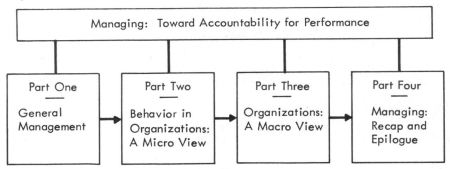

Part One

General Management. Part One consists of this introductory chapter, four other chapters and several "supplements." (We use chapter supplements throughout this book to discuss in depth

specific topics that are related to the *general* topic of the chapters.)
The four remaining chapters in Part One deal with goals, planning,
controlling, and decision making. We view these four topics as a
"functional foundation" for the rest of our discussion of managing.
All four involve important functions performed by managers in
meeting their accountability for performance. We view *goal setting*
as the strategically important managerial function—strategic because goals provide the rationale for managing. (Another topic
that could be included in this functional foundation is organizing.
We devote all of Part Three to a discussion of organizing.)

Part Two

Behavior in Organizations: A Micro View.   "Every problem we
have gets back to what I call a 'people problem.'" That comment
from the CEO of the world's largest automobile firm is one way of
making an important point: Managing is primarily concerned with
the behavior of people. You already know a lot about the behavior of
people. You may have taken one or two psychology or sociology
courses. In addition, human behavior is discussed in courses such
as economics, marketing, philosophy, literature, and history. Furthermore, you have accumulated your own unique understanding of
human behavior through personal experience and relationships. All
of this knowledge is part of your "management education." In this
book we make an effort to build on your present understanding of
human behavior. You will find that some of the material is a review
of what you already know, but most of it should be new and of particular interest to your efforts to become a manager. The major topics in Part Two are job performance and motivation, perception,
attitudes, values, behavioral consequences, interpersonal behavior,
behavior in groups, managerial leadership, managerial communication, conflict, and stress.

Part Three

Organizations: A Macro View.   Whereas Part Two is a micro view
—the focus is on types and contexts of individual behavior, Part
Three is a macro view—the focus is on the organization as an entity. Since managing occurs within organizations, knowledge about
organizations is potentially useful to managers in their efforts to
meet their accountability for performance. The major topics discussed in Part Three are foundations of contemporary thought
about organizations, the organization as a system, the organization–
environment relationship, the organization–technology relationship, several topics dealing with the general area of organizational
design, organizational change, organizational development, and
organizational effectiveness.

Part Four

Managing: Recap and Epilogue.   The last full chapter in this
book is an overview and recap of the major ideas discussed throughout the book. It should prove useful to you as an aid in integrating
the book's broad coverage and diverse set of ideas. Finally, the
book ends with an Epilogue—a personal statement concerning organizations and managing.

WHAT YOU CAN EXPECT TO LEARN

Reasonable expectations

It is important to begin the study of a subject with reasonable expectations about what your effort might yield. Of course, it is never possible to know exactly what you will learn, how well you will learn it, whether you will ever use it, or whether the learning is worth all your effort. Nevertheless, there are some things that are known.

Role of experience

Managing is a multi-dimensional skill. Like all other skills, you learn how to do it by studying, observing, practicing, succeeding, and failing. Managerial skills are acquired largely by personally experiencing the work of creating and maintaining environments in which people attempt to accomplish goals efficiently and effectively. On-the-job and real-life experiences are the primary ways of learning how to be an effective manager.

> For a discussion of several approaches to the study of managing see Supplement 1A.

No guarantee

Formal study of managing can make experience more meaningful. But managerial experience does not necessarily lead to acquiring managerial skills; experience is no guarantee of effectiveness. Nevertheless, without actual personal experiences that are meaningful to the work of managing, you cannot expect to be a good manager. "You can teach the rudiments of cooking, as of management, but you cannot make a great cook or a great manager."[16]

Limitation of books

There is no book or set of books that can teach you all there is to know about being a manager. There is no point in believing in magic, even though there are dozens of tricks that some claim lead to executive success. Some books are better than others in what they can teach you about managing, some are more "practical," and some are written better than others. But there is no book that can make a manager out of you. There is no course or executive training program that can assure your effectiveness.

An assumption

The fundamental assumption of this book is that there is some knowledge about managing that, *if learned and applied appropriately*, increases the probability of your managerial effectiveness. The key linkage is that the knowledge you acquire leads to more effective managerial behavior. All the knowledge in the world is useless if you don't use it in some way. "Book learning" about managing can increase your chances of managing effectively. It can give you an advantage over those who do not have the learning. But it cannot guarantee anything.

---

[16] Robert Heller, *The Great Executive Dream* (New York: Delacorte Press, 1972), p. 11.

*Expect
to learn*

What, then, can you expect to learn about managing from this book? First, you can expect to be exposed to a comprehensive and contemporary discussion of the academic discipline of managing. Second, you can expect to learn some managerial language, concepts, and theories that serve as a foundation for your further study of managing. Third, you can expect to become acquainted with a few managerial techniques that can be used to solve managerial problems. Fourth, through study and discussion with others, you can expect to learn material that will serve as a background for developing your own personal philosophy and theory of managing. Fifth, regardless of your major field of study or your career plans, you can expect to be exposed to information applicable to personal and managerial problems you will encounter in the "real world."

*Think like
a manager*

Finally, and perhaps most important, careful study of this book should help you to "think like a manager." This means thinking of goals and plans, of responsibilities and accountabilities, of relationships among the parts of an organization, and of probabilities and trends. It means understanding the complexity of systems involving human, technical, and economic components. Thinking like a manager means appreciating the complexity and mystery of human behavior at work. It means thinking of leadership opportunities and of ways to implement those opportunities. In the final analysis, this book will have a measure of success if it contributes to your ability to *think*—like a manager!

Supplement 1B, "Two Management Radicals,"
discusses two men who made early and original
contributions to our understanding of what it
means to think like a manager.

CHECK YOUR UNDERSTANDING

Managing   Efficiency
Supervising   Effectiveness
Administering   Managing as a universal activity
Narrow view of accountability   Test of managerial positions
Broad view of accountability   Business functions
Performance   Basic theme of this book
                                      Major parts of this book

STUDY QUESTIONS

1. How would you have defined managing before reading Chapter 1? What is the function of a definition? (The definition of "definition" is "a word or phrase expressing the essential nature of a person or thing.") Is it essential to define a subject in order to study it? (There are management textbooks that do not formally define management.)

2. Discuss what it means to say that managing occurs in all *types* of organizations. How, in your opinion, might the job of a business manager differ from the job of a hospital administrator?

3. Discuss what it means to say that managing occurs in all *levels* of organization. In what ways might the types of problems that a foreman encounters differ from those encountered by the president of an organization?

4. Discuss what it means to say that managing occurs in all *functions* of an organization. In your opinion, how might the task of a production manager differ from a marketing manager's?

5. The text takes the view that managing occurs by and through people. What is your interpretation of that view? Contrast it with the view that computers can manage or that money is managed.

6. As a professional person, how might your accountability to your profession conflict with your accountability to your immediate superior? Make a list of these kinds of conflicts and consider how you would go about resolving them.

7. Presumably, the main rationale for most college courses in management is that the subject matter covered in the course will be beneficial to you as a manager. What, in your opinion, can be learned in a classroom about management? What are some aspects of the manager's job that, in your opinion, cannot be learned in a classroom or from books?

8. What, in your opinion, is the value of work experience in the study of management? Can you think of ways in which work experience could be a hindrance to your professional study of management?

APPLICATION: MANAGING VERSUS NONMANAGING

Managing is the work of creating and maintaining environments in which people can accomplish goals efficiently and effectively. Which of the following actions do you think are examples of managing?

1. Presenting the results of a research project you have just completed to the national meeting of the Academy of Management.

2. Going to a dinner party with your spouse at the home of your superior's boss.

3. Helping your subordinates rearrange the physical facilities in their office.

4. Phoning your superior to ask his opinion about a new compensation system you have developed for your subordinates.

5. Going over the budget with one of your subordinate managers as part of a final budget review process.

6. Interacting with your seven subordinates in a session devoted to setting goals for your area of responsibility.

7. Trying to figure out how you are going to be evaluated by your superior.

8. Listening to complaints one of your subordinates has about a co-worker.

9. Taking a university course, Contemporary Managerial Issues, as part of an evening Master of Business Administration (M.B.A.) degree program.

10. Assessing who in your organization are the "rising stars" for key executive positions so that you can hitch your wagon to a star.

11. Firing two employees because their constant horseplay annoys you.

12. Attending your department's annual Christmas party.

13. Answering the telephone because none of your subordinates is present.

14. Playing golf with a good customer in order to assure that he remains a good customer.

15. Deciding on a new way to organize the relationships among people in your area of responsibility.

16. Developing, with the aid of a planning committee, an overall "strategic" plan for achieving the goals for which your area of responsibility will be held accountable.

17. Comparing progress reports of the actual job performance of your subordinates against performance standards.

18. Approving a new plan your subordinates have suggested for the redesign of jobs so that their performance and satisfaction will improve.

19. Discussing with a disappointed subordinate your decision to promote another subordinate to a highly prized executive position.

20. Filing papers that have piled up in your "To File" box.

APPLICATION: WOMEN MANAGERS—A JOB OR A CAREER

Mary Margaret and Jacqueline can't help but feel somewhat fortunate. They both have good jobs as general supervisors of important functions in a large manufacturing firm. They earn good salaries (about $15,000 per year), have competent supervisors that work for them, and have budget responsibility for their function.

Even though Mary and Jackie are very competent and have superior job performance histories they realize that, as women, they have at least one strike against them. Mary and Jackie are aware of statistics like these:

Women account for about 40 percent of the total labor force but for under 3 percent of those earning more than $25,000.

About 19 percent of all women in business are in managerial positions and, of these, one in five is either self-employed or an unpaid family worker.

About 60 of every 100 women workers is a clerk, saleswoman, waitress, or hairdresser. Twenty-five years ago the ratio was around 52 to 100.

Three years ago the average female college graduate earned less than the average male high-school dropout.

Somehow Mary and Jackie had been able to escape the "underpaid and underemployed" trap that is the lot of millions of women workers. Mary and Jackie had been given very challenging and responsible assignments on their first job after graduation from college. In fact, it has been one demanding job after another for both of them over the past six years. The question is, What does the future hold? There are some signs that Mary and Jackie may find their career paths going in different directions.

As in many well-managed companies, the careers of young, promising supervisors are watched closely by senior executives, human resource managers, and by immediate superiors. This was the case with Mary and Jackie—not because they were women, but because they were potential executives.

Until now both Mary and Jackie had met every challenge placed before them. Their job attitudes and performance were outstanding. However, now they were being thought of for promotion to a higher-level executive position. This position requires a serious career commitment and considerable conceptual and human relations skills. It is on this commitment and these skills that the firm feels Mary and Jackie differ. The consensus of their superiors seems to be that:

Mary thinks more in terms of a job than of a career. A job is short-term, here and now, and "earning-a-living" oriented. A career is long-run, future, and "part-of-a-life-style" oriented. Jackie views her job as a step in her career.

Jackie seems to want to avoid risks. She views risk strictly in the negative terms of losing what she has worked so hard to earn. Mary, on the other hand, thrives on risk; she sees the possibility of winning as well as that of losing.

Unlike Mary, Jackie seems to recognize the importance of "knowing what your boss wants." She feels that it is important to find out the expectations of her superior. This allows Jackie to be alert to cues from her superior and to adapt her performance to those cues. Mary gives the impression that such behavioral flexibility is really just hypocrisy.

Neither Mary or Jackie appears to be sensitive enough to the value of teamwork and to the need to win the support and cooperation of others. They appear to feel that "we got where we are by our own efforts and we intend to keep on going that way." The problem is that the higher-level executive position requires a lot of interdepartmental cooperation.

1. Identify some of the specific ways in which women are discriminated against in jobs and careers. What are some of the "myths" associated with the career orientations of women? (An example of one of these myths is that women work for "pin-money"—just a little extra spending money.)

2. Discuss the differences between Mary and Jackie. Can you think of reasons for these differences? Are they important factors in deciding on the promotion of Mary or Jackie?

Objective of Supplement 1A

To discuss briefly six ways that the study of managing can be approached and to indicate how they fit into the approach used in this book.

SUPPLEMENT 1A

Approaches to the Study of Managing

No matter how one approaches the subject, dealing with people emerges as an important aspect of managerial work.

John B. Miner

This supplement

Every academic discipline can be studied in a variety of ways. One management author notes that "In the century-and-a-quarter that marks the history of formal study of the subject, a good many schools of thought have emerged."[1] We will briefly examine the following "schools" or approaches to studying managing: traditional, case-method, behavioral, decision-making, quantitative, and contingency.

TRADITIONAL APPROACH

Two major ideas

The so-called classical, or traditional, approach to the study of managing is the approach that has characterized management education for over 50 years and is still dominant. Two major ideas running through the traditional approach are managerial functions and principles of management.

Managerial functions

The idea of "managerial functions" is that managers perform certain tasks that differentiate them from nonmanagers. The original concept of managerial functions is credited to Henri Fayol, an early contributor to management thought.[2] In response to the question, What do managers do? the traditional answer is that they perform functions such as planning, organizing, directing, and controlling. Specifically, managers plan, organize, direct, and control *the activities of other people.* The overall process of performing these functions is often called the "managerial process."

Basic rationale

The basic rationale for considering an activity a managerial function is that it is unique and essential to accomplishing goals

[1] John A. Beckett, *Management Dynamics: The New Synthesis* (New York: McGraw-Hill Book Company, 1971), p. 2.

[2] See Supplement 1B for a brief discussion of Henry Fayol's contributions to the development of management thought and for more on the ideas of managerial functions and principles of management.

efficiently and effectively. In this book, we discuss managerial functions—planning, organizing, controlling, and so forth, but we do not adopt the idea as our framework.

Principles of management

The second major idea in the traditional approach to studying managing is that there are "principles of managing" that serve as general guides for managerial behavior. Some textbooks are titled *Principles of Management* and emphasize principles applicable to the managerial functions of planning, organizing, controlling, and directing. Because so many of the so-called principles of management are violated in practice, are not necessarily true in theory, and are difficult to apply in rapidly changing environments, they have been criticized widely during the past 15 years.[3] Even writers who stress principles of management seem to do so with diminishing conviction. We do not emphasize in this book principles of management, even though we discuss many ideas associated with those principles.[4]

CASE-METHOD APPROACH

Diagnose, analyze, decide

Many colleges and universities use the case-method approach to the study of managing. Harvard's School of Business Administration is known for this approach. "Cases" are write-ups of actual problem situations in real organizations. The students diagnose and analyze the problem situation and are required to make decisions based on their analysis. The process of doing this many times is supposed to develop in the student the skill to analyze real problem situations and the ability to make decisions. Analytical and decision-making skills are the main objectives of this approach. The student also acquires knowledge about different types of business organizations and processes. In addition, the student is responsible for acquiring an understanding of theories relevant to any particular case.

Main thrust

The case-method approach is not necessarily in conflict with other approaches to the study of managing. For example, one can analyze and make decisions about a case dealing with managerial functions or human behavior. This book contains several cases that may be used to implement the case-method approach. The cases provide opportunities for you to relate ideas and theories to concrete situations. They can be useful as a means of applying knowledge and as a vehicle for validating your understanding of that knowledge.

---

[3] For example, see Orlando C. Behling, "Who Killed 'Principles of Management' and Why We Did It," The Ohio State University, College of Administrative Sciences, *Partners Journal*, vol. 2, no. 3 (Fall 1976), pp. 4–5.

[4] For a current discussion of principles of management and managerial functions see Harold Koontz and Cyril O'Donnell, *Management: A Systems and Contingency Analysis of Managerial Functions*, 6th ed. (New York: McGraw-Hill Book Company, 1976). It is interesting to note that in this revision, Koontz and O'Donnell dropped the term "principles" from the title of their textbook.

BEHAVIORAL APPROACH

Individuals,
interpersonal
relations,
groups, and
organizations

The behavioral approach focuses on people and the relationships among people while working. Some writers focus primarily on *individual* personality and the problems of integrating the individual's goals with those of the organization. Others focus on *interpersonal* relationships and communication. Still others place primary attention on effective *work groups* and their development. The work group is seen as the basic organizational unit, and the way groups function and interact will determine, in large part, organizational effectiveness. Finally, other writers focus on the *total organization* and look at problems of authority, decision making, leadership, motivation, communication, and change from an organizational viewpoint.

Our major
emphasis

Behavioral understanding is extremely important in managing. The attempt to communicate some knowledge of human needs, of how people adapt to organizations, of how groups function and what needs they fill has been a characteristic of managing courses since the late 1950s. In some cases, traditional topics such as goals, planning, controlling, and organization were ignored, and management courses became quasi-behavioral science courses. In most cases, however, traditional management material has been complemented by newer knowledge of the behavioral sciences. Our major emphasis in this book is on the behavioral approach.

DECISION-MAKING APPROACH

Logical
approach

Another way of approaching the study of managing is through decision making. Some writers use the terms "managing" and "decision making" synonymously. Managing, like any other form of behavior, is goal-directed; managers move toward goals by choosing among alternative courses of action. Therefore, focusing attention on decisions, decision makers, and the decision-making process is a logical and useful way of approaching the study of managing.

Descriptive
and normative
decision
making

This approach emphasizes not only acquiring a better understanding of how decisions are made in organizations, but also understanding how decisions should be made. Thus, a decision-making approach has a "descriptive" (how decisions are made) as well as a "normative" (how decisions should be made) dimension. Further, an emphasis on decision making tends also to emphasize the *information* needed for decisions, the problems and costs of acquiring the information, and the *system* needed to assure that decisions will be made. We devote one chapter to decision making and emphasize it in other chapters. However, we do not consider "decision making" as synonomous with "managing," nor do we view it as the central task of managers.

QUANTITATIVE APPROACH

*Three
quantitative
tools*

There are some colleges and professors who feel that the most productive approach to management education is one that emphasizes managerial problems that can be modeled, quantified, and solved. Emphasis on quantitative aspects of managing has been present in management education since World War II, and especially since the late 1950s. The computer, which became a useful educational and operational tool of managers in the late 1950s, plays an important role in quantitative management education. In recent years, information theory and systems analysis have been associated with quantitative managerial problems. More traditional quantitative areas, such as cost accounting, statistics, and industrial engineering, have long been sources of information for managers. This book does not emphasize quantitative approaches to managing, although it contains brief discussions of three quantitative decision-making tools: linear programming; decision matrices; and network analysis.

CONTINGENCY APPROACH

*Growing use
of term
"contingency"*

In recent years the word "contingency" has invaded the field of management. It started, modestly, as an adjective describing a specific "contingency theory of leadership," and a "contingency theory of organization."[5] In the 1970s, the general utility of the term became widely apparent, and now there are contingency theories or views of planning, organizing, controlling, leadership, goal setting, and so on. Furthermore, the entire managerial process can be and is viewed in a contingency context.[6] What is this contingency idea? How will we use it?

*The con-
tingency idea*

At one level of understanding, the contingency idea is extremely vacuous. It simply means "depends." To say, for example, that "leadership is contingent on factors in the situation" means that the type of leadership that will be effective depends on the particular circumstances in the specific situation. If that is all contingency theories had to offer, then they would be of little interest to anyone. However, there is a good reason for the widespread interest in the contingency idea.

*Strength of
the idea*

The strength of the contingency idea derives from two sources. First, the concept of contingency focuses attention on specific situa-

[5] Fred E. Fiedler, *A Theory of Leadership Effectiveness* (New York: McGraw-Hill Book Company, 1967); Paul R. Lawrence and Jay W. Lorsch, *Organization and Environment: Managing Differentiation and Integration* (Boston: Harvard University, Graduate School of Business Administration, Division of Research, 1967).

[6] See Henry L. Tosi and Stephen J. Carroll, *Management: Contingencies, Structure, and Process* (Chicago: St. Clair Press, 1976), and Gary Dessler, *Organization and Management: A Contingency Approach* (Englewood Cliffs, N.J.: Prentice-Hall, 1976).

tional factors that influence the appropriateness of one managerial strategy over another. Second, emphasis on the contingency idea highlights the importance to managers of developing skills in situational analysis. Such skills will help managers identify and evaluate critical contingency factors that directly influence their approach to managing.

Leadership example

To use again the example of leadership, one contingency theory asserts that the most effective leadership style is contingent upon the need for a high-quality decision or a decision that is accepted by those who must implement it.[7] (We will discuss this theory more fully later.) Thus, the theory attempts to relate two contingency factors, quality and acceptance, to the type of leadership style that is likely to be most effective.

Managerial process example

Another example of the use of the contingency idea is "managerial process contingency theory." This theory argues that the specific way that managers carry out the managerial process (which includes such functions as planning, coordinating, evaluating, and staffing) depends on: (1) the structure of the organization; and (2) the personnel in the organization. "The management process is performed within the constraints imposed by these two factors."[8]

Our use of the contingency approach

How will we use the contingency idea? First, we recognize the practical value of a contingency viewpoint. Specifically, the application of managerial knowledge and techniques must always be adapted to the demands of specific, concrete situations. There is no such thing as applying knowledge in the abstract. "Effective management is always contingency, or situational, management."[9] It is good intellectual discipline to always think of the way that knowledge and understanding about managing must interact with situational factors (including the manager's personality and behavioral skills) in order to arrive at appropriate managerial strategy. Second, we will discuss specific contingency theories—most of which pertain to leadership. Third, we do not try to develop a contingency theory but, where appropriate, we identify situational factors relevant to specific topics being discussed.

CONCLUSION

No one best way

There are additional approaches to the study of managing other than the ones mentioned.[10] However, the approaches we have

[7] Victor H. Vroom and Philip W. Yetton, *Leadership and Decision-Making* (Pittsburgh: University of Pittsburgh Press, 1973).

[8] Tosi and Carroll, *Management: Contingencies, Structure, and Process*, p. 18.

[9] Koontz and O'Donnell, *Management: A Systems and Contingency Analysis of Managerial Functions*, p. 23.

[10] See Henry Mintzberg, *The Nature of Managerial Work* (New York: Harper & Row, Publishers, 1973), chap. 2.

noted are enough to suggest that there is no one best way to study managing. There is nothing wrong with having a variety of ways of thinking about the task of getting people to work productively and with satisfaction in an efficient and effective manner. There is no need to search for one correct approach. The test is: Is a particular approach useful to you? If all are useful, use them all; if none is useful, find some other approach. The chances are that you will find the perspective of each of the above-described approaches useful to you in your study.

Summary box

There are several approaches to the study of managing. A few are discussed in this supplement. The *traditional* approach emphasizes managerial functions and principles of management. The *case-method* approach emphasizes acquiring diagnostic, analytical, and decision-making skills through the discussion of cases. The *behavioral* approach focuses on people and the relationships among people while working.

The *decision-making* approach focuses on how decisions are and should be made. The *quantitative* approach concentrates on managerial problems that can be modeled, quantified, and solved. The *contingency* approach emphasizes sensitivity to specific situational factors influencing the choice of the most effective managerial strategies.

Our approach in this book is a combination approach. Major emphasis is on human behavior in organizations. We provide some cases and discuss three quantitative techniques. In addition, we devote considerable attention to the managerial functions of goal setting, planning, controlling, and decision making.

CHECK YOUR UNDERSTANDING

Six approaches to studying managing
Managerial functions
Basic rationale for a managerial function
Principles of management

Different focuses within behavioral approach
Descriptive and normative decision making
Strength of the contingency idea

STUDY QUESTIONS

1. In this supplement, the six ways of studying managing were discussed as if they are complementary rather than contradictory. Why, in your opinion, do the advocates of any one of these approaches sometimes view the other approaches with suspicion, ridicule, and contempt?

2. To what extent, in your opinion, is the contingency view of managing compatible with the idea of a *theory* of managing? To what extent is it incompatible?

APPLICATION: APPROACHES TO STUDYING MANAGING

Bill Cazalas, Dave Spencer, and Sarah Ryan all attended the same high school and college. All three majored in a nonbusiness subject. On graduating, each decided to enter a graduate program in order to earn a Master of Business Administration degree. Bill went to Stanford University, Dave went to the University of Chicago, and Sarah went to Harvard's School of Business Administration.

At the end of their first year of graduate school, Bill, Dave, and Sarah returned to their hometown and to the summer jobs they had had while undergraduates. After they talked for a while, it became clear that, although each was part of a management program, all three were following different approaches.

Bill and Dave had heard of the case-method approach that Sarah talked about. It seemed to them like a lot of wasted effort to devote time to the study of cases that they were never likely to encounter in real life. Sarah, on the other hand, felt that all the theory, concepts, and mathematical tools that Dave and Bill were studying were unrealistic and boring: "What do they have to do with managing people?" "How many managers actually use any of those models and theories?"

Sarah was determined to convince Bill and Dave of the value of "Harvard's approach." Bill and Dave took up the competitive challenge, promising Sarah she would see the light and come over to their view. (Bill and Dave also had some differences but agreed to present a united front against the case-method approach.)

1. What are some ways that Bill, Dave, and Sarah can go about winning their challenge?
2. Is it possible that different approaches to the study of managing can reflect different values and learning theories? If so, how might this apply to Bill, Dave, and Sarah?

SUPPLEMENT 1B

Two Management Radicals

Objectives of Supplement 1B

1. To convince you that it is useful to you to become familiar with two pioneers in the development of management thought.
2. To summarize three major contributions of Henri Fayol.
3. To discuss Frederick W. Taylor and identify his four fundamental principles of scientific management.

It is not what you can do with history but what history does to you is its use.

Source unknown

This supplement   This supplement introduces you to two men who have been very important to the development of management thought. Every field of study has its major pioneers and, although many others could be mentioned, we will discuss two.[1] Henri Fayol and Frederick Winslow Taylor are uniquely important for their original impact on management theory, education, and practice. No college-level course in basic management would be complete without acknowledging the field of management's debt to Frederick W. Taylor and Henri Fayol.

Who cares?   Why should today's students of managing devote their time to learning what a supervisor at Bethlehem Steel Company and an executive of a French mining company had to say in the early part of this century? After all, the best of what they had to say—if still relevant—is integrated into modern management education and practice. Furthermore, there is no evidence whatever that a study of Taylor and Fayol has made anyone a more successful manager. Finally, much of their writing is simply irrelevant to the management problems of today. What, then, *is* the point of learning about Taylor and Fayol?

Original thinkers   First, Taylor and Fayol were original thinkers. They broke with tradition and began developments that have influenced managerial education and practice for over 75 years. Both Taylor and Fayol

---

[1] The best single reference on the history of management thought is Daniel A. Wren, *The Evolution of Management Thought* (New York: Ronald Press Company, 1972). For a shorter and more descriptive view, see Claude S. George, Jr., *The History of Management Thought* (Englewood Cliffs, N.J.: Prentice-Hall, 1968).

are a delight to read. Their writings not only have the clarity and freshness characteristic of original writing, but also reveal the difficulties faced by those who advocate and are committed to change. In one sense, Taylor and Fayol were the management radicals of their day. They both advocated basic changes in management practice and theory. Taylor, especially, experienced hostile and even violent resistance to his ideas, and he was ridiculed by his peers. Since many of the problems of implementing change tend to be similar wherever and whenever encountered, Taylor and Fayol provide useful case studies of two very influential management "change-agents."

Sense of history

Second, your professional study of any field of study involves, in part, acquiring a sense of the historical development of the field. This allows you to place yourself at some point in time in the development of major ideas and practices. When you study management today, you benefit from many years of managerial thought and practice. A sense of history about the field of management is one of the factors that distinguishes a professional approach from a purely vocational approach to management study. This supplement is a start in acquiring a sense of management history.

The critics' role

Third, some knowledge of Taylor and Fayol is important if you are to critically and fairly evaluate the most modern managerial and organization theories. A large amount of modern writing about managing and organizations is devoted to criticism of earlier theories; and Taylor, especially, has been the target of a substantial part of that criticism. Fayol's approach to management is also widely criticized, even though it remains the most common approach to formal management education.

HENRI FAYOL

Father of administrative management

"More than any other European who has lived in this century, Henri Fayol is responsible for directing minds to the need for studying administration scientifically."[2] That is how Lyndall Urwick in 1934 described the man who was to become known as the "father of administrative management thought." Henri Fayol's book, *General and Industrial Management*, presents the earliest statement of a general theory of management and is a singularly important contribution to management thought.[3]

Fayol's purpose

Fayol's purpose in writing his book was to communicate the idea that management could be taught and a theory of management

[2] Lyndall Urwick, "The Function of Administration," in Luther Gulick and L. Urwick, eds., *Papers on the Science of Administration* (New York: Institute of Public Administration, 1937), p. 117.

[3] New York: Pitman Publishing Corporation, 1949. First published in France in 1916 as *Administration industrielle et générale* and translated into English in 1928 for limited distribution in Great Britain before its publication in this country.

could be developed. In fact, Fayol held that the idea of teaching management depends on developing a theory. Both of these ideas were new although today they are simply part of accepted management thinking. Fayol devoted his later years to furthering ideas of management theory and teaching, and from 1918 until his death in 1925, presided over the Centre of Administrative Studies. As part of its emphasis on the teaching of management and on the development of a theory of management applicable to all forms of human endeavor, Fayolism contained three specific contributions that you should know about: generic activities, managerial elements, and general principles of management.

Six activities of industrial firms

Generic Activities.   Fayol was the first to articulate the idea that all organizations have certain common activities. Specifically, he identified six activities of industrial undertakings: technical, commercial, financial, security, accounting, and managerial. Note here that Fayol identified managing as an activity "quite distinct from the other five essential functions."[4] This particular insight reveals something about Fayol's frame of reference: That is, as a top executive of Comambault, a large mining company in France, he tended to take a view that encompassed the entire organization. This "macro" view has been the perspective of administrative management and organization theory for almost 50 years and, in some respects, is the view of modern "systems" theory.

Organic functions

Fayol's idea of activities or functions essential to all organizations has taken several forms over the years. Some writers have referred to "organic functions" in identifying those activities without which an organization could not exist.[5] Commonly, production, sales, and finance are identified as organic functions of a business organization. In addition, this idea of organic functions has been the basis for the historically important concepts of line and staff (to be discussed in a later chapter). In sum, Fayol's contribution here was the original abstraction of essential organizational functions. Such an abstraction was an important step in the direction of an administrative theory applicable to all types of organizations.

Plan, organize, command, co-ordinate, control

Managerial Elements.   In Supplement 1A, we mentioned that the idea of managerial functions is one of the themes of the traditional approach to the study of managing. Fayol originated this idea (he used the term elements rather than functions): "Therefore, I have adopted the following definition: To manage is to forecast and plan, to organize, to command, to co-ordinate and to control."[6] This conception of managing has had, and continues today to have, a decisive impact on managerial thought, education, and practice.

---

4 Ibid., p. 6.

5 See, for example, Ralph C. Davis, *The Fundamentals of Top Management* (New York: Harper Bros., 1951).

6 Fayol, *General and Industrial Management*, p. 5.

POSDCORB

One early adaptation of Fayol's managerial elements was suggested in 1936.[7] In answer to the rhetorical questions, "What is the work of the chief executive? What does the chief executive do?" one author responded, "POSDCORB." POSDCORB is an acronym for Planning, Organizing, Staffing, Directing, Co-ordinating, Organizing, Reporting, and Budgeting. POSDCORB thus became a management byword and was used for years. A recent management textbook uses a slight variation of POSDCORB as its framework for discussing management;[8] many other management textbooks use some variation of Fayol's basic idea of managerial elements.[9]

Business application

The idea of managerial functions is not just for textbooks. Many business organizations view management as a set of elements. Examples include Chrysler Corporation's planning, organizing, guiding performance, and appraising results; General Electric's planning, organizing, integrating, and measuring; and Texas Instrument's planning, organizing, controlling, and motivating. These firms find the functional view of managing useful for purposes of inhouse managerial training and development.

To focus discussion

General Principles of Management. In order to get a discussion going on management theory, Fayol identified 14 general principles of management. In so doing, he said, ". . . it seems to me particularly useful at the moment to endow the theory of administration with about a dozen well-established principles, on which public discussion can conveniently be focused."[10]

General and flexible guides

Every field of study involves a search for principles—general statements of cause-and-effect relationships that tend to be true under specified conditions. Fayol deserves credit for his initial formulation of (what he considered to be) principles. Unlike some who followed him, Fayol recognized that management principles must be flexible guides:

> For preference I shall adopt the term principles whilst dissociating it from any suggestion of rigidity, for there is nothing rigid or absolute in management affairs, it is all a question of proportion. . . .

---

[7] Gulick and Urwick, eds., *Papers on the Science of Administration*, p. 13.

[8] Ernest Dale, *Management: Theory and Practice*, 3d ed. (New York: McGraw-Hill Book Company, 1973).

[9] Some management scholars feel that the Fayol view of the manager's job is too simplistic and not very useful. See, for example, Henry Mintzberg, "The Manager's Job: Folklore and Fact," *Harvard Business Review*, vol. 53, no. 4 (July–August 1975), pp. 49–61.

[10] A detailed discussion of Fayol's 14 principles is not included here. Some of these principles will be discussed in the context of the text material on organization. A sense of the nature of Fayol's principles can be gained from a listing of the titles Fayol gave them: division of work, authority and responsibility, discipline, unity of command, unity of direction, subordination of individual interest to the general interest, remuneration, centralization, scalar chain, order, equity, stability, initiative, and esprit de corps. The quotation is from *General and Industrial Management*, p. 41.

Therefore principles are flexible and capable of adaptation to every need; it is a matter of knowing how to make use of them, which is a difficult art requiring intelligence, experience, decision and proportion.[11]

Summary box

> This supplement discusses Henri Fayol and Frederick Winslow Taylor. We feel it is worthwhile for you to learn about these two men because: they were original in their thinking about managing; they help you acquire a sense of the history of management thought; and their writings continue to be important in managerial education and practice.
>
> Henri Fayol is known as the "father of administrative management thought." We cited three major contributions credited to Fayol: (1) the idea that all organizations have certain *generic activities*, (2) the idea that managing consists of a set of *managerial elements* or functions, and (3) the idea of *general principles of management*.

FREDERICK WINSLOW TAYLOR

Father of scientific management

If Henri Fayol was the primary European responsible for the initial development of management thought, his American counterpart was Frederick W. Taylor, "father of scientific management." As you will see, while their approach to management differed, both have had an enormous impact on managerial practice.

Most significant role

In the early development of modern management thinking, no one man played a more significant role than Frederick W. Taylor. It is unlikely that any other individual will equal Taylor's impact on worldwide management education and practice. His "methods became standard practice throughout industry."[12] His original ideas and methods helped launch the careers of numerous later contributors to management thought. More than that, Taylor's emphasis on a systematic, rational, deliberate, scientific approach to *all* jobs and problems encountered in organized effort completely altered the foundation of prevailing managerial ideology. In terms of the history of ideas, Frederick W. Taylor may be only a footnote; in terms of the history of management thought, Taylor is a substantial part of the main story.[13]

---

[11] Ibid., p. 19.

[12] Paula Smith, "The Masterminds of Management," *Dun's Review*, vol. 108, no. 1 (July 1976), p. 18.

[13] A primary source of information on scientific management is Frederick Winslow Taylor, *The Principles of Scientific Management* (New York: Harper & Bros., 1911). Also see his *Shop Management* (New York: Harper & Bros., 1947).

*Taylor's
key idea*

The key idea for understanding Taylor is science. A scientific approach—later to become known as "scientific management"—to problem solving was Taylor's cardinal principle and his overriding obsession. At a time when the relationships among owners, managers, and workers were based on Darwinian concepts of survival of the fittest, Taylor advocated basing these relationships on scientifically determined personnel selection and training and on the determination of appropriate work methods. In this new conception of relationships, previous concepts became obsolete. The worth of the employee could no longer be ascertained by his success in the struggle for survival or by his docility. Employers could no longer be seen as the natural leaders who had proven their natural superiority simply by virtue of their success in business. Rather, under scientific management, both employers and employees would be placed in the "highest class of work for which [their] natural abilities fit [them]."[14]

*Before
scientific
management*

You might ask, "What was management practice like before Taylor's scientific approach was introduced?" The basic answer to that question is that management, as it is known today, was not widely practiced. At the turn of the current century, the most common approach to the production of economic goods was what Taylor called the approach of "initiative and incentive"—an approach Taylor argued resulted in gross inefficiencies. There were few standard methods for doing jobs. Workmen trained themselves or learned under an apprenticeship system. The idea that certain people in an organization—management—had responsibility to select and train workmen was not generally accepted. One view of the differences between scientific and ordinary management is given by Taylor and summarized in Figure 1B–1.

*Mental
revolution
versus bag of
tricks*

The four fundamental principles of scientific management shown in Figure 1B–1 may not impress you as radical or revolutionary. However, think of them in terms of the cultural context of the early 1900s and as new ideas *at that time*. The central idea that gives unity to the four principles is the idea of the scientific method. Taylor was calling for a complete "mental revolution." Scientific management was not to be a mere bag of tricks, techniques, or gimmicks: "The mechanisms [time study, functional foremanship, standardization, exception principle, et cetera] of management must not be mistaken for its essence, or underlying philosophy. . . . Scientific management, in its essence, consists of a certain philosophy which results in a combination of the four great underlying principles."[15]

---

[14] Reinhard Bendix, *Work and Authority in Industry* (New York: John Wiley & Sons, 1956), p. 279.

[15] Taylor, *The Principles of Scientific Management,* p. 128.

FIGURE 1B–1
Ordinary and Scientific Management

The common practice under ordinary management	The four fundamental principles of scientific management
1. No standard times, methods, or motions, for any job. Jobs were performed by rule of thumb methods.	1. Develop a science for every job.
2. Management played little direct part in personnel selection and training. Workmen selected other workmen. Training, at best was under an apprentice system.	2. Scientifically select, train, teach, and develop the workmen.
3. Employers and employees were essentially in competition for a larger slice of the surplus. Employees reasoned that employers benefited at the expense of the employees. The size of the surplus was seen as relatively constant and thus the two factions were competing for a larger slice.	3. Cooperation between management and the workmen. Taylor argued that the two leading objects of management are to maximize the prosperity of the employer and every employee. He felt the true interests of employers and employees were basically in harmony. Furthermore, the entire country would benefit from this harmony and cooperation.
4. Almost all of the work and most of the responsibility was given to the workmen. The idea of management, as a group performing unique duties, was not widespread.	4. An equal division of the work between management and workers. Management should plan, train, select, control; workers should perform. The essential idea here is that management, as a group, has unique duties that *only* management can accomplish. Under scientific management there was to be a theoretical 50–50 sharing of the work between management and the worker.

Misinterpretation and employee resistance

Unfortunately, scientific management was often mistaken for its mere mechanisms. Misapplications and abuses were common.[16] For one thing, it is much easier to adopt mechanisms and learn techniques than to participate in a mental revolution. Furthermore, employers were not always eager to participate in a mental revolution that altered fundamentally their relative position vis-à-vis workers: ". . . the employers resisted Taylor's approach in many cases, because they opposed this substitution of techniques for judgment and discretion. After all, Taylor had questioned their

_____
[16] Bendix, *Work and Authority in Industry*, p. 280.

good judgment and their superior ability. . . . Hence, many employers regarded his methods as an unwarranted interference with managerial prerogatives."[17]

Criticism of management

Taylor was often critical of the top management of American business firms. He attacked management for its failure to improve efficiency and its reluctance to pay workers according to their productivity. Taylor's mental revolution, with its emphasis on scientific analysis, could require substantial cost outlays that employers were hesitant to make in the absence of certain and beneficial results. And at a time when employers were looking for more effective means for preventing trade unionism, scientific management did not impress employers as an effective new tool. For this and other reasons, ". . . most managements of the time kept him out of their plants as a 'dangerous radical' and 'troublemaker.' "[18]

No overnight success

In view of the above factors, it would be inaccurate to say that scientific management became an overnight success. Taylor had unreasonably high expectations for scientific management and appeared oblivious to its limitations. Employers and employees alike were hostile toward it. The American Federation of Labor opposed Taylorism on the grounds that it treated workers like machines. Taylor's system was investigated by a special committee of the House of Representatives.[19] The rational and harmonious relationship between employers and employees that Taylor visualized never did come to pass. It could be said that Taylor's idealistic version of scientific management never yet has been tried in all of its dimensions.

Continuing mental revolution

Nevertheless, scientific management changed the basic foundations of managerial thought and practice. Taylor's mental revolution is still going on today. It is a revolution that has as its main thrust the idea that systematic, rational, and scientific approaches can be applied to the solution of managerial problems. Taylor's guiding rule was: "When starting an experiment in any field, question everything, question the very foundation upon which the act rests, question the simplest, the most self-evident, the most universally accepted facts; prove everything."[20]

---

[17] Louis W. Fry, "The Maligned F. W. Taylor: A Reply to His Many Critics," *Academy of Management Review*, vol. 1, no. 3 (July 1976), pp. 124–29.

[18] Peter F. Drucker, "The Coming Rediscovery of Scientific Management," *Conference Board Record*, vol. 13, no. 6 (June 1976), p. 24.

[19] Taylor's testimony before the Special House Committee can be found in his *Scientific Management* (New York: Harper & Bros., 1947). Taylor gave his testimony in 1912 and it is also contained in the public document, *Hearings before Special Committee of the House of Representatives to Investigate the Taylor and Other Systems of Shop Management under Authority of H. Res. 90;* vol. 3, pp. 1377–508.

[20] Robert B. Downs, *Molders of the Modern Mind* (New York: Barnes and Noble Books, 1961), p. 349.

Summary box

> Frederick W. Taylor is known as the "father of scientific management." Without question, his ideas and methods have had more impact on industrial management than those of any other person. Science is the key idea for understanding Taylor. Through the application of the scientific management as a *mental revolution* and identified *four fundamental principles of scientific management* (see Figure 1B–1).

CONCLUSION

They suggested a guiding philosophy

It is impossible to gain a full perspective on the contributions of Frederick W. Taylor and Henri Fayol from this brief discussion. However, it is reasonable to conclude two points. First, both Taylor and Fayol made significant contributions to the development of modern management thought. The significance and influence of their continuing contribution lies not so much in the specific details of their writings, but in the guiding philosophy suggested. Both men favored the development of theory and principles as the surest way to improve managerial practice. Taylor was more empirical in his approach; he advocated extensive data collection in the process of developing a "science" for every job. Fayol, however, was equally insistent on validating principles and developing new principles. "Both men gave the devotion of their later lives to putting science into management."[21]

They were only human

Second, it is possible to recognize their contributions without insisting that Taylor and Fayol were correct and comprehensive enough in all things. They were, after all, only humans. It would be unreasonable to expect that these two men would be able to anticipate modern behavioral and systems thinking. Although both were ahead of their times, to some extent they took what is now called a "closed system" view of management and organizations. They had little to say about the role of the environment in influencing managerial practice. Their views were inadequate in recognizing complex behavioral processes that occur in organizations. Taylor, in particular, has been criticized for placing too much emphasis on financial and economic incentives. In conclusion, we need to recognize both the limitations *and* the contributions of the two management radicals, Henri Fayol and Frederick W. Taylor.[22]

[21] Urwick, "The Function of Administration," p. 118.

[22] For a psycho-historical analysis of Taylor, See Sudhir Kakar, *Frederick Taylor: A Study in Personality and Innovation* (Cambridge, Mass.: M.I.T. Press, 1970). For a criticism of Taylor's most often-cited experiment, see Charles D. Wriege and Amedeo G. Perroni, "Taylor's Pig-Tale: A Historical Analysis of Frederick W. Taylor's Pig-Iron Experiments," *Academy of Management Journal*, vol. 17, no. 1 (March 1974), pp. 6–27.

CHECK YOUR UNDERSTANDING

Father of administrative management
Idea of generic activities of industrial firms
Idea of managerial elements or
functions
POSDCORB
Idea of general principles of management

Father of scientific management
Key idea for understanding Taylor
Ordinary versus scientific man-
agement
Four fundamental principles of
scientific management

STUDY QUESTIONS

1. If you use Henri Fayol's idea of generic activities, what, in your
    opinion, are the generic activities of a—
    a. Hospital   *c.* Manufacturing firm
    b. University   *d.* Retail department store
    What decision rule are you using to classify an activity as generic?

2. Does it make sense to you to think of the manager's job in terms of
    certain elements or activities? Is this idea of what managers do
    supported by what you actually see managers doing? Discuss.

APPLICATION: FREDERICK W. TAYLOR*

For three days last November, I sat in the court room of the In-
terstate Commerce Commission at Washington, listening to one of
the most remarkable cases ever presented before that distinguished
body. On one side were the powerful Eastern railroads, present in
the persons of some half a hundred attorneys, and pleading permission from the government to raise their rates; on the other side
were the Eastern shippers, disputing the demands of the railroads.
Upon the issue hung vast commercial and financial interests.

The railroads pleaded that they must have more money from
the people to meet the "increased cost of living," especially the
wages of their employees. The shippers responded by boldly attack-
ing the railroads at the point where they have always felt strongest
—that of managerial efficiency. The shippers declared that the
railroads were not efficiently managed, and that if they would "look
within," they could save more money than they now demanded in
increased rates.

To support this bold response Mr. Louis D. Brandeis, the shippers' attorney, placed on the stand 11 witnesses who told of a
singular new system or method of securing a marvelous degree of
efficiency in all manner of industrial operations. This new system,
or philosophy, which they said, frankly, was revolutionary in its
aims, they called Scientific Management.

. . . It was even asserted with confidence by one witness, Mr.

* Source: Ray Stannard Baker, "Frederick W. Taylor: Scientist in Business Management," *The American Magazine,* vol. 71, no. 5 (March 1911), pp.
564–65.

Emerson, that, if applied to the railroads, Scientific Management could be counted upon to save at least $1 million a day.

To those who heard this testimony there seemed at first something almost magical about the new idea; but as one sober, hardheaded business man after another testified as to what had actually been accomplished in his plant, the spirit of incredulity changed to one of deep interest. Another factor in carrying conviction to the hearers was the extraordinary fervor and enthusiasm expressed by every man who testified. Theirs was the firm faith of apostles: It was a philosophy which worked, and they had the figures to show it.

"This," said Mr. Commissioner Lane to one of the witnesses, "has become a sort of substitute for religion with you."

"Yes, sir," responded Mr. Gilbreth.

Mr. Taylor himself was not present at the hearing, but he was constantly referred to as the originator of the system; and he has since become a man of whom the world wishes to know more. What is this Scientific Management, and who is Mr. Taylor?

Examine a business-related periodical of the period from 1908 to 1912. See if you can get a feel for why Taylor's work was referred to in phrases such as these: "the most important advance in industry since the introduction of the factory system"; the most remarkable practical researches ever published"; and "almost staggers the mind to comprehend."

Objectives of Chapter 2

- To identify and emphasize the role of goals as the most important concept in the study and practice of managing.
- To define goals and differentiate goals and motives. To explain how we use the terms "group" and "organizational" goals and to suggest ways in which goals change.
- To recognize the potential uses and the limitations of goals.
- To discuss several criteria that goals must meet if they are to be useful to managers.
- To suggest a particular view of the multiple interacting goals that enter into managerial accountability for performance.
- To outline a way of thinking about the problem of conflict between individual and organizational goals.
- To describe the complex human behavioral process that leads to goals in organizations.

Outline of Chapter 2

2

GOALS: THE STRATEGIC MANAGING VARIABLE

There is one quality more important than "know-how"
. . . this is "know-what" by which we determine
not only how to accomplish our purposes, but what
our purposes are to be.

Norbert Wiener

What the hell is going on around here?

Almost everyone

President Carter

Look again at the title of this chapter. What does it mean? What is a *strategic* variable? An example from the world of politics can help answer these questions. In American political experience, Jimmy Carter's election as president of the United States is an outstanding example of what dedication to a goal can achieve. Carter's worst enemies acknowledge his personal success story.

Strategic goal

For almost four years prior to being elected, Carter and those around him pursued the goal of his election with an almost unparalleled singleness of purpose. The goal was *strategic* in that it was the ultimate basis for all plans, policies, procedures, organization, staffing—for practically everything in Carter's personal and professional life for almost four years. With all the odds against his final success, it is unlikely he would have made it without a confident and unshaking commitment to his goal.

The how and the what

But haven't other politicians had this degree of commitment without the result that President Carter enjoys? Yes! Which is just another way of saying that a goal is not enough. The "how" is as important as the "what." In President Carter's case, personality and style were important. Entering all the primaries and winning most of them was a crucial feature. Effective organization and a sophisticated information–communication system may have made the decisive difference. Talented and committed helpers, including his family and friends, all were part of Carter's "how" that led to his "what"—the presidency of the United States.

Goals—
necessary but
not sufficient

President Carter's success story helps us make two points. First, goals are *necessary* for political or managerial success. They provide the basis for a coherent set of plans and policies, for effective organization, and for purposeful behavior. In that sense, we say that goals are the "strategic" managing variable. Second, goals are not *sufficient* for political or managerial success. All the ingredients that make up the means for achieving the ends (goals) are also crucial. This chapter focuses on goals; the rest of the book focuses on the means of achieving goals.

Meaningful
goals are rare

Goals that are meaningful in guiding the behavior of managers are the exception rather than the rule in organizations. Many managers do not give goals the attention they deserve. Goals are commonly ambiguous, unattainable, overly conflicting, unconscious, and nonmeasurable. It is a lot easier to talk about goals than it is to formulate and implement them. As a student of managing, you will want to develop the skill to set and use goals as an important tool in efficient and effective managing. Goals should be the starting point of managerial thought and action. They are the key to managerial accountability for performance.

This chapter

In this chapter, we define goals and several related terms and recognize the potential uses and limitations of goals in managing. We discuss several criteria goals should meet and suggest a view of the manager's goal system. Then we examine the issue of integrating individual and organizational goals. The chapter ends with a discussion of the goal-setting process.

SOME BASIC GOAL CONCEPTS

Our definition
and other
terms

What Are Goals? Goals are desired results toward which behavior is directed. We use the terms "goals," "purposes," "missions," "aims," and "objectives" interchangeably.[1] In *business organizations,* desired results include attaining a desired profitability level, achieving personal satisfaction from job performance, learning a new skill, and complying with a new law regulating business activity. In *hospitals,* desired results include improving patient care, broadening patient services, community education, and fi-

---

[1] In some business firms and other types of organizations, these words have different meanings. A *mission* or *aim* is a very broad, general statement such as, "The mission of our automobile firm is to provide passenger transportation." An organizational *objective* may be "low-cost cars," and a specific *goal* may be to have the lowest-priced model among competing models. There is no standard way of using these terms and, for our purposes, there is no value in differentiating them.

nancial solvency. In *schools*, desired results include expanding course offerings, introducing educational innovations, having a good football team, and offering students and faculty opportunities to discover new knowledge.

> For a brief discussion of two important goals of business firms, see Supplement 2A: "Profit and Social Responsibility."

Test of a goal

Note that in our definition of goals behavior *is* directed toward desired results. Simply identifying a desired result as a "goal" does not make it a goal. Our view is that the test of a goal is its real impact on organizational policies, structure, operations, and, in general, on the behavior of people. You might ask, "Aren't some goals simply statements of desired results or desired future states of affairs?" This question can be answered by distinguishing between stated and real goals.[2]

Stated and real goals

Stated or *official* goals are simply statements about desired results. Such statements are found in a variety of places—in corporate charters, on posters in the lobby of a business office, and in the public pronouncements of organization leaders. *Real* or *operative* goals are behaviorally supported goals. Our definition of goals is consistent with the terms "real" and "operative" goals. How can this distinction be useful to you in managing?

Differences between stated and real goals

In actual work environments, you may find that stated and real goals are almost identical. In other words, behavior *is* directed toward results which were *said to be* desired. However, you may also find work environments in which there is a major difference between stated and real goals. A business firm may say it wants to sell a high-quality product (stated goal), but if it does not adequately finance a quality-control operation, its goal cannot be said to be selling a high-quality product. A political administration may say it wants to have an "open" administration (one in which there is a free flow of communication and a receptiveness to different viewpoints). However, it may actually follow policies that restrict communication and reject ideas.

Analyzing differences

Why might there be differences between stated and real goals? It could be because the stated goals are too difficult or because certain key personnel are not committed to them. Stated goals are sometimes just public relations gimmicks. Stated goals may be

---

[2] Amitai Etzioni, "The Organization Goal: Master or Servant," in *Modern Organizations* (Englewood Cliffs, N.J.: Prentice-Hall, 1964), p. 7. A similar distinction is that between "official" and "operative" goals: See Charles Perrow, *Organizational Analysis: A Sociological View* (Belmont, Calif.: Wadsworth Publishing Company, 1970).

outdated in a changing environment. Skill in analyzing these and other reasons for stated and real goal variance is a useful skill for helping managers meet their accountability for performance.

Motives are
inner states

Goals and Motives.   A "motive" is an inner state (that is, it is internal to a person) that activates and directs behavior toward goals. Goals and motives are related, but different, concepts. The distinction between goals and motives can be useful to you as a manager.

One goal can
satisfy several
motives

In the first place, a single goal can satisfy a variety of motives. (See Figure 2–1A.) The goal of getting a college education can satisfy motives of achievement, affiliation, security, and personal development. The goal of producing 500 subassemblies can satisfy motives of achievement, self-esteem, recognition, and job security.

FIGURE 2–1
Goals and Motives

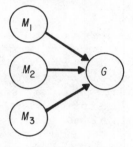

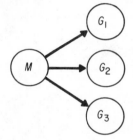

A. A single goal can satisfy
a variety of alternative
or complementary motives

B. A single motive can
activate and direct
behavior toward a
variety of alternative
or complementary goals

One motive
can serve
several goals

In the second place, a single motive can activate and direct behavior toward a variety of goals. (See Figure 2–1B.) For example, it is one thing to know that your employees have high-achievement motives, but it is another to know what kind of goals will satisfy those motives. Some may fulfill their need for achievement by producing more, whereas others may fulfill their need by producing higher-quality products. Still others will seek off-the-job opportunities for achievement.

Common
terms

Group and Organizational Goals.   It is common in managerial education and practice to refer to "group" and "organizational" goals. We use these terms throughout this book, but here we want to make three observations about them.

*Only
individuals
have goals*

First, in a literal sense, only individuals have goals. Only individuals can engage in the directed, purposive behavior that is necessary for goal achievement. The motives that activate and direct behavior toward goals are in individuals only; the satisfaction that comes from achievement is internal to individuals. "It is the individual who possesses values, makes choices, and, if given the freedom, takes actions."[3] We are arguing here that it is not *literally* correct to associate the term "goal" with groups, organizations, nations, and so on. We cannot, (should not) refer to these social entities as if they are living things capable of having goals and being satisfied by achievement.

*How are the
terms used?*

Second, the fact is, however, that the terms "group" and "organizational" goals are widely used. The terms are intuitively acceptable and are part of managerial vocabulary. How are they used in managerial education and practice? In general, they refer to goals the individuals in groups and organizations agree on (in varying degrees) as guides to their behavior.[4] An organizational goal of a business firm may be to earn a 20 percent rate of return on its total invested capital. This goal *may* guide the behavior of employees throughout the firm, even though it actually represents results directly sought only by top management and stockholders. Or, five students may share the goal of having a party. This goal *may* guide the behavior of the five students because the party is a result desired by each student individually.

*The derived
nature of
group goals*

Third, group and organizational goals are necessarily derived from individual goals. The derived nature of these goals is a useful point for managers to keep in mind. Why? For one reason, it is easy to think that once a group or organizational goal has been stated, all individuals are committed to it. In fact, there almost always will be wide variance in commitment because the group or organizational goal is not equally relevant to the personal goals of the individuals. Reflection on the derived nature of goals should help managers think of the relationship between individual and organizational goals. Further, group or organization goals do not, and cannot, fully account for all the goals, interests, and motives of individuals.

*Changes in
internal
environment*

Goal Changes. Goals in organizations are in a continuous process of change. This process is required by changes in the internal and external environment of the organization. One of the major internal environmental changes is personnel turnover. As new people enter an organization, they will have an impact on the

[3] Richard B. McKenzie and Gordon Tullock, *The New World of Economics: Explorations into the Human Experience* (Homewood, Ill.: Richard D. Irwin, 1975), p. 7.

[4] One widely-quoted definition of organizational goal is "the constraint sets and criteria of search that define roles at the upper levels" of a business firm. See Herbert A. Simon, "On the Concept of Organizational Goal," *Administrative Science Quarterly*, vol. 9, no. 1 (June 1964).

goals selected for attention. Another major internal environmental change is the new information obtained as people acquire experience in attempting to achieve goals. This experience may suggest radical change in the specific goals or in the priorities assigned to goals.

Changes in external environment

An organization's external environment—customers, suppliers, consumer groups, community-interest groups, and so on—can also put pressure on organizations to change their goals. For example, significant changes in their operating environment are forcing retailers to change their goals and strategies. Slower population growth, specialty and narrow-focus apparel stores, the emergence of more career women, the growing "singles market, and family formation at a later age are operating environment changes that are moving department stores toward goals and strategies of market penetration and away from being 'all things to all customers.' "[5]

Goal displacement or means-ends inversion

Changes in goals can reflect normal operating responses to changes in the internal and external environment of the organization. However, two relatively nonroutine types of changes are "goal displacement" and "goal succession." Goal displacement occurs when the means that are being used to achieve goals become, in fact, the real goals. Thus, what were the real goals become only stated goals. This means-ends inversion[6] runs counter to the original goals, may be intentional or unintentional, and is usually not publicly announced, for obvious reasons.

Examples

An example of goal displacement is when an athletic program disproportionately dominates the total environment of a university instead of being simply one, among many, means of creating a total university environment. Another example of goal displacement is when a government agency engages in activities that are directed only to the survival of the agency rather than to some socially desirable result.

Goal succession

Goal succession occurs when new goals are adopted that add to or replace old goals but which are consistent with the old goals. The most common example cited is that of the National Foundation for Infantile Paralysis changing its goal in the 1950s from the treatment of poliomyelitis to the reduction and treatment of birth defects and arthritis. This change became necessary because of the discovery of vaccines which provided immunization against polio. If the Foundation were to survive and continue to be useful to society, it had to find another worthy goal, one consistent with its original health-related mission. To some degree, all organizations

---

[5] "Department Stores Redefine Their Role," *Business Week,* December 13, 1976, p. 47–48.

[6] Lyman W. Porter, Edward E. Lawler III, and J. Richard Hackman, *Behavior in Organizations* (New York: McGraw-Hill Book Company, 1975), p. 85.

must engage in the goal-succession process, "but not all of them will do this fast enough or in a way that will ensure continued viability of the organization."[7]

Summary box

> There is no idea more important to managing than goals. We consider goals to be *the* strategic managing variable. Nevertheless, managers do not always give goals the attention they deserve.
>
> *Goals* are desired results toward which behavior is directed. *Stated* goals and *real* goals are not necessarily the same. The *test* of a real goal is its impact on organizational policies, structure, operations and, in general, on the actual behavior of people.
>
> *Motives* are the inner states that activate and direct a person's behavior. A single goal can satisfy a variety of motives; a single motive can direct behavior toward a variety of goals.
>
> In a literal sense, only individuals can have goals; groups and organizations cannot. However, in the sense that collections of individuals can agree on and be guided by goals, it is reasonable to use the phrases "group goals" and "organizational goals." *Group and organizational* goals are derived from individual goals.
>
> Goals change continuously. They are not static and inflexible guides to behavior. Rather, organizational goals are dynamic guides that respond to changes in both the internal and external environment.
>
> *Goal displacement* is a type of goal change in which there is a *means-ends inversion* that runs counter to an organization's stated goal. *Goal succession* occurs when new goals are adopted that add to or replace old goals, but which are consistent with the old goals.

GOALS: USES AND OVEREMPHASIS

Practical question

Simply stating goals does not guarantee they will make any contribution to effective managing. All the benefits of goals derives from their influence on behavior. If the influence is minor, then the benefits will be minor. Goals do not automatically contribute to managerial effectiveness. Managers must make goals serve their uses. The uses of goals are stated below. The practical question for a manager is: Are goals *actually* serving these uses in my area of managerial accountability?

---

[7] Ibid., p. 87.

Motivate and focus attention

Targets.   One potential use of goals is as targets for behavior. As targets, goals provide motivation and focus attention. For example, one well-known electronics firm set a goal of $1 billion in sales, to be reached in six years. This goal served as a target for operations in the firm and was the foundation for plans and strategies. The existence of the goal, set by top management, contributed to bringing about the behavior necessary to achieve the goal. Targets do more than provide direction for behavior. They also provide an incentive to do what is necessary to reach the target. This, of course, assumes that the people involved have a need for goal achievement.

Appraisal against standards

Standards.   Goals provide standards against which performance can be measured. Your performance as a manager and the performance of your employees will be appraised in terms of goal accomplishment. Your employees will evaluate you in terms of the help you give them in accomplishing their work-related goals. The company you work in will be judged by the community according to how well it fulfills its role as a responsible citizen in the community. As standards against which to measure performance, goals serve an important purpose in the manager's efforts to be accountable for performance. Goals, as standards, provide the primary basis for evaluating overall managerial and organizational effectiveness.

Basis for evaluating change

Evaluating Change.   Goals also serve as a basis for evaluating change. Change in business is continuous and pervasive. Nevertheless, a proposed change in business performance is desirable or not, depending on its relationship to goals. A proposed change can also suggest that goals should be changed and activities redirected toward new goals. For example, suppose it is being proposed that a petroleum products business firm enter the newspaper publishing business. A decision about this proposal involves, among other things, an analysis of the impact of the new business on the present goals of the firm and an appraisal of the desirability of new goals.

Foundation of planning and controlling

Plans and Controls.   Goals are the foundation of the planning and controlling functions of managers. The essence of planning is determining the "what–where–when–how–who" of achieving goals. The essence of controlling is assuring that performance contributes to desired results. If a hospital has a goal of servicing emergency-room patients within ten minutes, then specific plans and controls must be used to assure that the goal will be achieved. Managerial planning and controlling are impossible without goals, and both of these functions are essential to efficient and effective managing.

Over-commitment

Goal Overemphasis.   Although they can serve an important role in managing, goals can be *over*emphasized. We will discuss three ways in which this overemphasis occurs. First, it is possible for managers to be overcommitted to a particular goal or set of goals. This overcommitment may result in failing to achieve some goals because all the effort and resources are directed toward one particular goal. For example, the personal-development goals of employees may lose out in a big push for higher production. Overcommitment can also blind managers to the need for new goals that are more relevant to current conditions. One suggestion for avoiding overcommitment to specific goals is to establish processes that will assure that goals are continually reevaluated.

Goals partially explain behavior

A second way in which goals can be overemphasized is to expect too much from them. For example, the behavior of individuals cannot be fully understood in terms of their goals. Could you understand your own behavior solely by reference to your goals? Although the thoughts and actions of an individual may partially reflect goals, behavior is not fully determined by goals. Understanding behavior involves not only an understanding of goals, but also of perceptions, attitudes, motives, environmental conditions, and many other variables.

Goal model, systems model

In a similar way, groups and organizations cannot be understood solely in terms of goal-directed behavior. Such a "goal model" view of organizations can be contrasted with a "systems model" view. "The system model explicitly recognizes that the organization solves certain problems other than those directly involved in the achievement of a goal, and that excessive concern with the latter may result in insufficient attention to other necessary organizational activities."[8] In other words, people in organizations devote time to normal routines and habitual activities that, although important, do not involve conscious goal-seeking behavior.[9] (We have more to say about the systems model later in the book.)

All goals cannot be achieved

Finally, even the most successful people and organizations do not accomplish all their goals, all the time, to every "stakeholder's" satisfaction.[10] If Jimmy Carter had lost the election, then it could be said that he failed to achieve his goal; it was a win-or-lose situation. However, such situations are seldom characteristic of managing. Managing is more like "win-some, lose-some" situations. An organization is not ineffective if it does not achieve all of its goals. It is in this sense that one can say that "most organizations most of the time do not attain their goals in any final sense. . . . Low effectiveness is a general characteristic of organizations."[11]

---

[8] Etzioni, *Modern Organizations*, p. 17.

[9] Porter, Lawler, and Hackman, *Behavior in Organizations*, p. 79.

[10] George F. Wieland and Robert A. Ullrich, *Organizations: Behavior, Design, and Change* (Homewood, Ill.: Richard D. Irwin, 1976), p. 109. Stakeholders are "those groups of individuals which have a legitimate interest in determining the behavior of" organizations.

[11] Etzioni, *Modern Organizations*, p. 16.

CRITERIA GOALS SHOULD MEET

Five criteria

The final result of the goal-setting process should be goals that are measurable, attainable, acceptable, congruent, and compared against alternatives.

Appropriate degree of precision

Measurable. Goals should be measurable. It is difficult to know when a goal has been accomplished if there is no way to measure the goal. Although it is often difficult to measure precise progress toward goal accomplishment, there is a degree of precision appropriate to every goal. Goals should not be selected *because* they can be measured precisely. They should be selected because of their suitability to the situation and then should be stated with the appropriate degree of precision. A humorous example of trying to impose more precision than warranted is shown in Figure 2–2.

Quantity, quality, time, and cost

Goals can be measured in terms of four dimensions: quantity; quality; time; and cost. For example, suppose that a business firm states that its goal is "customer service." Some legitimate questions about this goal might be: How much service and what type? What quality of service will be provided? At what cost to the customer? When and how frequently will the service be available?

Precision is not an end in itself

Although measurement is important, one goal is not better than another simply because it has a higher degree of precision. Some trivial goals may be measured with a high degree of precision; some worthwhile goals may be difficult to measure. It is important to mention this because goals that are precisely set and measurable tend to be more powerful competitors for the time of those who are responsible for achieving them.

Reach versus realism

Attainable. Although a certain amount of reach or stretch should be built into goals, they should be realistic enough so that achievement is practical. Goals that are too difficult may lead to frustration for those who try to achieve them. Goals that are too easy may fail to provide the satisfaction that comes from successfully achieving a difficult goal.

Goal difficulty studies

"Goal difficulty" is related to motivation by having an impact on the level of effort expended by a person. "The harder the goal, the more effort the individual knows he must exert to attain the goal."[12] This would tend to be true when attaining the goal is a desired outcome for the person involved.[13] Other goal-setting studies suggest "that when goals for high performance are set, performance in-

---

[12] James R. Terborg, "The Motivational Components of Goal Setting," *Journal of Applied Psychology,* vol. 61, no. 5 (October 1976), p. 619.

[13] R. D. Pritchard and M. I. Curtis, "The Influence of Goal Setting and Financial Incentives on Task Performance," *Organizational Behavior and Human Performance,* vol. 10 (1973), pp. 175–83.

FIGURE 2–2
An Example of Forcing Too Much Precision*

Dear Mr. Jefferson:

We have read your 'Declaration of Independence' with great interest. Certainly, it represents a considerable undertaking, and many of your statements do merit serious consideration. Unfortunately, the Declaration as a whole fails to meet recently adopted specifications for proposals to the Crown, so we must return the document to you for further refinement. The questions which follow might assist you in your process of revision:

1. In your opening paragraph you use the phrase 'the Laws of Nature and Nature's God.' What are these laws? In what way are they the criteria on which you base your central arguments? Please document with citations from the recent literature.

2. In the same paragraph you refer to the 'opinions of mankind.' Whose polling data are you using? Without specific evidence, it seems to us, the 'opinions of mankind' are a matter of opinion.

3. You hold certain truths to be 'self-evident.' Could you please elaborate. If they are as evident as you claim, then it should not be difficult for you to locate the appropriate supporting statistics.

4. 'Life, liberty, and the pursuit of happiness' seem to be the goals of your proposal. These are not measurable goals. If you were to say that 'among these is the ability to sustain an average life expectancy in six of the 13 colonies of at least 55 years, and to enable newspapers in the colonies to print news without outside interference, and to raise the average income of the colonists by 10 percent in the next 10 years,' these could be measureable goals. Please clarify.

5. You state that 'Whenever any Form of Government becomes destructive of these ends, it is the Right of the People to alter or to abolish it, and to institute a new Government . . . .' Have you weighed this assertion against all the alternatives? What are the trade-off considerations?

6. Your description of the existing situation is quite extensive. Such a long list of grievances should precede the statement of goals, not follow it. Your problem statement needs improvement.

7. Your strategy for achieving your goal is not developed at all. You state that the colonies 'ought to be Free and Independent States,' and that they are 'Absolved from All Allegiance to the British Crown.' Who or what must change to achieve this objective? In what way must they change? What specific steps will you take to overcome the resistance? How long will it take? We have found that a little foresight in these areas helps to prevent careless errors later on. How cost-effective are your strategies?

8. Who among the list of signatories will be responsible for implementing your strategy? Who conceived it? Who provided the theoretical research? Who will constitute the advisory committee? Please submit an organization chart and vitas of the principal investigators.

9. You must include an evaluation design. We have been requiring this since Queen Anne's War.

10. What impact will your problem have? Your failure to include any assessment of this inspires little confidence in the long-range prospects of your undertaking.

11. Please submit a PERT diagram, an activity chart, itemized budget, and manpower utilization matrix.

We hope that these comments prove useful in revising your 'Declaration of Independence.' We welcome the submission of your revised proposal. Our due date for unsolicited proposals is July 31, 1776. Ten copies with original signatures will be required.

Signed: *Management Analyst to the British Crown*

* Source: Unknown.

creases as goal difficulty increases, provided the goal is *specific and accepted by the individual* [emphasis added]."[14]

Role of individual differences

It is interesting to note that level of goal difficulty is somewhat a matter of perception and can depend on personality, experience, and other individual differences. For example, "Hard goals are more likely to be perceived as challenging rather than impossible if the employee has a high degree of self-assurance and has previously had more successes in goal attainment than failures."[15] Finally, one study of 133 first-line supervisors found a significant and positive relationship between goal difficulty, job satisfaction, and job involvement.[16]

Target dates, subgoals

Goals should be attainable in a specified time period; target dates should be set. In order to make goals more attainable, they can be broken down or divided into subgoals. In terms of the psychology of behavior, people are more likely to accomplish long-term goals if they can see, and are rewarded for, subgoals that represent progress toward the long-term goal. Accomplishing subgoals provides an incentive for additional goal accomplishment

Factors affecting goal acceptance

Acceptable. Goals should be accepted by those who are expected to achieve them. How is goal acceptance obtained? To that question there is no single, definite answer. Whether or not goals will be accepted can depend on the manner in which the goals were set, the perceived importance and reasonableness of the goal, the perceived relationship between achieving the goal and receiving desirable outcomes,[17] the expectations of those who are involved with the goals, and so on. In other words, there is no simple key to goal acceptance.

Participation and acceptance

One way of trying to obtain goal acceptance is to involve employees and other interested personnel in the goal-setting process. Participative goal setting is time-consuming, may not always be practical, and may not always lead to higher levels of goal acceptance. For example, employees ". . . with an authoritarian orientation and low need for independence react positively where little participation is used."[18] However, greater acceptance *can* result

[14] Manuel London and Greg Oldham, "Effects of Varying Goal Types and Incentive Systems on Performance and Satisfaction," *Academy of Management Journal,* vol. 19, no. 4 (December 1976), p. 537.

[15] Gary P. Latham and Gary A. Yukl, "A Review of Research on the Application of Goal Setting in Organizations," *Academy of Management Journal,* vol. 18, no. 4 (December 1975), p. 835.

[16] Richard M. Steers, "Factors Affecting Job Attitudes in a Goal-Setting Environment," *Academy of Management Journal,* vol. 19, no. 1 (March 1976), p. 11.

[17] Latham and Yukl, "A Review of Research on the Application of Goal Setting in Organizations," p. 835.

[18] Arlyn J. Melcher, "Participation: A Critical Review of Research Findings," *Human Resource Management,* vol. 15, no. 1 (Spring 1976), p. 20. For a study that found no relationship between the need for independence

from participative goal setting if those involved in the process place value on participation. Further, by investing some of their own time and thought in goals, employees can view the goals as their own and, ". . . in our culture most people seem to be more ready to believe and act on ideas they regard as their own, than on the recommendations or commands of others."[19]

Conflict versus congruence

Congruent. Goals should be congruent. That is, the specific goals that compose a manager's system of goals should be compatible with each other. They should support each other and not be in direct conflict. Conflict may result from the failure to define goals precisely enough in terms of quantity, quality, time, and costs.

Conflict is inevitable

A certain amount of conflict between goals in organizations is inevitable because the interests and goals of all an organization's members are not perfectly identical or compatible. For example, the wage goals of employees are, to some extent, in conflict with the profit goals of owners. Even the goals of the professional managers of a firm can be in conflict with the owner's goals. The desire of top executives to be free to manage their organizations may be partially in conflict with society's desire to regulate organizations through laws. Most complex organizations are pursuing so many different systems of goals that it would be unreasonable to expect that they could all be in harmony with each other.

Limited span of attention

Additionally, a degree of conflict between goals inevitably arises because of the inability of organizational leaders to keep track of all the goals at one time. It simply is not possible, because of the limited span of human attention, to know all the goals being pursued at any one time. Thus, it is very likely, in organizations, that two or more goals which are in conflict with each other, will be pursued simultaneously. In spite of the inevitability of some goal conflict, however, congruence is a criterion that should characterize goals to the degree that is possible and practical.

Internal and external congruence

A distinction between "internal" and "external" goal congruence is useful. Internal congruence refers to the compatibility of the system of goals (personal, group, performance) *within* the manager's immediate area of accountability. External congruence refers to the compatibility of the manager's goal system with those of *other parties* in the organization. For example, suppose that you manage a department of 15 employees. The goals that directly apply to the 15 employees and yourself must be consistent (internal congruence). They should also be consistent with the goals of other departments in the organization (external congruence).

and participation in goal setting, see Gary P. Latham and Gary A. Yukl, "Effects of Assigned and Participative Goal Setting on Performance and Job Satisfaction," *Journal of Applied Psychology,* vol. 61, no. 2 (April 1976), pp. 166–71.

[19] David A. Emery, *The Compleat Manager* (New York: McGraw-Hill Book Company, 1970), p. 37.

Tradeoffs,
opportunity
costs

Compared with Alternatives. The choice of one goal implies fore-going other goals. "Tradeoffs" are required and "opportunity costs" are incurred. Opportunity costs are the costs (which can be measured in time and effort, for example, as well as in dollars) of opportunities lost because of selecting a specific goal. For example, a business firm that adopts a one-product and fixed-price strategy reduces its flexibility to adapt to a change in the market environment. This reduced flexibility is an opportunity cost, or tradeoff, accepted in order to achieve the advantage of the chosen strategy.

State the
goals not
selected

The point is, "the concept of goals implies aims foregone as well as those which are sought."[20] In selecting goals you need to be sensitive to the tradeoffs involved. It may be useful to actually state, in explicit terms, those goals which are *not* being selected. Such a practice may assure a more careful comparison of alternatives.

Useful
technique

Opportunity-cost analysis can be extremely complex and time-consuming. However, the most informal examination of alternative goals can yield crucially important results. Opportunity-cost analysis can be one of the most generally useful techniques you can use in managing.

Summary box

> All of the benefits of goals to managing are only potential benefits. One of the manager's tasks is to make goals realize their potentialities. All the benefits of goals derive from their influence on job behavior.
>
> *Potential uses* of goals are as targets, standards, a base for evaluating changes, and a foundation for planning and controlling.
>
> In spite of their strategic role in managing, goals can be *overemphasized*. Managers can become too committed to a set of goals. Goals cannot be used to explain all behavior in an organization because some behavior is not consciously purposive or goal-seeking.
>
> Organizations should not be judged too harshly just because they do not achieve all their goals. In your own approach to managing, give a strategic role to goals but do not consider them the only important variable.
>
> *Five criteria* that goals should meet are: (1) measurable; (2) attainable; (3) acceptable; (4) congruent; and (5) compared with alternatives. These criteria serve to make goals more operational and thus help assure that they will provide meaningful direction for behavior in your area of accountability.

---

[20] Perrow, *Organizational Analysis*, p. 133.

THE MANAGER'S GOAL SYSTEM

Multiple goals

The situation facing most managers is one of responsibility for achieving multiple goals at a satisfactory level. It is seldom the case that a management situation has only one relevant goal, although particular goals may rank higher in importance and intensity than others. For example, even though business managers may be evaluated primarily in terms of profitability criteria, they are also accountable for accomplishing goals in other areas—such as employee turnover, absenteeism, training, job attitudes, and customer relations. Further, there are times when improving job attitudes may be more important than immediate improvement in profitability. Reducing absenteeism may be a manager's major concern *at a particular time.*

Interacting goals

The multiple goals that managers are responsible for achieving interact with and influence each other. At times, the various goals may seem incompatible with each other. For example, progress toward greater productivity may conflict with higher quality: That is, in their efforts to increase the quantity of output, employees may become less concerned about the quality of their output. Or, an emphasis on higher productivity may mean lower levels of job satisfaction for employees. Our point is that managers' goals are not only *multiple*, but they are also *interacting*.

Goal system

The term "system" connotes the idea of a set of interacting and interdependent elements. Therefore, we will use the term "goal system" to refer to the set of multiple goals for which a manager is responsible. Specifically, what are these goals? We answer that question by identifying three *types of goals* with which every manager must be concerned: performance goals, group goals, and individual goals. The idea of these goals as a goal system is shown in Figure 2–3.

FIGURE 2–3
A Manager's Goal System

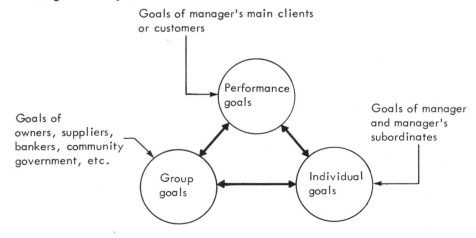

Main rationale for individual jobs

Performance Goals. "Performance goals" are the goals that justify or explain the reason for creating and continuing jobs. The performance of a dishwasher in a restaurant is measured by the quantity, quality, time, and expense of washing dishes. If you are the supervisor of the dishwasher, you are accountable for the quantity, quality, time, and expense of the dishwasher's job performance. Presumably, the dishwasher's performance will be better because of your supervision, and it is this improved performance that justifies your continued presence on the payroll. Performance goals are the main rationale for jobs.

Main rationale for organizational units

Suppose you are managing the personnel department of a large business firm. Your performance goals are the results the firm seeks from the personnel department. These results will have to be identified for each major performance area in the personnel department. These areas may include recruitment, selection, training and development, organizational planning and development, compensation, labor relations, affirmative action, public relations, and so on. The goals set for these performance areas are the main rationale for the existence of the personnel department. Similar goals constitute the rationale for other units (sections, departments, divisions) within the firm.

Main rationale for organizations

Let's move our level of thinking from jobs and departments to organizations. Performance goals are also the main rationale for organizations. The continued existence of business firms, for example, depends on their ability to meet their customers' expectations in terms of the quantity, quality, time, and cost dimensions of economic products and services. Customers want these products and services *when* they want them and at a *price* they are willing to pay, given their *quantity* and *quality* needs. This line of reasoning does not apply only to business firms. Every type of organization has customers or clients. Performance goals dealing with the needs of these clients are the main rationale for organizations of all types.

Drucker's key result areas

One popular and broad view of the areas in which a business firm must set performance goals is suggested by Peter F. Drucker. He considers that the survival of a business depends on performance in eight "key result areas": marketing; innovation; human organization; financial resources; physical resources; productivity; social responsibility; and profit requirements. Drucker argues that the specific goals set in any one of these key result areas will vary from one business firm to another. However, the key result areas are common to all business firms because "all businesses depend on the same factors for their survival"[21]

---

[21] Peter F. Drucker, *Management: Tasks, Responsibilities, Practices* (New York: Harper and Row, Publishers, 1974), pp. 100–101.

Two
exceptions

Group Goals. We include in this category the goals of groups with which the manager's area of accountability must interact, with two exceptions: (1) the manager's main clients or customers; and (2) the manager and the manager's subordinates. The goals of the manager's main clients we call "performance goals"; the goals of the manager and the manager's subordinates we call "individual goals."

Examples of
group goals

"Group goals" include the goals of groups inside and outside the organization. For example, in business firms, earning a competitive rate of return on investment is a goal of the *owners*. Receiving prompt payment of invoices is a goal of the firm's *suppliers*. *Communities* expect the firm to contribute to the general community welfare. *Banks* expect the business firm to pay interest on loans. *Government agencies* expect (or insist on) active cooperation with government regulations and with programs that are receiving popular support. All these groups, and others, have expectations of a business firm's performance, and these expectations must be met. They are group goals of the firm. They must be achieved in a satisfactory manner, just like the firm's performance goals and the goals of its individual employees.

Private
individual
goals

Individual Goals. Managers and their subordinates have "personal," or "individual goals." Some of these goals may not be explicitly formulated or consciously stated. Nevertheless, individuals do direct their behavior toward certain desired results; thus, they have goals. Some of these goals are private, or not job-related. For example, goals for spiritual, intellectual, and social development may be goals that individuals do not seek to achieve while at work or in an organizational setting.

Job-related
individual
goals

For some employees, job-related individual goals include: financial progress and security; career advancement and development; job satisfaction and achievement; opportunities for creative and challenging work; and the opportunity for congenial social relations. For other employees, job-related individual goals include: job security with minimum performance; the opportunity to do a job that requires no initiative, challenge, or change; and a work environment that makes no demands or requests that they "get involved." Still other employees, including managers, have some combination of these goals even though they appear to be contradictory. During the work life of any particular employee, job-related goals can and do change radically. In Part Two of this book, we will have much more to say about individual goals and motives. However, one interesting issue that is useful to discuss here is the issue of individual versus organizational goals.

Summary box

> Managers are accountable for the efficient and effective accomplishment of a *system* of *performance, group,* and *individual* goals.
>
> Performance goals are the *main rationale* for jobs and organizations. Nevertheless, over time, the entire system of goals must be achieved in a satisfactory manner.

INDIVIDUAL "VERSUS" ORGANIZATIONAL GOALS

Integrating goals

The individual "versus" organizational goals issue is concerned with the nature of the result when individual employees try to integrate or harmonize their individual goals with those of the organization in which they work. For example, how can the desire of some employees for jobs that are meaningful and creative be integrated with the organization's need for repetitive and standardized behavior? How can the employee's desire for more fringe benefits be harmonized with the owner's desire for greater profits?

Three possibilities

For purposes of our discussion, we argue that attempts to integrate individual and organizational goals can result in: no conflict; destructive conflict; or workable conflict and cooperation. The basic issue is diagrammed in Figure 2–4.

FIGURE 2–4
Results of Attempts to Integrate Individual and
Organizational Goals

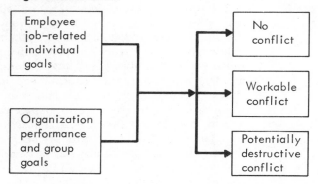

Early management theory

No Conflict. The argument that there is not, or need not be, a conflict between individual and organizational goals is an argument characteristic of early management theory. In general, this theory holds that conflict between individual and organizational goals is a temporary deviation from a normal state of harmony—a state that should exist if management has done a good job of organization design and of creating a cooperative spirit within the organization. Needless to say, this state of harmony does not always exist.

There may be no conflict

For some people in work organizations, there actually is no conflict between individual and organizational goals. It is possible to so match your own goals with those of the organization in which you work that no meaningful distinction can be drawn between the two. In such cases, all goals are job-related, and achieving individual goals is the same as achieving organizational goals. This uncommon situation is undoubtedly more characteristic of top executives than of managers and employees at lower levels of the organization.

Three points

Destructive Conflict.   The argument that individual and organizational goal conflict can be destructive is based on these three points:[22]

Developmental trends

1. Human beings in American culture share certain basic developmental trends as they move from infancy to maturity. Such trends include developing from being passive to being active, from being dependent to being relatively independent, from having a short-time perspective to having a longer-time perspective, and from having limited behavioral responses to having a varied behavioral repertoire.

Organization interference

2. On the other hand certain types of organizations tend to interfere with these developmental trends through such devices as rules, policies, authority relationships, controls, and close supervision.

Coping with conflict

3. The incongruence between the needs of a mature person and the requirements of formal organization lead to frustration, failure, and conflict for the employee. In order to cope with this conflict, employees adapt to it in several ways. Some employees simply leave the organization and attempt to find one more agreeable to their personality needs. Others work to move up the organizational ladder, assuming that higher-level jobs are less restrictive of mature behavior. Still others increase their absenteeism, decrease their productivity, become apathetic, and withdraw from active involvement in the affairs of the organization. In a few cases, employees cope with conflict by overt acts of sabotage and violence.

Central life interest

One of the factors that may influence the degree of conflict between individual goals and the goals of the organization is the extent to which employees view their work as a central life interest.

[22] The argument in this section is based primarily on the views of Chris Argyris, "Personal vs. Organizational Goals," in Robert Dubin, *Human Relations in Administration*, 3d ed. (Englewood Cliffs, N.J.: Prentice-Hall, 1968), pp. 80–89. For a full discussion of Argyris's views, see his *Integrating the Individual and the Organization* (New York: John Wiley & Sons, 1964).

"Work, for probably a majority of workers, and even extending into the ranks of management, may represent an institutional setting that is not a central life interest for its participants." In other words, if work were to represent the main vehicle through which individuals achieve their goals, then the worker would rebel against the tyranny of organizational controls and restrictions. However, if the worker considers work "only a necessary part of his round of life, but not central to his interests,"[23] he will be relatively indifferent to the various forms of control by the organization.

For some, work is less important

Some changes may be occurring in the importance people attach to work as one of their life interests. Some argue that work is becoming less important as a central life interest to millions of workers. Reasons often cited for this include more off-the-job time in which to pursue fulfilling activities, the failure of jobs to meet rising expectations of employees, and increased awareness of and opportunities for other types of need-fulfilling activities.

For others, work is becoming more important

However, for others, work may be becoming more, rather than less, of a central life interest. Many organizations are successfully redesigning jobs to allow employees more self-control, provide them with meaningful responsibilities and opportunities for personal growth and development, and to enable them to work toward goals and on projects that they consider worthwhile. We need to recognize that the status of work may be shifting from what it was 20 years ago. We should, however, avoid generalizations about the direction or intensity of this shift.

A basic congruence

Workable Conflict and Cooperation.   Individuals and organizations need each other! Organizations are collections of individuals, and the organizational goals *derive from* the goals of individuals. Therefore, there is, on one hand, a basic congruence between the goals of particular individuals and the goals of the organization. There are times when this congruence is minimal. There are other times when this congruence reaches maximum proportions. Mostly, the degree of congruence is sufficient for the organization's survival and growth.

A basic incongruence

There is, on the other hand, a basic incongruence between the goals of particular individuals and the goals of the organization in which they work. Inevitably, there will be times when individual goals must be sacrificed to those of the organization. This basic incongruence is the foundation for conflict between individuals and the organization. Once again, however, most of the time the degree of conflict is not enough to threaten or damage the organization's survival and growth. It is from the mutual need for each other that individuals and organizations are able to coexist in a state of workable conflict and cooperation. It is because of this mutual need that

---

[23] Robert Dubin, "Person and Organization," in Dubin, *Human Relations in Administration,* pp. 90, 91.

individuals recognize the need to give as well as to receive from organizations. Organizations do the same.

Summary box

> The individual "versus" organizational goals issue is concerned with the nature of the result when individual employees try to *integrate* or harmonize their individual goals with those of the organization in which they work. We discussed *three possible results:* no conflict, destructive conflict, and workable conflict and cooperation.
>
> Several early management theories suggest that there need be no conflict between individual and organizational goals. When conflict does occur, it is viewed as temporary.
>
> It is possible for the conflict between individual and organizational goals to be destructive. This can be true if organizational rules and controls are incompatible with the needs of mature employees. In such situations, employees cope with the conflict in several ways, including increased absenteeism, withdrawal, lower productivity, and sabotage. The manner and extent of coping may depend on, among other things, the extent to which work is viewed as a central life interest.
>
> It is because individuals and organizations need each other that a workable level of conflict and cooperation characterizes most organizations.

THE GOAL-SETTING PROCESS

A behavioral process

Goal setting is a managerial *responsibility* but not an exclusive managerial *activity*. It is a process that involves the behavior of employees throughout the organization. This behavioral process is not as logical and rational as you might think. It is a give-and-take process that is both logical and illogical, rational and irrational, thought-provoking and emotion-generating. It is, in other words, a *human* process. Three ideas that will help us think about the goal-setting process are: the ends-means chain, imperfect rationality, and coalition formation.

Hierarchy or cascade of goals

The Ends-Means Chain. Goal setting in organizations is a process of translating general statements of organizational purpose into meaningful behavioral guides for people at each level of the organization's structure. The goal-setting process starts with the organization's top management. This group formulates goals applicable to the organization's top level, and these goals provide the basis for goals at the second level. The goals at the second level are the *means* used for achieving the *ends*, or goals set at the top level. This "ends-means chain" continues throughout the organizational structure. The goals at each level are derived, more or less logically, from those of the level above, and they collectively form a hierarchy, or cascade, of goals.

Each goal is also a means to a goal

Thus, "Except for the broadest, most encompassing objective, each goal that develops in an organization can be considered to be both a goal in itself and a *means* of reaching some other goal."[24] Figure 2–5 illustrates the idea of a goal-setting ends–means chain that links goals at the top level with the goals of individual salespeople at the bottom level.

> For a discussion of one widely used goal-setting process see Supplement 2B: "Management by Objectives."

FIGURE 2–5
The Marketing Function Ends–Means Chain

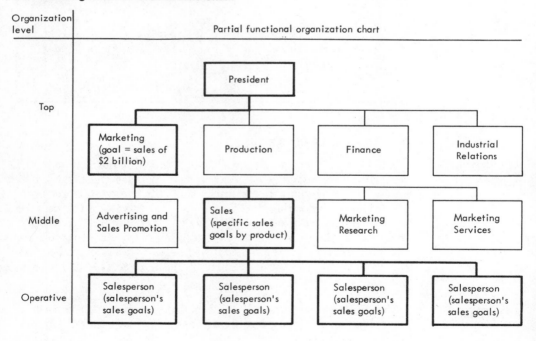

---

[24] Porter, Lawler, and Hackman, *Behavior in Organizations,* p. 83.

Various approaches are used

Most organizations develop their own process for formulating their hierarchy of goals. The process may be so informal and routine that organizational members are hardly aware of it. In other organizations, goal setting is a highly formalized process involving personnel at all levels in meetings, feedback and critique sessions, and paperwork processing. Regardless of the specific process used, organizations should have some process for arriving at a hierarchy of goals.

Conditions for perfect rationality

Imperfect Rationality. We do not want to give the impression that the ends-means chain results in a hierarchy of goals that are related in a perfectly rational way. Perfect rationality is an impossibility in organizational goal setting or in any type of organizational behavior. It would require that those involved in goal setting have full knowledge of opportunities and constraints, have similar goals, and have the capacity and willingness to focus attention on the entire goal-setting process. It is not likely that these conditions can be fully met in any complex organization; most organizations must be satisfied with an imperfectly rationalized goal-setting process.

Goals are compromises

What does it mean to say that the goal-setting process is imperfectly rational? It means that many goals will be compromises. These compromises result from the fact that, when *people* get involved in the ends–means chain, goals must accommodate a variety of needs and motives that are not always in harmony, or congruent with each other.

Incongruence

Complete congruence of all goals in an organization is not possible. For one thing, it may be impossible to resolve even the known goal conflicts among parts of an organization; the organization will then, in effect, pursue, or act as if it is pursuing, conflicting goals. For another thing, it is almost impossible in an organization to observe behavior to the extent that you can know all the goals that are being pursued. People in organizations have a limited attention focus—they cannot see all behavior; they cannot always link particular behavior with specific goals; and they cannot always see that some goal-directed behaviors conflict with each other.

Temporary alliances

Coalition Formation. One of the tactics that individuals in organizations use to increase their influence is "coalition formation."[25] A coalition is a temporary alliance formed by two or more persons for the purpose of promoting a common interest. The coalition enhances the bargaining power or influence of each coalition member—in unity there is strength.

Negotiated consensus

When coalition formation enters into goal setting, the process must accommodate the interests and goals of various individuals

[25] Richard M. Cyert and James G. March, *A Behavioral Theory of the Firm* (Englewood Cliffs, N.J.: Prentice-Hall, 1963), p. 27.

and coalitions. Since the interests of coalitions are seldom identical, goals often represent a negotiated consensus. "Therefore, what we have been calling the objectives of the organizations are, in essence, no more than a negotiated consensus of the individuals who play major roles in the organization's affairs."[26]

Coalitions
are useful

Coalition formation should not be considered a devious way for individuals to thwart organizational purposes and to enhance their own position. Although that may and does happen, coalition formation is a typical and useful part of the goal-setting process. At their best, coalitions are an attempt to combine the influence of several people and channel it toward constructive organizational goals that are integrated with individual goals.

Example of
failure to
establish a
coalition

Effective coalitions can have a major impact on organizational functioning. The failure to establish effective coalitions in organizations can have serious consequences. An illustration of what can happen when an effective coalition fails to materialize follows:

> The "palace revolt," which led to Semon Knudsen's departure from Ford Motor Company, is an illustration of the failure in the formation of a coalition. While it is true that Henry Ford II named Knudsen president of the company, Knudsen's ultimate power as a newcomer to an established power structure depended on forming an alliance. The particular individual with whom an alliance seemed crucial was Lee Iacocca. For some reason, Knudsen and Iacocca competed for power and influence instead of using cooperatively a power base to which both contributed as is the case with most workable coalitions. In the absence of a coalition, the alternative postures of rivalry and battle for control erupted. Ford ultimately responded by weighing his power with one side over the other.[27]

Example of
successful
coalition

In a similar vein, an apparently effective coalition was one between American Motors Corporation's board chairman, Roy D. Chapin, and AMC's former president, William V. Luneburg. For a decade these two helped keep AMC viable by operating as a policy-making and policy-executing team:

> While Chapin is the velvet glove of AMC management, Luneburg is the iron fist. . . . Chapin and Luneburg operate much more as a team than any other pair of top executives in Detroit.[28]

[26] Wieland and Ullrich, *Organizations: Behavior, Design, and Change,* p. 99.

[27] Abraham Zaleznik, "Power and Politics in Organizational Life," *Harvard Business Review,* vol. 48, no. 3 (May–June 1970), p. 52. The Ford Motor Company was subsequently managed by a three-man "Office of the Chief Executive" including Henry Ford II, Lee Iacocca, and Philip Caldwell, with Ford being "first among equals." "A Ford Triumvirate, but Henry's Still the Boss," *Business Week,* May 2, 1977, p. 31.

[28] "Can American Motors Survive Its Huge Losses?" *Business Week,* December 20, 1976, pp. 42–43. Mr. Luneburg retired as president of AMC. On June 1, 1977 Gerald C. Meyers assumed the position and in October Mr. Meyers became AMC's CEO, replacing Mr. Chapin.

Summary box

> The goal setting process in organizations is a complex *human behavioral process*. We viewed the process in terms of an ends–means chain, imperfect rationality, and coalition formation.
>
> Viewing goal setting as an *ends–means chain* conveys the idea that goals at any level of an organization are the means for achieving the goals at the next higher level. This chain links the goals at all organization levels into a hierarchy, or cascade, of goals.
>
> To say that goal setting is *imperfectly rational* means that goals will be compromises and, to some extent, incongruent.
>
> *Coalition formation*—the formation of temporary alliances by two or more persons for the purpose of promoting a common interest—is a typical and useful goal-setting tactic. The failure to form effective coalitions can be detrimental to an organization.
>
> The final result of the goal-setting process is a *negotiated consensus* about goals that will guide the behavior of organization members.

CHECK YOUR UNDERSTANDING

Goal
Test of a goal
Stated goal
Real goal
Motive
Organizational goal
Derived nature of group goals
Goal displacement
Means-ends inversion
Goal succession
Goal uses
Goal model
System model
Goal criteria
Four dimensions for measuring goals

Goal congruence
Internal congruence
External congruence
Tradeoffs
Opportunity costs
Goal system
Performance goals
Group goals
Key result areas
Central life interest
Ends-means chain
Hierarchy of goals
Imperfect rationality
Coalition formation
Negotiated consensus

STUDY QUESTIONS

1. The basic theme of this book is the manager's accountability for performance. What role do you see goals playing in managerial accountability? What role do goals serve in creating an environment for effective job performance?

2. Give an illustration of your own of how a single goal can satisfy a variety of motives. Give an illustration of how a single motive can activate and direct behavior toward a variety of goals.

3. What is your opinion of the author's view that, in a literal sense, only individuals have goals? Many authors take the contrary view, that groups and organizations can have goals. Other writers choose not to make this point. Do you think it is important to emphasize that only individuals have goals? Why, or why not?

4. Suppose that one of your goals is to graduate from college. Evaluate this goal in terms of the five criteria discussed in the text.

5. Explain the statement: "A certain amount of conflict between goals in organizations is inevitable."

6. Identify and explain three ways in which goal overemphasis can occur.

7. What dimensions are important in making goals measurable? Explain: A goal is not "better" because it has a higher degree of precision than some other goal.

8. What is the relationship between goal difficulty, goal acceptance, and job performance?

9. Discuss fully the idea of a manager's goal system consisting of performance, group, and individual goals.

10. Discuss fully the individual versus organizational goals issue, and the possible outcomes.

APPLICATION: COALITION FORMATION*

When Donna saw the nine members of the Batty Batters walk in the door she knew she was in for another one of those nights. Everytime the wild nine won a game they all stopped at the Pizza Palace to celebrate. Unfortunately, the Batty Batters were No. 1 in their softball league.

The problem for Donna is that the girls can never agree on what kind of pizza to order. But they always insist on ordering just one pizza for the entire group.

With vivid memories of their last visit, Donna approached the jammed booth, gave each girl a glass of water, and asked, "May I take your order?" Each girl replied by making two demands"

Ann: Any pizza (except pepperoni) with regular sauce.
Patty: Pepperoni pizza with green peppers.
Carol: Giant thin and crispy pizza.
Dana: Giant pizza with green peppers.
Susan: Thick and chewy pizza with extra spicy sauce.
Mary: Thick and chewy pepperoni pizza.
Marianne: Any pizza with regular sauce and green peppers.

---

* Adapted from Richard M. Cyert and James G. March, *A Behavioral Theory of the Firm,* © 1963, Prentice-Hall, Englewood Cliffs, N.J., p. 31.

Joyce: Pepperoni pizza with extra spicy sauce.
Jana: Giant thin and crispy pizza.

The nine girls agreed that they would order any pizza on which any five of them could agree. After forming their coalitions, they found there were four different pizzas they could order.

1. What are the four?
2. Which of the nine girls is in the best position in terms of coalition formation? That is, which one has the best chance of being in one of the four coalitions?
3. What do you feel this example has to do with goal setting in an organization?

APPLICATION: PERSONAL GOAL SETTING

Goals are viewed in Chapter 2 as *the* strategic managing variable. Our interest in goals derives from their potential contribution to the manager's accountability for performance. However, goals are also important to managers as persons, and personal goal setting can be a useful activity for managers (and nonmanagers); This application offers some suggestions about the process of personal goal setting.

First, affirm the importance of goals. In order for any approach to personal goal setting to be effective, you need to be convinced that a set of personal goals is important to you. You may think that the importance of goals is recognized by everyone. Actually, very few people have consciously determined a set of goals for themselves. It is often estimated that only 5 percent of the general American public have set explicit goals for themselves and have a plan for achieving those goals.

Second, make an inventory of your goals. The purpose here is to identify all goals that are important to you. It may be helpful to:

1. Identify major goal areas. For example, you may want to identify personal goals in each of these areas: financial, social, spiritual, family, physical, professional, life-style, and intellectual.
2. Select from the total list of goals those that you can do something about right now and that are most important to you. For example, select the top ten goals that are most important to you. Then, rank these ten goals in order of their overall importance to you. This selection and ranking of goals is a very difficult but essential part of the personal goal setting process.
3. Check your goals against the following criteria (see Chapter 2): measurable; attainable; acceptable; congruence; and comparison with alternatives.

Third, develop a plan for goal achievement. The idea here is to come up with a systematic approach to attaining your goals. It may be helpful to:

1. Specify specific steps to take daily, weekly, and monthly. Set target dates. Write out your plan and refer to it regularly. Many writers suggest keeping daily records of your progress in carrying out your plan. Identify the obstacles and aids you expect to encounter in achieving your goals. Determine who else will be involved in your goal achievement.

2. Build into your plan specific mechanisms or events that serve to support your personal goal-attainment efforts. For example, some writers suggest affirming to yourself daily the importance of your personal goals. Another mechanism that supports personal goal setting is to visualize the goal as already attained and visualize the rewards you receive as part of the goal attainment.

Finally, stay flexible. There is a risk of becoming obnoxious about attaining goals. Some balance needs to be reached between, on the one hand, a genuine commitment to a set of personal goals, and, on the other hand, a single-mindedness that is blind to aspects of life that are unrelated to goals and to the need to adapt personal goals to changing conditions.

SUPPLEMENT 2A

Profit and Social Responsibility

. . . the only foundation of real business is service.

Henry Ford, Sr.

Profit as a goal

One idea firmly entrenched in the American experience is that business firms exist in order to make as much money as they possibly can. Even those who disagree with American business values and practices often accept implicitly the reasonableness of the profit objective of business firms. If asked, "What is the goal of a business firm?" they are likely to respond, incredulously, "To make money!"

Social responsibility as a goal

Another idea that is gaining acceptance is that business firms must be socially responsible. Sometimes the idea is discussed as if it were opposed to the profit goal of business firms. Thus, the issue becomes conceptualized as profit *versus* responsibility. That is unfortunate because, over the long run, profit and social responsibility are two complementary goals of business firms.

This supplement

The overall purpose of this supplement is to stimulate you to think about the relationship between profitability and social responsibility. To that end, we first discuss several points that are useful for thinking about the role of profits. Second, we identify the social responsibility issue as one of means rather than ends. Third, we discuss two approaches often suggested for meeting social responsibilities.

PROFIT

Seven points

This section discusses seven points about profit that are helpful in understanding its role in business and the relationship between profit and social responsibility.

69

Profit is a
dollar amount

Profit versus Profitability. If American Telephone and Telegraph, one of the country's largest corporations, earned a profit of
$1 in a year, no one would say it was a good year for AT&T. Al-
though $1 represents a profit, it would be considered inadequate
because of the total assets available to AT&T. for the purpose of
generating profit.

Profitability
is a ratio

The idea of profitability relates the absolute amount of profit to
an investment base. Investment may be considered as total assets,
owner's total investment, or any of several other bases. The profitability of a business organization is measured, therefore, in terms
of a ratio of dollar income to dollar investment. It is possible for
the profits of a business firm to be at record levels while profitability is declining or is inadequate. The adequacy or inadequacy
depends on such factors as the type of firm, the availability of
alternative investments, and the overall evaluation of the firm's
long-run prospects. We leave for textbooks in economics the debate
on the question, "How much profitability is enough?"

Estimates
versus actual

Opinions about Profitability. How profitable are business firms?
A recent survey of almost 7,000 of the nation's household heads
revealed that more than one-fourth estimated that profits are 25¢
or more on every sales dollar. When asked what profits out of
every sales dollar *should be,* the median estimate was 13¢. These
figures are interesting, compared to the actual after-tax profits per
dollar of sales—under 6¢.[1] Corporate profit margins have averaged
less than 6 percent for years.[2] Figures like these do not indicate
how much profit business firms should make. Furthermore, the
figures are averages and, as such, hide the rather extraordinary
profit levels of some firms. The figures do, however, reveal that
there is a large difference between the profits corporations make
and the profits people think they make. This difference may account
for much of the heat in the debate over whether profits are too high.

Name of
the game

Profitability Is Essential. There is no tenable argument that
denies the crucial role of profitability in business firms. Profitability is the "name of the game" in business, but it is not the entire game. Whatever else business executives do, they must operate
their firms profitably. This requirement constantly presses on business excutives. Even though managerial accountability is broadening and expanding into new areas, future managers will have one
thing in common with their counterparts of yesterday: responsibility for the bottom line on the profit and loss statement. The
nature of this bottom-line responsibility may be changing, but the
responsibility remains. There is one simple reason for this: profits

---

[1] *1976 Study of American Opinion: Summary Report.* Available from
Marketing Department, *U.S. News & World Report,* 2300 N St., N.W., Washington, D.C., 20037.

[2] "Profits: The Quality Is Higher," *Business Week* (November 15, 1976),
pp. 87–108. Four times a year, *Business Week* publishes a survey of the
financial performance of more than 1,000 corporations.

are ultimately the source of funds for survival and growth of the business firm.

Not the only essential

To say that profitability is essential to business firms is not to say that it is the only essential goal of business firms. It is also essential that a business firm obey laws, pay competitive wages, offer working conditions accepted in the community, pay bills, and provide incentives for managers. In other words, it is essential that a business firm satisfy its entire system of performance, group, and individual goals.

Essential to all types of organizations

The argument that profitability is essential is applicable to all types of organizations. If hospitals, for example, are to survive and grow in an expanding society, they require an excess of income over expenses just as business firms do. Although hospitals may receive their income from gifts, endowments, subsidies, government agencies, and insurance companies, as well as directly from patients, they must operate profitably or else they will not survive. The same is true of universities or other nonprofit organizations. Whatever the source of funds, income must be greater than expenditures in the long run. In this sense, there is no such thing as a nonprofit organization.

Energy income versus outgo

A more general way of stating this point is to say that all organizations, if they are to survive and grow, must take in more "energy" than they expend. Profits represent one form of energy for organizations. Other forms include favorable employee attitudes, public support, customer satisfaction, and new product development. Thus, profit and other forms of energy are essential to *all types* of organizations.

One group goal of the firm

Profitability as a Goal. Profitability is a goal of the business firm's owners. Indirectly, of course, all participants in the firm have an interest in profitability because their goals are met through profits. However, it is inaccurate to speak of profitability as *the* goal, or the primary goal, of the firm because it is actually a goal of only one group associated with the firm. The owner's goal is not the firm's goal. In terms of the goal system idea discussed in Chapter 2, profitability is but one group goal of the firm.

Imperfect measure

Profitability as a Measure. Profits also serve as a measure of the firm's success in meeting the goals of customers, employees, creditors, and the general public. The long-run profitability of a business firm is, at best, an imperfect measure of the overall effectiveness of the firm. There is no simple or single way to evaluate the effectiveness of a business organization. Even firms that make no profits can be effective in other ways. (However, profits are never more effective as a measure of a firm's success as when they do not exist.) Effectiveness must be measured in terms of accomplishment of the firm's total goal system and in terms of the total social welfare.

*Conditions
for serving
as a measure*

It is very possible for a firm to sustain, over the long run, a competitive profit position while at the same time engaging in illegal activities, evading taxes, paying inadequate wages, and polluting the environment. This is particularly true under conditions of imperfect competition and when the various claimants on the organization have unequal bargaining power. However, to the extent that the competitive market system is working and to the extent that claimants can make their demands known and can enforce them, profits can serve as *one* measure of organizational effectiveness.

*The firm as
an optimizer*

Optimizing versus Satisficing. You often will hear it said that business firms "maximize" or "optimize" profits. If this means that the firms simply try to make as much profit as they can, then the statement is acceptable. Business firms do act *as if* they are trying to optimize profits. However, if a more technical and precise meaning of "optimize" is implied, then the statement is less acceptable. Referring to the difficulty of knowing how to maximize profits, one business executive remarked, "In the real business world you're lucky if you've got a plus or minus 10 percent fix on things."[3]

*The firm as
a satisficer,
aspiration
level*

Rather than thinking of a business firm as a profit optimizer, it is more realistic to think of the business firm as a "satisficer" of an entire system of goals. At particular times, some of these goals will be more important than others. "Most organizational objectives take the form of an *aspiration level* rather than an imperative to *maximize* or *minimize*, and the aspiration level changes in response to experience."[4] In other words, people in organizations strive to achieve goals at a level that will satisfy the aspiration of those with influence in or on the organization. These aspiration levels change, depending upon, among other things, the level of goal achievement. The higher the level of achievement, the greater the tendency of aspiration levels to rise. The converse is also true.

*Observing
behavior*

Role of Profits in Understanding Behavior. When you observe what people in business firms are actually doing, you can seldom explain it in terms of profit seeking. Why do some employees work hard and others hardly work at all? Why is absenteeism so high? Why is the quality of work declining? Why are some willing to assume new responsibilities while others try to escape their present responsibilities? Answers to questions such as these cannot be found by reference to the profit goal.

*Indirect
relationship*

Of course, certain key decisions can be analyzed primarily in terms of profit, and the direct acts of a few participants can be interpreted as profit-related. Nevertheless, such decisions and acts

[3] Eli Goldston, as quoted in "The 'Responsible' Corporation: Benefactor or Monopolist?" *Fortune*, vol. 88, no. 5 (November 1973), p. 56.
[4] Richard M. Cyert and James C. March, *A Behavioral Theory of the Firm* (Englewood Cliffs, N.J.: Prentice-Hall, 1963), p. 28.

are few, compared to the total number of decisions made and acts performed in a business firm. Decisions by personnel and maintenance managers, public relations directors, advertising executives, and accountants can seldom be directly related to profits. Furthermore, the everyday behavior of the vast majority of organizational participants is only indirectly related to the profit-seeking goal of the firm.

*Limited
source*

Actual behavior in organizations is determined by multiple goals and expectations about the consequences of behavior. It is asking too much of the profit goal to expect it to explain much of the behavior in organizations. In spite of what might be said about the role of profit in the business firm, it is a limited source of information about actual behavior. Later we shall discuss several organizational and behavioral theories that provide managers with alternative ways of understanding behavior in organizations.

THE ISSUE OF SOCIAL RESPONSIBILITY

*The common
good*

All social organizations, including business firms, have responsibilities to society for the common good. They must meet these responsibilities; otherwise they have no social right to exist. Contributing to the total common good is the essence of the responsibility of every legitimate social organization.

*Nebulous
concept*

The idea that business firms should be socially responsible seems reasonable enough. No one advocates the opposite position. However, the idea is nebulous. "Social responsibility" has many meanings; it lacks the clarity of the profitability idea. In corporate annual reports, social responsibility is discussed under such headings as "social action," "public service," "beyond-the-profit-motive," and "corporate citizenship."[5] Social responsibility means something, but what?

One view

One way of thinking about the responsibilities of business firms is shown in Figure 2A–1.

*Inner-circle re-
sponsibilities*

The *inner* circle A includes the clear-cut basic responsibilities for efficiently and effectively executing the economic function. These are the responsibilities commonly associated with producing and distributing economic goods and services. That is the *basic role* of business firms in our, and any other, society.

*Intermediate
circle respon-
sibilities*

The *intermediate* circle B includes the inner-circle responsibilities and also additional responsibilities that reflect changing social values and priorities. For example, during the 1980s, business will be expected to continue to promote the employment of blacks,

[5] Edward H. Bowman and Mason Haire, "A Strategic Posture toward Corporate Social Responsibility," *California Management Review,* vol. 18, no. 2 (Winter 1975), p. 50.

FIGURE 2A–1
Responsibilities of Business Firms

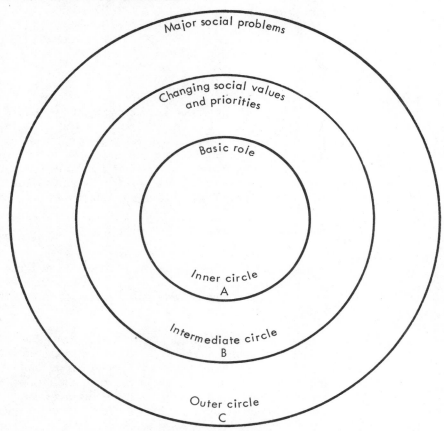

Source: Research and Policy Committee, Committee for Economic Development, *Social Responsibilities of Business Corporations* (New York: Committee for Economic Development, 1971).

women, and other minorities. Business will be expected to contribute to a cleaner environment, to respond positively to the interests of consumer groups, to take necessary steps to conserve energy and scarce resources, and so on. Many of these intermediate responsibilities are now required by law.

Outer-circle responsibilities

The *outer* circle C includes those responsibilities that business should assume in order to help solve major social problems. Examples include the responsibility for the renewal of deteriorated urban areas, for the reduction of poverty, for massive training programs for those who lack job skills, and for long-term solutions to problems related to energy.

Using the framework

Using the above framework of concentric circles, we can say that all business firms must be directly involved with the inner-circle responsibilities. In addition, all firms must meet intermediate and outer-circle responsibilities required by law or other pressures. The extent to which business firms can or will voluntarily become actively involved in meeting intermediate and outer circle responsibilities depends on their resources, the public's expectations, and competitive factors. We expect more of American Telephone and Telegraph and General Motors Corporation than of Pizza Hut and Jack-in-the-Box.

A question of means

The "issue" of social responsibility is not whether or not business firms should have goals for meeting responsibilities in each of the three circles. They should have such goals, or *ends*. The issue is, What is the best *means* for meeting these responsibilities and *to what extent* can they be met?[6] About that question, there is considerable debate. The debate is over the appropriate degree of direct participation by business in intermediate and outer-circle responsibilities. On one side is the view that business can best meet intermediate and outer-circle responsibilities by *focusing on its inner-circle responsibilities*. On the other side is the view that business must positively and actively *focus on all three circles of responsibilities*. We shall examine each of these views in more detail.

FOCUSING ON THE INNER CIRCLE

Traditional social contract

In American society, the traditional contract between society and business has been that the greatest social good results when business concentrates on efficient and effective performance of its economic function. Such concentration results in greater productivity, profits, and economic growth. These results increase the capacity of society to handle its problems. Furthermore, employees, owners, suppliers, and all other direct participants in the economic process benefit.

Pursue self-interest

This argument is essentially that business firms should pursue their own self-interest, free of interference from extraneous forces, and the result will be the maximum good for the most people: "The objective of the profit-maximizing ethic . . . is to promote efficient use of resources, so there will be a bigger pie to split among profits, wages, and lower prices, to the benefit of the entire community."[7] And, "The business of business is profits. . . . In the end, business has only two responsibilities—to obey the everyday face-to-face civility (honesty, good faith, and so on) and to seek material gain."[8]

---

[6] Archie B. Carroll, "Social Responsibility and Management," *Personnel Administrator,* vol. 4, no. 2 (April 1975), p. 46.

[7] "Some Thinking to Do," *Wall Street Journal,* vol. 50, no. 118 (December 18, 1972), editorial, p. 4.

[8] Theodore Levitt, "The Dangers of Social Responsibility," *Harvard Business Review,* vol. 36, no. 5 (September–October 1959), pp. 41–50.

Agents versus principals

This traditional argument maintains that corporate business executives are the agents of the owners of the corporation. It is their duty, within legal limits and sociocultural norms and values, to promote the interests of the owners. If, in order to act "socially and responsibly," corporate executives take action that reduces profit, they are acting as principals rather than as agents of the owners. If the executive's socially responsible action results in higher prices, it penalizes consumers; if lower wages result, it hurts employees.

Survey of CEOs

In a recent survey, 96 percent of a large sample of CEOs of the nation's leading business firms agreed that to "gain a satisfactory return on stockholder equity" is the primary corporate objective. Eighty-nine percent of the CEOs agreed that they owe their greatest responsibility to stockholders. In what they *say* and *do*, business executives recognize their role as agents of the owners.[9]

Other arguments

There are other arguments supporting this traditional view of how business should meet its responsibilities to society: conflict with the profit goal of business; prohibitive costs of social involvement; lack of necessary skills to solve social problems; dilution of business's purpose of economic productivity; weakening of competitive position in international trade; business already has enough social power; lack of broad support; and lack of accountability of business executives for their action in social areas.[10]

Persuasive and logical argument

All the above points can be made to support the argument that business firms should meet their social responsibilities by simply doing a good job of their economic function. The argument is persuasive and logical. Indeed, many complaints against business from the general public and consumer groups are concerned primarily with the basic economic task of business. Consumers want better products, more product information, safer and longer-lasting products, meaningful warranties, improved customer services, and lower prices.

Not a denial of social responsibility

It is important to emphasize that this view does not deny that business has social responsibilities. Rather, the view argues for a particular approach to solving social problems and enhancing the general welfare. The approach focuses on inner-circle responsibilities and, through that focus, hopes to fulfill intermediate and outer-circle responsibilities.

FOCUSING ON ALL THREE CIRCLES

New view

A different view of the social responsibility of business is that business should be actively involved in all three circles of responsi-

---

[9] Charles P. Edmonds III and John H. Hand, "What Are the Real Long-run Objectives of Business?" *Business Horizons,* vol. 19, no. 3 (December 1976), p. 77.

[10] Keith Davis, "The Case for and against Business Assumption of Social Responsibilities," *Academy of Management Journal,* vol. 16, no. 2 (June 1973), pp. 317–21.

bilities. This view is reflected in the suggestion that large corporations not only *may* become more socially responsible, but that they *must* become more active.[11] To some, ". . . corporate social responsibility is no longer unique, startling, or . . . controversial. Social responsibility has become part of the business of business."[12]

Specific arguments

There are several specific arguments that can be made in support of the view that business should focus on all three circles of responsibilities. These arguments include: long-term self-interest; improved public image; long-run viability of business as an institution; avoidance of government regulation; the existence of sociocultural norms and constraints; stockholders' interest; business has the resources and the innovative ability; prevention is better than curing; and social responsibilities can become profit opportunities.[13]

New social contract

Most of the above arguments derive from the changing expectations that people have of business firms. These expectations may be leading to a new social contract for business—". . . there is a new social contract emerging that increasingly involves business in broader social roles."[14] An acceptance of this new social contract is implied in this statement by the CEO of Prudential Insurance Company of America: "Business belongs to the people. Business has, in effect, a franchise granted to it by society, and the franchise will be continued only as long as society is satisfied with the way it is handled."[15]

Public institutions

Society's changing expectations of business may be leading to the view that large business firms are, in effect, public institutions and, consequently, "management's political [social] role is precedent to its economic function, rather than vice versa. . . . Or, at the least, that the political and economic functions are concomitant, each reinforcing—or undermining—the other."[16] As you can see, this view is quite different than the traditional view of the business firm as a basically economic institution whose purpose is to maximize its profits. From the viewpoint of managing, this broader social contract increases the variables on which managers must focus their attention.

Public interest

Consistent with the view of business firms as public institutions is the view that firms must promote the public interest: "Where

[11] Gilbert Burck, "The Hazards of Corporate Responsibility," *Fortune,* vol. 87, no. 6 (June 1973), p. 115.

[12] "How Business Tackles Social Problems," *Business Week,* May 20, 1972, p. 95.

[13] Davis, "The Case for and against Business Assumption of Social Responsibilities," pp. 313–17.

[14] Melvin Anshen, "Changing the Social Contract: A Role for Business," *Columbia Journal of World Business,* vol. 5, no. 6 (April 1972), pp. 6–14.

[15] Donald S. McNaughton, "Managing Social Responsiveness," *Business Horizons,* vol. 19, no. 6 (December 1976), pp. 19–24.

[16] Neil W. Chamberlain, *The Limits of Corporate Responsibility* (New York: Basic Books, Publishers, 1973), p. 203.

the public interest . . . is at issue, there is no natural right to be left alone."[17] One writer asserts that, "A democracy is not likely to permit huge and powerful institutions . . . to define their interests in a limited way or to go about pursuing them in a single-minded way. It insists that such institutions show a proper attentiveness to . . . the 'public interest.' "[18]

Efficiency and choice

If this attentiveness to the public interest somehow hurts a business firm's economic performance, then that is a choice the people in a democracy make. Some argue that direct involvement in intermediate and outer-circle responsibilities leads to economic inefficiency. If that is the case, then others counterargue that economic efficiency is not necessarily the major value desired by society. The values to which society gives highest priority change, and society's major institutions must change with them.

Summary box

> In thinking about the profits of a business firm the idea of *profitability* is useful because it relates dollar profit to an investment base. Most people think business firms are more profitable than they actually are.
>
> Profitability is *one* of the essential ingredients of a business firm; it is *one* goal of a firm; it is *one* measure of success; and it is *one* source of behavioral understanding.
>
> Business firms are *goal satisficers* rather than goal optimizers.
>
> The responsibilities of business firms can be thought of in terms of *three concentric circles of responsibilities:* inner, intermediate, and outer.
>
> The social-responsibility issue is primarily one of *means* rather than *ends.* Two views of the best means for achieving social responsibility goals are: (1) to focus on inner-circle responsibilities; and (2) to become directly involved in all three circles of responsibilities. The first view represents the traditional social contract that business has with society. The second view represents a new social contract that places emphasis on business as a public institution that contributes to the public interest.

---

[17] John K. Galbraith, "On the Economic Image of Corporate Enterprise," in Ralph Nader and Mark Green, eds., *Corporate Power in America* (New York: Grossman Publishers, 1973), p. 7.

[18] Irving Kristol, "The Corporation and the Dinosaur," *The Wall Street Journal*, vol. 53, no. 32 (February 14, 1974), p. 16.

MANAGERIAL CONCERNS

New activism

Many business firms are taking a more active role in meeting intermediate and outer-circle responsibilities. This new activity often is in response to the requirements of laws. Much of the time, also, the activity reflects the pragmatic view that a broader view of social responsibility is in the best interest of business firms. Sometimes the activity is forced on business firms by pressure from outside groups.

Beyond tokenism

Whatever the motivation, more American business firms are going beyond social "tokenism" and are putting their resources and skills behind such social issues as training of the physically and mentally handicapped; prison reform and hiring of ex-convicts; energy conservation; pollution control; cure of alcoholics; upgrading the job skills and opportunities of blacks, women, migrant workers, and Indians; corporate codes of conduct; psychological counseling; and restoring deteriorating urban neighborhoods.

Disclosure of social responsibility

It is becoming more common for large business firms to discuss their socially responsible activities in their annual reports along with traditional types of financial information for stockholders. For example, 85 percent of the Fortune 500 industrial corporations provided some disclosure of socially responsible activities in their 1975 annual reports.[19] Some of these disclosures may be for appearances sake only; talk is cheap and not necessarily evidence of behavior. Other disclosures, however, may be the reflection of a progressive managerial strategy that is sensitive to both profit and social responsibility.[20]

Major variable

The major variable influencing business's participation in social issues is likely to be the commitment of key managers throughout business organizations. A recent survey concludes that ". . . a growing number of executives believe that social involvement is necessary, even though short-run profit returns are reduced and no long-run returns are probable."[21] Such statements of belief may never materialize into social involvement behavior. Managerial commitment is likely to go to those activities that make a contribution to the firm's goals, including its profitability.

Issues

As a manager you may have to confront issues that fall in the social responsibility area. A few issues for you to consider are:

---

[19] *Social Responsibility Disclosure: 1976 Survey of Fortune 500 Annual Reports.* Available from Ernst & Ernst, 1300 Union Commerce Building, Cleveland, OH 44115.

[20] Bowman and Haire, "A Strategic Posture toward Corporate Social Responsibility," p. 57.

[21] Sandra L. Holmes, "Executive Perceptions of Corporate Social Responsibility," *Business Horizons,* vol. 19, no. 3, (June 1976), p. 37.

*Defining
social respon-
sibility*

1. What, precisely, does social responsibility mean in your unique area of accountability? What specific actions can be included within its boundaries?

*Relate to
profit*

2. How will you rationalize a "call for social responsibility to the traditional business pursuit of sales and profits?"[22]

*Goals and
plans*

3. What socially responsible goals will be included in the goal system you will be held accountable for achieving? What specific plans and controls will support these goals?

*Personal
philosophy*

4. How does your personal philosophy toward social responsibility mesh with the philosophy of your supervisors? To what extent can you be an advocate of activities that are not encouraged by your superiors?

Your career

5. How does your performance in the area of social responsibility enter into your own job performance appraisal? How will socially responsible activity affect your career?

CHECK YOUR UNDERSTANDING

Profit versus profitability
Optimizing versus satisficing
Aspiration level
Concentric circles of
  responsibilities
Social responsibility issue

Traditional social contract
Agents versus principals
New social contract
Business as a public institution
Social responsibility disclosure

STUDY QUESTIONS

1. Argue, pro and con:

    a. Profit is no more essential to the business firm than any other of its goals.
    b. Profit is no more essential to the business firm than it is to hospitals.
    c. Profit is a limited source of understanding about behavior in business firms.

2. How much profit do you think business firms should be allowed to earn? What criteria are you using in answering this question?

3. What type of information would be required to demonstrate that the direct involvement of a business firm in intermediate and outer-circle responsibilities reduces the firm's economic efficiency?

4. To what extent, in your opinion, is a business firm such as General Motors Corporation free to decide what its responsibilities to society are?

---

[22] Arthur Elkins, "Some Observations on the Training and Evaluating of Business Managers in the Meeting of Social Issues," *Management Research*, vol. 9, no. 4 (July–August 1976), p. 112.

APPLICATION: POLLUTION PREVENTION*

The odor on his clothes kept other passengers from sitting next to Jack Grady on his return flight from 3M Co.'s Cordoba, Illinois plant. Jack found that the smell of the experimental herbicide he had helped to develop repelled people as well as retarded weeds.

Fortunately, Jack's unpopularity on the airplane turned into a plus for 3M. The company launched a two-year project to reformulate the herbicide and make it virtually odor-free. The project was one of several in 3M's "3P Program"—Pollution Prevention Pays!

The 3P Program illustrates how one company combined socially responsible behavior (pollution prevention and control) with profitability. The Environmental Protection Agency (EPA) calls 3M's program one of the most thorough pollution prevention programs it has seen.

How does the 3P Program work? First, the company blitzed all of its divisions with the message: Stop thinking about pollution removal and start thinking about pollution prevention.

Second, top management at 3M made its commitment to the program clear to all personnel. Third, departments submit pollution-prevention proposals on a one-page form to a 3P coordinating committee. The committee reviews each project for environmental benefit, cost effectiveness, individual effort required, and technical accomplishment.

What have been the results of the 3P program? Not all submitted proposals are approved by the coordinating committee. However, the 3P program has already saved 3M several million dollars in lower costs and deferred capital expenditures. The company's annual pollution of water, air, and sludge have been drastically reduced. In some cases, 3P projects have resulted in a better or less costly product.

1. Does this illustration suggest other ways in which business firms can take a *preventive* approach to meeting certain social responsibilities?

2. 3M uses a *program* approach to its pollution prevention goals. Can you think of other organizational mechanisms that could be used to achieve their goals?

3. 3M's experience illustrates the complementary relationship between profitability and social responsibility. Are there contingencies that may result in a conflict between profitability and social responsibility goals? Discuss.

* Source: "3M Gains by Averting Pollution," *Business Week,* November 22, 1976, p. 72.

SUPPLEMENT 2B

Management by Objectives

Advocates argue that it [MBO] is the successor to Taylor's "Mental Revolution"—a new way of thinking about, and engaging in, collective effort.

F. P. Sherwood and W. J. Page, Jr.

Different meanings

One approach many organizations use for goal setting is management by objectives (MBO). MBO is more than just an approach to goal setting: It ranges in use from simple goal setting to a comprehensive overall managerial organizational philosophy.[1]

Nonbusiness uses

In addition to its widespread use in business firms (one study reports that 83 percent of business firms in the United States are using MBO)[2] MBO has received increasing acceptance by medical, educational, and governmental administrators. MBO is not merely a *business* tool; it is a *general managerial* tool.

Various names

MBO goes by various names:[3] management by results (MBR), work planning and review (WPR), charter of accountability (COACH), objectives-strategies-tactics (OST), individual goal setting (IGS), improving business performance (IBP), and goal setting and self-control. By whatever name, MBO is a managerial tool of potential importance to your managing.

Fraud or innovation

Some business managers will tell you, on the basis of their experience, that MBO is a joke and a fraud, a gimmick for justifying

[1] Heinz Weihrich, "The MBO Jungle: And What to Do about It," *Proceedings* of the Eighteenth Annual Meeting of the Southwest Division, Academy of Management, March 1976, pp. 243–47.

[2] R. Henry Migliore, "A History of Management by Objectives," *Proceedings* of the Eighteenth Annual Meeting of the Southwest Division, Academy of Management, March 1976, pp. 131–35.

[3] Daniel M. Glasner, "Patterns of Management by Results," *Business Horizons*, vol. 12, no. 1 (February 1969), pp. 37–40.

the existence of personnel departments, a fad that will go away, and a paper-shuffling hassle that won't stop. Others, of course, think it's the greatest managerial innovation in years.

This supplement

Which view proves to be right *for you* will depend, in part, on your understanding of what MBO is, of its basic ideas, and of its limits and benefits. We discuss these aspects of MBO in this supplement, as well as give two examples of MBO in practice.

DEFINITION

Meaning varies

The exact meaning of MBO varies from organization to organization. In some, MBO is nothing more than a phrase used to show that they are using the latest management jargon. In other organizations, MBO is the foundation of their overall approach to managing. In-between these two extremes, MBO means different things in different organizations. In spite of this diversity, however, it is possible to define MBO in a way that communicates its essential meaning.

MBO defined

MBO is ". . . . a process whereby the superior and subordinate managers of an organization jointly identify its common goals, define each individual's major areas of responsibility in terms of the results expected . . . , and use these measures as guides for operating the unit and assessing the contributions of each of its members."[4]

THREE BASIC IDEAS

The above definition brings out three ideas basic to most applications of MBO: interactive goal setting; implementing; and appraising performance. Figure 2B–1 shows the relationship of these three MBO ideas. A brief discussion of each idea will provide additional insight into MBO.

Basic characteristic— in theory

Interactive Goal Setting. MBO implies an active give-and-take between managers and their subordinates in goal setting. The purpose of this interaction is to identify clear and measurable results to be accomplished in a specified time period, for example, three months. In theory, the basic characteristic of this interactive goal-setting process is that subordinates are actively involved in formulating goals for which they will be held accountable. In practice, the extent and nature of their involvement varies.[5]

---

[4] George S. Odiorne, *Management by Objectives: A System of Managerial Leadership* (New York: Pitman Publishing Corporation, 1965), pp. 55–56.

[5] For example, the degree of subordinate involvement can vary with the managerial style of the superior. If the superior's style is autocratic, subordinate involvement is minimal. The reverse is true if the superior's style is participative. See Wendell L. French and Robert W. Hollmann, "Management by Objectives: The Team Approach," *California Management Review*, vol. 17, no. 2 (Spring 1975), pp. 13–22.

FIGURE 2B–1
The MBO Process

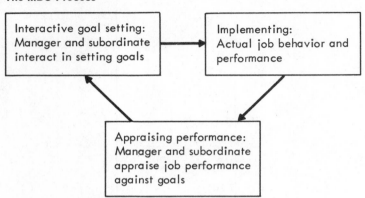

<table>
<tr><td>Interactive goal setting:
Manager and subordinate
interact in setting goals</td><td>→</td><td>Implementing:
Actual job behavior and
performance</td></tr>
</table>

Appraising performance:
Manager and subordinate
appraise job performance
against goals

Practice
varies

In many cases, the superior–subordinate goal-setting sessions are occasions in which the superior, in effect, says to the subordinate, "Here are your goals. Take them or leave them." In other cases, however, the goal-setting sessions are authentic opportunities for subordinates to contribute to goal setting, to seek clarification and explanation of goals, to make positive contributions to goal setting, and to integrate their personal goals with those of the organization. This type of goal-setting session may increase the commitment of superiors and subordinates to the MBO approach and may contribute to goal acceptance, clarity, and achievement.

One
approach to
setting goals

How might you, as a manager, go about setting goals with your subordinates by using MBO? Here is one approach you can use in your managing.

Know your
own goals

1. Know your own goals. Before meeting with subordinates, it is important to know your own individual job-related goals, the goals of groups relevant to your area of accountability and performance, the performance goals which you are going to be held accountable for by your immediate superior, and the goals of your superior. Determining what all of these goals are is going to take a considerable amount of time, effort, and skill.

Meet with
subordinates

2. Meet with your subordinates. In this initial meeting, you can explain the purpose of the meeting, emphasize the importance of goals to the organization, communicate your own goals, explain the process that led to them, emphasize the two-way nature of the goal-setting process, and ask for some tentative statements of goals that your subordinates might set for their own organizational units.

Climate for goal setting

This initial meeting helps to set the climate for goal setting. If subordinates sense that you are serious about the interactive process and that the organization will be supportive of it, then a favorable climate for goal setting may develop. In this initial meeting (more than one may be required), subordinates can check their understanding of the performance goals for which you will be held accountable. They can be given the opportunity to question those goals. Your subordinates can use this initial meeting to get a better idea of how their goals derive from the overall performance of the department in which they work.

Specific output

A specific result of this initial meeting is an agreement about when to meet individually with subordinates in order to go over the goal proposals that they develop. These written proposals can be reviewed by you prior to the meeting. The purpose of such a review is to allow you to check their goals for congruence with other goals. In addition, the review offers the opportunity to check their proposals against other criteria (measurability, attainability, opportunity cost) and to observe if any areas of responsibility have been omitted.

Meet individually with subordinates

3. Meet individually with your subordinates. The purpose of the individual meeting is to "work through" the specific goal proposals and arrive at a set of actual goals that are mutually acceptable. Additionally, target dates are set where applicable, goals are ranked according to relative importance, and some agreement is reached on the general means that will be followed in accomplishing the goals. The goals agreed on during the meeting can include not only specific performance goals, but also personal-development goals of the subordinate.

Six ideas

Implementing MBO. Even the best MBO program on paper can be a disaster in practice. MBO does not always work out as well as expected. Here are six ideas to keep in mind concerning implementing MBO.

Top management support

1. Have the active support of the top managers who have a direct influence on your area of accountability. "The most effective manner to implement MBO is to allow the top-level executives to explain, coordinate, and guide the program."[6] Having top managers actively involved in MBO helps convey the message that MBO is not just another gimmick thought up by a training clerk. It is not uncommon for management consultants to refuse to install an MBO program if it does not have the *active* support, involvement, and commitment of top managers.

---

[6] James H. Donnelly, Jr., James L. Gibson, and John M. Ivancevich, *Fundamentals of Management: Functions, Behavior, Models* (Dallas: Business Publications, 1975), p. 161.

Mechanics

2. Take care of the necessary mechanics. There may be a need for a guideline manual of procedures to follow in MBO.[7] There is usually need for forms to be used in goal setting and performance appraisal. (One management writer suggests that "Management by objectives' effectiveness is inversely related to the number of MBO forms.")[8] It is also important to assign authority and responsibility for initiating and overseeing the MBO program.

Training

3. An additional requirement for implementing MBO is to provide adequate training in MBO philosophy and procedures. Managers and subordinates may require technical and conceptual skill training in order to engage in effective interactive goal setting and performance appraisal.

Time

4. Allow sufficient time for MBO to work. In a small organization, MBO can yield benefits in a relatively short time—six months to one year. However, a well-conceived MBO program cannot be installed overnight. In a large organization, it may take three to five years of operation before the MBO program is yielding significant companywide performance results.

Monitor,
modify

5. Monitor MBO as it is being implemented. This means comparing the actual progress of MBO with the planned progress. This comparison may suggest a need to modify the MBO procedures that are being used. MBO systems can become so formalized and rigid that they become ends in themselves rather than means for effective managing. When this occurs, "the system tends to take precedence over the people who use it."[9] Monitoring also provides opportunities for feedback, counseling, and encouragement to subordinates at times other than the regular performance appraisal sessions.

Politics

6. Be sensitive to "the politics of implementing MBO."[10] For example, MBO potentially can redistribute power in an organization and not all managers will welcome this possibility. Their response to threats to their power may be obstructive tactics. Another political reality is resistance to change. If MBO is seen as a significant change, then it will generate resistance in the form of jokes, infighting, and overt conflict. Finally, MBO can alter the status of an organization, can influence salary and promotion decisions, can affect budgets, and can cause the creation of coalitions

[7] Michael J. Etzel and John M. Ivancevich, "Management by Objectives in Marketing: Philosophy, Process, and Problems," *Journal of Marketing,* vol. 38, no. 4 (October 1974), pp. 47–55.

[8] Quoted in Robert A. Howell, "Managing by Objectives: A Three Stage System," *Business Horizons,* vol. 13, no. 1 (February 1970), p. 42.

[9] John B. Lasagna, "Make Your MBO Pragmatic," *Harvard Business Review,* vol. 49, no. 6 (November–December 1971), p. 64.

[10] George S. Odiorne, "The Politics of Implementing MBO," *Business Horizons,* vol. 17, no. 3 (June 1974), pp. 13–21.

to fight it. All these possibilities have political implications. "MBO has failed in many organizations because those in charge ignored the political considerations included in the implementation."[11]

Three purposes of appraisal

Appraising Performance. The third basic idea of MBO is appraisal of actual performance against the goals and other appraisal criteria agreed on in the goal-setting phase.[12] Performance appraisals can serve three purposes: (1) feedback to personnel concerning their actual performance; (2) provide the basis for identifying more effective job behavior; and (3) supply information to managers relevant to future job assignments and to compensation decisions.[13] In practice, formal performance appraisal seldom reaches its potential value.

Playing God

For example, in some cases appraisal sessions are nothing more than awkward and uncomfortable sessions in which managers "play God" with their subordinates. The emphasis in such appraisals is on judging the personal worth, not the job performance, of subordinates. Are they loyal? Are they reliable? Are they of good moral character? Do they comb their hair right? One writer has referred to this type of performance appraisal as a violation of the integrity of the subordinate's personality.[14] Another author argues that, as typically practiced, MBO appraisal sessions are ". . . inherently self-defeating over the long-run because they are based on a reward-punishment psychology that serves to intensify the pressure on the individual while really giving him a limited choice of objectives."[15]

Working through problems

In other cases, however, performance appraisals are give-and-take sessions in which managers and their subordinates "work through" problems encountered in efforts to achieve predetermined goals. This type of performance-appraisal session is extremely difficult to achieve. It requires that adequate information be available on which to appraise performance. It requires that the involved people have the necessary interpersonal skills. And it requires that a reasonable level of trust and mutual respect exists between managers and their subordinates. Managers must create a climate

---

[11] Ibid., p. 21.

[12] "Other appraisal criteria" include proper allocation of time to given objectives, type and difficulty of objectives, creativity in overcoming obstacles, coordinative and cooperative behavior, and so on. See Henri L. Tosi, John R. Rizzo, and Stephen J. Carroll, "Setting Goals in Management by Objectives," *California Management Review*, vol. 12, no. 4 (Summer 1970), p. 76.

[13] Harry Levinson, "Appraisal of What Performance?" *Harvard Business Review*, vol. 54, no. 4 (July–August 1976), p. 30.

[14] Douglas McGregor, "An Uneasy Look at Performance Appraisal," *Harvard Business Review*, vol. 35 (May–June 1957), pp. 89–94.

[15] Harry Levinson, "Management by Whose Objectives?" *Harvard Business Review*, vol. 48, no. 4 (July–August 1970), p. 134.

in which subordinates feel free to communicate honestly and openly without fear of retaliation.[16]

Three stages

The role of performance appraisal in MBO has evolved over the past 20 years. In the early years of MBO, performance appraisal received major, and perhaps primary, emphasis. As MBO evolves in a business firm, one author suggests it goes through three stages. Stage 1 is the performance-appraisal stage. Stage 2 integrates MBO with the firm's short-term planning and budgeting cycle. In Stage 3, MBO becomes a part of the firm's long-range and strategic planning. Through these stages, performance appraisal remains important but receives *relatively* less emphasis.[17]

EXAMPLES

Examples, not ideals

Two practical examples will help make some of the ideas in this supplement more meaningful. The first example identifies a five-step approach used by a large food product firm. The second example focuses on the performance appraisal part of an overall performance management system used in another large business firm. A word of caution: We are not suggesting that these are ideal approaches that can be used in any situation. They are approaches that work, more or less, for these two firms. Even within these firms, these approaches are continually being revised and are flexible enough to accommodate varying managerial styles.

Accountabilities and an action plan

General Mills.[18]   First, a manager and his or her boss review the manager's accountabilities. Accountabilities are the long-term results that a specific job should produce. They are listed in the manager's "position guide" and on an Action Plan form. The main purpose of this first step is to review the list of accountabilities to see if they are still current and complete. The outcome is that the manager agrees on the set of accountabilities for which he or she is responsible.

Determine priorities

Second, the manager considers the first accountability. The specific objectives that must be achieved in order to meet the accountability are listed on the Action Plan. For example, if one of the accountabilities is to assure that product quality improves, the specific objective of implementing a new approach to quality management may be listed on the Action Plan. In this second step,

---

[16] There are many approaches to performance appraisal that are not part of MBO programs. For a concise discussion of several performance-appraisal methods and procedures, see Larry L. Cummings and Donald P. Schwab, *Performance in Organizations: Determinants and Appraisal* (Glenview, Ill.: Scott, Foresman and Company, 1973).

[17] Howell, "Managing by Objectives: A Three-Stage System," pp. 41–45.

[18] Information for this illustration comes from two sources: Walter S. Wikstrom, *Managing by—and with—Objectives*, Personnel Policy Study No. 212 (New York: The National Industrial Conference Board, Inc., 1968), pp. 27–37, and Ernest C. Miller, *Objectives and Standards of Performance in Financial Management*, AMA Research Study 87 (New York: American Management Association, 1967), pp. 17–19.

the manager determines priorities for each of the specific objectives listed. A primary priority means that the objective is part of the basic core of the job. A secondary priority means that the objective supports primary objectives and is shared with other individuals. An administrative priority means that the objective is one that will usually be achieved in the normal course of time.

Determine degree of involvement

In addition to assigning priorities to objectives, the manager indicates on the Action Plan the degree of involvement of the boss or others in attaining a specific objective. General Mills uses a three-way classification (important, moderate, and light) to identify the degree of involvement of others in achieving the manager's objective. This second step of listing objectives, attaching priorities, and judging the degree of involvement of others is completed for each of the manager's accountabilities.

Checking against criteria

Third, the manager checks the list of specific objectives against a set of criteria. General Mills suggests these criteria: supportive of an accountability; specific; measurable; limited in time; attainable; and a commitment between the employee and the supervisor. The last criterion is achieved by means of the fourth step in the overall MBO procedure.

Basis for control

Fourth, the manager sends the Action Plan to the boss. The boss studies the Action Plan and then discusses it with the manager. When agreement is reached, the Action Plan is prepared in final form and it becomes the manager's principal basis for control. The Action Plan "specifies what is to be done, in what degree, and by what time; and it specifies the means by which progress shall be measured."[19] As such, the Action Plan allows managers to control their own work rather than having to be controlled by high-level managers.

Appraisal

The fifth step in General Mills' approach to MBO is the appraisal process. This process involves continual review of progress whenever warranted. More formal reviews and appraisals may take place at midyear and year-end. General Mills has adopted an appraisal process suited to its needs. The company emphasizes, however, that goal setting and performance review is a continuous process of planning and controlling. This process is more important than the appraisals.

Corning's approach to performance appraisal

Corning Glass Works.[20] An interesting approach to performance appraisal is the one used by Corning Glass Works for almost 4,000 managerial and professional personnel. Corning's performance management system (PMS) includes MBO, performance development and review, and placement and salary review. Our discussion

---

[19] Wikstrom, *Managing by—and with—Objectives,* p. 34.

[20] This discussion is based on information in Michael Beer and Robert A. Ruh, "Employee Growth through Performance Management," *Harvard Business Review,* vol. 54, no. 4 (July–August 1976), pp. 59–66.

here concerns Corning's approach to performance development and review. Corning found that some of their managers were having difficulty in helping their subordinates improve their performance. Consequently, to assist managers in their *helping role,* Corning took three actions.

Performance description questionnaire

The company first developed a 76-item performance-description questionnaire. Sample items include: gives poor presentations; takes the initiative in group meetings; objects to ideas before they are explained. Each of the 76 items are significantly correlated with effective job performance and with potentiality for management throughout Corning. In completing the questionnaire, managers are asked to indicate, on a six-point scale, the extent to which their subordinates behave in ways similar to each of the 76 items.

Performance profile

Corning also developed a performance profile which identifies 19 performance dimensions, which are summarized from the 76 items on the performance-description questionnaire. Each manager is provided with a computer-developed performance profile for each subordinate. The profile identifies the subordinate's performance strengths and weaknesses. For example, a subordinate might be weak on the "work accomplishment" dimension but strong on the "cooperation" dimension. This summary statement can then be used in a developmental interview.

Developmental interview

Third, Corning created some tools to help managers and subordinates come out of the developmental interview with specific plans and objectives. These tools include an "interview guide" and a "developmental matrix." The interview guide ties developmental needs to identified training programs. The developmental matrix relates general improvement needs to several improvement strategies. For example, if a subordinate needs to improve in-job knowledge, then possible strategies include training in job-related skills, coaching, job redesign, and job rotation.

OVERALL PERSPECTIVE

Limits

MBO is not applicable in all management situations. It appears to be more appropriate for managing managerial and professional personnel than operative or clerical workers.[21] However, MBO *can* work in any situation in which there is some discretion in setting performance and personal development goals. If the manager and subordinate have no discretionary influence on goals (for example, when the output of the job is governed by the rate at which a machine operates), then genuine interactive goal setting is impossible for performance goals.

---

[21] MBO has been used with "blue-collar" employees at Continental Can Company, Texas Instruments, and Ohio Bell. See Migliore, "A History of Management by Objectives," p. 135.

Requirements   MBO requires setting clear and measurable performance goals, something that is not always possible or practical. Further, to be effective, MBO requires considerable managerial expertise and skill, a substantial commitment of time and effort, and a willingness to make some difficult, data-based career and compensation decisions. MBO assumes that those involved are interested in participating in the goal-setting process and are capable of such participation. The approach is time-consuming and requires a genuine commitment to an interactive relationship between managers and their subordinates. Finally, some managers, either because of their basic managerial style, time limitations, or inadequate support from their superiors, will not be able to use MBO.

Management philosophy   Some organizations encounter difficulties with their MBO programs because the programs are essentially inconsistent with the basic management philosophy and style dominant in the organization. MBO is an approach to management that involves a recognition that both superiors and subordinates can make a worthwhile contribution to goal setting. It involves the active participation of employees in the goal-setting process. Organizations that operate with an autocratic philosophy and management style may have difficulty implementing MBO. Employees in such organizations may lack the necessary experiences and skills for collaborative organizational relationships. MBO cannot be "plugged in" to an otherwise hostile environment; it must be congruent with other important organizational characteristics.[22]

Assumed benefits   Some of the assumed benefits of MBO are: improving short and long-range planning; providing a basis for checking progress; improving motivation and commitment of managers; providing a results orientation; improving the clarity of a manager's role; providing feedback to managers; and increasing and improving the interaction between superiors and subordinates.[23]

Potentiality versus reality   The above benefits are not always realized in practice. One study of 120 of the Fortune 500 largest industrial firms found that 50 percent of the respondents thought lack of understanding of the MBO program was a serious problem. Fifty-two percent of the respondents indicated only moderate or passive support for the program. The study concluded with the "educated and considered guess" that "less than 10 percent of the Fortune 500 companies have successful applications of MBO." However, a positive conclusion of the study is that MBO has great potentialities, even though it is difficult to implement.[24]

[22] Heinz Weihrich, "MBO in Four Management Systems," *MSU Business Topics,* vol. 24, no. 4 (Autumn 1976), pp. 51–56.

[23] John M. Ivancevich and James H. Donnelly, Jr., "The Present and Future of MBO: Research and Application," Paper presented before the Southwest Academy of Management, Dallas, Texas, March 29, 1974.

[24] Fred E. Schuster and Alva F. Kindall, "Management by Objectives: Where We Stand—A Survey of the Fortune 500," *Human Resource Management,* vol. 13, no. 1 (Spring 1974), pp. 8–11.

*Research
support*

There is little research support for the assumed benefits of MBO. There are some studies that suggest that MBO is associated with improved planning and organization of work.[25] Additionally, there is some support for the role of specific goals in MBO programs in improving performance.[26] On the whole, however, it cannot be said that research evidence verifies the excellence of MBO. This observation is neither surprising nor unique to MBO. There are very few studies that verify the value of *any* particular approach to managing. Management research and practice are not at that stage of development at the present time.

*First use
of term*

The first person to use the phrase "management by objectives" was Peter F. Drucker. In 1954, Drucker noted that: "The first requirement in managing managers is management by objectives and self-control."[27] Drucker then went on to describe his view of the MBO philosophy and process. Twenty years later, Drucker offered this perspective:

> . . . it's now past the fad stage. It's been oversold and over-promoted. . . . But in an amazingly large proportion of institutions they have found that it works. . . . In another five to eight years it will become another very important management tool.[28]

[25] For example, see Herbert H. Meyer, E. Kay, and John R. P. French, Jr., "Split Roles in Performance Appraisal," *Harvard Business Review*, vol. 43, no. 1 (January–February 1965), pp. 123–29. Also, for some evidence of the impact of MBO on managerial performance and attitudes, see Stephen J. Carroll, Jr. and Henry L. Tosi, *Management by Objectives: Applications and Research* (New York: The Macmillan Company, 1973).

[26] Gary P. Latham and Gary A. Yukl, "A Review of Research on the Application of Goal Setting in Organizations," *Academy of Management Journal*, vol. 18, no. 4 (December 1975), p. 832.

[27] Peter F. Drucker, *The Practice of Management* (New York: Harper & Row, Publishers), p. 119.

[28] "Conversation with Peter F. Drucker," *Organizational Dynamics*, vol. 2, no. 4 (Spring 1974), p. 46.

Summary box

> MBO is more than an approach to goal setting. In some organizations it is the overall approach to managing. *Three ideas* are basic to most MBO applications.
>
> First, MBO is an *interactive approach to goal setting.* Managers and subordinates are both actively involved in setting goals for which they will be held accountable.
>
> Second, MBO must be *carefully implemented.* Implementation benefits from top management support, careful attention to necessary mechanics, political considerations, training programs, careful monitoring, and sufficient time to allow the MBO program to work.
>
> Third, MBO involves *appraisal of actual job performance against goals.* This appraisal can serve three purposes: feedback, basis for identifying more effective job behavior; and information for career and compensation decisions.
>
> MBO is not applicable to every management situation, nor have the assumed benefits of MBO been scientifically validated. Nevertheless, the MBO approach to managing is logical, appeals to managerial common sense, and enjoys widespread popularity.

CHECK YOUR UNDERSTANDING

Definition of MBO
Three ideas basic to MBO
Limits and requirements of MBO
Assumed benefits of MBO

MBO at General Mills
Performance review at Corning
  Glass Works

STUDY QUESTIONS

1. What is the basic characteristic of interactive goal setting? How might you engage in this process with your subordinates?

2. Identify and discuss several factors that need to be considered in implementing MBO. What are some of the limits, requirements, and benefits of MBO?

3. In Chapter 2, the problem of possible conflict between individual and organizational goals was discussed. How do you think MBO could contribute to the integration of individual and organizational goals?

4. Chapter 2 discussed three aspects of the goal-setting process: the ends-means chain, imperfect rationality, and coalition formation. How do you see these three aspects entering into the MBO process?

APPLICATION: MBO IN THE FEDERAL GOVERNMENT*

April 18, 1973, was "MBO Day" for the federal government. On that day, President Nixon issued a memorandum to cabinet members and agency heads calling for certain steps that would contribute to excellence in government. The steps included preparing an outline of major goals and objectives to be accomplished during the year.

This presidential request was followed on April 19, 1973, by a memorandum from the Office of Management and Budget (OMB). The OMB memo asked the cabinet members and agency heads to identify those objectives that were of presidential-level significance. They were also to indicate how the objective fit into a longer-term goal, if it did so fit. In addition, the OMB memo suggested that it would be useful to convene progress-review meetings on a bimonthly basis with appropriate White House staff.

The initial and longer-term impact of these two memos was both favorable and unfavorable. Some federal agencies were able to absorb MBO into their ongoing managing process. Others were less fortunate. An examination of several governmental MBO programs in the fiscal year of 1975 reveals opposition to MBO, both as an idea and as an administrative program. Sample complaints include: "MBO is a fad and won't last"; "it was forced on us"; "it was poorly administered by OMB"; and "it was a source of frustration for managers."

One device that some agencies used to cope with an unwanted MBO program was to ignore the program or various parts of it. The Civil Service Commission and the Food and Drug Administration essentially adopted planning systems only indirectly related to MBO. Other agencies only selectively followed the general guides for MBO that were set down by its originators. For example, the Department of Justice (DOJ) simply did not implement 12 of the 14 guides. The Bureau of Outdoor Recreation (BOR), on the other hand, implemented all 14.

1. Do you feel there are factors unique to the federal sector which influence the effectiveness of MBO as a managerial tool?
2. Can you think of any reasons why MBO implementation in the DOJ and BOR differed so much?
3. What are some of the critical contingencies that may have influenced the success of MBO during the period 1973–75?

* Source: Edward J. Ryan, Jr., "Federal Government MBO: Another Managerial Fad?" pp. 35–43, *MSU Business Topics,* Autumn 1976. Reprinted by permission of the publisher, Division of Research, Graduate School of Business Administration, Michigan State University.

Objectives of Chapter 3

- To define planning, and to relate it to goal setting, controlling, budgeting, and forecasting.
- To identify four characteristics of plans.
- To discuss the idea of planning premises.
- To recognize several approaches to organizing for planning.
- To describe and illustrate the formal planning process.
- To recognize a major managerial problem: Finding time to plan.

Outline of Chapter 3

MANAGERIAL PLANNING

The best laid schemes o' mice and men
Gang aft-a-gley.

Robert Burns

The problem is not simply that we plan too little;
we also plan too poorly.

Alvin Toffler

Some reasonable questions

It is difficult to relate to the idea that *planning* can be exciting. How can it be *the* "turn-around" ingredient in a business firm's success? How can planning be the basis of a managerial philosophy that brings forth enthusiastic and effective cooperation from a firm's operating managers? At a personal career level, how can effective planning for achieving goals be the crucial difference between effective and ineffective managing?

Wheels spinning?

These are reasonable questions, because to action-oriented, today-oriented people, planning does not mean anything spectacular. As the governor of our most populous state said: "Planning is just wheel spinning."[1] The governor may be right about planning. Such statements often are. But a specific example will help us see that planning can be more than wheel spinning, and planning can be all those things implied by the questions in our first paragraph.[2]

Example

In 1970 an executive recruiting firm asked Richard B. Madden to become president of Potlatch Corporation. Madden had reason to be less than 100 percent receptive, because the large forest products firm was in a grim and desperate financial situation. The firm was also getting some bad national publicity about its alleged foot-dragging about pollution control. The board of directors agreed to go outside of the firm for its new CEO, and the recruiting search led to Madden, who was then a group vice president of Mobil Chemical Company.

[1] Attributed to Edmund G. Brown, Jr., governor of California. See Alan L. Otter, "Politics and People," *The Wall Street Journal*, May 13, 1976, p. 18.

[2] This example is based on "At Potlatch, Nothing Happens without a Plan," *Business Week*, November 10, 1975, pp. 129–34.

*A strategy
based on
planning*

When Madden accepted the presidency of Potlatch, he decided to build his strategy for Potlatch around planning. Further, he was determined that the firm's operating managers would fully commit themselves to the planning process. In order to elicit this commitment, Madden became a planning evangelist. He traveled to operating units in Idaho, Arkansas, and Minnesota to explain his ideas. He saw to it that everyone, from vice presidents to plant managers, got a crash course in long-range planning.

*Operational-
izing the
strategy*

Help from outside management consultants was purchased to make sure that line managers actually used plans. Recent MBA graduates were hired on an intern basis to spread current management theory into all levels of Potlatch. Madden held long consensus-building sessions with his top operating managers, a few of whom were reluctant to accept his ideas. Additionally, planning effectiveness became a factor considered in promotions. All these tactics served to make operational a managerial philosophy and strategy based on planning.

Results

What have been the real results of all the tactics mentioned above? *As of this writing* (disaster may strike tomorrow), Potlatch has "turned around" its financial situation, although the entire improvement cannot be attributed to planning. Nevertheless, planning, and the effective coordination of strategic planning with annual profit planning, were major ingredients in the turnaround. Of course, not all managers became 100 percent converts to Madden's planning philosophy, nor were all managers equally able to contribute to strategic planning. However, these comments appear typical: "What planning did," said one division manager, "was to get us off our duffs." A group vice president actually said, and meant, "It was exciting."

*Planning is
important
to you*

The main reason for citing the Potlatch Corporation example is to help *you* relate to the importance of planning. Whether you are president of a large forest-products company like Potlatch or the manager of a three-person department, planning for goal achievement is crucial to your effective managing and to your accountability for performance.

*Primacy of
planning*

The phrase "primacy of planning" is often used in managerial education and practice to convey the importance of planning (and goal setting) to everything else managers do. A convincing case for the importance of planning was stated over 450 years ago by Niccolo Machiavelli:

> . . . it may be true that fortune is the ruler of half our actions, but she allows the other half or thereabouts to be governed by us. I would compare her to an impetuous river that, when turbulent, inundates the plains, casts down trees and buildings, and removes earth from this side and places it on the other. Everyone flees before it and everything yields to its fury without being able to

oppose it; and yet . . . when it is quiet, men can make provisions against it by dikes and banks so that when it rises it will go into a canal where its rush will not be so wild and dangerous. So it is with fortune which shows her power where no measures have been taken to resist her, and directs her fury where she knows no dikes or barriers have been made to hold her.[3]

This chapter

Our overall purpose in this chapter is to help you get a feel for the role of planning in meeting your accountability for performance as a manager. First, we define planning and distinguish it from some other terms. Second, we identify some characteristics of plans and discuss the idea of planning premises. Third, we recognize several approaches to organizing for planning. The formal planning process is then discussed and illustrated. Finally, we suggest a strategy for assuring that managers will take time to plan.

PLANNING: SOME BASIC CONCEPTS

Who, what, where, when, how

Definition. "Planning" is the process or activity of determining in advance specifically what should be done in order to achieve particular goals, how it should be done, when and where it should be done, and who should do it. Goals are the why of planning. Planning without goals doesn't make a whole lot of sense, although the process of planning can be beneficial even if the resulting plans are not.

Actual guides to behavior

A plan is simply a predetermined set of actions toward a goal or goals. Plans that are in the process of being implemented or executed are intended to be actual guides to the behavior of people. Nevertheless, a large number of plans in organizations are never implemented and, thus, do not serve as a pattern of influence on the actions of organizational participants. Perhaps the frequent failure to implement plans is behind Governor Brown's statement: "The reason why everybody likes planning is because nobody has to do anything."[4]

Strategic planning

Goal Setting, Planning, and Controlling. You will notice that in this book we have divided our discussion of goals and planning into two chapters. We did this simply for the convenience of dealing with them sequentially and to reflect our emphasis on goals as the strategic managing variable. Some authors view goal setting as part of planning. For example, one places "choosing company objectives" at the top of his list of strategic planning activities.[5] Others

---

[3] Quoted in George H. Dixon, "An Objective Look at Management by Objectives," *Managerial Planning*, vol. 19, no. 1 (January–February 1970).

[4] Alan L. Otter, "Politics and People," p. 18.

[5] Robert N. Anthony, *Planning and Control Systems: Framework for Analysis* (Boston: Harvard University, Graduate School of Business Administration, Division of Research, 1965) pp. 15–21.

consider goal setting as the first of several planning phases.[6] It is fairly common practice for the term "strategic planning" to include the work of formulating goals and broad policies.[7]

OST
Texas Instruments, a progressive and successful electronics firm, uses a management system that appears consistent with our view that planning assumes the existence of goals. Its system, called "OST," uses three basic concepts: Objectives or goals, Strategies, and Tactics. "Objectives" are the overall results toward which behavior is directed. They result from an explicit consideration of the firm's environment and management philosophy. "Strategies" are the general courses of action to meet objectives. "Tactics" are specific, shorter-range programs for implementing strategies.[8]

Planning and controlling
What is the relationship between planning and controlling? Although planning and controlling are discussed in this and the next chapter as separate ideas, the distinction is somewhat arbitrary. Some activities are uniquely planning, some are uniquely controlling, and some overlap both areas. It is not always possible to tell from observing the behavior of managers whether they are planning or controlling. They may be doing one, both, or neither. As one planning expert notes, even though planning and controlling call for different types of mental activity, ". . . they do not relate to separable major categories of activities actually carried on in an organization, either at different times, or by different people, or for different situations."[9] Planning and controlling are two sides of the same coin. Nevertheless, it is useful to separate them, and we do so here.

Not all plans require budgets
Budgeting. Planning "cannot be equated with only one of its elements, or it will suffer."[10] Budgeting is one of the elements that may contribute to a firm's total planning activity. A budget is a concrete, although partial, expression of plans in financial terms. In some firms, the budget may be the only plan the firm has. Nevertheless, planning is broader than budgeting. Planning specifies the "what-how-when-where-who" of action toward goals. Furthermore, not all plans require financial expression. It is possible, for example, to have plans for the future structure or design of an organization without supporting those plans with a budget.

---

[6] W. Warren Haynes and Joseph L. Massie, *Management: Analysis, Concepts, and Cases* (Englewood Cliffs, N.J.: Prentice-Hall, 1969), p. 259.

[7] David W. Ewing, *The Practice of Planning* (New York: Harper & Row, Publishers, 1968), p. 21.

[8] David Allison, "Can A System Perform Like a Hero?" *Innovation*, no. 8 (1969), pp. 16–31.

[9] Anthony, *Planning and Control Systems: Framework for Analysis*, p. 10.

[10] E. Kirby Warren, *Long-Range Planning: The Executive Viewpoint* (Englewood Cliffs, N.J.: Prentice-Hall, 1966), p. 18.

Not all budgets reflect plans

Conversely, not all budgets reflect plans. It is easy to put together a budget—a simple estimate of income and allowable expenses. However, those budgets are not always preceded by conscious goal setting and planning activity. Managers should view budgeting as a useful and widely used tool or technique of planning, but they should understand that their responsibility for planning is more comprehensive than budgeting.

ZBOP

It is outside the scope of this book to discuss the technology of budgeting. That is the province of accounting and financial management textbooks. However, managing the budgeting process is within our scope. One interesting, new, and generally useful approach to managing the process of budgeting is "Zero-Base Budgeting." In an "Application" at the end of this chapter, we discuss Zero-Base Operational Planning and Budgeting (ZBOP), a budgeting approach used by Southern California Edison.

Three forecasting strategies

Forecasting. Like budgeting, forecasting is only one element of planning. It is possible to have forecasts without plans and plans without forecasts. "Forecasting" is the process of predicting future environments; it can be a help to managers when they form judgments and make assumptions about the future. Three forecasting strategies that involve different assumptions about the relationship of the present to the future are: deterministic; symptomatic; and systematic.

Causal relation

The "deterministic" strategy assumes that there is a close causal relation between the past and the future. When the deterministic strategy applies, there is greater reliance on forecasting techniques that utilize information about past performance. Thus, the past is used to predict the future. For example, past sales are used to predict future sales; past hospital admissions are used to predict future admissions

Present signs indicate future

The "symptomatic" strategy looks at present signs as indicators of the future. The widely used economic "leading indicators" are examples of measures of present economic activity that business firms use as signs of future levels of business. The symptomatic approach to forecasting is based on the concept that the sequence of events in a business cycle is consistent enough to warrant using the leading indicators as a basis for forecasting.

Underlying regularities

The "systematic" forecasting strategy looks for underlying regularities in the real world. The way to find these regularities is ". . . to block out much of reality and hold only to the abstractions that make up a system, such as a solar system, or a nuclear system, or an economic system." The econometric model of the U.S. economy developed by the Wharton School of Business at the University of Pennsylvania is an example of systematic forecasting.[11]

Forecasting methods

The methods used by business organizations to arrive at their forecasts range from informal guesses to very sophisticated methods that use statistical and quantitative techniques. A recent survey of corporate forecasting practices in 127 large business firms found that over half use one or more of the following seven methods: jury of executive opinion, regression analysis, time series smoothing, sales force composite, index numbers, econometric models, and customer expectations.[12] A discussion of these methods is outside the scope of this book. They are usually discussed in marketing textbooks or specialized books on forecasting.[13] However, in an "Application" at the end of this chapter, we discuss briefly a relatively new technique known as Delphi forecasting.

Factors influencing the choice of forecasting method

Several factors influence a firm's decision to use a particular forecasting method. The factors include: cost, user's technical ability, degree of accuracy required and availability of required statistical information, and problem-specific characteristics (such as degree of top-management support, time horizon to be forecast, and the functional area involved).[14] In general, the planning and forecasting methods used by a firm will be a mixture of informal and formal methods that meet the specific needs, requirements, and abilities of the firm.

---

[11] Leonard S. Silk and M. Louise Curley, *A Primer on Business Forecasting* (New York: Random House, 1970), pp. 3–17.

[12] Steven C. Wheelwright and Darral G. Clarke, "Corporate Forecasting: Promise and Reality," *Harvard Business Review,* vol. 54, no. 6 (November–December, 1976), pp. 40–42+.

[13] For example, E. Jerome McCarthy, *Basic Marketing: A Managerial Approach* (Homewood, Ill.: Richard D. Irwin, 1975), chap. 5. For a survey of the use of planning models, see Thomas H. Naylor and Daniel R. Gattis, "Corporate Planning Models," *California Management Review,* vol. 18, no. 4 (Summer 1976), pp. 69–78. And, for further study, see S. C. Wheelwright and Spyros Makridakis, *Forecasting Methods for Management* (New York: John Wiley & Sons, 1973).

[14] Steven C. Wheelwright and Darral G. Clarke, "Corporate Forecasting: Promise and Reality," pp. 41–42.

Summary box

> The phrase *primacy of planning* is used to convey the importance of planning and goal setting to everything else managers do.
>
> *Planning* is the process of determining the who-what-where-when-how of achieving goals. A *plan* is a predetermined set of actions toward a goal or goals.
>
> For purposes of discussion, we separate the related activities of planning and *controlling*. In order to emphasize the strategic importance of *goals*, we separate goal setting from planning. In practice, *strategic planning* often refers to the formulation of goals and broad policies.
>
> *Budgeting* and *forecasting* are elements or techniques of planning. Three *forecasting strategies* are deterministic, symptomatic, and systematic. A variety of forecasting methods is used in organizations, ranging from very informal, *ad-hoc* methods to sophisticated, formal methods.

CHARACTERISTICS OF PLANS

Dimensions

Plans have several dimensions or characteristics, including scope, repetitiveness, flexibility, and time span.[15]

Organizational space affected

Scope. "Scope" refers to the total amount of organizational space affected by plans. "Strategies" or "strategic plans" affect the total organization's direction and priorities. They are the result of an organization's attempt to match its resources and capabilities to the specific opportunities and risks in its environment. "Policies" are broad guides to behavior that contribute to goals and strategic plans. "Programs" or "tactics" are detailed courses of action aimed at carrying out strategic plans. "Functional plans" represent specific areas of the organization, such as sales, personnel, advertising, and production control. "Procedures," "methods," and "rules" are plans that are very limited in scope, but which serve as specific guides to behavior. Within a single area of managerial responsibility, plans vary according to their scope.

One-time or recurring activities

Repetitiveness. The "repetitiveness" dimension refers to whether plans are one-time projects or are behavioral guides for activities which recur. "Standing plans" refer to policies, procedures, methods, and rules that organizations use as guides to behavior. These guides are meant to assure consistent behavior in situations that

---

[15] Richard A. Johnson, Fremont E. Kast, and James E. Rosenzweig, *The Theory and Management of Systems* (3d ed., New York: McGraw-Hill Book Company, 1973), pp. 59–66.

occur with sufficient frequency to warrant formulating a predetermined behavioral response. Many well-managed organizations have policy and procedures manuals that spell out, in writing, various standing plans. "Single-use plans" are predetermined courses of action designed to fit a specific and nonrepetitive situation. Terms commonly used for such plans are "programs," "projects," and "special tasks." Part of the skill of managers is their ability to determine the best mix of standing plans and single-use plans.

Balance

Flexibility. The "flexibility" characteristic refers to the idea that plans can vary according to their responsiveness to change. This dimension is a matter of balance between stability and flexibility. On the one hand, every plan has to be flexible enough to adapt to the realities of the situation. A budget, for example, based on a sales forecast of $4 million cannot be implemented when sales are significantly above or below the forecast. "Variable" budgets provide a means of adjusting actual performance to changes in sales levels. On the other hand, if a plan is to be beneficial, it cannot be altered every time something occurs that does not conform to the plan or the assumptions on which the plan is based.

Planning horizon

Time Span. "Time span" refers to the different time periods represented by plans. Sometimes this time period is referred to as the "planning horizon." A common planning horizon in business organizations is one year; even then, the year is divided into smaller time segments. In effect, "long-range" or "strategic" planning covers any time period longer than one year, and "short-range" or "tactical" planning is for one year or less. A three-way set of terms for plans with various time spans includes strategic plans (five years and beyond), development plans (one to five years), and operational plans (one year).[16]

Contingencies

The role of contingencies is important in determining the appropriate time span. For example, a firm in the fashion industry has a planning horizon of only a few months. Public utilities have planning horizons of 20 years or more; since their sales volume is linked to population changes. Firms in the forestry industry may have to plan for a tree-life cycle of over 75 years.

Few guides

Obviously, the time-period covered influences and is influenced by the need for precision in planning, and it has important implications for the commitment of resources. Ideally, an organization has a mix of interrelated strategic and tactical plans for the accomplishment of goals. There are few known general guides for determining the most appropriate time span for an organization's plans. One general guide is that "Logical planning covers a period

[16] David I. Cleland and William R. King, *Management: A Systems Approach* (New York: McGraw-Hill Book Company, 1972), p. 270.

of time in the future necessary to foresee . . . the fulfillment of commitments involved in a decision."[17]

Practical value

The idea of planning dimensions or characteristics can be useful to you as a manager if you evaluate your plans against these characteristics. Do your plans cover the most appropriate time span? Have you provided for flexibility in the implementation of the plans? Are they comprehensive enough in scope? Do you have a useful mix of standing and single-use plans?

PLANNING PREMISES

Assumptions about environment

"Planning premises" are assumptions about the environment in which plans are to be implemented. From the viewpoint of planning for a total organization, the external and internal environments of the organization need to be assessed, and relevant assumptions made.

External environment premises

Premises for the Total Organization. Premises are needed—about external environment factors such as legislation, political climate, general economic conditions, industry trends, consumers' attitudes, interest rates, money supply, gross national product, social norms and values, competition, court decisions, consumers' behavior, relevant government and industry statistics, population characteristics, and technological developments.

Internal environment premises

Premises also need to be made about internal environment factors such as expected changes in key management personnel, cash flows and capital budgeting, organizational structure, advertising expenditures, research and development, production technology, product line, existing and anticipated policies, and management philosophy.

Sales forecast

The sales forecast is one of the major planning premises in business organizations. It is the result of numerous assumptions made about the *external* (industry sales, competitor's actions, for example) and *internal* (costs, technology, personnel, for example) environments of the firm. It is, in turn, a major premise affecting plans throughout the entire organization. Among other things, the sales forecast is the basis for capital planning, cash-flow analysis, personnel planning, production planning and controlling, and advertising and sales promotion planning.

A manager's environments

Premises for Organizational Subunits. Planning premises are not only required in planning for the *total* organization. All managers involved in planning and the planning process must give explicit consideration to premises about their own external and

---

[17] Harold Koontz and Cyril O'Donnell, *Management: A Systems and Contingency Analysis of Managerial Functions* (New York: McGraw-Hill Book Company, 1976), p. 266.

internal environments. That is, the *external* environment of managers of departments within an organization includes other parts of the organization with which the managers interact or which influence their accountability for performance. Their *internal* environment is their immediate area of responsibility.

Example

For example, suppose that you are the manager of the personnel department of a hospital. How does the idea of planning premises relate to your planning? In the first place, you need to establish *internal* premises—assumptions about people in your department, facilities, activities, and so on. Second, you need to establish *external* premises. Some of these premises are determined by the plans of other departments in the organization that are served by you. If the medical-records department is planning to expand, that expansion is one of your external premises. In addition, you have to establish premises about the labor market for medical-records technicians. The point is that all managers—those who plan for the *total* organization and those who plan for *subunits* within the organization—must establish premises about the external and internal environments.

Assessing the environment

Organization-Environment Interaction.   In order to establish planning premises managers must be able to assess their environment. At a minimum, this requires that firms: (1) identify relevant environmental groups; (2) determine the form, focus, and intensity of the groups' expectations; and (3) find a measurement scheme to predict the impact of the demands of the various groups.[18] In other words, if an organization is to respond and adapt to its environment, it must first of all identify those forces in the environment that are relevant to its operations. General Motors' environment includes almost the entire world, but the entire world is not necessarily relevant to the operations of General Motors. In addition, the organization must have some way of knowing what the environment expects, and some way of gauging the force of its demands.

Scanning process

How do organizations obtain information about their external environment? One answer to this question is called the "scanning process." It consists of four modes of scanning: "undirected viewing," "conditioned viewing," "informal search," and "formal search."[19]

Four scanning modes

Undirected viewing is defined as general exposure to information, when the viewer has no specific purpose in mind except, possibly, exploration. Conditioned viewing is defined as directed exposure, not involving active search, in which the viewer is sensi-

---

[18] Walter Hill, "The Goal Formation Process in Complex Organizations," *Journal of Management Studies,* vol. 6 (May 1969), pp. 198–206.

[19] Francis Joseph Aguilar, *Scanning the Business Environment* (New York: Macmillan Company, 1967).

tive to particular kinds of data and is ready to assess their significance as they are encountered. Informal search is an effort to actively seek out information for a specific purpose, but the effort is relatively limited and unstructured. Formal search is a structured, deliberate effort to secure specific information. It implies that the organization knows what kind of information it needs, and that it is organized to get that information.

Contingencies

Which scanning mode will an organization use? Perhaps all four will be used on a selective basis, depending on such contingencies as: time available for scanning; adequacy of existing information; importance of the problem; availability of resources, cost-benefit considerations, and so on. Regardless of which scanning mode is used, the idea of the scanning process is a realistic and useful one for managers to consider. Its output can provide the basis for negotiating with the external environment.[20]

Negotiating strategies

In negotiating with the external environment, an organization can use a variety of strategies. One view of these strategies is that they can range from competition to coalition. "Competition" is a strategy that is least costly to the organization in terms of the organization's control over decisions. That is, when a business firm competes with another firm, it does not give up any of its control over decision making in the firm. On the other hand, "coalitions," such as mergers and consolidations, are very costly ways for an organization to adapt to an environmental force. When a business firm merges with another firm, the decision-making processes in both firms are altered. Between competition and coalition, organizations can choose negotiating strategies that vary in cost as measured by control over decision making.[21]

ORGANIZING FOR PLANNING

Individual managers

How is formal planning integrated into organizations? There are several approaches, and many organizations use all of them, depending upon the demands that are perceived in their unique situation. Some organizations, particularly small organizations, place most of the authority and responsibility for effective planning in the hands of individual managers. The production manager, for example, will be held accountable for planning for the overall production activity.

Specialized assistance

Other organizations provide managers with specialized assistance in performing their planning activity. Although the individ-

[20] For additional information, see Charles W. Hofer, "Research on Strategic Planning: A Survey of Past Studies and Suggestions for Future Efforts," *Journal of Economics and Business,* vol. 28, no. 3 (Spring–Summer 1976), pp. 264–66.

[21] James D. Thompson and William J. McEwen, "Organizational Goals and Environment: Goal-Setting as an Interaction Process," *American Sociological Review,* vol. 23 (February 1958), pp. 23–31.

ual managers are still held accountable for effective planning in their area of responsibility, they have available the help of sales forecasters, accountants, schedulers, recruiters, and trainers. These planning specialists do not *do* the planning, but they provide services to assure effective planning processes.

Planning groups, departments

Formal Planning Units.   Still other organizations establish formal organizational units to assure coordination of all planning activities and to engage in overall organizational planning. These organizational units can take the form of formal planning departments, planning groups or committees, or even an individual planning director. Such formal planning units are becoming more common, especially in large-scale organizations, where planning is a complex process requiring extensive coordination among units within the organization. One study of long-range planning in 250 firms in varied industries reported that 55 percent of the firms utilized, in some capacity, a planning department or a planning specialist.[22]

Formal planning will become more common

Formal planning units are likely to become even more common in various types of organizations. Hospitals, for example, are "strongly encouraged" by the Joint Commission on Hospital Accreditation to have planning committees for long-range planning. Formation of planning advisory groups is a requirement of the Community Mental Health Centers Act and of several other laws affecting community planning.

What do planning groups do?

In business firms, planning groups or departments are growing in popularity. Such groups assist management by making environmental forecasts, helping in goal setting and strategy formulation, monitoring planning activities throughout the organization, being available to management for planning consulting, and coordinating and consolidating the planning efforts of others. Sometimes planning groups perform special functions such as evaluating capital expansion proposals, project development, and serving as an organizational "think tank."[23] Another activity of planning groups and departments is to propose "planning guides" or manuals that managers can use for guidance in their planning efforts.[24]

Need to avoid isolation

One study of 58 business organizations with identifiable formal planning functions (not necessarily planning departments) found that the individuals responsible for formal planning spend half their time working alone, reading and writing reports. The study

[22] Leslie W. Rice, "The How and Who of Long Range Planning," *Business Horizons,* vol. 16, no. 6 (December 1973), p. 29.

[23] Robert J. Litschert and Edward A. Nicholson, "Corporate Long-Range Planning Groups: Some Different Approaches," *Long Range Planning,* vol. 7, no. 4 (August 1974), pp. 62–66.

[24] Rochelle O'Connor, "Corporate Planning Guides: Roadmaps to the Future," *Conference Board Record,* vol. 13, no. 9 (September 1976), pp. 29–31.

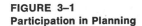

FIGURE 3–1
Participation in Planning

"Things must be going badly--he keeps referring
to it as my plan."

The Wall Street Journal, March 18, 1974.

suggests that the formal planners' relative isolation from meetings with managers and other organization members may be one factor contributing to a lack of planning effectiveness. The danger of such isolation can be reduced if planning is not separated from the implementation of plans.[25]

Range of participation

Planning Participation. Organizing for planning is also concerned with the extent of employee participation in the planning process. Even when individual managers do most of their own planning, they often seek the participation of peers and subordinates. The participation may range from a minimal opinion-seeking to giving subordinates a voice in the actual decision making that goes into planning. What degree of participation is best? There is no simple answer to that question. We will have much more to say about it in Chapter 11.

Contingencies

The optimum degree of participation depends on such contingencies as time, cost, importance of the plans, interest and knowl-

[25] Larry E. Greiner, "Integrating Formal Planning into Organizations," in F. J. Aguilar, R. A. Howell, and R. F. Vancil, eds., *Formal Planning Systems: 1970* (Cambridge, Mass.: Harvard University, Graduate School of Business Administration, 1970), p. 88.

edge of potential participants, the manager's style, the manager's relation with subordinates and peers, the type of problem, and so on. The importance of one of these contingencies, the knowledge of the participants, can be illustrated by a study in the area of health planning. The study found that "planning groups with *consumer* members identified solutions with significantly lower quality than planning groups with *expert* members [emphasis added]." In other words, it helps if the participants are knowledgeable about the planning problem.[26]

Summary box

> Plans may be characterized in terms of several characteristics: scope, repetitiveness, flexibility, and time span. A term commonly used to refer to the time-span of plans is *planning horizon.*
>
> *Planning premises* are assumptions about the environment in which plans are to be implemented. Whether from the viewpoint of the total organization or of subunits within the organization, managers must make premises about both their *internal* and *external* environments.
>
> In order to establish planning premises managers must be able to assess their environment. A *four-mode scanning process* is one view of how firms obtain information about their environment for purposes of developing negotiating strategies. One view of these strategies is that they range from *competition* to *coalition.*
>
> Various approaches to *organizing for planning* are currently in use—assigning responsibility for planning to individual managers, planning specialists, formal planning units, and various combinations of these. There are several contingencies that influence the appropriate *degree of participation* that should be used in the planning process.

THE FORMAL PLANNING PROCESS

Informal planning

Some managerial planning is nothing more sophisticated than making snap judgments about what action to take tomorrow. Right or wrong, "seat-of-the pants" planning characterizes much managing. Planning in a small manufacturing plant that produces only to customers' specifications is largely limited to responding to customers' actual orders. This type of informal, *ad-hoc,* planning is important, not only in small companies, but also as a complement to more formal planning in moderate and large-size organizations. For our purposes here, we want to examine the idea of planning as

---

[26] Paul C. Nutt, "The Merits of Using Experts or Consumers as Members of Planning Groups: A Field Experiment in Health Planning," *Academy of Management Journal,* vol. 19, no. 3 (September 1976), p. 392.

a formal process in organizations, while still recognizing the importance and pervasiveness of informal approaches.

Formal planning

One writer suggests that ". . . most, or perhaps virtually all, businesses and organizations of any size and history have some sort of formal planning process."[27] There is some evidence that even moderate-size companies take a formal or systematic approach to planning. In a survey of 93 companies, most of which had fewer than 2,000 employees, The Conference Board found that all but 4 used a formal approach to planning, that 42 of the companies plan five years ahead, and that 6 plan as much as ten years ahead. Of course, the degree of the formality of the planning process varies.[28]

Contingencies

Variations in the Planning Process. Clearly, the planning process must be adapted to the needs of the organization in which it is used. In other words, various contingencies affect the planning process that will be used in an organization. Some of these contingencies include the managing style of the CEO, the degree of uncertainty in the organization's external environment, the stage of development of the firm, and the firm's interest in diversification. By way of illustration, we will discuss the latter two contingencies.[29]

Three stages of development

One way of looking at the stages of development of a firm is in terms of moving from a single product firm (Stage 1), to a firm in several related areas (Stage 2), to a firm that has diversified into unrelated areas. An example of a firm in stage 1 is the Adolph Coors Company; examples of firms in stage 2 are U.S. Steel Company and Eastman Kodak; a firm in Stage 3 is International Telephone & Telegraph.

Diversification interest

In terms of their diversification, firms can be classed as having a broad or narrow interest. A "broad interest" refers to an interest in diversification outside the current product-mix of the firm. A "narrow interest" reflects a predisposition to concentrate on the present product line. These two ideas can be placed into a planning matrix (Figure 3–2).

Cell A firms; Cell F firms

Firms characterized by Cell A would use the simplest planning process. Their primary planning tool is the capital budget; the president of the firm may be the primary planning officer, and planning decisions may heavily reflect his judgment, experience, and intuition. Firms characterized by Cell F require the most comprehensive planning process. The process relies on sophisticated

[27] George H. Dixon, "Planning: Is It Mostly an Exercise?" *Managerial Planning,* vol. 22, no. 5 (September–October 1973), p. 4.

[28] Jeremy Bacon, *Planning and Forecasting in the Smaller Company* (New York: The Conference Board, Inc., 1971), pp. 3–5.

[29] This section is based on Milton Leontiades, "Planning: A Reexamination of Fundamentals," *Journal of Economics and Business,* vol. 28, no. 3 (Spring–Summer 1976), pp. 189–94.

FIGURE 3–2
Planning Matrix

Stage of Development	Interest in Diversification	
	Narrow	Broad
1. Single-product	A	D
2. Related products	B	E
3. Diversified	C	F

planning tools and must provide for the considerations of essentially different types of planning units. Thus, the planning system must be suited to two contingencies: the firm's stage of development and its interest on diversification.

Main point

Our main point in presenting Figure 3–2 is to emphasize that a firm's planning process must be responsive to the contingencies that press on it. Our examples suggest two contingencies, but they are only two and, for particular firms, may not be the most crucial ones.

A conceptual process

Similarities in the Planning Process. Although planning processes vary with firm-related contingencies, there are similarities among firms. In other words, there is such a thing as a general, or "conceptual" planning process that can be followed, but which much be adapted to specific contingencies.

An eight-step planning process

Some years ago, a prominent management author suggested an eight-step planning process that is a variation of the scientific method of problem solving and decision making. These steps represent a conceptual approach to the planning process. That is, although the manner of implementing the steps depends on contingencies in the immediate situation, the basic process remains the same. The eight steps are as follows:

1. Recognize the problem and determine its difficulties.
2. Preliminary observation, analysis, and determination of limiting factors.
3. Develop tentative solutions or plans.
4. Evaluate proposed solutions.
5. Develop preferred solution.
6. Final evaluation of the solution.
7. Intelligent compromise.
8. Installation and activation of the agreed-on plan.[30]

[30] Adapted from Ralph C. Davis, *The Fundamentals of Top Management* (New York: Harper & Bros., 1951), chap. 3.

AN ILLUSTRATION OF A PLANNING PROCESS

One approach

This section illustrates an approach to planning used by a multidivisional business organization that produces and distributes electronic consumer products. The illustration is not intended to serve as an example of the best or ideal approach to planning. It is simply the approach actually used by one very successful American business firm.

Profits, products, markets

A Dynamic Feedback Process.   The firm views planning as an orderly process by which management rationally decides both the amount of profit growth it intends the business to achieve and the product and market directions through which it intends to achieve that growth. Ideally, the firm bases its planning on what it considers to be a realistic appraisal of the prospects of the outside environment and on a sound evaluation of the company's present strengths and weaknesses. Planning is viewed as one way to sharpen management's ability to realistically conceptualize the future and to identify the best courses of action to follow in that future. Planning is seen as a dynamic process, in which each step has a feedback effect on every other step. This "feedback effect" is illustrated in Figure 3–3.

Four strategies

Products–Markets Analysis.   A products–markets analysis of the question, "What must we do differently?" suggests four different strategies. As shown in Figure 3–4, introducing new products into

FIGURE 3–3
Planning as a Dynamic Process with Feedback at Each Step

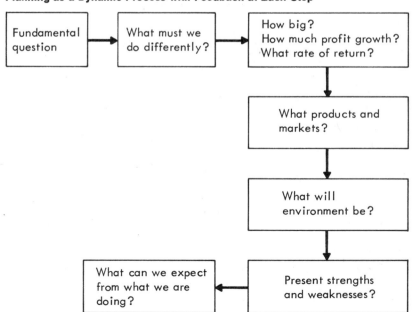

new markets requires additional diversification and is probably the most risky of the four strategies. On the other hand, better distribution of existing products in existing markets is the least risky of the four strategies in terms of profit growth.

FIGURE 3–4
Products–Markets Strategies

Products \ Markets	New	Existing
New	Strategy 1: Additional diversification	Strategy 2: Product development
Existing	Strategy 3: Market development	Strategy 4: Operational planning

Total planning program

Steps Followed in Planning. The total planning program followed by the firm involves several steps which are performed sequentially, but which also are characterized by the feedback effect mentioned in connection with Figure 3–3. The steps followed by the firm in its overall approach to planning are:

1. Determine profit-growth goals.
2. Prime assumptions (premises).
3. Divisional assumptions (premises).
4. Divisional five-year forecasts—tentative.
5. Challenge and review meetings.
6. Divisional five-year forecasts—final.
7. Corporate five-year forecast.
8. Planning gap—corporate.
9. Corporate plans to fill gap.
10. Assigned divisional profit goals.
11. Planning gap—divisional.
12. Divisional objectives and goals.
13. Strategies and plans.

Profitable growth

Step 1 in the process is to determine profit-growth goals. This is a specific illustration of the idea that "The success of any business is measured by the extent to which the resources of that business are kept in profitable growth balance with the customer needs served by those resources."[31]

Planning premises

The premises noted in steps 2 and 3 are assumptions about the internal and external environments of the firm. These assumptions

[31] Robert W. Ferrell, *Customer-Oriented Planning* (New York: American Management Association, 1964), p. 24.

are often called "planning premises." Steps 4, 5, 6, and 7 provide for the development, testing, and redevelopment of proposed solutions.

Planning gap, seven goal areas

The term "gap," noted in steps 8, 9, and 11, refers to the difference between goals and expected results. Thus, plans at both corporate and divisional levels are required to fill the gaps. Finally, steps 12 and 13 refer to divisional objectives and goals that are the basis for specific strategies and plans. The firm under discussion establishes divisional objectives and goals in seven areas: profits; products and technology; markets and service; operations; international; people and facilities; and business strategy and development.

FINDING TIME TO PLAN

The pressure of time

Invariably, when managers talk about planning the conversation will come around to something like this: "Planning is great and should be done, but I don't have time to do it." Managers often have time only for handling each day's operating problems, sometimes not even enough time for those. Of course, it is easy to say that "finding time for planning is part of the manager's job," but there is only so much time available, and there is usually a waiting list of things for managers to do with that time. Planning is easy to put off. It is not exciting to action-oriented managers, and it often results in plans that are never implemented.

Reward planning

Is there some way to assure that managers have and take time to plan? There are some minor steps they can take, such as working longer hours and learning how to manage their time better. These steps may get some useful results. However, a more useful approach exists. If an organization wants its managers to plan, planning must be an activity that is rewarded. This general approach applies to much of the behavior desired of managers, such as controlling, decision making, communicating, goal setting, and motivating. However, we want to mention rewards now, early in the book, because it is a very simple and generally useful idea.

Reason why managers do not plan

One important reason why managers do not plan in necessary and sufficient ways is that the organization's reward structure does not encourage and demand good planning. Although there are many exceptions, managers tend to behave in ways that lead to rewards that they desire. Some managers do an excellent job of planning in spite of the organization's design and reward system. The important point, however, is that the design of the organization and its reward structure either encourages good planning or it does not. If planning is essential to the effective and efficient accomplishment of goals, then the organization's design and reward system must assure that good planning is one of the organization's outputs.

Hold
managers
accountable

If managers know they will be held accountable by their immediate superiors, not only for current performance but also for their *preparation for future performance*, they will be more likely to prepare for that future performance. This is what was done at Potlatch Corporation, as we noted at the beginning of this chapter. Actual goals that relate to the preparation for future performance must be set. Such preparation can include manpower planning, forecasting of capital requirements, developing new product opportunities, planning for necessary changes in the organization, and planning for training and development of personnel.

Example

An example of how one organization assures that managers take time to plan is provided by Texas Instruments (TI). TI holds annual planning meetings that run for a week or more. At these meetings, every corporate objective and strategy is evaluated by key executives. Managers prepare for these meetings throughout the year, because they must defend their strategy statements and their estimates of commitments required to assure strategy success. Managers at TI take these planning meetings seriously, and they know that their careers are affected by their performance at these meetings. Therefore, TI, through the organizational mechanism of an annual planning meeting, assures that its managers find time to plan.

Summary box

Informal planning activities are necessary complements to formal planning processes used in organizations. The particular planning process used varies with several contingencies. Several of these contingencies were noted in this chapter. However, there is such a thing as a general or *conceptual planning process*. One view of this process is a variation of the scientific method of problem solving and decision making.

An illustration was given of the planning process used in a multidivisional business organization that produces and distributes electronic consumer products.

The problem of managers finding *time* to do necessary planning is basically the problem of finding time to do anything. If planning is essential to the effective and efficient accomplishment of goals, then the design of the organization and its reward structure must assure that good planning will be one of the organization's outputs.

CHECK YOUR UNDERSTANDING

Plan

Planning

Primacy of planning

Strategic planning

Budgeting

Forecasting

Forecasting strategies

Forecasting methods

Scope variations in plans

Repetitiveness variations in plans

Time span variations in plans

Planning horizon

Planning premises

Four-mode scanning process

Negotiating strategies

Approaches to organizing for
   planning

Variations in the planning process

Idea of a conceptual planning
   process

Planning gap

Strategy for assuring that
   managers will plan

Zero-base budgeting

Distinguishing characteristics of
   Delphi forecasting

STUDY QUESTIONS

1. How, in your opinion, can plans enhance an organization's capacity to adapt to changing conditions? Under what circumstances might plans restrict an organization's adaptability?

2. Arrange an interview with a top executive or administrator. Determine if a formal planning process is followed in the organization. What are the specific steps in the process? How do they relate to the eight-step process suggested in the text? Who participates in the process? How does the organization assure that its executives take the necessary time to plan? What specific premises does the organization use in its planning? How is the planning integrated into the organization design?

3. Arrange an interview with a foreman or a supervisor of a small department within an organization. Determine the type of planning the supervisor does. Contrast planning at this level with that at the top level of the organization.

4. Give examples of internal and external planning premises that are important to an organization with which you are now associated.

5. What is the "external" environment of a department within an organization? How does it differ from the external environment of the entire organization?

6. Give examples of the four modes of scanning included in the scanning process that organizations use to gain information about their environment.

7. Identify several contingencies that could influence the way that a firm organizes for planning and the way that it approaches the planning process.

8. To what extent are the ideas of a planning process, planning characteristics, and planning premises applicable to your personal planning? Discuss.

```
┌─────────────────────────────────┐
│                                 │
│                                 │
│    P L A N   A H E A            │
│                          ◠      │
│                                 │
└─────────────────────────────────┘
```

APPLICATION: ZERO-BASED BUDGETING*

Budgeting is one of the elements that may contribute to a firm's total planning activity. In some firms the budget may represent the only type of formal plan; in almost every business firm, budgets are an important planning goal. "Zero-base budgeting" is a relatively new approach to budgeting for general and administrative costs, special programs, or clearly identifiable projects. The way it works can be illustrated by reference to ZBOP, used by Southern California Edison (SCE).

When ZBOP is used, each project and each continuing work activity is broken down into smaller "elements." The elements represent some meaningful minimum cost, say, $10,000. For each element, a "decision package" is prepared; it summarizes the element's scope of work, cost, personnel requirements, time schedule, anticipated benefits, and expected consequences if the element is not performed.

Each decision package is then *ranked* against packages for other current and proposed elements and projects. This priority ranking continues throughout the various SCE divisions. As it proceeds, each higher-level manager merges and reranks the lower-priority packages of all the subunits of SCE that report to that manager.

This ranking process leads to one *organization-wide* list of prioritized and priced-out decision packages built from the ground up, or "zero-base." These packages, in turn, provide the base for establishing individual department and total company budget levels.

SCE initiated ZBOP on a trial basis in six staff departments reporting to the financial vice president. Later, the ZBOP process was extended throughout the entire company. Like any approach to operational planning and controlling, ZBOP requires sufficient time before it can be fairly evaluated. Not all managers responded to ZBOP with equal enthusiasm or understanding, nor did all managers experience the same degree of success with it.

Nevertheless, SCE feels that the ZBOP process has yielded good results. Compared to the traditional budgeting process (which must still be used in certain parts of SCE's operations), ZBOP forces managers to critically examine activities and projects for their

---

* Source: Adapted by permission of the publisher from "Zero-Base Budgeting: How to Get Rid of Corporate Crabgrass" by Donald N. Anderson, *Management Review*, October 1976, © by AMACOM, a division of American Management Association.

cost effectiveness; places projects in competition with others throughout the company; encourages grassroots participation in the budgeting process; and develops a professional, cost-reduction oriented spirit among managers.

1. What do you see as the essential idea of zero-base budgeting that differentiates it from traditional budgeting?

2. What, in your opinion, are some indirect benefits of a process like ZBOP? What are some problems that might be encountered during the (a) introduction and (b) continuance of ZBOP?

APPLICATION: DELPHI FORECASTING*

Delphi forecasting is an interesting, though not yet widely used, approach for obtaining and refining the opinions of a group of persons about the future. It was developed in the 1960s by personnel of the Rand Corporation. Since then, it has been used in the areas of personnel, transportation, environmental, marketing, and hospital planning, to name a few. An example will be useful in identifying the distinguishing characteristics of Delphi forecasting.

Corning Glass Works wanted to forecast future sales of electronic products. The firm decided to use Delphi as one procedure for gathering information. Here is how Corning proceeded. First, it identified and obtained the cooperation of over 40 experts on electronic businesses. Since electronics is such a broad field, the experts were from three areas: consumer products, industrial products, and government programs. The experts, divided into three different "panels," were unknown to each other.

Next, Corning, by mail, asked each panel member to identify important future events that might be important to the electronics business. From their responses, the Delphi administrator prepared a structured first questionnaire asking about specific electronics-related events.

Then the questionnaire was mailed to the panel members, asking them to indicate the extent to which each event might occur five or ten years in the future. When these questionnaires were returned, about nine weeks after they were mailed, the Delphi administrator prepared a *statistical summary* (the median, and the upper and lower-quartile dates) of the responses. In addition, a narrative summary was prepared of the reasons given for the responses. The narrative and statistical summaries, plus the original list of events mentioned on the first questionnaire, became the basis for the second questionnaire. Thus, each panel member received *controlled feedback* about the opinions of all other panel members. This feedback was used by the panel members when they responded to the second questionnaire.

This procedure was repeated for a third questionnaire. In theory, such an *iterative procedure* can continue until a consensus about

---

* Source: Jeffrey L. Johnson, "A Ten-Year Delphi Forecast in the Electronics Industry," *Industrial Marketing Management,* vol. 5, no. 1 (March 1976), pp. 45–55.

all questions is reached. In practice, there is little additional information to be gained beyond the third iteration. Corning found that the first-round responses differed from those of the third round on less than 2 percent of the questions.

The net result of Corning's using the Delphi procedure was that it obtained a large amount of information about electronic sales events. Further, it obtained some degree of consensus about these events.

1. Identify the distinguishing characteristics of the Delphi forecasting procedure.

2. What, in your opinion, are some problems that might be encountered if you were administering a Delphi forecast?

Objectives of Chapter 4

- To define managerial controlling and recognize its increasing importance.
- To identify the four fundamental elements in the control process.
- To propose a framework for thinking about what can be controlled by managers.
- To distinguish three types of control systems.
- To assess the potential influence on behavior of control systems, both positive and negative.
- To express three views about managerial controlling.

Outline of Chapter 4

Controlling: Some Basic Concepts
Definition
Increasing Importance
Elements of the Control Process
What Can Managers Control?
Four Controllable Aspects
Pareto's Law
Cost Points
The Idea of Control Tolerances
Types of Control Systems
Internal and External Control
Proactive and Reactive Control
Open and Closed-Loop Control
The Human Side of Controlling
Positive Potentialities of Control Systems
Negative Potentialities of Control Systems
Controlling: Managerial Perspectives
Overcontrol versus Undercontrol
Costs versus Benefits
Means versus Ends

MANAGERIAL
CONTROLLING

Theorists as well as practicing executives agree that good management requires effective control.

Earl P. Strong and Robert D. Smith

Organizational control systems often produce unintended consequences.

Cortlandt Cammann and David A. Nadler

Nick

Nick is the owner and manager of the Showboat, a popular restaurant and bar located in a large Midwest city. Like most other small business operators, Nick's major problem is finding and keeping good "help"—cooks, bartenders, waitresses, dishwashers. Nick's most recent problem employee was Hobby, the nightwatchman.

Hobby

Hobby liked to drink, and Nick suspected that Hobby was doing most of his drinking on the job. Apparently, Hobby felt that helping himself to the bar whiskey was one of the fringe benefits of being alone all night at the Showboat. Nick disagreed, and decided to implement a control process.

First control system

Before leaving the restaurant at night, Nick placed every two whiskey bottles behind the bar at a 45° angle to each other. When he returned the next day, he looked at the collection of about 100 bottles and could tell exactly which one had been moved. Hobby never replaced the bottle that he had used at the proper angle to the adjacent bottle. For several days, Nick confronted Hobby with statements like, "Hobby, I see you had two drinks of Canadian Club last night," or "How was the Seagram's 7 last night, Hobby?"

Behavioral flexibility

Completely perplexed, Hobby finally altered his behavior. Illustrating his flexibility and his capacity to beat Nick's control system, Hobby quit drinking whiskey and switched to beer. However, Nick had a control system for beer, too.

Second control system

Every night, just before leaving the Showboat to go home, Nick completely emptied the containers that caught the bottletops when the bartender opened a bottle of beer. When Nick arrived at the Showboat the next day, he examined the bottletop containers. On several occasions, Nick was able to say, "Hobby, who did you sell a Budweiser to last night?" or "There seem to be two bottles of Pabst Blue Ribbon missing, Hobby."

Result

Hobby never did figure out how Nick always managed to know exactly what he had drunk the night before. Nick finally fired Hobby for drinking on the job—but for drinking whiskey he had purchased elsewhere. Although his control system did not stop Hobby's drinking, it did stop Hobby's drinking of Nick's whiskey and beer.

This chapter

This true incident may seem like a trivial way to introduce the subject of managerial control. But it raises questions that are basic to even the most sophisticated control systems. What is controlling? What are its basic elements? What are some types of control systems? What can managers control? How do control systems affect behavior? Is there a range of performance within which behavior can be viewed as "in control?" We shall try to answer these and other questions in this chapter. Before we go on, however, we want to indicate how this chapter relates to the chapters on goals and planning.

Tie-in to last two chapters

Goals (discusssed in Chapter 2) are the foundation for plans. Since planning and controlling activities of managers are so interrelated, much of the discussion of *planning* (in Chapter 3) is important to our discussion of *controlling*. Specifically, the *premises* made when formulating plans influence the process of controlling. Significant changes in any of the major planning premises can cause performance to go "out of control." The *characteristics* of plans influence the control process. Long-range plans, for example, require the application of different control techniques than short-range or standing plans. Plans of a broad scope require more coordination to control than plans of limited scope. Finally, the discussion of *organizing for planning* also applies to the controlling activity. As with planning, some organizations use specialized departments for control purposes—such as production control, credit control, internal auditing, inventory control, and quality control.

CONTROLLING: SOME BASIC CONCEPTS

Controlling: What and why

Definition. Managerial controlling is the process of assuring that actions are in line with desired results. The objective of controlling is not to assure that actions conform to plans; sometimes it is necessary to change plans in response to information acquired in the process of controlling. The objective of controlling is to assure that actions contribute to *goal accomplishment*. The ultimate justification of both planning and controlling is their contribution to goals. Both activities are essential to efficient and effective managerial performance. Both help managers meet their accountabilities.

Larger firms

Increasing Importance. Control has always been important to effective managing. The failure to support goals and plans with adequate control systems, behavior, and resources explains why managers are so often ineffective. Control is becoming an ever more important managerial function.[1] One reason for this is the trend toward larger organizations. In general, larger firms require more complex control systems. Steak and Ale requires a somewhat more elaborate control system than Nick's Showboat.

Changing environment

Another reason for the growing importance of control is the rapidly changing and uncertain environment. Nothing illustrates this point better than the changes created in the world economy by the energy crisis. The huge price increases in crude oil imposed (they more than quadrupled between 1974 and 1977) by the Organization of Petroleum Exporting Countries (OPEC) brought about permanent changes in cost-price relationships.[2] In one way or another these changes affect managing in *all types* of organizations. One executive puts it this way: "Everything [before the oil embargo] is history . . . the future is a whole new game."[3]

Four fundamental elements

Elements of the Control Process. Four elements are necessary to a control process: (1) a predetermined goal, standard, or plan; (2) measurement of performance; (3) comparison of performance with the goal; and (4) corrective action when required. The corrective action may take the form of attempting to bring performance into line with plans, or to bring plans into line with performance.

Control process terms

The above four elements are often referred to as: (1) a "characteristic" or condition to be controlled; (2) a "sensor"—a way to sense or measure the characteristic or condition; (3) a "comparator"—an individual, unit, or device that compares measurements with the plan or standard; and (4) an "activator"—an individual, unit, or mechanism that directs action to bring about a change in the operating system.[4] These four terms are in common use in today's automated and computerized control processes. Figure 4–1

[1] Philip Kotler, *Marketing Management: Analysis, Planning, and Control,* 2d ed. (Englewood Cliffs, N.J.: Prentice-Hall, 1972), pp. 752–53.

[2] One estimate of the impact in 1977 alone of the OPEC-induced oil price increases is that they will cost the United States $75 billion in gross national product, 3 million jobs, and $90 billion in disposable income. See "The Cartel's New Blow to the World Economy," *Business Week,* January 10, 1977, pp. 61–62.

[3] Attributed to Irving Shapiro, DuPont Company in H. Igor Ansoff, "Managing Strategic Surprise by Response to Weak Signals," *California Management Review,* vol. 18, no. 2 (Winter 1975), p. 21.

[4] Richard A. Johnson, Fremont E. Kast, and James E. Rosenzweig, *The Theory and Management of Systems,* 3d ed. (New York: McGraw-Hill Book Company, 1973), p. 75.

FIGURE 4–1
The Four Elements in the Control Process

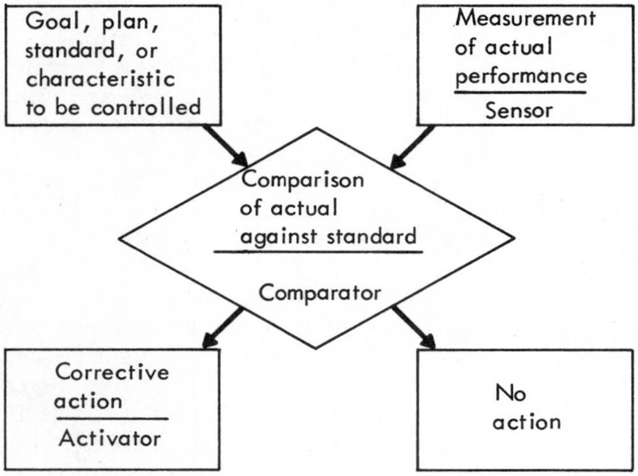

shows the interaction of the four elements or steps in the control process.

Universal process

The elements of the controlling process are "universal" in the sense that controlling any process, activity, or behavior involves, to some degree, these four elements. That is, the basic nature of the control process is always the same, even though its application varies. "The control process is a basic one and remains essentially the same regardless of the activity involved or its location in the organization."[5] Can you identify the four elements in the incident used to open this chapter?

WHAT CAN MANAGERS CONTROL?

Performance factors

In Chapter 1, we took the position that managers manage people rather than things, such as money or machines. Another way of stating that idea is to say that, through managing *people*, managers indirectly manage all other types of *things* that enter into performance—for example, materials, computers, supplies, money, equipment, and information. Performance factors may be thought of, therefore, as falling into one of two categories: people and things. Clearly, both these performance factors must be managed and controlled. But what is it about performance factors that can be controlled?

Quantity, quality, time, and cost

Four Controllable Aspects.   There are four aspects of performance factors that can be managed and controlled: quantity, quality, time, and cost. When we speak of "controlling people," we mean

---

[5] Gary Dessler, *Organization and Management: A Contingency Approach* (Englewood Cliffs, N.J.: Prentice-Hall, 1976), p. 360.

simply that efforts are made to regulate the quantity, quality, timing, and cost of their work performance. You can readily see how Nick tried to do this with Hobby. Similarly, nonhuman performance can be controlled: When we refer to "controlling machines," we simply mean that the quantity, quality, and costs of the output are regulated in some way and attempts are made to efficiently use available machine time.

Relating performance factors to controllable aspects

Figure 4–2 illustrates the idea of performance factors and their controllable aspects. There are control techniques applicable to each of the cells shown in Figure 4–2. For example, in controlling

FIGURE 4–2
Performance Factors and Their Controllable Aspects

	Performance Factors	
Controllable Aspect	*People*	*Things*
Quantity	A	E
Quality	B	F
Time	C	G
Cost	D	H

the *quality* of the performance of employees, cell B, the following resources are used: written job instructions, policies that assure consistent job behavior, organization manuals, promotion policies based on quality of performance, wage and salary plans that reward quality, training programs designed to increase skills and raise quality levels, and systematic quality control procedures that compare performance with standards. Cell E refers to the control of the *quantity* of things. If inventories are used as an example, common techniques include: economic order quantity buying, use of statistical reorder points, buying as a hedge against inflation, and hand-to-mouth buying when prices are expected to fall.[6]

Relating organizational functions to performance factors

The four controllable aspects can also be related to the major functions of an organization. For example, Figure 4–3 applies the idea to several major functions of a business organization. Each of these functions may be very specialized in its use of control techniques. Cell C is illustrated by the practice in some large business firms of investing excess cash for as short a time period as one day in order to earn interest. Cell B is illustrated by policies that require investment portfolios to have a mix between stocks and bonds. In controlling the timing of production, cell G, some firms use very sophisticated scheduling techniques so as to assure the best time schedule. Finally, the timing of marketing activities,

---

[6] We do not discuss in this chapter specific control techniques such as budgeting, ratio analysis, break-even analysis, and return on investment. Control techniques are discussed in more specialized books.

FIGURE 4–3
Major Functions of a Business Organization and Their Controllable
Aspects

	Sample Functions			
Controllable Aspect	Finance	Production	Marketing	Engineering
Quantity.................	A	E	I	M
Quality.................	B	F	J	N
Time...................	C	G	K	O
Cost...................	D	H	L	P

cell K, is controlled through test marketing, advertising campaigns, and special promotions.

A little means a lot

Pareto's Law. An interesting concept that can be useful in controlling quantity and cost is Pareto's law. This law states that "the significant elements in a specified group usually constitute a relatively small portion of the total items in the group."[7]

Pareto curve

Figure 4–4 is an example of a curve based on Pareto's law. Figure 4–4 shows that 20 percent of the inventory accounts for 80 percent of the value of the inventory. Additional examples of Pareto's law are: 10 percent of a firm's employees may account for 80 percent of the grievances filed, and 90 percent of a firm's orders may come from 5 percent of its customers. Five percent of a firm's executives may account for 50 percent of the new ideas.[8] When Pareto's law applies, the lesson for managers is clear: identify the significant elements and concentrate control efforts on those elements. See the "Application" at the end of this chapter for an illustration of Pareto's law.

Four cost point categories

Cost Points. The basic idea of Pareto's law is contained in the idea of "cost points." A "cost point" is an activity within a manager's area of responsibility that accounts for a significant portion of total costs. There may be several cost points in any one responsibility area or cost center. Major cost points fall into four main categories: "productive," "support," "policing," and "waste." Productive costs contribute directly to the value of the product or service. Support costs provide no direct value to the customer but are necessary to support production. Policing costs aim at preventing things

---

[7] Pareto's law is named after Vilfredo Pareto (1848–1923), an Italian economist and sociologist. Pareto noted in 1897 that the relation between income and population was significantly skewed; that is, a large percent of income was earned by a small percent of the population. The quoted definition is from C. J. Slaybough, "Pareto's Law and Modern Management," *Price Waterhouse Review*, vol. 2, no. 4 (Winter 1966), p. 27.

[8] Earl P. Strong and Robert D. Smith, *Management Control Models* (New York: Holt, Rinehart, and Winston, 1968), p. 15.

FIGURE 4–4
A Pareto Curve

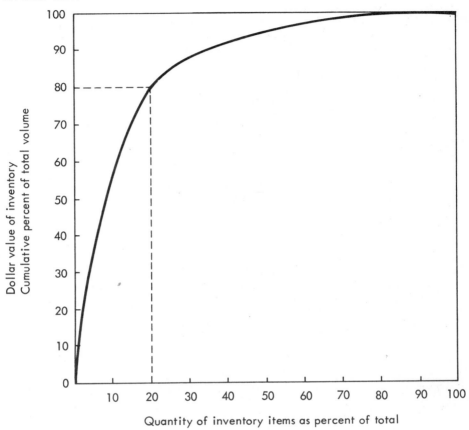

from going wrong. Waste is the cost of efforts that produce no productive, support, or policing results.[9]

*Broadening
the idea*

The idea of cost points is, of course, particularly relevant to a manager's effort to control the aspect of cost. However, the idea can be applied to other controllable aspects. That is, a manager might identify quality points, quantity points, and time points. Such points would represent activities within a manager's area of responsibility that account for a significant portion of total quality, quantity, and time, respectively. Thus, the idea of cost points can be broadened to include quantity, quality, and time.

---

[9] Peter F. Drucker, *Managing for Results* (New York: Harper & Row, Publishers, 1964), pp. 78–84.

Essential idea

The Idea of Control Tolerances. In controlling quantity, quality, time, and cost, the idea of control tolerances can be useful. The essential idea of control tolerances is that limits set on both sides of a standard serve to establish a range within which performance can occur and still be considered in conformance with the original plan. This idea can be visualized as in Figure 4–5.

FIGURE 4–5
The Idea of Control Tolerances

————————————————	UCL
Upper Control Limit	
————————————————	Standard
Goal, Plan, or Standard	
————————————————	LCL
Lower Control Limit	

Deviations are normal

Actual performance seldom conforms to plans in a perfect manner. Deviations from plans are to be expected and are the normal state of affairs. The question is, how far can actual performance deviate from planned performance before the system is judged "out of control"? What deviations are allowable within the flexibility dimension of plans? What deviations are considered abnormal? The idea of control tolerances suggests that deviations are normal or allowable as long as they fall within the UCL and LCL tolerances. Two illustrations will help clarify this idea.

Budget tolerances

In the implementation of budgets in business firms, individual departments may be allocated a specific dollar amount for expenses. This dollar amount represents the middle line in Figure 4–5. Actual expenditures during a given period will fluctuate around the allocated expenditures. As long as actual expenditures fall within the upper and lower limits established for the control range, the department will be considered "in control."

Responding to deviations

When expenditures fall outside of the control limits, specific steps may be taken to bring expenditures back in control. For example, if the department is exceeding its budget, UCL restrictions may be placed on additional expenditures. If the department is falling below its LCL, it may be neglecting essential purchases. Sometimes it may be necessary to set new control limits in response to higher expenditures. If the higher expenditures are the result of greater-than-expected sales volume, then the overall budget must be adjusted. Trends in expenditures will also be watched. If expenditures are consistently within the UCL region and are trending in an upward direction, it may indicate they are moving toward being out of control.

*Quality
control
tolerances*

Another common application of the control tolerance idea is in the area of quality control.[10] Statistical quality-control charts are widely used in manufacturing operations. The center line of such a chart could be a characteristic of a part being produced, for example, diameter in inches. The UCL and the LCL represent the outer limits of the diameter that will be considered acceptable. These limits are based on such factors as knowledge of the production process, customer specifications, and cost considerations. As production occurs, samples of the item being produced are measured to determine if their diameters fall within the allowable tolerances. If they do not, corrective action is taken.

*Other
applications*

Statistical control charts are applicable to a variety of repetitive operations, including billing errors, printing errors, customer complaints, sales returns, and travel expenses.[11] One author provides an illustration of the application of control charts to the control of the ratio of advertising expenses to the dollar value of sales.[12] See the "Application" at the end of this chapter for an illustration of the idea of a statistical control chart.

*Imprecise
control limits*

Commonly, it is not possible to set exact upper and lower control limits. Rather, the limits are intuitively established or based on a combination of judgment, past experience, and available current information. How can precise upper and lower control limits be established for the plan of a large, multiplant manufacturing firm to install antipollution devices in its operations? Or, what are the upper and lower limits of allowable behavior in a business organization's plan to be more active in meeting its social responsibilities? In cases such as these, the idea of control tolerances is applicable even though precise, measurable limits cannot be established.

---

[10] See Elwood S. Buffa, *Modern Production Management,* 4th ed. (New York: John Wiley & Sons, 1973), pp. 659–65.

[11] Charles T. Horngren, *Cost Accounting: A Managerial Emphasis* (Englewood Cliffs, N.J.: Prentice-Hall, 1962), p. 750.

[12] Philip Kotler, *Marketing Management: Analysis, Planning, and Control,* p. 763.

Summary box

> *Managerial controlling* is the process of assuring that actions are in line with desired results The *objective* of controlling is to assure that actions contribute to goal accomplishment.
>
> The *four elements* in the control process are: a predetermined standard (characteristic), measurement (sensor), comparison (comparator), and corrective action (activator).
>
> Managers work with two types of *performance factors:* people and things. There are four aspects of performance factors that can be controlled. These *controllable aspects* are: quantity, quality, time, and cost.
>
> *Pareto's law* is useful in controlling quantity and cost. It states that the significant elements in a specified group usually constitute a relatively small portion of the total items in the group.
>
> A *cost point* is an activity within a manager's area of responsibility that accounts for a significant portion of total costs. Four major categories of cost points are: production; support; policing; and waste.
>
> The essential idea of *control tolerances* is that limits (UCL and LCL) are set on both sides of a standard. As long as performance is within these limits, it is "in control." The idea of control tolerances is generally applicable to the control of quantity, quality, time, and cost.

TYPES OF CONTROL SYSTEMS

Three ideas

In this section we discuss control systems in terms of their *source* (internally or externally imposed), their *relationship to error* (proactive or reactive), and the extent to which all of the *control elements* are built into the system (open or closed-loop).

Self-imposed and externally imposed

Internal and External Control. When we think of the source of the controls on our behavior, we can easily relate to the idea that some controls are self-imposed and others are externally imposed. This distinction can be useful as a way of thinking about the on-the-job behavior of managers and employees. To the extent possible and practical, it is desirable for people to control the quantity, quality, time, and cost of their own work.

Self-control

Self-control can provide immediate responsiveness to changes in job requirements. It allows job holders to be, or perceive themselves to be, somewhat autonomous in their work environment. In the final analysis, a minimum degree of self-control on the job is a *necessary condition* for organizational survival.

Other people and things

However, not everyone is capable or desirous of self-control on the job. Furthermore, self-control alone is an *insufficient* means for meeting the control requirements of organizations. Therefore, externally imposed controls are essential. These controls are in the form of *other people* who are in a position of authority, or of *other things*—such as policies, rules and procedures, specified job methods, the organization structure or design, compensation systems, retirement plans, budgets, accounting and financial reporting systems, and so on. The point is that every work environment needs both self-imposed and externally imposed controls on job behavior.

Relation to error

Proactive and Reactive Control. Proactive control systems anticipate variations from standards and take corrective action *before* an error or some crucial event occurs. Reactive control systems respond to errors *after* they occur.

Examples of proactive control

An example of a proactive control system is an inventory control system that automatically identifies the need to reorder an item when the amount on hand reaches a statistically determined reorder point. Such a system is designed to prevent a shortage by ordering far enough in advance to assure that sufficient quantities will be on hand. Another example of a proactive control system is a variable budget system which allows operations throughout a business firm to adjust to changes in actual or predicted sales volume. In general, proactive control tries to prevent dysfunctions or errors, by anticipating them and taking compensatory action.

Examples of reactive control

Examples of reactive control systems are plentiful in business firms. One example is the common practice of quality control inspection after all production of an item has occurred. If the inspection reveals that the item falls below predetermined standards, the "rejects" are reworked and the reasons for their causes for the existence are investigated. Similar after-the-fact control systems characterize budgetary control, absenteeism and labor turnover control, control of disruptions caused by the loss of key personnel, and so on. In general, reactive control systems respond to error after it occurs. Like self-imposed and externally imposed controls, every organization requires both proactive and reactive controls.

Based on control elements

Open and Closed-loop Control. The distinction between open and closed-loop control systems is based on the extent to which all four elements of control (standard, sensor, comparator, and activator) are built into the system.

Example of a closed-loop system

A closed-loop control process utilizes a sensor, comparator, and activator which operate simultaneously with a performance system. One example often given of a closed-loop control process is the thermostat in home heating units. The thermostat is set at a desired temperature or standard. The heating unit is the performance system. The thermostat contains a sensor, comparator, and activator that respond automatically to the healing unit's performance. The ideal or perfect closed-loop process requires no human intervention; it is a self-contained process. As such, there are not many closed-loop control processes that are significant to managers.

Example of open-loop control

Open-loop control requires varying degrees of environmental and human intervention. Any process that relies on people to perform the sensor, comparator, or activator steps of the control process is open-loop. Quality control inspectors who perform measurements on production work by using "go–no-go" gauges are part of an open-loop control system. Accountants who engage in variance analysis when comparing actual income and expenses with budgets perform an important comparator function. Managers who make corrective decisions are part of open-loop control processes.

Main point

The point of our distinction between open and closed-loop control is that control processes fall on a continuum from closed to open. Very few significant managerial control problems can be solved with a closed-loop process. It is often possible, however, to build into open-loop processes various automatic controls, or automatic-decision rules, and thereby reduce the openness of the control process. Closed-loop systems are not necessarily better than open-loop systems simply because they are more automatic. They are also less flexible and more limited in application. The form that the basic control process should take depends on the nature of the control problem and on the goals to which the control process contributes.

Real-time control and feedback

Computers have made "real-time" control possible and practical. Real-time or "on-line" control means essentially that the control process allows for "immediate feedback" concerning operations. Feedback is information received by a system about the actual performance of that system. Immediate feedback allows an operating system to perform within established tolerances as the system moves through time. The concept of immediate feedback, however, is independent of computers. That is, it is possible to design systems that will allow for immediate feedback without relying on computers. Nevertheless, computers have vastly widened the possibilities for real-time control.

Examples of real-time control

An example of real-time control is the reservation system used by most major airlines. These systems allow airport managers and technical personnel to know exactly and immediately the passenger-load status of any and all airplanes. Similar systems are used by major hotel and motel chains. Another example of real-time control is that used by some retail establishments, such as large department stores or supermarkets. These systems enable managers to keep accurate and timely records of inventory levels over a wide geographic area as the inventories are sold and restocked. Some large business firms have developed real-time control processes that provide information about the firm's cash flow.

Most control
processes

The overwhelming majority of control processes used in organizations are simple, unsophisticated, and not computerized. They are not real-time processes, and they are more often open than closed-loop systems. Some very effective managerial control is the result of imagination and personal experience rather than formal knowledge about control processes. That was the case in the control system Nick applied to Hobby. It was an externally imposed, reactive, open-loop, simple, nonreal-time control system. It was effective in some respects—Hobby stopped drinking Nick's whiskey and beer, and ineffective in others—Hobby kept on drinking and was finally fired.

THE HUMAN SIDE OF CONTROLLING

Acceptance
is essential

Managerial controlling makes a contribution to effective managing through its influence on the behavior of people. The best control system can prove to be useless unless it is accepted as a behavioral guide by individual job holders.

Communica-
tion and
understanding

Acceptance of a control system by employees is initially contingent on adequate communication and understanding of the control system. Understanding of the control system is promoted when employees are actively involved in the design and administration of the system. Such participation also may improve the employee's perception of the fairness of the system and, thus, further enhance the system's acceptance by other employees.[13]

Contingencies

Several contingencies will determine whether initial acceptance of a control system will be sustained over time. Among these contingencies are: the manner of administering the system, the continued appropriateness of the system to goals, the perceived equity of the system vis-à-vis other controls, and the consequences of the system for the employee's perceived job needs.

Ambivalent
attitudes

In general, the attitudes of managers and employees toward control systems will vary. Since every organization uses multiple controls, attitudes toward each of them may differ. On the one hand, the need for some controls is apparent to most employees. On the other hand, controls tend to restrict behavior and can pose threats to employees. "It is probably safe to assume that most employees in most organizations will have ambivalent attitudes toward control systems—seeing some degree of threat but also recognizing that both the individual and the organization can gain something from them."[14]

---

[13] Dessler, *Organization and Management: A Contingency Approach,* p. 364.

[14] Lyman W. Porter, Edward E. Lawler III, and J. Richard Hackman, *Behavior in Organizations* (New York: McGraw-Hill Book Company, 1975), p. 268.

Integral part
of managing

Positive Potentialities of Control Systems. Well-designed control systems are an integral part of effective managing. Goals and plans cannot be achieved without the sensing, comparing, and activating elements of control. Thus, control systems are a positive and essential feature of managing, and managing is indispensable to efficient and effective goal accomplishment.

Clear
guidelines

Control systems can encourage improved job performance by providing clear guidelines for employees of what is expected of them in terms of the quantity, quality, time, and cost of their work. In addition, the control systems can be motivational if they challenge employees to stretch in order to meet the standards used in the system.

Directs energy

Further, "when an area is covered by a control system, organization members concentrate on improving their performance in the measured area."[15] This tends to be true because employees may perceive that performance in the measured area will be taken into account in determining their rewards. Of course, employees do not always perceive that this performance-reward contingency exists.[16] Even when they do perceive it, it is not always a valid perception. Nevertheless, control systems can serve to direct energy toward performance areas that are measured.

Dysfunctional
behavior

Negative Potentialities of Control Systems. There is no doubt that control systems can activate behavior that is "dysfunctional" from an organization's viewpoint. We will examine two types of potentially dysfunctional behavior: control-system-oriented behavior and production of invalid information.[17]

Control-
system-
oriented
behavior

Control systems can cause control-system-oriented behavior rather than *goal-oriented* behavior. The system may generate behavior that makes employees look good on the control system's measures. This type of behavior can be useful if the measures are goal-related; it can be dysfunctional if they are not. For example, some professors require their students to attend class every day; some portion of each student's grade may be based on attendance. In order to look good (get a better grade), students may attend class. However, unless the attendance policy is a contributor to the learning goals of the course and is perceived as such by the students, their learning may suffer as a result of their negative attitude toward the attendance policy.

[15] Cortlandt Cammann and David A. Nadler, "Fit Control Systems to Your Managerial Style," *Harvard Business Review*, vol. 54, no. 1, (January–February 1976), p. 67.

[16] One study of 400 accountants' reaction to a management office control system concludes that effective systems contribute to successful performance by (1) allowing the employee to exercise personal control, (2) clarifying what is expected, and (3) relating rewards to performance. See John T. Todd, "Small Business Control Systems in a Dynamic Environment," *Journal of Small Business Management*, vol. 14, no. 4 (October 1976), pp. 1–6.

[17] Edward E. Lawler III and John Grant Rhode, *Information and Control in Organizations* (Pacific Palisades, Calif.: Goodyear Publishing Company, Inc., 1976), pp. 83–94.

Invalid data about what can be done

Control systems can produce invalid data about what can be done.[18] Budgeting control systems provide an example of the first type of invalid data. In the budgeting process, it is common for managers to underestimate revenues and overestimate costs in order to try to build some slack into their budgetary control system. One way to avoid this type of invalid data is for the organizational reward system to hold managers accountable for the accuracy of their budget estimates. Zero-base budgeting and controlling is another way of trying to insure the validity of budgetary estimates.

Invalid data about what has been done

Some performance-appraisal systems provide examples of control systems that encourage invalid data reporting about what has been done. Recently, we discussed this with the labor-relations manager of a large firm in the aerospace industry. The manager said that the firm's performance-appraisal system was tied directly into wage and salary recommendations. There are times when an employee might have deserved a salary increase but not have been doing too well in the short run on specific performance measures. Since the appraisal system required that salary-increase recommendations be accompanied by favorable performance appraisals, the result was an upward bias in the appraisals. The resulting invalid appraisal reports led to a separation of the firm's performance appraisal from salary recommendations.

Need for well-designed controls

We have cited just two of the ways that control systems can have a negative or dysfunctional effect on behavior. In both cases, it is not the control, *per se*, that causes the dysfunctional behavior. It is the particular *system* that is being applied. People can respond to controls in a positive, goal-oriented way, but unless the controls are well-designed and well-accepted, they can cause dysfunctional behavior.

CONTROLLING: MANAGERIAL PERSPECTIVES

Managers must control

Overcontrol versus Undercontrol. The statement that managers must control, means largely that managers must measure, compare, and correct, when necessary, the activities of people. Managers manage people. Managers plan the activities of their subordinates, they design and implement organizational behavioral systems, and they establish controls to assure that behavior contributes to goals. Managerial control, therefore, involves the planning and control of human behavior. Some like to avoid use of the word "control" when it refers to people. Other more pleasant-sounding terms, such as "influence" or "coordination," seem more acceptable. Whatever term is used, however, managers are accountable for getting employees to behave in ways that contribute to efficient and effective goal accomplishment.

---

[18] Ibid., p. 88.

Overcontrol   Sometimes managers "overcontrol," in the sense of overdirecting and overregulating behavior. Many employees are controlled from the time they "punch in" until the time they "punch out." Their every move is regulated by methods, procedures, rules, policies, and the watchful eyes of supervisors. Overcontrol can stifle the employee's initiative and encourage them to find ways to "beat the system." There is no system yet developed that cannot be beaten by imaginative, overcontrolled employees. Beating the system leads to further controls that, in turn, need to be escaped. Thus, overcontrol and control over the wrong things lead to a *lack* of control.

Example of   An example of the consequences of overcontrol at the top-man-
overcontrol   agement level is the case of Genesco, Inc., a large firm in the apparel and retailing fields.[19] Genesco's former CEO was a strong believer in tight financial controls and in his own personal involvement in even minor, routine decisions. These beliefs led to a centralization of management which, in turn, led to decision-making delays, "paperwork paralysis," and frustration of executives. The result for the former CEO was a "palace revolt" that led to his ouster. Such revolts are seldom explained by a single cause, but an obsession with controls appears to provide a partial explanation.

Undercontrol   On the other hand, it is possible to "undercontrol" and, thereby, increase the chances of goal failure. Undercontrol can result from a failure to operationalize the basic control process. It can result from failure to obtain and use feedback, failure to make adequate comparisons of actual performance against plans, or failure to correct deviations from plans. The ultimate result of undercontrol is inefficiency and ineffectiveness. Undercontrol can lead to frustration and dissatisfaction resulting from actions not corresponding to plans. It can create poor job attitudes, expectations, and behavior. And it can create financial disaster.

Example of   An absence of strategic planning and financial controls partially
undercontrol   explains the difficulties of Westinghouse Electric Corporation. Lack of clear plans and adequate managerial controls has cost Westinghouse millions of dollars. General Electric Company, on the other hand, is known for a system of strong corporate controls within which managers operate. These differences in management philosophy and practice, and in the resulting performance, illustrate what undercontrol can do to a large-scale business firm.[20]

Main question   Examples of overcontrol and undercontrol are found everywhere, in all types of organizations. The effective control of complex human-technical-economic systems is extremely difficult. Even with the best of intentions and sophisticated knowledge, it is difficult

---

[19] "What Undid Jarman: Paperwork Paralysis," *Business Week*, January 24, 1977, pp. 67–68.

[20] "The Opposites: GE Grows while Westinghouse Shrinks," *Business Week*, January 31, 1977, pp. 60–66.

to determine the most appropriate amount of control in a management situation. It is neither desirable nor possible to completely control all the behavior of employees in work organizations. Control must be selective, and there are definite limits on what can be controlled. The question is whether controls will contribute to the efficient and effective accomplishment of goals, *and at the same time* be consistent with, and contribute to, the personal development and goals of the employees.

Guiding principle

Costs versus Benefits.   As in any managerial activity, a guiding principle in controlling is that the costs—direct and indirect—incurred should be justified by the benefits received. Ideally, the level of expenditures for control is determined by "marginal analysis." That is, the cost of the last control expenditure should be equal to the revenue received from that expenditure. This easily stated general guide to managerial behavior is difficult and sometimes impossible and impractical to apply. In some cases, it is possible to analyze the costs and benefits of controlling. Usually, however, a costs-benefits analysis of controlling must rely on inexact data and a large amount of personal judgment.

Customer service policy

Additional expenditures for controlling do not always result in equal additions to value gained. For example, a policy of always being able to fill customer orders from inventories may require a prohibitive inventory-carrying cost, whereas a "95 percent customer service policy" (that is, being able to fill 95 percent of customer orders from inventories) may lower total inventory investment by an amount greater than the value gained from a 100 percent customer service policy.

Quality control

Another example is in the area of quality control. It is an unusual case in business operations where a policy of no-defects can be justified on a costs–benefits basis. The common case is that the cost of eliminating the last defects exceeds the benefits gained. Part of the concern of quality control management is with determining optimum quality levels. The optimum level is seldom a no-defects level, although there are cases where that level is essential—various parts of the Apollo program, for example.

Types of costs and benefits

The costs–benefits of controlling should not be thought of simply in financial terms. "Costs" of controlling also can take the form of lost time, negative attitudes, lowered job expectations, dysfunctional job behavior, and adverse customer relations, among others. "Benefits" of controlling can take many forms, such as time savings, improved morale, higher job expectations, improved customer and public relations, cleaner air and water, and quality improvements.

Controls are instrumental

Means versus Ends.   The contribution of controls to effective managing in an instrumental one; that is, controlling is a mana-

gerial activity that follows logically and necessarily from goal setting and planning. Once a system of performance, group, and
individual goals is established, and once plans are formulated for
achieving these goals, then controls are instruments or means that
contribute to goals. Control is not an end in itself, but it is one
means of assuring goal accomplishment.

Sometimes
controls
are viewed
as ends

Most managers and students of management agree with the
idea that controls have no value in themselves. Their value, as
with plans and organization, is instrumental to goals. In practice,
however, controls are often viewed as having intrinsic value. Long
after they serve any useful purpose, controls are retained "for their
own value." Like plans that are obsolete and organizations that are
unresponsive to peoples' needs, controls can hinder goal accomplishment.

Orientation
toward results

It is common in business management education and practice
to say that controls should be "results-oriented." That is, managers
should not be overly concerned with particular methods and procedures used in order to get results; rather, "It is the results that
count." Presumably, the results referred to are in terms of contribution to goals. One of the main features of management by objectives is that it is a results-oriented approach to management.
The focus is on the objectives—the ends—and not on the specific
means used in accomplishing the objectives.

The end does
not justify
the means

The value of a results orientation is self-evident; however, it
can be exaggerated. A concentration on ends may make managers
insensitive to the inappropriateness of the means used to accomplish the ends. In managing, as in other types of behavior, the end
does not justify the means. The specific mechanisms used to obtain control can make the difference between ethical and unethical
management practices.

Both ends and
means are
important

Some control mechanisms are illegal even though they may assure that actions conform to desired results. Other control mechanisms may be legal but, at the same time, degrade human beings
and violate their human rights. At least part of the Watergate trag-
edy was caused by a preoccupation with ends, or results, without
regard to the means used. On a lesser scale, there are similar pre-
occupations in almost all organizations. Thus, managers should
not be results-oriented any more than they should be methods-
oriented. Both ends and means contribute to overall managerial
effectiveness. Particularly in the means used to control human
behavior, managers must recognize the dignity and rights of individuals.

Summary box

Three types of control systems were discussed in this chapter. One type is based on the source of the control: internally or externally imposed. Another type is based on the relationship to error: proactive and reactive. The third type is based on the presence or absence of the four control elements that differentiate open from closed-loop control. Most control processes used by managers are externally imposed, reactive, and open-loop.

Real-time or *on-line* control is control that allows for immediate "feedback" concerning operations. *Feedback* is information received by a system about the performance of that system.

In order for control systems to be effective, they must be *communicated, understood,* and *accepted* by the people who are affected by them. Control systems are an integral part of managing, can provide guidelines for behavior, and can direct energy.

Control systems can also have a negative influence on behavior by encouraging *control-system-oriented behavior* and by promoting the reporting of *invalid data* about what can be and has been done.

Too much control of the employees' behavior can stifle initiative and stimulate behavior designed to "beat the system." *Too little control* increases the probability that the desired results will not be achieved. A difficult problem for managers is to determine the most appropriate amount and kind of controls to use in their area of accountability.

A *guiding principle* in controlling is that the costs incurred should be justified in terms of the benefits received. Cost and benefits are not limited to monetary measures.

The contribution of controls to effective managing is *instrumental.* Controls are not ends: They are instruments or means that contribute to goal accomplishment.

See Supplement 4A for a discussion of network analysis, a popular managerial planning and controlling technique.

CHECK YOUR UNDERSTANDING

Controlling
Objective of controlling
Four control process elements
Performance factors
Four controllable aspects
Pareto's law
Cost points
Cost point categories
Control tolerances

UCL and LCL
Three types of control systems
Real-time control
Overcontrol versus undercontrol
Overcontrol leads to lack of
  control
Costs versus benefits of control
Controls as means versus ends

STUDY QUESTIONS

1. Explain the statement: The objective of controlling should not be thought of as assuring that actions conform to plans.

2. Can you think of other aspects of performance that can be controlled other than the four mentioned in the chapter (quantity, quality, time, cost)? Explain.

3. Refer to Figure 4–3. Examine the current literature to determine some control techniques used in one of the major functions of a business.

4. Read a current article (dealing with marketing, production, or a personnel-related field) that discusses the application of Pareto's law.

5. Be able to illustrate, through an example of your own and a diagram, the idea of control tolerances.

6. What are some of the contingencies that will influence the choice of a control system? What are some contingencies influencing the acceptance of a control system by employees?

7. Explain the statement: "Additional expenditures for controlling do not always result in equal additions to value gained."

8. It is often suggested that, in human affairs, immoral, unethical, or illegal means of accomplishing an end cannot be justified even by the most noble and worthy goal. The end cannot justify the means. How, in your opinion, would you argue the proposition that the end does, in fact, justify the means? How, in your opinion, is this idea relevant to management practice?

9. Think about and be able to give your personal interpretation of: Even with the best of intentions and sophisticated knowledge, it is difficult to determine the most appropriate amount of control in a management situation. What, in your opinion, are some of the factors for the manager to consider in determining the extent of control that should be implemented in a management situation?

10. The manager's job can be thought of, broadly, as one of exerting influence over the behavior of human beings at work. The manager exerts this influence in numerous ways, including goal setting, planning, organization design, and controlling efforts.

What, in your opinion, are some of the moral issues for managers to think about relevant to their job of influencing the behavior of subordinates?

APPLICATION: CONTROL TOLERANCES

Pam Jillespie is the supervisor of the Cutting Department in the TAMU Paddle Plant. One of the products produced in the plant is the TAMU paddle. This paddle was originally designed for the initiation rites of a popular student organization at a large university in the Southwest. Over the years, however, it has become widely accepted all over the country as a generally useful, all-purpose paddle.

One of the important specifications of the TAMU paddle is that it be 20 inches long. It doesn't have to be *exactly* 20 inches, but it cannot vary too much. In the past, customers have complained that their paddling is less satisfying when the paddle exceeds 20 inches. Consequently, Pam decided to use the idea of control tolerances in order to assure uniformity in the length of the paddles produced.

Using 20 inches as the standard, Pam decided that a variance of 0.075 inches would be acceptable to customers and to the management of the TAMU plant. Knowing the cutting operation, Pam also knew that the actual lengths of the cut paddles would fall outside of the acceptable range (20 inches ± 0.075) less than 1 percent of the time.

Twice every hour, Pam selects a sample of five paddles. She measures the lengths of the five paddles and then computes the arithmetic mean of their lengths. The means during one day of production are as follows:

Sample Number	Mean
1	19.980
2	19.965
3	19.980
4	20.030
5	20.070
6	20.070
7	20.105
8	20.040
9	20.005
10	19.960
11	19.960
12	19.975
13	20.030

1. What does the control chart that Pam is using look like? Plot the above data on the chart.

2. Would you judge the cutting process to be "in control?" What action might you take after observing the means of samples 3, 4, 5, and 6?

APPLICATION: PARETO'S LAW

Tom McEwan also works at the TAMU Paddle Plant. Tom is in charge of all marketing-related activities of the firm. One of these activities is sales analysis. In trying to obtain an overall picture of the sales of TAMU paddles, Tom gathered the following information:

Customer Identification	Dollar Amount of Customer Orders, 1977
Group A customers	
UCLA....................................	$30,000
USC.....................................	25,000
OSU.....................................	20,000
UM......................................	15,000
UT......................................	15,000
PSU.....................................	12,500
MSU.....................................	12,500
UI......................................	10,000
Group B customers (8).....................	30,000
Group C customers (16)....................	20,000
Group D customers (48)....................	10,000

Tom wants to use a visual aid when he presents the above sales analysis summary to his boss. He wants the visual aid to highlight the fact that a small percentage of TAMU Paddle Plant's customers account for a very large percent of the plant's total dollar sales of TAMU paddles.

1. Prepare a Pareto curve using the sales information provided.
2. What does the curve imply about Tom's managing?

SUPPLEMENT 4A

Planning and Controlling with Network Analysis

There has been much notable success and much notable wreckage ascribed to the application to PERT.

F. S. Hillier and G. J. Lieberman

Planning approach depends on nature of the problem

The approach that managers use to plan and control depends on the nature of the problem. If managers are planning and controlling the activities of people involved with routine problems, they use planning and controlling techniques appropriate to routine problems. For example, planning of normal production operations in a manufacturing plant involves the use of devices such as flow-process charts, bills of materials, operation sheets, and route sheets. Other common approaches to routine planning are sales forecasting, budgeting, and manpower forecasting.

NPC

One approach to the planning and controlling of unique problems is Network Planning and Controlling (NPC). Examples of problems that lend themselves to NPC include installing a large machine, changing a plant's location, introducing a new product, constructing a building, planning and controlling an advertising campaign, planning and controlling of large-scale projects such as the Polaris missile project, and changing the layout of the physical facilities of a manufacturing plant. Such problems involve the coordination of many activities and people. They are nonroutine problems about which there is an insufficient backlog of past experience useful in planning and controlling.

This supplement

This supplement discusses a general approach to NPC and then discusses in detail one widely used NPC technique, PERT.

GENERAL APPROACH TO NPC

Time is a constraint

Suppose that you were given a project to manage. Part of your managerial task would be to plan and control *over time* the activities involved in the project. If the project is unique, you may have a minimal understanding of what major activities it involves. You may know even less about the sequence of these activities, and less still about the time to allow for the activities. Time, however, is normally a relevant constraint in the management of special projects. Thus, you have some interest in completing the project within acceptable time constraints.

Major steps

How might you use NPC to help you manage the project to which you have been assigned? The major steps are: determine the project goal; identify the events; sequence the events; determine the activities; estimate activity times; prepare the network; and use the network. The following paragraphs discuss the meaning of these steps in a general approach to NPC.

Step One

Determine the Project Goal. If, for example, the project is to introduce a new product into a test market, a target date for the completion of the project must be established. Sometimes these target dates are contractually specified, as in construction projects. Clauses that provide for penalties if the project is not completed by the target date are often included in construction contracts. The target date is not the only aspect of the goal that needs to be considered explicitly. The manager also needs to have an understanding of what resources—human, financial, materials, equipment—are available for the project. Further, quality and cost dimensions of the goal need to be specified.

Step Two

Identify the Events. Events in a project are significant points in time in the life of the project. The beginning of the project and the end of the project are always two of the major events. The manager's problem is to determine the major events between the start and the end event. For example, in introducing a new product into a test market, major events include: completion of product design, market survey, product pricing, start of production, beginning of advertising campaign, and arrival of the product at the retail outlet. Identifying the events is an important part of NPC. The fragmentation, or degree of detail, of the network has an effect on the probability of completing the project on time. Some projects are so large that several networks of events, or "fragnets," have to be used. The Polaris submarine project involved the coordination of over 70,000 parts, and several networks were used in the project.

Step Three

Sequence the Events. Some events in a project can occur simultaneously, whereas others must be performed in a sequential manner. For example, in constructing a large building, completing the rough plumbing occurs independently of completing the rough wiring. Both these events, however, precede the interior finishing work, such as plastering and painting. Or, in introducing a new product into a test market area, the beginning of production does not occur until after the final design of the product. However, the beginning of the advertising campaign can occur simultaneously with the beginning of production. The sequencing of events is a critical step in NPC. Proper sequencing reduces the total time required for the project. In general, the idea of "sequencing" is to determine the arrangement of events that results in completing the project within the allowable constraints of cost, time, and quality.

Step Four   **Determine the Activities.**   The activities are the tasks that enter into the completion of an event. If beginning an advertising campaign is one of the events in a network, then the activities leading to that event include all the specific tasks involved in getting the advertising campaign started. Activities take up time, whereas events do not; events are instantaneous. Recall that network planning is primarily useful for special projects, as opposed to routine problems. Thus, identifying events and determining activities is difficult. Commonly there is no backlog of experience that is used as the basis for activity and event determination.

Step Five   **Estimate Activity Times.**   The goal of activity-time estimating is to get a precise estimate of the time required for all of the activities that link the events in the network. This step plays a large part in the success of NPC. At the same time, it is a difficult step because the time estimates are of activities about which there is little knowledge. If a production supervisor is asked how long it takes to process a typical production order, he can give a reasonably accurate estimate. If the same supervisor is asked how long it takes to move a major piece of equipment out of one department and into another department, the estimate is likely to be somewhat less accurate.

Step Six   **Prepare the Network.**   An example of a network is shown in Figure 4A–1. A network is a linear graph consisting of a set of nodes or junction points, here called "events" (10, 20, 30, 40, 50), and a set of branches, here called "activities" (*a, b, c, d, e*). A

FIGURE 4A–1
A Network Showing Events, Activities, Paths, and Direction of Flow

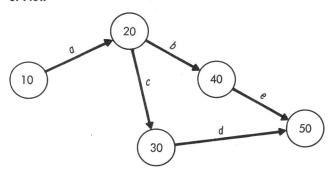

sequence of activities that connects an event with another event is called a "path." The paths in Figure 4A–1 connecting events 10 and 50 are *a-b-e* and *a-c-d*. The path on the network that requires the longest time to complete is called the "critical path." Identifying the critical path is a major feature of NPC. Knowing the critical path allows the manager, among other things, to know which path of activities that is most likely to delay the completion of the project. The direction of flow in the Figure 4A–1 network is indicated by the arrows.

Step Seven

Use the Network. A network is simply a drawing on a piece of paper. It frequently takes the form of a computer printout because NPC is often practical only when a computer is available to handle the mechanics. In any case, if a network is to be useful, it has to be an actual guide to behavior. As such, it has to be accepted by the people involved as a reasonable guide for their work performance, communicated to all relevant participants, kept up-to-date, and integrated into the normal processes of the organization.

Managerial control

The network provides a basis for comparing actual performance against plans. If, for example, activities exceed the estimated times, it may be necessary to shift resources to different paths, extend the project's target date, or live with the performance deviation. A major advantage of NPC is that, through identifying the critical path in a network, managers know where to devote control efforts. Time and money spent on expediting activities on the critical path may pay off in terms of shortening the total time required for the project. Elaborate computer programs have been developed to facilitate the use of NPC. These programs make it possible to keep the network up-to-date and, as a result, are an aid in furthering managerial control.

Perspective

It is clear that NPC is a generally useful managerial technique for the management of special projects and unique problems. Its utility to managers depends on how well it is used; a good technique requires competent people to apply it. Furthermore, the value of NPC depends on the contribution it makes to the *total managerial job* and to the goals of the *total performance system* for which the manager is accountable. For example, whatever its theoretical merit, if NPC significantly disrupts the established behavioral patterns in an organization, it can have a negative net effect on managerial performance.

Summary box

> NPC is an approach to managerial planning and controlling that is generally applicable to nonroutine problems about which there is an insufficient backlog of experience. The *major steps in a general approach* to NPC are:
>
> 1. Determine the project goal.
> 2. Identify the events.
> 3. Sequence the events.
> 4. Determine the activities.
> 5. Estimate activity times.
> 6. Prepare the network.
> 7. Use the network.

PERT/TIME

CPM, PERT

The acronyms for the most widely used and discussed NPC techniques are PERT (Program Evaluation and Review Technique) and CPM (Critical Path Method). CPM and PERT were developed independently at about the same time. Since PERT encompasses most aspects of all approaches to NPC, it will be used here as the basis for discussion of some of the specific "mechanics" associated with the technique. The mechanics discussed include expected time for an activity, earliest completion time for an event, latest completion time for an event, slack of an event, and probability of completing the project on time.

Three time estimates

Expected Time for an Activity (t_e). Pert involves the use of three time estimates for each activity in the network: an optimistic time; a pessimistic time; and a most likely time. The "optimistic" time is the shortest projected time for completion of an activity; the "pessimistic" time is the longest projected time for activity completion; and the "most likely" time is the modal value of the activity time distribution.

Beta distribution

The activity time distribution is approximated by the beta distribution and is illustrated in Figure 4A–2.[1]

Expected time, standard deviation, variance

The expected time (t_e) of an activity is assumed to be the weighted mean of the beta distribution and is estimated according to the following formula:

$$t_e = (a + 4m + b)/6$$

---

[1] The beta distribution is a unimodal distribution with finite end points. It is not necessarily symmetrical, and its shape is determined by the optimistic, pessimistic, and most likely time estimates.

FIGURE 4A–2
An Example of a Beta Distribution

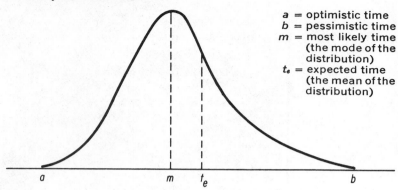

a = optimistic time
b = pessimistic time
m = most likely time
      (the mode of the
      distribution)
t_e = expected time
      (the mean of the
      distribution)

The standard deviation of the expected activity time is estimated as follows:

$$s = (b - a)/6$$

and the variance of the expected activity time is $s^2 = [(b - a)/6]$.[2]

Assumptions   The optimistic time estimate is based on the assumption that there is no more than one chance in a hundred of completing the activity in less than the optimistic time. The pessimistic time estimate is based on the assumption that there is no more than one chance in a hundred of completing the activity in more than the pessimistic time.[2]

Example of t_e,   Example: Given $a = 2$ days, $m = 4$ days, and $b = 6$ days.
s, s^2

$$t_e = \frac{2 + 4(4) + 6}{6} = \frac{24}{6} = 4 \text{ days}$$

$$s = \frac{6 - 2}{6} \qquad\qquad = \tfrac{2}{3} \text{ days}$$

$$s^2 = \left(\frac{6 - 2}{6}\right)^2 \qquad = \tfrac{4}{9} \text{ days}$$

Sample   In PERT, you may encounter a network like the one in Figure
network   4A–3. The optimistic, pessimistic, and most likely times for each activity are used (as in the formula above) to compute the expected time, t_e, for each activity. The result is a network as shown in Figure 4A–4.

Critical path   The critical path of the network in Figure 4A–4 is

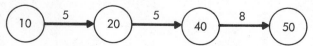

---

[2] Elwood S. Buffa, *Operations Management: The Management of Productive Systems* (New York: John Wiley & Sons, 1976), p. 546.

The time required to complete the critical path = 18 (weeks). The time represented by the critical path is longer than the time represented by path

TE   **Earliest Completion Time for an Event (*TE*).** The earliest completion time for an event is equal to the sum of all the expected times (t_e) on the path leading up to that event. If there is more than one path of activities leading up to the event, *TE* equals the sum of the expected times on the *most* time-consuming path. For

FIGURE 4A–3
PERT Network Showing Events and Activities with Optimistic, Pessimistic, and Most Likely Times

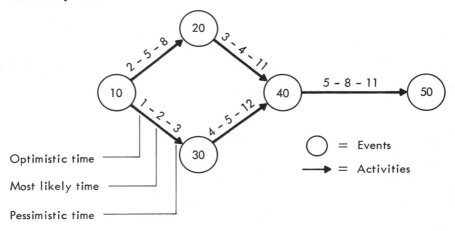

FIGURE 4A–4
PERT Network Showing Events and Activities with Expected Times (t_e) Computed from Time Data from Figure 4A–3

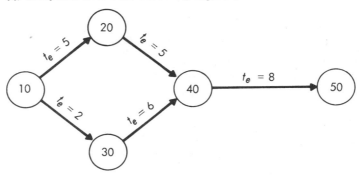

example, in Figure 4A–5, the TE for event $40 = 10$ $(5 + 5)$, not 8 $(2 + 6)$.

FIGURE 4A–5
Network Showing Earliest Completion Time for Events

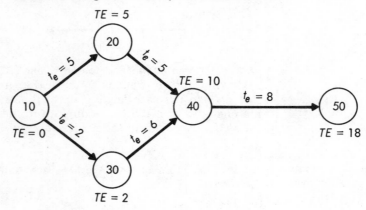

TL, TS

Latest Completion Time for an Event (TL). This refers to the latest completion time for an event if the project is to be completed within the time allowed. In computing TL for a particular event, it is necessary to work backward from TS, the scheduled completion time for the entire project. Working backward from TS to compute the TLs is sometimes called the "backward pass." The TL for event 40 is equal to TS minus the expected time (t_e) of the activity immediately preceding event 50.

TLPE, TLSE

In general, if the event for which TL is to be computed is referred to as $TLPE$ (the latest completion time for a predecessor event), and the event immediately succeeding $TLPE$ is referred to as $TLSE$ (the latest completion time for a successor event), then,

$$TLPE = TLSE - t_e$$

For example, Figure 4A–6 shows the TLs for the events in a project with a scheduled completion time (TS) of 20 days.

When an event has more than one immediate SE

The TL for event 10 illustrates an important point. If an event has more than one immediate successor event, $TLPE$ is calculated for each of the $TLSE - t_e$ combinations, and the *smallest TLPE* is used. For example, event 10 has two successor events, 20 and 30. Therefore, $TLPE$ for event 10 is equal to the smallest $TLPE$ resulting from the following computations:

$$TLPE_{10} = TLSE_{20} - t_e = 7 - 5 = 2$$
$$TLPE_{10} = TLSE_{30} - t_e = 6 - 2 = 4$$

Thus, $TLPE_{10} = 2$.

FIGURE 4A–6
Network Showing Latest Completion Time for Events

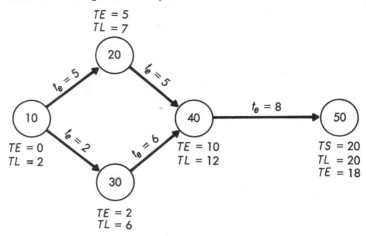

$S = TL - TE$

Slack of an Event (S). The slack of an event is an estimate of the excess time available to reach that event. Slack can be positive, negative, or zero. The formula for computing the slack of an event is $TL - TE$. For example, using the data in Figure 4A–6, the slack for event 40 is 2 $(12 - 10)$. The path in a PERT network with the *least* slack is the critical path. In Figure 4A–6, path

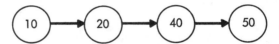

is the critical path. In this case, slack $= 2$ for each event on the critical path because the TS is 2 days longer than the TE.

Slack is neither good nor bad

In networks with several paths, it is possible for paths with little slack to become critical paths. Further, paths with high variance estimates that parallel the critical path can themselves become critical.[3] A *positive* slack represents the amount of time that the time estimates leading up to an event can slip without causing a delay in the completion of the total project. Slack is neither good nor bad; it depends on why it exists. For example, slack can indicate poor time estimates for activities, and it can be a sign that materials and equipment have been overallocated to activities. However, slack can also offer managers some flexibility and looseness in managing projects.

---

[3] Kenneth R. MacCrimmon and Charles A. Ryavec, "An Analytical Study of the PERT Assumptions," *Operations Research,* vol. 12, no. 1 (1964), pp. 16–37.

PR

Probability of Completing the Project on Time (*PR*). When the three time estimates are used to calculate t_e, it is possible, given the beta distribution assumption, to estimate the probability of completing a project within the allowed time. The validity of the probability estimate is directly dependent on the accuracy of the three time estimates. This probability (PR) is estimated as follows:

Steps in estimating PR

1. Determine TS − TE where TS = scheduled project completion time and TE = earliest completion time of the final event in the project. For example, in Figure 4A–6, $TS - TE$ for event

    is equal to 2.

2. Divide $TS - TE$ by $\sqrt{S_v}$, the square root of the sum of all the variances in the critical path. Recall that the variance of an expected activity time is equal to $[(b - a)/6]^2$ and that the expected times for the activities shown in Figure 4A–6 are computed from the time estimates shown in Figure 4A–3. The $\sqrt{S_v}$ for the critical path in Figure 4A–6 is 1.94. This is computed by using the optimistic and pessimistic times shown in Figure 4A–3.

3. The result of steps 1 and 2 is Z, the standard normal random variable.

$$Z = \frac{TS - TE}{\sqrt{S_v}}$$

Thus,

$$Z = \frac{20 - 18}{1.94} = 1.03$$

4. Z is interpreted by referring to a Z table, a table of area under the normal distribution curve is found in most elementary statistics textbooks. A portion of a Z table is shown in Table 4A–1.

TABLE 4A–1
Values of Cumulative Proportions of Area under the Normal Curve for Selected Values of Z

Z	PR
−2.00	0.023
−1.50	.067
−1.00	.159
0	.500
1.00	.841
1.03	.848
1.50	.933
2.00	.977

Source: J. P. Guilford, *Fundamental Statistics In Psychology and Education* (New York: McGraw-Hill Book Company, 1965), pp. 569–73.

Measuring
of Z

The Z of 1.03 means that there is a .848 probability that the project will be completed within the 20-day scheduled completion time. A Z of -1.00 means that there is only a 0.159 probability that the project will be completed on time. It is not necessarily true that "the higher the *PR* the better." Although there may be cases where that is true, a high *PR* may result from errors in the various time estimates, or from an unnecessarily extended *TS*. The value of *PR* that managers consider acceptable is determined for each situation. Although a $PR = 0.50$ is often an acceptable risk, such "rules of thumb" are of little value in specific cases.

PERT/COST

Essential idea

The above discussion of PERT is concerned only with the *time* dimension. The critical path is defined in terms of time required to complete the project. All other calculations mentioned above are based on time. PERT/Cost is an attempt to relate the two dimensions of time and cost. Although PERT/Cost has not been as widely applied as PERT/Time, the general idea of PERT/Cost is useful.[4] The essence of the idea of PERT/Cost is that there are different costs associated with the different estimated times.

Example

For example, an activity that requires 10 days to complete at a cost of $500 may cost $600 to complete in 8 days, and $350 to complete in 12 days. This example assumes that *cost is a function of time*—a reasonable assumption in a wide variety of cases. The minimum-cost conditions for completing a project may result in a total project time that is too great. However, a significant reduction in project time may result in prohibitive cost conditions.

Costs-benefits
comparison

PERT/Cost analysis involves a costs-benefits comparison. Suppose that reducing the time to complete an activity from ten days to eight days costs an additional $100. The question then is, What is the benefit of reducing the required time by two days? If the benefit is less than $100, then presumably there is no financial advantage in reducing the time required to complete the activity. Of course, there may be nonfinancial reasons for the shorter completion time. The general point, however, is that PERT/Cost involves a costs-benefits comparison of the consequences of the different time-cost combinations. This type of comparison can occur before the project starts, to determine the time-cost tradeoffs, and it can occur during the project as a means of controlling costs.

PERT AND MANAGERS

Useful
technique

PERT is one of several techniques that managers use in planning and controlling. It is particularly useful as an aid in man-

[4] John Fertakis and John Moss, "An Introduction to PERT and PERT/Cost Systems," *Managerial Planning*, vol. 20, no. 1 (January–February 1971), pp. 24–31.

aging special projects. Actual applications of PERT often involve hundreds of activities and events and require the use of computers in order to keep managers informed about the current status of projects. However, simple PERT networks that utilize the mechanics discussed in this supplement can also be useful to managers. The necessity of identifying key events in the life of a project, of specifying the activities necessary to achieve those events, of sequencing the events, and of obtaining time estimates for activities, is a discipline that facilitates managerial planning and controlling.

*Tradeoff
thinking*

The ideas of slack and critical path are valuable for managers because they enable managers to think in terms of tradeoffs. For example, a reduction in the critical path time reduces the slack for events on all paths in the network. In order to reduce the critical-path time, managers can shift resources from paths with large amounts of slack to the critical path if they decide that additional resources can reduce the project time. Another alternative is to obtain additional resources—labor, materials, equipment—rather than shift them from paths with slack. Another possibility is to subcontract part of the project so as to bring about a reduction in the total project time. Rather than reducing the critical-path time, managers may want to reduce the resources allocated to events on noncritical paths.

Summary box

> *PERT/Time* is a widely used NPC technique. It involves the use of all seven steps in the general approach to NPC.
>
> A unique feature of PERT/Time is its use of *three time estimates* to compute the expected times for activities. When these three estimates are consistent with assumptions of the beta distribution, PERT/Time allows *probability calculations*. These probabilities enable managers to make estimates of the chances of completing a project on time.
>
> *PERT/Cost* adds the cost dimension to PERT/Time. The essential idea of PERT/Cost is that there are different costs associated with the different estimated times. In general, for any particular activity, the lower the estimated time, the higher the cost.
>
> The concepts of PERT/Time and PERT/Cost are useful to managers. Actual applications of the two techniques often require the use of computers.

CHECK YOUR UNDERSTANDING OF THE FOLLOWING:

NPC	Optimistic time (a)
Steps in a general approach to NPC	Most likely time (m)
	Pessimistic time (b)
Network	Standard deviation of t_e
Target date	Variance of t_e
Events	Earliest completion time (TE)
Fragnets	Latest completion time (TL)
Sequencing of events	Scheduled completion time (TS)
Activities	Slack (S)
Path	Probability of completing by TS (PR)
Critical path	
PERT/Time	Standard normal random variable (Z)
CPM	
Expected time (t_e)	PERT/Cost
Beta distribution	

STUDY QUESTIONS

1. What, in your opinion, are some difficulties you might encounter in introducing and using PERT as a managerial planning and controlling tool?

2. In the computation of TE, explain why the sum of the expected times on the *most* time-consuming path is used rather than the sum of the expected times on the *least* time-consuming path.

3. In calculating TLPE when an event has more than one immediate successor event, why is the *smallest* TLPE used rather than the *largest*?

4. For further study of PERT, see Elwood S. Buffa, *Operations Management: The Management of Productive Systems,* chap. 17, and David R. Anderson, Dennis J. Sweeney, and Thomas A. Williams, *An Introduction to Management Science: Quantitative Approaches to Decision Making,* St. Paul, West Publishing Company, 1976, chap. 8.

APPLICATION: PERT/TIME

Suppose that you are the supervisor of a small construction project. You have decided to use PERT on the project as a planning and controlling technique. Your *goal* is to complete the construction project in 72 days ($TS = 72$). You have identified 8 major *events* in the life of the project, including the beginning and end events, A and H, respectively.

After *sequencing the events*, you determined the *activities* that enter into the completion of each event. Activities are identified by referring to the events that initiate and terminate the activity. For example, activity A–B starts with the beginning event and ends at the point represented by event B.

A summary of the activities and their expected times in days (t_e) is given in the table below.

Activity	Expected Time
A–B......................	9
A–E......................	18
B–C......................	21
B–F......................	2
E–F......................	6–12–36*
E–G......................	18
C–D......................	12
F–D......................	21
F–H......................	24
G–H......................	30
D–H......................	15

* Compute the t_e given these three time estimates.

1. Prepare the network using the data in the above table.

2. Identify all of the paths. For example, one of the paths is A–B–C–D–H.

3. Which of the paths is the critical path? Which is the next most critical path?

4. Determine the *TE*, *TL*, and *S* for each *event*. (Remember, *TS* = 72).

5. If $\sqrt{S_v} = 3$, what is the value of *Z* and what is its corresponding *PR*? What is the interpretation of this *PR*?

6. Suppose that Activity *E–G* took 20 days and, because of new time estimates, Activity *G–H* is projected to take 37 days instead of 30 days. Assuming everything else remains the same, what implications do these changes have on the critical path and on *PR*? Assume $\sqrt{S_v} = 3$.

Objectives of Chapter 5

- To define decision, identify its main elements, relate it to managing, and recognize two basic types of decisions.
- To describe the decision matrix framework for thinking about decision problems.
- To contrast two approaches for evaluating the correctness of a decision.
- To discuss several aspects of the question, How good should decisions be?
- To recognize the role of groups in decision making.
- To emphasize the value of developing your own decision-making process.
- To suggest a useful model for thinking about problem-solving styles.

Outline of Chapter 5

MANAGERIAL
DECISION MAKING

I'll think of it all tomorrow, at Tara . . . After all,
tomorrow is another day.

Scarlett, in *Gone with the Wind*
by Margaret Mitchell

Men are not gods. They are not going to be Olympian
in their judgments, and they are not going to be fully
guided by qualities of mercy and justice and right in
making their decisions.

Dwight D. Eisenhower

Star Trek

Have you ever thought of *Star Trek* as a dramatization of the dilemma of decision making? Almost every show is about some decision Captain Kirk must make. He always seems to make the right decision, balancing the advice of his two right-hand men, Science Officer Spock and Ship Surgeon Lt. Commander McCoy.[1]

Spock and
McCoy: two
styles

Spock and McCoy have opposing problem-solving and decision-making styles. Spock offers Kirk analytical data and advice—unemotional, logical, and computer-like. McCoy provides emotional inputs—warm, caring, people-oriented. Spock and McCoy represent the pull between cold, objective, rationality and warm, subjective, humane judgment.

Essential roles

Both Spock and McCoy play essential roles in Kirk's decision process. Spock examines huge amounts of data that might bear on a decision problem, separates out all that is unimportant, and passes the rest on to Kirk. McCoy provides a counterbalance for Kirk that recognizes environmental uncertainty and the anxieties of people. Kirk somehow manages to get all of this together and makes the right decision.

---

[1] This anecdote is adapted from Rick Hesse and Steve Altman, "Star Trek: An Optimum Decision Making Model," *Interfaces*, vol. 6, no. 3 (May 1976), pp. 60–62.

This chapter

The *Star Trek* example raises several questions about decision making for us. What are the elements of a decision? When are decisions right and how should they be evaluated? Are there different styles that people use in problem solving and decision making? What is the relationship of decision making to managing? What is the process of making decisions? These are some of the questions we discuss in this chapter.

DECISION MAKING: SOME BASIC CONCEPTS

Definition

What Is a Decision? A decision is a choice from among a set of alternatives. Managerial decision making involves decisions made within an organization by those accountable for the job-related activities of organizational participants. In thinking about managerial decisions, it is useful to recognize that they are just one phase of a process that begins with problem recognition and ends with implementation and follow-up. We have more to say later in this chapter about the decision-making *process*.

Choice is a continuum

Elements of a Decision. Every decision involves three elements: choice, alternatives, and goals. "Choice" is a relative concept. It is always present to some degree, but it is always limited. That is, the extent of choice can be thought of as a continuum ranging from extremely restricted to extremely unrestricted. This idea that choice is a continuum is an important concept for managers. Every manager makes decisions within a context of human, technical, and economic constraints. These constraints are present regardless of the level of the manager. It is often said that the higher up one goes in an organization, the more the limits on choice are felt. The stereotype of top executives of large corporations having complete freedom of choice is a myth. These executives do have substantial power and authority to make decisions, but their decisions reflect important limits on their authority.

Alternatives

A "decision problem" requires more than one alternative. There are significant management problems that have only one practical solution. For example, there are problems for which the only solution is to do nothing. Such a problem is not a "decision problem" because no choice of alternatives is involved. Although some problems may appear to have only one solution, such a view is commonly the result of inadequate analysis and a short-term perspective. More commonly, more alternatives exist than can possibly be known or evaluated. Managerial decision making involves the process of limiting, as well as generating, alternatives.

Goals

Finally, decisions imply goals. A major point about managerial decision making is that decisions are supposed to contribute to the efficient and effective accomplishment of consciously formulated real goals. Presumably, the motive behind particular decisions is goal achievement. Of course, it is not always possible to justify or interpret every decision in terms of some predetermined purpose or goal. Nevertheless, decisions are made to achieve *some* purpose, outcome, or goal. Managers must test their decisions by their contribution to achieving the system of goals for which the managers are accountable.

Synonymous with managing?

Relationship to Managing. Some authors feel that "managing" and "decision making" are synonymous. For example, one suggests that "Management is the process of converting information into action. The conversion process we call decision-making." Another states, "I shall find it convenient to take mild liberties with the English language by using 'decision making' as though it were synonymous with 'managing.'" Another considers that "the central role of management is to make decisions which determine the future of the organization."[2]

Synonymous with planning?

Other writers consider "decision making" synonymous with "planning." For example, one popular textbook author indicates that "decision" and "plan" mean the same thing when he states, "A manager can improve his ability to plan—to make decisions —by. . . ." Another views decision making as "at the core of planning," implying that it is not at the core of organization or controlling.[3]

Our view

We prefer to view decision making as a type of behavior that pervades all of the manager's functions. Decision making is not the entirety of management, because it represents only one of the ways in which managers can influence the efficient and effective accomplishment of goals. Neither is decision making synonymous with planning nor a subset exclusively of planning, because organizing and controlling also involve decision making.

Programmed decisions

Types of Decisions. The decisions that managers make can be roughly grouped into two classes, programmed and nonprogrammed.[4] Programmed decisions are those made in response to repetitive and routine problems. They are often made by means of a specific, predetermined procedure. The goal of a programmed decision is usually clear to and accepted by involved decision mak-

---

[2] Jay W. Forrester, "Managerial Decision Making," in Martin Greenberger, ed. *Management and the Computer of the Future* (Cambridge, Mass., and New York: The M.I.T. Press and John Wiley & Sons, 1962), p. 37; Herbert A. Simon, *The Shape of Automation for Men and Management* (New York: Harper & Row, Publishers, 1965), p. 53; Elwood S. Buffa, *Operations Management: The Management of Productive Systems* (Santa Barbara, Calif.: John Wiley & Sons, 1976), p. 26.

[3] William H. Newman, Charles E. Summer, and E. Kirby Warren, *Process of Management: Concepts, Behavior, and Practice,* 3d ed. (Englewood Cliffs, N.J.: Prentice-Hall, 1972), p. 243; Harold Koontz and Cyril O'Donnell, *Management: A Systems and Contingency Analysis of Managerial Functions* (New York: McGraw-Hill Book Company, 1976), p. 196.

[4] Herbert A. Simon, *The New Science of Management Decision* (New York: Harper & Row, Publishers, 1960), pp. 5–6.

ers. Every organization requires large numbers of programmed decisions.

> For an illustration of one computational technique for solving programmed decision problems, see Supplement 5A, "An Introduction to Linear Programming."

*Unpro-
grammed
decisions*

Unprogrammed decisions are unique and involve creative approaches to their solution. Decision problems for which there is no predetermined solution procedure (known or agreed on by the decision makers), whose precise goals are either unclear or unaccepted, and which are difficult to define or structure require unprogrammed decisions. Such decision problems often have to be resolved by parties with opposed goals, methods, or both.[5] Unprogrammed decisions are often important or strategic in terms of ". . . the actions taken, the resources committed, or the precedents set."[6]

*Practical
value*

Of what practical value is the distinction between programmed and unprogrammed decisions? First, it suggests the idea of trying, whenever possible, to build structure or program into the decision-making process. There are undoubtedly thousands of managers who treat each purchase order for paper clips as if it were a unique, nonrecurring problem requiring a creative solution. Second, the two classes of decisions are only rough categories. There are few managerial problems that can be called "fully programmable." There probably are no managerial problems that are completely nonprogrammable. Managers should be sensitive to the need for flexibility and creativity in solving programmed decision problems and look for opportunities to put programming into nonprogrammed decision problems.

A DECISION FRAMEWORK

*Decision
matrix*

Sometimes it is useful to think about decision problems in terms of a "decision matrix." As shown in Figure 5–2, there are three main components of a decision matrix: strategies; states of nature; and outcomes, or pay-offs.

---

[5] The presence of this opposition and conflict is the basis for what Andre L. Delbecq calls a *negotiated decision-making strategy*. This strategy involves the use of personnel who represent the opposing factions and who try to protect their interests while negotiating an acceptable compromise solution to the decision problem. See Andre L. Delbecq, "The Management of Decision Making within the Firm: Three Strategies for Three Types of Decision Making," *Academy of Management Journal*, vol. 10, no. 4 (December 1967), pp. 329–39.

[6] Henry Mintzberg, Duru Raisinghami, and André Théorêt, "The Structure of 'Unstructured' Decision Processes," *Administrative Science Quarterly*, vol. 21, no. 2 (June 1976), p. 246.

FIGURE 5-1
How to Make a Decision

"After much deep thought, careful consideration, close scrutiny and flipping of a coin, we've come to a decision."

The Wall Street Journal, July 9, 1973

Examples of strategies

Strategies. Strategies are the alternatives available to the decision maker. For most decision problems there are several possible strategies, shown in Figure 5–2, as $S_1, S_2 \ldots S_i$. To illustrate the idea of strategies, an investment decision problem can be used. Possible strategies open to an investor include investing in com-

FIGURE 5-2
A Decision Matrix

Strategies	States of Nature			
	N_1	N_2	$N \ldots$	N_j
S_1	O_{11}	O_{12}	$O \ldots$	O_{1j}
S_2	O_{21}	O_{22}	$O \ldots$	O_{2j}
. . .	. . .	. . .	. . .	. . .
S_i	O_{i1}	O_{i2}	$O_i \ldots$	O_{ij}

O = outcomes or payoffs.

mon stocks, bonds, treasury notes, commercial paper, and combinations of stocks and bonds. Another example of strategies is the choice of a product that a manufacturing plant produces. Different combinations of products produce different profits for a firm.

Examples of states of nature

States of Nature.   The conditions or expected future environments in which strategies are implemented are called "states of nature," shown in Figure 5–2 as $N_1, N_2 \ldots N_j$. These conditions are not directly under the control of the decision maker, and their occurrence is assumed to be independent of the strategy selected by the decision maker. For example, in deciding on a strategy of investing in stocks or bonds, an investor is interested in knowing the probabilities of inflation, depression, or recession. Each of these possible states of nature influences the choice of a strategy. Common stocks, for example, may be a better hedge against inflation than bonds. Bonds, on the other hand, may be a better choice if a period of recession or depression is anticipated. These oversimplifications illustrate the influence of states of nature on the choice of a strategy.

> See Supplement 5B, "An Introduction to Quantitative Decision Criteria," for several illustrations of the use of the decision matrix framework.

Three classes of decision problems

Knowledge of States of Nature.   Decision problems are sometimes grouped according to the decision-maker's knowledge about the probability of the occurrence of the states of nature. Although this represents only one way to classify decision problems, it is a useful approach. Three classes of decision problems are—decision making under conditions of certainty, risk, and uncertainty.

Certainty

"Certainty" means there is only one state of nature for each strategy. The probability of that state of nature occurring is assumed to be equal to one. When the state of nature is, in effect, known, then the decision involves choosing the strategy with the largest pay-off. Sometimes, however, it would be impractical to calculate pay-offs for all possible strategies; the number of different strategies may be so large as to make a separate calculation for each strategy infeasible.

Risk

"Risk" involves more than one state of nature, but the decision maker knows the probability of each state of nature occurring. Past experience may allow a business firm to collect data on the probability of some event occurring. For example, data about the time it takes a supplier to deliver an order for materials can be the basis for determining the probability of delivery in six days, seven days, eight days, and so forth.

Uncertainty

"Uncertainty" also involves more than one state of nature, but the decision maker has little or no basis for estimating their likelihood of occurrence. In the case of extreme uncertainty, the decision maker may not even know what states of nature to consider. The more common case, however, is that the decision maker knows something, but not everything, about the possible states of nature. Some specific criteria for making decisions under conditions of uncertainty are introduced in Supplement 5B.

Examples of outcomes

Outcomes. The outcomes, or pay-offs, shown in Figure 5–2 as O_{11}, O_{22} . . . O_{ij}, represent the expected result of implementing a strategy–state of nature combination. For example, O_{22} represents the outcome of implementing strategy S_2 when the state of nature is N_2. Outcomes in a decision matrix can be expressed in dollars, pounds, points, utilities, or some other common and comparable measure of value.[7] For example, the outcome of a strategy of investing in common stock under a state of nature of inflation can be projected in terms of actual dollars.

Summary box

A *decision* is defined as a choice from among a set of alternatives. Every decision involves *three elements:* choice, alternatives, and goals.

Choice is a relative concept. It is rarely completely determined or free. It is limited by the decision maker's peers, superiors, subordinates, and forces and groups outside the organization.

Alternatives range from restricted to unrestricted. All alternatives are seldom known. Most significant management decision problems involve a consideration of multiple alternatives.

Decision making is related to management in the sense that it pervades all of the manager's functions.

Decisions may be classified as either programmed or unprogrammed. *Programmed decisions* are those made in response to repetitive and routine problems. *Unprogrammed decisions* are unique and involve creative approaches to their solution.

A *decision matrix* is a useful way to think about problems. It has *three components:* strategies or action alternatives; states of nature, or expected future environments; and outcomes, or payoffs.

Decision problems can be classified according to the decision maker's knowledge about the likelihood that states of nature will occur: One common classification is decision problems involving *certainty, risk,* or *uncertainty.*

---

[7] Decision theorists contend that outcomes are best expressed as utilities. See Supplement 5B for a brief discussion of the rationale for expressing outcomes as utilities.

WHEN IS A DECISION RIGHT?

The trap of
being right

Managerial decision problems seldom have one correct solution. Most decision problems have several alternative solutions, each of which has some advantages and disadvantages. Effective decision making is not aided by the assumption that there is a "right" solution and that all others are, therefore, "wrong." Nor is it helped by assuming that "I'm right; you must be wrong." One writer refers to these assumptions as "the trap of being right."[8]

Two
approaches

Nevertheless, managerial decisions will be and must be evaluated in terms of their rightness, correctness, or appropriateness. What should be the basis for this evaluation? There are two distinctly different approaches to evaluating decisions. One is to examine the decision in terms of its results. The other is to examine the decision in terms of the process used in reaching the decision.

Consequences
of the
decision

What Were the Results? The most obvious and common approach to evaluating decisions is to ask what the consequences were. If the consequences are acceptable, then the decision is "right." The practicality and realism of this approach to evaluating decisions is obvious and requires very little discussion. One factor that must be considered in this approach is the time period in which to make the judgment. Decisions that lead to desirable short-run consequences may not lead to acceptable consequences in the long run.

Evaluating
consequences

Evaluating decisions and decision makers in terms of how the decisions "turn out" may require considering factors over which the decision makers may have had no control. Furthermore, when decisions turn out right or wrong, the credit or blame may be due to events—even random events—that could not be foreseen at the time the decisions were made. The results of a decision may be very favorable, even though the decision was not right for the situation at the time. Conversely, a decision may turn out disastrous even though it was right at the time it was made.

Evaluating
the process

What Was the Process? The other approach to evaluating decisions is to examine the process used in reaching the decision. Was the process appropriate to the decision problem? Was the process used effectively? This approach recognizes that the skill of decision makers must be evaluated in terms of the situation, the information, the resources, and the technology existing at the time the decision maker was required to make the decision. Furthermore, ". . . good results can best be encouraged by fostering and rewarding good decision making processes."[9]

---

[8] Peter F. Drucker, *Management: Tasks, Responsibilities, Practices* (New York: Harper & Row, Publishers, 1974), p. 474.

[9] Douglas R. Emery and Francis D. Tuggle, "On the Evaluation of Decisions," *MSU Business Topics*, vol. 24, no. 2 (Spring 1976), p. 47.

Example

Suppose that you are to decide how to invest $100,000 of some-one else's money. Assume that you are a qualified investment ana-lyst and that you know what steps to take in order to reach a rea-sonably good decision. After making an analysis of alternatives, you invest the money in common stock. Three months later the Dow Jones Average is down 100 points, and the stock you invested in is doing even worse. Did you make the correct decision? You did if, *at the time of the decision,* you took all reasonable steps in the decision process. You may not be able to convince your client that you made the correct decision, but *you* should be convinced.

You cannot prove you were right

Since the evidence to support decisions can seldom take the form of uncontestable proof of reasonableness, there are often dif-ferences of opinion about the reasonableness of decisions. Most decisions involve personal judgment, and accuracy of judgment cannot be proven. Managers are always vulnerable to the claim, often supported by hindsight, that they neglected important fac-tors that should have been considered when the decision was made. And very often these claims are valid.

Results count

A Dilemma.   There is an apparent dilemma here for managers. On the one hand, the correctness of a decision is established at the time the decision is made. On the other hand, managers are actu-ally evaluated in terms of how decisions turn out. If executives make too many decisions that are disadvantageous for their or-ganization, they won't be around long enough to defend the cor-rectness of their decisions. In practice, this is not a real dilemma. Most managers understand that they are evaluated primarily in terms of results. Of course, they try to make decisions that will turn out well, and they try to improve their skill in estimating the consequences of alternatives.

Don't cry over . . .

At the same time, managers, who may make hundreds of deci-sions every week, need to understand that when a decision is made and implemented there is no point worrying about factors over which they have no control. Such worry serves no purpose and diminishes the manager's effectiveness. This idea is dramatically illustrated by an example from World War II. It is said that when President Truman was asked what he did after deciding to drop the atomic bomb on Japan, his reply was that he forgot about it. He meant that once the decision was made there was no point in worrying about whether it should have been made. President Tru-man was, of course, concerned about the consequences, but he evaluated his decision in terms of the conditions existing and the process used at the time the decision was made.

THE QUALITY OF DECISIONS

Anything worth doing—

Costs versus Benefits.   The idea of making the very best deci-sion possible is a variation of an idea ingrained in most of us since

childhood: "Anything worth doing is worth doing well." We all
know from our own experience that many things we do we *could*
do a lot better. We may even *want* to do them better. We do not
do so for a very good reason—the additional cost. Cost can take
many forms: money; time; inconvenience; embarrassment; and
so on.

—may not be
worth doing
well

What should be the level of quality that a person seeks? It is
that level where the benefit received from an additional unit of
quality is equal to the costs incurred. From the viewpoint of decision making, the quality of decisions should be only as high as
justified by costs. At least from the viewpoint of costs-benefits
analysis, "Anything worth doing is not necessarily worth doing
well."[10]

Five ideal
conditions

The Best Decision Is Seldom Possible.   What are the ideal conditions for making the best possible decision? Any manager faced
with a significant decision problem would like to have the following conditions present:

1. An accurate, precise, and comprehensive definition of the
    problem.
2. An accurate and complete understanding of the multiple goals
    relevant to the problem.
3. An accurate understanding of all feasible alternatives and a
    reliable way of predicting the consequences of each alterna-
    tive.
4. A way of relating consequences to goals. That is, an "opti-
    mality criterion" is needed, so that the decision maker will
    know which consequence is best.
5. The freedom to choose the alternative that best optimizes the
    decision.

Conditions
seldom
present

Most of the above conditions are seldom present in significant
managerial decision-making situations. It is often impossible to
define or structure the problem accurately. Relevant goals may not
be fully understood or may be in conflict with each other. It is almost never possible to know all alternatives, the probabilities of
their occurrence, and their consequences. Further, because of restrictions on their choice, managers may not be free to choose the
best alternative. Since the ideal conditions are seldom present, the
goal of managers should be to make decisions that are "good
enough," rather than best or optimal in terms of ideal conditions.

Boundaries to
rationality

Decisions Should Be "Good Enough."   In any significant management decision problem, there are always limits to the ability
and capacity of decision makers to consider the complexities and
to process information relevant to the problem. There are always

[10] Richard B. McKenzie and Gordon Tullock, *The New World of Economics: Explorations into the Human Experience* (Homewood, Ill.: Richard
D. Irwin, 1977), chap. 2.

"boundaries to rationality" in any organization. That is, there are always elements in problem situations—policies, personalities, costs, technology, competition—that must be taken as given and which do not enter into decision making as variables.[11]

Subjective versus objective rationality

The intuitively acceptable idea of "bounded rationality" means simply that decision makers seldom try to find the optimum solution to a decision problem. Such "objective rationality" is unrealistic: ". . . people simply don't have such an irrational passion for dispassionate rationality."[12] Rather, they define the problem in a limited way, accepting as given many aspects of the situation, and they select a course of action whose consequences are "good enough." This more realistic type of rationality is sometimes called "subjective" rationality to contrast it with "objective" rationality.

Simplifying decision situations

You can see that the essential requirement of simplifying decision situations presents managers with a problem. On the one hand, in order to make a perfectly correct decision, managers need to know practically everything about anything that affects the decision: "The manager cannot manage well unless he in some sense manages all."[13] In order to manage well some small part of an organization, managers need to understand all aspects of the organization. On the other hand, as a practical matter, managers cannot know everything about an organization that can influence their decisions. Thus, "The key to understanding . . . decision-making . . . is to discover the ways in which the decision-maker simplifies the complex fabric of the environment into workable conceptions of his decision problems."[14]

Internal and external limitations

In their efforts to simplify or "model" decision problems, managers are subject to both internal and external limitations or constraints. "Internal limitations" include personal background, education, perceptions, attitudes and beliefs, values, and motivation. "External limitations" include the influence of subordinates, superiors, and peers on the way a decision situation is modeled. Choice is also limited by forces and groups outside of the organization. "Forces" include time, competition, degree of certainty, type of industry, and social values. "Groups" include labor unions, citizens' groups, government agencies, contractors, suppliers, and the local community.

The effective decision

Quality and Acceptance. An interesting view of decisions is that every decision has two distinct ingredients: quality and ac-

---

[11] James G. March and Herbert A. Simon, *Organizations* (New York: John Wiley & Sons, 1958), p. 170.

[12] David W. Miller and Martin K. Starr, *The Structure of Human Decisions* (Englewood Cliffs, N.J.: Prentice-Hall, 1967), p. 49.

[13] C. West Churchman, *Challenge to Reason* (New York: McGraw-Hill Book Company, 1968), pp. 23–26.

[14] William T. Morris, *The Analysis of Management Decisions*, rev. ed. (Homewood, Ill.: Richard D. Irwin, 1964), p. 10.

ceptance.[15] Both these ingredients influence the ultimate effectiveness of a decision. The highest-quality decision, if not accepted by those affected by it, may not be the most effective. For example, in determining new procedures for performing a job, business firms often hire methods-study specialists. These specialists are trained in the techniques of methods, time, and motion study; they *know* how to arrive at the best method of doing the job. However, the best method is of no value if those who are to use it do not understand and accept it.

*Three
possibilities*

Decision makers should determine the relative requirements of a decision's quality and acceptance. Three possibilities are: high-quality–low-acceptance; high-acceptance–low-quality; and high-acceptance–high quality. Of course, there are variations of these possibilities. A significant point for managers to think about is that not all decisions fall into the high-acceptance–high-quality category; that is, the "ideal" solution (even if possible to find) is not as effective as one that is "good enough" and highly accepted by those who implement it.

GROUP DECISION MAKING

Role of groups

Most significant decisions in organizations are made in a group or committee context. The decisions are not necessarily made *by* the group, but they are made *within* the context of group interaction. Groups play an important role in decision making, not only in organizations and political structures, but also in social, religious, judicial, educational, and family situations.

*Canceling
individual
errors*

Two Heads Better Than One—Sometimes. An important step in developing the decision-making resource of a group is to make sure that the group is aware of the rationale for group decision making. The common-sense axiom that "two heads are better than one" derives its validity from two sources. First, when several people are involved in making a decision, individual errors are canceled out; statistical averaging occurs. Thus, if you sought ten *individual* opinions about a decision problem and weighed them equally, your final decision would eliminate extreme opinions—good and bad.

*Group
interaction*

Second, the validity of the "two heads are better than one" axiom stems from the process of people interacting with each other— that is, the dynamics of the group process adds to the quality of decisions. When people interact in a group decision-making process, the result is often superior than when those same people offer individual opinions.

Two lessons

Two lessons for managers are implied by the rationale that "two heads are better than one." First, managers need to understand

---

[15] Norman R. F. Maier, "Fit Decisions to Your Needs," in *Keys to Better Business Planning* (*Nation's Business,* 1965), pp. 8–11.

groups, group processes and, particularly, various approaches to group decision making. (Groups are the subject of a later chapter.) Second, managers need to understand that two, or more, heads are *not* always better than one. It depends on the particular heads involved and the group skills of those participating in the decision making, and also on the type of decision problem and the means needed to carry out the decision.

Decision by consensus

The Japanese Approach. An interesting example of group decision making is provided by Japanese organizations. The *typical* approach to decision making in many Japanese institutions is decision by consensus. Although such an approach takes time, it leads (for the Japanese) to effective solutions. Rather than emphasizing the *answer* to a decision problem, the Japanese process emphasizes *defining* the problem.[16]

"Ringi"

Two methods of reaching a consensus are *ringi* and *matomari*.[17] Ringi is a process in which middle and lower-level employees initiate the decision process by drafting a paper on the decision problem. The paper is circulated and discussed by other departments, and eventually passed up to higher levels in the organization. Higher-level executives are, thus, under pressure to approve the paper because of its broad consensual support at the lower levels of the organization.

"Matomari"

Matomari differs from ringi in that it refers to a meeting that is attended by employees of all departments or levels within the organization. Matomari is an unhurried process of securing a consensus. Decisions are rarely based on voting, an approach the Japanese refer to as the "tyranny of the majority." Rather, individual views are presented, feelings are explored, and views are altered in an inoffensive, cautious climate.

General idea

Ringi and matomari are customary in many Japanese organizations. They are not used only for exceptional decisions or on infrequent occasions. As such, they do not have an institutionalized counterpart in American organizations, even though other types of group decision making are common here. The specifics of the Japanese approach to decision making have evolved out of and are in harmony with the Japanese culture. They cannot be directly transplanted to other environments.[18] Nevertheless, the general idea of decision by consensus can be adapted to American, as well as other, cultures.

---

[16] Drucker, *Management: Tasks, Responsibilities, Practices,* pp. 466–70.

[17] S. I. Hayakawa, "Maintaining Employee Morale," syndicated column, *The Eagle,* April 23, 1972. For a more extended discussion of Japanese management, see Herman Kahn, *The Emerging Japanese Superstate: Challenge and Response* (Englewood Cliffs, N.J.: Prentice-Hall, 1970).

[18] "Drawbacks of Japanese Management," *Business Week,* November 24, 1973, p. 12.

*Group
formation*

General Requirements.[19]   In order to establish and effectively use a decision-making group, managers should consider requirements for group formation, cohesion development or coalescing, processes, and control. In "forming" a decision-making group it is important to take into account the type of group members needed in order to meet the task, and the political and social demands of the group. Increasingly, decision-making groups in organizations are required to include members who represent the public, consumers, unions, and others who have a vested interest in the decisions of the group.

*Coalescing,
processes,
and control*

"Coalescing" refers to the need to develop sufficient cohesion in groups so that the task requirements of the group can be achieved and so that the group can provide social–emotional rewards—recognition and affiliation, for example. Group "processes" must be appropriate to the decision task of the group. Processes can vary from highly interactive, face-to-face processes to those that minimize interaction ("nominal groups") and that eliminate face-to-face processes ("Delphi groups"). The "control" of group performance involves the application of the control process (see Chapter 4). In controlling group performance, a special problem arises in connection with the distribution of rewards. Giving equal rewards to all members of the group places emphasis on the overall group task, but it fails to reward differences in individual performance.

---

[19] Material in this section is drawn from Paul C. Nutt, "Models for Decision Making in Organizations and Some Contextual Variables which Stipulate Optimal Use," *Academy of Management Review*, vol. 1, no. 2 (April 1976), pp. 88–90.

Summary box

> A decision problem rarely presents a manager with a choice between pure right and pure wrong. Nevertheless, the correctness of decisions is evaluated. One approach to evaluating decisions is to examine the decision's *consequences*. Another approach is to evaluate the *process* used to reach the decision and how well it was used. Both these approaches have a role to play in managing.
>
> How good *should* decisions be? They should be good enough so that the benefits received are equal to the costs incurred. Further, decision acceptance must be considered along with decision quality. The best quality decision may not meet requirements for acceptance.
>
> How good *can* decisions be? The conditions for a perfect, ideal, or objectively rational decision are seldom present. Therefore, managers must make decisions that are subjectively rational. This means that the decisions are "good enough" within boundaries of rationality.
>
> In making decisions, managers must simplify or "model" the decision situation. The purpose of this modeling is to abstract from the total reality of the situation a workable conception of the decision problem. In modeling decision situations, managers are subject to both internal and external constraints.
>
> Groups or committees often are used in the process of making a decision. The logic of this practice, from the viewpoint of decision quality, is that sometimes "two (or more) heads are better than one." When this is true, it is because of the canceling out of individual errors and because of the dynamics of the group process. The need to consider requirements for group formation, coalescing, processes, and control were noted. We discuss groups again in Chapter 10.

THE DECISION-MAKING PROCESS

Variety of approaches

Approaches to Decision Making. Some decisions represent snap judgments made by executives on the spur of the moment. Other decisions are made on the basis of the manager's intuitive judgment about the right decision to make at the time. When time and cost considerations permit, some decisions are deferred until after an examination of relevant information. Still other decisions are made only after an exhaustive analysis of all major decision parameters. Very sophisticated analytical techniques and electronic equipment may be used in decision making. In such cases, relevant experience and good judgment are still important.

Contingencies   The point of these statements is that there are numerous approaches to decision making *and all of them may be appropriate at certain times.* The more rigorous, scientific, and analytical approaches to decision making are not always the "best." The "best" approach depends on such contingencies as the nature of the decision problem, time available, the state of technology applicable to the problem, skill and knowledge of the decision makers, cost-benefit considerations, and the degree of certainty in the problem situation.

Continuum of   Approaches to decision making can be thought of as ranging on a
approaches   continuum as shown in Figure 5–3.

FIGURE 5–3
Continuum of Approaches to Decision Making

Judgment, intuition	Common sense	Logic	Scientific analysis

Nonrational   Rational

Fit the   Rather than thinking of one or more of these approaches as be-
approach to   ing better than others, think of them in terms of their appropriate-
the problem   ness to specific decision problems. Although intuition, judgment, and common sense may be the most common approaches to managerial decision making, they also share another characteristic: they are not readily taught in a classroom situation or discussed in a managing textbook. In the formal study of managing, the emphasis is on approaches that can be learned through classroom experience. These approaches emphasize a systematic, quasi-rational *process* of making decisions.

Sequence   **The Idea of a Process.**   The idea of a "process" implies a series
of phases   or sequence of steps or elements that lead to a particular goal or result. A decision-making process is a series of steps or phases, generally sequential, that facilitates decision making. Some examples of decision-making processes are shown in Figure 5–4.

General idea   The examples shown in Figure 5–4 are specific cases of a general idea. The general idea worth learning here is that of a systematic, sequential approach to stages in problem solving and decision making. There are numerous different views about the decision-making process, but most are a variation of the general and useful idea of following a systematic approach.

Develop your   You can develop your own list of phases that you feel should be
own process   included in the process. You can use the list to check the correctness and completeness of your approach to reaching a decision. In

FIGURE 5–4
Examples of Decision-Making Processes

Example A*
1. What is the problem?
2. What are the alternatives?
3. Which alternative is best?

Example B†
1. Immediate pressures on the decision maker.
2. Analysis of the type of problem and its basic dimensions.
3. Search for alternative solutions.
4. Consideration of the consequences of alternative solutions, anticipation of post-decisional conflict, and final choice.

Example C‡
1. Recognition of a situation that calls for a decision about what action should be taken.
2. Identification and development of alternative courses of action.
3. Evaluation of the alternatives.
4. Choice of one of the alternatives.
5. Implementation of the selected course of action.

Example D§
1. Identification phase
   a. Decision recognition
   b. Diagnosis
2. Development phase
   a. Search
   b. Design
3. Selection phase
   a. Screen
   b. Evaluation—Choice
   c. Authorization

* John Dewey, *How We Think* (New York: D. C. Heath and Company, 1910), pp. 101–105.
† Daniel Katz and Robert L. Kahn, *The Social Psychology of Organizations* (New York: John Wiley & Sons, 1966), p. 274.
‡ Joseph W. Newman, *Management Applications of Decision Theory* (New York: Harper & Row, Publishers, 1971), p. 3.
§ Mintzberg, Raisinghami, and Théorêt, "The Structure of 'Unstructured' Decisions," pp. 252–59.

that way, you can be more confident that your decision is "right" at the time it is made. There is no intrinsic value to such a list; its value lies in the *actual behavior* that the list provokes. For example, most approaches to a decision-making process include the notion of "recognizing and defining the problem." To be useful, however, this notion must elicit certain behavior, such as: searching behavior to identify problems; analyzing behavior to distinguish symptoms from problems; and evaluating behavior to determine the importance of the problem.

Degrees of sophistication

Implementing a Process. Implementing a decision-making process may be very casual or intuitive, or it may be very sophisticated and systematic. Managers, for example, may go through a decision-making process in a matter of minutes. They may recognize and define the problem in their mind, analyze it, reflect on several alternatives, reach a decision, and implement it. Other decisions may call for a more elaborate set of behaviors. Mathematical analysis, models, and computers may be utilized at several stages of the process.[20] Our main point is that the nature of the decision problem and the action desired determine the appropriate degree of sophistication in implementing a decision-making process.

People implement processes

The logic of a decision-making process becomes operational through the behavior of people. Individuals define and indentify problems and evaluate alternatives. Furthermore, these individuals behave in an interpersonal, group, and organizational context, and this context influences how the process is implemented. If decisions are not made as logically as implied by a decision-making process, the explanation is found in the fact that people do not behave in a totally logical and rational way. It is important to emphasize this "obvious" point of the influence of people on decision making. An executive can easily lose sight of the fact that all management and organizational processes are accomplished through the behavior of individuals. That is why the major emphasis in this book is on the behavioral dimension of management.

PROBLEM-SOLVING STYLES

The idea of style

Our final topic in this chapter deals with the differing styles that can be used in problem solving and decision making. The idea of style is easily captured by comparing *Star Trek*'s Spock and McCoy. These characters personify opposite approaches to the task of gathering information about a decision problem and of using that information in order to make a decision. Captain Kirk, of course, always gleans out the best from these two approaches and comes up with the decision that is exactly right.

Carl Jung

Four Psychological Functions. In this section, we briefly discusss a model of problem-solving styles that is based on the work of psychologist Carl Jung.[21] Jung identified four psychological functions: sensing, intuiting, thinking, and feeling. According to Jung, these four functions interact with a person's orientation toward extraversion or introversion. This interaction determines the "self" of a person.

Perceiving and judging

Our discussion deals only with the four psychological functions. Sensing and intuiting represent opposite ways of *perceiving*, or be-

---

[20] For an interesting article on the use in business of pocket-size, programmable computers, see "Tiny Computers that Speed Business Decisions," *Business Week*, January 10, 1977, pp. 40–44.

[21] Carl G. Jung, *Psychological Types* (London: Rutledge and Kegan Paul, 1923). Also see J. Campbell, ed., *The Portable Jung* (New York: Viking Press, 1971).

coming aware; thinking and feeling represent opposite ways of *judging,* or of deciding. Brief statements of the meaning of these four psychological functions are given in Figure 5–5.

FIGURE 5–5
Carl Jung's Four Psychological Functions

Perceiving Functions

Sensing. A tendency to search for facts, to be realistic, and to look at things in an objective, impartial manner. Places high value on facts that can be verified by appeal to the five senses. Shuns sentiment and wishful thinking. Likes routine and precision.

Intuiting. A tendency to try to discover new possibilities for changing a situation and for changing the way a situation is being handled. Likes new and unique situations, dislikes routines, details, and precision.

Judging Functions

Thinking. A tendency to look for systematic, cause and effect relationships, to analyze fully, and to impersonally differentiate between true and false. Relies on cognitive processes.

Feeling. A tendency to consider how you and others will feel as a result of decisions. Discriminates between what is good and bad, valued and not valued. Relies on affective processes.

Combining the perceiving and judging functions

Four-Quadrant Model. The four psychological functions can be shown as in Figure 5–6.[22] The model reflects the four combinations of the perceiving and judging functions. Each quadrant represents a particular approach to becoming aware of an environment or situation (perceiving) and for reaching conclusions based on that awareness (judging). Thus, the model deals with problem-solving

FIGURE 5–6
A Model of Problem-Solving Styles

Judging Functions	Perceiving Functions	
	Sensing	Intuiting
Thinking	ST	NT
Feeling	SF	NF

---

[22] For applications of the model to organizational problems, see Ian I. Mitroff and Ralph H. Kilmann, "Stories Managers Tell: A New Tool for Organizational Problem Solving," *Management Review,* vol. 64 no. 7 (July, 1975), pp. 18–28. Also see Don Hellriegel and John W. Slocum, Jr., "Managerial Problem Solving Styles," *Business Horizons,* vol. 18, no. 6 (December 1975), pp. 29–37.

and decision-making styles. These styles can be "measured" with the Myers-Briggs Type Indicator.[23]

ST

People who fall into the *ST* quadrant are fact-oriented and analyze these facts in an impersonal manner. They tend to be oriented toward the practical and to develop technical skills for dealing with the practical world. We would expect engineers, accountants, applied scientists, and many business professionals to be in the *ST* category.

SF

SF people also emphasize facts but tend to bring a personal and warm dimension to the analysis of these facts. They are sympathetic and friendly toward people and direct their talents to people-related activities, such as teaching, sales, and hospital service.

NT

Possibilities and opportunities, rather than facts, are the emphasis of an *NT* person. Like an *ST*, an *NT* analyzes possibilities in an impersonal, logical manner. An *NT* ought to be good at concept formation and theory development. We would expect to find examples in research work and in top-level management positions.

NF

The opposite of an *ST* is an *NF*, who combines personal warmth and concern for people with an emphasis on possibilities and opportunities. *NFs* do not like details or routine, preferring instead to focus on broad, people-oriented issues.

Each style can be appropriate

Use of the Model. In terms of aiding our understanding of decision making, the model we have presented serves several purposes. First, it recognizes the existence of several problem-solving styles. No one of these styles is better than the other. Each is appropriate, depending upon the decision problem.

Identifying your own style

Second, the model is an aid in identifying your own style and in suggesting how you might broaden your style. For example, if the *ST* quadrant describes you best, then you might want to make an effort to develop *NF* skills that will complement your *ST* orientations.

Match style with problem

Third, the model may help you to utilize personnel better by matching problem-solving styles and decision problems. For example, for decision problems requiring programmed decisions, an *ST* may be most appropriate. Solutions to problems requiring creative, unprogrammed decisions may benefit from the skills of an *NF* problem solver.

---

[23] Isabel Briggs Myers, *The Myers-Briggs Type Indicator* (Palo Alto, Calif.: Consulting Psychologists Press, 1962).

Summary box

There is *no one best approach* to making decisions. Approaches can range on a continuum from judgment and intuition to scientific analysis. Which approach is best depends on specific contingencies in the decision situation.

The general idea of a decision-making *process* is that of a systematic, sequential approach to making decisions. You can develop a process that suits your needs. The process will be useful to the extent that it provokes actual behavior that contributes to effective decision making.

One way of thinking about *problem-solving styles* is in terms of *four psychological functions:* sensing (S), intuiting (N), thinking (T), and feeling (F). These four functions can be combined into *four basic styles:* ST, SF, NT, and NF. Each style has specific characteristics and can be an appropriate style, depending on the situation and the problem.

CHECK YOUR UNDERSTANDING

Decision
Elements of a decision
Choice continuum
Relation of decision making to managing
Programmed decisions
Unprogrammed decisions
Decision matrix
Components of a decision matrix
Three classes of decision problems
Ideal conditions for a decision

Boundaries to rationality
Objective versus subjective rationality
Ringi
Matomari
Approaches to decision making
Decision-making process
Perceiving functions
Judging functions
Four problem-solving styles
Uses of problem-solving styles model

STUDY QUESTIONS

1. Which of the four problem-solving styles best fits *Star Trek*'s Spock? Dr. McCoy? Where would you fit Captain Kirk into the model of problem-solving styles? Which style best fits you?

2. What are some examples of decision problems that you have that can be resolved by programmed decisions? What is a recent decision problem that required an unprogrammed decision?

3. Suppose that you plan to purchase a car. Can you use a decision matrix framework for the decision problem? If so, what are the strategies, states of nature, and outcomes?

4. Cite examples of decision making involving certainty, risk, and uncertainty.

5. Select a major political or business decision and evaluate it in terms of its correctness. Examples:
   a. The Watergate break-in.
   b. President Nixon's decision to participate in the Watergate coverup.
   c. General Motors Corporation's decision to introduce a 1977 shortened version of its full-size cars.

6. In order to make decisions that are "good enough," managers must construct conceptual simplifications of decision problem realities. What are some ways in which *you* simplify decision problems? What are some important internal and external limitations on your ability to consider decision problems?

7. In your opinion, what are some examples of decision problems that would not benefit from a group decision-making process? What are some of the "costs" and "benefits" of group decision making?

8. What is the "best" approach to decision making? What are some contingencies to consider in determining the best approach to any specific decision problem?

9. The text states that "anything worth doing is not necessarily worth doing well." Why is this true?

10. Identify the problem-solving characteristics that you think are important for a person planning for a career in public accounting. Which quadrant of the problem-solving styles model do you think best fits the characteristics you have identified?

APPLICATION: AN UNPROGRAMMED DECISION*

"It will be studied as a classic episode in Britain's political history," predicts a senior government official. It can also be used as an illustration of almost every topic discussed in Chapter 5.

What is "It?" It is the 1975 decision of the British government to enter into a limited partnership with Chrysler U.K., the British subsidiary of Chrysler Corporation. The partnership was designed to keep Chrysler operations in Britain. The decision was one element of a process of high-level decision-making drama that has not yet played out its final act.

On November 3, 1975, in London, Prime Minister Harold Wilson met with Mr. John J. Ricarrdo, chairman and CEO of Chrysler Corporation, along with other top Chrysler officials. The issue: Chrysler U.K.'s future in Britain. The climate for this initial meeting had not been helped by Wilson's publicized allusion to Chrysler's holding a "pistol to the government's head." Ricarrdo was privately referred to as "the godfather" by government officials. Additional hostility was felt by various members of Parliament because of the British subsidiary's subservience to the Detroit-based parent company. An example: Chrysler U.K. had to consult Detroit before making expenditures over $40,000.

---

* Reprinted with permission of *The Wall Street Journal*, © Dow Jones & Company, Inc. (1976). All Rights Reserved.

The "pistol" referred to by Wilson was Chrysler's public announcement in Detroit of its intention to dispose of its British operations. The announcement was all the more shocking because Chrysler U.K. officials had not been told of the plan.

Chrysler U.K., with heavy losses during six of the previous nine years, had seen, within the year, its share of the new-car market drop from 12 to 4 percent. From Chrysler's viewpoint, the economic facts of life were that it would not sustain additional losses. Chrysler was willing to leave Britain "honorably" by paying all of its obligations and arranging for the transfer of operations to the government. Britain, however, did not want to take over Chrysler U.K. But the message was clear—Chrysler wanted out.

From Britain's viewpoint, Chrysler's departure could lead to serious consequences. Unemployment was already high and Chrysler's closing could increase it another 50,000. The Labor Party's position in Scotland was precarious and could be made worse by the Chrysler move. In addition, the shah of Iran was concerned about the effect of Chrysler's closing on a $200 million contract Iran had with Chrysler, U.K. Failure to deliver on that contract could adversely affect Britain's position in the Middle East.

Talks between Chrysler and British government officials continued for about four weeks. The discussions were relatively fruitless and, according to one source, badly handled: "I watched this bloody, idiot negotiation going on with great distaste." With the talks at an impasse, it looked as if Chrysler was going to pull out.

Then, on December 2, a crucial event took place. In two minor elections, Scottish Nationalists defeated Labor Party candidates, suggesting a political mood in Scotland that threatened the Labor Party's power base. This election shook the British Cabinet. On December 5, Wilson ordered Harold Lever, his economic advisor, to enter the talks. By the time the Cabinet met on December 6, a new British position had taken shape. Some phrases used to describe the proposal were: "Unbelievably good" for Chrysler, "flabbergasted," "amazement over the plan." Despite some bitter opposition, the new plan was approved by the Cabinet and, subsequently, by Parliament.

The new plan called for Britain to make substantial cash contributions and loan guarantees to Chrysler U.K. In addition, Chrysler received assurances that a cut in its work force would not be met by strikes, a reversal of the previous position taken by union officials. For its part, Chrysler promised to increase production and investment in Britain. The result of the new plan was that Chrysler remained in Britain.

But for how long? The plan may have only postponed the inevitable. Few were certain that Chrysler could remain viable in the British auto market. Clearly, the future was uncertain. Chrysler U.K. was known to have some internal management problems —the worst labor record among the auto companies, for example.

1. Discuss this unprogrammed decision in terms of:
   a. The three elements of a decision.
   b. The decision matrix framework.
   c. Ideal decision conditions.
   d. A decision-making process.
2. Was the decision right?

APPLICATION: PROBLEM-SOLVING STYLES AND CAREER DEVELOPMENT

Refer back to the section in Chapter 5 that discusses problem-solving styles and review Figures 5–5 and 5–6.

This application presents data that show how a group of 426 students were divided into the four problem-solving styles. The 426 were members of a university-level introductory course in management. A shortened version of the Myers-Briggs Type Indicator was used in order to get a general idea of the students' problem-solving styles (The complete Myers-Briggs Type Indicator should be used for more accurate measures.)

Figure 5–7 divides the 426 students by problem-solving style and classifies them into categories according to (a) academic major and (b) sex. Within each category, the *observed* number of students having each of the four problem-solving styles is shown. This is the top number in each cell. For example, Table 5–7 shows

FIGURE 5–7
Number of Students Having Each of Four Problem-Solving Styles (total students = 426)

Method of Classifying Students	Sensing/ Thinking (ST)	Sensing/ Feeling (SF)	Intuitive/ Feeling (NF)	Intuitive/ Thinking (NT)	Total
By Academic Major					
Accounting	34 (23)*	25 (29)	33 (38)	17 (19)	109
Finance	9 (9)	13 (11)	11 (14)	8 (7)	41
Managing	9 (15)*	15 (19)	31 (24)*	15 (12)	70
Marketing	5 (14)*	28 (18)*	22 (22)	11 (12)	66
Nonbusiness	33 (29)	33 (37)	50 (49)	24 (25)	140
Total	90	114	147	75	426
By Sex					
Male	72 (64)*	72 (81)	98 (104)	60 (53)	302
Female	18 (26)*	42 (33)*	49 (43)	15 (22)*	124
Total	90	114	147	75	426

* See text.

that the number of students majoring in managing who have an *ST* style is 9. There are 49 females who have an *NF* style.

Figure 5–7 also contains a second number in each cell. This number is in parentheses and represents the number of students that would be *expected* to be in that cell. This number is determined by a procedure known as chi-square analysis. The mechanics of the procedure need not concern us here. The general idea is that we can use the *observed frequencies* in order to compute the *expected frequencies*, and then we can compare the two. Sometimes the difference between observed and expected frequencies is very small or zero, and at other times it is relatively large, as in the cells with an asterisk.

1. Is there any particular significance, in your opinion, to the way the total number of students divide into the four problem-solving styles?

2. Given your own perceptions of the characteristics of careers in accounting, managing, and marketing, do the figures in Figure 5–7 suggest anything concerning career development?

3. Are the figures in Figure 5–7 consistent or inconsistent with common stereotypes about males and females? Do you see any implications for career development?

SUPPLEMENT 5A

An Introduction to Linear Programming

Why not the best?

Jimmy Carter

LP—For allocation problems

Linear programming (LP) is a way of finding the "best solution to a problem. "It is a useful and popular aid to decision making developed during the last 30 years. From its initial applications during World War II, LP has become an important aid to managers in the solution of linear "allocation problems." Allocation problems involve the distribution of limited resources to competing uses.

LP—An optimization technique

LP is an example of an optimization technique. That is, it is a technique for finding the one best decision, given certain assumptions about the parameters of the decision problem. For example, LP is used in business firms to find the combination of products to produce and sell in order to obtain the maximum profit. It is also used to find the schedule of machine utilization that results in the minimum idle time, and in production scheduling to determine the schedule that results in the minimum labor turnover. LP systematically finds the best, or optimum, solution in a set of feasible solutions. Prior to LP, trial-and-error methods were used to test solutions, and there was no certainty that the best solution was found.

This supplement

In the paragraphs that follow, we look at LP in terms of the decision matrix framework discussed in Chapter 5, note briefly the names of the three most common LP methods, define several basic LP concepts, and identify the two major characteristics or assumptions of LP problems. Then we go through an illustration of the mechanics of the graphical method of LP and conclude with a discussion of how managers can use LP.

AN LP DECISION MATRIX

LP—Decision making with certainty

Linear programming generally is associated with the class of problems discussed in Chapter 5 as decision making with "certainty"—that is, a situation in which there is assumed to be only one state of nature for each strategy. The probability of occurrence of the state of nature is assumed to be equal to one. The problem in such a situation is to select that strategy with the best outcome or payoff. This problem is not as simple as it appears, because the large number of possible strategies makes it difficult to evaluate each strategy.

Select best payoff

The general idea of LP can be visualized in a decision matrix. As shown in Figure 5A–1, an LP decision matrix has one state of

FIGURE 5A–1
An LP Decision Matrix

Strategies	State of Nature $P = 1$
S_1	Outcome of S_1
S_2	Outcome of S_2
S_3	Outcome of S_3
. . .	. . .
S_t	Outcome of S_t

nature with an assumed probability of occurrence equal to one $(P = 1)$. In addition, the matrix contains a theoretically infinite number of strategy alternatives. The decision problem is to select that alternative with the best payoff.

State of nature

An example of a state of nature in an LP decision matrix is the set of conditions that characterize a product's supply and demand. For example, the decision maker may know that all products produced can be sold at predetermined prices and produced at predetermined costs. Thus, the decision maker is certain about potential sales, the selling price, and the production cost. These three elements make up part of the decision problem's state of nature.

Strategies

The strategies in this illustration are the possible combinations of quantities of products that can be produced within the limitations of available resources. Even when the number of different products produced by the firm is very small, the number of combinations of different quantities of the products can be very large. LP is one way of handling this "product-mix" decision problem.

THREE MAIN LP METHODS

Graphical

There are three main linear programming methods: graphical, simplex, and transportation. This supplement illustrates the graphical method. The primary value of the graphical method of LP is its capacity to quickly convey the essential idea and power of LP. It illustrates graphically how LP searches out, from a large number of alternative solutions, the one that is best. The graphical method, however, has almost no practical value for managers because, as this supplement shows, it is unable to handle multiple-variable problems.

Simplex

The most versatile and widely used of the LP methods is the "simplex" method, a method that can handle problems containing hundreds of variables. The simplex method is an iterative process in which various combinations of variables are tested for their feasibility and payoff. The process proceeds, systematically testing variable combinations that yield better and better payoffs. The process ends when the "best" payoff is determined, or when the decision maker decides that a "good enough" payoff is achieved. Although the simplex method is not difficult to comprehend, it does require considerable time and effort to learn. Such an investment of your time and effort is more appropriate in a textbook dealing primarily with quantitative decision-making approaches.

*Transpor-
tation*

The "transportation" method of LP is uniquely applicable to a problem that can be thought of as a "source-destination" problem in which the supply provided by the sources equals the demand required by the destinations. For example, the transportation methods can be used in problems concerned with shipping products from a factory to a warehouse, or transporting materials from one part of a plant to another. The transportation method is less flexible than the simplex method, but, where the restricting assumption can be met, it offers a useful approach to the solution of source-destination problems.[1]

BASIC LP CONCEPTS

Six concepts

The basic concepts that we need to illustrate the graphical method of solving LP problems are: constraints, variables, feasible solution, feasibility area, objective function, and optimum solution. These terms are also basic to the simplex method of solving LP problems.

Constraints

The "constraints" in an LP problem are the restrictions on the production of variables. They are the scarce resources that the

---

[1] For discussions of the simplex and transportation methods of LP, see Harvey M. Wagner, *Principles of Operations Research with Applications to Managerial Decisions* (Englewood Cliffs, N.J.: Prentice-Hall, 1969), chaps. 2, 3, 4, and 5. Also, see Frederick S. Hillier and Gerald J. Lieberman, *Introduction to Operations Research* (San Francisco: Holden-Day, 1967), chaps. 5 and 6.

decision maker is trying to allocate in an optimal manner. Examples of constraints in LP problems include materials, labor time, labor skills, money, warehouse space, available land, sales quotas, and equipment time.

Variables

The "variables" in an LP problem are the factors or products to which the constraints are being allocated. For example, in the product-mix problem previously mentioned, the variables are the products being produced. The graphical method of LP is limited to two-variable problems (one for each axis on the graph), whereas the simplex method is, in theory, unlimited.

Feasible solution

An LP "feasible solution" is any combination of variables that is technically possible in terms of the constraints in the problem. The number of feasible solutions can be very sizable in a large, multiple-variable LP problem. Each of these solutions is a "strategy" that the decision maker can choose. Each of these strategies has a payoff. The LP procedure searches among a potentially large set of feasible solutions and finds the best solutions.

Feasibility area

The "feasibility area" is the total set of feasible solutions. In Figure 5A–3, the feasibility area is shaded. Any solution within the feasibility area is a feasible solution. The boundaries of the area are determined by the constraints.

Objective function

The "objective function" is the equation that the LP problem is attempting to optimize. Common symbols used to identify the objective function are Z and Θ. In a product-mix problem, for example, the objective function consists of the variables produced and their corresponding profit coefficients. LP finds the optimum value of the objective function. Another way of thinking about the meaning of the objective function is as the standard against which feasible solutions will be compared. Each feasible solution has a value in terms of the objective function.

Optimum solution

The "optimum solution" is that feasible solution that causes the objective function to have its optimal value. We show in the following illustration that it is possible, in LP problems, for the optimum value of the objective function to be arrived at by means of several combinations of the variables. In other words, there can be several optimum solutions. It is important to remember that the optimal solution to an LP problem is optimal only in terms of the constraints included in the problem.

BASIC CHARACTERISTICS OF LP PROBLEMS

Two characteristics

Before a decision problem can be thought of in terms of an LP solution, it is necessary that the problem have two characteristics: linearity and certainty.[2] These characteristics concern the rela-

---

[2] R. Stansbury Stockton, *Introduction to Linear Programming*, 2nd ed. (Boston: Allyn & Bacon, 1963), pp. 5–6.

tionship between the variables and the constraints in the decision problem.

Linearity

"Linearity" means that the relationships between all variables and constraints in the decision problem are linear; that is, it must be possible to express the relationship between all constraints and variables in the form of a linear equation (an equation in which terms to the first power are all related in an additive manner).

Example of linearity

For example, suppose that the production of a bicycle requires the use of three materials (A, B, C), labor (D), and machine time (E). These constraints are expressed in units of one kind or another (labor and machine time in hours, materials in pounds). Linearity requires that the expression for the composition of the bicycle using the five constraints be a linear equation, such as:

$$\text{One bicycle} = 3(A) + 2(B) + 6(C) + 1(D) + 0.5(E).$$

The coefficients (3, 2, 6, 1, and 0.5) of the five constraints in the above equation are arbitrary values selected for the purpose of this illustration. In general, linearity requires that the decision problem can be stated in the form of a set of linear equations that relate all variables and constraints in the problem.

Certainty

"Certainty" means that all the coefficients in the linear equations are known and constant. For example, in the above linear equation, certainty requires that each bicycle does, in fact, require three units of A, two units of B, and so forth. Certainty also requires that the coefficients in the objective function equation be known and constant. In general, LP requires certainty of its coefficients in the linear equations. Sometimes, certainty is referred to as the "deterministic characteristic."

AN ILLUSTRATION OF THE GRAPHICAL METHOD OF LP[3]

The situation

Suppose that you are the production manager of a very small manufacturing plant. Your plant produces two types of dolls, Tams and Tamettes. Each doll requires three inputs: labor, materials, and machine time. Each Tam that is sold provides a net contribution to profit and overhead of $4 (contribution to profit and overhead is equal to the doll's selling price minus the variable costs of making the doll). The contribution to overhead and profit of each Tamette sold is $5. Assume that you can sell all the Tams and Tamette dolls your present plant capacity can produce.

Two variables

Variables and Constraints. In this illustration, the Tams and the Tamettes are the variables. The Symbol X is used to identify Tams; the symbol Y is used to identify Tamettes. Figure 5A–2

---

[3] For additional background on the graphical method see C. West Churchman, Leonard Auerbach, and Simcha Sadan, *Thinking for Decisions: Deductive Quantitative Methods* (Chicago: Science Research Associates, 1975), chap. 10.

FIGURE 5A-2
Quantities of Inputs Required to Make One Tam and One Tamette

Variable	Input		
	Labor	Materials	Machine Time
Tam (1X)........................	5	3	4
Tamette (1Y)...................	4	5	12

shows the quantities of each of the three inputs that are required to make one Tam (1X) and one Tamette (1Y). These unit quantities are the same regardless of the number of dolls produced.

Input quantities available

The available quantities, expressed in a standard unit of measure, of the three inputs are:

$$\text{Labor} = 200 \text{ units}$$
$$\text{Material} = 150 \text{ units}$$
$$\text{Machine time} = 240 \text{ units}$$

Three constraints

These three limited quantities represent the constraints in this illustration. The symbol A is used to identify the labor constraint, B to identify material, and C to identify machine time. The use of the three inputs can be accounted for by the following linear inequations:

$$\text{Labor} = A = 5(X) + 4(Y) \leq 200$$
$$\text{Material} = B = 3(X) + 5(Y) \leq 150$$
$$\text{Machine time} = C = 4(X) + 12(Y) \leq 240$$

Three constraint inequations

For example, the total quantity of labor used must be equal to or less than 200 units. Although it is not essential to use the full amount of labor, it is essential that no more than 200 units be used. The total quantity of labor actually used will be determined by the quantities of Tams and Tamettes produced. Each Tam requires 5 units of labor (5A) and each Tamette requires 4 units of labor (4A). Thus, the inequality, $5(X) + 4(Y) \leq 200$, expresses the constraint for the labor input. The same reasoning applies to the material and the machine time inputs.

Objective function = $\$4(X) + \$5(Y)$

Objective Function. The objective function is $Z_{\max} = \$4(X) + \$5(Y)$; that is, in this illustration we want to optimize the total contribution to overhead and profit. "Optimize," in this case, means maximize—we want the largest possible contribution to overhead and profit. For every Tam sold there is a net contribution of $4; for every Tamette sold there is a net contribution of $5. Remember that the best solution to an LP problem depends on what the objective function is. Suppose, for example, that in this problem we want to maximize the use of the material. In that case, the objective function is $Z_{\max} = 3(X) + 5(Y)$. The best solution to the $3(X) + 5(Y)$ objective function could be different than the best solution to the $4(X) + 5(Y)$ objective function.

Constraints

Graph. The relationships between variables and constraints are shown graphically in Figure 5A–2. The constraints are shown by lines *A, B,* and *C.* These lines can be drawn by determining, for each constraint, the value of X when Y is zero, and the value of Y when X is zero. (See tabular insert in Figure 5A–3.)

FIGURE 5A–3
The Graphical Method of Linear Programming

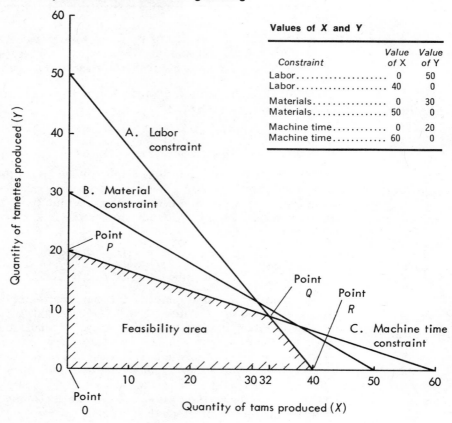

Values of X and Y		
Constraint	Value of X	Value of Y
Labor....................	0	50
Labor....................	40	0
Materials................	0	30
Materials................	50	0
Machine time...........	0	20
Machine time...........	60	0

Variables

The variables in the problem are represented by the two axes. You can see that the graphical method quickly becomes useless as the number of variables increases. Problems with more than two variables are cumbersome to solve using the graphical method because each variable requires one axis. The simplex and transportation methods of LP can handle multivariable problems.

Feasibility area

The shaded area in Figure 5A–3 is the feasibility area, the total set of technically feasible solutions. Any combination of X and Y values that is outside the feasibility area is not technically possible. For example, a decision to produce 20X and 20Y is not possible because there is not enough machine time or materials. In plotting the three constraint inequations on the graph, the extreme condition of equality is plotted. For example, the labor constraint (line A) is plotted as $5(X) + 4(Y) = 200$. All space *on* or *below* the line is potentially part of the feasibility area.

Basic and optimum feasible solutions

The feasible solution are *in* and *on* the feasibility area bounded by points, O, P, Q, and R. The feasible solutions represented by points O, P, Q, and R are sometimes called "basic feasible solutions." The "optimum feasible solution" for this problem is point Q. Point Q provides a contribution to overhead and profit of $173 because it represents a decision to produce approximately 32 Tams ($32X$) at $4 each and 9 Tamettes ($9Y$) at $5 each. There is no other combination of quantities of X and Y that will, within the restrictions of this problem, yield a higher value for the objective function. Point R yields a contribution of $160 ($40 \times$ 4), point O a contribution of $0, and point P a contribution of $100 ($20 \times$ 5). All other solutions within the feasibility area result in less than $173.

Optimum in terms of constraints

The optimal figure, $173, is optimal only in terms of the three constraints included in the LP problem. All that can be said of the product-mix of 32 units of X and 9 units of Y is that it is the best product-mix in terms of constraints A, B, and C. In the final decision making, the manager may want to consider other constraints. For example, perhaps the manager has a personal preference for Y over X. Or, a different product-mix may be chosen in order to optimize the operations of a larger or different department of the organization. The general point is that optimization techniques, such as LP, optimize only in terms of the constraints included in the model of the problem.

Must test all boundary points

In *this* problem, point Q turned out to be the optimum solution because the contribution to overhead and profit yielded by point Q is greater than that yielded by points O, P, and R. When working an LP graphical problem, you must compare the value of the objective function given by *each* of the boundary points of the feasibility area. The optimum solution is the boundary point that gives the optimum (either a maximum or a minimum depending on the problem) value of the objective function.

Relevant constraint

The optimum solution is always either a boundary point of the feasibility area, similar to points O, P, Q, and R, or it is between two of the boundary points. The latter occurs when the slope of the objective function equation is the same as the slope of one of the relevant constraint equations. A "relevant constraint equation" is one that contributes to forming the boundaries of the feasibility area. In Figure 5A–2, machine time and labor are relevant constraints, but material is not because the plotted material constraint does not touch the feasibility area.

Slope

The *slope* of the objective function in the Tam and Tamette problem is −4/5.[4] Since the −4/5 slope is not the same as the slopes of the labor constraint (−5/4) or the machine time constraint (−1/3), the optimum solution will be at one of the feasibility area boundary points (*O*, *P*, *Q*, or *R*). However, if the slope of the objective function were −1/3, for example, instead of −4/5 then the optimum solution in the Tam and Tamette problem would be at point *P*, point *Q*, or any point in-between points *P* and *Q*. The practical significance of this condition is that the manager can decide from more than one product-mix and yet reach an optimal solution. This provides the manager with additional flexibility in decision making.

FIGURE 5A–4
Decision Matrix Showing Payoffs of the Four Basic Feasible Solutions

Strategy	Point	Quantity Sold		State of Nature
		Tams	Tamettes	
S_1	O	0	0	$0 (Payoff of S_1)
S_2	P	0	20	$100 (Payoff of S_2)
S_3	Q	32	9	$173 (Payoff of S_3)
S_4	R	40	0	$160 (Payoff of S_4)

Strategy S_3 is best

Decision Matrix. To return to the decision-matrix framework discussed earlier, the decision problem in this illustration of the graphical method is shown in Figure 5A–4. Strategy S_3 is best because it gives the highest payoff.

LP AND MANAGERS

Technical versus managerial skill

You may be wondering how or whether managers use LP. We noted before that there is very little practical application for the graphical method of LP. In fact, the chances are poor that you ever encounter a managerial problem to which you would apply the LP technique. Furthermore, confronted with an LP decision

---

[4] The objective function = $4(X) + $5(Y). Convert the objective function to the slope intercept from of the linear equation. That is, solve the equation for Y, as follows:

$$\$4(X) + \$5(Y) = ?$$
$$(Y) = ? - \$4(X)/\$5$$
$$(Y) = ?/5 - 4/5(X)$$

The slope = −4/5. The ? represents any dollar value of the objective function. No specific value is needed to compute the slope. In the Tam and Tamette problem, the optimal value of the objective function is $173. Thus, when $X = 32$ and $Y = 9$, $4(X) + $5(Y) = $173. (Note: The values of 32 and 9 are approximate values, read from the graph. More precise values may be computed by setting the equations for labor and machine time equal to each other and solving for X and Y. This procedure yields $X = 32.7$ and $Y = 9.1$.)

problem, most managers seek the advice of a specialist in applied quantitative decision-making techniques. Facility in the use of LP and other operations-research management techniques is a highly specialized skill. Such skills are technical, not managerial.

Why know about LP?

Nevertheless, you should know about LP for several reasons: First, although LP is restricted to certain types of problems, it cannot be used, even in those problems, if you are not aware of the technique. Second, LP and other quantitative decision-making aids require a disciplined approach to decision problems. LP requires that the parameters of the problem be expressed in mathematical relationships; the set of these relationships represents the LP model of a decision problem. As such, LP is an excellent example of the important managerial skill of modeling. This modeling discipline forces you to think more precisely and concretely about the relationships of the variables in a decision problem. In addition, the discipline helps you understand what can and what cannot be included in a mathematical model. Finally, you should know something about LP so that you can communicate with LP specialists about the limitations, advantages, and assumptions of LP as it applies to problems affecting your accountability for performance.

Summary box

> LP is a managerial decision-making aid. It is an *optimization* technique applicable to the solution of *allocation* problems. LP is generally associated with decision making under conditions of *certainty*. As such, it can be thought of in terms of the main components of a decision matrix: strategies, state of nature, and outcomes.
>
> There are *three main LP methods*: graphical, transportation, and simplex. Of these, the simplex method has the greatest applicability. For purposes of illustration, however, we discussed only the graphical method.
>
> *Six concepts* important to the graphical method are: constraints, variables, feasibility area, feasible solution, objective function, and optimum solution.
>
> *Linearity* and *certainty* are two basic characteristics that must be present in a problem in order for LP to be applicable to it.

CHECK YOUR UNDERSTANDING OF THE FOLLOWING:

Allocation problem   Feasible solution
Optimization technique Feasibility area
Graphical method   Objective function
Simplex method   Optimum solution
Constraints   Linearity
Variables   Certainty
Transportation method Basic feasible solution

STUDY QUESTIONS

1. With which class of problems is LP generally associated? Why?

2. If LP is thought of in terms of a decision matrix, what do the strategies represent? What can you say about the states of nature?

3. For further study see James L. Riggs, *Production Systems: Planning, Analysis, and Control* (Santa Barbara: John Wiley & Sons, 1976), chap. 5 and Appendix C.

4. Refer to the Tam and Tamette problem:

    a. What is the effect on the optimum solution to the problem if each Tam contributes $5 to overhead and profit and each Tamette contributes $4?
    b. What is the effect on the feasibility area and the optimum solution of the amount of material required for each Tam increases from 3 to 6?
    c. If a decision is made to produce at the optimum solution point (32X, 9Y), how much labor and machine time will remain idle? How many units of material will not be used? What questions are raised for the manager by these unused units of material?

APPLICATION: LP

Manuel Solik is the sales manager of a small plant that produces and sells a wide variety of consumer products. Manuel is trying to decide what to tell the production manager, Frank Huffa, to produce. His immediate decision concerns two products that go by the names "Grits" and "Fritz." Since both products have become very popular recently, Manuel knows that he can sell as many as Frank can produce.

Manuel wants his decision to be the one that is most profitable for the business. On each Fritz sold, the company makes a $40 contribution to overhead costs and profits. The corresponding figure for each Grits sold is $70. These contribution margins are certain, regardless of the number of Grits and Fritz sold.

In order to make each Grits and Fritz, three inputs are required. The amount of input required for each product is the same regardless of the number of products made. Moreover, the "recipe" for each product can be expressed as a linear combination of the three inputs.

		Input	
Product	A	B	C
Fritz..........................	0	5	5
Grits..........................	10	8	5
Amount available (in standard units)...........	60	80	70

1. What are the *variables* and *constraints* in this problem?

2. On a graph similar to Figure 5A–3, plot the constraint inequations and identify the total set of *feasible solutions*—the *feasibility area.*

3. What is the *objective function* in this problem?

4. Which of the feasible solutions is the *optimum* solution?

5. What is the maximum quantity of Fritz that can be produced? Of Grits?

6. Suppose that the contribution margin on Fritz and Grits changed to $50 and $80, respectively. What would be the optimum product-mix of Fritz and Grits? What specific point made in the text does the change in contribution margin illustrate?

7. When Manuel tells Frank the optimum product-mix, Frank responds by saying he doesn't want to produce that particular combination. What are some possible explanations for Frank's response?

Objectives of Supplement 5B

1. To introduce you to some specific approaches to making decisions under conditions of risk and uncertainty.
2. To introduce you to the idea of gaming as an approach to making decisions under conditions of conflict.
3. To encourage you to pursue further study of quantitative techniques and their role in managerial decision-making.

SUPPLEMENT 5B

An Introduction to Quantitative Decision Criteria

Nothing goes more against my grain than blinking at plain facts.

Admiral Elmo R. Zumwalt

This supplement

This supplement expands on the Chapter 5 discussion of decision making under risk, uncertainty, and conflict. Specifically, the supplement discusses several quantitative criteria useful in decision making: expected value, utility, LaPlace-Bayes, Hurwicz, Wald, Savage, and maximax criteria. In addition, zero-sum games and nonzero-sum games are discussed briefly.

EXPECTED VALUE

Expected value problem

The expected value of a decision strategy is the sum of the products of each outcome associated with the strategy, times the probability of that outcome occurring. For example, suppose that a manager wants to determine what size plant to build in order to

FIGURE 5B–1
A Decision Matrix for Illustrating Expected Value

Decision Strategy	States of Nature		
	Low Product Demand .50	Medium Product Demand .25	High Product Demand .25
Small plant = S_1	30	30	30
Large plant = S_2	−14	68	68
Very large = S_3	−30	28	100

produce a new product.[1] Three sizes are under consideration: small, large, and very large. In terms of a decision matrix, each of these sizes represents a decision strategy. The most appropriate plant size depends on the level of the demand for the new product. Assume that three demand levels are possible: low, medium, and high, and assume that the probability of each demand level occurring is .50, .25, and .25, respectively. This combination of decision strategies, states of nature, and probabilities along with projected payoffs is shown in Figure 5B–1.

Computation of expected values

The expected value of each decision strategy is computed as follows:

$$S_1 \text{ expected value} = \tfrac{1}{2}(30) + \tfrac{1}{4}(30) + \tfrac{1}{4}(30) = 30$$
$$S_2 \text{ expected value} = \tfrac{1}{2}(-14) + \tfrac{1}{4}(68) + \tfrac{1}{4}(68) = 27$$
$$S_3 \text{ expected value} = \tfrac{1}{2}(-30) + \tfrac{1}{4}(28) + \tfrac{1}{4}(100) = 17$$

The strategy with the highest expected value is S_1. In the absence of additional information, S_1 is selected as the best of the three strategies. In general, decision makers should choose the decision strategy with the best expected value, assuming that the appropriate payoffs are used; that is, when the proper measure is used in the payoff cells the most rational decision criterion is to select the strategy with the highest expected payoff. As we will see in the next section, payoffs should be expressed in terms of utility.

UTILITY

Important to measure payoffs accurately

Suppose that you were offered the alternatives of (1) accepting a $100,000 tax-free gift or (2) if heads come up after the toss of a fair coin, you get nothing, but if tails come up, you receive a tax-free $300,000 gift. At first glance it appears that, using the expected-value criterion, you should choose the coin toss; that is, the expected value of the coin toss, 0.50 ($0) + .50 ($300,000) = $150,000, is greater than the expected value of the certain gift, 1.0 ($100,000) = $100,000. However, this conclusion assumes that a certain $100,000 is less desirable to you than a 50–50 chance of earning $300,000. Since many people would rather have a certain $100,000 than have a chance at $300,000, it is sometimes concluded that the expected-value criterion is inappropriate. However, that conclusion is incorrect. What we need to emphasize is that the strategy with the highest expected value is the most rational *so long as the payoffs are accurately measured.*

Measuring payoffs

In order to measure payoffs accurately, we need to express them as utilities. Simply put, "the utility," or satisfaction; or desirability of a $100,000 certain gift is subjectively different for each individual. It appears reasonable to suppose that the utility of a $100,000

---

[1] Example based on Richard J. Tersine, "Organization Decision Theory: A Synthesis," *Managerial Planning*, vol. 16, no. 4 (July–August 1967), p. 23.

gift for a poor person is higher than for a millionaire. Daniel Bernoulli hypothesized in 1730 that "the utility of additional sums of money to an individual must be inversely proportional to the amount of money he already has."[2]

Dollars and utility

There are several other hypotheses consistent with the idea of the diminishing utility of additional sums of money. They are not important for our purposes, but it is important to emphasize that utility is subjective. Further, dollar amounts are not necessarily an accurate measure of utility. The utility to you of $1 is not necessarily the same as the utility of $1 to another person.

Computing utilities

How are utilities computed? Utilities are stated in units of measure called "utiles." In general, the procedure for determining the utility curve for an individual decision maker is a trial-and-error procedure based on the basic principle that if a decision maker is indifferent between two alternatives, the expected utility of the alternatives is the same. In the above example, suppose that you prefer a certain $100,000 to a 50–50 chance of earning $300,000. However, if you are indifferent about it, then the utility of the two alternatives is the same. With this knowledge, other points on a decision maker's utility curve can be determined.[3]

THE LAPLACE-BAYES CRITERION

Rationale

The LaPlace-Bayes criterion for decision making under uncertainty states that if the probabilities of occurrence of states of nature are truly unknown they should be assigned equal probabilities of occurrence. The rationale behind this criterion is that if there is no basis for estimating probabilities of states of nature, then the only reasonable assumption is that their probabilities are equal.

Example

For example, in the problem shown in Figure 5B–1, assuming the three states of nature have equal probabilities of occurrence, the expected values are as follows:

$$S_1 = (30 + 30 + 30)/3 \quad = 30$$
$$S_2 = (-14 + 68 + 68)/3 \quad = 40\tfrac{2}{3}$$
$$S_3 = (-30 + 28 + 100)/3 = 32\tfrac{2}{3}$$

Principle of insufficient reason

Thus, using expected value and the LaPlace-Bayes criterion, S_2 will be selected. The LaPlace-Bayes criterion, named after the 18th-century mathematicians Reverend Thomas Bayes and Pierre Simon de LaPlace, is also called the "principle of insufficient reason."

[2] David W. Miller and Martin K. Starr, *The Structure of Human Decisions* (Englewood Cliffs, N.J.: Prentice-Hall, 1967), p. 74.

[3] For an illustration of the computation of utility curves, see Ralph O. Swalm, "Utility Theory: Insights into Risk-Taking," *Harvard Business Review*, vol. 44, no. 5 (November–December 1966), pp. 123–36.

THE HURWICZ CRITERION

Index of optimism

Another guide to decision making under uncertain conditions is named after Leonid Hurwicz. Using the Hurwicz criterion, the decision maker chooses that strategy with the highest weighted average of the best and worst outcomes that can result from a strategy. The computation of this weighted average involves the use of an index of relative optimism and pessimism.

Example

For example, in the problem shown in Figure 5B–1, suppose that the decision maker tends to be optimistic. He does not know the probabilities of the three states of nature but is willing to admit that all three are possible. The decision maker's indices of relative optimism and pessimism must add up to one. Since he tends to be optimistic, his index of optimism will be considered as .8 and his index of pessimism as .2. Since,

$$\text{Hurwicz criterion} = H = \alpha(\min) + (1 - \alpha)(\max)$$

where,

$$\alpha = \text{index of pessimism} = 0.2$$
$$1 - \alpha = \text{index of optimism} = 0.8$$
$$\min = \text{minimum payoff of a strategy}$$
$$\max = \text{maximum payoff of a strategy}$$

Therefore,

$$H(S_1) = (0.2)(30) + (0.8)(30) = 30.0$$
$$H(S_2) = (0.2)(-14) + (0.8)(68) = 51.6$$
$$H(S_3) = (0.2)(-30) = (0.8)(100) = 74.0$$

Optimist's criterion

Using the Hurwicz criterion, S_3 will be chosen. The Hurwicz criterion is also called the "optimist's criterion." Note that the Hurwicz criterion is not completely optimistic since it does take into account the largest and the smallest payoffs of each strategy.

THE WALD CRITERION

Pessimist's criterion

A pessimistic approach to decision making is suggested by Abraham Wald. The Wald criterion, also called the "maximin criterion," is guided by the maxim: if the worst can happen, it will. In using the maximin criterion, the decision maker first selects the minimum (worst) payoff associated with each strategy choice. He then chooses that strategy with the best minimum pay-off. If the decision matrix is in terms of profits, then the maximum minimum ("maximin") is chosen; if the matrix is written in terms of costs then the minimum maximum ("minimax") is chosen. In Figure 5B–1 the three strategies with their minimum payoffs are as follows:

$$S_1 = 30$$
$$S_2 = -14$$
$$S_3 = -30$$

Following the maximin criterion, S_1 will be chosen because it is the best strategy, assuming that the worst is going to happen. This assumption can be a reasonable one: "At high decision levels, when one mistake may be the last, the notion of getting at least the best of the worst appears to be quite tenable."[4]

Summary box

> The *expected value* of a decision strategy is the sum of the products of each of the strategy's outcomes times the probability of that outcome occurring.
>
> The *utility* of a decision strategy outcome is its subjective satisfaction to the decision maker.
>
> The *LaPlace-Bayes* criterion (principle of insufficient reason) states that when the probabilities of occurrence of states of nature are truly unknown, they should be assigned equal probabilities of occurrence.
>
> The *Hurwicz* criterion (optimist's criterion) chooses that decision strategy with the highest weighted average of the best and worst outcomes of a strategy.
>
> The *Wald* criterion (pessimist's or maximin criterion) selects the minimum pay-off associated with each decision strategy and then chooses that strategy with the best minimum. The Wald criterion is a special case of the Hurwicz criterion in which the index of optimism = 0.

MAXIMAX CRITERION

The complete optimist

The "maximax criterion" is essentially the opposite of the maximin criterion. The maximin criterion represents the pessimistic view that the decision maker should choose that strategy with the maximum minimum (thus, "maximin") pay-off. Conversely, the maximax criterion chooses that strategy with the maximum-maximum (thus, maximax) pay-off. The maximin criterion is pessimistic; the maximax criterion is completely optimistic.

Example

The maximin criterion leads to the selection of strategy S_1 given the data in Figure 5B–1. Conversely, the maximax criterion leads to the selection of strategy S_3 since the payoff of 100 associated with S_3 is larger than the payoffs of 30 and 68 associated with S_1 and S_2, respectively.

Relation to Hurwicz criterion

From this discussion you can see that the Hurwicz criterion is a kind of compromise between the maximin and the maximax criteria; that is, the Hurwicz criterion takes account of both the maximum *and* the minimum pay-off associated with each strategy.

[4] Martin K. Starr, *Management: A Modern Approach* (New York: Harcourt Brace Jovanovich, 1971), p. 153.

On the other hand, the maximax criterion can be viewed as a special case of the Hurwicz criterion in which the decision maker's index of optimism $= 1$. Similarly, an index of optimism $= 0$ leads to the maximin criterion because the effect is to make the index of pessimism $= 1$.

THE SAVAGE CRITERION

Minimize regret

The Savage criterion is named after Leonard J. Savage and is also called the "regret criterion." The basic idea of the regret criterion is that decision makers try to minimize the regret experienced when, after the selection of a decision strategy and the occurrence of one of the states of nature, they discover they selected the wrong strategy.

Regret matrix

The use of the regret criterion requires the conversion of the usual type of decision matrix into a "regret matrix." In order to prepare a regret matrix from a decision matrix, do the following: for each state of nature, subtract from the highest pay-off value each of the pay-off values associated with the state of nature.

Example

The regret matrix derived from the decision matrix shown in Figure 5B–1 is shown in Figure 5B–2. The regret matrix shown in Figure 5B–2 is an opportunity-cost matrix. This is true when the

FIGURE 5B–2
Regret Matrix Derived from Decision Matrix Shown in Figure 5B–1

		States of Nature		
		Low Demand	Medium Demand	High Demand
Small	$= S_1$	0	38	70
Large	$= S_2$	44	0	32
Very large	$= S_3$	60	40	0

original decision matrix from which the regret matrix was derived (in this case, the decision matrix shown in Figure 5B–1) is expressed in dollar profits or dollar costs. The $60 opportunity cost or regret means that $60 is the decision maker's cost of choosing S_3 over S_1, when low demand occurs.

Explanation of calculations

Explanation of Figure 5B–2, Second Column. For each state of nature, subtract from the highest pay-off value each of the pay-off values associated with the state of nature. (See Figure 5B–3.) The same procedure is used to compute the regrets shown in the third and fourth columns of Figure 5B–2. The three regrets shown

FIGURE 5B–3
Calculation of Figures in Second Column of Figure 5B–2

Strategies	Information from Decision Matrix in Figure 5B–1	Calculation of Regret	Regret
S_1.....................	30*	$(30 - 30)$ $=$	0
S_2.....................	−14	$(30 - (-14)) =$	44
S_3.....................	−30	$(30 - (-30)) =$	60

* Highest pay-off.

in Figure 5B–3 are interpreted as follows: If S_1 is chosen and low demand occurs, the highest payoff is received. If S_2 is chosen and low demand occurs, an actual loss of $14 is incurred and an opportunity cost of $44 is incurred. If S_3 is chosen and low demand occurs, the actual loss is $30 and the opportunity cost or the regret is $60.

Minimax

Once the regret matrix is determined, you can apply either the LaPlace, Wald, or Hurwicz criteria to it. Savage, however, proposes the use of something like the Wald criterion; that is, he chooses to be pessimistic about the state of nature that will occur. Thus, what is the worst that can happen if each of the strategies is selected? Data from the regret matrix in Figure 5B–2 shows:

Strategy	Maximum Regret
S_1............................	70
S_2............................	44
S_3............................	60

The decision maker protects himself from experiencing some regret by selecting the strategy with the minimum maximum, or the minimax. Thus, in this case he would select S_2.

Minimize sum of regrets

A variation in the use of the Wald criterion is for the decision maker to select that strategy which minimizes the *sum* of the regrets involved. Using the information shown in Figure 5B–2, the decision maker would select S_2 $(44 + 0 + 32 = 76)$.

ZERO-SUM AND NONZERO-SUM "GAMES"

Decision making when there is conflict

Up to this point the discussion of decision making when there is certainty, risk, and uncertainty has treated states of nature as independent of the strategy choice. For example, in the problem shown in Figure 5B–1, the occurrence of the states of nature is in no way dependent on the choice of S_1, S_2, or S_3. In many decision problems, however, strategies and states of nature are not independent of each other.

Game theory

A common case of such a problem is when one decision maker is in competition with another or several other decision makers. The decision makers can be thought of as opponents in a game involving conflict of interest. In fact, this area of decision theory is called "game theory," and it represents a highly sophisticated body of knowledge dealing with decision making. Two types of game situations are discussed here: the two-person, zero-sum game and the two-person, nonzero-sum game.

Gain offset by loss

Two-Person, Zero-Sum Game. A situation in which the gain of one decision maker is directly offset by the loss of other decision makers is called a zero-sum game. When only two decision-making opponents are involved in a zero-sum game, it is called a "two-person, zero-sum game."

Example

In a two-person, zero-sum game, the payoffs add to zero for each pair of strategies. For example, given the following decision matrix showing strategies available to two decision makers, each pair of strategies results in a zero sum. If decision maker A chooses S_3 and decision maker B chooses S_2 the net payoff is $0 ($10 − $10). That is, as shown by the heavily outlined middle "cell" in the last row of Figure 5B–4, when A pays B $10 and,

FIGURE 5B–4
Two-Person, Zero-Sum Decision Matrix

Decision Maker A Strategies	Decision Maker B Strategies		
	1	2	3
1	A pays B $4	B pays A $20	A pays B $12
2	B pays A $5	B pays A $10	B pays A $8
3	A pays B $8	A pays B $10	B pays A $16

consequently, B receives $10 from A, the net payoff between A and B is $0.

Applying maximin

The previously discussed maximin criterion can be applied to the two-person, zero-sum situation shown in Figure 5B–4. Suppose that the two decision makers are to select their strategies independently; that is, decision maker A selects a strategy without knowledge of what strategy B will select. If decision maker A selects his maximin strategy (in this case, decision maker A's maximin strategy is S_2), the worst he can do is gain $5 from B. If decision maker B selects his maximin strategy (in this case, decision maker B's maximin strategy is S_1), the best he can do is lose $5 to A.

Maximin is most rational for both decision makers

The main point of the above paragraph is to emphasize that in a two-person, zero-sum decision situation, the most rational decision criterion for *both* decision makers is the maximin criterion; that is, if one decision maker chooses his maximin strategy, the best the other decision maker can do is to choose his maximin strategy.

Additional explanation

If you do not understand the above two paragraphs, then the following additional explanation may help:

If Decision Maker A Chooses	*The Worst That Can Happen Is*	*The Payoff for A Is*
S_1....................	A pays B $12	−$12
S_2....................	B pays A $ 5	+$ 5
S_3....................	A pays B $10	−$10

Thus, S_2 is decision maker A's maximin strategy because S_2 is the "best of the worst" payoffs. In the same way, you can compute the maximin strategy for decision maker B. The payoffs that he has to choose from are: $S_1 = -\$5$, $S_2 = -\$20$, and $S_3 = -\$16$. Thus, S_1 is the maximin strategy for decision maker B. Notice that decision maker B is forced to choose from three negative payoffs—all three strategies result in a loss to B. Naturally, B wants to select that strategy that will minimize his loss. Since all three strategies result in a loss to B, his best strategy is the *minimax* strategy.

Noncompetitive situation

Two-Person, Nonzero-Sum Game. In the "two-person, nonzero-sum" problem, a noncompetitive situation exists. It is possible for both decision makers to gain, lose, or break even. For example, assume the following decision matrix.

FIGURE 5B–5
Two-Person, Nonzero-Sum Decision Matrix

Decision Maker A Strategies	*Decision Maker B Strategies*	
	1	2
1	Both get $5	Both get $3
2	Both get $0	Both get $8

If both decision makers use the *maximax* (maximize the maximum payoff) criterion, they will both receive $8. If only one decision maker uses maximax, then both are worse off than if they both use maximax. If both decision makers use maximin, they will each get $3. Thus, in this specific case, the best decision criterion is maximax.

Summary box

> The *maximax* criterion chooses that decision strategy with the maximum maximum payoff. It is a special case of the *Hurwicz* criterion in which the index of optimism $= 1$.
>
> The *Savage* criterion (regret criterion) tries to minimize the regret that will be experienced by the decision maker if the wrong strategy is chosen.
>
> A *zero-sum game* is a competitive situation in which the gain of one decision maker is directly offset by the loss of other decision makers. A *nonzero-sum game* is one in which all decision makers can gain, lose, or break even.

CHECK YOUR UNDERSTANDING

Expected value
Utility
Utiles
Principle of insufficient reason (LaPlace-Bayes)
Optimist criterion (Hurwicz)
Pessimist criterion (Wald)
Maximax

Maximin
Minimax
Regret criterion (Savage)
Regret matrix
Opportunity-cost matrix
Zero-sum game
Nonzero-sum game

STUDY QUESTIONS

1. Contrast the maximax criterion with the maximin criterion. Compare the maximax and maximin with the Hurwicz criterion.

2. Why, in your opinion, is the use of *monetary* gains or losses not always a valid guide for making decisions?

3. What, in your opinion, are some of the problems that you would expect to encounter in any effort to apply the several criteria discussed in this supplement? Do these criteria have any value for the decision maker even when they are not directly applicable to a specific decision situation? Explain.

4. For further study, see the following references:
   William C. Emory and Powell Niland, *Making Management Decisions* (Boston: Houghton Mifflin Company, 1968).
   David W. Miller and Martin K. Starr, *The Structure of Human Decisions* (Englewood Cliffs, N.J.: Prentice-Hall, 1967).

APPLICATION: DECISION MATRICES

You've just been asked to advise your first client about an investment decision. You don't know much about your client's risk preference so, anxious to be prepared, you decide to be prepared for both an optimist and a pessimist.

Your client has identified three possible investments. All are fairly good, but which is best depends on what occurs after the investment is made. From the information your client has given you, you conceptualize the decision problem in terms of the following framework.

Investment	Possible Future Circumstances		
Alternative	Good	Better	Best
A.........................	$ 800	$1,100	$4,500
B.........................	2,000	2,500	4,100
C.........................	2,100	2,300	2,400

1. Suppose your client turns out to be very pessimistic, which investment alternative would you recommend? Which would you recommend if she turns out to be very optimistic? Support your recommendation.

2. After talking with your client for awhile, you detect that she is neither very pessimistic or optimistic. She seems to lean toward being optimistic. On an "optimism scale" of 1 to 10, you would rate her 7. Which one of the decision strategies will you recommend to her. Explain your answer.

3. Which alternative will you recommend if your client tells you that each of the possible future circumstances has an equal chance of occurring and that she wants to select the alternative with the highest expected payoff? Explain your answer.

4. Your client is positive that she is going to make the wrong decision and wants to select the one that is the "least wrong." Which one would you recommend? Explain your answer.

part two

Behavior in Organizations: A Micro View

Where we've been

Before presenting an overview of Part Two, we want to recall briefly some elements from Part One. First, we defined "managing" as the work of creating and maintaining environments in which people can accomplish goals efficiently and effectively. Managers manage *people, not things*. We view managing as a *universal activity*. The essence of a manager's job and the *basic theme* of this book is the accountability of managers for the performance of their subordinates.

Functional foundation

After recognizing *goals* and goal setting as the *strategic* managing variable, we discussed three important managerial functions: *planning, controlling*, and *decision making*. Part One, then, is a functional foundation for our understanding of organizations and of behavior in organizations.

Part One
General
Management

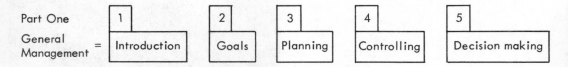

A micro view

Part Two is a "micro" view of behavior in organizations. By that we mean that the focus is on the individual and on specific *types* of individual behavior (such as leadership and communication) and on specific *contexts* of individual behavior (such as the interpersonal and group contexts and the context of a conflict or stress situation).

Chapter 6

Chapter 6 presents a way of thinking about *individual behavior* as a function of both the individual and the individual's environment. One type of individual behavior is *job performance*. Chapter 6 views job performance behavior as depending on environmental or *situational factors* and on three characteristics of the individual job holder: *role perceptions; abilities and skills;* and *motivation*. The "expectancy theory" of motivation is used to discuss the motivation process; the discussion is developed around two ideas: *valence* and *expectancy*. Supplement 6A extends the discussion of the motivation process by introducing several viewpoints about *motives*.

Chapter 7

Chapter 7 deals with three *cognitive variables* that play a role in determining an individual's behavior. "Perception" is the process by which individuals attach meaning to their experiences. "Attitudes" are internal states of a person that are focused on objects, events, or other people. "Values" are beliefs about what is good and bad. Each of these three variables—perception, attitudes, and values—is discussed in some detail in Chapter 7. In addition, Supplement 7A deals with another cognitive variable, *assumptions about people*, and Supplement 7B discusses one important job-related attitude, *job satisfaction*.

Chapter 8   Chapter 8 switches the focus of our examination of behavior from "cognitive variables," which are characteristics of the person, to the consequences of behavior. The major proposition of Chapter 8 is that if managers want improved job performance from their employees, this is what they must do: Make the rewards of performance (such as higher pay, promotion, and so on) *contingent* on improved performance. The key idea is to establish desired behavior–desired consequences contingencies. Chapter 8 discusses five types of contingencies and three basic ways of scheduling the contingencies.

> Chapters 6, 7, and 8 are particularly important to our discussion in Part Two. They provide a foundation for thinking about the specific types and contexts of behavior that we will discuss: behavior in interpersonal and group contexts; leadership; communication; and behavior in conditions of conflict and stress.

Chapter 9   Chapter 9 deals with behavior in an *interpersonal context*. The chapter opens with several *general observations*. Examples and characteristics of *interpersonal response traits* are discussed, and three models of *interpersonal attraction* are introduced. Chapter 9 also discusses the roles of *congruence* and *self-disclosure* in growth-facilitating interpersonal relations and introduces the *Johari window*.

Chapter 10   Chapter 10 deals with behavior in a *group context*. Both formal and informal groups are important to managerial effectiveness. Chapter 10 introduces the idea of *stages* of group development and identifies two types of *stimuli* that groups use in order to influence the behavior of group members. *Four variables*—size, composition, norms, and cohesiveness—that influence performance in groups are noted. Additional topics discussed in Chapter 10 include observing groups, rational behavior in groups, a process model for describing behavior in groups, and intergroup competition.

Chapter 11   *Leadership* is a subject that has fascinated and intrigued people since the beginning of recorded history. We are interested in leadership because of the role it plays in effective managing. We discuss *six approaches* to understanding leadership: great-man, personality trait, leader behavior, contingency, path-goal, and participation in decision making. Chapter 11 ends with a discussion of *leadership styles*, including introductions to Systems 1–2–3–4 and the Managerial Grid®.

Chapter 12   *Communication* is sometimes viewed as the source of most managerial problems or as "Management's Number One Problem."

Chapter 12 defines communication and distinguishes it from *information* and *data*. The need for organizations to restrict the flow of communication as well as to maintain open channels of communication is identified. One-way and two-way communication are contrasted and the idea of *noise* in the communication process is introduced. Chapter 12 discusses both formal and informal *communication networks* and makes suggestions for *improving personal communication*.

Chapter 13

Conflict and *stress* are inevitable features of life in organizations. Chapter 13 defines and contrasts conflict and stress and presents a view of conflict as a *process*. Five *conflict-management styles*, based on the two dimensions of cooperativeness and assertiveness, are discussed. The chapter ends by relating stress to health, identifying some job-related stressors, and noting several approaches to coping with stress.

Objectives of Chapter 6

- To identify the factors influencing individual behavior
- To introduce a general framework for thinking about job performance.
- To introduce the concept of role, to relate how role perceptions enter into job performance, and to suggest a way of thinking about the process of role taking.
- To use expectancy theory as a way of explaining the process of motivation and to assess its usefulness to managers.

Outline of Chapter 6

6

JOB PERFORMANCE AND THE MOTIVATION PROCESS

I spend 40 hours a week here
—am I supposed to work too?

From a sign on a tavern wall
near an auto assembly plant

Set me anything to do as a task, and it is incon-
ceivable the desire I have to do something else.

George Bernard Shaw

An actual
incident

Jessica: Boy, those garbage collectors do a terrible job! Every time they empty the trashcan they spill half of the trash in the yard and street. They ought to be reported.

Bob: Well, what do you expect? Why should they be careful about spilling stuff in our yard? They get paid the same one way or another.

Jessica: But that's their job. They're supposed to be careful.

Example from
The Wall
Street Journal

Grim Warnings: A jolting film asks "What killed the Bell System?"

Seeking to shock employees into more productive habits, Ohio Bell shows simulated TV newscasts depicting events in 1984, when the phone system is broke and about to be nationalized by Congress, and when it takes six months to get a telephone installed. Executives in the film talk of sloppy work, waste, and theft; workers complain about managers "who can't even find the men's room." The anchorman concludes the cure is "a full day's work for a full day's pay."

Ohio Bell figures the film has saved $29 million in three years through increased productivity.[1]

Common
concern

These two examples illustrate that job performance is a concern of almost everyone—from homemakers who are dissatisfied with

---

[1] Reprinted with permission of *The Wall Street Journal,* © Dow Jones & Company, Inc. (1977). All Rights Reserved.

the way garbage collectors do their job to the corporation executive who tries to shock and shame employees into doing a better job. Improving job performance is not just another task of managers; it is the *most* important task. Accountability for the performance of others is the essence of managerial positions.

This chapter

This chapter deals with four objectives. First, three approaches to understanding individual behavior are identified and behavior is viewed as being influenced by personal and environmental factors. Next, a general framework for thinking about job performance is suggested and discussed. Third, the concept of role and a way of thinking about the process of role taking are introduced. Last, the motivation process is discussed in terms of expectancy theory and its two major variables, valence and expectancy.

INDIVIDUAL BEHAVIOR

Where to look for an understanding of behavior

Where would you look for an explanation of your own behavior or that of others? The sources of information are numerous and include personal background and experience, knowledge of the situation in which behavior occurs, the behavior of others, and knowledge about what behavior "works" and what does not. Additionally, an understanding of individual behavior can be acquired from music, poetry, literature, and art. Some academic disciplines are rich in their potential contribution to understanding behavior —philosophy, economics, history, sociology, genetics, political science, and industrial engineering, to name several.

Psychology

All the above sources of understanding are potentially useful to managers. However, they do not all lend themselves to systematic study nor can they all be studied in a basic textbook on managing. Thus, choices have to be made concerning the source of understanding that will be emphasized. This text looks primarily to the discipline of psychology for its main point of departure. It is in the field of psychology that the study of individual behavior takes its most systematic form. It is in psychology that one can find the most clearly delineated models of behavior.

Psychoanalytic approach: personality

Even within the discipline of psychology there are distinctly different approaches to the understanding of behavior. One book identifies and summarizes three approaches—psychoanalytic, cognitive, and reinforcement.[2] In the "psychoanalytic approach," originated by Sigmund Freud, personality is the core concept, and somewhat mysterious and mystical notions such as the id, the ego, the superego, and the libido are important. The psychoanalytic approach has made important contributions to the understanding

[2] H. Joseph Reitz, *Behavior in Organizations* (Homewood, Ill.: Richard D. Irwin, 1977), chap. 3.

of behavior, but we do not utilize it to any great extent in this book.[3]

Cognitive approach: mental processes

The "cognitive approach" places heavy reliance on "internal" variables—that is, the person's mental processes. Examples of these include perceptions, attitudes, values, needs and motives, expectations, and assumptions we make about human nature, people, and their behavior. We discuss most of these variables in Chapter 7. However, there are features of the cognitive approach that run through this chapter as well as Chapter 8.

Reinforcement approach: behavioral consequences

The "reinforcement approach" to understanding behavior places major emphasis on external determinants of behavior. The major external determinant is considered to be the consequences of behavior. Specifically, behavior is seen as determined largely by the environmental contingencies that link behavior and its consequences. These ideas will become more meaningful when they are discussed at length in Chapter 8.

$B = f(P,E)$

The overall view we take in this book is that individual behavior (B) in organizations is a function (f) of the person (P) and of his or her environmental situation (E). That is, $B = f(P,E)$. This behavioral formulation serves the useful purpose of identifying the two major variables in understanding job performance: the employee and the employee's job environment. Additionally, the relationship or *interaction* between P and E is important to understanding specific behavior; that is, people *act on* as well as *react to* their environment.

A general model

Figure 6–1 shows schematically the relationship between personal (P) and environmental (E) factors as determinants of behavior. The interaction of these two factors is symbolized by a comma (,). The three approaches to understanding behavior noted above—psychoanalytic, cognitive, and reinforcement—are all consistent with the $B = f(P,E)$ formulation, but they place differing emphases on the person and the environment.[4]

---

[3] For a management-related book that approaches the study of motivation from the viewpoint of psychoanalytic theory, see Harry Levinson, *Psychological Man* (Cambridge, Mass.: Levinson Institute, 1976).

[4] Reitz, *Behavior in Organizations*, p. 50.

FIGURE 6–1
Factors Influencing Individual Behavior

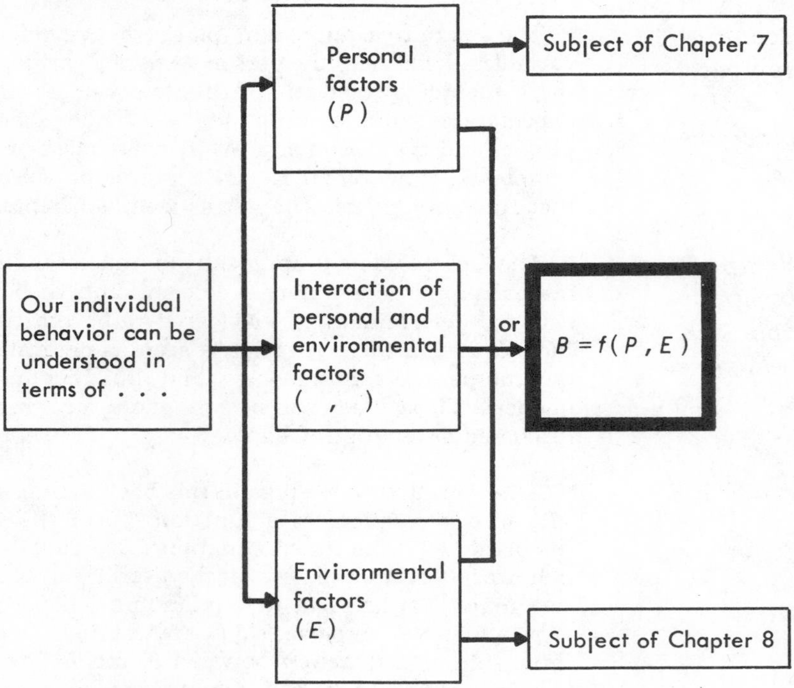

Summary box

> So far in this chapter we have discussed *one major idea* —individual behavior.
>
> In psychology, there are *three main approaches* to the understanding of individual behavior: psychoanalytic, cognitive, and reinforcement. We do not discuss the psychoanalytic approach; the other two approaches are discussed in this and the next two chapters.
>
> All three of the approaches are consistent with our overall view of individual behavior. This view is that an individual's behavior (B) is a function (f) of the *interaction* ($,$) between characteristics of the *person* (P) and of the person's *environment* (E) or situational context. $B = f(P,E)$.

JOB PERFORMANCE

Factors in job performance

Think about how you have performed on various jobs. At first glance it may seem as if there are an infinite number of factors that could contribute to your job performance. Many come readily to mind: money, working conditions, availability of necessary materials and equipment, the scope and depth of the job, the nature of your formal organizational relationships, your "know-how" and "know what," and your compatibility with others—particularly your supervisor. There appear to be so many variables influencing job performance that it is almost impossible to make sense of them.

Four variables   We can make our discussion of job performance more manageable by identifying four different types of variables that influence a person's job performance: situational factors; role perceptions; abilities and skills; and effort, or motivation. In our discussion of job performance, we are interested primarily in the role of motivation. Nevertheless, for a complete discussion, we have to recognize the role of situational factors, role perceptions, and abilities and skills in determining job performance.

A general framework   Figure 6–2 is a general framework for thinking about job performance. The dashed-line box conveys the idea that job performance takes place within a context of situational factors (SF). As

FIGURE 6–2
A General Framework for Thinking about Job Performance

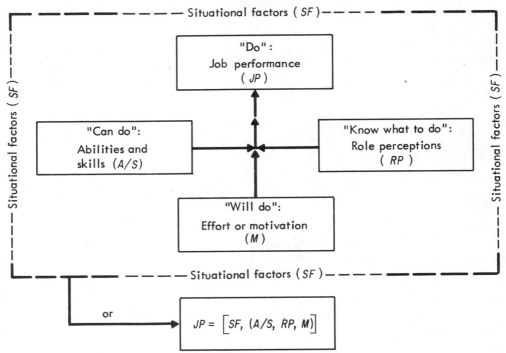

such, those factors are not part of the individual, as are abilities and skills (A/S), role perceptions (RP), and effort, or motivation (M).

Can do, supposed to do, and will do

In Figure 6–2, situational factors represent the "doing" context. Abilities and skills represent what a person can do; role perceptions represent the person's understanding of what he or she is supposed to do; and effort or motivation represents what a person will do. The model shown in Figure 6–2 is primarily designed to help us think about and understand job performance—our own and that of others.

SITUATIONAL FACTORS

Contingencies

Everything from working conditions to luck fits into the category of situational factors or contingencies affecting job performance. Managers influence some of these factors directly, and others are out of their control. A large part of managerial work is concerned with providing employees with the factors they need in order to work. For example, meaningful performance goals (see Chapter 2) and appropriate task and organization design (see Chapters 16 and 17) are two factors that influence the capacity of employees to be effective on the job.

Situational factors, ability and motivation

The ability to perform a job depends on the presence of necessary materials and equipment. The ability to operate a machine is of no value in the absence of the machine. The machine is of no value in the absence of materials. Motivation, in turn, can be adversely influenced by the continued absence of necessary equipment and materials. If these shortages cause employees to be *unable* to work, they may soon become *unwilling* to work.

Situational factors and role perceptions

Similarly, employees may begin to wonder about their perception of what they are supposed to do, if they are continuously unable to do it. Thus, situational factors influence what employees *can do* (ability and skill), how much effort they *will* exert doing it (motivation), and their understanding of what it is they are *supposed* to do (role perception).

Mediating role

Our view of situational factors is that their influence on job performance is mediated by abilities, role perception, and motivation. We do not consider situational factors as variables that enter directly into an individual's performance. That is, it is the *individual* that performs in an organizational and situational context. This view is in line with most discussions of job performance and is illustrated by showing situational factors as a dashed-line box in Figure 6–2.

ABILITIES AND SKILLS

Individual differences

Individuals, of course, differ to some extent on almost every physical and psychological dimension. These individual differences account partially for differences in job performance. An individual's capacity to perform is determined by such factors as physical size and body type, manual dexterity, verbal and mathematical skills, and other genetically determined or learned characteristics.

Character- istics of individuals

Abilities are characteristics of individuals.[5] Many of them are learned during childhood and adolescence. Employees bring abilities with them when they begin to learn new tasks. For example, spatial visualization may be considered a human ability. "It has been found to be related to performance on such diverse tasks as aerial navigation, blueprint reading, and dentistry."[6]

Level of proficiency

Skills refer to the level of proficiency in specific tasks. A person may have spatial-visualization ability but may not have the skill to fly an airplane. An employee may have manual dexterity but not know how to operate a machine. There is a relationship between abilities and skills, however. Presumably, the skills involved in complex activities can be described in terms of their more basic abilities. In addition, persons who have certain basic abilities are supposed to be able to learn associated skills more readily.

Short run versus long run

Changing Abilities and Skills. In the short run, the abilities and skills of employees are relatively stable. They are not affected by situational factors. Over the long run, abilities and skills can be changed through employee selection, training, and development. Part of the manager's responsibility is not only to assure adequate training and development for present needs, but also to anticipate future needs.

Selection procedures

No one knows how much employee performance would improve as a result of more systematic approaches to selection, training, and development. Frederick W. Taylor's scientific management principle, "scientifically select, train, teach, and develop the workmen," (see Supplement 1B) has never been fully implemented by managers.

Effects of selection and training

The goal of effective selection and training is as follows: "Selection seeks to enhance ability levels through a process of elimination. Valid selection procedures enable an organization to hire a greater proportion of high-ability employees than would otherwise

---

[5] For reviews of research in the field of human abilities, see George A. Ferguson, "Human Abilities" in *Annual Review of Psychology*, vol. 16 (1965), pp. 39–62; and Edwin A. Fleishman, "Human Abilities," *Annual Review of Psychology*, vol. 20 (1969), pp. 349–80.

[6] Edwin A. Fleishman, "On the Relation between Abilities, Learning, and Human Performance," *American Psychologist*, vol. 27, no. 11 (November 1972), p. 1,018.

be possible. Training, alternatively, seeks to achieve the objective by increasing the ability levels of the existing work force."[7]

"Can do"
affects
"will do"

Ability and motivation may not have *independent* effects on performance. As ability is increased by experience, motivation may also be increased. What we *can* do may influence what we *will* do and our perceptions of what we are *supposed* to do. It is not surprising that people who are good at golf want to play golf a lot. At work, we often want to do those parts of our job that we can do well, and we put off doing what we cannot do well.

"Will do"
affects
"can do"

Similarly, what we want to do partially may determine what we can do. Those who are good at golf often are those who most wanted to be good. The so-called positive mental attitude approach to motivation comes down to one principle: If you think you can, you can! "Whatever you vividly imagine, ardently desire, sincerely believe, and enthusiastically act upon . . . must inevitably come to pass."[8] To an advocate of a positive mental attitude "can't" is a dirty word.

Multiplicative
relationship

Interaction with Motivation and Role Perceptions. Precisely, how do abilities and skills interact with motivation and role perception to influence job performance? The answer is not clear. One view is that they interact "multiplicatively." What does that mean? It means that if you could assign numerical values to skills, role perceptions, and motivation, you could estimate job performance by multiplying the three variables. The multiplicative relationship takes care of the extreme case of ability equal to 0. Zero ability means zero performance; zero motivation means zero performance regardless of ability; zero role perception equals zero performance regardless of ability or motivation.

Manager's
concern

Why should managers care about the relationship among ability, role perceptions, and motivation? Why should they care whether it is multiplicative, additive, or anything else? First, the most important point for managers is to recognize performance as a function of *individual* ability, role perception, and motivation. Each of these variables is a potential source of difficulty for managers in meeting their accountability for the performance of their subordinates. Second, the precise way in which these three variables interact can be important for aggregate predictions of job performance. Such predictions can be useful in estimating output levels and training requirements, and in determining selection procedures. At the present time, however, our ability to make such predictions is very poor.

---

[7] From *Performance in Organizations: Determinants and Appraisal* by L. L. Cummings and Donald P. Schwab, p. 20. Copyright © 1973 by Scott, Foresman and Company. Reprinted by permission.

[8] Paul J. Myer, "The Million Dollar Personal Success Plan," *Thoughts for Increased Personal Power* (Waco, Texas: Success Motivation Institute, 1971).

ROLE PERCEPTIONS

*Accuracy
of role
perception*

Meaning. As we use the term here, "role perception" refers to "the way in which the individual defines his job—the types of effort he believes are essential to effective job performance."[9] Our main concern is with the accuracy of role perception. The role perception referred to here is "how-to-do-it" perception—the employees' perception of the kinds of activities and behavior they *should* engage in to perform their jobs.

Example

Suppose an employee perceives that performance will be evaluated primarily in terms of the *quantity* of production. The employee may devote considerable effort to producing more. However, if the evaluation actually emphasizes the *quality* of production, the employee may not be judged a good performer. Even though the employee's ability and motivation may be high, performance, *as defined by the organization or the immediate supervisor*, may be poor.

*Usefulness of
the concept
of role*

Role is an especially useful concept for understanding individual job performance. Roles prescribe the behavior expected from someone occupying a specific position in an organization (or in a family, a group, a political office, et cetera). For the person occupying it, role is supposed to give accurate direction and guidelines for behavior.

*The process
of coming to
terms with
the demands
of a role*

A problem associated with role is that the expectations, requirements, and demands of a role do not automatically make themselves known to the person who occupies the role. The process by which individuals come to terms with their roles is a very interesting one, and one with which students of managing should have some familiarity. A useful way of thinking about this process is the "role episode."

*Focal person,
behavior,
received role*

The Role Episode.[10] Figure 6–3 shows the many factors that contribute to the way a role occupant defines and responds to role demands. We refer to the role occupant as the "focal person" (*A*). The focal person's actual role behavior (*B*) is a behavioral response to the received role (*C*).

*Sent role, role
expectations*

The "received role" is the focal person's perception of the sent role (*D*) and includes his or her own conception of what the role should be. The "sent role" is presumably related to but not identical with the expectations (*E*) of the various role senders (*F*). "Role expectations" include the behavior, beliefs, and values expected of the focal person by the role senders.

---

[9] Lyman W. Porter and Edward E. Lawler III, *Managerial Attitudes and Performance* (Homewood, Ill.: Richard D. Irwin, 1968), p. 24.

[10] This section is based on the discussion in Daniel Katz and Robert L. Kahn, *The Social Psychology of Organizations.* (New York: John Wiley & Sons, 1966), chap. 7.

FIGURE 6–3
The Role Episode

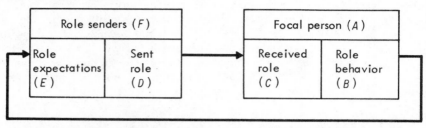

Source: Daniel Katz and Robert L. Kahn, *The Social Psychology of Organizations*: (New York: John Wiley & Sons, 1966), p. 182.

Role senders,
role set

"Role senders" include peers, superiors, subordinates, and any others who have expectations of the focal person's role. Such role senders are part of the focal person's "role set"—the set of interlocking roles that has relevance to the focal person's role. One difficulty is that, for one reason or another, role senders do not always let the focal person know what their expectations are. In such cases, there is discrepancy between the role expectations and the sent role.

Three
contingencies

As you can see from our discussion of Figure 6–3, the process of role taking is quite involved. It takes on additional complexity when you consider that the process must be responsive to particular characteristics of the organization, of the focal person, and of the interpersonal relations between the focal person and the role senders.

Role
ambiguity

Role Ambiguity and Conflict. The role-taking process we have described has ample opportunities in it for ambiguity and conflict. "Role ambiguity" results from an actual or perceived inadequacy or inconsistency in the role expectations communicated to the focal person by the role senders. When employees experience role ambiguity, job performance is adversely affected because they literally do not know what they are supposed to do. Role ambiguity is a common result of the role-taking process, and it may be particularly common in managerial roles.[11]

Role conflict,
contingencies

"Role conflict" results from "The simultaneous occurrence of two or more role sendings such that compliance with one would make more difficult compliance with the other."[12] The severity of role conflict may depend on several contingencies, such as the extent to which the role sendings are incompatible, the extent to

---

[11] Andrew D. Szilagyi, Henry P. Sims, Jr., and Robert T. Keller, "Role Dynamics, Locus of Control, and Employee Attitudes and Behavior," *Academy of Management Journal*, vol. 19, no. 2 (June 1976), p. 261.

[12] Katz and Kahn, *The Social Psychology of Organizations*, p. 184.

which role senders will be inflexible in enforcing their expectations, and the personality and coping capabilities of the focal person.[13] In addition, the potential for conflict is greater in some roles than in others. For example, some people occupy roles concerned primarily with coordinating. They may experience conflict that arises out of the different goals and processes of the specific functions (marketing and production, for example) that are being coordinated.[14]

Relation to work outcomes　　Role ambiguity and conflict are important ideas for managers. Many research studies have shown them to be inversely related to job satisfaction and directly related to job tension and anxiety and to the inclination of job holders to quit their jobs.[15]

Summary box

This section of the chapter discussed *four major ideas*: job performance, situational factors, abilities and skills, and role perceptions.

Our *general framework for thinking about job performance (JP)* contains four components: situational factors (*SF*), role perceptions (*RP*), abilities and skills (*A/S*), and effort or motivation (*M*). We can express this as follows:

$$JP = f[SF,(A/S,RP,M)]$$

Situational factors include all types of contingencies that can influence job performance but which are not part of the individual. They include working conditions, type of supervision, luck, company policies, et cetera.

Abilities are relatively enduring characteristics of an individual; *skills* refer to the level of proficiency on specific tasks. Abilities and skills represent the "can do" part of job performance.

Role perceptions are "how-to-do-it" perceptions about a job. If these perceptions are inaccurate, then performance is adversely affected. We extended our discussion of role perceptions by introducing several dimensions of the role concept and by using the *role episode* as a way of describing the process of role taking.

---

[13] Jerry W. Koehler, Karl W. E. Anatol, and Ronald L. Applbaum, *Organizational Communication: Behavioral Perspectives* (New York: Holt, Rinehart and Winston, 1976), pp. 129–30.

[14] Robert J. House and J. R. Rizzo, "Role Conflict and Ambiguity as Critical Variables in a Model of Organizational Behavior," *Organizational Behavior and Human Performance*, vol. 17, no. 3 (June 1972), pp. 467–505.

[15] Robert H. Miles, "Role Requirements as Sources of Organizational Stress," *Journal of Applied Psychology*, vol. 61, no. 2 (1976), p. 172.

THE MOTIVATION PROCESS

Refer to
Figure 6–2

Refer back to Figure 6–2, "A General Framework for Thinking about Job Performance." Recall that our view of job performance is that it is explained by four variables: situational factors, role perceptions, abilities and skills, and motivation. In this section we focus on the final variable in that framework—motivation. The motivation process is "the mechanism which gets the individual from the motivated state to some specific form of behavior. As such, motivational process refers to the *direction* of behavior."[16]

Expectancy
theory

In our examination of the motivation process we use the general approach of expectancy theory. "Expectancy theory" is an example of what was referred to earlier as a *cognitive* approach to understanding behavior. Since the 1960s, expectancy theory has become a popular way of thinking about the motivation process as it applies to job performance behavior.[17]

> Supplement 6A at the end of this chapter deals with an important cognitive variable affecting motivation—motives.

Assumptions
of expectancy
theory

There are several versions of expectancy theory but most share these basic assumptions:

1. They assume that behavior is *voluntary*.

2. They assume that a person will *choose* to behave in a *rational* way so as to optimize actual or perceived desired "outcomes," or consequences.[18] An outcome is any "potential need-related consequence of behavior."[19] In any work environment there are multiple outcomes associated with each behavioral alternative.

3. They assume that the person's voluntary, rational choice of behavior can be explained largely in terms of two cognitive variables: valence and expectancy. It is these two variables that we examine next. Figure 6–4 shows the role of valence and expectancy in a general expectancy theory of motivation.

---

[16] From *Performance in Organizations: Determinants and Appraisal* by L. L. Cummings and Donald P. Schwab, p. 27. Copyright © 1973 by Scott, Foresman and Company. Reprinted by permission.

[17] See, for example, Victor H. Vroom, *Work and Motivation* (New York: John Wiley & Sons, 1964); Lyman W. Porter and Edward E. Lawler III, *Managerial Attitudes and Performance* (Homewood, Ill.: Richard D. Irwin, 1968); and L. L. Cummings and Donald P. Schwab, *Performance in Organizations: Determinants and Appraisal* (Glenview, Ill.: Scott, Foresman and Company, 1973).

[18] A recent study that tested the assumption of optimizing against alternative assumptions of satisfying and a type of minimizing found no support for the optimizing assumption. See Jack M. Feldman, H. Joseph Reitz, and Robert J. Hilterman, "Alternatives to Optimization in Expectancy Theory," *Journal of Applied Psychology*, vol. 61, no. 6 (1976), pp. 712–20.

[19] Kenneth N. Wexley and Gary A. Yukl, *Organizational Behavior and Personnel Psychology* (Homewood, Ill.: Richard D. Irwin, 1977), p. 82.

FIGURE 6–4
A General Expectancy Theory of Motivation

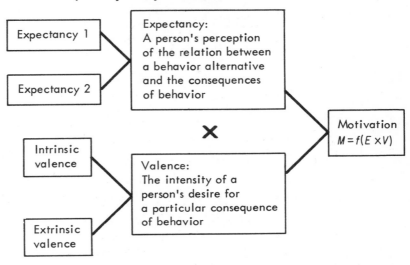

VALENCE

What is
valence?

"Valence" refers to the attractiveness or the intensity of desire for some expected behavioral consequence. It is a measure of the desirability a person attaches to the occurrence of some expected behavioral consequence. These measures can be positive or negative, depending on the desirability of the behavioral consequence.

Two types
of valence

As a factor in the motivation process, valence is simply a way of handling the obvious truism that we are motivated to behave in ways that lead to consequences we find attractive—the more attractive, the better. There are two types of valence, intrinsic and extrinsic.[20]

Internally
imposed

Intrinsic Valence. "Intrinsic valence" refers to the intensity of desire for consequences that are intrinsic or internal to the person; they are internally imposed but are derived from the job itself. Examples include the valence of the desire for job satisfaction, self-esteem, self-fulfillment, a sense of achievement, and satisfying interpersonal and social relationships. All of these are potential work outcomes; they are controlled by and internal to the person. For example, only you decide whether your job is satisfying.

---

[20] The terms *intrinsic* and *extrinsic* are used in the motivation–literature as adjectives modifying consequences, motivation, and valence. There is lack of agreement on the precise meaning of the terms. See Lee Dyer and Donald F. Parker, "Classifying Outcomes in Work Motivation Research: An Examination of the Intrinsic-Extrinsic Dichotomy," *Journal of Applied Psychology*, vol. 60, no. 4 (1975), pp. 455–58. Also see Laurie A. Broedling, "The Uses of the Intrinsic-Extrinsic Distinction in Explaining Motivation and Organizational Behavior," *Academy of Management Review*, vol. 2, no. 2 (April 1977), pp. 267–76.

Behavior
versus
achievement

Intrinsic valences may be associated with both task behavior and task achievement.[21] For example, a person may gain great satisfaction from performing a task (like climbing Mt. Everest), but the actual achievement of the task may be an anticlimax (like reaching the top of Mt. Everest). Another person, however, may view the achievement of the task as the only source of satisfaction.

Externally
imposed

Extrinsic Valence. "Extrinsic valence" refers to the intensity of desire for consequences that are extrinsic or external to the person; they provide satisfaction that is independent of the job itself; and they are externally imposed and controlled by the organization. Examples include pay, fringe benefits, promotions, office furnishings, assignment to desirable jobs, parking privileges, and so on. These are the types of job-related consequences over which the manager has some discretionary influence and which can be utilized as means for improving job performance.

Positively
valent
consequences

Use to Managers. For practicing managers, the concept of valence is an aid to thinking about the complexity of motivation. *First,* it emphasizes that if consequences are to be useful in motivating individual behavior, they must be "positively valent" to the individual. Consequences the organization thinks are positively valent are not necessarily the same as those the employees view as positively valent.

Measures
of valence

Second, the concept of valence calls attention to the need for some measure of the attractiveness and importance of different consequences of behavior. These measures are difficult to obtain. A common approach is simply to ask individuals to give self-report measures of valence. However, self-reports are not always accurate. For one thing, they require the reporters to be aware of what is important to them. For another, self-report measures often report what individuals perceive they are supposed to report.

Nonadditive
valence

Third, there is evidence that intrinsic and extrinsic valence are not additive.[22] That is, it is possible for extrinsic valence to increase at the expense of intrinsic valence. A work environment that emphasizes extrinsic valence may cause employees to find *less* satisfaction and fulfillment in the job itself.

Multiple
consequences
of behavior

Fourth, valence helps managers reflect on the multiple consequences of behavior. The employee's behavior can have positive, negative, or neutral consequences. In order to understand the motivation process, it is necessary to determine the valence of *all*

[21] Robert J. House, "A Path Goal Theory of Leader Effectiveness," *Administrative Science Quarterly,* vol. 16, no. 3 (September 1971), pp. 321–38.

[22] William W. Notz, "Work Motivation and the Negative Effects of Extrinsic Rewards," *American Psychologist,* vol. 30, no. 9 (September 1975), pp. 884–91.

consequences that are relevant to any particular level of job performance. No practicing manager has the time, money, or skill to do that. Nevertheless, an accurate understanding of motivation requires it. Understanding the motivation of human behavior is not a simple undertaking—particularly for managers who have other responsibilities.

EXPECTANCY

*What is
expectancy?*

"Expectancy" refers to a person's perception of the relationship between behavior and its consequences. There are two types of expectancies: expectancy 1 and expectancy 2.

*The effort–
performance
expectancy*

Expectancy 1.   Expectancy 1 is a person's perception of the chances that a given level of effort will lead to good job performance, *as defined by the organization.* A person may exert a great deal of effort but, in the absence of necessary skills or accurate role perceptions, may never be a high-level performer. Further, a person may increase level of effort and still get a poor performance evaluation from a superior. Additionally, it is possible that, in the short run, intense levels of effort may lead to poorer performance. This seems to be implied by the statement, "You're trying too hard."

*Perception is
important;
measures*

For purposes of motivation, it is the person's perception of the effort–performance expectancy that is important. The *actual* contingency relationship between effort and performance is not as important initially as the *perceived* contingency relationship. Presumably the actual relationship will influence the perceived relationship. When attempts are made to *measure* expectancies, the measures usually take the form of subjective probability estimates ranging from -1 to $+1$.

*The per-
formance–
consequences
expectancy*

Expectancy 2.   Expectancy 2 is a person's perception of the chances that a given level of job performance will lead to certain consequences. Sometimes this type of expectancy is referred to as "instrumentality." Once again, it is the *perception* that is important in motivating behavior. There actually may be a perfect contingency relationship between performance and desired consequences or "reinforcers." But if the person does not perceive this contingency relationship, it will not positively influence the person's motivation.

*Importance of
perceptions
and attitudes*

Use to Managers.   Like valence, expectancy is an aid in thinking about the motivation process. *First,* it emphasizes for managers the importance of perceptions and attitudes. The employees' perceptions of expectancy relationships partially determine their attitudes toward those relationships. The facts are not as important as the perceptions and attitudes determining the direction of behavior.

Importance
of both
contingency
relationships

Second, the concept of expectancy identifies for managers the importance to motivation of *both* effort–performance and performance–consequence relationships. For purposes of motivating behavior, it is not enough to identify consequences that appear to satisfy some need or motive. It is also important to evaluate the *contingency* relationships among effort, performance, and desired consequences.

Suggestions
for action

Third, the concept of expectancy suggests some managerial behavior. Managers can positively influence employee motivation by: identifying the type and amount of behavior that will be judged good performance; classifying the performance criteria that will be evaluated; assuring that employees have appropriate job skills; actually making desired consequences contingent on good performance; and communicating those contingencies. In other words, managers can direct some of their efforts toward increasing the employee's probability estimates of expectancy 1 and expectancy 2.

AN ASSESSMENT OF EXPECTANCY THEORY

Current status

In our general framework for thinking about job performance, motivation is one of the four components. We have used expectancy theory as our approach to understanding the motivation process. What is the actual and current status of expectancy theory?

Practice

In terms of managerial *practice* it can be said unequivocally that expectancy theory is not commonly applied in American work organizations. Only a very small minority of managers have even heard of expectancy theory. It is a relatively new theory; it is complex; it is still developing; and it would be very difficult to apply in a practical situation. Expectancy theory is not a managerial household word.

Research

In terms of *research,* expectancy theory is currently dominant in studies of work-related motivation.[23] What does this research have to say? The *bad news* is that there are numerous studies that, taken together, call into question the assumptions,[24] the relationships, and the hypotheses[25] of expectancy theory. There is a definite need for expectancy theory research to take into account the

[23] For excellent reviews of research on expectancy theory see Terrence R. Mitchell, "Expectancy Models of Job Satisfaction, Occupational Preference and Effort: A Theoretical, Methodological, and Empirical Appraisal," *Psychological Bulletin,* vol. 81, no. 12 (1974), pp. 1,053–77, and Robert J. House, H. Jack Shapiro, and Mahmoud A. Wahba, "Expectancy Theory as a Predictor of Work Behavior and Attitude: A Reevaluation of Empirical Evidence," *Decision Sciences,* vol. 5, no. 3 (July 1974), pp. 481–506.

[24] Orlando Behling and Frederick A. Starke, "The Postulates of Expectancy Theory," *Academy of Management Journal,* vol. 16, no. 3 (September 1973), pp. 373–88. Also see Behling and Starke, "A Test of Two Postulates underlying Expectancy Theory," *Academy of Management Journal,* vol. 18, no. 4 (December 1975), pp. 703–14.

[25] Herbert G. Heneman and Donald P. Schwab, "Evaluation of Research on Expectancy Theory Predictions of Employee Performance," *Psychological Bulletin,* vol. 78, no. 1 (July 1972), pp. 6–7.

contingencies of individual and environmental differences.[26] The *good news* is that these and other contingencies are entering into research;[27] attempts are being made to clarify many issues related to expectancy theory;[28] and it "has been at least as successful as any alternative theory in predicting variability in employee performance."[29]

Education

In management *education,* expectancy theory is one important cognitive approach to learning about job performance. It is an intuitively acceptable way of thinking about the motivation process. It is useful in identifying the choices that affect performance. Our conclusion is that expectancy theory is valuable as a theory for examining the motivation process within a general framework for thinking about job performance.

Summary box

> The final section of this chapter discussed *three major ideas:* the motivation process, valence, and expectancy.
>
> We examined the *motivation process* from the viewpoint of a cognitive approach known as "expectancy theory of motivation." This theory attempts to explain voluntary behavior in terms of a rational process of choice designed to maximize the benefits a person receives from behavior. Expectancy theory has two main variables: valence and expectancy.
>
> *Valence* refers to the intensity of desire for an expected behavioral consequence. There are two types of valence: intrinsic and extrinsic. Intrinsic valences may be associated with both task behavior and task achievement.
>
> *Expectancy* refers to a person's perception of the relationship between behavior and its consequences. There are two types of expectancy. Expectancy 1 is an effort–performance expectancy, and expectancy 2 is a performance–consequences expectancy. Measures of expectancy 1 and 2 usually take the form of subjective probability estimates.

---

[26] Leon Reinharth and Mahmoud A. Wahba, "Expectancy Theory as a Predictor of Work Motivation, Effort Expenditure, and Job Performance," *Academy of Management Journal,* vol. 18, no. 3 (September 1975), pp. 520–37.

[27] Henry P. Sims, Jr., Andrew D. Szilagyi, and Dale R. McKemey, "Antecedents of Work Related Expectancies," *Academy of Management Journal,* vol. 19, no. 4 (December 1976), pp. 547–59.

[28] Terry Connolly, "Some Conceptual and Methodological Issues in Expectancy Models of Work Performance Motivation," *Academy of Management Review,* vol. 1, no. 4 (October 1976), pp. 37–47.

[29] From *Performance in Organizations: Determinants and Appraisal* by L. L. Cummings and Donald P. Schwab, p. 29. Copyright © 1973 by Scott, Foresman and Company. Reprinted by permission. For a discussion of other theories of work motivation see Orlando Behling, Chester Schriesheim, and James Tolliver, "Alternatives to Expectancy Theories of Work Motivation," *Decision Sciences,* vol. 6, no. 3 (July 1975), pp. 449–61.

CHECK YOUR UNDERSTANDING

Psychoanalytic approach   Role expectations
Cognitive approach   Role senders
Reinforcement approach   Role set
$B = f(P,E)$ Role ambiguity
$JP = f(SF,A/S,RP,M)$ Role conflict
Abilities versus skills   Content of motivation
Multiplicative relationships   Process of motivation
Role   Expectancy theory assumptions
Role perceptions   Intrinsic valence
Role episode   Extrinsic valence
Focal person   Expectancy 1
Received role   Expectancy 2
Sent role

STUDY QUESTIONS

1. In a poll of 4,059 Americans, 57 percent of the respondents said they *could* produce more each day if they tried. An additional result of that poll was that less than 40 percent said they think they *should* produce more. What, in your opinion, is the significance of this latter poll result and what effect might it have on a manager's concern for motivation?

2. In what ways can managers influence the situational factors, abilities and skills, and role perceptions that enter into job performance? What, in your opinion, are some nonmanagerial influences on these three variables?

3. What, in your opinion, are some of the abilities and skills that are essential to *managerial* work?

4. What does it mean to say that ability and motivation do not have *independent* effects on performance? What does it mean to say that role perceptions, ability, and motivation interact *multiplicatively* to determine job performance?

5. Use expectancy theory to analyze your level of motivation in one of your present situations (for example, in a job you now hold or in a college course you are now taking).
   a. What are the relevant expected consequences of your behavior?
   b. How might you calculate the net (positive and negative) valence of these consequences? What value can you put on this valence calculation?
   c. What is your estimate of expectancy 1?
   d. What is your estimate of expectancy 2?
   e. What is your level of motivation?

6. For the situation you analyzed in Question 5, use the role episode as a different approach to analyzing the situation.

7. What, in your opinion, are some reasons why the *perceived* probabilities employees associate with expectancy 1 and expectancy 2 might be lower than justified by the *actual* effort–performance–rewards relationships?

8. The term "role overload" is sometimes used to refer to a situation in which a focal person simply cannot handle all of the legitimate demands of role senders within time, quality, quantity, and cost limits. How does the role-overload idea apply to your current situation?

APPLICATION: PAY, VALENCE, AND EXPECTANCY

Pay is important! It is *very* important to some people (like the man shown in Figure 6–5); it is of *some* importance to almost everyone; but it is rarely *all-important.*

FIGURE 6–5
Money Is Important to Employee Behavior

Source: *The Wall Street Journal.*

The role of pay in work organizations is actually very complex. The desire for money can be viewed as a *motive,* and the receipt of money can be viewed as a reinforcing *consequence* of behavior. Money can be seen as a form of *concrete feedback* about job performance, or it can be considered as an ingredient of the work environment that is necessary in order to *prevent job dissatisfaction.*

What conditions must be present in an organization if a pay program is to have a direct effect on our motivation? Let's answer that question by applying the ideas of valence and expectancy. We can identify three conditions:

1. Valence. In order for pay to be a motivator of our behavior, we must attach a positive valence to pay. We must view it as attractive and desirable. Just how attractive and desirable pay will be to us depends on the valence we attach to other consequences (feeling tired, possible social disapproval, missing a hunting trip) that result from our job performance.

It is reasonable to say that most of us are positively valent toward pay. Even without considering expectancies, pay has been shown to be predictive of job performance. A pay program must ensure that there is more incentive for good performance than for poor or average performance.

2. Expectancy 2. In order for a consequence of behavior to be a motivator of behavior, the consequence must be perceived as contingent on the behavior. Our job performance can be influenced by pay if we perceive that our pay is contingent on our performance. "When individual pay is clearly dependent upon individual performance, job performance is higher than when pay and performance are not related."[30]

3. Expectancy 1. If pay is perceived as contingent on performance and if pay is to affect our level of motivation or effort, we must perceive that a change in our level of effort will bring about a change in our job performance. If we do not perceive that a change in effort will directly affect the quality or quantity of our job performance, then we will not associate effort with the pay that is contingent on performance.

1. What are some of the difficulties that managers might encounter in their attempts to make the level of pay a person receives contingent on the level of performance?

2. Is it always desirable to have the level of pay contingent on the level of performance? Discuss.

APPLICATION: HOW IMPORTANT IS EQUITY?[31]

Until two weeks ago, Jerrold would not have hesitated to tell anyone who would listen that he was very satisfied with his job. He felt fortunate to have a job that challenged him and that provided self-fulfillment. He got along very well with Katherine, his supervisor, and felt that she looked out for his career interests. In fact, Jerrold liked everything about his job—his new office, his co-workers, his chances for promotion, and his pay, especially his pay!

When Jerrold and Ernest went on a coffee break together two Wednesdays ago, Jerrold wasn't prepared for the shock he was about to receive. Ernest and Jerrold were "talking shop" and the subject of the recent pay increases came up. Since they were fairly close friends and had similar jobs, they decided to tell each other what their pay increases had been.

Jerrold couldn't believe it. Neither could Ernest. How could Katherine have given Ernest a pay increase so much larger than

---

[30] Edward E. Lawler III, *Pay and Organizational Effectiveness: A Psychological Review* (New York: McGraw-Hill Book Company, 1971), p. 132.

[31] For background information see Paul Goodman and Abraham Freedman, "An Examination of Adams' Theory of Inequity," *Administrative Science Quarterly*, vol. 16, no. 3 (September 1971), pp. 271–88; and E. E. Walster, E. Berscheid, and G. W. Walster, "New Directions in Equity Research," *Journal of Personality and Social Psychology,"* vol. 25 (1973), pp. 151–76.

Jerrold? What possible reason could there be? Jerrold knew that he worked just as hard and was as smart as Ernest. They both had almost identical backgrounds except that Jerrold already had his M.B.A. degree and Ernest was still about 20 hours short of receiving his.

Ernest couldn't help noticing Jerrold's astonishment and dismay. In fact, he sympathized with Jerrold. Ernest wasn't about to suggest to Katherine that an adjustment should be made in the pay increases. Ernest was no fool! Nevertheless, he wished that something could be done to help him feel less uneasy about this situation.

Jerrold's attitude toward his job changed immediately. Somehow it seemed less exciting, and certainly his relationship with Katherine had taken a turn for the worse. Jerrold's job behavior also began to change. He seemed to be more of a loner now. Several people commented that Jerrold's productivity wasn't up to par. He was frequently late in getting projects completed and several projects had to be sent back to him for correction of errors.

1. What are some steps that Ernest *could* take to reduce the inequity that he perceives to exist? Do you think he will take these steps?

2. What are some steps that Jerrold *could* take to reduce the inequity that he perceives to exist? Do you think he will take these steps?

3. How can the situation described here be related to the ideas of valence and expectancy?

SUPPLEMENT 6A
Motives

. . . embarrassment. I am easily embarrassed by myself. No single emotion is more responsible for whatever I have achieved.

Jack Nicklaus

Swimming is the only sport where *before* an athlete competes he stands on a pedestal, is introduced, and applauded. He hasn't even done anything. Instant recognition. That's so much of what an athlete wants. Then he gets rewarded immediately afterward. It would be terrible if he got the award the next day; he might forget what he got it for.[1]

Motives vary

In the above quotation, Mark Spitz expresses his opinion about *what* motivates athletes (instant recognition), and about the preferred *timing* of rewards (before and immediately after the competition). For Mark Spitz, the desire for recognition may be (or, in his case, may have been) one of his important motives. For Jack Nicklaus, the need to avoid embarrassment is important. As we will see, a variety of motives are needed to explain behavior. "Indeed it seems that there is nothing that does not serve as an incentive for someone, given the right set of circumstances."[2]

---

[1] Quoted in George Plimpton, "A Golden Fish Out of Water," *Sports Illustrated*, vol. 45, no. 1 (July 5, 1976), p. 58.

[2] Orlando Behling and Chester Schriesheim, *Organizational Behavior: Theory, Research, and Application* (Boston: Allyn and Bacon, 1976), p. 57.

Central role of motives

The idea of motives has played a central role in the attempt of management educators, researchers, and practitioners to understand *what* motivates job performance behavior. The idea that our behavior can be explained in terms of our needs and motives is intuitively acceptable to many managers and students of managing. It is an idea that has dominated the study of job performance behavior for the past 25 years.

This supplement

First, we define motives, note how difficult it is to identify motives, and differentiate primary from secondary motives. Second, we discuss and critique two influential views of human needs, Maslow's need-hierarchy theory and Herzberg's two-factor theory. Third, a new and as yet untested framework of social motives is introduced. Fourth, three specific motives—affiliation, power, and achievement—are singled out for discussion.

WHAT IS A MOTIVE?

Definition

A motive is an inner state that activates, directs, sustains, and stops behavior toward goals. The study of motives is concerned with what it is inside a person that causes the person to engage in goal-directed behavior. No one has ever seen a motive; they always remain inside people. In that sense, motives, like perceptions, attitudes, and values, are cognitive variables. Trying to understand job performance by looking at motives is a cognitive approach.

Difficult to identify motives

We sometimes infer what people's motives are from observations of their behavior. We also learn something about people's motives by asking them about their motives. We can ask them indirectly, through psychological tests, or directly. We need to be cautious in doing these kinds of things, remembering that it is often difficult to identify motives. If you infer a person's needs or motives from behavior, remember that "Between a need and its satisfaction may be interposed almost any behavioral demand."[3] This idea was discussed in Chapter 1, where we noted that a single goal can explain a variety of motives and a single motive can explain a variety of goals.

Primary and secondary motives

In an attempt to give some order to the diversity of motives that are said to explain behavior, many classifications have been suggested. One of the most basic classifications used by psychologists is the two-way classification of primary and secondary motives. "Primary motives" derive from the survival needs of a person to maintain biological processes. To some extent it is possible to measure primary motives directly. For example, a person's need for water or food can be determined. "Secondary motives" derive

---

[3] Daniel Katz and Robert L. Kahn, *The Social Psychology of Organizations.* (New York: John Wiley & Sons, 1966), p. 344.

from association with the primary motives. They are learned; can be measured only in indirect ways; and include such motives as achievement, recognition, affiliation, power—the need to influence other people, and effectance—the need to influence or manipulate nonhuman aspects of the environment.[4]

MASLOW'S NEED HIERARCHY

Popularity of the model

Needs and Desires. A well-known classification of motives, or needs, and one that has had a major impact on management education and practice is Abraham H. Maslow's "need-hierarchy" theory.[5] As shown in Figure 6A–1, Maslow suggests that human needs can be arranged into five levels.

Two basic desires

In addition to the five needs noted in Figure 6A–1 Maslow suggests that people have two basic desires: (*a*) the desire to *know;* to be aware of reality; to get the facts; and to satisfy curiosity; and (*b*) the desire to *understand;* to systematize and to look for relations and meanings. Taken together, Maslow's view of five basic needs and two basic desires is a comprehensive way of looking at the diversity of human motives present in work environments.

Sequencing of needs

Maslow asserts that the five needs usually (not always) emerge *sequentially.* For example, in order for the *social* needs of a person to become dominant, it is first necessary for the person to satisfy *safety* needs. The safety needs would have to be "relatively" satisfied before the next higher level of needs can become "prepotent," or dominant. As a person satisfies safety needs their capacity to motivate the person is weakened, and social needs then become the strongest motivator of behavior.

A satisfied need is not a motivator, except . . .

A common way of expressing this idea is to say that a satisfied need is not a motivator; that is, according to Maslow, as a need is increasingly satisfied it decreases in importance as a motivator of behavior. The exception to this is the self-actualization need. Maslow argues that increased satisfaction of self-actualization needs leads to *increased* rather than decreased importance of that need in motivating behavior.[6] The more one gets a taste of becoming what one is capable of becoming, the more an additional taste is desired.

The hierarchy idea

Perspective. The idea of a "hierarchy of needs" is appealing because it suggests an orderly progression which should aid predic-

---

[4] Behling and Schriesheim, *Organizational Behavior: Theory, Research, and Application,* p. 55.

[5] Abraham H. Maslow, *Motivation and Personality* (New York: Harper & Row, Publishers, 1954).

[6] Abraham H. Maslow, *Toward a Psychology of Being,* 2d ed. (New York: Van Nostrand Reinhold, 1968), p. 30.

FIGURE 6A–1
Abraham H. Maslow's Hierarchy of Human Needs

General Idea

Maslow's classification includes five "levels" of human needs: physiological, safety, social, esteem, and self-actualization. These needs are arranged in a "hierarchy of prepotence." That is, the needs at a particular level must be relatively satisfied before the needs at the next higher level become operative. This proposition is generally *not* supported by tests of Maslow's model.

Maslow does not argue that all people's needs are arranged in this particular order: He allows for many differences. However, he does argue that this particular order of needs seems to have general validity.

Hierarchy of Human Needs (listed in order from lowest to highest)

Physiological. This classification includes such motives as hunger, thirst, and sex. These needs are the most prepotent of all. The man who is extremely hungry has no interest in anything other than food. Man lives for bread alone—when there is no bread.

Safety. This classification refers primarily to freedom from bodily threat, but it is also broader than that. Maslow argues that much adult resistance to change derives from the safety need. In addition, he suggests that much contemporary conflict may be traceable to the feeling of insecurity resulting from questioning so many "safe" things (church, family, marriage, country, flag).

Social. These needs are concerned with love, affection, and belongingness. A question you might ask is, What happens at the workplace if the need for love, affection, and belongingness is thwarted?

Esteem. This need is concerned with self-respect and self-esteem based on real personal capacity and achievement. Esteem needs can be classified into *two sets*. One set is concerned with the desire for achievement, strength, adequacy, independence, and confidence. The other set is concerned with reputation, attention, prestige, recognition, importance, and appreciation.

Self-actualization. This is the desire for self-fulfillment. It is the desire or need to become what one is capable of becoming. Self-actualization is not particularized. Rather, it is a general need that must be defined individually. What self-actualizes an artist will likely be different from what self-actualizes an assembly-line worker.

tion of behavior. That is, knowledge about which need is currently most important suggests that increased satisfaction of that need will *decrease* its importance and *increase* the importance of needs at the next higher level. The imagery here is of a person climbing a ladder to higher levels of human fulfillment. The problem with the hierarchy-of-needs idea is that there is very little evidence to support it, and there is some evidence against it.

Supportive
evidence

The evidence in support of the need hierarchy model is primarily concerned with "lower-level" needs. For example, when physiological needs such as hunger and thirst are unsatisfied, people are relatively unconcerned about higher-level needs. When these needs are satisfied, they become, as Maslow asserts, less important in motivating behavior.

Nonsuppor-
tive evidence

The evidence against Maslow's theory is primarily concerned with *higher-level* needs. By "higher-level needs" is meant the social, esteem, and self-actualization needs noted in Figure 6A–1. These needs play an important role in managerial positions. However, concerning the higher-level needs, there is almost no evidence to support Maslow's proposition of a hierarchy.[7]

Conclusions
for managers

What are managers to conclude about Maslow's theory? First, the theory is useful because of its rich and comprehensive view of human needs. Second, there is some evidence to support the theory's predictions that satisfaction of physiological and safety needs *causes* the strengths of those needs to decrease. Third, the hierarchy idea is of little value to managers. Rather than thinking of the five needs as a hierarchy, it may be more useful to think of them as a *system* of interacting needs having different degrees of importance at different times.

HERZBERG'S TWO-FACTOR THEORY

Major
influence

Another view of human needs that has had a major influence on managerial education and practice is the "two-factor," or "two-need," theory suggested by Frederick Herzberg and his associates.[8]

Critical-
incident
procedure

The theory originally was derived by analyzing "critical incidents" written by 200 engineers and accountants. These incidents were supposed to describe times when the engineers and accountants felt particularly happy and particularly unhappy at work. This approach has been repeated numerous times with a variety of job holders. The data from analyzing such incidents was interpreted by Herzberg to reveal that there are two types of needs in the work environment: "hygienes and motivators."

Hygienes and
job dissatis-
faction

Hygienes and Motivators. Hygiene needs represent the need to avoid pain in the work environment. The need is met by hygienes or dissatisfiers in the environment, such as the type of supervisor, fringe benefits, and working conditions. Herzberg considers money to be the most important hygiene factor in the work environment. What is the role of hygiene factors? In general, they have their

---

[7] John B. Miner, *The Management Process: Theory, Research, and Practice* (New York: The Macmillan Company, 1973), p. 319.

[8] F. Herzberg, B. Mausner, and B. Snydermann, *The Motivation to Work*, 2d ed. (New York: John Wiley & Sons, 1959). Also, F. Herzberg, *Work and the Nature of Man* (Cleveland: World Press, 1966).

greatest impact on preventing employees from being *dissatisfied* or unhappy with their jobs. They do not, Herzberg asserts, have an important role in making people feel satisfied or happy in their jobs. That is the role of motivators.

Motivators and job satisfaction

Motivator needs include the need for employees to use their talents and to grow. This need is met by motivators or satisfiers, such as recognition, responsibility, advancement, personal growth, and the nature of the job itself. Herzberg considers achievement to be the most important motivator. What is the role of motivators? They make people *satisfied* with their job. And what is the consequence of that satisfaction? Improved job performance, Herzberg asserts.

Different roles of hygienes and motivators

Figure 6A–2 outlines the Herzberg two-factor theory. In general, the theory alleges that *high* levels of job dissatisfaction have a negative influence on job performance, but *low* levels do not have a positive influence. Additionally, the theory holds that higher levels of job performance are obtained when the level of job satisfaction is high and that high job satisfaction happens primarily through motivators. Thus, hygienes are necessary to keep job dissatisfaction low; motivators are necessary to keep job satisfaction and job performance high. (A discussion of job satisfaction and its relation to job performance is the main subject of Supplement 7B, "Job Satisfaction.")

Herzberg debate

Perspective. Herzberg's theory is widely know by management educators and by managers. A considerable amount of research and debate has revolved around it, and it has had a major impact on managerial practice. The major debate concerning Herzberg's theory centers on Herzberg's insistence that hygienes influence

FIGURE 6A–2
Hygienes and Motivators and Their Influence on Job Satisfaction, Job Dissatisfaction, and Job Performance

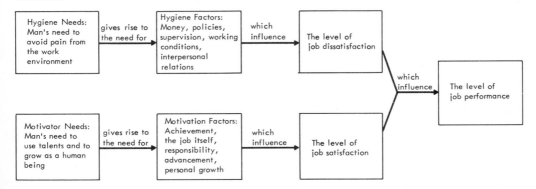

only job dissatisfaction, not job satisfaction. In general, there is little support for this position.[9]

Conclusion for managers

Concerning Herzberg's theory, many agree with the following observation: "The most meaningful conclusion that we can draw is that the two-factor theory has now served its purpose and should be altered or respectfully laid aside. Theories are never true or false, but exhibit varying degrees of usefulness."[10] Our conclusion is that Herzberg's theory has been very useful in stimulating thought and discussion about motivation in the work environment. One can only speculate about what this discussion would have focused on over the past 20 years had it not been for Herzberg and Maslow. Nevertheless, our expectation is that the insights of Maslow and Herzberg will, in the future, be viewed as minor but still useful contributions to the understanding of job-performance behavior.

---

[9] For a defense of two-factor (hygienes and motivators) theory of motivation, see D. A. Whitsett and E. K. Winslow, "An Analysis of Studies Critical of the Motivator-Hygiene Theory," *Personnel Psychology,* vol. 20, no. 4 (Winter 1967), pp. 391–15. For a critical review of two-factor theory, see Robert J. House and Lawrence A. Wigdor, "Herzberg's Dual-Factor Theory of Job Satisfaction and Motivation: A Review of the Evidence and a Criticism," *Personnel Psychology,* vol. 20, no. 4 (Winter 1967), pp. 369–90.

[10] John P. Campbell, Marvin D. Dunnette, Edward E. Lawler III and Karl E. Weick, Jr., *Managerial Behavior, Performance and Effectiveness* (New York: McGraw-Hill Book Company, 1970), p. 381.

Summary box

> The idea of motives has played a central role in attempts to understand and predict job performance behavior. *A motive* is an inner state that activates, directs, sustains, and stops behavior toward goals. The use of motives to understand behavior is an example of a *cognitive approach*.
>
> *Primary motives* derive from the survival needs of a person. *Secondary* motives are learned and derive from association with primary motives.
>
> Abraham H. Maslow's classification of human needs has had an important influence on managerial education and practice. He identifies *five levels of needs* (physiological, safety, social, esteem, and self-actualization) and *two basic desires* (to know and to understand). There has been considerable discussion about whether the five needs should be viewed as a *hierarchy*. Our view is that they are a system of interacting needs having different degrees of importance at different times.
>
> Frederick Herzberg's two-factor theory suggests that there are two types of needs in the work environment: hygienes and motivators. *Hygiene needs* represent the need to avoid pain in the work environment. *Motivator needs* represent the need for employees to use their talents and to grow. The two-factor theory identifies hygiene factors which influence the level of job *dissatisfaction* and motivator factors that influence the level of job *satisfaction*. Both factors can have an influence on job performance.

A FRAMEWORK OF SOCIAL MOTIVES[11]

The simplest social situation

A newer framework of motives is intended to aid our understanding of a social situation in which only two social units are involved. The social units could be individuals or different-size groups. We shall discuss individuals.

Three types of concern

In this framework, a "social motive" is defined as one in which an individual takes the outcomes of others into account when making a choice. In the simple social situation involving two individuals, an individual can be concerned with the payoffs or consequences to (1) only him*self* or her*self*, (2) only the *other* individual, or (3) *both self* and *other*.

Concern only for self

In the first case (concern only for self), two basic motives are self-interest and self-sacrifice. The "self-interest" motive is mani-

[11] This section is based on Kenneth R. MacCrimmon and David M. Messick, "A Framework for Social Motives," *Behavioral Science*, vol. 21, no. 2 (March 1976), pp. 86–100.

fested when the individual behaves to increase his or her own benefits. The "self-sacrifice" motive is manifested when the individual behaves to as to decrease his or her own benefits.

Concern only for other

In the second case (concern only for other), two basic motives are altruism and aggression. The "altruism" motive is manifested when the individual behaves so as to increase the benefits to the other person. The "aggression" motive is illustrated when the individual behaves so as to decrease the benefits to the other person.

Concern for both

In the third case (concern for both self and other), two basic motives are cooperation and competition. The "cooperation" motive is manifested by behavior which increases the sum of self's and other's benefits. The "competition" motive works to increase the difference between self's and other's benefits.

Potential value of framework

This framework of social motives has not as yet received much attention from management educators or practitioners. Only the basic framework is described here. For our purposes, the framework provides insight into motives that may operate in simple social situations. Managers often find themselves in such situations in the contexts of interpersonal and intergroup behavior. The framework is a different type than that of the Maslow and Herzberg models. In the latter cases, the models identify what motivates behavior. In the framework of social motives, the emphasis is on six motives having differing impacts on the payoffs to an individual.

THREE SPECIFIC MOTIVES

TAT procedure

The achievement, power, and affiliation motives have been researched extensively over the past 25 years.[12] One common procedure in this research has been to utilize a Thematic Apperception Test (TAT). This "projective" test asks persons to write imaginative stories in response to a series of pictures. A large number of these stories have been analyzed over the years. The analysis suggests, among others, the three motives discussed here.

n Aff

The Affiliation Motive. The motive or need for affiliation (n Aff) is the desire to be with other people regardless of whether anything else is gained thereby. Positive attitudes toward social relationships and being concerned about the happiness of others are evidence of n Aff. It has been suggested that the number of groups to which an individual belongs can be taken as a measure of n Aff. Further, it has been suggested that merely being in the presence of others seems to reduce unhappiness, especially when the others are unhappy too. "Misery loves miserable company."

---

[12] See David C. McClelland, J. W. Atkinson, R. A. Clark, and E. L. Lowell, *The Achievement Motive* (New York: Appleton-Century-Crofts, 1953); J. W. Atkinson and N. T. Feathers, eds., *A Theory of Achievement Motivation* (New York: John Wiley & Sons, 1966); and David C. McClelland, *Power: The Inner Experience* (Boston: Irvington Publishers, 1975).

n Pow

The Power Motive. To a greater extent than *n* Aff, the need for power (*n* Pow) is important for understanding managers,[13] because *n* Pow refers to the desire to have influence over other people. There is a positive and a negative side to power.[14] Some seek power for personal aggrandizement, and such "personalized power" is obtained at the expense of others.[15] Others seek "socialized power," in order to serve the institution of which they are a part. There is some research evidence that suggests that effective managers are high in the need for socialized power, as opposed to the need for personalized power.

n Ach

The Achievement Motive. The achievement motive (*n* Ach) is "a relatively stable disposition, or potential behavioral tendency, to strive for achievement or success."[16] Presumably, the achievement motive is aroused in response to incentives in the environment that a person perceives as enhancing feelings of achievement.[17]

Three characteristics of high n Ach

There are three major characteristics of a self-motivated achiever. *First,* they like to set their own goals. They do not want to drift "goal-less" and they want to have a high degree of control over goal achievement. *Second,* self-motivated achievers will set goals that are neither too easy nor too difficult to accomplish. High achievers want to win; they will not set goals too difficult to reach. However, goals that are too easy would provide inadequate satisfaction. The *third* characteristic of those high in *n* Ach is that they like frequent and concrete feedback about their performance. High achievers like to know how well they are doing.

Determining achievement motivation

David C. McClelland, a prominent researcher of the achievement motive, estimates that only about 10 percent of the general American population have a strong achievement motive. This 10 percent, however, can be very important to management and business

---

[13] David C. McClelland and David H. Burnham, "Power Is the Great Motivator," *Harvard Business Review,* vol. 54, no. 2 (March–April 1976), pp. 100–10.

[14] David C. McClelland, William N. Davis, Rudolf Kalin, and Erie Warner, *The Drinking Man* (New York: The Free Press, 1972). Also, David C. McClelland, "The Two Faces of Power," *Journal of International Affairs,* vol. 24, no. 1 (1970), pp. 29–43.

[15] McClelland and Burnham, "Power Is the Great Motivator," p. 103. Also, McClelland and Burnham, "Good Guys Make Bum Bosses," *Psychology Today,* vol. 9, no. 7 (December 1975), pp. 69–70.

[16] Campbell, Dunnette, Lawler, and Weick, *Managerial Behavior Performance and Effectiveness,* p. 351.

[17] The following formulation is sometimes suggested: The tendency to approach a task with the intention of performing it successfully (T_s) is equal to the strength of the achievement motive (M_s) times the subjective probability of success (P_s) times the strength of desire for success (I_s). $T_s = (M_s \times P_s \times I_s)$. Similarly, the tendency to approach a task with the intention of avoiding failure (T_f) is equal to the strength of the motive to avoid failure (M_f) times the subjective probability of failure (P_f) times the strength of the desire to avoid failure (I_f). $T_f = (M_f \times P_f \times I_f)$. It is further suggested by achievement motivation researchers that the potential strength of motivation is equal to T_s minus T_f.

organizations. McClelland suggests that a most convincing sign of a strong achievement motive is the tendency of a person, who is not being required to think about anything in particular, to think about ways to accomplish something difficult and significant.

Developing
achievement
motivation

The work by McClelland and others can help managers identify the major characteristics of achievers and suggest approaches to increasing achievement motivation. McClelland feels that "achievement characteristics" can be built into jobs—characteristics such as personal responsibility, allowing more participation by employees in goal setting, moderate goals, and concrete and frequent feedback.

Relation of
n Ach to job
performance

A recent study of a sample of first-level supervisors found a relationship between *n* Ach and job performance. Supervisors with high *n* Ach were found to have better job performance than low *n* Ach supervisors. A possible explanation for this finding is that high *n* Ach supervisors may view superior job performance as a means of satisfying their *n* Ach and as leading to rewards from the organization in which they work. Supervisors with low *n* Ach ". . . apparently do not view good performance as being instrumental to need satisfaction."[18]

Summary box

> The simplest social situation is one in which only two individuals are involved. A *framework of social motives* applicable to such a situation is one in which an individual shows concern only for *self*, only for the *other* person, or for *both* self and other. *Two basic motives* for each of these three types of concern were identified.
>
> The need for *affiliation* (*n* Aff) is the desire to be with other people regardless of whether anything else is gained thereby. It has not been found to be characteristic of effective managers.
>
> The need for *power* (*n* Pow) is the desire to have influence over other people. This need can take two forms: need for *personalized* power and need for *socialized* power. The need for socialized power has been found to be characteristic of effective managers.
>
> The need for *achievement* (*n* Ach) is the desire to strive for achievement or success. *Three characteristics* identify a person with high *n* Ach: like to set their own goals; will set moderately difficult goals, and like frequent and concrete feedback about their performance.

---

[18] Richard M. Steers, "Effects of Need for Achievement on the Job Performance-Job Attitude Relationship," *Journal of Applied Psychology*, vol. 60, no. 6 (December 1975), pp. 678–82.

CHECK YOUR UNDERSTANDING

Motive
Primary motives
Secondary motives
Maslow's need hierarchy model
  Five levels of needs
  Two basic desires
  Sequential emergence of needs
Herzberg's two-factor model
  Hygiene needs
  Motivator needs
  Hygiene factors
  Motivator factors
  Different role of two factors

Framework of social motives
  Social motive
  Three types of concern
  Self-interest and self-sacrifice
  Altruism and aggression
  Cooperation and competition
Affiliation motive (n Aff)
Power motive (n Pow)
  Personalized power
  Socialized power
Achievement motive (n Ach)

STUDY QUESTIONS

1. As a manager, how could you go about determining the job-important motives of your subordinates?

2. What suggestions for managing do you think are implied by the three characteristics of those who are high n Ach?

3. What does it mean to say that a satisfied need is not a motivator?

4. What are the implications of Herzberg's view that money is the most important hygiene factor and that achievement is the most important motivator factor?

APPLICATION: USING KNOWLEDGE OF MOTIVES*

You are the supervisor of a group of 12 skilled and semi-skilled employees. Your employees are competent in their work and have an accurate perception of the nature and requirements of their jobs. This competence and perception is due, in part, to a personnel selection process that attempts to match job requirements with the basic abilities of job holders. Additionally, once hired, employees are placed in an on-the-job training role in which they have the opportunity to develop job skills and to learn methods and procedures that are important to their performance.

Some of your employees seem to have a "motivation problem." Although this problem is somewhat of a mystery, you have decided to attempt to find a solution. As luck would have it, you recall reading an article in your basic management course dealing with the measurement of human needs. After looking up the article, talking with the professionals in the personnel department of your company, and laying some groundwork with your own employees, you decide to administer the "Need Fulfillment Questionnaire for Management." This questionnaire, although intended primarily for use

---

* The questionnaire referred to in this application may be found in Lyman W. Porter, *Job Attitudes in Management: Perceived Satisfaction and Importance of Needs* (Berkeley, Calif.: University of California, Institute of Industrial Relations, Reprint no. 229, 1964).

with managers, will, you believe, provide you with some useful knowledge of the needs and motives of your employees.

After administering the questionnaire and analyzing the data collected, you're not sure exactly what to do with the information. When you average out the responses of all 12 employees you find that the mean value of scores on security, social, and esteem need importance is about equal (scores of about 5 on a scale having a maximum value of 7). The mean values of scores on autonomy and self-actualization need importance are a full point higher than the mean values of the other three need categories. Another finding is that, on the average, your employees feel that their autonomy and self-actualization needs are more unsatisfied than the other three needs. This finding resulted from comparing the perceived degree of satisfaction of a need that a job *is* giving against the perceived degree of satisfaction the job *should* give.

Now that you have opened the "motives pandora box" some practical questions that come to your mind are:

1. How will you know *how* those needs can be satisfied? *When* should they be satisfied? To what extent?

2. How will you handle similarities and differences between the needs of your subordinates?

3. What might be some constraints on your ability to use your knowledge of employee needs?

4. What steps should you take to assure yourself that you have the skills required to manage more highly motivated employees?

Objectives of Chapter 7

- To underline the importance of the role of three cognitive variables—perceptions, attitudes, and values—in the understanding of job performance behavior.

- To describe the two basic aspects of the perceptual process: selectivity and organization.

- To distinguish two views of attitudes and to identify important characteristics of attitudes.

- To characterize the process of forming attitudes as a learning process and to question the assumed relationship between job attitudes and job performance behavior.

- To introduce cognitive dissonance theory as an approach to understanding attitude change.

- To discuss two approaches that are used to measure values of managers.

Outline of Chapter 7

Perception
  What Is Perception?
  Perceptual Similarities and Differences
  Perceptual Selectivity
  Perceptual Organization
Attitudes
  What Is an Attitude?
  Attitude Components
  Attitude Characteristics
  Role of Groups in Forming Attitudes
  The Process of Forming Attitudes
  Measuring Attitudes
  Changing Attitudes
  Attitudes and Behavior
Values
  What Are Values?
  Values Are Changing
  Personal Value Systems of Managers
  The "Study of Values"

7

COGNITIVE VARIABLES

I'll see it when I believe it.

Robert E. Ornstein

The divergent scales of values scream in discordance, they dazzle and daze us, and so that it might not be painful we steer clear of all other values . . . and we confidently judge the whole world according to our own home values.

Alexander Solzhenitsyn

The dean and the anthropolgist

A recent newspaper article provides an interesting illustration of one of the ideas we discuss in this chapter—frame of reference. The article, written by the dean of Stanford University's Graduate School of Business and former president of Ford Motor Company, discusses and critiques a new book about corporation executives.[1] The author of the book is a social and clinical psychologist and director of the Harvard Project on Technology, Work and Character.

The gamesman

According to the book's author, the new corporate executives are sharp, likable, confident "gamesmen." Their goals in life are career advancement and winning. To these goals they bring many qualities: a sense of fairness, an absence of hostility, an openness to new ideas, a willingness to take risks, and an unbigoted, non-ideological, liberal view of the world. But the emphasis on advancement and winning takes its toll: "shallowness," "manipulative tendencies," "lack of courage and conviction," and "lack of compassion" are all terms used by the book's author to describe the new corporate leaders.

The teamsman

In commenting on the above view of corporate executives, the author of the newspaper article suggests that, rather than "gamesmen," the new corporate executives could be called "teamsmen."

---

[1] The article referred to is Arjay Miller, "Analyzing the Corporate Executive," *Wall Street Journal,* Southwest Edition, vol. 59, no. 19 (January 27, 1977), p. 14. The book referred to is Michael Maccoby, *The Gamesman: The New Corporate Leaders* (New York: Simon & Schuster, 1976).

This difference in labeling connotes a more substantive and positive view and one that is also accurate. Cooperation and teamwork are important dimensions of the corporate environment. Lamenting the book's failure to recognize the corporate executive's effective role in managing useful work, the dean and former Ford Motor Company president observes that:

> Often the cultural anthropologist has difficulty appreciating the logic of behavior dictated by the necessary goals of an unfamiliar social system, therefore he evaluates it within an inappropriate frame of reference. Such may be the case, in part, here.[2]

Which should it be?

Which should it be—gamesman or teamsman? Which should be emphasized—the alleged failure of corporate environments to be emotionally supportive or the useful work that is done in those environments? We don't have to choose sides; both sides describe perceived views of reality. However, the illustration does show how our perceptions, attitudes, and values are influenced by the frame of reference from which we view the world.

Tie-in to last chapter

Recall the framework we developed in Chapter 6 for understanding job performance. It contained four components: situational factors; abilities and skills; role perceptions; and motivation. Our view of motivation was developed around two variables: valence and expectancy. These two variables are cognitive, or covert, variables; they are variables that are internal to a person that are used to explain and understand observable, or overt, behavior. Valence and expectancy are specific types of *attitudes* or beliefs. They are formed, in part, as a result of the *perceptions* and *values* of a person. This chapter develops more fully these three cognitive variables: perceptions; attitudes; and values.

This chapter

First, we define perception and describe the perceptual process in terms of two basic aspects: perceptual selectivity and perceptual organization. Second, we discuss the components and characteristics of attitudes; deal briefly with the processes of forming and changing attitudes; and evaluate the issue of the relationship between job attitudes and job performance behavior. Third, we recognize that in today's society values are changing, including job-related values, and we note an approach to measuring the personal value systems of managers.

PERCEPTION

Three umpires

What Is Perception?   There is a short incident that illustrates the idea of perception. It is about three baseball umpires discussing the problems of their work. First umpire: "Some's balls and some's strikes, and I calls 'em as *they is*." Second umpire: "Some's balls

---

[2] Miller, "Analyzing the Corporate Executive," p. 14.

and some's strikes and I calls 'em as *I sees 'em."* Third umpire, with an air of confidence: "Some's balls and some's strikes, but they ain't nothing till *I calls 'em."*[3]

Simple view

Perception is the process by which individuals attach meaning to their experience. It is the process by which persons transform, organize, and structure information arising from experiences of the senses or memory.[4] The simple view of this process is that there are objects, people, and events, such as balls and strikes, in the "real world" that somehow move directly into our consciousness. All we have to do is "call 'em as they is" or "as I sees 'em." The real world is simply there, and its objective reality is transfered directly to us. We have all met people who insist that their view of an event is *the* truth. Their view is the way it *is*, and everyone else is crazy.

Complex view

A more complex view of the perceptual process is represented by the third umpire's statement, "they ain't nothing till I calls 'em." This view recognizes the existence of objects, people, and events in the real world, but realizes that they do not move directly into our awareness. Rather, we interpret the real world by processing its reality in our own way. There are forces in *ourselves,* in the *en-vironment,* and in the *stimuli* being perceived that cause percep-tions of reality to differ. In short, the contemporary view of the perceptual process is that it is an inherently complex and active process by which people attach meaning to the experiences of their senses.[5]

Perception tolerance zone

Perceptual Similarities and Differences. Although no two per-sons have completely identical perceptions of the world, the dif-ferences are not always significant on the job. It might be helpful to think of a "perception tolerance zone" within which perceptions can vary without significantly affecting performance. Managers are interested in perception as a possible influence on work be-havior—their own and that of superiors and subordinates. Per-ceptual processes are always operating in every work situation. However, there are forces in work situations that encourage per-ceptual *similarities.* For example, work groups share common experiences, norms, expectations, and goals that contribute to perceptual similarity.

Two basic aspects

Nevertheless, the role of perceptual differences can be an im-portant influence on job performance. For example, the extent to

---

[3] Hadley Cantril, "Perceptions and Interpersonal Relations," *American Journal of Psychiatry,* vol. 114, no. 2, pp. 119–26. Copyright 1957 the American Psychiatric Association. By permission.

[4] Edward C. Carterette and Morton P. Friedman, eds., *Handbook of Per-ception,* vol. 1 (New York: Academic Press, 1974), p. xiii.

[5] A. R. Luria, *Cognitive Development: Its Cultural and Social Foundations* (Cambridge, Mass.: Harvard University Press, 1976), p. 21.

which employees are satisfied with their work is partially determined by perceptual processes. The effectiveness of various rewards
(money, promotion, and so on) associated with job performance
is influenced by the employee's perceived need for those rewards.
The degree to which the employee sees rewards as associated with
performance is a matter of perception. Employees' perceptions of
where they stand in an organization as compared to others are important influences on job satisfaction and behavior. Clearly, an
understanding of perception can be important to managers. We will
discuss two basic aspects of the perceptual process: perceptual
selectivity and perceptual organization.

Cognitive map   **Perceptual Selectivity.**   Each person has a personalized image
of the world, a "cognitive map." This image is not a camera picture
of the "real" world. It is, rather, a construct influenced by such
things as personal experience, attitudes, beliefs, knowledge, physical and social environment, and personal characteristics. The cognitive maps of all people are similar in some respects and unique
in others. They are learned, perceptual "models"—abstractions of
reality—that help people understand and get along in the world.

Selectivity is   In constructing our cognitive map, a process of perceptual se-
forced on us   lectivity occurs. Perceptual selectivity is a process of letting into our
cognitive map some perceptions and keeping out others. Selectivity
is forced on us by our limited *span of attention* and our limited
span of immediate memory. The world does not come at us one
stimulus at a time. Further, we are often bombarded by stimuli of
varying degrees of clarity.

Stimulus   Which things will be selected for inclusion in our cognitive maps
factors: depend on stimulus and personal factors. "Stimulus factors" include
contrast,   contrast, frequency, change, movement, and intensity. One in-
frequency   formally dressed executive stands out in a shirt-and-tie group. One
high producer in an otherwise mediocre work group will be no-
ticed. In these cases it is the contrast that draws attention to the
executive and the high producer. Further, a communication that
is repeated frequently is more likely to be noticed by managers and
employees than the communication made only once. The frequency
of the communication is what attracts our attention to it.

Stimulus   The physical arrangement of office facilities is more likely to
factors: enter our consciousness if the arrangement represents a change
change, move-   from a previous layout. A flashing light or moving signal on a
ment, and   machine stands out. A supervisor shouting instructions may get
intensity   more attention than usual (although the increased intensity of the
supervisor's voice may yield poorer results). Stimulus factors can
have an influence on work performance through the role they play
in perceptual selectivity. They help determine what will be "seen"
and will become a part of the perceiver's cognitive map.

Personal factors: selective sensitization

Personal factors also determine what will be included in our cognitive map. "Personal factors" are those influencing perception that are in the perceiving individual. Perception is clearly a transactional process between stimuli and the perceiver. Two personal factors already mentioned are span of attention and span of immediate memory. Others include selective sensitization, selective distortion, and perceptual defense. "Selective sensitization" refers to our state of readiness to perceive objects or events in a certain way. A manager, for example, may see a work group in terms of abilities and motivations that contribute to productivity. Members of the work group may see the same abilities and motivations in terms of contribution to job satisfaction and social needs. The abilities and motivations have different meanings to the manager and the employees.

Personal factors: selective distortion

"Selective distortion" refers to the process by which a perception, although congruent with the individual's emotions and motives, represents a distortion from a more objective interpretation of the object or event. For example, in the presence of a rumor of layoffs employees may perceive almost any event as support for the rumor. An executive who feels "passed by" for promotion perceives the most minor event as confirmation. In each of these cases, the perception is congruent to the perceiver (that is, the perception is consistent with the perceiver's motivational state), but is a distorted interpretation of events.

Personal factors: perceptual defense

"Perceptual defense" refers to the tendency to resist information or facts that would cause us to change our perceptions. We, in fact, create constancies, so that we do not have to always make guesses about people and their behavior. These constancies, if they are accurate, help us to behave more effectively. We want to pigeonhole people and events in order to enhance our capacity to cope with them. In order to protect these constancies in our perceptions we are capable of denying conflicting facts, reinterpreting the facts to be consistent with our perception, recognizing but ignoring the facts, and suppressing or magnifying information.

Do we see only what we want to see?

It is common to say that people perceive what they want to perceive and block out everything else. People do perceive on the basis of their own personalized history and motivations and do block out certain objects and events that threaten their present cognitive maps. On the other hand, that view can be carried too far. To some extent, we may perceive what is significant for us for purposes of personal growth and development. The perception may be uncomfortable, distasteful, and in conflict with our cognitive map. Nevertheless, we accept the perception because we recognize it as accurate:

> We do not agree with those who hold that people selectively distort their cognitive functioning so that they will see, remember and think only what they want to. Instead we hold to the view

that people will do so only to the extent that they have to and no more. For we are all motivated by the desire which is sometimes strong and sometimes weak, to see reality as it actually is, even if it hurts.[6]

Cognitive system

Perceptual Organization. A second basic aspect of the perceptual process is "perceptual organization," or categorization.[7] This second aspect is concerned with the way we pick up information "out there" and categorize or "place" it in our own cognitive systems. A "cognitive system" is an interrelated set of perceptions and cognitions about objects, people, or events. When we cannot categorize information into one of our cognitive systems, we basically do not know what to do with it.

Categories

Most of the categories into which we place perceptions are learned. The manager uses such categories as "productive," "ambitious," "loyal," "creative," "leader," "competitor," and "teamwork." When managers perceive behavior, they can categorize it into one or more of these sample categories. Certain categories can be interrelated, becoming a category or cognitive "system." Thus, "leader," "ambitious," and "creative" can be part of one cognitive system.

Perceptual tendencies

There are several perceptual tendencies that can influence the way in which we organize our perceptions and categorize them into cognitive systems. The perceptual tendencies we will discuss include category accessibiiity, frame of reference, adaptation level, stereotyping, halo effect, implicit personality, first impressions, and projection.

Category accessibility

Some categories are more accessible at a given moment than others. "Category accessibility" reflects two sets of factors: need and interest state, and the need to avoid disruptive mistakes. For example, when we are unemployed and looking for a job we are much more alert to the "want ads" section of the newspaper, because we associate want ads with finding a job. Further, we expect to find these want ads in the classified section of the newspaper and not in the sports section.

Frame of reference

The vantage point, or "frame of reference" from which you view objects, events and people partially determines how you will categorize it. When a company profit figure is cited, unions may categorize it as "high," investors may categorize it as "competitive," and top management may put it in the "we're progressing toward our goals" category. As suggested by the incident described at the opening of this chapter, the perception of a particular event is

---

[6] Milton Rokeach, *The Open and Closed Mind* (New York: Basic Books, 1960), p. 400.

[7] Jerome S. Bruner, *Beyond the Information Given* (New York: W. W. Norton & Company, 1973), p. 7.

dependent upon the context in which the event takes place and on the vantage point, or frame of reference, of the perceiver.

Adaptation level: women's liberation

"Adaptation level" refers to "the point, as it were, on the range or continuum of opinion which is the neutral point for the individual."[8] For example, suppose that all opinions about women's liberation could be arranged on a continuum from extremely pro-"women's lib" (point 1) to extremely anti-"women's lib" (point 7). Shades of opinions between the two extremes are represented by the numbers 2 through 6. This continuum of opinion is illustrated in Figure 7–1. A person may perceive him or herself as in the

FIGURE 7–1
Continuum of Opinions toward Women's Liberation

(1)	(2)	(3)	(4)	(5)	(6)	(7)
Extremely	Quite	Slightly	Neutral	Slightly	Quite	Extremely
Pro-women's liberation				Anti-women's liberation		

middle of the continuum (point 4). However, he or she actually may hold opinions consistent with a slightly anti-women's liberation bias (point 5). The person's adaptation level is at point 5. Other views toward women's liberation will be classed by the person as on one or the other side of point 5.

Adaptation level: collective bargaining

Another example of adaptation level is in the area of collective bargaining. Historically, organized labor and management lined up somewhere on a continuum of pro or anti-collective bargaining. Initially, management was extremely anti-collective bargaining. Almost any statement supporting the idea of collective bargaining was seen as bad. Over the years, the adaptation level of management has moved somewhat more toward the center. If compulsory arbitration were introduced as an alternative to collective bargaining, it is likely that management's adaptation level to collective bargaining would shift dramatically toward the center and perhaps toward the pro-collective bargaining position.

Stereotyping

"Stereotyping" involves the act of judging an individual according to a predetermined formula arrived at without even considering the personal characteristics of the individual being judged. Some common stereotypes include "hard-core unemployed," "blue-collar worker," "Theory X manager," and "bureaucrat." Stereotyping is one way of avoiding perceptual and cognitive effort; however, it often results, not only in loss of information (the simplifying of a complex of personal characteristics into the simple category of "blue-collar worker," for example), but also possibly in misinforma-

---

[8] David J. Lawless, *Effective Management: Social Psychological Approach* (Englewood Cliffs, N.J.: Prentice-Hall, 1972), p. 38.

tion (we tend to see the blue-collar worker represented by our personally created category).

Stereotyping: costs and benefits

It is possible that stereotypes have some basis in fact, and that they do serve a sometimes necessary function in economizing the perceptual process. From a managing viewpoint, the question is, Does the potential loss of information and addition of misinformation due to stereotyping have an effect on work performance? In concrete situations, the question is one of balancing the benefits of stereotyping against such costs as loss of information, misinformation, inaccurate perception, unfairness, and possibly ineffective behavior based on a stereotype.

Halo effect

"Halo effect" is the tendency to generalize from an impression of one characteristic or dimension to all dimensions or to a general impression. Halo effect can work both for and against a person. For example, if we have specific cause to distrust a man, we might conclude he is also lazy, irresponsible, and dumb. Or, if we have a specific reason to like a woman, we may attach several other favorable characteristics to her.

Implicit personality

"Implicit personality" is the idea that how an individual perceives another is influenced by the individual's theory of personality and the interrelation of traits. Some people perceive others as honest and trusting, and others perceive the same people as suspect. Some employees have a theory of supervisory personality that influences their perception of particular supervisors. Similarly, some managers view all other managers in terms of competition, power, and distrust. Some people associate a friendly disposition with honesty, trustworthiness, and high moral character.

First impressions

"First impressions" about a person may be formed on the basis of an inadequate behavioral sample (inadequate not only in terms of quantity but also in terms of relevance to the traits about which impressions are formed) and on the basis of surroundings rather than on the person (our first impression of a person may be different if we see the person in an executive office rather than at home). Nevertheless, first impressions *will* be formed. They are not always inaccurate, and they serve the useful function of helping to categorize new information and make maximal use of sparse incoming data. Of course, their usefulness, in the final analysis, depends on their accuracy. "Too often in forming impressions the perceiver does not know what is relevant, important, or predictive of later behavior."[9]

Projection

"Projection" means that we ascribe our own characteristics to other people and use ourselves as the norm for judging others.

---

[9] Sheldon S. Zalkind and Timothy W. Costello, "Perception: Some Recent Research and Implications for Administration," in W. E. Scott, Jr. and L. L. Cummings, *Readings in Organizational Behavior and Human Performance*, rev. ed. (Homewood, Ill.: Richard D. Irwin, 1973), p. 84.

There is some evidence that our own characteristics influence what we are likely to see in others. The better we know ourselves, the more accurately we may perceive others. Accuracy in perceiving others is not a single skill (you might be accurate sometimes and inaccurate other times), and it is not necessarily one that can be learned through training. A good question for the manager to consider in viewing another person is, "Am I looking at him, and forming my impression of his behavior in the situation, or am I just comparing him with myself?"[10]

Summary box

> *Perception* is the process by which individuals attach meaning to their experiencing of objects, people, and events.
>
> In any work environment there will be both perceptual *similarities* and *differences*. Not all of these differences will significantly influence job performance. The idea was suggested of a *perception tolerance zone* within which perceptions can vary without significantly affecting performance.
>
> *Two basic aspects* of the perceptual process are perceptual selectivity and perceptual organization. *Perceptual selectivity* is the process of letting some perceptions into our *cognitive map* and keeping out others. Perceptual selectivity depends on two types of factors: stimulus and personal.
>
> *Stimulus factors* include contrast, frequency, change, movement, and intensity. *Personal factors* include span of attention, span of immediate memory, selective sensitization, selective distortion, and perceptual defense.
>
> *Perceptual organization* is a process concerned with the way we gather information and categorize it into our cognitive systems. The process is influenced by several *perceptual tendencies* including: category accessibility, frame of reference, adaptation level, stereotyping, halo effect, implicit personality, first impressions, and projection.

ATTITUDES

An internal state

What Is an Attitude?   An attitude is an internal state of a person that is focused on objects, events, or people that exist in the person's psychological world.

Opinions, written responses

By referring to an attitude as an "internal state," we mean that an attitude always remains inside a person. A person may express an opinion about an object, but that opinion is only a verbal ex-

---

[10] Ibid., p. 88.

pression of an attitude toward the object. Opinions are supposed to reflect attitudes, but they do not always do so accurately. Further, a person may respond in writing on a questionnaire designed to "measure" attitudes, but these responses are, at best, indirect approximations of attitudes. The point to remember is that attitudes remain inside a person.

Focused on objects

Attitudes are focused on objects which have existence in the psychological world of the attitude holder. Everyone's psychological world is limited, and thus everyone has a limited number of attitudes. For example, supervisors may not have attitudes about certain objects in the psychological world of their superior because the objects do not exist for the supervisor. Clearly, if managers want to attempt attitude measurement, a first step is to determine if the attitudes exist. We only have attitudes about persons, objects, or events that exist in our own psychological world.

Affective component

Attitude Components. An attitude is often viewed as having three components: affective, cognitive, and conative. The "affective" or feeling component refers to the emotions associated with an attitude object. An object is felt to be good or bad, pleasing or displeasing, favorable or unfavorable. It is this affective feature or component that is most commonly associated with the idea of attitude.

Cognitive component

The "cognitive" or belief component represents the beliefs of a person about an attitude object. You may believe that managers are intelligent or stupid, ethical or unethical, and good or bad. These beliefs may be based on a variety of learning experiences, rumors, misunderstandings, and other information. It is useful to note that it is possible for beliefs and feelings to be incongruent. For example, you may have a positive feeling toward a person but still believe that the person has negative characteristics.

Conative component

The "conative" component of attitudes is the behavioral component. In 1935, after reviewing more than 100 different definitions of attitudes, one researcher concluded that there was widespread agreement that an attitude is a "learned predisposition to respond to an object or a class of objects in a consistently favorable or unfavorable way."[11] Not all attitude theorists would agree with that statement today, but many still consider the predisposition to respond or act as a component of attitudes. The assumption is that if you have negative feelings or beliefs toward an object, you will be likely to behave negatively toward the object.

Two views

So far we have suggested a "three-component" view of an attitude. This view is shown in Figure 7–2. There is another way of

---

[11] Researcher referred to is Gordon Allport. See Martin Fishbein, "Attitude and the Prediction of Behavior," in Martin Fishbein, ed., *Readings in Attitude Theory and Measurement* (New York: John Wiley & Sons, 1967), p. 477.

—FIGURE 7–2

Two Views of the Relationship between Attitudes, Feelings, Beliefs, and Behavioral Intentions

A. Three-component view

B. Single-component view

(attitude)

Beliefs ⟷ Feelings ⟶ Behavioral intentions

(attitude)

thinking about the way these three components are related to each other.[12] This alternative view is also shown in Figure 7–2. The logic of the "single-component" view—the view that attitude refers only to feeling—is based on two points. *First,* most actual attempts to measure attitudes usually measure only the affective component. *Second,* there is considerable evidence that a person's feeling toward an attitude object is determined by beliefs.[13] Feelings also can influence beliefs. The dual relationship between beliefs and attitudes is represented by the two-directional arrow in Figure 7–2.

Knowing, feeling, and acting

One prominent attitude theorist makes the interesting observation that the three components of attitude correspond to various stances that may be taken with respect to the human condition: "Philosophers at diverse times and places have arrived at the same conclusion, that there are basically three existential stances that man can take with respect to the human condition: knowing, feeling, and acting."[14]

A systems view

It is useful to view the three attitude components as a "system" in order to emphasize their interrelatedness. That is, one component affects the other; a change in one component may bring a change in one of the others. For example, suppose that we acquire more favorable feelings toward labor unions. These feelings can make us more receptive to factual information about unions, and, as a result, we may change some of our beliefs about unions. These

[12] Martin Fishbein and Icek Ajzen, *Belief, Attitude, and Behavior: An Introduction to Theory and Research* (Reading, Mass.: Addison-Wesley Publishing Company, 1975), pp. 5–18.

[13] Fishbein, "Attitude and the Prediction of Behavior," pp. 478–79.

[14] Reprinted by special permission of William J. McGuire, "The Nature of Attitudes and Attitude Change," in *The Handbook of Social Psychology,* 2d ed. Gardner Lindzey and Elliot Aronson, eds. (Reading, Mass: Addison-Wesley, 1969), vol. 3, p. 155.

changed feelings and beliefs may cause us to change our behavioral intentions—and our actual behavior—toward unions.

Valence or magnitude

Attitude Characteristics. Attitudes can be characterized in terms of their valence, multiplexity, relation to needs, and centrality. The "valence," or "magnitude" of an attitude refers to the degree of favorableness or unfavorableness toward the attitude object. Most attempts to measure attitudes are concerned with valence. If you are relatively indifferent to an attitude object then your attitude has low valence; if you are extremely favorable or unfavorable toward an attitude object, then your attitude has high valence.

Multiplexity, relation to needs

The "multiplexity" characteristic refers to the number of elements making up the attitude. For example, one employee may feel simply loyal to a company, but another may feel loyal, respectful, fearful, and dependent. Attitudes can vary according to their "relation to needs." For example, attitudes of a person toward work may serve strong needs for security, self-esteem, achievement, and self-fulfillment. On the other hand, attitudes of a person toward the movies may serve only social or entertainment needs. One reason that attitudes toward work may be so resistant to change is that they serve such varied human needs.

Centrality or salience

The "centrality," or "salience," attitude characteristic refers to the importance of the attitude object to the person. Presumably, attitudes which have high centrality for a person will be more resistant to change.

Determinant attitudes

Somewhat related to, but not identical with, the centrality characteristic of attitudes is the idea of attitude determinance. "Determinance" refers to the extent to which attitudes are decisive in influencing behavior or intentions. A "determinant attitude" is one that is closely related to behavior or to intentions.[15]

Determinant attitude example

The idea of determinant attitudes can be related to job behavior. Employees have two types of attitudes toward their jobs. *First,* they have an *overall* attitude—they like it or they don't like it. This overall attitude is one factor that influences job behavior. *Second,* employees have attitudes toward *each of the job's components.* Common job components that are attitude objects include: the work itself, pay, people involved, prospects for promotion and self-development, type of supervision, and working conditions. Suppose that employees attach importance to these six job components in the order listed above—the work itself is most important and working conditions least important. The idea of determinant attitudes suggests that when no variations between jobs are perceived on the job components rated as *most* important by employees

---

[15] The idea of determinant attitudes is discussed further in James H. Myers and Mark I. Alpert, "Determinant Buying Attitudes: Meaning and Measurement," *Journal of Marketing,* vol. 32 (October 1968), pp. 13–20.

(the work itself, pay, people involved) then attitudes toward job components rated *lower* (type of supervision, working conditions) can become determinant in influencing job behavior.

Factors affecting role of groups

Role of Groups in Forming Attitudes. Attitudes relevant to job performance are determined, in part, by the group affiliations of employees and managers. Attitudes are learned in a social context. How groups affect the attitudes of an individual depends on such things as distance of the group from the individual, the importance attached to the group, the role of the group in satisfying the individual's needs, and the pressures exerted on the individual by the group.

Primary group, work group

"Primary groups," such as the family, can play a very important part in the formation of attitudes about work, success, management, and unions. The family may be the most influential of all forces shaping attitudes. The immediate work group can influence attitudes toward the company and overall work performance. The immediate work group satisfies many needs for the employee. New employees may adopt, as their own, attitudes of the work group in order to gain acceptance by the group. Group pressures to accept the attitudes and norms of the groups contribute to attitude formation. In addition, some of our group affiliations can be explained in terms of the function the group serves in supporting attitudes we already hold.

Culture group

The fact that individuals are part of the same "culture group" means that many beliefs will be held in common and much common information is shared. For example, "Protestant ethic" beliefs about work are rather common among Americans, but not among Indians. Such beliefs are, of course, not shared by all Americans. Nor are they likely to be understood in exactly the same way by many Americans.

Reference group

Another important group for attitude formation among professionals is the "reference group." A reference group for accountants might be the American Institute of Certified Public Accountants. The attitudes and norms of this professional society may be more influential than the immediate work group in forming attitudes. Reference groups and other types of groups are more or less important for job attitudes, depending on the extent to which the individual identifies with the group.

Learning

The Process of Forming Attitudes. The process of forming attitudes is a learning process. Attitudes are learned, and their formation is subject to basic principles of learning. "Learning" refers to "changes in response tendencies due to the effects of experience."[16] Some response tendencies are not commonly considered as learned,

[16] James F. Engel, David T. Kollat, and Roger D. Blackwell, *Consumer Behavior*, 2d ed. (New York: Holt, Rinehart and Winston, 1973).

for example, instinctive behavior, maturational changes, and changes caused by temporary conditions of the individual, such as fatigue, sickness, or hunger.

Drive

The basic learning process can be thought of in terms of four concepts: drive, cue stimuli, response, and reinforcement. "Drive" is a convenient way of referring to a state of tension or disequilibrium in an individual that impels the individual to action. Drive is a condition within the individual that influences the probability that the individual will make a response to a cue stimulus. If you are hungry, you are more likely to make a behavioral response to food.

Cue stimuli

"Cue stimuli" are objects, people, or events in the individual's environment and that are perceived by the individual. Any object about which an individual could have an attitude could be, for that individual, an "attitude cue stimulus."

Response

"Response" refers to the individual's reaction to cue stimuli. The formation of an attitude is one type of response. Every new cue stimulus does not evoke from an individual a new response. We tend to see the similarities in stimuli, and, to that extent, we respond to them as we have responded before. This process of making the *same* learned response to similar cue stimuli is called "generalization." The process of making a *different* learned response to similar cue stimuli is called "discrimination."

*Reinforce-
ment*

"Reinforcement" is a consequence that serves to increase the probability of a response being repeated when the individual is confronted with the same cue stimulus. For example, a newly formed attitude can be thought of as being reinforced if, on giving a verbal expression of the attitude, an individual is complimented by members of an important reference group. Although reinforcement is not necessary for learning to occur, it does affect the retention of a behavioral response and the rate of learning of responses. We discuss reinforcement at greater length in the next chapter.

*Measurement
is imperfect*

Measuring Attitudes. It is logical to seek measures of attitudes in order to give more precision to understanding them. Thus, various tests and scales have been developed to measure attitudes. Such scales are beyond the scope of this book.[17] The entire complexity of an attitude cannot be wholly described, for example, by the number 6 on a 7-point scale. Clearly, something is lost in the attempt to express an internal state in the form of a number. Nevertheless, this is a problem in all psychological measurement. Furthermore, any measurement is inexact to some extent; the measurement does not wholly describe the object measured.

------

[17] For an extended discussion of attitude measurement, see William A. Scott, "Attitude Measurement," in Lindzey and Aronson, eds., *The Handbook of Social Psychology,* chap. 5, pp. 204–73.

Attitude
surveys

However, attitudes *can* be measured and they *are* measured in industry. The most common approach to attitude measurement in industry is the employee attitude survey. Such surveys usually utilize questionnaires on which the employees are asked to indicate attitudes toward a variety of job-related objects. The results of such questionnaires are usually averaged to obtain an aggregate measure of a group departmental attitude. These surveys, if handled in a professional manner, can yield useful information for managers and employees.[18]

Consistency

Changing Attitudes. Why would you change your attitude toward an object, event, or person? One approach to answering that question is known as "consistency theory." The basic idea of most consistency theories is that you adjust your attitudes so as to maintain harmony *among* attitudes and *between* attitudes and behavior. We will confine our discussion of consistency theory to one particular theory known as "cognitive dissonance theory."[19]

Cognitive
dissonance

A central assumption of cognitive dissonance theory is that there are definite limits to the amount of psychological inconsistency human beings can tolerate. In line with other consistency theories, cognitive dissonance theory contends that a person will attempt to establish internal harmony or consistency among opinions, attitudes, knowledge, and values. The main ideas that enter into the theory are dissonance, cognitive overlap, pressure to reduce dissonance, and dissonance reduction. We will illustrate these four ideas by means of an example.

Dissonance

Whenever you make a decision between two or more alternatives you may experience "dissonance." In other words, if you chose A you may think or feel that you *over*emphasized the advantages of A and the disadvantages of B and that you *under*emphasized the disadvantages of A and the advantages of B. How much dissonance you will experience depends on several factors, including how important the decision is to you, how attractive the unchosen alternative was compared to the chosen alternative, and the extent to which the alternatives are similar in their cognitive elements. This last factor is called "cognitive overlap."

Cognitive
overlap

Cognitive overlap can be illustrated as follows: Suppose that you are a salesperson and are offered the free choice[20] of accepting

[18] Charles W. Eisenmann and Charles L. Hughes, "Have Your People Talked Lately—Candidly?" *Personnel Administrator,* vol. 20, no. 6 (October 1975), pp. 13–16+.

[19] Robert A. Wicklund and Jack W. Brehm, *Perspectives on Cognitive Dissonance* (Hillsdale, N.J.: Lawrence Erlbaum Associates, Publishers, 1976).

[20] Postdecision dissonance is allegedly greater under conditions of free choice. That is, you are more likely to experience dissonance after a decision if you were free to make or not to make it. However, the evidence for this role of free choice is somewhat ambiguous. See David O. Seas and Ronald P. Abeles, "Attitudes and Opinions," *Annual Review of Psychology,* vol. 20 (1969), p. 267.

another sales position or accepting a sales-manager position. You are likely to have knowledge, opinions, and beliefs (cognitive elements) more similar to the sales position than to the sales-manager position; the two sales positions presumably share more comparable features. If you choose the sales-manager position, there is a greater potential for dissonance because of the dissimilarity between the sales position and the sales-manager position. Or, in the jargon of cognitive dissonance theory, there is a "low cognitive overlap" between the two positions.

Dissonance reduction

When you experience dissonance you will want to take action to reduce the dissonance. You can reduce postdecision dissonance, and your superior can help you reduce postdecision dissonance in three ways: by minimizing the importance of the decision to yourself; by increasing the attractiveness of the alternative you chose, thus decreasing the attractiveness of the unchosen alternative; and by perceiving greater cognitive overlap in the alternatives. For example, if you choose to remain a salesperson, you could tell yourself that the career choice is not really a significant one; emphasize the advantages of remaining in sales and the disadvantages of becoming a manager; and weigh more heavily those aspects of the two jobs that are similar.

Pressure to reduce dissonance

The above points can be illustrated as in Figure 7–3. Almost any decision between meaningful alternatives will result in dissonance. The pressure to reduce dissonance depends on how much dissonance the decision maker experiences. The general tendency is for the decision maker to try to reduce dissonance through one of the three dissonance reduction approaches. In other words, the decision maker is trying to justify the decision by reducing perceived dissonance. This, in turn, will help establish internal consistency among attitudes toward the decision.

FIGURE 7–3
Sequence of Events in Postdecision Dissonance Reduction

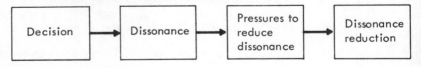

Unclear relationship

Attitudes and Behavior.   The relationship between attitudes and behavior is unclear. In general, research attempts to establish the nature, if any, of this relationship have not been successful.[21] What

---

[21] A. H. Brayfield and W. H. Crockett, "Employee Attitudes and Employee Performance," *Psychological Bulletin*, vol. 52, no. 5 (1955), pp. 396–424. See also Martin Fishbein, ed., *Readings in Attitude Theory and Measurement* (New York: John Wiley & Sons, 1967), p. 477, and A. W. Wicker, "Attitudes versus Actions: The Relationship of Verbal and Overt Behavioral Responses to Attitude Objects," *Journal of Social Issues*, vol. 25, no. 4 (1969), p. 65.

are we to make of this observation? If we interpret it literally, we pretty well undermine the justification for managers studying attitudes. For if we cannot relate an employee's job attitudes to performance, then managers had better spend their time studying other variables that can be related to performance. Managers, as managers, are *accountable for performance*. However, before giving up their study of the role of attitudes on job performance behavior, managers might consider the following two points:

Complexity of job performance

First, as we noted in Chapter 6, job performance is the result of several factors. It is difficult to measure precisely the role of any one of these factors in determining job performance. Clearly, however, a person's job attitudes cannot be viewed as the only determinant of the person's job performance. Rather than concluding that there is no relationship between job attitudes and job performance, it is preferable to conclude that the relationship has not yet been determined, that behavior and attitudes are difficult to measure, and that the relationship is complex because of the interaction of many other variables.

Need to get specific

Second, attempts to relate employee attitudes and performance must make every effort to link a specific attitude with specific behavior or intention. Most studies of the relationship between attitudes and behavior have measured *general* attitudes.[22] For example, we cannot expect to get good predictions of employee behavior simply from knowing the employees' general feelings toward work. Actual job behavior occurs in a *particular* context of job requirements, expectations, and environmental rewards and punishments. In order for knowledge of attitudes to be useful to managers in understanding and predicting employee behavior, the knowledge must be about specific behavior in a specific situation.[23]

---

[22] Herbert C. Kelman, "Attitudes Are Alive and Well and Gainfully Employed in the Sphere of Action," *American Psychologist,* vol. 29, no. 5 (May 1974), p. 313.

[23] Martin Fishbein, "The Search for Attitudinal-Behavioral Consistency," in Joel B. Cohen, *Behavioral Science Foundations of Consumer Behavior* (Glencoe, Ill.: The Free Press, 1972).

Summary box

An *attitude* is an internal state of a person that is focused on objects, events or people that exist in the person's psychological world.

The *three-component view* of attitude is that an attitude is a system containing an affective, a cognitive, and a conative component. The *single-component view* is that an attitude is a person's affect or feeling toward an attitude object.

Attitude *characteristics* include valence, multiplexity, relation to needs, and centrality or salience. A *determinant* attitude is one that is closely related to behavior regardless of its centrality.

Groups play an important role in attitude formation. Specific types noted were primary, immediate work, culture, and reference groups. The *process of forming attitudes* is essentially a learning process. The basic learning process can be thought of in terms of *four concepts:* drive, cue stimuli, response, and reinforcement. Responses to cue stimuli can be described by the processes of *generalization* and *discrimination.*

In discussing *attitude change,* we focused on *consistency theory* in general, and *cognitive dissonance theory* in particular. This latter theory was discussed in terms of four main ideas: dissonance, cognitive overlap, pressure to reduce dissonance, and dissonance reduction.

Managers should avoid the casual assumption that there is a direct and consistent link between employee job attitudes and performance. There is very little research to support the assumption. However, managers should not abandon their interest in attitudes. Attitudes need to be seen as one of the many variables influencing performance. In addition, efforts need to be made to relate specific job attitudes to specific performance.

VALUES

Values and norms defined

What Are Values? "Values" provide a general "guidance system" for a person's behavior. They are different than attitudes in that they transcend specific objects, events, or people.[24] Values may be defined as beliefs about what is "good" (freedom, justice, charity) and what is "bad" (war, poverty, disease).[25] Sometimes values and

[24] Martha A. Brown, "Values: A Necessary but Neglected Ingredient of Motivation on the Job," *Academy of Management Review,* vol. 1, no. 4 (October 1976), p. 16.

[25] David Krech, Richard S. Crutchfield, and Egerton L. Ballachey, *Individual in Society: A Textbook of Social Psychology* (New York: McGraw-Hill Book Company, 1962), p. 102.

norms are contrasted. "Norms" refer to specific expectations about how people are supposed to behave in particular situations. In a work group, there may be a norm that all members of the group are expected to contribute their fair share to getting the group's work accomplished. This group norm may be supported by a value —justice, for example—shared by the group members. Values are general ideas about good and bad that support norms.

*Values
diversity;
value gap*

Values Are Changing.   A common observation made about values today is that they are changing. There appears to be a "values diversity" and a contemporary acceptance of the right of individuals to believe and act in accordance with these diverse values. Since the rate and direction of value change differs among people, there is often a "value gap" that characterizes employees in any work environment.[26] For example, the work values of 1,058 (nonindustrial) workers were studied in order to investigate differences in values related to age and education.[27] The findings in the study were that younger workers place a higher value on self-expression and the opportunity to develop their abilities than older workers. Age, however, did not differentiate between workers on the value of pride in work. Educational level was related to the value of trust in economic system, the less educated workers expressing less trust.

*Business administration
students*

On the basis of a study of the occupational values of business administration students, one author concludes:

> . . . contemporary students are no longer interested in conventional careers, working their way through an administrative hierarchy of an organization, especially a bureaucratic organization. They reject authoritarian supervision and instead have a strong preference for a consultative-participative relationship with their supervisor. They reject narrow, closely defined jobs and prefer work situations which allow a strong sense of independence, individual responsibility, achievement, and recognition. Finally, they prefer to work with co-workers with skill and competence equal to theirs in a co-operative team relationship or as a group of colleagues rather than in an interpersonal competitive relationship.[28]

*Careful of
generalizations*

A word of caution is in order about the above quotation. Because of the great diversity of values reflected in American society, it is always a good idea to be skeptical of generalizations about the values of "youth," "students," "managers," "middle America" and any other classification of people. For example, there are very few meaningful generalizations that can be made about the values of

[26] Douglas T. Hall, "Potential for Career Growth," *Personnel Administration,* vol. 34, no. 3 (May–June 1971), pp. 18–30.

[27] Ronald N. Taylor and Mark Thompson, "Work Value Systems of Young Workers," *Academy of Management Review,* vol. 19, no. 4 (December 1976), pp. 522–36.

[28] D. A. Ondrack, "Emerging Occupational Values: A Review and Some Findings," *Academy of Management Journal,* vol. 16, no. 3 (September 1973), p. 430.

managers. Managers do not represent a homogeneous group in terms of values held to be important.

Point for managers

The point of this discussion of changing values is to suggest that managers need to be aware of their own values and the values of those who have an influence on their accountability for performance. Furthermore, it is significant to managers, not only that values are changing, but that multiple, and sometimes conflicting, scales of values characterize work environments.

What is a personal value system

Personal Value Systems of Managers.   Personnel at the Industrial Relations Center at the University of Minnesota have assessed the personal values of thousands of managers from several countries. A "personal value system" may be defined as "a relatively permanent perceptual framework which shapes and influences the general nature of an individual's behavior."[29]

FIGURE 7–4
Framework for Categorizing PVQ Responses

Value Role	Importance to Individual		
	High	Average	Low
Successful	My company Customers Ability	Power Risk Labor unions	Force Prejudice
Right	Trust Loyalty Dignity	Social welfare Obedience Caution	Tolerance Compassion
Pleasant	Religion	Leisure Prestige Security	Conformity

PVQ

In assessing values, an instrument known as the Personal Values Questionnaire (PVQ) was used.[30] The PVQ asks the person to score 66 different concepts on four dimensions: "importance," "successful," "right," and "pleasant." The responses are then categorized by degree of importance assigned (high, average, low) and whether the respondents view the 66 values as aesthetically pleasant, ethically right, or as having a role in success. This approach to categorization is shown in Figure 7–4 along with some examples of the 66 values shown in the cells in which they frequently fall.[31]

[29] George W. England, *The Manager and His Values: An International Perspective from the United States, Japan, Korea, India, and Australia* (Cambridge, Mass.: Ballinger Publishing Company, 1975), p. 1.

[30] Ibid., pp. 131–139.

[31] Edward J. Lusk and Bruce L. Oliver, "American Managers' Personal Value Systems—Revisited," *Academy of Management Journal*, vol. 17, no. 3 (September 1974), pp. 549–54.

Results
of PVQ

The results of research using the PVQ suggests that the personal value systems of managers are relatively *stable* (they did not change much when a 1966 sample was compared to a 1972 sample) and are related to managerial *career success*. Specifically:

> Viewing the value-success relationships of American managers provides the following picture. Successful managers favor pragmatic, dynamic, achievement-oriented values' while less successful managers prefer more static and passive values, the latter forming a framework descriptive of organizational stasis rather than organizational and environmental flux. More successful managers favor an achievement orientation and prefer an active role in interaction with other individuals useful in achieving the managers' organizational goals. They value a dynamic environment and are willing to take risks to achieve organizationally valued goals. Relatively less successful managers have values associated with a static, protected environment in which they take relatively passive roles and often enjoy extended seniority in their organizational positions.[32]

Six basic
values

The Study of Values. In addition to the PVQ, another instrument that sometimes is used to obtain a measure of a person's values is the Allport-Vernon-Lindzey Study of Values.[33] "The Study of Values" attempts to measure the relative prominence in a person of six basic values: theoretical, economic, aesthetic, social, political, and religious. This six-way classification is based directly on Edward Spranger's *Types of Men*.[34] A brief description of the six values is given in Figure 7–5.[35]

Scores on
Study of
Values

A "score" on the Study of Values reveals the *relative* importance to a person of each of the six values; a high score on one value can be obtained only by reducing correspondingly the scores on one or more of the other values. The Study of Values is designed to yield a total score of 240 points distributed over the six value dimensions.

Application
of Study
of Values

The Study of Values has been used to measure the values of high-level U.S. executives, research managers, and industrial scientists. The value profiles of these three groups are shown in Figure 7–6. The value profiles represent averages and, therefore, hide individual differences within each of the three groups.

[32] George W. England, "Personal Value Systems of Managers—So What?" *Personnel Administrator,* vol. 20, no. 2 (April 1975), pp. 20–22.

[33] Gordon W. Allport, Philip E. Vernon, and Gardner Lindzey, *Study of Values,* 3d ed. (Boston: Houghton Mifflin Company, 1960).

[34] Edward Spranger, *Types of Men: The Psychology and Ethics of Personality* (New York: Johnson Reprint Corporation, 1928).

[35] Several investigators feel that the six values measured by the Study of Values are, in fact, only three or four distinct value factors. See Allan R. Buss and Wayne Poley, *Individual Differences: Traits and Factors* (New York: *Gardner Press,* 1976), p. 117.

FIGURE 7–5

A Brief Description of the Six Values in Edward Spranger's *Types of Men*

Theoretical. The dominant interest of the theoretical man is the discovery of truth. . . . Since the interests of the theoretical man are empirical, critical, and rational, he is necessarily an intellectualist, frequently a scientist or philosopher. His chief aim in life is to order and systemize his knowledge. . . .

Economic. The economic man is characteristically interested in what is useful. . . . This type is thoroughly "practical" and conforms well to the prevailing stereotype of the average American business-man. . . .

Aesthetic. The aesthetic man sees his highest value in form and harmony. Each single experience is judged from the standpoint of grace, symmetry, or fitness. He regards life as a procession of events, each single impression is enjoyed for its own sake. . . .

Social. The highest value for this type is love of people. . . . The social man prizes other persons as ends, and is therefore himself kind, sympathetic and unselfish. He is likely to find the theoretical, economic, and aesthetic values cold and inhuman.

Political. The political man is interested primarily in power. . . . Leaders in any field generally have high power value. . . . There are certain personalities in whom the desire for a direct expression of power is uppermost, who wish above all else for personal power, influence and renown.

Religious. The highest value of the religious man may be called unity. He is mystical, and seeks to comprehend the cosmos as a whole, to relate himself to its embracing totality. . . .

A person does not belong exclusively to one or the other of these types of values. That is, the six areas represent "ideal types"; no person is fully explained by any one type.

Source: Edward Spranger, *Types of Men. The Psychology and Ethics of Personality* (New York. Johnson Reprint Corporation, 1928)

FIGURE 7–6

Value Profiles of Samples of Executives, Research Man-agers and Industrial Scientists Based on Scores on the Study of Values

Value	653 Executives	178 Research Managers	157 Industrial Scientists
Theoretical...................	44	49	51
Economic.....................	45	44	41
Aesthetic....................	35	37	38
Social.......................	33	32	34
Political....................	44	42	41
Religious....................	39	36	35
	240	240	240

Source: William D. Guth and Renato Tagiuri, "Personal Values and Corporate Strategy," *Harvard Business Review*, vol. 43, no. 5 (September–October 1965).

The value
of values

Undoubtedly, we could all benefit in a variety of ways by having better knowledge of our value systems. More specifically, managers, who are professional decision makers, could benefit from a more explicit understanding of the role of personal values in decision making. Such an understanding would not only help the manager clarify decision making, but it may allow for an *increase* in the influence of values on decisions. The Study of Values is one way for managers to become more aware of their values.

What are
your values?

What are your values? What role are they playing in decisions you are now making? Can any of your present conflicts with others be made more understandable by conscious reflection on value profiles? How do you expect your values to coincide with the values of the organization in which you will work?[36]

Summary box

> *Values* are beliefs about what is good and what is bad. *Norms* are specific expectations of behavior in specific situations.
>
> Contemporary American society is characterized by *changing values* and acceptance of *values diversity*. The different rates and direction of value change among people gives rise to a *value gap* in work environments.
>
> A *personal value system* is a relatively permanent perceptual framework which shapes and influences the general nature of an individual's behavior. The *PVQ* has been used in research to measure the personal value systems of managers. An overall conclusion of this research is that personal value systems are relatively stable and related to career success.
>
> The Allport-Vernon-Lindzey *Study of Values* is another instrument for measuring values. It is based on a six-way classification of values: theoretical; economic; aesthetic; social; political; and religious values. Use of the Study of Values makes it possible to determine and compare value profiles of managers.

---

[36] For practical help in understanding the process of values formation and the techniques of value clarification, see Maury Smith, *A Practical Guide to Value Clarification* (La Jolla, Calif.: University Associates, 1977).

> So far in our discussion of behavior in organiza-
> tions, we have focused on four cognitive varia-
> bles: motives (Supplement 6A), and perceptions,
> attitudes, and values (Chapter 7).
> Supplement 7A deals with another type of cogni-
> tive variable—assumptions about people.
> Supplement 7B discusses a specific job-related
> attitude—job satisfaction.

CHECK YOUR UNDERSTANDING

Perception
Perception tolerance zone
Two basic aspects of the percep-
    tual process
Cognitive map
Limited span of attention
Limited span of immediate
    memory
Stimulus factors
Personal factors
Selective sensitization
Selective distortion
Perceptual defense
Cognitive system
Category accessibility
Frame of reference
Adaptation level
Stereotyping
Halo effect
Implicit personality
First impressions
Projection

Attitude versus opinion
Three-component view of attitude
Single-component view of attitude
Valence
Multiplexity
Centrality or salience
Determinant attitude
Reference group
Learning
Four-concept learning process
Generalization
Discrimination
Consistency theory
Cognitive dissonance theory
Cognitive overlap
Values
Norms
Value gap
Value diversity
Personal value system
PVQ
Study of Values

STUDY QUESTIONS

1. What does it mean to say that the view that "people see what they want to see" can be carried too far?

2. How can perceptual defense serve a useful function to a person?

3. Cite examples from your own experience that illustrate how, in your opinion, the "right" attitude made the difference between good and bad performance.

4. Cite examples from your own experience that illustrate the application of the idea of determinant attitudes.

5. Cite examples from your own experience that illustrate Leon Festinger's theory of cognitive dissonance.

6. How accurate do you feel. D. A. Ondrack is in his conclusions about the values of contemporary business administration students?

7. Can you identify an important value that you now have that repre-
    sents a change from a previous value? If so, what process brought
    about the value change?

8. How would you rate yourself on the six values shown in Figure
    7–5? Do these six values adequately reflect your values? Explain.

APPLICATION: EXECUTIVE DROPOUT*

In 1970, Tony Rousellot, a 36-year-old successful stockbroker in
New York City, quit his job, sold his co-operative apartment and
his country home, and headed west to the ski slopes of New Mexico.
Six years later, he is still in New Mexico and can't think of anything negative to say about it.

Last winter, Tony was outdoors every day of the ski season. He
and his wife designed their own home and formed a landscape
company. Tony is also involved in raising tropical plants and is
planning to go into it full-time.

For Tony, New York was "the salad days—when you wanted
something you bought it." Now there is less money—but less is
needed. "If I had to have eight suits in New York, out here I have to
have eight pairs of blue jeans. And blue jeans last longer than
suits."

Tony is one of a small but growing number of executive dropouts. Although executives are not dropping out in large numbers,
the trend, which began several years ago, is quietly continuing. A
spokesman for an executive search firm links the minor trend
to "the loosening up of career planning that stems from the youth
movements of the 1960s." One of the assumptions prodding dropouts is that success need not, or perhaps cannot, be defined in corporate or institutional terms.

According to one management educator, the yearning for a
completely different type of life on the other side of the rainbow
is common among executives. "Between [the ages of] 38 and 50,
men are most vulnerable to stopping and asking that tough question, 'What am I doing here?' It's like you've been slumbering for
20 years, and suddenly you see what you want to do, and see
you've been doing everything but what you want."

1. What, in your opinion, is the relationship between job satisfaction and life satisfaction?

2. How would you evaluate Mr. Rousellot's decision in terms of
value change?

* Source: "Dropouts Revisited," *Wall Street Journal*, Vol. 58, no. 125
(December 27, 1976), pp. 1, 2.

SUPPLEMENT 7A

Assumptions about People

Objectives of Supplement 7A

1. To outline several points of difference between two views of man: behaviorism and phenomenology.
2. To suggest four views of human nature and recognize their possible impact on managing.
3. To discuss and evaluate Douglas McGregor's Theory X and Theory Y.

In spite of everything, I still really believe that people are good.

Diary of Anne Frank

An actual incident

A very successful executive was having lunch one day with an author of several best sellers dealing with contemporary American society. The author was an extremely articulate critic and observer of American life since World War II.

The executive asked the author, "Would you explain to me your view of the nature of man?"

The author made a gesture indicating bewilderment and replied, "I never really thought about it."

The executive later said that the author's reply seemed equivalent to an aeronautical engineer saying that he had never thought about the nature of aircraft. The point is that the author's writings undoubtedly were influenced by some concept of the nature of man, *whether or not he ever thought about it.*

Central premise

The central premise of this supplement is that preconceived notions about the nature of people can influence a person's behavior. In particular, assumptions that managers make about themselves and other organization members can directly influence their behavior as managers.

This supplement

Our concern in this supplement is with two specific ideas. The first idea is that of the nature of man. We note two models of man and suggest four views of human nature. Our second idea is Douglas McGregor's Theory X and Theory Y. This idea has been very influential in getting managers to think about and discuss their assumptions about people at work.

THE NATURE OF MAN

Rationale

Two Models. The basic rationale for discussing the nature of man in a managing textbook is that the way a person manages may be influenced by the person's views about the nature of man. How can we deal with this broad subject? One approach is to view man in terms of two opposing "models": behaviorism and phenomenology. Figure 7A–1 identifies ten points on which these two models can be compared.

FIGURE 7A–1
Two Models of Man

Behaviorism	*Phenomenology*
Man can be described meaningfully in terms of his behavior.	Man can be described meaningfully in terms of his consciousness.
Man is predictable.	Man is unpredictable.
Man is an information transmitter.	Man is an information generator.
Man lives in an objective world.	Man lives in a subjective world.
Man is a rational being.	Man is an arational being.
One man is like other men.	Each man is unique.
Man can be described meaningfully in absolute terms.	Man can be described meaningfully in relative terms.
Human characteristics can be investigated independently of one another.	Man must be studied as a whole.
Man is a reality.	Man is a potentiality.
Man is knowable in scientific terms.	Man is more than we can ever know about him.

Source: William D. Hitt, "Two Models of Man," *American Psychologist*, vol. 24, no. 7 (July 1969).

Behaviorism

The behaviorism model is based on the *reinforcement* approach to understanding individual behavior that was mentioned in Chapter 6 and that will be discussed further in Chapter 8. The behaviorist places primary emphasis on the role of external determinants of behavior.

> The behaviorist views man as a passive organism governed by external stimuli. Man can be manipulated through proper control of these stimuli. Moreover, the laws that govern man are essentially the same as the laws that govern all natural phenomana; hence it is assumed that the scientific method used by the physical scientist is equally appropriate to the study of man.[1]

Phenomenology

The phenomenology model is consistent with the *cognitive* approach to understanding behavior. The phenomenologist tends to

---

[1] William D. Hitt, "Two Models of Man," *American Psychologist*, vol. 24, no. 7 (July 1969), p. 652.

place importance on the role of the person's awareness and consciousness.

> The phenomenologist . . . views man as the source of acts; he is free to choose in each situation. The essence of man is inside of man; he is controlled by his own consciousness. The most appropriate methodology for the study of man is phenomenology, which begins with the world of experience.[2]

Compatible views

The relative merits of these two models of man is a subject of a continuing debate that began during the mid-1950s.[3] We consider the two views compatible. They are incompatible only if interpreted in their extreme form. The extreme behaviorist position is that *all* behavior is determined by the consequences of behavior. The extreme phenomenologist position would almost have to deny the deterministic influence of environmental consequences. Such a denial would be untenable.[4]

No universal view

Four Views of Human Nature.   There is, of course, no universally accepted view of the essential characteristics of human nature. Our approach is to identify four different views.

Human nature is good

The *first* is that human nature is basically good. This view seems implicit in much of the social legislation of recent years. That is, if you provide people with the right kind of opportunities (medical, employment, education), they will respond in positive and constructive ways. Some views of management appear to reflect this view of human nature. For example, managers that use participative or democratic approaches to managing may be showing evidence of a basic faith in the "goodness" of people. That is, give employees the opportunity to involve themselves in the managerial process, and they will respond with constructive contributions. This view of human nature is consistent with phenomenology and with what we later describe as Theory Y.

Human nature is evil

The *second* view is that human nature is basically evil. This view seems implicit in some religions and in much everyday behavior. Many managers—effective managers—clearly behave as if people are basically evil (irresponsible, lazy, indifferent, untrustworthy, incapable of self-direction and self-control). As one executive who had served as president of several business firms said, "I notice that when I let things go they tend to fall apart." This second view of human nature is consistent with what we later describe as Theory X.

---

[2] Ibid.

[3] Carl R. Rogers and B. F. Skinner, "Some Issues Concerning the Control of Human Behavior: A Symposium," *Science*, vol. 124, no. 3,235 (November 1956), pp. 1,057–66.

[4] For discussions of several issues relevant to the controversy between behaviorism and phenomenology see Floyd W. Matson, ed., *Without/Within: Behaviorism and Humanism* (Monterey, Calif.: Brooks/Cole Publishing Company, 1973).

*Human
nature is
a blank
slate*

The *third* view is that human nature is neither good nor evil. Rather, it is whatever the existing human condition is. This is the "blank-slate" view. If such is the case, men *ought* to do whatever it is they *are* doing, there is no concept of what is normal, and notions of good and bad are geographically determined with each passing day. According to this view, "Any concept of human nature which implies something permanent, independent, and tending to revert to a norm is dismissed as a myth, since the so-called human nature could not be anything more than what the inevitable human condition at any moment has made it."[5]

*There is no
such thing as
human nature*

The *fourth* view is that there is no such thing as human nature. This view is consistent with the behaviorist position that "if you can't see it, it isn't there." Because behaviorists are interested only in what they can observe, they cannot use the concept of human nature. The idea of human nature does not play any role in the behaviorist model of man.

*Use for
managers*

For managers, the main point of these views of human nature is not that one is more right than the other. The main point is that, whatever your view of the nature of man, your managerial behavior may be influenced by it. "The quality of human relations in any organization, from the political state to the business enterprise, reflects first of all its members', and particularly its leaders', views of the essential character of humanity itself."[6]

*Success,
individual
dignity*

The Western Civilization View. The Western civilization image of the human race has tended to stress such things as success, materialism, belief in immortality, belief in the dignity of the individual, belief in rational processes, and belief in the superiority of the Western image of people and freedom.

*Stress on
natural
problems
and rational
solutions*

One author suggests that Western civilization has specialized in solving *natural* problems by means of rational solutions. China has specialized in the person's attempt to *get along with others;* and India has specialized in people's *inner conflicts.*[7] One problem with such specialization is that the other approaches are neglected. For example, Western cultures may not be as sensitive to personal and interpersonal concerns as many Eastern cultures.

*The public
philosophy*

As an illustration of the Western belief in the usefulness of rational processes, the influential notion of the "public philosophy" is a good source:

---

[5] Joseph Wood Krutch, *Human Nature and the Human Condition* (New York: Random House, 1959), p. 18.

[6] Henry P. Knowles and Borge O. Saxberg, "Keeping Informed," *Harvard Business Review,* vol. 45, no. 2 (March–April 1967), p. 178.

[7] Huston Smith, "Accents of the World's Philosophies," *Philosophy East and West,* vol. 7, no. 1 (April–July 1957), p. 7.

> The sovereign principle of the public philosophy: that we live in a rational order in which by sincere inquiry and rational debate we can distinguish the true and the false, the right and the wrong. There is no set of election laws or constitutional guarantees which are unchangeable. What is unchangeable is the commitment to rational determination.[8]

*Rational
from whose
viewpoint?*

This Western emphasis on rational processes is interesting from a management and organization viewpoint. The assumption of rational behavior of people at work has often hindered management's understanding of actual behavior in organizations. Managers and employees *do* behave in ways they *perceive* as rational from their own viewpoints. But the behavior may be quite irrational from other viewpoints, such as from the viewpoint of contributing to organizational performance goals.

Adaptive man

Behavioral Science Man. How does the image of man that emerges from the behavioral sciences compare with other images developed in the Western world over the ages? As the following quotation suggests, "behavioral-science man" is characterized by adaptive behavior; he is a seeker of both reality and deception.

> Perhaps the character of behavioral science man can best be grasped through his orientation to reality. He is a creature who adapts reality to his own ends, who transforms reality into a congenial form, who makes his own reality. And he does this in two ways. First, he is extremely good at adaptive behavior—at doing or learning to do things that increase his chances for survival or for satisfaction. . . . But there is another way in which man comes to terms with reality when it is inconsistent with his needs or preferences; and it is here that the behavioral-science model departs most noticeably from the others. In his quest for satisfaction, man is not just a seeker of truth, but of deceptions, of himself as well as others. . . . When man can come to grips with his needs by actually changing the environment, he does so. But when he cannot achieve such realistic satisfaction, he tends to take the other path: to modify what he sees to be the case, what he thinks he wants, and what he thinks others want. . . . In short, man lives not only with the reality that confronts him but with the reality he makes.[9]

THEORIES X AND Y

*The human
side of
enterprise*

Douglas McGregor. Without doubt, one of the most significant discussions of the nature of man as related to management is contained in Douglas McGregor's book *The Human Side of Enterprise*. The part of this classic book that ultimately became so popular

---

[8] Walter Lippman, *The Public Philosophy* (New York: New American Library of World Literature, 1956), p. 102.

[9] From *Human Behavior: An Inventory of Scientific Findings* by Bernard Berelson and Gary A. Steiner, © 1964, by Harcourt Brace Jovanovich, Inc., and reprinted with their permission, pp. 662–67.

was his identification of two distinct sets of assumptions about people. McGregor labeled these sets of assumptions "Theory X" and "Theory Y" and argued that the assumptions managers make about employees influence their attempts to manage. A summary of theories X and Y is given in Figure 7A–2.

FIGURE 7A–2
An Outline of Douglas McGregor's Theory X and Theory Y Assumptions

Two sets of assumptions or propositions concerning management's task of harnessing human energy to organizational requirements

Conventional view: Theory X	*A new view: Theory Y*
1. *A Proposition Common to Theories X and Y.* Management is responsible for organizing the elements of productive enterprise—money, materials, equipment, people—in the interest of economic ends.	
2. With respect to people, this is a process of directing their actions, modifying their behavior to fit the needs of the organization.	2. People are *not* by nature passive, or resistant to organizational needs. They have become so as a result of experience in organizations.
3. Without this active intervention by management, people would be passive—even resistant—to organizational needs. They must therefore be persuaded, rewarded, punished, controlled— their activities must be directed. This is management's task. We often sum it up by saying that management consists of getting things done through people.	3. The motivation, the potential for development, the capacity for assuming responsibility, the readiness to direct behavior toward organizational goals are all present in people. Management does not put them there. It is a responsibility of management to make it possible for people to recognize and develop these human characteristics for themselves.
4. The average man is by nature indolent—he works as little as possible.	4. The essential task of management is to arrange organizational conditions and methods of operation so that people can achieve their own goals *best* by directing *their own* efforts toward organizational objectives.
5. He lacks ambition, dislikes responsibility, prefers to be led.	
6. He is inherently self-centered, indifferent to organizational needs.	
7. He is by nature resistant to change.	
8. He is gullible, not very bright, the ready dupe of the charlatan and the demagogue.	

Source: Douglas McGregor, *The Human Side of Management* (New York: McGraw-Hill Book Company, 1960).

Neither view is always correct

The Theory X set of assumptions is a rather pessimistic view of man. The Theory Y assumptions, on the other hand, view man in more optimistic terms. Although McGregor did not argue that either view is always correct, he did suggest that managers adopt Theory X assumptions more often than is justified by the characteristics of employees. McGregor felt that prevailing management practices were unreasonably influenced by Theory X assumptions. He argued that, when appropriate, management practices consistent with Theory Y assumptions would yield greater personal and organizational benefits.

Impact of McGregor

Perspective. From today's perspective, several observations about theories X and Y can be made. *First*, McGregor's views have had a tremendous impact on management education. Theory X and Theory Y represent a good point of departure for discussing views about employees and managers. Theories X and Y are common vocabulary among executives. In a Conference Board poll of businessmen, Douglas McGregor was named most often in answer to the question, "Which behavioral scientist has influenced you personally?"[10] McGregor's influence is largely due to his Theory X and Theory Y.

Misinterpretations of X and Y

Second, McGregor's views have been widely misinterpreted. An "either-or" type of thinking emerged that tended to classify managers as either Theory X or Theory Y managers. In addition, McGregor was incorrectly presented as dogmatically for Theory Y assumptions and against Theory X assumptions. Perhaps worst of all, real managers were led to believe that if they were not sympathetic to Theory Y assumptions, then they were "out of style." Managers tried to give the appearance of sharing Theory Y assumptions even though they actually were uncomfortable with them.

X and Y are not managerial strategies

Third, Theories X and Y are not strategies of managing; they are *assumptions* about the nature of people which influence the adoption of a strategy for managing. It is meaningless to refer to a manager as a "Theory X manager" or a "Theory Y manager" unless the reference is to the set of assumptions that appears to guide the manager's strategy of managing. Both Theory X and Y can be operationalized using several different strategies of managing.

Y not better than X

Fourth, Theory Y assumptions are not "better" than Theory X assumptions. The best assumptions about people are those that most accurately fit the particular group of people. These assumptions will vary, not only among situations, but also with time and individuals.

---

[10] Harold M. F. Rush, *Behavioral Science: Concepts and Management Application,* Personnel Policy Study no. 216 (New York: National Industrial Conference Board, 1969), p. 10.

*X and Y not
opposites*

Fifth, Theory X and Y are not opposites. A common simplification was to suggest that, on a continuum of managerial strategies, Theory X would be at one end and Theory Y at the other. On this point McGregor comments:

> It was not my intention to suggest more than that these were *examples* of two among many managerial cosmologies, nor to argue that the particular beliefs I listed represented the whole of either of these cosmologies. . . . Cosmologies do not lie on a continuous scale. They are qualitatively different. The belief that man is essentially like a machine that is set into action by the application of external forces differs in more than degree from the belief that man is an organic system whose behavior is affected not only by external forces but by intrinsic ones. Theory X and Theory Y therefore are not polar opposites; they do not lie at extremes of a scale. They are simply *different* cosmologies.[11]

*They served a
useful purpose*

Finally, and in retrospect, it appears that too much has been made of the Theory X and Y part of Douglas McGregor's work. Not only did he make numerous other good points in his writings, he also must have been disturbed by the tendency to oversimplify his views. In any case, Theory X and Y have served a useful purpose in stimulating thinking about the assumptions managers make about themselves and about employees. It is the general idea of examining these underlying assumptions that is important.

---

[11] Douglas McGregor, *The Professional Manager* (New York: McGraw-Hill Book Company, 1967), p. 80.

Summary box

> *Two models of man* were briefly noted. Behaviorism
> places major emphasis on behavior and its external deter-
> minants. Phenomenology places major emphasis on per-
> sonal awareness and consciousness. The two models are in-
> compatible only if interpreted in their extreme forms.
>
> *Human nature* may be viewed as (1) good, (2) evil, (3)
> a blank slate, or (4) nonexistent or useless.
>
> The *Western civilization image* of people emphasizes
> success, individual dignity, and rational solutions to hu-
> man problems, especially problems dealing with the con-
> quest of nature. These types of emphases, although very
> legitimate, may lead indirectly to insufficient attention to
> personal and social problems.
>
> The *behavioral-science* person is characterized by adap-
> tive behavior—confronting reality when possible and cre-
> ating it when necessary.
>
> Douglas McGregor's *Theories X and Y* have had an im-
> portant impact on managerial education and practice. They
> are essentially sets of assumptions about people at work.
> Neither set is right or wrong; each set can be useful if it ap-
> proximates reality. X and Y are not managerial strategies
> nor are they polar opposites. McGregor referred to them as
> "simply different cosmologies."

CHECK YOUR UNDERSTANDING

Behaviorism

Phenomenology

Four views of human nature

Western civilization image of
  people

The public philosophy

Behavioral-science view of people

Douglas McGregor

Theory X

Theory Y

STUDY QUESTIONS

1. How, in your opinion, can a particular view of human nature
   operate as an influence on a person's behavior?

2. Can you infer a person's view of human nature from observing
   behavior? Explain.

3. What does it mean to say that Theories X and Y:
   a. Are not managerial strategies?
   b. Are not polar opposites?

APPLICATION: VIEWS OF MAN AND MANAGERIAL STRATEGIES

"Doug, my first impression of them was that they seemed like
perfect examples of those two theories we heard about in the
Supervisor Development Program. But maybe first impressions can
be wrong."

"Who and what are you talking about, Larry?"

"I'm talking about Theory X and Theory Y, Doug. When we heard about them in the Program, the lecture went in one ear and out the other. But it must have made some impression because I was able to relate the two theories to those three supervisors we met last week—well, maybe only two of them."

"I think I see what you mean. Let's check out our impressions, Larry, to see if we both see them in the same way."

"OK. I'd say that Loretta, the medical-records supervisor, is about as close to Theory X as a person can get; she's a sure 'Ms. X.' She talked about all the deadweight in her department and how she felt lucky if they made it through the day. Remember, she said her 'losers' can't understand simple instructions and, as for coping with change, they wouldn't know how to change their minds.'"

"That's pretty close to my view. What puzzles me, Larry, is that Loretta has this big reputation as a 'softie.' Last week when I talked to a couple of her 'losers' they said that Loretta was never on their back; did practically everything for them; let them have a lot of time off; and gave them plenty of chances to goof off. They seemed happy enough."

"I've heard that too, Doug. That doesn't seem to fit with the Theory X idea. Then there's Carlton, the business-office manager. He and Loretta seem to have a contest going to see who can say the worst things about their workers. According to Carlton, he'd be better off if they all stayed home. I heard he's trying to get all ten of them to take their vacation at the same time so that he can get some rest."

"But, at least, his reputation matches the view of his workers. He's 'Mr. Hardnose.' He tells everyone exactly what they're supposed to do; stands over them while they're doing it; and lays it on them if they don't do it right. He's a regular Captain Queeg."

"The one I can't figure out is Manuel. I get the impression that he'd win anyone's 'Mr. Y' contest. What a beautiful person! He seems to think everyone's as pure as Snow White, as committed as Joan of Arc, as smart as Einstein, and as capable as O. J. Simpson. The guy doesn't seem real. He seems to feel that he's got twelve future hospital administrators in his department. That would be some achievement for a maintenance department."

"It's funny, though, Larry, how Manuel is known to be a pusher and a no-nonsense type guy. He drives his workers and asks them to do things that really aren't part of their job description. He also stays somewhat aloof from his people, even when they are socializing. I hear he expects a lot from them and won't put up with mediocrity. He gives his workers the chance to stretch, and they'd better stretch, or else!"

1. How can you reconcile the apparent contradictions between the *assumptions* and the managerial *strategies* of Loretta, Carlton, and Manuel?

2. What contingencies do you feel might enter into the choice of a managerial strategy?

SUPPLEMENT 7B
Job Satisfaction

Objectives of Supplement 7B

1. To recognize job satisfaction as a managerial problem and a general social concern.

2. To identify ways to define and measure job satisfaction and to evaluate the relationship between satisfaction and dissatisfaction.

3. To note three views of the relationship between job satisfaction and performance and to relate job satisfaction to the concepts of valence and expectancy.

Work is work,
And can be fun.
But when it's not,
Must still be done.

> Auren Uris
> in *The Executive Deskbook*

I savor the joy of dull work.

> Eric Hoffer

I ride the bus, the Michigan Boulevard Bus in Chicago, and I look at people's faces. I see the bank teller, the elevator operator, the secretaries, the guys who work on the assembly lines, when they come home at night. They're tired. They're beaten. There's a fatigue. It isn't the satisfying tiredness of a day well spent, but the fatigue of another day killed.[1]

A common opinion

In the above quotation, Studs Terkel, author of the bestseller *Working*, expresses a commonly held opinion—people do not like their work![2] Terkel believes that the "great majority" of people get no satisfaction from their work. And he includes in that great majority the managers, executives, and bosses of those people on the Michigan Boulevard bus.

There is a job-satisfaction problem

Is Studs Terkel right in his view that the majority of people get little or no satisfaction from their jobs? We have to answer that question by saying that there is no "scientific evidence" to support

---

[1] "Studs Terkel Loves His Work, But He Says You Don't," (an interview with Studs Terkel by Claudia Driefus), *MBA*, vol. 10, no. 6 (June 1976), p. 41. Reprinted with permission from the June 1976 MBA Magazine. Copyright © 1976 by MBA Communications, Inc.

[2] New York: Pantheon Books, 1972.

such a sweeping statement. Nevertheless, there is a job-satisfaction problem of sufficient magnitude to warrant the attention of managers everywhere. It is not only a managerial problem, but also a worldwide problem with social, political, and economic implications. It is not a new problem, but our awareness of it and our sensitivity to the need to confront it is a characteristic of today's society.

This supplement

This supplement examines job satisfaction from the viewpoint of its importance to managers in meeting their accountability for the job performance of others. That viewpoint, of course, restricts the scope of our examination. First, we discuss several general questions about job satisfaction. Second, we evaluate three propositions concerning the relationship between job satisfaction and job performance.

JOB SATISFACTION: GENERAL QUESTIONS

Three components

What Is Job Satisfaction?   Job satisfaction is an *attitude*. It is both a general attitude that a person has toward an overall job, and it is a set of specific attitudes a person has toward particular components of a job, such as its pay or its working conditions. Recall from Chapter 7 that an attitude can have three components: cognitive, affective, and conative. The cognitive component of the job satisfaction attitude is the set of *beliefs* that a person has toward the job. The affective component is the *feeling* of like or dislike of the job. It is the affective component that is most commonly used in identifying job satisfaction. The conative component is the *action-tendency* aspect of the job satisfaction attitude. For example, it has been common to argue that job satisfaction brings about improved performance. As we shall see, that argument is not always valid.

Conceptual approach

What Approaches Can Be Used to Define JS?   There are two approaches to defining job satisfaction: conceptual and operational. The "conceptual" approach is to compare a person's perceived needs or expectations with the person's perceived outcomes from working. This approach is illustrated by the following quotation:

> Job satisfaction and dissatisfaction are a function of the perceived relationship between what one wants from one's job and what one perceives it as offering or entailing.[3]

Operational approaches

In any systematic study of job satisfaction, conceptual definitions must be translated into operational definitions. Operational definitions allow job satisfaction to be "measured." For example, an approach to defining job satisfaction operationally is to: (1) identify job-satisfaction components, (2) develop a way of measuring

---

[3] Edwin A. Locke, "What Is Job Satisfaction?" *Organizational Behavior and Human Performance,* vol. 4, no. 4 (November 1969), p. 316.

satisfaction on each component, and (3) obtain job-satisfaction scores for each component.

Summation measures

These scores provide a job-satisfaction measure for each component. The summation of the scores provide an overall measure of job satisfaction. When component scores are summed, it is known as the "summation" approach.

Discrepancy measures

Sometimes two types of component scores are obtained. For each component, job holders might be asked to indicate how satisfied they are *now* and how satisfied they perceive they *should be* or *would like to be*. The discrepancy between these two scores is taken as a measure of job satisfaction on that component. This operational approach to measuring job satisfaction is known as the "discrepancy" approach.

Five components

What Are Job Satisfaction Components? Almost any job-related factor can influence a person's level of job satisfaction or dissatisfaction. Over the years, efforts have been made to identify categories of such factors. These categories are referred to as "job-satisfaction components." In a review of several studies of job-satisfaction components, it was concluded that, "the main components of general job satisfaction are (1) attitude toward work group, (2) general working conditions, (3) attitude toward company, (4) monetary benefits, and (5) attitudes toward supervision."[4] These five components may not be applicable to all work environments, but they are general components of job satisfaction in many work environments.

Single continuum view

Are Job Satisfaction and Job Dissatisfaction Opposites? How do job-satisfaction components enter into a person's level of job satisfaction or dissatisfaction? The traditional way of answering that question is to view job satisfaction and dissatisfaction as polar opposites on a single continuum. This idea is shown in Figure 7B–1.

FIGURE 7B–1
The Single Continuum of Job Satisfaction and Job Dissatisfaction

Job Dissatisfaction _____ Job Satisfaction

Example of role of money

Figure 7B–1 suggests that a person's job satisfaction can be thought of as falling along a continuum that has, as its extreme points, satisfaction and dissatisfaction. A person shifts along this continuum in response to any and all job-related factors. Traditional thinking about job satisfaction is that the kinds of factors that affect job satisfaction also affect job dissatisfaction. For ex-

---

[4] Philip B. Applewhite, *Organizational Behavior* (Englewood Cliffs, N.J.: Prentice-Hall, 1965), p. 22.

ample, money is considered to have an impact on both: if you are satisfied with the money you receive for your work, you are "job satisfied"; if you are not satisfied with the money you receive for your work, you are "job dissatisfied."

Two
continuum
view

An alternative view of the relationship between job satisfaction and dissatisfaction is shown in Figure 7B–2. This view is associated with Frederick Herzberg's two-factor model of work-related needs (see Supplement 6A). Herzberg argues that there are two continuums. A person's level of job dissatisfaction is influenced by hygiene factors. A person's level of job satisfaction is influenced by motivator factors. Using this view, money, a hygiene factor, affects the level of job dissatisfaction, but not the level of job satisfaction.

FIGURE 7B–2
The Two Continuums of Job Satisfaction and Job Dissatisfaction

Job Dissatisfaction	_____(Hygiene Factors)_____	No Job Dissatisfaction
No Job Satisfaction	_____(Motivator Factors)_____	Job Satisfaction

Practical
implication

If the two-continuums view is correct, the practical point is that the kinds of actions that management might take to prevent or reduce job dissatisfaction are basically different than the actions that might maintain or increase job satisfaction. In the first case, the actions would be aimed at improving the work hygienes in the *environment*. In the second case, the actions would be aimed at improving the motivators in the *job itself*.

Which view
is correct?

Of the two views noted here, the single-continuum view is more generally accepted. Several tests have been made of the two-continuum view and, in general, the view has not been supported. However, the lack of support does not mean the two-continuum view should be rejected. Job satisfaction and job dissatisfaction may, in fact, be qualitatively different.

MSQ

How Can Job Satisfaction Be Measured?   A large number of instruments exist for measuring job satisfaction, although not many of them are commonly used.[5] The Minnesota Satisfaction Questionnaire (MSQ) is designed to measure satisfaction with several aspects—ability utilization, working conditions, co-workers, for ex-

---

[5] For brief descriptions of five job-satisfaction measuring instruments, see Karlene H. Roberts and Frederick Savage, "Twenty Questions: Utilizing Job Satisfaction Measures," *California Management Review*, vol. 15, no. 3 (Spring 1973), pp. 82–90.

ample—of an individual's work environment.[6] The MSQ is based on a theory of work adjustment that proposes that job satisfaction depends on the correspondence between an individual's work environment and needs. Although the MSQ has been extensively researched and is considered a reliable and valid instrument for measuring job satisfaction, it is currently undergoing continuing research and revision. "Until the results of these changes have been assessed, the Minnesota Satisfaction Questionnaire can best be described as promising but not yet ready for commercial use."[7]

JDI

Perhaps the most widely used measuring instrument for job satisfaction is the Job Descriptive Index (JDI). It has been referred to as "without doubt the most carefully constructed measure of job satisfaction in existence today."[8] Because of its common usage and good properties as a measuring instrument, we will discuss the JDI more fully.

Five components

The JDI measures job satisfaction in terms of five components: the work itself, the supervisor, the co-workers, pay, and opportunities for promotion. For each of these five components, there is a list of adjectives or short phrases. The list of adjectives and phrases for the "work" component is shown in Figure 7B–3. There is a similar scale for the other four components. The instructions for each scale ask the employee to put "Y" beside an item if it applies to his job, "N" if the item does not apply to his job, or "?" if the employee is undecided about the applicability of the item to his job. A score for each of the five scales is then obtained. When these scores are added, an overall measure of job satisfaction is obtained.

A measure is not an attitude

It is important not to confuse any measurement with the attitude measured. Studies that purport to show a relationship between job satisfaction and some other variable are always concerned with some *measure* of job satisfaction, and not with job satisfaction itself. Attitudes are inner states; measurements of attitudes are not the attitudes themselves. This is not a criticism of attempts to measure job satisfaction—research studies have no alternative but to measure the variables studied. However, in interpreting such studies, the distinction between job satisfaction and its measurement is important.

---

[6] David J. Weiss, Rene V. Dawes, George W. England, and Lloyd H. Lofquist, *Manual for the Minnesota Satisfaction Questionnaire,* Bulletin 45 (Minneapolis: University of Minnesota, Industrial Relations Center, 1967).

[7] Quoted in Oscar Krisen Buros, ed., *The Seventh Mental Measurements Yearbook,* vol. 2 (Highland Park, N. J.: Gryphon Press, 1972), p. 1,494.

[8] Victor H. Vroom, *Work and Motivation* (New York: John Wiley & Sons, 1964), p. 100. For a full discussion of the development of the JDI, see Patricia C. Smith, Lorne M. Kendall, and Charles L. Hulin, *The Measurement of Satisfaction in Work and Retirement* (Chicago: Rand McNally & Company, 1969).

FIGURE 7B–3
The Work Scale of the Job Descriptive Index

	Work
_____	Fascinating
_____	Routine
_____	Satisfying
_____	Boring
_____	Good
_____	Creative
_____	Respected
_____	Hot
_____	Pleasant
_____	Useful
_____	Tiresome
_____	Healthful
_____	Challenging
_____	On your feet
_____	Frustrating
_____	Simple
_____	Endless
_____	Gives sense of accomplishment

Summary box

> *Job satisfaction is an attitude.* Like any attitude, it can have cognitive (belief), affective (feeling), and conative (action-tendency) components.
>
> There are *two approaches to defining job satisfaction:* conceptual and operational. *Conceptually*, job satisfaction involves a comparison between a person's perceived needs or expectations and the perceived outcomes of performance.
>
> *Operationally*, however, job satisfaction is sometimes viewed as the *sum* of the satisfactions on several job components. Job satisfaction is also defined operationally as the sum of scores of the discrepancy between how satisfied employees perceive they are now compared to how satisfied they perceive they should be or would like to be.
>
> *Job-satisfaction components* are factors that can have an influence on the level of a person's job satisfaction. Examples include attitudes toward the work group, the company, supervision, working conditions, and monetary benefits.
>
> Job satisfaction and job dissatisfaction are most commonly viewed as polar opposites on a *single continuum*. An alternative but less accepted view is that there are *two continuums*—one for job satisfaction and one for job dissatisfaction.
>
> The most widely used instrument for measuring job satisfaction is the *JDI*, which can be used to obtain an overall measure of job satisfaction as well as separate measures of satisfaction toward the work itself, the supervisor, co-workers, pay, and promotion.

THE JOB SATISFACTION–JOB PERFORMANCE RELATIONSHIP

Reviews of research

A review of over 50 studies of employees' attitudes and performance concludes, "There is little evidence in the available literature that employee attitudes of the type usually measured in morale surveys bear any simple—or, for that matter, appreciable relationship to performance on the job."[9] Another review of 155 studies of job attitudes also failed to show strong satisfaction and performance relationships.[10] Still another review of 23 field studies concluded that satisfaction explained less than 2 percent of the

---

[9] Arthur H. Brayfield and Walter H. Crockett, "Employee Attitudes and Employee Performance," *Psychological Bulletin*, vol. 52, no. 5 (1955), pp. 396–424.

[10] F. Herzberg, B. Mausner, R. Peterson, and D. Capwell, *Job Attitudes: Review of Research and Opinion* (Pittsburgh: Psychological Services of Pittsburgh, 1957).

variance in performance.[11] These reviews call into question the common-sense notion that job satisfaction and job performance are related.

Satisfaction →performance view

Three views.   Three major "theoretical propositions concerning the relationship between satisfaction and performance" can be identified.[12] One view is that high job satisfaction leads to or causes improved job performance. This view is reflected in the statement, "A satisfied worker is a productive worker." The "satisfaction→ performance view" is implied in any managerial strategy that is aimed at improving job performance by increasing the level of a person's job satisfaction. Herzberg's two-factor model is an example of a view that implies that an increase in the level of job satisfaction will lead to an increase in the level of job performance. In general, it is not safe to make this assumption. A lot depends on whether the job satisfaction derives from factors that are consistent with job performance—factors such as Herzberg's *motivators.*

Example

Caution should be exercised in assuming a causal relationship between the job satisfaction and job-related behavior. For example, a commonly held view is that dissatisfaction is a major cause of absence from work. In some cases, this may be true. However, a study of 1,222 male and female blue-collar production workers failed to demonstrate the existence of this relationship. The study concludes that "Absence itself may take a multitude of forms and may be caused and constrained by a host of diverse factors: the person, the workplace, and the outside world."[13]

Satisfaction — ? → performance view

A second view of the job satisfaction–job performance relationship is that different variables can intervene to moderate or influence the relationship between the two. Some intervening variables that have been suggested are the employee's skill and ability, motivational differences, and pressure for production. For example, in certain cases the greater the pressure for production, the lower the job satisfaction but the higher the job performance. Again, the satisfaction–performance relationship is moderated by the extent to which an employee perceives improved performance as a way of reducing the dissatisfaction that is being experienced.

Performance →satisfaction view

The third view of the satisfaction–performance relationship is the opposite of the other two. This view is that job performance leads to improved job satisfaction. In order for this to be the case, a person would have to view improved job performance as intrinsically desirable or as leading to rewards—pay, promotion, recog-

---

[11] Vroom, *Work and Motivation.*

[12] Donald P. Schwab and Larry L. Cummings, "Theories of Performance and Satisfaction: A Review," *Industrial Relations,* vol. 9, no. 4 (October 1970), pp. 408–30.

[13] Nigel Nicholson, Colin A. Brown, and J. K. Chadwick-Jones, "Absence from Work and Job Satisfaction," *Journal of Applied Psychology,* vol. 61, no. 6 (December 1976), pp. 728–37.

nition, and so on. Further, these rewards must be perceived by the person as equitable.

Recall job performance model

Applying Expectancy Theory.   Recall the framework of job performance presented in Chapter 6. Job performance was viewed, in that framework, as dependent on situational factors, role perceptions, abilities and skills, and motivation. These four components are not independent of each other. Nevertheless, it appears reasonable to say that job satisfaction is most related to motivation. Thus, if job satisfaction and performance are related, it must be through the motivation component.

Valence and expectancy

We suggested in Chapter 6 that motivation depends on the desirability (valence) of various consequences and on the beliefs (expectancies) about the relationships between effort and performance and between performance and consequences. In order to influence motivation, therefore, job satisfaction must affect valences and expectancies.

Job satisfaction can decrease valence

On the one hand, job satisfaction can have a *negative* impact on valence. Suppose that one of the consequences you desire is pay. Pay is an external consequence of your performance. Since there is a tendency for satisfaction to decrease the importance of most rewards (a satisfied need is not a motivator), the valence of pay ought to decrease as you become satisfied with your pay. To that extent, your motivation declines and, in turn, your job performance.

Job satisfaction can increase valence

On the other hand, job satisfaction can have a *positive* impact on valence. The tendency of a satisfied need to decrease in importance does not always operate consistently or equally. This may be true, in particular, for the self-fulfillment need. Maslow argued that, as this need is satisfied, it increases in importance as a motivator of behavior. Thus, satisfaction should increase the valence of self-fulfillment, motivation should increase, and performance should improve.

Job satisfaction and expectancy

What about the effect of job satisfaction on expectancies, the second component of motivation? Expectancies are concerned with the relationships between performance and consequences. Job satisfaction results from the positive consequences of job behavior— pay, promotion, and recognition. As we noted in Chapter 6, however, it is the *contingency* relationship between behavior and consequences that is important.

Contingency relationship

If desired consequences are contingent on performance, we would expect there to be a *positive* relationship between satisfaction and performance. We would expect this because good performance leads to more desired consequences, and these consequences lead to greater satisfaction. Thus, the good performers would attach a higher value to expectancy, and that higher value would have a positive impact on motivation and performance.

Size of
difference in
consequences

In addition to the contingency relationship between consequences and behavior, the size of the difference in the rewards received by good and poor performers is important. "If the difference is small, then it is not likely that a substantial positive relationship will exist, because good performers have higher aspirations than poor performers, and it will take more than a small difference in reward level to make them more satisfied."[14] It appears that the key idea here is that the good performers must perceive the contingent rewards as equitable. That is, they must perceive that they are receiving rewards equal to what they feel they *should* receive.[15]

No
contingency
relationship

If desired consequences are not contingent on performance, we would expect there to be a *negative* relationship between job satisfaction and performance. We would expect this because the good performers see that they are not differentiated from poor performers and that they are not receiving the desired consequences they perceive they should receive. Therefore, they attach a lower value to expectancy. This lower expectancy value has a negative impact on motivation and performance.

No inherent
relationship

Conclusion. We have seen that job satisfaction can have both a negative and a positive influence on *valence.* Similarly, depending upon the nature of the contingency relationship, job satisfaction can have both a negative and a positive influence on *expectancy.* In view of these complex influences, we can conclude that there is no inherent relationship between job satisfaction and job performance. Satisfaction can cause performance to increase or decrease, and performance can cause satisfaction to increase or decrease. However, even these relationships may not occur; satisfaction may have no effect on performance, and vice versa.

Key idea
for managers

For managers, the key idea here is contingency. If managers want to have a positive influence on the job satisfaction of their employees, the best practice is to establish contingency relationships between job behavior and consequences desired by employees: "If rewards are not positively contingent, then the administration of rewards will not only fail to encourage performance increments, it may also increase dissatisfaction."[16] To this we can add that the positively contingent rewards must be perceived by the good performers as equitable.

---

[14] Edward E. Lawler III, *Pay and Organizational Effectiveness: A Psychological Review* (New York: McGraw-Hill Book Company, 1971), p. 268.

[15] In the context of expectancy theory of motivation, the importance of the perceived equity of rewards was first suggested in Lyman W. Porter and Edward E. Lawler III, *Managerial Attitudes and Performance* (Homewood, Ill.: Richard D. Irwin, 1968), p. 29.

[16] David J. Cherrington, H. Joseph Reitz, and William E. Scott, Jr., "Effects of Contingent and Noncontingent Reward on the Relationship between Satisfaction and Task Performance," *Journal of Applied Psychology,* vol. 55, no. 6 (1971), p. 536.

PERSPECTIVE ON JOB SATISFACTION

A means and
an end

Managers and management educators are concerned with the job-satisfaction attitude primarily because it is assumed to be related to job behavior. Job satisfaction is seen as a means to better performance. Although the precise nature of this relationship is unclear, a relationship is still assumed to exist. In addition, some managers are interested in improving the job satisfaction of their employees as an end in itself. They place a high priority on job satisfaction as a characteristic of the work environment.

Downward
trend

A recent study reported job satisfaction measures of over 98,000 workers over a ten-year period. The data reported in the study ". . . establish the existence of a general downward trend in job satisfaction over the ten years studied for workers who are fairly representative of United States industrial workers."[17] This downward trend shows up regardless of the worker's tenure, function, or geographic location.

Job satis-
faction is
important

Job satisfaction may not be important to everyone, but it is important to millions of people who work. The lives of these employees and managers are organized around their jobs. Their jobs are important to them, not only while they work, but also off the job. Their jobs can influence where they live; who they associate with; what they read, think, and talk about; what they eat; what they wear; what they buy; and how they will "spend" their leisure time. Their jobs can have an important impact on those interpersonal and group relationships that importantly determine the quality of their lives and the development of their personalities.

Psychology of
entitlement

Of course, some job dissatisfaction is inevitable, and perhaps even desirable. Also, certain causes and conditions that result in job dissatisfaction are beyond the control of managers. For example, the employee's level of job satisfaction may depend as much on total outlook on life and life style as on the job.[18] Furthermore, the spreading "psychology of entitlement" has an impact on job satisfaction.[19] More and more workers believe they are entitled to a meaningful and satisfying job and to one that matches their abilities and skills.

Managerial
challenge

Creating and maintaining work environments that are *productive and satisfying* may be the most important and difficult challenge facing managers today and in the future.

---

[17] Frank Smith, Karlene H. Roberts, and Charles L. Hulin, "Ten Year Job Satisfaction Trends in a Stable Organization," *Academy of Management Journal*, vol. 19, no. 3 (September 1976), pp. 462–69.

[18] Bonnie Carroll, *Job Satisfaction* (Ithaca, N.Y.: New York State School of Industrial and Labor Relations, 1973), pp. 15–16.

[19] John Hoerr, "Worker Unrest: Not Dead, but Playing Possum," *Business Week* (May 10, 1976), p. 134.

The world of work is caught up in the cross currents of rapid change. Problems of the work place including job satisfaction demand immediate attention and action.

Three distinct forces are involved: the institutions and the jobs they provide, the society at large, and the individual worker. Each is changing at different rates of speed and with different degrees of responsiveness. The individual workers and the society are changing much faster than the institutions and the quality of the jobs they provide.

Disaffection and discontent are a reflection of increasing education and rising aspirations rather than of alienation. . . .

The society must take a larger view of work and examine how it relates to increased or decreased satisfaction with life, both on and off the job. The issue is made clear by focusing on the expectations workers bring to the job and on the distinction between economic and psychological work satisfaction. While the employer is primarily motivated to create and maintain a productive work place, this is not incompatible with a high quality of working life, provided there is a balanced relationship among human, technical, and economic factors.[20]

Summary box

Concerning the job satisfaction–job performance relationship:

1. One view is that improving job satisfaction will lead to higher levels of job performance (job satisfaction→ performance).

2. Another view is that the relationship between the two is moderated by variables such as pressure for production and the degree of dissatisfaction being experienced (job satisfaction— ? →job performance).

3. A third view is that improved job performance leads to higher levels of job satisfaction (job performance→ job satisfaction).

4. Our conclusion is that there is *no inherent relationship* between job satisfaction and job performance. We reached this conclusion by illustrating how job satisfaction can have both a negative and a positive influence on valence and expectancy, the two variables that enter into motivation.

5. A key idea for managers is to establish *contingency* relationships between a person's job performance and the person's desired job outcomes or consequences.

---

[20] *The Changing World of Work.* Final Report of the 43d American Assembly, November 1–4, 1973, Arden House, Harriman, New York, p. 4.

CHECK YOUR UNDERSTANDING

Job satisfaction	JDI
Conceptual approach	Satisfaction→performance
Operational approach	Satisfaction—?→performance
Summation	Performance→satisfaction
Discrepancy	Psychology of entitlement
Job satisfaction components	
Single-continuum view	
Two-continuum view	
MSQ	

STUDY QUESTIONS

1. As a manager, you have decided to make a concerted effort to improve the level of job satisfaction of your subordinates. What choices are available to you? Develop your answer around the model of job performance presented in Chapter 6.

2. To what extent, in your opinion, is it possible for managers to be instrumental in increasing job-satisfaction levels of their employees? Discuss.

3. Suppose that there is conclusive evidence that the more satisfied employees become with their jobs, the *less* productive they become. As a manager, how would you react to such evidence? Discuss.

4. Using the concepts of valence or expectancy, explain how increasing job satisfaction can both increase and decrease motivation.

APPLICATION: MEASURING JOB SATISFACTION

The Job Descriptive Index (JDI) views job satisfaction in terms of five components. Figure 7B–3 is the "work" scale of the JDI. The four other JDI scales attempt to measure satisfaction with supervision, co-workers, pay, and opportunities for promotion.

1. Do you agree that these five components are sufficient to tap the multiple dimensions of the job satisfaction attitude?

2. If not, what other components would you suggest?

3. How independent do you think the five components are?

The JDI uses adjectives or descriptive phrases as "stimuli" to elicit perceptions of satisfaction with each of the five components.

4. What do you think of this approach? Are there alternative approaches that might be used to obtain measures of the components of job satisfaction? Explain.

5. Develop a list of adjectives and descriptive phrases that would, in your opinion, apply to the pay component. Compare your list with those used in the JDI.[21]

6. How could the JDI be used to obtain measures of the discrepancy between perceived job satisfaction and the degree of satisfaction that employees perceive should be characteristic of the job?

---

[21] See Patricia C. Smith, Lorne M. Kendall, and Charles L. Hulin, *The Management of Satisfaction in Work and Retirement* (Chicago: Rand McNally and Company, 1969).

Objectives of Chapter 8

- To highlight the role of behavioral consequences as an influence on job performance behavior.

- To distinguish a "motives" from a "consequences" approach and to identify types of behavioral consequences.

- To define a contingency and to discuss five types of contingencies that link behavior and consequences.

- To recognize the roles of scheduling, timing, and shaping processes in attempts to influence behavior by behavioral consequences.

- To present a critique of the consequences approach to understanding behavior.

Outline of Chapter 8

The Role of Behavioral Consequences
  Motives versus Consequences
  The Law of Effect
Types of Behavioral Consequences
  Positive, Negative, or Neutral
  Intrinsic and Extrinsic
  Reinforcers and Punishers
  Motives and Reinforcers
Using Contingencies to Link Behavior and Consequences
  What Is a Contingency?
  Avoidance
  Negative Reinforcement
  Positive Reinforcement
  Punishment
  Extinction
Scheduling Behavioral Consequences
  Continuous Schedules
  Ratio Schedules
  Interval Schedules
  Concurrent Schedules
Two Influencing Processes
  Timing
  Shaping
A Brief Critique
  Vocabulary
  Limited Scope
  Fear of Control

8

BEHAVIORAL CONSEQUENCES

I am proceeding on the assumption that nothing less than a vast improvement in our understanding of human behavior will prevent the destruction of our way of life or of mankind.

B. F. Skinner

Boy, have I got this guy trained. Every time I press the pedal, he gives me some food.

A rat in a Skinner box

Fran Tarkenton

Fran Tarkenton is an extraordinary quarterback for the Minnesota Vikings. He is also CEO of a firm that specializes in training. In an interview with *Training,* Fran emphasized the important role of *behavioral consequences* in obtaining good job performance:

> Back when I worked for Coca-Cola Company in Atlanta, the training field turned me off. Millions were being spent on motivational speakers and so forth but little of what I saw happening seemed to rub off on productivity and performance.
>
> It's frustrating to be the head of a training or personnel department and to be told "Congratulations, fella, you're now responsible for motivating my people." Sure it might sound good at first, but training and personnel people don't have control of the performers' *consequences.*
>
> If, say, the marketing vice president is interested in improving performance, he has got to get involved and accept and acknowledge his responsibility for the performance he wants. . . . He is going to have to learn about behavior—to control *consequences,* to use positive reinforcement, to give feedback. . . . He's got to take responsibility for the total performance picture.
>
> You've got to remember that on the football field I'm labor, not management. I'm only involved with one-half of the game, the offense. But yes, we do have a performance feedback system.
>
> Managing behavior through *consequences* is an important part of managing the Viking's offense. Extensive data is collected on 20 variables which . . . bear directly on the offensive team effort. During the Wednesday showing of Sunday's game films, the offensive unit is evaluated on those 20 variables. . . . We

get feedback on the variables, we get reinforced on the variables, and it gets our people to concentrate on the things that are important to us winning.[1]

Chapter's major theme

Fran Tarkenton's recognition of the relationship between controlling *behavioral consequences* and good job performance behavior ties right in to the major theme of this chapter. That theme is that managers can increase the effectiveness of job performance by focusing on behavioral consequences.

This chapter

The chapter begins with a brief discussion of the role of behavioral consequences in influencing behavior. Second, it identifies types of consequences and types of contingencies used to link behavior with its consequences. Then we discuss three processes— scheduling, timing, and shaping—that have an effect on behavior–contingency–consequence relationships. The chapter ends with a brief critique of the consequences approach.

THE ROLE OF BEHAVIORAL CONSEQUENCES

Motives approach

Motives versus Consequences. In the preceding two chapters and in their supplements we discussed several cognitive variables —motives, perceptions, attitudes, values, assumptions about people, and job satisfaction. These are variables that are internal to a person and which influence behavior *before* it occurs. In effect, we were looking inside the person for variables that would allow us to understand and predict behavior. For convenience, we refer to this as a "cognitive" or "motives approach" to understanding behavior.

Consequences approach

In this chapter we take a different viewpoint—the viewpoint of behavioral consequences. Specifically, the underlying assumption of this chapter is that behavior can be understood and predicted by its consequences and the contingencies that link behavior to consequences. In a sense, this means that we focus on an explanatory variable, consequences, that occurs *after* the behavior. For convenience we refer to this as a "reinforcement" or "consequences approach" to understanding behavior.

A behavioral law

The Law of Effect. The consequences approach is based on the idea that behavior that is reinforced is likely to be repeated, and behavior that is not reinforced or that is punished is likely to be avoided or eliminated. This basic idea is called the "law of effect" or the "law of reinforcement." Calling this idea a "law" suggests that it applies all the time. Its application does not require that people are aware of how reinforcement is working. For managers, this means that job behavior—their own and that of their employees —is influenced largely by reinforcing consequences. These conse-

---

[1] "PF/PR: Fran Tarkenton Uses It on the Gridiron—and Sells It in the Boardroom," *Training, The Magazine of Human Resources Development* (Lakewood Publications, Minneapolis), vol. 13, no. 12 (December 1976), pp. 26–27. (Emphasis added.)

quences influence job behavior, whether or not employees are aware of them.

How does the law of effect operate?

Just how can the consequences of a behavior explain that behavior? How can we explain behavior by looking at something that occurs *as a result of the behavior*? In short, how does the law of effect work? Consequences influence behavior by conveying information to a person about what behavior can be expected to be reinforced or punished.[2] "People behave on the basis of the outcomes they *expect* to prevail on future occasions (emphasis added)."[3] The law of effect works, then, by a process of providing *information* and influencing a person's *expectations* concerning future behavior.

TYPES OF BEHAVIORAL CONSEQUENCES

Different reactions to praise

Positive, Negative, or Neutral. An employee's job behavior leads to consequences that are positive, negative, or neutral *for that employee*. A particular consequence may seem positive to one person and negative or neutral to another. For example, receiving praise from a supervisor for good performance may be viewed positively by employees if they are positively valent toward doing a good job and toward receiving recognition from their supervisor. Conversely, receiving praise from a supervisor may be viewed negatively by employees if the praise makes them "look bad" in the eyes of their peers, work group, or other reference groups. Still other employees may receive praise with nonchalence.

Praise and expectations

Praise is a form of feedback to a person regarding his or her behavior, and it is evaluated by a person in terms of that person's expectations. That is part of the reason why the same degree of praise affects people in different ways. "In order for praise to be experienced as highly positive, it must, by definition, be above and beyond the person's expectations."[4] Feedback in the form of praise that is inconsistent with or unequal to a person's expectations can create tension in the person, which, in turn, may be reduced by the manner in which the praise is perceived by the person.

Intrinsic consequences

Intrinsic and Extrinsic. "Intrinsic consequences" are internal consequences of job behavior that are *controlled by the person*. They result from actual job performance or achievement. In Chapter 6, we referred to valence toward intrinsic consequences as "intrinsic valence." The satisfaction felt from good job performance is an example of a positive intrinsic consequence. The absence of a sense of achievement is an example of a negative intrinsic conse-

---

[2] W. K. Estes, "Reinforcement in Human Behavior," *American Scientist*, vol. 60, no. 6 (November–December 1972), p. 723.

[3] Albert Bandura, "Behavior Theory and the Models of Man," *American Psychologist*, vol. 29, no. 12 (December 1974), p. 860.

[4] Frank P. Bordonaro, "The Dilemma Created by Praise," *Business Horizons*, vol. 19, no. 5 (October 1976), pp. 76–81.

quence. (It is negative if the employee would prefer to experience a sense of achievement.) Managers can influence intrinsic consequences by appropriate person–job matching, by improving the design of jobs, and by job training, among other ways.

Extrinsic consequences

"Extrinsic consequences" are external consequences of job behavior that are largely *controlled by the organization*. Their source is the person's environment. Examples include pay, promotions, disciplinary layoffs, interpersonal relationships, and type of supervision. In Chapter 6 we referred to valence toward extrinsic consequences as "extrinsic valence." The intensity of the valence will depend on the perceived need of employes for those consequences.

Manager's role

Managers play a key role in establishing the system of extrinsic consequences of behavior. However, managers have to be careful not to place exclusive emphasis on the use of extrinsic consequences. Of course, an effective system of such consequences is an essential ingredient in an organization in order to elicit good job performance. However, exclusive or too much emphasis on extrinsic consequences may tend to reduce an employee's desire for intrinsic consequences that satisfy needs for competency and autonomy.[5]

Effect on behavior

Reinforcers and Punishers. If the consequence of a behavior tends to *increase* the probability of that behavior recurring, the consequence is called a "reinforcer." If the consequence of a behavior tends to *decrease* the probability of that behavior recurring, the consequence is called a "punisher."

Reinforcers and rewards

Reinforcers are not quite the same as rewards. The word "rewards" has a positive connotation for most people. A reward is something "good." A reinforcer, however, is *any* consequence of behavior that tends to increase the probability of that behavior recurring. Such a consequence could be something generally thought of as a reward (such as a pay bonus) or it could be something generally thought of as punishing (such as a reprimand by a supervisor). What one person considers a reinforcer may not be considered a reinforcer by another person. The key to determining whether a consequence is a reinforcer is to observe the effect of the consequence on the person's behavior.

Primary and secondary reinforcers

Consequences that satisfy basic, unlearned needs such as food, water, and shelter are called "unconditioned" or "primary" reinforcers. Consequences that indirectly satisfy basic needs or that satisfy learned needs are called "conditioned" or "secondary" rein-

---

[5] There is considerable difference of opinion on this point. See W. E. Scott, Jr., "The Effects of Extrinsic Rewards on 'Intrinsic Motivation,'" *Organizational Behavior and Human Performance*, vol. 15 (1975), pp. 117–29. In the same issue is a reply to the Scott article: Edward L. Deci, "Notes on the Theory and Metatheory of Intrinsic Motivation," pp. 130–45.

forcers. Social approval and the sight of food are examples of secondary reinforcers. Money is a prime example of a secondary reinforcer; some people "are reinforced by it even when they do not exchange it for other things."[6]

Tie-in to Supplement 6A

Motives and Reinforcers. How are motives related to reinforcers? Motives are *inner states* that influence a person's behavior. Reinforcers are *consequences* of behavior that increase the probability of that behavior recurring.

Motives determine reinforcers

On the one hand, we can say that "motives determine reinforcers." If employees have a desire for money, then money will be a reinforcer. If employees have a need for security, then things which contribute to security will be reinforcers. If employees have a need for self-actualization at work, then jobs that they find self-fulfilling and that give them a sense of achievement will be reinforcing. In this line of reasoning, we *infer* what reinforcers will be effective from a knowledge of motives. Of course, our inferences may not be correct.

Reinforcers indicate motives

On the other hand, we can say that "reinforcers tell us what motives a person has." If people are reinforced by food, then we can infer that they are hungry. If someone is reinforced by recognition, then we can infer that the person has a need for recognition. If employees are reinforced by money, we can infer that they are motivated by money. In this line of reasoning, we *infer* what a person's motives are by observing what reinforcers are effective for that person. Once again, the accuracy of our inferences may be less than perfect. A single reinforcer can satisfy a variety of motives.

---

[6] B. F. Skinner, *Contingencies of Reinforcement: A Theoretical Analysis* (New York: Appleton-Century-Crofts, 1969), p. 68.

Summary box

> We refer to the approach taken in this chapter as a *con-sequences* approach, as contrasted to a *motives* approach.
>
> The *law of effect* is that behavior that is reinforced is likely to be repeated and that behavior that is not reinforced or that is punished is likely to be avoided or eliminated.
>
> The law of effect works through the effect behavioral consequences have on a person's *expectations* concerning future behavior. Thus, behavioral consequences convey *information*.
>
> An employee's job behavior may lead to consequences that are *positive, negative,* or *neutral* for that employee.
>
> Behavioral consequences may be intrinsic or extrinsic. *Intrinsic* consequences are internal and are controlled by the person. *Extrinsic* consequences are external. They have their source in the environment, and are largely controlled by the person's organization.
>
> A *reinforcer* is any consequence of behavior that increases the probability of that behavior recurring. A *punisher* is any consequence of behavior that decreases the probability of that behavior recurring.

USING CONTINGENCIES TO LINK BEHAVIOR AND CONSEQUENCES

Prior emphases on contingent relationships

In our discussion of expectancy theory of motivation (see Chapter 6), we stressed the importance of making desired outcomes contingent on good job performance. In our discussion of job satisfaction (see Supplement 7B), we again noted the importance of a contingent relationship between job satisfaction and job performance.

An "If . . . then" relationship

What Is a Contingency? A "contingency" is the link that connects behavior with the consequences of that behavior. A contingency establishes an "If . . . then" relationship—If (behavior), then (consequences). A contingency must specify three things: (1) the antecedent events or the setting within which the behavior is to occur; (2) the desired behavior; and (3) the consequence that will follow the behavior.

$A \rightarrow B \rightarrow C$ model

The three-part contingency can be referred to as the $A \rightarrow B \rightarrow C$ model. That is, given a particular environmental setting or or antecedent event (A), behavior (B) will occur that leads to a consequence (C).[7]

---

[7] Fred Luthans and Robert Kreitner, *Organizational Behavior Modification* (Glenview, Ill.: Scott, Foresman and Company, 1975), p. 44.

Five types   There are five types of contingencies for managers to consider in their efforts to establish desirable job behavior–consequence relationships that contribute to efficient and effective performance. The five contingencies are: avoidance; negative reinforcement; positive reinforcement; punishment; and extinction. Examples of these contingencies are shown in Figure 8–1.

FIGURE 8–1
Types of Contingencies and Examples of Behavior–Consequences Relationship

Type of Contingency	Behavior Intended to Be Elicited by the Contingency	Major Behavioral Consequence of Person's Behavior
Contingencies designed to increase desirable behavior		
Avoidance............	Promptness in arriving at work	*Avoid* deduction from pay due to late arrival at work
Negative reinforcement	Completion of a supervisory training seminar	*Elimination* of one obstacle to promotion. (Assume that the business firm requires completion of the seminar as a condition for promotion.)
Positive reinforcement	Increase in the quantity and quality of job performance	*Receiving* praise, recognition, and a pay increase
Contingencies designed to decrease undesirable behavior		
Punishment...........	Reduction of frequent and unexcused absence from work	*Receiving* a three-day disciplinary layoff and *denial* of opportunity to work overtime for additional pay
Extinction............	An executive wants a subordinate to stop relying on him for advice on solving problems. Therefore, the executive sees that he is "out" when the subordinate calls.	*Elimination* of subordinate advice-seeking behavior.

Avoidance learning   **Avoidance.** An "avoidance contingency" is an attempt to elicit desired behavior by linking the behavior to a consequence that a person wants to avoid. Learning by means of avoidance contingencies is sometimes called "avoidance learning" because the learned behavior results in the avoidance of a particular consequence.

Getting to work on time

An example of an avoidance contingency is, "If you get to work on time then you will not have your pay reduced." The behavior (getting to work on time) avoids the consequence (reduction in pay). Not having pay reduced (consequence) is contingent on getting to work on time (desired behavior). Note that an avoidance contingency is designed to reinforce the behavior of getting to work on time. The consequence (avoiding reduction in pay) is designed to increase the probability of the behavior (getting to work on time). In this example, avoiding the reduction in pay is a consequence that most employees would consider a reinforcer. However, it may not be a reinforcer for some employees or, more commonly, it may be a relatively weak reinforcer.

Avoiding the supervisor's temper

Another example of an avoidance contingency is when employees get to know the behavioral patterns of their superior. The employees may know, for example, that when their superior gets unfavorable feedback about work performance, he or she reacts violently and blames the employees for the poor performance. In order to avoid the superior's violent reaction (consequence), the employees simply withhold from the superior any feedback that may be viewed as unfavorable (behavior). From the viewpoint of the *employees*, in order to avoid a bad consequence they must engage in a certain type of behavior. From the viewpoint of the *superior* and the *organization*, the employees' behavior may be undesirable.

Escape learning

Negative Reinforcement. A "negative reinforcement contingency" is one in which the termination, or elimination, of a consequence is contingent on some desired behavior. Learning by means of negative reinforcement is sometimes called "escape learning" because the desired behavior leads to escape from a negative reinforcement event.

Why called negative?

The reason negative reinforcement is called "negative" is that it takes the form of termination or elimination of some event. "Negative" does not imply punishment or something to be avoided. A negative reinforcement event is a reinforcer because its termination tends to increase the probability of behavior.

Example

An example of a negative reinforcement contingency is one in which employees know they are ineligible for promotion to a supervisory position unless they complete a supervisory training course. In such a contingency, the completion of the course is the desired behavior and the elimination of the obstacle to promotion is the consequence of the desired behavior. The supervisory training course can be viewed as a negative reinforcement event; that is, it increases the probability of a response (attending and completing the training course) when its *termination* or *elimination* is contingent on the response.

Obtaining
something
desired

Positive Reinforcement. A "positive reinforcement contingency" is one in which the occurrence of a consequence is contingent on some desired behavior. If managers know that if they perform at a certain level they will receive a bonus of $500, then the bonus (consequence) is contingent on the behavior (high level of performance). "Positive reinforcement" is obtaining something desired as a result of engaging in certain behavior. The bonus of $500 can be viewed as a positive reinforcement event; that is, it increases the probability of the desired behavior when the event's *occurrence* is contingent on that behavior.

Stimulus and
response
events

Positive reinforcement can be either stimulus or response events. A "stimulus event" is something that is actually received as a result of performing behavior on which the event is contingent. Examples include a promotion, an increase in salary, praise from a respected person, and the awarding of a prize. A "response event" is the opportunity to engage in some desired behavior. For example, the opportunity for an engineer to work on a desirable project (project *A*) may be made contingent on the completion of a project on which he or she prefers not to work (project *B*).

Premack
principle

In the above example, working on project *A* can be referred to as "high-probability behavior" (HPB), and working on project B can be referred to as "low-probability behavior" (LPB). When two events are compared and one is preferred over the other, the preferred behavior is the HPB and the less-preferred behavior is the LPB. The idea that any HPB can reinforce any LPB on which it is contingent is sometimes called the "Premack principle."[8]

Managers and
the Premack
principle

The Premack principle opens up many possibilities for managers in their search for positive reinforcers. It is not always possible for managers to find stimulus events to serve as positive reinforcers. For example, foremen and supervisors in unionized manufacturing plants have little direct control over wage levels, wage increases, fringe benefits, working conditions, or working hours. Even top executives are not always free to offer additional pay or benefits to middle managers, because salaries and benefits must conform, to some extent, to the firm's overall salary administration program. Thus, managers often have little control over those variables that normally would serve the function of *stimulus events*. However, managers may have more flexibility in making available *response events* that provide the opportunity to engage in preferred activities which can serve as reinforcers for certain required but less preferred job assignments.

---

[8] D. Premack, "Toward Empirical Behavioral Laws: 1. Positive Reinforcement," *Psychological Review,* vol. 66, no. 4 (July 1959), p. 219.

*Increasing
the role of
positive
reinforcers*

If managing is the work of creating and maintaining environments in which people can accomplish goals efficiently and effectively, much of the actual work of managing is going to center on finding and implementing positive reinforcers. At a time when organizations are staffed with sophisticated and knowledgeable employees, when there is a growing cultural norm recognizing the need for personal growth and development, and when there is an urgent need for more efficient and effective work organizations, reliance on positive reinforcers will inevitably become more important.

*Decreasing
undesirable
behavior*

Punishment. A "punishment contingency" attempts to *decrease* the likelihood of particular behavior occurring by making the punishment contingent on the behavior. Common punishment contingencies used in work organizations include disciplinary layoffs, discipline for rule infractions, transfer to undesirable jobs, and withholding salary increases.

Two forms

Punishment contingencies can take two forms. One is the *awarding* of a punisher for the undesirable behavior, such as a disciplinary layoff for absenteeism. A second form of punishment is the *denial* or *removal* of a positive reinforcer. If, for example, a person views the possession of a carpeted office with a window and a mahogany desk as a positive reinforcer, then a punishment contingency would link certain undesirable behavior with the removal of the reinforcer.

*Reinforce-
ment and
punishment*

The major difference between punishment and reinforcement is that punishment attempts to *decrease* the probability of behavior and reinforcement attempts to *increase* the probability of behavior. Thus, the major difference is in the *direction* of behavioral change. Reinforcement tries to facilitate behavior, and punishment tries to suppress it: "Reinforcement and punishment are therefore opposite sides of the same operation; the conditions which make one possible also make the other possible."[9]

*Different
results of
punishment*

Although reinforcement and punishment may be opposites in what they attempt to do, research on reinforcement and punishment does not always yield results consistent with that notion. There is research that shows punishment can: increase the occurrence of undesired behavior, cause it to last longer, be only a short-lived deterrent, bring about even less-desired behavior or other negative side effects, or even improve behavior by calling the individual's attention to the undesired behavior.[10] For managers,

[9] D. Premack, "Catching up with Common Sense or Two Sides of a Generalization: Reinforcement and Punishment," in Robert Glaser, ed, *The Nature of Reinforcement* (New York: Academic Press, 1971), p. 149.

[10] Hoyt N. Wheeler, "Punishment Theory and Industrial Discipline," *Industrial Relations,* vol. 15, no. 2 (May 1976), pp. 235–43. Also see Richard L. Solomon, "Punishment," *American Psychologist,* vol. 19, no. 4 (April 1964), p. 254, and James M. Johnston, "Punishment of Human Behavior," *American Psychologist,* vol. 27, no. 11 (November 1972), p. 1,051.

one of the implications of this research on punishment is to suggest that punishment can have diverse and unpredictable outcomes.

Effect of punishment is complex

The effect of punishment on behavior is complex and depends on multiple and interacting factors:

> Even a mild form of punishment can be effective if it is delivered without delay, for a short period of time after *each* occurrence of the behavior, when the positive reinforcer supporting the behavior is removed, and when alternative behaviors are positively reinforced. Conversely, a very intense punishing stimulus may fail to eliminate behavior that is being consistently maintained by a powerful reward.[11]

Important variables

The effectiveness of punishment as a controller of behavior varies with a wide number of parameters, including the *intensity* of the punishment, the *proximity* in time of the punishment to the punished behavior, the *contingency* between the behavior and the punishment, the *strength* of the behavior to be punished, the *familiarity* of the subject with the punishment being used, and the *age* of the subject.

Managers and punishment contingencies

The reason we are emphasizing the complexity of the role of punishment in influencing behavior is to encourage managers to be cautious in their use of punishment contingencies. Like other types of contingencies, managers use them in order to contribute to the efficient and effective accomplishment of goals. As we have seen, however, the effect of punishment is complex and depends on many parameters. Nevertheless, managers can hardly avoid using punishment contingencies; they are an inevitable part of the physical, psychological, and sociological dimensions of work environments: "Throughout our daily activities we are constantly barraged by a variety of stimuli which have punishing effects, whether it be someone's frown or bumping into a chair we did not see."[12]

Ignoring behavior

Extinction. In an "extinction contingency," a particular behavior is followed by a consequence that is neither reinforcing nor punishing. The purpose is to decrease behavior by ignoring it. Sometimes extinction contingencies are used unknowingly, as when the job-related suggestions of an employee are inadvertently but consistently ignored. At other times, extinction contingencies are used knowingly to eliminate undesirable behavior. An example would be when a supervisor ignores the mild "horseplay" of an employee who is intentionally trying to upset the supervisor.

---

[11] Everett E. Adam, Jr., and William E. Scott, Jr., "The Application of Behavioral Conditioning Procedures to the Problems of Quality Control," *Academy of Management Journal*, vol. 14, no. 2 (June 1971), p. 183.

[12] Johnston, "Punishment of Human Behavior," p. 1,051.

Summary box

> A *contingency* is the link that connects job behavior with consequences of that behavior. A contingency establishes an "if . . . then" relationship. The *three parts of a contingency* are an antecedent event or an environmental setting (A), specification of a behavior (B), and specification of the consequences that will follow the behavior (C). This is referred to as the $A \rightarrow B \rightarrow C$ model of a contingency.
>
> There are *five types* of contingencies: avoidance, negative reinforcement, positive reinforcement, punishment, and extinction.
>
> The essential idea of an *avoidance* contingency is to increase the probability of particular behavior occurring by making the avoidance of a consequence contingent on the behavior. Learning by means of avoidance contingencies is called *avoidance learning*.
>
> The essential idea of a *negative reinforcement* contingency is to increase the probability of particular behavior occurring by making the termination of the negative reinforcement event contingent on the behavior. Learning by means of negative reinforcement contingencies is called *escape learning*.
>
> The essential idea of a *positive reinforcement* contingency is to increase the probability of particular behavior occurring by making the occurrence of the positive reinforcement event contingent on the behavior.
>
> Positive reinforcers can be either *stimulus events* or *response events*.
>
> The *Premack principle* states that any HPB can reinforce any LPB on which it is contingent.
>
> The essential idea of a *punishment* contingency is to decrease the probability of particular behavior occurring by making the punishment contingent on the behavior. Punishment can take two forms: *punishers* and *denial of a positive reinforcer*.
>
> The essential idea of an *extinction* contingency is to decrease behavior by ignoring it.

SCHEDULING BEHAVIORAL CONSEQUENCES

Types of scheduling

So far, our discussion has implied that when a consequence is contingent on desired behavior, the consequence will follow the desired behavior. Actually, behavioral consequences can "follow" behavior in a variety of ways. Three basic types of schedules are: continuous; ratio; and interval. Managers ought to be familiar with these schedules because they can influence the effectiveness of behavioral contingencies.

Consequence occurs after each response

Continuous Schedules. A "continuous schedule" is one in which the consequence follows the behavior every time. In a general sense, it could be said that when an employee receives intrinsic reinforcement from job performance he is on a continuous reinforcement schedule. However, that is not the sense in which the term is commonly used. In work organizations, there are almost no examples of continuous schedules. It would be extremely difficult to design and administer such schedules.

Example

A far-fetched example might be where an employee who performs a job with limited scope and depth is reinforced, through some automatic device, after each successful repetition of a work cycle. The reward could take the form of money, tokens, "green stamps," bonus points, and so on. Continuous schedules have very limited application in work organizations. Some form of intermittent reinforcement is usually required. The remaining two types of reinforcement schedules are intermittent.

Schedules based on number

Ratio Schedules. "Ratio schedules" are schedules based on the relationship between the *number* of behavioral responses and the frequency of occurrence of the behavioral consequence. Two types of ratio schedules occur—fixed and variable.

Fixed ratio

A "fixed ratio schedule" is one in which the consequence occurs after a fixed number of behavioral responses. For example, in a work organization an employee may receive wages (reinforcer) for producing a predetermined number of units of production (behavior).

Variable ratio

A "variable ratio schedule" is one in which the consequence occurs after an established average number of behavioral responses. For example, a variable ratio 15 (VR-15) means that a specific behavior is reinforced, on the average, 1 out of 15 times. On one occasion, the employee may receive extra pay after producing 10 units, on another occasion after producing 20 units and, on the average, after producing 15 units. Laboratory studies suggest that variable ratio schedules are very effective in maintaining high performance levels. However, such results cannot as yet be generalized to behavior in the "real world."[13]

Schedules based on time

Interval Schedules. "Interval schedules" are schedules based on the relationship between a *time period* and the frequency of occurrence of the consequence. Two types of interval schedules occur—fixed and variable.

---

[13] Gary Latham, Elliott Purseli, and Gary Yukl, "The Effectiveness of Performance Incentives under Continuous and Variable Ratio Schedules of Reinforcement," *Personnel Psychology*, vol. 29, no. 2 (July 1976), pp. 221–31.

Fixed interval   A "fixed interval schedule" is one in which the consequence occurs after a fixed period of time. Most work organizations pay employees on a fixed interval schedule. Most employees are paid once
a week, whereas managerial personnel are commonly paid every
two weeks or once a month. It is interesting to note how often the
consequence (wages or salary) is not clearly contingent on the behavior (work performance) supposedly being reinforced. That is,
the pay is received regardless of the quantity or quality of the performance. In such a case, the contingency relationship between
performance and pay is only a very general one and may amount
to nothing more than the requirement of physical presence at
work during the time period.

Variable   The "variable interval schedule" is one in which the consequence
interval   occurs after a variable period of time. A variable interval schedule
"is approximately the situation that might be faced by a worker
employed by a company that is having difficulty meeting its payroll."[14]

Comparison   Fixed and variable interval schedules have been compared as
follows:

> Performance on a fixed-interval schedule often shows a decline
> after the occurrence of a reinforcer followed by an accelerated
> increase until the next reinforcer occurs. The decline is of longer
> duration when the fixed interval is long, but it may disappear
> with extended practice. . . .
>   Performance on a variable-interval schedule is characterized
> by rather constant rates of responding over long periods of time.
> Very often, social reinforcement from significant others takes
> place on a variable interval basis not because it is planned that
> way but simply because the supervisor is too busy to provide
> it on a systematic basis.[15]

Combinations   **Concurrent Schedules.** Concurrent schedules are combinations
of continuous, ratio, or interval schedules. Designing a behavioral
system would be significantly easier if all schedules could be controlled and isolated. However, human behavioral systems do not
work that way. In any organization, for example, multiple schedules, some planned and others unplanned and even unknown, may
be operating at the same time. An employee may be on a fixed-
interval pay schedule, a fixed-ratio coffee-break schedule, a continuous reinforcement schedule resulting from intrinsic job satisfaction, and a variable interval social reinforcement schedule from
other employees. One of the operational problems that makes managing so complex is the problem of concurrent schedules which
influence behavior.

---

[14] Owen Aldis, "Of Pigeons and Men," *Harvard Business Review,* vol. 39,
no. 4 (July–August 1961), p. 60.

[15] Adam and Scott, "The Application of Behavioral Conditioning Procedures," p. 181.

Summary box

> Three basic types of *schedules* can be used in following behavior with behavioral consequences. The different types of schedules influence the way in which consequences influence behavior.
>
> *Continuous* schedules are those in which the consequence occurs after each behavioral response.
>
> *Ratio* schedules are based on the ratio of the number of behavioral responses to consequences. A *fixed ratio* schedule is one in which the consequence occurs after a fixed number of behavioral responses. A *variable ratio* schedule is one in which the consequence occurs after an established average number of behavioral responses.
>
> *Interval* schedules are based on time. A *fixed interval* schedule is one in which consequences occur after a fixed period of time. A *variable interval* schedule is one in which consequences occur after a variable period of time.
>
> At any point, most people are behaving in response to various combinations of schedules. We referred to these combinations as *concurrent* schedules.

TWO INFLUENCING PROCESSES

Unifying idea

The unifying idea of this chapter is that behavior that is reinforced is likely to be repeated, and behavior that is not reinforced is likely to be avoided. We have referred to this idea as the "law of effect" or the "law of reinforcement." The way in which this law works, however, is influenced by the contingencies and schedules that are used. Two additional influencing factors are timing and shaping.

Immediate and certain consequences

Timing. Consequences that are immediate and certain tend to be more effective than those that are distant and uncertain.[16] For consequences to have their greatest effect, they should come immediately after the behavior occurs. Delay in administering a consequence may allow unrelated or noncontingent consequences to intervene. When this happens the person may "lose sight of the behavior-consequence contingency which was established."[17]

---

[16] Frederick W. Taylor recognized this idea many years ago by saying, "A reward, if it is to be effective in stimulating men to do their best work, must come soon after the work has been done. But few men are able to look forward for more than a week or perhaps at most a month, and work hard for a reward which they are to receive at the end of this time." *The Principles of Scientific Management* (New York: Harper & Bros., 1911), p. 94.

[17] Robert I. Lazer, "Behavioral Modification as a Managerial Technique," *Conference Board Record*, vol. 12, no. 1 (January 1975), p. 24.

Differing
need for
immediacy

Just how consequences influence a particular person depends on a variety of factors. Some people are able to take a long-range view of things. "Humans can cognitively bridge delays between behavior and subsequent reinforcers without impairing the efficacy of incentive operations."[18] This ability to defer immediate gratification is alleged to be one sign of maturity in a person.

Example

Nevertheless, in general, immediate and certain reinforcers are most effective. For example, although most college students are motivated by a college degree (a distant reinforcer for most students), their everyday behavior is not significantly influenced by that goal. Rather, the everyday behavior of college students is a matter of taking and passing specific courses and completing assignments that are due "next period." Much behavior on a particular day depends to a great extent on whether there is a test to pass the next day (immediate consequence).

Salary and
reinforcement

Possibly one of the least effective compensation plans in terms of influence on actual job behavior is the once-a-month salary plan. Although there is a certain amount of status associated in some companies to being paid monthly and there may be other advantages to such a pay plan, it is unlikely that the monthly salary serves as much of a reinforcer for work during the month. Even though salary is a certain consequence of job behavior, many employees may consider it too distant from performance to effectively reinforce the behavior.[19]

Key idea:
timing

The key idea to keep in mind about the timing of consequences is that behavior is influenced by consequences. Behavior at any particular time leads to consequences that are reinforcing, punishing, or neutral. If managers want particular consequences of behavior—pay, for example—to effectively reinforce behavior, then those consequences must compete with other consequences—the satisfaction that comes from arriving at work late, for example—that are reinforcing for the person. In this competition, immediate and certain reinforcers *tend* to *be* more powerful in influencing behavior than distant and uncertain reinforcers.

Definition

Shaping. "Shaping" is the process of reinforcing successive approximations of the behavior that is ultimately desired. When parents praise the initial piano-playing efforts of a child, they are engaging in shaping. If the parents wait until the child becomes a concert pianist before praising the child, they may have to wait forever. Similarly, if a manager requires perfect job performance

---

[18] Bundura, "Behavior Theory and the Models of Man," p. 862.

[19] For a discussion of the effect of various pay and other types of reward systems see Edward E. Lawler III, "Reward Systems," in J. Richard Hackman and J. Loyd Suttle, *Improving Life at Work: Behavioral Science Approaches to Organizational Change* (Santa Monica, Calif.: Goodyear Publishing Company, 1977), pp. 163–226.

before reinforcing an employee's behavior, the reinforcement may never take place.

When to
shape

In shaping, reinforcement is given only for behavior that *more nearly* approximates the desired behavior. However, since reinforcement may be needed simply to keep the person interested, it may be necessary at times to reinforce behavior even though it does not represent progress.

Shaping and
managers

Shaping is an extremely important idea for managers. Sometimes it may be almost impossible for managers to find approximations of desired behavior to reinforce. For example, an employee who consistently arrives late at work and who, after repeated warnings, continues to arrive late may give the manager no "approximations" to reinforce. Performance that is consistently and continuously below standard may offer no opportunity for reinforcement other than that minimally required. Cases such as these require that managers imaginatively seek out any approximations that can legitimately be reinforced, as in the following example.

> One of the most courageous examples reported to us was from a manager who had a man working for him who just couldn't seem to do anything he was told. However, the manager remembered that he occasionally initiated very small projects of his own and carried them out very well. Deciding that initiative and self-reliance were good, . . . the manager began encouraging the man who couldn't follow instructions to do things on his own. Over a period of a few weeks, the man's performance changed so much that the manager was considering promoting him rather than firing him. He still had a weakness in following direction, but his work was so good that it was only a very minor problem.[20]

A BRIEF CRITIQUE

Reinforce-
ment theory

The psychological theory that supports most of the ideas discussed in this chapter is known as "reinforcement theory" or, more specifically, "behavior modification." It is a theory and behavioral technology popularly associated with B. F. Skinner.[21] It is also a theory that generates fear, anger, and other negative emotions in many people.

A theory
ignored

During the 1950s and the 1960s, the work of B. F. Skinner and other reinforcement theorists was almost totally ignored in management education and practice. Only in recent years has rein-

---

[20] From *Behavioral Analysis in Business and Industry: A Total Performance System* by Dale N. Brethower. Copyright © 1972 by Behaviordelia, Inc. Used by Permission of Behaviordelia.

[21] B. F. Skinner, *Science and Human Behavior* (New York: Macmillan Company, 1953) and *Contingencies of Reinforcement, A Theoretical Analysis* (New York: Appleton-Century-Crofts, 1969). Skinner discusses his psychology through the medium of a novel in *Walden Two* (New York: The Macmillan Company, 1948). For a recent statement of Skinner's philosophy of behaviorism, see his *About Behaviorism* (New York: Alfred A. Knopf, 1974).

forcement theory been given attention in management literature.[22] In contrast, the work of such men as Douglas McGregor, Abraham Maslow, Chris Argyris, and Frederick Herzberg has been popular and, in fact, has virtually dominated management education in the area of human behavior and motivation.

Reasons

Some of the reasons for the lack of attention to reinforcement theory compared to more popular ways of attempting to understand human behavior are vocabulary, limited scope, and fear of control.

Mechanistic and manipulative terms

Vocabulary. The vocabulary of reinforcement theory does not sound "right." The vocabulary—"conditioning, contingencies, reinforcement, punishment, escape learning, operants, schedules, cumulative records, stimulus, and response"—has a mechanistic and manipulative ring to it. Much of reinforcement theory and its vocabulary is derived from experiments with rats, monkeys, and pigeons. Many people are repelled by the implication that human behavior can be explained, however indirectly, in terms of concepts relevant to animal experiments.

People terms

The vocabulary of more popular explanations of human behavior, such as those of Abraham Maslow and Douglas McGregor, is dominated by such terms as "self-actualization, fulfillment, esteem, enrichment, achievement, personal development, self-direction, needs, motives, recognition, and peak experiences." These terms sound appealing and are terms to which most people can relate—they are "people" terms, not animal terms.

Managers and the vocabulary

Although the vocabulary of reinforcement theory is an obstacle to managers it becomes less of an obstacle as knowledge and understanding of the theory and its language is acquired. Behind the mechanistic-sounding vocabulary is a developing and scientific body of knowledge that managers can use. The concepts of reinforcement theory can be useful to managers in their efforts to create work environments in which people can "self-actualize" *and* be productive. Managers may have to learn some new language.

Complex social situations

Limited Scope. Reinforcement theory is often viewed as applicable only to jobs with very limited scope and depth, and where there is a clear and precise relationship between behavior and

---

[22] See, for example, Walter R. Nord, "Beyond the Teaching Machine: The Neglected Area of Operant Conditioning in the Theory and Practice of Management," *Organizational Behavior and Human Performance,* vol. 4 (1969), p. 377; Richard W. Beatty and Craig Eric Schneier, "A Case for Positive Reinforcement," *Business Horizons,* vol. 18, no. 2 (April 1975), pp. 57–66; Robert Kreitner, "PM: A New Method of Behavior Change," *Business Horizons,* vol. 19, no. 6 (December 1975), pp. 79–86; and "Reinforcement Analysis in Management—Concepts, Issues, and Controversies: A Symposium," *Organization and Administrative Sciences,* vol. 6, no. 4 (Winter 1975–1976), pp. 38–72.

consequences. However, this limited view of the applicability of reinforcement theory is not justified.[23]

*Difficult
to apply
any theory*

There is no doubt that the application of reinforcement theory to organizations requires considerable skill. Anyone who has experience with behavior in organizations understands the difficulty of applying any theory of behavior. Various types of behavior occur simultaneously, expectations concerning consequences of behavior change, actual contingencies and consequences of behavior are multiple, and several reinforcement schedules are operating at the same time. Furthermore, the variables in a work environment can never be controlled as completely as the variables in experimental laboratories.

*The law of
effect is
operating*

Nevertheless, the law of effect or reinforcement is operating whether or not managers are consciously attempting to apply the principles of reinforcement theory. We may not be aware of *how* it is operating, but it is operating. The argument that reinforcement theory is too limited in scope for organizations misses the important point that the theory *is* operating in organizations. That is, behavioral contingencies *are* influencing job behavior and performance. It does not matter whether these contingencies are intentionally arranged or whether they reflect the conscious application of reinforcement theory principles.

*Limited ability
to apply the
theory*

It is not reinforcement theory that is limited in scope. It is our ability to apply the theory that is limited. B. F. Skinner has commented on the embryonic stage of the understanding of the behavioral contingencies that will be effective in complex human behavioral situations:

> Only very recently, and then only under rigorous experimental conditions, have the extraordinary effects of contingencies been observed. Perhaps this explains why it has not been possible to design effective contingencies simply with the help of common sense or of practical skill in handling people or even with the help of principles derived from scientific field observations of behavior. The experimental analysis of behavior thus has a very special relevance to the design of cultures. Only through the active prosecution of such an analysis, and the courageous application of its results to daily life, will it be possible to design those contingencies of reinforcement which will generate and maintain the most subtle and complex behavior of which men are capable.[24]

---

[23] For additional information on this point, see S. F. Jablonsky and D. L. DeVries, "Operant Conditioning Principles Extrapolated to the Theory of Management," *Organizational Behavior and Human Performance*, vol. 7 (1972), pp. 340–58.

[24] B. F. Skinner, "Contingencies of Reinforcement in the Design of a Culture," *Behavioral Science*, vol. 11, no. 3 (1966), p. 166.

The real
question

From the viewpoint of managers, the question is not whether reinforcement theory is too limited in scope for work environments. The theory is applicable, and the basic law of effect is working all the time. The real question for managers is, How can they best *use* that law and its accompanying theory? How can managers *broaden* its scope of application?

Freedom
versus
control

Fear of Control. Reinforcement theory has come to be associated with the wrong side of a debate often seen in terms of freedom versus control. Reinforcement theory is seen as manipulative and unethical. Fears that reinforcement theory will be used to control human behavior without the knowledge, awareness, or consent of those being controlled are often expressed. Reinforcement theory is sometimes viewed as treating people as *objects* rather than as purposive, self-directing, personally responsible *subjects* who make choices.

> The rather widespread resistance on the part not only of laymen but of many psychologists to accepting the reinforcement principle and the technique of operant conditioning as the main approach to the modification of human behavior is based largely on intuitive distaste for the rather mechanical conception of human action that seems to be implied.[25]

Apparent
implications

What "seems to be implied" by reinforcement theory is a view of the behavior of human beings as totally predictable, "determined," or controlled by *external* consequences. Such a view appears to deny the importance of individual choice, of internal cognitions, and of consciousness. It appears to make the individual human being passive in any behavioral transaction. It raises the "specter of predictable man"[26]—wholly predictable and deterministic, like a machine.

Skinner's
response

In response to the allegation that reinforcement theory is designed to totally control the behavior of people, B. F. Skinner argues that controls over people exist regardless of whether reinforcement theory is used. Control is everywhere! "So any man-made design to control people does not suddenly change the world of human experience from one of freedom to one of control."[27] Further, he observes that, although every act is controlled, control is seldom complete and need not be concealed or manipulative. In response to those who say that he views people as controlled *by* their environment, Skinner observes that people have a great deal of control *over* their environment. When Skinner talks about people being "controlled," he is not implying that "some person is

[25] W. K. Estes, "Reinforcement in Human Behavior," *American Scientist,* vol. 60, no. 6 (November–December 1972), p. 723.

[26] Andrew Hacker, "The Specter of Predictable Man," *Antioch Review,* vol. 14, no. 2 (June 1954), pp. 195–207.

[27] Finley Carpenter, *The Skinner Primer: Behind Freedom and Dignity* (New York: The Free Press, 1974), p. 91.

trying to control and force them to behave as he wishes."[28] Rather, Skinner's "controls" are more "causes" or factors in the environment that influence behavior.

Environment control versus people control

Some of the fear of control of people that is associated with reinforcement theory is unfounded:

> Behavior technology is a science concerned with the changing of environments, not people; actions, not feelings; and, in general man's external condition rather than his outlook or philosophy. In a society where we are dithered by computers, traffic jams, pollution, fast food, aerosol cans, etc., an environment which *responds positively* to human results will contribute to the reinforcement—rather than the destruction—of human autonomy.[29]

Managing requires control

Any approach to management implies control. Control of human behavior is an essential aspect of management. Rather than being repelled by this thought, we should consider the alternative. If managers do not exercise some control over the behavior of their subordinates, then in what sense can it be said that managing is taking place? The question for managers is not *whether* the performance of employees will be controlled. The question is *how* can controls be made more reasonable, less arbitrary, and more effective from the viewpoint of both the employee and the organization.

Cannot force reinforcement

The success of reinforcement theory depends on the link between behavior, contingencies, and consequences. Reinforcement theory cannot *make or force* an employee to find a particular consequence reinforcing or rewarding. It requires that managers find behavior–contingency–consequence relationships that employees *will* find reinforcing. Reinforcement theory's potentialities for manipulation of human behavior is real, but it is no greater than alternative approaches to effective managing.

It is one approach that can work

Managing is the work of creating and maintaining environments in which people can accomplish goals efficiently and effectively. This work will be more and more concerned with applications of reinforcement theory. It is, of course, possible that reinforcement theory will be applied in ways inconsistent with the progressive development of human personality. *Any approach to management can be abused.* On the other hand, reinforcement theory offers to professional managers an approach to the design of work environments that *can be* consistent with the personal-development needs of employees and with the need for greater organizational effectiveness.

---

[28] Anna E. Friedman, *The Planned Society: An Analysis of Skinner's Proposals* (Kalamazoo, Mich.: Behaviordelia, 1972), p. 5–5.

[29] Harry Wiard, "Why Manage Behavior? A Case for Positive Reinforcement," *Human Resource Management,* vol. 11, no. 2 (Summer 1972), p. 20.

Not a panacea   In spite of reinforcement theory's potential use to managers, however, it is not a panacea. An article on the application of reinforcement theory to work environments contains this word of caution:

> Don't oversell the idea. . . . It's not this year's new technology that should cause a manager to drop everything else in favor of it. There is always the danger . . . that business will treat the technique as a solution in search of a problem. If that happens, a high failure rate is almost a certainty.[30]

For the future, the following prescription is useful for managers:

> For those interested in the application of behavior modification to work behavior, the task for the future is two-fold: to develop and test techniques for application in ongoing organizations and to continue the already imaginative efforts toward identifying the range and scope of such applications.[31]

Summary box

> The *timing* of behavioral consequences is important. In general, consequences that are immediate and certain tend to be more effective than those that are distant and uncertain. However, individual differences must be considered. One of these differences is the ability to defer immediate gratification.
>
> *Shaping* is the process of reinforcing successive approximations of behavior that is ultimately desired. Since there are times when these approximations may be difficult to find, managers may have to be active in seeking out evidence of approximations that can be legitimately reinforced.
>
> The psychological theory supporting the discussion in this chapter is known as *reinforcement theory*. This theory has only recently received attention by managers and management educators. Some reasons for this belated attention are its *vocabulary*, its alleged *limited scope*, and the *fear of control* that the theory generates. Our view is that reinforcement theory will become more important to managerial work.
>
> Considered together, the discussions in Chapters 6, 7, and 8 and in the supplements accompanying those chapters provide a foundation for thinking about behavior. It is a foundation consisting of both *cognitive variables and processes* and *reinforcement variables and processes*.

---

[30] "Where Skinner's Theories Work," *Business Week*, December 2, 1972, p. 65.

[31] Craig Eric Schneier, "Behavior Modification in Management: A Review and Critique," *Academy of Management Journal*, vol. 17, no. 3 (September 1974), p. 544.

CHECK YOUR UNDERSTANDING

Motives approach
Consequences approach
Law of effect
Types of behavioral consequences
    Intrinsic and extrinsic
    Reinforcers and punishers
    Primary and secondary reinforcers
Relation of motives and reinforcers
Reinforcers versus rewards
Contingency
Three parts of a contingency
$A \rightarrow B \rightarrow C$ model
Types of contingencies
    Avoidance
    Negative reinforcement
    Positive reinforcement
    Punishment
    Extinction

Avoidance learning
Escape learning
Negative reinforcement event
Positive reinforcement event
    Stimulus event
    Response event
Premack principle
    High-probability behavior
    Low-probability behavior
Two forms of punishment
Schedules
    Continuous
    Fixed ratio
    Variable ratio
    Fixed interval
    Variable interval
    Concurrent
Timing of consequences
Shaping

STUDY QUESTIONS

1. What, in your opinion, are some practical problems that would confront managers if they attempt to influence job performance by managing behavioral contingencies and consequences?

2. Precisely how do behavioral consequences influence future behavior?

3. The chapter suggests that the "motives" and "consequences" approaches are not incompatible. Explain.

4. What, in your opinion, does it mean to say that the law of effect applies *whether or not* people are aware of it?

5. What contingencies are affecting your present behavior? What kinds of schedules are you on? Evaluate your reinforcers in terms of their immediacy and certainty.

6. Do you agree with the statement that there is nothing intrinsic about work that dictates a small role for positive reinforcement? Why or why not?

7. Do you agree with the statement that managers can hardly avoid using punishment contingencies? Discuss.

8. Evaluate the argument that the application of reinforcement theory (behavior modification, positive reinforcement) is dangerous because it "manipulates" people. Argue pro and con.

APPLICATION: POKER CHIPS*

Alcoholics Anonymous (AA) is an organization that is very successful in helping individuals cope with alcoholism. AA meetings are known for their low-pressure tactics, soft sell, relaxed atmosphere, and supportive climate. AA is self-supporting and relies largely on money that comes in by "passing the hat" at the end of each meeting. This Application describes how AA uses behavioral consequences as one small part of its total approach to treating alcoholics.

Some AA clubs use red, white, and blue poker chips as a technique for modifying behavior. When a prospective member comes to a first meeting the member is told about "passing the hat." However, instead of putting *in* a contribution, the member is told to take *out* a red poker chip and to place it in the pocket where drinking money is kept. When the member enters a bar (antecedent event) and reaches for money to buy a drink (behavior), his or her fingers will find the red poker chip (consequence).

Finding the red poker chip *may* help the member recall AA's "one day at a time" abstinence philosophy, and it may be a sufficient incentive to remain sober for another 24 hours. If it is not a sufficient incentive, the member is supposed to take the red poker chip out of the pocket, conspicuously break it, and throw the particles away before putting any money down on the bar. If desired, the member returns to a subsequent AA meeting in order to get another red poker chip.

If the member abstains from alcohol for one month, he or she turns in the *red* poker chip and picks up a *white* chip. After abstaining for three additional months, a *blue* chip is held for eight long months. Now the AA member is entitled to a first anniversary celebration.

With great fanfare, the member's sponsor rewards the member with a silver dollar into which a ⅛ inch hole has been drilled. The silver dollar is a memento of a year's abstinence. At the conclusion of every alcohol-free year, the ceremony is repeated and another hole is drilled in the silver dollar. All this symbolism occurs within an atmosphere of support, understanding, and human involvement.

1. What type of behavioral contingencies and consequences are used in the poker-chip technique? What schedules are used?
2. Can you think of ways in which this technique might be used to improve job performance behavior in traditional work environments?

APPLICATION: CHITA CHIP COMPANY

Arturo, Bruce, Carmen, and Debra are employed by Chita Chip Company (CCC), a medium-sized single-plant firm that produces

---

* Adapted from Alexander Bassin, "Red, White, and Blue Poker Chips: An AA Behavior Modification Technique," *American Psychologist*, vol. 30, no. 7 (July 1975), pp. 695–96. Copyright 1975 by the American Psychological Association. Reprinted by permission.

Chitas, a food product for distribution in retail stores. CCC is a wholly owned subsidiary of one of the country's largest business firms that produces and distributes food products for industrial and retail customers. CCC is the only plant that produces Chitas.

CCC has a policy of placing management trainees in a responsible position in order to see how they perform on the job. Their performance is watched closely, and they receive continuous coaching from their supervisor–sponsor. In addition to their on-the-job training, management trainees also receive formal training through their participation in CCC's assessment center.

In the assessment center, various training techniques are used in order to assess the trainee's managerial strengths and weaknesses. Examples of these techniques are role playing, in-basket exercises, decision-making simulations, and critical-incident analyses. At one of the assessment center exercises, Arturo, Bruce, Carmen, and Debra, were given a critical incident to analyze. They were to prepare their analysis independently and were to present it, one at a time, to a group of CCC first-line supervisors.

The critical incident to be analyzed concerns Earle Gibson, a former CCC management trainee. Earle came to CCC about one year ago full of enthusiasm for a job that he felt matched his needs perfectly. All of the job's "hygienes" were more than satisfactory to Earle and prospects for promotion were excellent. In addition, he felt that the immediate on-the-job experience would itself provide him with the kind of responsibility that he desired. Earle had no doubts about his abilities to meet difficult job assignments. From past experience, he knew how much he valued the sense of accomplishment and the recognition that comes from a "job well done." All in all, Earle entered CCC with confidence in himself and with great expectations for the future.

Everything went downhill for Earle from that point on. Earle's job did not really provide him with opportunities to show his superiors what he could really do. He felt he was being held back by a lot of "busywork" like listening to employee's complaints and keeping daily records. He became impatient with the lack of objectivity of other supervisors and with their failure to examine problems in a systematic, analytical manner. He noticed that the other supervisors were neglecting to ask for his views about problems that he knew he could solve by himself—if anyone would let him.

The harder Earle worked, the less he seemed to get anywhere. His general supervisor never gave him the time of day, and he was getting the cold shoulder from the other manager trainees. Earle's wife was upset by the long hours he was working without additional pay. Besides, she wanted him to be home more.

Gradually, Earle began to withdraw from his job. He offered fewer ideas, worked fewer hours, and communicated less with the other trainees. The performance of his subordinates, already poor, declined further. The straw that broke the camel's back was when Farrah was selected for a supervisory position—a sign that Farrah was considered the best trainee in the group that Earle had started with. '

Earle decided he did not want to work for a company that couldn't recognize his obvious talents. He didn't care that much about the supervisory position but he felt that, by passing him by, CCC had shown they could not recognize superior managerial talent when they saw it. Earle quit his job with CCC eleven months after he began it. He entered the job with confidence, and he left it with confidence—the confidence that CCC was a lousy place to work.

1. Take the role of Arturo and analyze this incident from the viewpoint of perception, attitudes, and values.

2. Take the role of Bruce and analyze this incident from the viewpoint of motives.

3. Take the role of Carmen and analyze this incident from the viewpoint of the components that enter into job performance, including motivation.

4. Take the role of Debra and analyze this incident from the viewpoint of behavioral consequences.

Objectives of Chapter 9

■ To underline the importance to managers of the interpersonal context within which individual behavior occurs.

■ To identify ten observations about interpersonal relationships that have a high degree of generality.

■ To introduce the idea of inter-personal response traits and to provide examples of such traits.

■ To discuss and illustrate two approaches to explaining interpersonal attraction.

■ To discuss and assess the roles of congruence and self-dis-closure in growth-facilitating interpersonal relations.

Outline of Chapter 9

INTERPERSONAL BEHAVIOR

My only regret in life is that I'm not someone else.

Woody Allen

*I don't hate anybody, but if I ever change my mind
I've got a couple of people picked out.*

Sam Gillespie

Trust you?
Sure I trust you!
(I wonder what he's after now.)
Be open with you?
Of course, I'm open with you!
(I'm as open as I can be with a guy like you.)
Level with you?
You know I level with you!
(I'd like to more, but you can't take it.)
Accept you?
Naturally I accept you—just like you do me.
(And when you learn to accept me, I might accept you more.)
Self-direction?
I've always believed in self-direction!
(And someday this company may let us use some.)
What's the hang-up?
Not a damn thing!
What could ever hang-up
   Two self-directing,
   Open, trusting,
   Leveling and accepting
   Guys like us.[1]

*Some
questions*

Trust, openness, acceptance, leveling (and their opposites) are all possible dimensions of our personal and interpersonal relationships. What do we know about such relationships? How would you rate yourself on the interpersonal rating scale shown in Figure 9–1?

---

[1] Reproduced by special permission from *The Journal of Applied Behavioral Science*, "Of Course I Believe," by Lyman K. Randall. Volume 5, Number 1, p. 110. Copyright 1969 by NTL Institute for Applied Behavioral Science.

FIGURE 9–1
Interpersonal Rating Scale

Performance Factor	Performance Level				
	Outstanding	*High Satisfactory*	*Satisfactory*	*Low Satisfactory*	*Unsatisfactory*
Quality...........	Leaps tall buildings with single bound	Needs running start to jump tall buildings	Can only leap small buildings	Crashes into buildings	Cannot recognize buildings
Timeliness........	Is faster than a speeding bullet	Only as fast as a speeding bullet	Somewhat slower than a bullet	Can only shoot bullets	Wounds self with bullets
Initiative.........	Is stronger than a locomotive	Is stronger than a bull elephant	Is stronger than a bull	Shoots the bull	Smells like a bull
Adaptability.......	Walks on water consistently	Walks on water in emergencies	Washes with water	Drinks water	Passes water in emergencies
Communication.....	Talks with God	Talks with the angels	Talks to himself	Argues with himself	Loses those arguments
Relationship.......	Belongs in general management	Belongs in executive ranks	Belongs in rank and file	Belongs behind a broom	Belongs with competitor
Planning..........	Too bright to worry	Worries about future	Worries about present	Worries about past	Too dumb to worry

Source: Unknown.

This chapter

This chapter examines individual behavior as it occurs in an *interpersonal context*. We begin by identifying ten general observations about the nature of interpersonal relationships. Then, the idea of interpersonal response traits is introduced and examples given. Next, we discuss and illustrate approaches to understanding interpersonal attraction. The chapter ends with a discussion of the role of congruence and self-disclosure in growth-facilitating interpersonal relations.

GENERAL OBSERVATIONS

Systematic study is recent

People have been interested in interpersonal relationships since the beginning of history. However, systematic study of interpersonal relationships has been going on for less than 50 years. Building on the ideas that a person exists and develops as a "self" largely as a result of interactions with others, those who study interpersonal relations tend to agree on some general conclusions or observations.

Beginning point

Figure 9–2 summarizes several of these general observations. They are listed in descending order of generality and derive from more than one of many approaches to the study of interpersonal relations. Our view is that the ten general observations provide a good beginning point for our discussion of interpersonal behavior.

INTERPERSONAL RESPONSE TRAITS

Definition

Interpersonal response traits are relatively stable and consistent dispositions of a person to respond in distinctive ways to other people. These traits "channel" our behavior during interpersonal relationships even though we may not be aware of the important role they play.

Twelve primary traits

Examples of Traits. What are some examples of these traits? Twelve primary interpersonal response traits which are fairly representative of those discussed by various investigators are shown in Figure 9–3.

Main point

The main point about the 12 primary traits shown in Figure 9–3 is that they represent dispositions to respond behaviorally in a particular way. The traits do not exist in a person on an all-or-none basis; some degree of each of the traits is probably found in most individuals. However, the traits exist in different amounts. If a person regularly tends to exhibit the ascendence trait (defends personal rights, does not mind being conspicuous, not reticent, self-assured, forcefully puts self forward) in a variety of interpersonal situations more than others; we infer the "ascendence trait" in that person.

Trait learning

How are these traits learned? Important influences on the learning of interpersonal response traits are chance events, heredity,

FIGURE 9–2
Interpersonal Relationships: Ten General Observations

1. *Communications.* Communication—verbal and nonverbal—is an essential part of the interpersonal relationship. It includes everything that goes on between two or more people. Communication "communicates" three basic dimensions or messages: who is in control; who likes whom; and how strong are the feelings.

2. *Role of Parents.* There is a tendency for people to interact with other people in the same ways that they have observed their parents interact with other people. "Just as the twig is bent the tree's inclined."

3. *Role of Needs.* There is general agreement that people have needs. One of these needs is the need for satisfying relationships with others: "People need people."

4. *Self and Identity.* The conception we have of ourselves develops largely from our perception of how others perceive us.

5. *Basis of Attraction.* We are attracted to those who satisfy our needs, who provide us with a net pay-off in a reward–cost exchange, and who are like us or agree with us.

6. *Basic Dimensions.* Dominance–submission and acceptance–rejection are two basic dimensions in interpersonal relations.

7. *Role of Rewards.* There is general agreement that behavior that is rewarded will be repeated.

8. *Norms and Rules.* Norms and rules provide regularities to an interpersonal relationship. They reduce uncertainty and help satisfy people's need for predictability in their relationships.

9. *Reciprocity.* There is some evidence that we tend to treat other people the way they treat us.

10. *Social Intelligence.* A high ability to detect the cues that indicate what it is that another person feels or expects will contribute to satisfying interpersonal relationships.

Source: Clifford H. Swensen, Jr., *Introduction to Interpersonal Relations* (Glenview, Ill.: Scott, Foresman and Company, 1973), chapter 14.

FIGURE 9–3
Some Primary Interpersonal Response Traits and Their Polar Opposites

	Trait	*Polar Opposite*
1.	Ascendance	Social timidity
2.	Dominance	Submissiveness
3.	Social initiative	Social passivity
4.	Independence	Dependence
5.	Accepting of others	Rejecting of others
6.	Sociability	Unsociability
7.	Friendliness	Unfriendliness
8.	Sympathetic	Unsympathetic
9.	Competitiveness	Noncompetitiveness
10.	Aggressiveness	Nonaggressiveness
11.	Self-consciousness	Social poise
12.	Exhibitionistic	Self-effacing

Source: David Krech, Richard S. Crutchfield, and Egerton L. Ballachey, *Individual in Society: A Textbook of Social Psychology* (New York: McGraw-Hill Book Company, 1962), p. 106.

personal experiences, group memberships, and our personal self-concept. Undoubtedly, a very important source of trait learning is parental training. People interact with others in ways they have observed their parents interacting with others. "This is indicated by research that shows that a person in an interpersonal transaction is described in the same way by those others as the person describes his own parents."[2]

Use of knowledge of traits

What do you know about a person when you know the person's interpersonal response traits? Basically, you have some information about that person that can contribute to more effective interpersonal relations. With a knowledge of an employee's interpersonal response traits, managers are more informed about the employee's needs and wants. These traits of the individual have been referred to as "the end products of his characteristic experiences in satisfying his most intensely aroused wants."[3] In addition, knowledge of interpersonal response traits provides information about the types of interpersonal relations a person might find attractive. We will examine this idea more fully in the next section on interpersonal attraction.

Four trait characteristics

Response Trait Characteristics. What *don't* you know about a person when you know the person's interpersonal response traits? Quite a lot. The reason is that, between two persons, the traits may have differing degrees of stability, pervasiveness, consistency, and patterning.[4]

Stability

"Stability" refers to the continued presence of a trait. For example, if a new employee has the competitiveness trait, will that trait still be present five or ten years from now? There is some evidence that interpersonal response traits tend to be relatively stable.[5] Our understanding of the law of effect (see Chapter 8) suggests that insofar as these traits are reflected in behavior their stability will be lessened if they are not reinforced by behavioral consequences.

Pervasiveness and consistency

"Pervasiveness" refers to the extent to which the trait is exhibited in the interpersonal relations of the individual. For example, one individual may exhibit friendliness in all interpersonal relations, another may exhibit it only in the company of social equals. "Consistency" refers to the extent to which a trait is exhibited in differing situations. If a trait is of "low" consistency, the person's behavior is more influenced by situational factors than by the interpersonal response trait.

---

[2] Clifford H. Swensen, Jr., *Introduction to Interpersonal Relations* (Glenview, Ill.: Scott, Foresman and Company, 1973), p. 453.

[3] David S. Krech, Richard S. Crutchfield, and Egerton L. Ballachey, *Individual in Society: A Textbook of Social Psychology* (New York: McGraw-Hill Book Company, 1962), p. 115.

[4] Ibid., p. 111.

[5] Ibid., pp. 111–12.

Patterning

"Patterning" recognizes the common-sense notion that two people can have the "friendliness trait," for example, and yet exhibit it in quite different ways. Managers know something about employees when they know they share the "competitiveness trait" equally. However, each employee may manifest it differently.

Summary box

> *Ten general observations* about the nature of interpersonal relations are identified in Figure 9–2.
>
> *Interpersonal response traits* are relatively stable and consistent dispositions of a person to respond in distinctive ways to other people. Twelve interpersonal response traits are identified in Figure 9–3. These traits are learned. One very important source of trait learning is parental training.
>
> Knowledge of interpersonal response traits informs managers about employee needs and wants and about the types of interpersonal relations an employee might find attractive.
>
> *Four characteristics* of response traits are stability, pervasiveness, consistency, and patterning.

INTERPERSONAL ATTRACTION

Role of reinforcing consequences

Why are we attracted to some people and not to others? A very general answer to that question is that we are attracted to those who reinforce us in some way. That is the overall line of reasoning suggested by the behavior–contingencies–consequences framework discussed in Chapter 8. In other words, we will engage in a particular interpersonal relationship if we perceive that the behavior will lead to desired consequences and that the desired consequences are contingent on the behavior.

Two approaches

We can go one step further in answering the question of interpersonal attraction by examining the form of the reinforcer we receive from an interpersonal relationship. The reinforcer can take the form of: (1) satisfying our needs or of (2) providing us with a net gain in an exchange relationship. Each of these two reinforcers is the basis of an approach for explaining interpersonal attraction. We will examine each of these two approaches briefly.

Maslow

A Needs Approach. In Supplement 6A, we discussed Abraham H. Maslow's hierarchy of human needs. We will not repeat that discussion here, but we shall relate Maslow's theory to the subject of interpersonal attraction. Simply put, Maslow suggests that we will be attracted to another person if we see that person as a means of satisfying our needs (physical, safety, social, esteem, and self-actualization).

Satisfying a
deficiency

How can another person be a means of satisfying our needs? In two ways, according to Maslow.[6] *First,* a person can reduce a perceived "deficiency." The person can help us satisfy our unfilled needs. If we are hungry, another person can satisfy our deficiency by giving us food. We *need* to interact with the other person because of our deficiency of food. We are dependent on the other person. In a similar way, we can be deficient in safety and social needs.

Contributing
to self-esteem

Second, a person can be a means of satisfying our needs by contributing to our esteem and our "being"—our personal development and self-actualization. In this case, we do not need the other person for what the person can give us (food, clothing, safety). We are not dependent on the other person. Rather, we are attracted to the other person for what that person *is* and by being with such a person, we partially satisfy our self-actualization need. Thus, Maslow explains interpersonal attraction in terms of deficiency-satisfying and growth-satisfying relationships.

Complemen-
tary needs

Another view of the role of needs is that "complementary needs" can explain interpersonal attraction.[7] That is, people who *differ* in need structure are attracted to each other. For example, people who are dominant may form interpersonal relationships with those who are submissive. Those who have a need to take care of others form interpersonal relationships with others who have a need to be cared for.

Two reasons

Two suggested reasons for these types of attractions are: "First, each member of the dyad finds interaction . . . rewarding because . . . needs are expressed in behavior that is rewarding to the other member. . . . Second, persons are attracted to others who have characteristics they once aspired to but were prevented by circumstances from developing."[8]

Rewards
and costs

An Exchange Approach. The "exchange approach" to interpersonal attraction argues that people are attracted to each other because of the rewards and costs exchanged in the transaction. A "reward" can be anything the person finds reinforcing. A "cost" is anything the person has to give or acquire in order to get the reward. Examples of costs are punishments, giving up some preferred behavior, and fatigue. The difference between rewards and costs is the "outcome," or the profit.

Outcomes
or profit

The essence of the exchange approach lies in the outcomes, or profit. The key to a profitable exchange is "to give the other man

---

[6] Abraham H. Maslow, *Toward a Psychology of Being* (Princeton, N.J.: D. Van Nostrand Co., 1962).

[7] R. F. Winch, *Mate-Selection: A Study of Complementary Needs* (New York: Harper & Row, Publishers, 1958).

[8] Paul F. Secord and Carl W. Backman, "Theories of Interpersonal Attraction," in Fred Luthans, ed., *Contemporary Readings in Organizational Behavior* (New York: McGraw-Hill Book Company, 1972), pp. 311–12.

behavior that is more valuable to him than it is costly to you and to get from him behavior that is more valuable to you than it is costly to him."[9]

Comparison level

In addition to rewards, costs, and outcomes, the concept of "comparison level" is important in the exchange model. The comparison level is a kind of standard against which a person evaluates a relationship.[10]

Two types of comparison levels

There are two types of comparison levels. The "general comparison level" is a kind of average profit from all of a person's relationships. If profit from an interpersonal relationship falls below the general comparison level, the person will be dissatisfied with the relationship and vice versa. The "alternatives comparison level" is the profit a person could receive from other available interpersonal relationships. If profit from an interpersonal relationship falls below the alternatives comparison level, the person will drop the relationship and turn to the alternative,[11] and vice versa.

Role of perceived control

Why do the comparison levels of people differ? One suggested answer to this question is that they vary with the extent to which persons perceive that they have control over their own fate.[12] A perceived high degree of control allegedly makes people more aware of potential rewards than of costs. The result is a relatively high comparison level. A perceived low degree of control allegedly causes more concern with costs than rewards. The result is a relatively low comparison level.

Example of exchange model

In order to illustrate the exchange approach, Figure 9–4 will be used. Assume that persons C and D are subordinates of E. Both C and D are dissatisfied with their relationship with E because the outcomes (O) they receive from the relationship fall, in both cases, below the general comparison level (GCL),($O < GCL$). Person C may perceive that present outcomes are better than present alternatives ($O > ACL$ where ACL is the alternative-comparison level) therefore, even though dissatisfied, will continue the relationship with E. Person D, on the other hand, perceiving that alternatives are better than present outcomes ($ACL > O$), may discontinue the dissatisfying relationship with E. Although the actual alternatives available to C and D may be the same, their $ACLs$ may differ. Person C may emphasize the costs of those alternatives while Person D may emphasize the rewards. The difference between C and D may be due, among other factors, to differences in their perception of control over their own fates.

---

[9] George C. Homans, *Social Behavior: Its Elementary Form* (New York: Harcourt, Brace & World, 1961), p. 62.

[10] Swenson, *Introduction to Interpersonal Relatives,* p. 228.

[11] Ibid., p. 247.

[12] John W. Thibaut and Harold H. Kelley, *The Social Psychology of Groups* (New York: John Wiley & Sons, 1959), chap. 6.

FIGURE 9–4
Illustration of Exchange Approach

	Comparisons Made in an Exchange Relationship with Person E			
	Unfavorable			Favorable
Person C	ACL	O	GCL	
Person D		O	ACL	GCL

O = Outcome
GCL = General comparison level
ACL = Alternatives comparison level

Summary box

> Why are we attracted to some people and not to others? A general answer is that we are attracted to those who reinforce us in some way. This reinforcer may take the form of need satisfaction or of a net gain in an exchange relationship.
>
> The *needs approach* states that we will be attracted to another person if we see that person as a means of satisfying our needs. Maslow explains this in terms of two ideas: deficiency and personal growth. The needs approach also can be viewed in terms of complementary needs.
>
> The *exchange approach* has four basic concepts: rewards, costs, outcomes, and comparison levels. The approach says we will be attracted to a person if the rewards gained from the interpersonal relationship exceed the costs incurred and are consistent with relevant comparison levels.

INTERPERSONAL CONGRUENCE AND SELF-DISCLOSURE

Task relationships

The most important type of interpersonal interaction between a manager and a subordinate is concerned with the achievement of performance goals. Task performance, after all, is the basic reason for the existence of managers. Nevertheless, other types of interpersonal interactions are necessary and desirable. Some of these interactions serve to satisfy perceived needs for affiliation, tension release, job satisfaction, and recognition. Other interpersonal interactions serve to contribute to personal development and growth. It is these potentially growth-facilitating interpersonal relationships that we want to examine next.

Meaningful change

Growth-facilitating Relationships. By "growth-facilitating inter-actions" we mean those in which some meaningful change can emerge for those involved. These interactions aim at satisfying what Maslow calls "self-actualizing needs." They may not directly contribute to task accomplishment. They may even be an obstacle to task accomplishment in the short run. They are not necessarily "satisfying" in the sense of duplicating comfortable and stable in-terpersonal relations. "Over a longer period of time, growth, satis-faction, and productivity may be very much positively related, but at any instant of time in a relationship, they may well not be."[13]

Congruence

What is the dominant characteristic of a growth-facilitating in-terpersonal relationship? One answer to this question we have found intriguing is "congruence." Congruence may be defined as an accurate matching in a person of experience, awareness, and communication.[14] Let's examine congruence more closely.

An example

A person is behaving congruently when what the person is *ex-periencing* matches that person's *awareness* and *communication*. For example, when a baby is hungry (experience), the baby im-mediately communicates awareness of hunger by crying. At that instant, the baby is behaving congruently; the baby is completely integrated, genuine, and transparent.

Incongruence

On the other hand, many adults are unaware of what they are experiencing. For example, a person who is angrily involved in a discussion and communicates this anger, denies the anger and sin-cerely insists, "I'm not angry." This illustrates that an individual may not be the best judge of the level of congruence. Others may have to evaluate congruence.

Two sources of incon-gruence

When incongruence is the result of a disparity between experi-ence and awareness, it may be caused by a form of defensiveness. Our defenses prevent us from matching our experience with aware-ness. When incongruence is the result of a disparity between awareness and communication, it may be an example of deceit.

Honesty and congruence

When awareness and communication match, we say the person is behaving "honestly." However, honesty and congruence are not identical because an honest person may not be aware of many important feelings being experienced. "Truly congruent behavior must be consistent with the whole range of one's value system, as well as one's feelings."[15]

---

[13] Harold S. Spear, "Notes on Carl Rogers' Concept of Congruence and His General Law of Interpersonal Relationships," in Anthony Athos and Robert E. Coffey, *Behavior in Organizations: A Multidimensional View* (Englewood Cliffs, N.J.: Prentice-Hall, 1968), p. 190.

[14] Carl R. Rogers, *On Becoming a Person* (Boston: Houghton Mifflin Com-pany, 1961), p. 338–46.

[15] William G. Dyer, *Insight to Impact: Strategies for Interpersonal and Organizational Change* (Provo, Utah: Brigham Young University Press, 1976), p. 8.

*The growth-
facilitating
process*

How does congruence relate to interpersonal relationships? The basic connection is that the more two people perceive the relationship between them as characterized by congruence, the more the relationship facilitates interpersonal *growth and development*. The growth-facilitating process brings about the conditions for growth: "change in personality in the direction of greater unity and integration, less conflict and more energy utilizable for effective living, and change in behavior in the direction of greater maturity."[16]

Example

How does this growth facilitation occur? When A communicates with B, some degree of congruence is present. The greater the congruence in A, the more B will experience *clear* communication. The clearer the communication, the more B responds with clarity. Since A is behaving congruently and genuinely and without "facade," A is free to *listen* to B. B, therefore, feels positive toward A because A is making a genuine attempt to understand B. B's positive regard for A further reduces the barriers of communication between them. B, therefore, behaves more congruently and less defensively. B's congruence, in turn, causes A to continue behaving congruently. A and B are able to listen more accurately and with empathy.

*Self-
disclosure*

The Johari Window. An idea related to congruence is self-disclosure. "Self-disclosure" means that we communicate to another person something "private" about ourselves.[17] It is not a type of communication we engage in with everyone or in all situations. It involves a special kind of relationship with another person. A useful perspective about self-disclosure is provided by the "Johari window," named after its developers, Joseph Luft and Harry Ingham, is shown in Figure 9–5.

*Exposure and
knowledge*

The Johari window is a four-quadrant model of the interaction of two sources of information, "self" and "others." The *vertical* axis represents the degree of exposure of self to others; the *horizontal* axis represents the degree of knowledge self has of self. The total squared field represents self's interpersonal space in terms of exposure and knowledge.

*Quadrant size
and shape*

The four quadrants represent differing degrees of exposure and knowledge. In Figure 9–5, the size and shape of the four quadrants are equal. However, the size and shape can vary with the degree of exposure and knowledge. Figure 9–6 shows the Johari window for a person with a severely restricted open area. What kind of information is contained in the four quadrants? It can be any

---

[16] Rogers, *On Becoming a Person*, pp. 338–46.

[17] This section on interpersonal self-disclosure is based primarily on Samuel A. Culbert, *The Interpersonal Process of Self-Disclosure: It Takes Two to See One* (Washington, D.C.: National Training Laboratories, Institute for Applied Behavioral Science, 1968).

FIGURE 9–5
The Johari Window

Known to self   Not known to self

	Known to self	Not known to self
Known to others	I Open area	II Blind area
Not known to others	III Hidden area	IV Unknown area

Source: Reprinted from *Group Processes: An Introduction to Group Dynamics* by Joseph Luft by permission of Mayfield Publishing Company, formerly National Press Books, © 1963, 1970 Joseph Luft.

type—perceptions, values, attitudes, facts, assumptions, job knowledge, and so on.

Open area

Quadrant I of Figure 9–6 is the region of shared information and free exchange between individuals. It represents a person's "public self" or "open area." In an interpersonal relationship, the larger the size of Quadrant I, the more an individual can use personal resources for a productive and rewarding relationship.

Blind area

Quadrant II is the "blind area." It contains information that is known to others but not known by self. For self, the blind area is a limiting factor in interpersonal effectiveness. It gives others an advantage over self because they have information about self that self does not have. The blind area limits the size of the open area —the area directly related to interpersonal effectiveness.

FIGURE 9–6
The Johari Window—Restricted Open Area

Known to self   Not known to self

	Known to self	Not known to self
Known to others	I Open area	II Blind area
Not known to others	III Hidden area	IV Unknown area

Hidden area
Quadrant III contains data most relevant to the interpersonal process of self-disclosure. It is the "hidden area" containing information known to self but not known to others. Quadrant III is self's protective front, or facade. In an interpersonal relationship, "the question is not one of whether a facade is necessary but rather how much facade is required realistically."[18] How much facade can be allowed before the open area's space becomes so restricted as to inhibit interpersonal effectiveness?

Unknown area
Quadrant IV is the "unknown area"—unknown to self and others. It may represent resources and potentials of self which, when recognized by self or others, may increase the size of the open area.

Risk
Risking Congruence and Self-Disclosure. Why are not more potentially growth-facilitating interactions characterized by congruence and self-disclosure? Why do we sometimes choose not to be congruent? Why do we sometimes choose not to engage in self-disclosure? Answers to these questions center on the notion of "risk."

Rejection
What is the risk of congruence and self-disclosure? Essentially, it is the risk of rejection. This rejection is much more likely to hurt us if it is our congruent, self-disclosed self that is being rejected. It is easier to brush aside rejection when we can tell ourselves that it was not really I that was rejected; it was only my incongruent and public self. How can this risk of rejection be evaluated by a person? The following formula brings together three factors to consider.

Evaluating the risk
$$\frac{\text{Risk in}}{\text{self-disclosure}} = f\left[\frac{\text{Intensity}}{Pr(\text{intention}) \times Pr(\text{expected reaction})}\right]$$

"That is, the risk in self-disclosure is a function of the *intensity* or importance the communicator places on the disclosure divided by the product of the probabilities that the receiver will hear the disclosure as the communicator *intended* and that the receiver will react as the communicator *expected*."[19]

The self-disclosure process
The self-disclosure process may begin with one of the persons, A, making low-intensity disclosures to B. Depending on how B responds, A may increase or decrease the level of intensity of the disclosures. If B responds appropriately, B becomes more involved in the process. B may even reciprocate with self-disclosures and may exhibit increasing concern for A.

---

[18] Jay Hall, "Communication Revisited," *California Management Review*, vol. 15, no. 3 (Spring 1973), p. 58.

[19] Risk of self-disclosure equation and quotation reproduced by special permission from *The Interpersonal Process of Self-Disclosure: It Takes Two to See One* by Samuel A. Culbert, p. 8, © 1968 National Training Laboratories Institute for Applied Behavioral Science.

Trust

We can see that both congruence and self-disclosure assume a relationship of mutual trust between the participants in an interpersonal relationship. There must be a minimal initial level of trust in order to get processes characterized by congruence and self-disclosure started. The processes themselves must contribute to the progressive development of trust. This trust, in turn, reduces the chances for the perception of fear and threat—a perception that is a major barrier to effective interpersonal relations.

Usefulness to managers

A climate of mutual confidence and trust contributes to effective work environments. These environments facilitate the achievement of performance, group, and individual goals. The ideas of congruence and self-disclosure are useful in interpersonal relationships that are growth-facilitating. In that sense, they contribute primarily to the achievement of *individual* goals. However, interpersonal relations characterized by mutual confidence and trust provide a foundation for effective *performance* goal accomplishment.

Summary box

The ideas of congruence and self-disclosure are applicable to growth-facilitating interpersonal relationships.

Congruence refers to an accurate matching in a person of experience, awareness, and communication. One author suggests that the more two people perceive their relationship as characterized by congruence, the more the relationship facilitates interpersonal growth and development. One reason we choose not to behave congruently is that we do not want to take the risk of being rejected.

Self-disclosure means that we communicate to another person something private about ourselves. The *Johari window* is a way of visualizing data that is known and not known by ourselves and others. Like congruence, self-disclosure involves *risk*.

Congruent and self-disclosure processes are facilitated by an interpersonal relationship characterized by *mutual confidence* and *trust*. Trustful interpersonal relationships contribute to the achievement of performance, group, and individual goals.

CHECK YOUR UNDERSTANDING

Interpersonal response traits
Trait characteristics
Needs approach
   "Deficiency" satisfaction
   "Being" satisfaction
   Complementary needs
Exchange approach
   Outcomes
   General comparison level

Alternatives comparison level
Role of perceived control
Growth-facilitating relationships
   Congruence
   Self-disclosure
   The Johari window
   Risk of rejection
   Risk formula

STUDY QUESTIONS

1. How, in your opinion, might a knowledge of interpersonal response traits help managers become competent? How do the four characteristics of interpersonal response traits serve to caution managers about the usefulness of trait knowledge?

2. Is the idea of interpersonal response traits consistent with the view that behavior is determined by its consequences (see previous chapter)? Explain.

3. Contrast Maslow's notions of "deficiency" and "being" (D and B) motivation. How do they explain interpersonal attraction?

4. Does exchange theory seem to you to be "cold" or "inhuman" as a way of explaining interpersonal attraction? Discuss.

5. Which of the approaches to interpersonal attraction that are discussed in the chapter makes the most sense to you? Which do you feel might be the most useful for managers?

6. What is your personal opinion about Rogers' idea of congruence and Culbert's idea of self-disclosure? Can employees in business organizations "afford" to engage in congruent and self-disclosing behavior? How do they relate to managerial accountability for performance?

7. Identify ways in which the four quadrants of the Johari window can expand and contract. Discuss the Johari window as a static and a dynamic model of interpersonal processes.

8. In this chapter, the importance of mutual confidence and trust was emphasized. What are some factors that, in your opinion, make it difficult for managers and their subordinates to have a trusting relationship between them? What are some potential contributors to a trusting relationship?

APPLICATION: ANALYZING AN INTERPERSONAL RELATIONSHIP

Chapter 9 discusses several ideas that are potentially useful to managers in improving their understanding of work-related interpersonal relationships. This understanding could contribute to interpersonal competence. This application is concerned with relating some of the ideas discussed in Chapter 9 to one of your current interpersonal relationships.

1. Choose, for purposes of this exercise, a work-related or school-related interpersonal relationship that has major significance for you at the present time.

2. Select, from the 12 traits shown in Figure 9–3, those that you think are useful in characterizing your interpersonal relationship. Have the other person involved in the relationship do the same thing. Combine both sets of traits and rate (on a scale of 1 to 7) your perception of how the trait characterizes your own behavior and that of the other person.

3. Of the two approaches (needs and exchange) used in Chapter 9 to discuss interpersonal attraction, select the one that best relates to your interpersonal relationship. Write an essay on how the approach applies to your relationship and compare your essay with a similar one written by the other involved person.

4. Estimate (again, on a scale of 1 to 7) the level of congruence that you perceive in the interpersonal relationship. Compare your estimate with that of the other person. Are you satisfied with the congruence level? Try to apply the "risk of self-disclosure formula" to the interpersonal relationship being analyzed.

Objectives of Chapter 10

- To recognize the importance to managers of the group context within which individual behavior occurs.
- To define a group, differentiate formal and informal groups, and note the settings within which groups function.
- To present a viewpoint about the stages of group development and the nature of a group's influences on members.
- To discuss four variables (size, composition, norms, and cohesiveness) that directly affect behavior of groups.
- To suggest two aspects of the skill of observing a group.
- To introduce a particular view of rational behavior in groups.
- To describe a "process model" of behavior in groups.
- To assess the consequences of competition among groups.

Outline of Chapter 10

Groups at Work
Introduction
Group Development
Group Influences on Members
Performance in Groups
Size
Composition
Norms
Cohesiveness
Observing Groups
Content versus Process
Member's Roles and Behavior
Rational Behavior in Groups
Rational Behavior
The Free-rider Tendency
Counterforces to Free Riders
A Process Model for Describing Behavior in Groups
Three Major Elements
Two Systems
Intergroup Competition
Effects on Groups
Winners and Losers

10

BEHAVIOR IN GROUPS

The so-called common interest that group members share lies in sharing the benefits, not the costs, of group membership.

Mancur Olson

Experience with groups

One of the most common experiences we all have with groups is this: A *few* members do all the work, but *all* members share in the benefits. This chapter argues that such experiences are not only common but are to be expected as a consequence of the nature of groups. Another common experience with groups is this: The individual members seem to serve different functions. Some are good at raising questions, others at answering questions, others at summarizing discussion, and so on. In this chapter we recognize the variety of roles in a group that are necessary if the group is to be effective.

This chapter

This chapter is divided into six parts. *First,* several introductory observations about groups are made along with views about how groups develop and how they influence members. *Second,* the role of four specific variables on the performance of people in groups is discussed. Third, we identify three major types of group members. *Fourth,* we introduce the subject of rational behavior in groups. *Fifth,* a "process model" for describing behavior in groups is presented. Last, we discuss briefly some implications of intergroup competition.

GROUPS AT WORK

What is a group?

Introduction. A group is "two or more persons who are interacting with one another in such a manner that each person influences and is influenced by each other person."[1] Although most of us belong to many types of groups, we are concerned here with groups at work. Some managers take pride in not using groups of any

---

[1] Marvin E. Shaw, *Group Dynamics: The Psychology of Small Group Behavior* (New York: McGraw-Hill Book Company, 1971), p. 10.

347

kind; they feel that in order to be effective, individuals should act individually. Other managers say "with equal pride that they make all their major decisions in groups and rely heavily on teamwork."[2]

A context for behavior

Groups provide a context within which individual behavior occurs. Groups, as such, do not "behave" in the way that individuals do. "To take such a position would be reifying the concepts of groups in a way that is not congruent with the ways groups actually operate."[3] For this reason, we avoid use of the phrase "group behavior." We think of individual job-performance behavior (which depends on abilities and skills, role perceptions, and motivation—see Chapter 6) as occurring in the context of group influences. As we shall see, the group, like the interpersonal context, has important influences on individual behavior.

Formal groups

Groups at work can be formal or informal, and both types are found in all organizations. "Formal groups" are part of the official organization design, and their function is to accomplish specific goals as defined by the organization. Formal groups primarily serve the needs of the organization. Examples include boards of directors, project groups, task forces, work crews, and committees. Members of formal groups often are members as well of various informal groups.

Informal groups

"Informal groups" evolve out of the official organization primarily in order to satisfy needs of organization members that are not being satisfied by formal group membership. Informal groups help satisfy needs for security, attractive social relationships, and belongingness. Many groups at work serve *both* the needs of the organization and of its individual members.

Hawthorne studies

The role of informal groups as an influence on employees' job performance was first suggested in the 1930s by the Hawthorne studies. We will defer until Chapter 14 our full discussion of the Hawthorne studies. However, here we want to note that the role of informal groups in establishing performance standards that differ from formally established standards has been recognized since the 1930s. However, managers have been perplexed for almost 50 years about what to do with this information.

Four environmental settings

Groups at work function within several environmental settings: physical, personal, social, and task.[4] These settings affect group functioning. The "physical environment" refers to rooms, seating arrangements, chairs, tables, temperature, noise, and so on. The

---

[2] Edgar H. Schein, *Organizational Psychology*, 2d ed. (Englewood Cliffs, N.J.: Prentice-Hall, 1970), p. 80.

[3] Lyman W. Porter, Edward E. Lawler III, and J. Richard Hackman, *Behavior in Organizations* (New York: McGraw-Hill Book Company, 1975), p. 375.

[4] Shaw, *Group Dynamics: The Psychology of Small Group Behavior*, p. 118.

"personal environment" consists of the set of personal characteristics members bring to the group. The "social environment" is the whole set of relationships within the group. It includes such elements as group structure, roles, norms, means of distributing power and making decisions, and leadership processes. The "task environment" is the set of tasks and goals the group is supposed to perform and achieve.

Stages

Group Development.[5] The idea that a work or task group "grows" through a developmental process is a common one in managerial literature. Implicit in the idea is that there are "stages" in group development. One approach is to identify four stages: forming, differentiation, integration, and maturity.

Forming

The "forming stage" is concerned with initial attempts by individuals to identify with the group in terms of a give-and-take relationship. In addition, individuals focus on identifying the task of the group, the ways the group will serve to satisfy individual needs, the initial ground rules for behavior, and the "place" of the group and its task in the total organization of which it is a part. In the forming stage, "Much of the individual's conception of the group is based on selective attention to particular characteristics and behaviors of other group members."

Differentiation

The "differentiation stage" reflects the process of getting a better "feel" for the composition of the group and for its task. A major ingredient of this stage is the process of "nailing down" the means that will be used for accomplishing the group task and for satisfying individual members' needs. In the differentiation stage, it is not uncommon for conflict and competition to emerge. Coalitions of members may be formed in order to enhance the chances for need satisfaction. These conditions and individual members may compete with each other as they attempt to ". . . impose their definitions of the situation on the group and to obtain their desired position in the group's structure."

Integration

The "integration stage" reaps the benefits of the groping and imbalance that characterized the differentiation stage. The integration stage is a stage of balance in the life of a group. This balance comes from the influence of norms that regulate member behavior. To the extent that these norms are accepted and task-contributing, the group becomes a cohesive entity. One danger of the integration stage is that members can become mesmerized by the group's cohesiveness. This, in turn, can encourage "group think" and discourage those constructive variations from group norms that are essential to creative and effective behavior in the group.

[5] This section is based on J. Stephen Heinen and Eugene Jacobson, "A Model of Task Group Development in Complex Organizations and a Strategy of Implementation," *Academy of Management Review*, vol. 1, no. 4 (October 1976), pp. 98–111.

Maturity

The "maturity stage" is rather difficult to describe—a function of the fuzziness of the idea of maturity even when applied to individuals. Maturity in the life of a group refers to the group members' integration of the needs for both flexibility and stability. A mature group recognizes the necessary role of a stable system of norms, standards, and other regularities in guiding the behavior of individual members. At the same time, a mature group remains flexible enough so that it can adapt to changing tasks and contingencies in its environment.

Stimuli

Group Influences on Members.[6]   We have said that the group context influences individual behavior. How does this influence occur? One approach to answering that question is to identify two types of stimuli. "Stimuli" is an unpleasant-sounding word for some very ordinary things: other people, conversation, the furnishings of a room, paper, machines, and so on. Groups control many of the stimuli that a person encounters during the course of a work day.

Ambient stimuli

Simply being a member of a group makes certain stimuli available to a person. These stimuli are referred to as "ambient stimuli." They include the physical characteristics of the group's working environment, the people in the group, the characteristics of the group's task, and organizationally controlled rewards for group membership. "Ambient stimuli are part of the 'background' of group functioning. . . . The stimuli are just 'there' and they are always there." Nevertheless, they may be having a profound, if unnoticed, influence on behavior.

Discretionary stimuli

There is yet another class of stimuli that influences group members. "Discretionary stimuli" can be transmitted to group members by other group members on a selective basis. Group membership alone is not adequate reason for receiving discretionary stimuli. They are contingent on the behavior of the group member. Examples of discretionary stimuli include a supportive environment, social acceptance, social rejection, and information possessed only by group members.

Three types of impact

Both ambient and discretionary stimuli can influence a group member in three ways. *First,* the stimuli can serve as an important source of job-related or personal information. *Second,* the group, through both types of stimuli, can affect a group member's affective state, including attitudes, values, and motivations. *Third,* the group influences a member's behavior through its control over monetary and social rewards and other reinforcing consequences.

---

[6] This section draws heavily on J. Richard Hackman, "Group Influences on Individuals," in Marvin D. Dunnette, ed., *Handbook of Industrial and Organizational Psychology* (Chicago: Rand McNally College Publishing Company, 1976), chap. 33. © 1976 by Rand McNally College Publishing Company, Chicago.

Additionally, to the extent that behavior is influenced by group-supplied information and group-influenced affective states, the group influences its members' behavior.

Summary box

> A *group* is two or more persons who are interacting in such a manner that each person influences and is influenced by each other person. Groups do not behave; only individuals engage in behavior. Groups provide a *context* within which individual behavior occurs.
>
> Groups at work can be formal and informal. *Formal groups* are part of the official organization. *Informal groups* evolve out of the official organization as a response to individual needs.
>
> Groups are usually small (under 20 members) and function within several *environmental settings:* physical, personal, social, and task.
>
> The idea that a group "grows" suggests the notion of a group developmental process. Four stages in this process are: forming; differentiation; integration; and maturity.
>
> Groups control many of the stimuli that a person encounters on the job. *Ambient stimuli* are encountered simply as a result of membership in a group. *Discretionary stimuli* are distributed selectively by group members to other group members.
>
> Ambient and discretionary stimuli influence group members by altering their *informational and affective states* and by directly and indirectly influencing their *behavior.*

PERFORMANCE IN GROUPS

Four variables

What else is it about groups that can affect the performance of individuals in the group? We have already suggested several *indirect* factors: the four environmental settings, the developmental stage of the group, and the group's ambient and discretionary stimuli. In this section we discuss four variables that *directly* influence the performance of individuals in groups: size; composition; cohesiveness; and norms.

No optimum size

Size. There is no optimum group size, but group size can affect individual performance. Precisely *how* size affects performance is not clear. There is some evidence that size can affect the speed, quality, and quantity of group performance. However, it is difficult to isolate the effect of group size from the effect of other variables affecting performance.

Positive and negative influence

One author states that "as group size increases, contending forces are unleashed some of which foster performance while others hinder it."[7] An increase in group size may increase the resources that are available for performance, make it more "representative" of the population from which it is drawn, and provide more people with opportunities for affiliation with others. However, the larger size may also prevent the effective utilization of the group's resources. This may result if the larger group size makes group members feel inhibited. The larger size can also bring about the need for a more formal group structure with well-defined roles and tasks. As group size increases, members are less able to engage in eye contact and face-to-face communication. Depending on the problem, this can affect performance adversely.

Problem-solving groups

It has been suggested by two other authors that "for groups with the purpose of engaging in intensive problem-solving, it appears the maximum size should be around seven members." They note that "around seven" members may be a *necessary* condition for effective group problem-solving, but it is not a *sufficient* condition. In any case, managers should be aware that as a group increases in size there are both negative and positive influences on performance.[8]

Extreme cases

Composition. The effect of group composition on performance is brought into focus by this comment: "The extremes are obvious; five morons are unlikely to outperform five persons of evident brilliance, and five dedicated enemies are unlikely to outperform five friends on a problem requiring cooperative solution."[9] Between these extremes, the effect of such things as abilities, skills, motivations, personality, and other individual variables on performance in groups is less obvious.

Two points

We mention "composition" as a variable affecting performance primarily to emphasize two points. *First,* performance in a group is dependent on the capabilities of individual members. *Second,* the performance of an individual member can be enhanced or restricted by other group members. In terms of predicting the total performance of a group, we know surprisingly little about the influence of specific abilities and personality characteristics.

Problem-solving styles

We can relate the topic of group composition to that of problem-solving styles. Recall that in Chapter 5 we discussed four problem-solving styles that are based on the psychology of Carl Jung. Each of these styles emphasizes a different combination of information-gathering and decision-making orientations. The four problem-

---

[7] Reprinted by special permission from James H. Davis, *Group Performance,* 1969, Addison-Wesley, Reading, Massachusetts, p. 72.

[8] Don Hellriegel and John W. Slocum, Jr., *Management: A Contingency Approach* (Reading, Mass.: Addision-Wesley Publishing Company, 1974), p. 377.

[9] Davis, *Group Performance,* p. 75.

solving styles are: sensing-thinking (*ST*), sensing-feeling (*SF*), intuition-thinking (*NT*), and intuition-feeling (*NF*). (Refer back to Chapter 5 for a review of these styles.) There are times when potential group members can be classified according to their problem-solving styles. Since each of the four styles is appropriate for certain types of problems, and since the four styles complement each other, it could prove useful to base problem-solving group composition on a balanced mixture of the four problem-solving styles.

What are norms?

Norms. "Norms" develop in any group. They are ideas about how group members are supposed to behave in and outside of the group. Norms are standards against which the behavior of group members can be judged. They serve to regularize behavior and move it toward conformity.

Two purposes

In general, norms serve two purposes. *First,* they identify what behavior will be considered "appropriate." Appropriate behavior leads to positive consequences such as expressions of respect and approval from other group members. Second, norms define the "limits of behavior." As group members approach these limits, they are likely to receive signals from other members that they are violating group norms.

Formal standards and norms

A group of production workers may be expected to produce 500 items per hour. This is a formal performance standard set by someone outside the group. The group itself may establish its own production norm, say somewhere between 350 and 450 units, 400 units being considered the most appropriate average production.

Two types of norms

The effect of norms on performance depends on the *type* of norm and the *importance* of the norm in overall group functioning. Groups may have different types of norms. For our purposes, we identify two types: task-related and process-related. "Task-related norms" have the greatest effect on performance, positive or negative. In the example above, the group's norm is below the formal performance standard. However, task-related norms established by group members do not have to be in conflict with formally established standards. "Process-related norms" are norms about how group members should interact in developing and maintaining the group as a source of attractive and supportive interaction with others.

Importance of norms

The importance of norms also influences their effect on performance. The more important a norm is to a group, the more likely the group is to enforce the norm. The more important it is, the more likely that members will use the norm as a guide. Within any group, a norm may be considered important by most members but unimportant to a particular member. For that person, the important group norm may not be a guide for behavior.

Norms provide for range of behavior

Norms in a group can vary in the degree of deviance that will be tolerated. In the example given earlier, the production norm of 400 units has tolerances of plus or minus 50 units. However, if an employee produces, say, 300 units, that may be considered an unacceptable deviation from the norm. In that case, the other group members may transmit discretionary stimuli (pressure to increase production, social rejection) in order to correct the deviant behavior.

Norms are not always applied uniformly

Norms in a group can also vary in the uniformity of their application. Continuing with the same example, one employee may be allowed to produce 500 units, another employee may be allowed to produce only 300, and all others may be expected to produce between 350 and 450 units. One reason for the lack of uniformity in applying norms is that ". . . high-status members often have more freedom to deviate from the letter of the norm than do other people—that is, they build up so-called idiosyncrasy credits."[10]

Cohesiveness results from two forces

Cohesiveness. "Cohesiveness is generally regarded as characteristic of the group in which the forces acting on the members to remain in the group are greater than the total forces acting on them to leave it."[11] These cohesive forces may be grouped into two general categories: those that positively influence the achievement of the personal goals of group members, and those that satisfy group members' needs for attractive and supportive interactions with others.[12] Frequently, this latter category alone is used to identify group cohesiveness. For example, "When investigators have desired to manipulate the cohesiveness of groups, regardless of their nominal definition of the concept, the operations performed have typically involved telling the members of some groups that they would probably like each other, be congenial, etc., while telling others just the opposite."[13]

Performance affects cohesiveness

How does cohesiveness relate to performance? *First,* successful performance of group tasks can increase cohesiveness. Even failure can lead to a feeling of cohesiveness if the failure occurs in a threatening or a win-lose situation. If the group members see cohesiveness as an effective way of coping with threat or failure, the members may experience feelings of cohesiveness.

Cohesiveness affects performance

Second, cohesiveness can cause performance differences. In general, it can have a *positive* effect on performance if the reasons for the cohesiveness are consistent with group tasks and goals. Cohesiveness can have a *negative* effect on performance if the in-

---

[10] Porter, Lawler III, and Hackman, *Behavior in Organizations,* p. 393.

[11] Davis, *Group Performance,* p. 78.

[12] Based on D. Cartwright and A. Zander, *Group Dynamics: Research and Theory* (New York: Harper & Row, Publishers, 1968).

[13] Albert J. and Bernice E. Lott, "Group Cohesiveness as Interpersonal Attraction: Antecedents of Liking," *Psychological Bulletin,* vol. 64, no. 4 (October 1965), p. 259.

teractions within the group conflict with goal attainment. Too much cohesiveness can discourage needed deviation from norms and encourage an excessive sense of "groupthink."

Summary box

> Individual performance in work groups depends on situational factors, abilities and skills, role perception, and motivation. The group itself may be considered a situational factor.
>
> *Group size* can influence performance. As a group increases in size, negative and positive forces on performance result.
>
> *Group composition* refers to the performance capabilities of individual members. Individual performance capabilities can be enhanced or restricted by those of other group members.
>
> *Group norms* set standards for both appropriate and deviant behavior in groups. Group norms can be task and process-related. Both, if important in the group, can positively or negatively affect performance.
>
> *Group cohesiveness* can be caused by forces related to personal goals of group members and to forces that satisfy the members' needs for attractive and supportive interactions. Cohesiveness's effect on performance can be positive if the source of the cohesiveness is consistent with the group's task.

OBSERVING GROUPS

Observing behavior

A useful managerial skill is the skill to observe the behavior of people in groups. This skill may enhance the manager's effectiveness in groups and may provide a basis for counseling subordinates on how they might become more effective. But what is there to observe about behavior in groups? What is there to "see" in a group?

"What" versus "how"

Content versus Process. One of the things to observe in a group is "what" is taking place—what task is being worked on, what is being communicated, and what is being decided. These observations are related to content; they deal with what is happening in the group. In contrast, process deals with "how" the content items are being handled—how is the communication being handled (who talks? For how long? Who talks to whom? Who isn't talking)? And how are the decisions being made (majority voting, concensus, railroading by one person, and so on)?

Both provide useful data

Every group operates at both the content and process levels. Content and process norms evolve as the group develops and builds a record of influencing members through ambient and discretionary stimuli. However, explicit attention is seldom directed at the process level. Particularly, groups at work seem to avoid overt discussion of process issues. Perhaps that is because such groups are so predominantly task or content-oriented. In work groups there is often a norm that encourages "staying with the task." A person who deviates runs the risk of censure. Nevertheless, both content and process can be observed in a group. Both provide data useful in improving our effectiveness in groups.

Three types of roles

Members' Roles and Behavior. Behavior in a group can be roughly classified into three categories: task-related, maintenance-related, and individual-related.[14] These categories were identified over thirty years ago by researchers who were analyzing behavior in discussion groups. The "task" of the groups was to select, define, and solve problems. Most groups in work organizations are not discussion groups. Their task is commonly very specific, structured, and tied into the economic welfare of the group's members. Nevertheless, in our opinion, these three categories are a useful way of viewing behavior in groups at work.

Task and maintenance roles

"Task-related roles" call for behavior directly related to establishing and achieving the goals of the group. "Maintenance-related roles" call for behavior that is directly related to the well-being, continuity, and development of the group. Examples of both are shown in Figure 10–1. The behavior of a group member may fulfill one or more of these roles. In time, particular members may be-

FIGURE 10–1
Task and Maintenance Roles of Group Members

Group Task-Related Roles	*Group Maintenance-Related Roles*
Contributing new ideas or new approaches to the task	Encouraging others in the group by commendation and praise
Seeking or giving information	Mediating differences among members
Seeking or giving opinions	
Coordinating ideas and activities	Compromising in order to maintain group harmony
Energizing the group	
Orienting the group toward the task	Keeping communication channels open by encouraging broad participation
Recording necessary information	
Evaluating group performance	Setting standards of how the group will function
Elaborating on suggestions or new ideas	Observing group processes and providing group with feedback
Procedural technician—performs routine tasks, distributes materials	Following along with the movement of the group

---

[14] Kenneth J. Benne and Paul Sheats, "Functional Roles of Group Members," *Journal of Social Issues,* vol. 4, no. 2 (Spring 1948), pp. 42–47.

come known for their success (or lack of success) in filling specific roles.

Individual roles

All behavior in a group does not fit neatly into these two categories. Some behavior is oriented only to the individual needs of members, rather than to the group's needs. "Individual-oriented behavior" includes aggression, excessive resistance and opposition to the group, nonchalance, excessive "joking around" or horseplay, "soap boxing," soliciting sympathy, or catharsis of non-group-oriented feelings. Although these roles can at times be functional, they are, in general, dysfunctional in work groups.

Member versus leader roles

It is useful to reemphasize that the task and maintenance roles are member's roles. They are not roles that have to be filled by a leader. For example, if the group consists of a supervisor and subordinates, both the supervisor and the subordinates may fill any or all of the roles—depending on who is most qualified.

Shared leadership

If the official leader is the most qualified person to handle a specific role, then that leader should handle the role. If one of the group members is more qualified than the official leader, then that member should handle the role. In a sense, whoever is handling one of the task-related or maintenance-related roles is the "leader." Most of the time, the official leader of a work group is in a unique position to fill several roles. Furthermore, the leader's *accountability for results* assures that he or she will have more than a passing interest in how the roles are being filled and who fills them. Although this approach does not do away with the idea of the formal leader, it does emphasize a sharing, within the group, of duties often associated with a formal leader. The emphasis is on the roles to be filled and not on the leader's responsibility.

Summary box

> Behavior in groups occurs at both the *content* and *process* levels. The content level deals with what is taking place; the process level deals with how the group members handle such matters as communication and decision making.
>
> Roles in groups can be classed as group *task-related*, group *maintenance-related*, and *individual-related*. The first two roles are group-oriented, whereas the last role is oriented toward the individual's needs.
>
> In an effective group, the group-oriented roles are carried out by whoever is most qualified, regardless of whether the person is the group's official leader.

RATIONAL BEHAVIOR IN GROUPS[15]

Individual versus group interest

Some very useful insights about the behavior of individuals in groups can be gained by examining the relationship between the individual interest of a group member and the overall, collective group interest. This is an important relationship to examine because the most common—the almost universally present—condition in a small group is this: The individual members of the group have a stake in the group, but each also has individual interests different from the other members and which may be in conflict with the group's interest.

Benefits versus costs

Rational Behavior. What does it mean to say that each group member has a stake in the group interest? It means that each member wants to share in the benefits of achieving the group's interest. It does not mean that each member wants to share in the costs of achieving the group's interest. This is a simple idea to which most of us can relate. Haven't you been in a group where it seemed as if everyone in the group wanted a share of the benefits but expected *you* to do all of the work? This is such a common experience that there must be a good explanation for it. And there is. The explanation hinges on the idea of rational individual behavior in groups.

Rational behavior

What is "rational individual behavior"? One commonly held view of rational behavior is that it is behavior that attempts to achieve the best match between benefits and costs. For the moment, let us accept this "best match" view of rational behavior. A best match is one that is perceived to have a favorable balance of benefits over costs. At the extreme, some individuals might contend that behavior that results in "all benefits and no costs" is the best of all worlds. At the other extreme, there are few individuals that would contend that behavior that results in "all costs and no benefits" is a desired state of affairs. Such behavior is "irrational" from the viewpoint of the individual's self-interest.

The free-rider

The Free-Rider Tendency. Is it rational for a member to contribute to the group's interest? The answer is that sometimes it is and sometimes it isn't. Let's first consider when such behavior is *not* rational. A "free-rider tendency" operates within groups. A free rider is one who shares in the benefits of group effort without sharing in the costs. The free rider wants the other members of the group to bear all the costs. This situation can exist when individual rewards are not contingent on individual performance. A "pure" free rider may not be common, but there is a tendency operating in groups for individual members to be free riders *to some* extent. Why is this the case?

---

[15] We are indebted to Gerald Keim of the Department of Management, Texas A&M University, for calling the viewpoint of this section to our attention. In addition, this section draws heavily on Mancur Olson, *The Logic of Collective Action: Public Goods and the Theory of Groups* (Cambridge, Mass.: Harvard University Press, 1971).

Private goods   The tendency to be a free rider is due to the difference between private and public goods. When you work as an individual (rather than as a member of a group) it is possible for there to be a 1-to-1 relationship between your efforts and the results or "goods" produced by your efforts. Your individual efforts produce a private good. A "private good" is one whose benefits go in full to the individual who bore the costs of providing it. The commission earned when a salesperson completes a sale is a private good.

Public goods   However, when you work as a member of a group the results of your efforts lead to results or goods that are *shared by all members of the group*. If your costs = 1; your benefits = <1. Your individual efforts produce a collective or public good. A "public good" is one whose benefits are distributed to all members of a group even though all of the costs of providing the good were borne by fewer than all members of the group. A bonus earned by a work crew for increasing the productivity of the crew is a public good. The bonus may be distributed equally to all members of the work crew, even though it was the result of the extraordinary efforts of one member of the crew.

Effect of free-rider tendency   If all the group members share equally in the benefits, then the more an individual member contributes to those benefits, the *lower* that member's share of benefits *relative* to costs. This fact discourages individual members from putting forth effort to achieve the group interest. Furthermore, as the individual reduces effort, he or she may find that benefits are still received. This, in turn, further discourages the member from increasing effort. Why increase effort while benefits are still coming in?

Effect of group size   The free-rider tendency tends to increase with the size of the group. It is easier to be a free rider in a large group because one's lack of contribution is less noticeable and even less significant. This is an important point to keep in mind about group size. What it means from a practical point of view is that, as a group becomes larger, the more likely it is to fall short of achieving an optimal amount of the group's public good. As we noted in an earlier part of this chapter, group size is a variable that affects performance. The existence of the free-rider tendency is one additional reason for this. A group of ten is not just a group of five, grown twice its size.

Altruism; other incentives   **Counterforces to Free Riders.** There are several situations in which a group member may decide to bear what might *appear* to be a disproportionate share of the costs of achieving the group's interest. These situations represent counterforces to the free-rider tendency. *First,* an individual may not view rational behavior in terms of costs and benefits, strictly defined. There are individuals who are truly altruistic. They wish to contribute to the self-interest or welfare of others. *Second,* individual group members can be offered special incentives as a reward for bearing a larger share of the costs of the group interest. The effect of such incentives is to make a private good available to the individual in exchange for a contribution to the public good.

Special stake in group success

Third, individual members may have a special stake in the success of a group's effort. A career-oriented executive may want to make sure that any group she or he is associated with is successful in achieving its goal. The particular group's goal may not be that important to the executive, but the group's success may be very important, and the executive's interest in the group's success may spur her or him to provide up to all of the costs of achieving the group's goal.

Summary box

All members of a group have an interest in sharing in the *benefits* of membership in the group. However, they do not necessarily, and most likely will not, have an equal interest in sharing the *cost* of acquiring those benefits.

Individuals in groups act rationally when they attempt to achieve what is *for them* the best match between the benefits of group membership and the cost of that membership.

The *free-rider tendency* in groups is the tendency for individual members to achieve group benefits without sharing proportionately in the costs of achieving those benefits. The existence of the tendency is due to the difference between *private and public goods.* As a group increases in size, the free-rider tendency is likely to be more pronounced.

There are several situations in which individual group members may decide to bear what might appear to be a disproportionate share of the costs of achieving group benefits.

A PROCESS MODEL FOR DESCRIBING BEHAVIOR IN GROUPS

A-I-S model

A model for describing the process of behavior in groups is shown in Figure 10–2. It is referred to as "the *A-I-S* model" because it has three major elements: activities, interactions, and sentiments.

Activities, interactions, sentiments

Three Major Elements. "Activities" are what group members do (talk, operate machines, carry things, sleep, and so forth). "Interactions" are any communications or contacts between group members. Interactions involve an action and a reaction between two or more members. These interactions can have a positive, negative, or neutral effect on the persons involved. "Sentiments" are

FIGURE 10–2
The A-I-S Model for Describing Behavior in Groups

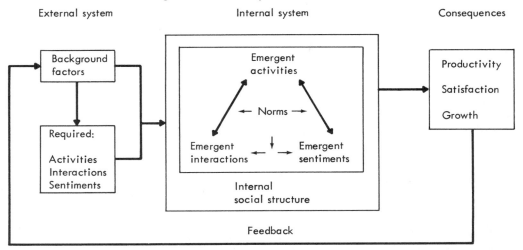

Source: Adapted from Arthur N. Turner, "A Conceptual Scheme for Describing Work Group Behavior," in Paul R. Lawrence and John A. Seiler, *Organizational Behavior and Administration* (Rev. ed.; Homewood, Ill.: Richard D. Irwin, Inc., 1965), p. 158.
     The above model is based on a model developed by George C. Homans. See his *Social Behavior: Its Elementary Forms* (New York: Harcourt, Brace & World, Inc., 1961).

ideas, beliefs, or feelings relevant to group tasks or processes. Sentiments, unlike activities and interactions, are not directly observable. Sentiments can be positive, negative, or neutral.

Required and emergent behavior

There are two kinds of activities, interactions, and sentiments: required and emergent. Those that are "required" are essential to the task assigned to the group. Some types of activities and interactions are essential to even minimal levels of performance. Examples of such required activities and interactions include being present at work, communicating with co-workers, processing paperwork, and acknowledging customers when they come into a store. Examples of "emergent" activities, interactions, and sentiments include more effective (although unauthorized) job methods and procedures, communicating with informal leaders about task-related problems, and informal group norms of job performance.

External system

Two Systems. The set of required activities, interactions, and sentiments along with background factors (task environment, task design, organizational policies, type of management, economic and social environment, personal backgrounds of group members, and so on) make up the "external system."

Internal system

The external system of background factors, required activities, interactions, and sentiments provides the raw material for forming the "internal system." The internal system is the set of activities.

interactions, and sentiments that emerges out of the external system. The internal system forms norms, about what behavior is desirable in the group. A norm is one type of sentiment that is held in common by group members. The internal system, then, produces *consequences* of three kinds: *productivity; satisfaction;* and *growth* for group members. These consequences, or information about them, become, through *feedback,* part of the external system.

Relation of sentiments and interactions

There are several ways in which the emergent activities, interactions, and sentiments might interrelate. For example, *all other things being equal,* group members who have favorable sentiments toward each other may interact more frequently than those who do not. Also, frequent interaction may lead to favorable sentiments between group members.

Relation of norms and sentiments

Additionally, norms serve as the basis for sentiment formation. Members who violate norms that are accepted by most members will have unfavorable sentiments directed toward them. These unfavorable sentiments lead to reduced interactions. Conversely, the more a member conforms to norms, the more the member will be viewed favorably and will engage in more frequent interactions. These relationships are only possibilities. They are suggestive, however, of how managers might use activities, interactions, and sentiments as elements for describing and predicting behavior in groups.

Summary box

> The *A-I-S* model provides managers with a way of describing behavior in groups. The model essentially involves three interacting elements: activities, interactions, and sentiments.
>
> There are two types of activities, interactions, and sentiments: *required* and *emergent.*
>
> Various background factors combine with the set of required elements to form the *external system.*
>
> Out of the external system develops the *internal system,* the set of emergent activities, interactions, and sentiments and the norms for behavior in the group.
>
> The operation of the internal system leads to *productivity, satisfaction,* and *growth consequences.*

INTERGROUP COMPETITION

Cooperation is the rule

The high degree of cooperation in business and almost all other types of organizations is a marvel to behold. "Cooperative" is the best word to describe the nature of most relationships between members of organizations. That is true whether we are referring to interpersonal, intragroup, or intergroup relationships. Nevertheless, "cooperative" does not accurately describe all intra or intergroup relations; "competitive" is sometimes an appropriate description. In this section we will suggest some of the consequences of intergroup competition and of win-lose situations.

Effect within competing groups

Effects on Groups.[16]   The consequences of intergroup competition are well known and generally constant. *First,* what is the effect of intergroup competition on the members within each competing group? The effects tend to be as follows: each group becomes more closely knit in the face of the "threat" from the competing group; each group becomes more task-oriented and less process-oriented; the groups become more organized, more willing to tolerate autocratic leadership; and conformity to group norm is demanded.

Effect on relations between groups

Second, what are the effects of intergroup competition on the relations between the groups? The effects tend to be: each group sees each other as an enemy, distorted perceptions result (we're good, they're bad), hostility between the groups increases along with a decrease in interaction and communication, and the quality of listening between groups declines.

Effect on the winner

Winners and Losers.   When groups compete, one of them ends up the winner and one the loser. What happens to the winning group? The group may become more cohesive, more relaxed and complacent, more concerned for member needs than for task accomplishment, and generally "satisfied" with itself. The result of this may be a decline in the group's performance and in its ability to compete.

Effect on the loser

What happens to the losing group? It may resist admitting defeat, look for a basis for denying defeat, look for scapegoats within the group, and look for ways to recoup its loss. The group may look for ways to reevaluate its performance. As a result, there may be an improvement in the group's ability to perform and compete.

Point for managers

These consequences are only tendencies, and "The gains of intergroup competition may under some conditions outweigh the negative consequences."[17] That is fortunate because there is no way that competition can be completely removed as an ingredient of intergroup behavior. Further, competition for scarce organizational resources and positions of influence can contribute to more effective member performance. However, the point is not that intergroup competition is bad. The point for managers is that they should be aware of the consequences of intergroup competition, and, where

[16] This section is based on Edgar H. Schein, *Organizational Psychology,* ed., © 1970, pp. 96–99. By permission of Prentice-Hall, Inc., Englewood Cliffs. N.J.

[17] Schein, *Organizational Psychology,* p. 99.

possible, they should attempt to base intergroup relations on co-operation and collaboration.

Summary box

> Interpersonal, intragroup, and intergroup relationships in organizations are often characterized as cooperative or competitive. Our opinion is that most of these relationships are most accurately characterized as *cooperative*. In this section, however, we examined the consequences of *competition* on groups and between groups.
>
> In general, there can be gains and losses from intergroup competition. Competition between groups tends to make *intra*group relations more cohesive and task-oriented. However, competition can negatively affect the character of the *inter*group relations. Competition creates a win-lose situation, and it leads to different consequences for the winning and losing groups.

CHECK YOUR UNDERSTANDING

Group
Formal group
Informal group
Group environments
Stages of group development
Ambient stimuli
Discretionary stimuli
Norms
Two types of norms
Cohesiveness
Content versus process
Group task-related roles
Group maintenance-related roles
Individual roles

Rational behavior
Free rider
Private good
Public good
A-I-S model
   Activities (required and
     emergent)
   Interactions (required and
     emergent)
   Sentiments (required and
     emergent)
   External system
   Internal system
   Group consequences

STUDY QUESTIONS

1. Why do informal groups evolve out of formal work groups in organizations?

2. Identify ways in which the four environmental settings might affect group functioning.

3. Discuss some probable characteristics of each of the four stages in group development.

4. Identify ambient and discretionary stimuli relevant to a group you are in at the present time.

5. The chapter suggests that the four problem-solving styles (discussed in Chapter 5) provide data useful in composing the membership of a group. Explain what is meant by this suggestion.

6. Identify and illustrate the ways in which group norms serve as behavioral guides for members.

7. What would be your basic approach to answering the question, does group cohesiveness contribute to individual performance in groups?

8. Discuss the free-rider tendency that operates in groups. Do you agree with the view of rational behavior on which the free-rider tendency is based? Explain.

APPLICATION: THE NOMINAL GROUP TECHNIQUE (NGT)*

Groups vary according to the degree of face-to-face interaction of group members. Our discussion of groups in Chapter 10 deals largely with *interacting groups*—groups characterized by a high degree of face-to-face interaction. Such groups fit more closely our definition of a group as two or more persons who are interacting with one another in such a manner that each person influences and is influenced by each other person.

Lower degrees of face-to-face interactions are illustrated by delphi groups and nominal groups. A "Delphi group" (see Chapter 3 "Application" on Delphi forecasting) literally has no face-to-face interaction. Such a group "interacts" only through mailed questionnaires. A "nominal group" is a face-to-face group but it interacts in a special way. We'll illustrate the way a nominal group operates through an example.

Assume that you are a supervisor of ten licensed vocational nurses (LVNs). Each LVN has from three to five subordinates— relatively unskilled workers who assist the LVNs with their duties with nursing home residents. As the supervisor, you feel there must be ways in which the job performance of the LVNs and their subordinates can be improved. Further, the LVNs are the best source of suggestions and ideas for job improvement. So you want to find an effective way of bringing forth these ideas and suggestions.

From your previous experience with the LVNs you know that bringing them together as an interacting group for a face-to-face, give-and-take session has mixed results. On the one hand, such sessions have helped synthesize information and crystalize thinking on specific problems, have led to better problem solutions, and have been enthusiastically received by the LVNs. You have a good working relationship with the LVNs and they are not bashful about coming forward with their opinions.

---

* This application is based on an actual use of the NGT. A nominal group proved to be a very successful mechanism for generating ideas and an interacting group was useful in identifying the requirements for implementing the ideas. For a thorough reference on NGT, see André L. Delbecq, Andrew H. Van de Ven, and David H. Gustafson, *Group Techniques for Program Planning* (Glenview, Ill.: Scott, Foresman and Company, 1975).

On the other hand, the group discussion is always dominated by a few of the more vocal and dynamic LVNs. Those who are less forceful seem to be intimidated into keeping quiet. Furthermore, it seems as if the discussion gets on one track and stays there. The result is that many dimensions of the problem never surface for discussion and never enter into the choice of a solution. Sometimes you end up with a solution to a problem that never has been adequately defined. In order to gain the above advantages without the disadvantages, you decide to use the *nominal group technique.*

First, you bring the LVNs together to sit around a U-shaped table. In front of each LVN is a sheet of paper on which is typed the *NGT question:* "What actions can we take to improve our service to the residents?" You request the LVNs not to talk to each other about the NGT question but to write down any ideas they have about the question. You request the LVNs to work in silence, and you allow about 10 to 15 minutes for this phase of the NGT.

Second, you ask one of the LVNs to read aloud to the group one of the ideas she has written on the paper. She reads: "Tell the night shift to keep the linen closet stacked with linen." You write this statement, or an abbreviated form of it, on a flip chart placed on the open end of the U-table. You identify the statement as no. 1. Without any discussion of the first idea, you ask a second LVN for one of her ideas. You write it on the flip chart and identify it as no. 2. This procedure continues until each LVN has had an opportunity to get her ideas up on the flip chart. This procedure assures that every LVN will contribute to the idea-generation; it assures that multiple dimensions of the NGT question will surface, and it assures that each LVN will feel like a participating member of the group.

The *third step* in the NGT is to allow some time for discussion of the items on this flip chart. This step is for clarification, not argumentation; it is to bring out the meaning and logic of each of the items. This step is also an opportunity for the LVNs to tell why they agree or disagree with one of the items. An advantage of this step is that it assures that each item will receive its fair share of consideration.

The *fourth step* in the NGT is to rank the numbered items on the flip charts. You ask each LVN to look at the flip charts and identify the five most important items. Further, you ask each LVN to assign a value of 5 to her most important item and a value of 4 to her next most important item, and so on. For example, say that there are 25 items in all, numbered 1 through 25. Say that LVN no. 1 thinks that items 3, 7, 9, 12, and 15 are the five most important. She thinks item no. 9 is most important so she assigns it a value of 5, then no. 15 is assigned a value of 4, item no. 3 a value of 3, item no. 12 a value of 2, and item no. 7 a value of 1. Each LVN performs this item ranking. In order to facilitate this process, it helps if the rankings are placed on separate cards—one numbered item per card. Thus, each LVN will have a set of five cards. The cards for LVN no. 1 would look as follows:

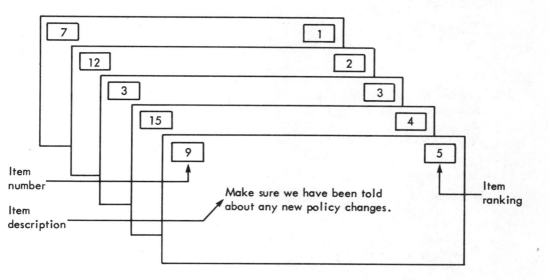

The *final step* in the NGT is to compile the results of the rankings. You collect the 50 cards (5 cards from each LVN), shuffle them (to assure anonymity), and record the results on the flip chart. The item that gets the largest total number of points is the highest priority item. This process will yield more than five priority items. For example, 15 of the original 25 items may receive some points, and 8 of them may receive a substantial number of points. These eight, rather than just the top five, may then be selected as the high-priority items. Subsequently, an *interacting group* session can be used as a way of generating action suggestions on these eight items.

Objectives of Chapter 11

■ To define managerial leadership, to relate leadership to the manager's role, and to identify defining characteristics of managing and leading.

■ To discuss three approaches to understanding leadership that seek universal truths about leadership.

■ To discuss three modern approaches to understanding leadership that attempt to place leadership within the context of a leader-follower-situation system.

■ To define leadership style and to identify several classifications of styles, including Systems 1, 2, 3, 4, and The Managerial Grid.®

Outline of Chapter 11

11

MANAGERIAL LEADERSHIP

When the best leader's work is done, the people say,
"We did it ourselves."

Robert Townsend

Arnold

Arnold Schwarzenegger could hardly be described as your typical "man-on-the-street." He has won the Mr. Universe contest five times and the Mr. Olympia contest six times. He is king of the bodybuilders. Arnold tells us something of his motivation when he says:

> I have always been very energetic, not satisfied with the things that satisfy most people. Ever since I was a child I would say to myself, "there must be more to life than this," and I found that I didn't want to be like everybody else. I wanted to be different. I wanted to be part of the small percentage of people who were leaders, not the large mass of followers. I think it was because I saw that leaders use 100 percent of their potential. And so do I. It all has to do with how hungry you are. I am very hungry.[1]

Arnold is a leader

The "hunger" to be a leader is, of course, only one of the factors in Arnold's success. He also has physical and psychological characteristics that support his motivation. There undoubtedly were family and other situational variables that contributed to his success in becoming someone "different." In any case, Arnold is one type of leader.

Low visibility of business leaders

Managers need to be leaders, too. They don't need to be bodybuilders like Arnold. They need to be organization builders, or more fundamentally, people builders. "The lack of leadership in industry and government is the chief difficulty in this country."[2] One area commonly unrepresented on lists of leaders is business. This low representation is illustrated by New York University's

---

[1] Diane K. Shak " 'Pumping Iron' Pumps Up Arnold," *National Observer*, vol. 16, no. 8 (week ending February 19, 1977), p. 25.

[2] William McCleery, "The Lack of Leadership Is the Chief Difficulty in the Country," *National Observer*, vol. 15, no. 32 (week ending August 7, 1976), p. 10.

Hall of Fame for Great Americans. Since it began in 1900, 99 men and women have been elected but only 10 were business leaders.[3] Somehow, the idea of leadership is not associated in popular thinking with business and managers.

Two reasons   As a student of managing, however, you should associate leadership with managing for at least two good reasons. *First,* effective managing requires leadership. *Second,* managers are given many unusual opportunities to be leaders. The need for effective and imaginative managerial leadership is a crucial one for groups and organizations in particular, and for American society in general.

This chapter   This chapter is divided into *four major parts.* The first part defines leadership and distinguishes it from managing. Three universalist approaches to understanding leadership are discussed in the second part of the chapter. Third, three situational approaches are discussed. The chapter ends by identifying several classifications of leadership styles.

MANAGING AND LEADING

Dux and rex   Although effective managing requires leadership, the two are not the same. As one author puts it, "there are many institutions I know that are very well *managed* and very poorly *led.*"[4] A popular way of distinguishing between leading and managing is brought out by the French terms *dux* ("leader") and *rex* ("ruler"). *Dux* is the activist and innovator, often an inspirational type. *Rex* is the stabilizer or broker or manager."[5] Managing is often associated with the more routine aspects of carrying out the inspirations and programs of leaders.

Managing: Managing and leading can be distinguished more systematically
three   in terms of certain characteristics common to each. In this con-
characteristics   text, managerial behavior has three characteristics. *First,* it implies the existence of manager-managed relationships. These relationships require an organizational context for their implementation. *Second,* managerial behavior owes its legitimacy to the authority vested in a job position in a formal organization. ("Legitimacy" refers to basic rationale or justification.) Managers acquire the opportunity to engage in managerial behavior because they have been placed in a position of "formal authority" in an organization. *Third,* the essence of manager-managed relationships is that managers are accountable for the job behavior of those managed as well as for their own behavior.

---

[3] Max Ways, "A Hall of Fame for Business Leadership," *Fortune,* vol. 91, no. 1 (January 1975), p. 64–73.

[4] Warren G. Bennis, *The Unconscious Conspiracy: Why Leaders Can't Lead* (New York: AMACOM, 1976), p. 154.

[5] "Leadership: The Biggest Issue," *Time,* vol. 108 no. 19 (November 8, 1976), p. 31.

Leading:
three
characteristics

Leadership behavior has three different characteristics. *First,* it can occur anywhere; it does not have to originate in an organizational context. A mob can have a leader even though a mob is the antithesis of an organization. (We normally do not think of a mob as being "managed.") Small, informal groups have leaders, not managers. Leadership can occur in organizations, but it does not have to occur there. *Second,* leadership does not owe its legitimacy to the authority vested in a formal job position. It is legitimate if it results in voluntary followers. *Third,* leadership implies no accountability relationship between leaders and followers. A leader is not accountable for the behavior of followers in the same sense that a manager is accountable for the job behavior of those managed.

Reasons for
following

Managing and leading are types of behavior. As types of behavior, they result in consequences that are positive, negative, or neutral. One clear consequence of managing and leading is that the behavior of other people—followers—becomes involved. The reason behind the responding action of followers tells us that managing and leading are not synonyms for the same type of behavior. People follow *managers* because their job description, supported by a system of rewards and punishments, *requires* them to follow. In contrast, people follow *leaders voluntarily* and for reasons of their own choosing. For example, they may like the personality of the leader and want to use it as a model for their own personal development.

Not always
possible to
distinguish
managing
and leading

Even though leading and managing are not synonymous, it is not always possible to distinguish between them in practice. When is particular behavior to be called "leadership" and when is it to be called "management"? One approach to answering this question is that ". . . every act of influence on a matter of organizational relevance is in some degree an act of leadership."[6] This statement could be interpreted to mean that every instance of managerial behavior has a leadership component in it. But how much of this behavior represents leadership is difficult to determine.

Managerial
leadership
defined

Our view is that, rather than trying to determine what behavior represents leadership and what behavior represents management, the concentration should center on the fact that *effective* managing requires leadership. Specifically, "managerial leadership" is behavior that elicits voluntary follower behavior beyond that associated with required performance on a job. Leadership is ". . . the influential increment over and above mechanical compliance with the routine directives of the organization."[7]

---

[6] Daniel Katz and Robert L. Kahn, *The Social Psychology of Organizations* (New York: John Wiley & Sons, 1966), p. 302.
[7] Ibid.

Why organizations need leadership

A manager's leadership behavior is what makes the difference between effective and ineffective organizations. No organization is so well designed and managed that it can delineate exactly what everyone must do on every occasion. All organizations rely and are dependent upon nonroutine behavior of which only human beings are capable. No organization can be effective if it relies only on minimal levels of performance. Effectiveness results from tapping the potential between adequate and superior performance. Additionally, leadership is needed in organizations so that they will be able to cope with the demands of changing internal and external conditions. Finally, and most important, managerial leadership is essential if organizations are to be more than "warehouses for machines." Leadership is necessary in order to create work environments in which human beings can live part of their day in a productive and satisfying manner.

Summary box

> *Managerial leadership* is defined here as behavior that elicits voluntary follower behavior over and above that associated with required minimal levels of job performance. This is the idea of leadership as an *influential increment*.
>
> Managing and leading are not synonomous although, in practice, it may be difficult to distinguish them. We distinguish managing and leading on the basis of three characteristics. On the one hand, *managerial behavior* (1) requires an organizational context, (2) owes its legitimacy to the authority vested in a formal job position, and (3) involves an accountability relationship between the manager and the managed.
>
> *Leadership behavior* on the other hand, (1) does not have to occur in organizations, (2) owes its legitimacy to the voluntary choice of others to follow, and (3) implies no accountability relationship between leader and followers.
>
> *Organizations require leadership* in order to tap the potential gain from raising adequate to superior job performance, in order to cope with changing internal and external environments, and in order to provide productive and satisfying work environments.

THREE UNIVERSALIST APPROACHES

Universalist approaches

In this section we discuss three approaches to studying leadership: "great man," "personality trait," and "leader behavior." These approaches are the forerunners of more modern approaches. They have one common thread—they are universalist approaches. That is, they search for a key to leadership that is independent of situational context and follower behavior and personality. To the degree that they are universalist in their approach, they have failed to cast much light on our understanding of leadership. However, when these approaches are combined with emphasis on situational and follower variables, they can be useful.[8]

Changing the course of history

The Great Man Approach. Thomas Carlyle, an influential Scottish historian, is given credit for the dictum: "The history of the world is but the biography of great men." We can easily relate to Carlyle's view, since specific examples of men who seem to have changed the course of history come readily to mind—de Gaulle, Hitler, Jesus Christ, Lincoln, Alexander the Great, Napoleon, Lenin, and Martin Luther King. Winston Churchill, a man who for many personifies the great man, is the subject of a book, *The Great Man.*[9] On a less grand scale, there have been great-man leaders in business and industry—Rockefeller, Carnegie, Ford, Mellon, Gould, Sloan, and Harriman.

Main emphasis

In the great man view, the emphasis is on the person—*who* the person is and what makes the person that way. Presumably, through studying the personality, behavior, and characteristics of these great persons, we can acquire greater awareness of leadership. This view implies that we can learn how to become effective leaders by studying great people and emulating those characteristics that seem to account for their success.

Where are the leaders?

Very often, when people lament the critical shortage of leadership in American society, they are referring to the absence of the great man type of leader. "Where have all the leaders gone?" asks one writer.[10] "Today's leaders seem to have less stature than their predecessors," comments another writer in an article describing the problems of leadership in the last half of the 20th century.[11] "There is a very obvious dearth of people who seem able to supply convincing answers, or even point to directions toward solutions," comments the president of Harvard University.[12]

Difficult times for great man leaders

What is often overlooked is that the demands on today's leaders have become incredibly complex and extremely broad in scope. Contemporary society is less responsive to the appeal of great-man leaders and is less willing to play a docile follower role, a role that is essential to the great-man leader. There may never be modern-

---

[8] For a comprehensive survey of approaches to studying leadership, see Ralph Stogdill, *Handbook of Leadership: A Survey of Theory and Research* (New York: The Free Press, 1974).

[9] Robert Payne, *The Great Man: A Portrait of Winston Churchill* (New York: Coward, McCann & Geoghegan, 1974).

[10] Bennis, *The Unconscious Conspiracy: Why Leaders Can't Lead,* chap. 10.

[11] A. James Reichley, "Our Critical Shortage of Leadership," *Fortune,* vol. 84, no. 1 (September 1971), p. 89.

[12] As quoted in "In Quest of Leadership," *Time,* vol. 104, no. 3 (July 15, 1974), p. 21.

day equivalents of the "captains of industry" that glamourized early American business history. The interplay of numerous forces —laws, taxes, administrative regulations, rapid change, widespread education and awareness, constant public exposure of leaders through television, raised expectations, and high priority on human freedom and personal development—makes the emergence of the great-man leader less probable.

Weakness of great man approach

Great men cannot be understood in isolation from the human and situational variables essential to leadership. *Leadership occurs as a result of the interaction of the behavior of leaders and followers within the context of concrete circumstances.* We will emphasize this point throughout this chapter. Great men leaders owe, at least, some of their greatness to circumstances and followers. Just as leaders exert influence on followers, so do followers influence leaders. The leader-follower relationship is a reciprocal one.[13] Winston Churchill is considered by some to be the greatest man of the 20th century. Nevertheless, it was the context of World War II and the siege of England and the condition of the British people that provided him the opportunity to show greatness. It was a unique combination of political and social circumstances that gave Charles de Gaulle the chance to return to power in the 1950s and to become almost synonymous with France.

What we can and cannot learn from great man leaders

We can learn something about leadership through the study of great people. We can learn examples of courage and persistence. We can find illustrations of approaches to problem solving, goal setting, planning, organizing, and controlling. We can learn, in essence, what worked in one leader-followers-situation combination. However, whether we can learn any general principles of leadership is doubtful. Moreover, there is the danger of trying to be like someone else. The coaching styles of Vince Lombardi, Woody Hayes, or Bear Bryant are not for everyone. Alfred Sloan would probably fail miserably as president of General Motors in the 1970s.

Main emphasis

The Personality Trait Approach. This approach to leadership is based on the premise that there are certain personality characteristics that are essential for a person to possess in order to be a leader. These traits are supposed to differentiate leaders and nonleaders. The main emphasis is on *what* the person is in terms of a single personality trait (leadership) or a constellation of personality traits. The search is for that set of universal leadership traits that will assure success. Numerous traits have been suggested: courage, integrity, loyalty, charisma, ambition, intelligence, honesty, clairvoyance, persistence, arrogance, health, political skill, confidence, and vision.

---

[13] David M. Herold, "Two-Way Influence Processes in Leader-Follower Dyads," *Academy of Management Journal*, vol. 20, no. 2 (June 1977), pp. 224–37.

Some traits do distinguish

There do appear to be a few traits that distinguish leaders from followers. Compared to followers, leaders tend to be slightly taller and heavier and tend to score slightly higher on tests of intelligence, extroversion, adjustment, dominance, and self-confidence. However, these differences are small and there is substantial overlap between the distributions of scores of leaders and followers. Furthermore, it is not clear whether these differences *caused* the leaders to become leaders or whether the differences were the *result* of occupying a leadership position. Finally, there is a lot of variation, across situations, in the magnitude and direction of the relation between personality traits and leadership status.[14]

No universal leadership traits

The major problem with the personality trait approach is that no one has ever found a set of leadership traits that could be supported as truly universal and essential to leadership. Years of leadership research have not led to the conclusion that there is any consistent pattern of situationally independent personality traits that characterize leaders.[15] Many factors have contributed to the failure to discover *the* leadership traits: difficulty in measuring and describing personality traits; problems in establishing cause-and-effect relations (Do traits cause leadership or does leadership cause traits?); and disagreement about the meaning of terms such as "loyalty," "courage," and even "leadership."

Limiting factor

However, the primary factor that accounts for the failure to establish a definite link between personality traits and leadership is the same factor that limits the value of the great-man view of leadership. The limiting factor is simply that *leadership cannot be examined in a vacuum;* it is always the result of the interaction of a leader, a group of followers, and situational variables. Leadership needs to be thought of as the result of an interaction system in which leaders exert influence on others in a particular situational context. Figure 11–1 illustrates this interaction influence system.

Some merit to trait approach

The personality trait approach has some merit. *First,* our capacity to measure personality variables is improving, and it may help to make the identification of traits more reliable. Some universal leadership traits may yet be discovered. *Second,* it is likely that certain traits are appropriate to the leadership demands of specific types of situations. Decisiveness, for example, may be essential in situations where decisions need to be made in a hurry. The ability to be a conciliator may be essential in cases of intergroup competition. The point is that, even though universal traits

---

[14] Information in this paragraph taken from Victor H. Vroom, "Leadership," in Marvin D. Dunnette, ed. *Handbook of Industrial and Organizational Psychology* (Chicago: Rand McNally College Publishing Company, 1976), p. 1,529.

[15] Ralph M. Stogdill, "Personal Factors Associated with Leadership: A Survey of the Literature," *Journal of Psychology,* vol. 25 (first half, January 1948), pp. 35–71.

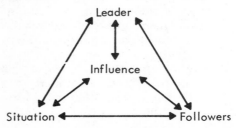

FIGURE 11–1
Leadership as an Interaction Influence
System

Source: Fred Luthans, *Organizational Behavior:*
A Modern Behavioral Approach to Management
(New York: McGraw-Hill Book Company, 1973),
p. 504.

cannot be found, it may be possible to find personality traits that are common to certain types of groups or situations.

Personnel selection

Third, for purposes of personnel selection in an organization, there will often be reliance on an appraisal of personality traits. Is John ambitious? Will Steve be able to bring these two conflicting groups together? Does Janet have the integrity needed to serve as comptroller? These kinds of questions are asked when people are being considered for jobs in specific companies. Therefore, there is some use in trying to determine what traits might be useful for particular jobs.

Popularity of trait approach

The personality trait approach is popular in general magazines and executive speeches. Hardly a week goes by that a magazine article does not proclaim a new list of "qualities of the successful leader." Speakers exhort listeners to develop those "characteristics of leadership" that guarantee success—courage, confidence, determination. The popularity of the personality trait view, however, should not mislead you as a student of managing. *There are no universal leadership traits.* Even if there were, it is questionable that a person could set out to develop a certain trait. The importance given personality traits must be viewed in proper perspective. In the study of leadership, personality traits—important as they are—are only one of the variables to be considered in a specific situation.

Main emphasis

The Leader Behavior Approach. What is it that leaders actually do? Do they inspire confidence? Do they lift the spirits of others? Do they raise performance levels to new heights? Do they simply behave in ways that reflect the wishes of a group? What kind of behavior distinguishes the leader from the follower? How can you tell when someone is "leading?" These questions suggest an approach to understanding leadership that is quite different than the great man and personality trait approaches. Here the emphasis shifts to actual behavior or dimensions of behavior that will be used to identify leadership. The main emphasis is not on *who* you are (great man approach) or on *what* you are (personality trait approach); the main emphasis is on *what you do* (leader behavior approach).

Examples of leadership behavior

There have been many attempts to identify the basic dimensions of leadership behavior.[16] These attempts have ranged from simple subjective analyses of the behavior of successful leaders to carefully designed empirical research studies. Behavior often cited as "leadership behavior" includes making decisions, giving directions, showing group belongingness and loyalty to the organization, planning, scheduling work, and accepting personal responsibility. "Hundreds of investigations have utilized various leader behavior dimensions in an attempt to determine which behaviors distinguish effective from ineffective leadership."[17]

The Ohio State University leadership studies

The most systematic and rigorous studies aimed at identifying the dimensions of leadership behavior originally were conducted at the Ohio State University.[18] These studies have influenced significantly the way in which leadership has been investigated over the past 25 years. Although the Ohio State Studies identified several leadership behavior dimensions, most research has centered on *two major dimensions* of leader behavior: initiating structure and consideration.

Initiating structure

"Initiating structure" refers to behavior that is aimed at getting the job done. It includes such behavior as scheduling work to be done, maintaining definite standards of performance, emphasizing deadlines, seeing that group members are working up to capacity, coordinating the work of group members, and assigning group members to particular tasks. The extent to which a leader initiates structure is measured by 15 items on the Leader Behavior Description Questionnaire (LBDQ).

Consideration

"Consideration" refers to behavior that indicates friendship, mutual trust, respect, and warmth in the relationship between the leader and group members. Consideration includes such behavior as doing personal favors for group members, listening to group members, explaining actions, and consulting group members as equals. The consideration behavior of a leader is measured by another 15 items on the LBDQ.

---

[16] Jeffrey Pfeffer, "The Ambiguity of Leadership," *Academy of Management Review*, vol. 2, no. 1 (January 1977).

[17] Jeffrey C. Barrow, "The Variables of Leadership: A Review and Conceptual Framework," *Academy of Management Review*, vol. 2, (April 1977), p. 233.

[18] Ralph M. Stogdill and Alvin E. Coons, eds., *Leader Behavior: Its Description and Measurement*, Research Monograph no. 88 (Columbus: The Ohio State University, Bureau of Business Research, 1957).

*Task and
people*

Initiating structure and consideration may be viewed as specific terms or labels that identify two general leader behavior dimensions —task and people. That is, the study of leadership over the past 25 years has tended to revolve around the idea that effective leadership requires task-oriented behavior and/or people-oriented behavior. As one writer has commented, "We are hooked on these two dimensions, by whatever name they are called."[19] The dominance of the task and people dimensions is present in leadership studies even when the studies appear to deal with more than these two dimensions. For example, one study suggests a four-factor theory of leadership. The four factors, or leader behavior dimensions, are: supportive, interaction facilitation, goal emphasis, and work facilitation. In general, the first two of these factors are parallel with consideration, and the last two are parallel with initiating structure.[20] Thus, although there are exceptions[21] to the exclusive emphasis in the study of leadership on task and people, and although future study of leadership undoubtedly will move in the direction of greater complexity and diversity,[22] it is accurate to say that until now task (initiating structure) and people (consideration) dimensions have been dominant.

*What do these
dimensions
tell us?*

After 25 years and numerous studies, what do initiating structure and consideration tell us about leadership? *First,* several studies have found that leaders with high scores on *initiating structure* are rated highly by their superiors and have high scores on performance measures such as productivity and cost. *Second,* several studies have found that leaders with high scores on *consideration* have satisfied subordinates, cooperative group members, and lower employee turnover and grievance rates.

*The Hi-Hi
leader*

Third, there are also several studies supporting the "Hi-Hi" leader behavior pattern.[23] A Hi-Hi leader is one who has high scores on *both* initiating structure and consideration. Such behavior is supposed to be correlated with measures of effectiveness. However, there are some researchers who believe this is an oversimplifica-

---

[19] Barbara Karmel, "Leadership: A Challenge to Traditional Research Methods and Assumptions," *Academy of Management Review,* in press.

[20] D. G. Bowers and S. Seashore, "Predicting Organizational Effectiveness with a Four-Factor Theory of Leadership," *Administrative Science Quarterly,* vol. 11, no. 2 (1966), pp. 238–63.

[21] G. Yukl, "Toward a Behavioral Theory of Leadership," *Organizational Behavior and Human Performance,* vol. 6, no. 2 (1971), pp. 414–40.

[22] Charles N. Greene, "Disenchantment with Leadership Research: Some Causes, Recommendations, and New Directions," in J. G. Hunt, ed., *Leadership: The Cutting Edge* (Carbondale, Ill.: Southern Illinois University Press, 1977).

Also see John B. Miner, "The Uncertain Future of the Leadership Concept," in J. G. Hunt and L. L. Larson, eds., *Leadership Frontiers* (Kent, Ohio; Kent State University Press, 1975), pp. 197–208.

[23] Stogdill, *Handbook of Leadership,* chap. 37.

tion[24] and some question the value of the Hi-Hi pattern as a predictive model.[25]

The all-important situation

So what is the final word on initiating structure and consideration? It isn't in yet, but one observation can be made. Just as we cannot identify universal leadership traits, we cannot identify universal leadership behaviors. In other words, we cannot separate leader behavior from follower behavior, from leader and follower personality,[26] and from the situational context. We need to keep before us the idea of leadership as an interaction influence system, as shown in Figure 11–1.

---

[24] S. Kerr, C. Schriesheim, C. Murphy, and R. Stogdill, "Toward a Contingency Theory of Leadership Based upon the Consideration and Initiating Structure Literature," *Organizational Behavior and Human Performance*, vol. 12 (1974), pp. 62–82.

[25] L. L. Larson, J. G. Hunt, and R. N. Osborn, "The Great Hi-Hi Leader Behavior Myth: A Lesson from Occam's Razor," *Academy of Management Journal*, vol. 19, no. 4 (December 1976), pp. 628–41. Abraham K. Korman, "Consideration, Initiating Structure, and Organizational Criteria: A Review," *Personnel Psychology*, vol. 19, no. 4 (1966), pp. 349–61.

[26] Douglas E. Durand and Walter R. Nord, "Perceived Leader Behavior as a Function of Personality Characteristics of Supervisors and Subordinates," *Academy of Management Journal*, vol. 19, no. 3 (September 1976), pp. 427–38.

Summary box

> **Three Universalist Approaches to Leadership**
>
> *Great Man Approach*
>
> Main emphasis: *Who* the leader is.
>
> Assumes that we can learn about leadership by studying great leaders.
>
> Conditions today are not conducive to the emergence of great-man types of leaders.
>
> *Personality Trait Approach*
>
> Main emphasis: *What* the leader is in terms of personality characteristics.
>
> Tries to identify leadership traits essential to leadership success.
>
> There is no known consistent pattern of universal leadership traits that can be shown to be essential to effectiveness.
>
> There is, however, some merit to this popular approach.
>
> *Leader Behavior Approach*
>
> Main emphasis: What the leader *does*.
>
> Tries to identify what behavior is essential to successful leadership.
>
> Initiating structure and consideration—two major dimensions of leadership behavior.
>
> Regarding these two behavioral dimensions, there are very few generalizations that can be made.
>
> The major problem common to the above three approaches is that they are *universalist approaches*. That is, they search for a key to leadership that is independent of situational context and follower behavior and personality.
>
> The idea of leadership as an *interaction influence system* is useful in approaching the study of leadership. This idea is diagrammed in Figure 11–1. The above three approaches can be useful *if* placed in the interaction influence system framework.

THREE SITUATIONAL APPROACHES

Interaction influence system context

In this section we discuss three approaches to studying leadership that make some attempt to place leadership in the context of the interaction influence system shown in Figure 11–1. The three approaches are: the contingency approach, the path goal approach, and the participation in decision making approach.

*Main
emphasis*

The Contingency Approach. The scholar most closely associated with the contingency approach is Fred E. Fiedler.[27] The main emphasis of the contingency approach is on (1) the interaction between a leader's style and (2) the favorableness of the situation for the leader. The idea is that the leadership style that will be most effective depends on, or is contingent upon, the favorableness of the situation for the leader.

Leader's style

The contingency approach measures a "leader's style" by means of a form known as the Least Preferred Co-worker (LPC) scale. The LPC is a set of 16 adjective pairs, such as "pleasant and unpleasant," "boring and interesting," "efficient and inefficient." The basic idea of the LPC is that if a leader describes the person with whom he or she can work *least* well in a *positive* way, the leader is considered "relationship-motivated" (a high LPC score). Conversely, if the description is *negative,* the leader is considered "task-motivated" (a low LPC score). The LPC, in theory, is supposed to identify a leader's style—a relatively stable personality characteristic of the leader that can be used to predict behavior. In practice, the precise meaning of LPC scores is not clear.

*Favorableness
of the
situation*

The contingency approach describes the "favorableness of the situation" in terms of three major dimensions of the group task situation: leader-member relations, task structure, and position power. "Leader-member relations" refers to the degree to which group members trust and like the leader and are willing to accept the leader's behavior as an influence on them. "Task structure" refers to the degree to which the task requirements are clearly defined, the correctness of a decision can be easily verified, and there are alternative correct solutions to task problems. "Position power" refers to the formal authority vested in a leadership position.

*Eight degrees
of favorable-
ness*

Using the above three dimensions, the *most favorable* situation for the leader is one in which there are good leader-member relations, high task structure, and strong position power. The *most unfavorable* situation is one in which there are poor leader-member relations, low task structure, and weak position power. Inbetween these two extremes, the contingency approach identifies 6 other degrees of situation favorableness. The eight degrees of situation favorableness are shown in Figure 11–2.

*Effective
styles*

In general, the contingency approach argues that a *task-motivated* leadership style is most effective in situations that are favorable (degrees 1, 2, and 3) and unfavorable (degrees 6, 7, and 8) to the leader. A *relationship-motivated* leader is most effective, the

---

[27] Fred E. Fiedler and Martin M. Chemers, *Leadership and Effective Management* (Glenview, Ill.: Scott, Foresman and Company, 1974). Also, Fred E. Fiedler, *A Theory of Leadership Effectiveness* (New York: McGraw-Hill Book Company, 1967), and "The Leadership Game: Matching the Man to the Situation," *Organizational Dynamics,* vol. 4, no. 3 (Winter 1976), pp. 6–16.

FIGURE 11–2
Eight Degrees of Situation Favorableness

Situation Dimension	Degree of Situation Favorableness							
	1	2	3	4	5	6	7	8
Leader-member relations........	Good	Good	Good	Good	Poor	Poor	Poor	Poor
Task structure....	High	High	Low	Low	High	High	Low	Low
Position power....	Strong	Weak	Strong	Weak	Strong	Weak	Strong	Weak

contingency approach argues, in situations with a moderate degree of favorableness (degrees 4, 5, and 6). The practical point of all this is to try to match the task and situation to the style of the leader. Or, as Fiedler suggests, in a very popular article, "Engineer the Job to Fit the Manager."[28]

Perspective

The contingency approach is a very nice way of emphasizing the importance of the *interaction* of the leader, followers, and the situation. The approach cautions against the simplistic notion that there is one best leadership style—regardless of the circumstances. Furthermore, information gathered from numerous studies suggests that the contingency approach can have practical implications for the recruitment, selection, and placement of leaders. Clearly, the contingency approach has made and continues to make a major contribution to our understanding of leadership.

Problems

However, there are problems with the contingency approach. A major problem is the LPC itself. There is a lack of consensus about precisely what it measures. That is a rather fundamental problem, considering the critical role of the LPC in the contingency approach. Another problem is that the contingency approach appears to assume that a leader's style is invariant and that it is a consistent predictor of behavior—regardless of the situation. This assumption appears questionable.[29] Style is learned and can be unlearned and changed. Further, it is unreasonable to think that a person uses the same style regardless of the demands of the situation. There are other problems with the contingency approach but a discussion of them would take us beyond the purposes of this book.[30] Our view,

[28] Fred E. Fiedler, "Engineer the Job to Fit the Manager," *Harvard Business Review*, vol. 43, no. 5 (September–October 1965), pp. 115–22.

[29] Stephen G. Green, Delbert M. Nebeker, and M. Alan Boni, "Personality and Situational Effects on Leader Behavior," *Academy of Management Journal*, vol. 19, no. 2 (June 1976), p. 192.

[30] For further study see the following three sources: (1) William M. Fox, "Reliabilities, Means, and Standard Deviations for LPC Scales: Instrument Refinement," *Academy of Management Journal*, vol. 19, no. 3 (September 1976), pp. 450–61; (2) Ahmed Sakr Ashour, "The Contingency Model of Leadership Effectiveness: An Evaluation," *Organizational Behavior and Human Performance*, vol. 9, no. 3 (June 1973), pp. 339–55; and (3) J. T. McMahon, "The Contingency Theory: Logic and Method Revisited," *Personnel Psychology*, vol. 25 (1972), pp. 697–710.

however, is that the problems with the contingency approach do not negate its value as a source of valuable knowledge about leadership.

Main emphasis

The Path-Goal Approach. The scholar most closely associated with the "path-goal approach" is Robert J. House.[31] This approach to leadership gets its name from the idea that if an employee sees high productivity as a *path* that leads to one or more personal *goals*, the employee will tend to be a high producer. Conversely, if low productivity is seen as a path leading to goals, the employee will tend to be a low producer.[32] The role of the leader, then, consists of "increasing the personal pay-offs to subordinates for work-goal attainment, and making the paths to these pay-offs easier to travel . . . , and increasing opportunities for personal satisfaction en route."[33] We will discuss the path-goal approach's view of leader behavior, situational variables, major propositions, and path instrumentalities.

Four types of leadership behavior

The path-goal approach identifies four types of leadership behavior: supportive, instrumental, participative, and achievement-oriented. "Supportive" leadership is similar to the consideration dimension discussed earlier in the chapter. "Instrumental" leadership is similar to the initiating structure dimension. "Participative" leadership is behavior that allows subordinates to influence decisions. "Achievement-oriented" leadership emphasizes excellence in performance along with confidence that subordinates will meet the high standards. The path-goal approach hypothesizes that each type of leadership behavior will be effective under certain conditions.

Two situational variables

In the path-goal approach, two important situational variables are (1) the personal characteristics of subordinates, and (2) the environmental pressures and demands. In other words, whether or not subordinates will perceive one of the four types of leadership behavior as an immediate source of satisfaction or as instrumental to future satisfaction is partially determined by the subordinates' personal characteristics. An example of one of these personal characteristics is the subordinates' perception of their own ability relative to their assigned task. Examples of the second situational variable, environmental pressures and demands, are the subordi-

---

[31] The discussion in this section is based primarily on Alan C. Filley, Robert J. House, and Steven Kerr, *Managerial Process and Organizational Behavior*, 2d ed. (Glenview, Ill.: Scott, Foresman and Company, 1976), pp. 252–60. Also see Robert J. House, "A Path Goal Theory of Leader Effectiveness," *Administrative Science Quarterly*, vol. 16, no. 3 (September 1971), pp. 321–38 and Robert J. House and Terrence R. Mitchell, "Path-Goal Theory of Leadership," *Journal of Contemporary Business*, vol. 5 (1974), pp. 81–97.

[32] See Basil S. Georgopoulos, Gerald M. Mahoney, and Nyle W. Jones, Jr., "A Path Goal Approach to Productivity," *Journal of Applied Psychology*, vol. 41, no. 6 (December 1957), pp. 345–53.

[33] Filley, House, and Kerr, *Managerial Process and Organizational Behavior*, p. 254.

nates' tasks, the formal authority system of the organization, and the primary work group.

Two propositions

The path-goal approach proposes that subordinates will find leader behavior acceptable and satisfying to the extent that they perceive it as an immediate source of satisfaction or as instrumental to future satisfaction. In addition, the path-goal approach proposes that leader behavior will increase subordinate effort to the extent that it makes satisfaction of subordinates' needs contingent on effective performance and to the extent that "it complements the environment of subordinates by providing the coaching, guidance, support, and rewards which are necessary for effective performance and which may otherwise be lacking in subordinates or in their environment."[34]

Two path instrumentalities

The path-goal approach states that employees make two probability estimates. *First,* they estimate the probability that their job behavior will lead to the accomplishment of some work goal. This is referred to as the "path-instrumentality" of work behavior for goal accomplishment. (Note resemblance to expectancy 1 in Chapter 6). *Second,* they estimate the probability that accomplishment will actually lead to desired extrinsic consequences. This is referred to as the "path instrumentality" of work goal accomplishment for desired consequences. (Note resemblance to expectancy 2.) The leader can influence the subordinates' estimates of these path instrumentalities. In addition to making the two path-instrumentality estimates, employees also place *subjective values* on the intrinsic consequences of the behavior required to achieve a work goal, and on the intrinsic consequences of achieving the work goal, and on the extrinsic consequences of achieving the work goal.

Leader's role

Bringing together the two path instrumentalities and the subjective values placed on intrinsic and extrinsic consequences, the path-goal approach suggests that the leader can play an important role in influencing all of the variables. For example, the leader partially determines what extrinsic consequences will follow achievement. By allowing employees the opportunity to exercise self-control over their work, the leader may enhance the intrinsic satisfactions of work and achievement. By assisting employees in their efforts to accomplish work goals, the leader may influence employees' estimates of the path instrumentality that efforts will lead to goal accomplishment. Finally, by being consistent and systematic in evaluating the performance of employees, the leader can positively influence estimates of the path instrumentality that goal accomplishment will lead to desired extrinsic consequences.

Perspective

You can see from this brief discussion that the path-goal approach is a relatively complex view of leadership. It attempts to

---

[34] Ibid.

relate four types of leadership behavior to subordinates' satisfaction and performance. Further, it attempts to show how this relationship is moderated by two situational, or contingency, variables: personal characteristics of subordinates and the work environment. Additionally, the path-goal approach views the leader as playing a role in influencing the subordinates' estimates of path instrumentalities and valences. All of this is much more sophisticated than trying to identify universally applicable leadership personality traits or behavior. With its foundation in expectancy theory of motivation (see Chapter 6), the path-goal approach is likely to yield important insights into the requirements for effective leadership.

Main emphasis

The Participation in Decision Making Approach. The scholars most closely associated with this approach are Victor H. Vroom and Philip W. Yetton.[35] Sometimes this intriguing approach is referred to as the Vroom-Yetton Model. Its main emphasis is on helping the leader identify the most appropriate behavior or style (or decision process) given the *quality* and *acceptance* requirements of a decision and the *time required* to make the decision. We will discuss these aspects of this approach: leadership methods or decision processes, diagnostic questions, and decision rules.

Leadership methods

Vroom and Yetton identify five distinct approaches that leaders can use in making decisions. These five approaches represent different degrees of autocratic (AI and AII), consultative (CI and CII), and group processes (GII). The five approaches are shown in Figure 11–3.

Problem attributes, diagnostic questions

Which of the five approaches is best? That depends on the attributes of the problem. Seven "problem attributes" deal with the quality and acceptance requirements of the solution and with the effect of participation on quality and acceptance. These problem attributes are put in the form of seven "diagnostic questions" to help the leader decide which of the five decision processes to use. The seven diagnostic questions are shown in Figure 11–3. Note that question A is concerned with quality, question D is concerned with acceptance, and the remaining five questions are concerned with the effects of participation on quality and acceptance requirements.

Rules

Once a leader has answered the diagnostic questions for a particular problem, there is need for a judgment about which leader-

---

[35] Victor H. Vroom and Philip W. Yetton, *Leadership and Decision-Making* (Pittsburgh: University of Pittsburgh Press, 1973). Vroom and Yetton did not originate, nor are they the basic advocates of, the general idea that employees should be allowed to participate in decision-making processes. However, Vroom and Yetton's model is developed around the idea that different degrees of participation are appropriate to different types of problems. Thus, we have labeled their approach the *participation in decision-making approach*.

ship method to use. The participation in decision making approach uses a set of seven rules to help the leader judge which of the leadership methods to use. For example, the "information rule" says that if quality is important and the leader does not possess adequate information, eliminate AI. The "goal congruence rule" says that if quality is important and subordinates do not share the organizations goals for the decision problem, eliminate GII. The "acceptance rule" says that when acceptance of the decision is important to subordinates and it is uncertain whether autocratic processes will result in acceptance, eliminate AI and AII.[36]

Feasible set, choice rule

The result of applying these rules is that a "feasible set" of alternatives is identified. The feasible set includes all of the leadership methods that are feasible for solving a problem. When a problem has more than one leadership method in its feasible set a "choice rule" is applied. An example of a choice rule is: choose the approach that requires the least investment in man-hours.

Perspective

Figure 11–3 is a summary of our discussion of the participation in decision making approach. The approach appears to be potentially useful to management and leadership practice, training, and research.[37] Vroom and Yetton have developed methods and procedures for applying their model in actual managerial and leadership situations. Several thousand managers have participated in research on the model. One conclusion Vroom and Yetton have reached as a result of their research is that differences in behavior *between* managers and leaders is less pronounced than differences *within*. That is, most managers say they use all five decision-making approaches some of the time. Consequently, Vroom and Yetton conclude, "It makes more sense to talk about participative and autocratic *situations* than it does to talk about participative and autocratic *managers* (emphasis added)."[38]

---

[36] The other four rules are: the unstructured problem rule, the conflict rule, the fairness rule, and the acceptance priority rule. See Vroom and Yetton, *Leadership and Decision Making*.

[37] See, for example, Arthur G. Jago and Victor H. Vroom, "Perceptions of Leadership Style: Superior and Subordinate Descriptions of Decision-Making Behavior," in James G. Hunt and Lars L. Larson, eds., *Leadership Frontiers*, pp. 103–20.

[38] Victor H. Vroom, "Can Leaders Learn to Lead?" *Organizational Dynamics*, vol. 4, no. 3 (Winter 1976), pp. 17–28.

FIGURE 11–3
A Schematic Interpretation of the Vroom-Yetton Model of Leadership and Decision Making

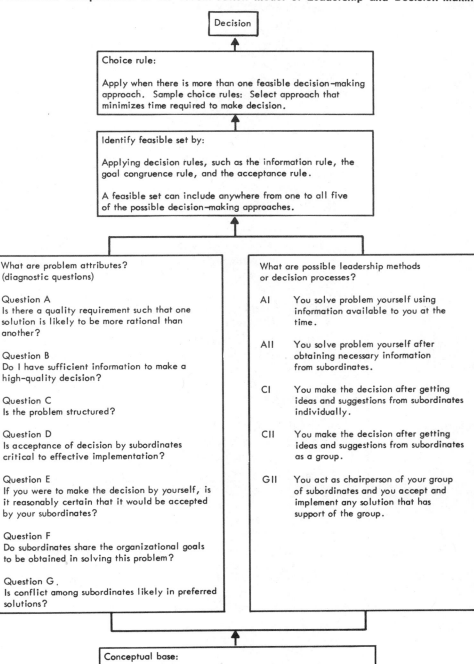

Summary box

Three Situational Approaches to Leadership

Contingency Approach

Main Emphasis: Interaction of style with situation favorableness.

Identifies, by means of LPC, two basic leader styles: task-motivated and relationship-motivated.

Focuses on the interaction of leadership style with three major situational variables: leader-member relations, task structure, and position power.

Combinations of the three situational variables yield eight degrees of situation favorableness for the leader.

Suggests that the most effective leadership style depends on the degree of situation favorableness.

Path-Goal Approach

Main emphasis: Interaction of leader behavior with personal characteristics and environmental variables.

Applies expectancy theory of motivation concepts to leadership.

Relates four types of leader behavior or styles to subordinates' satisfaction and performance.

Utilizes two situational variables as moderators of relationship between leader behavior and subordinates' satisfaction and performance.

Proposes conditions under which leader behavior will be effective.

Participation in Decision Making Approach

Main emphasis: Interaction of leadership method with decision requirements in terms of quality, acceptance, and time.

Based on need for quality and acceptance in a decision and the time required to make a decision.

Identifies five leadership methods and seven problem attributes.

Uses decision rules to help managers decide which leadership method is most feasible for a decision problem.

LEADERSHIP STYLES

What is style?

What is "style?" A leader's style is a reasonably stable mode of behavior the leader uses in efforts to exert the influential increment that is the essence of leadership. When someone is referred to as an "autocratic" leader or manager, it means that, on *most occasions*, the leader's approach to handling a situation is to unilaterally dictate what, how, and when things will be done. An autocratic leader may, however infrequently, ask opinions of others and even allow them to make some decisions. Nevertheless, if the primary behavioral disposition of the leader is to dictate and tell, then the leader can be described as "autocratic."

A 1938 study of leader styles

An Overview of Leadership Styles. It is impossible to pinpoint precisely the time when interest in leadership styles emerged. However, a set of experiments conducted by three social scientists in 1938 is a good time to begin. The researchers used groups of children to study different approaches to exercising control. Their classic study identified three types of control: autocratic, democratic, and laissez-faire. These three types of control came to be known as leadership styles.[39]

Conclusions of the study

The researchers were cautious in the conclusions they drew from this study. They noted that *autocratic* leadership does get results and is preferred over *democratic* leadership. However, they observed that autocratic leadership can create tension, apathy, frustration, and dependence by the group on the leader. Further, the researchers found that some of the differences in the behavior of the children were associated with the presence or absence of the leader. Specifically, constructive effort declined in the autocratically controlled children groups. Finally, they observed very little value in laissez-faire control—an essentially "no-leader" approach to leadership.

Significance

From our perspective, the 1938 study is important because it created an awareness of the possible effect on a group of the leader's style. In addition, it helped to make people more sensitive to the importance of the psychological atmosphere in the group. This atmosphere can influence not only productivity, but also psychological variables such as tension, frustration, and conflict. Thus, the specific findings of the study were not as important as the general awareness and sensitivity to the importance of leadership style that they encouraged.

Continuum of leadership styles

Since 1939, several studies of leadership styles have supported the importance of style to group behavior and have suggested several classifications of styles. These classifications generally fall somewhere on a continuum ranging from autocratic to democratic styles. One useful way of viewing leadership styles is shown in Figure 11-4. This continuum of leadership styles differentiates

[39] Kurt Lewin, Ronald Lippitt, and Robert White, "Patterns of Aggressive Behavior in Experimentally Created Social Climates," *Journal of Social Psychology*, vol. 10 (1939), pp. 271-99.

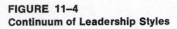

FIGURE 11-4
Continuum of Leadership Styles

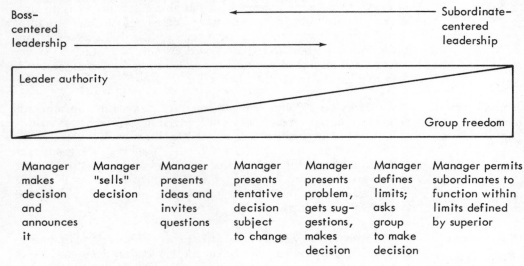

Boss-
centered
leadership

Subordinate-
centered
leadership

Leader authority

Group freedom

| Manager makes decision and announces it | Manager "sells" decision | Manager presents ideas and invites questions | Manager presents tentative decision subject to change | Manager presents problem, gets suggestions, makes decision | Manager defines limits; asks group to make decision | Manager permits subordinates to function within limits defined by superior |

"Tells"   "Persuades"   "Consults"   "Joins"   "Delegates"

Source: Robert Tannenbaum and Warren H. Schmidt, "How to Choose a Leadership Pattern."

seven styles of varying degrees of *leader* authority and *group* free-dom.[40]

Behavior, locus of power, and locus of information

Along the same lines as the continuum shown in Figure 11-4 is another classification of leader styles based on three elements: leader behavior, locus of power, and locus of information.[41] "Leadership behavior" is viewed as either authoritative (a_1), or democratic (a_2) Leader behavior occurs in a context of power and information distribution. The "locus of power" can either be with the leader (b_1) or with the subordinate (b_2). The "locus of in-

Leader Style	Profile		
Directive.....................	a_1	b_1	c_1
Negotiative..................	a_1	b_2	c_1
Consultative................	a_2	b_1	c_2
Participative................	a_2	b_2	c_1
Delegative..................	a_2	b_2	c_2

---

[40] Robert Tannenbaum and Warren H. Schmidt, "How to Choose a Leadership Pattern," *Harvard Business Review*, vol. 36, no. 2 (March–April 1958), pp. 95–101. For a retrospective commentary on this article, see *Harvard Business Review*, vol. 51, no. 3 (May–June 1973), pp. 166–68.

[41] Information in this paragraph is taken from two sources: B. M. Bass and E. R. Valenzi, "Contingent Aspects of Effective Management Styles," in J. G. Hunt and L. L. Larson, eds., *Contingency Approaches to Leadership* (Carbondale, Ill.: Southern Illinois University Press, 1974) and Zur Shapira, "A Facet Analysis of Leadership Styles," *Journal of Applied Psychology*, vol. 61, no. 2 (April 1976), pp. 136–39. Copyright 1976 by the American Psychological Association. Reprinted by permission.

formation" can be either with the leader (c_1) or the subordinate (c_2). Combinations of the above three variables lead to the following classification of leadership styles.

Major idea

The major idea to get from the above two classifications of leadership styles, is that each style can lead to different *behavioral* consequences. There is no implication in Figure 11–4 that styles at the left end of the continuum are "better" than styles at the right end. The best style depends on the criteria used to judge "best." If group productivity is the criterion, any of the styles could be effective. If optimizing group freedom is the criterion, styles at the right end are better than styles at the left. If quickness in decision making is the criterion, styles that maximize leader authority usually are best. Thus, the value of a leadership style must be evaluated in terms of desired outcomes.

Doing what comes naturally

Another important point can be seen in Figure 11–4. A leader's behavior at any one time falls somewhere on the continuum or within some range on it. This range may represent behavior that comes "naturally" to the leader. Even though leaders may know that another type of behavior would be more appropriate, it does not follow that they simply can change their style. Leaders acquire particular styles as a result of experience and training. They learn that their styles work for them on some occasions and do not work on others. Nevertheless, their styles are familiar to them, and they cannot be changed easily. *In theory,* the most appropriate leadership style is the one most responsive to the forces (in the leader, the followers, and the situation) determining behavior in concrete circumstances. *In practice,* few leaders are so flexible that they can adapt their behavior to all circumstances. New behavioral styles can be learned, but only with great effort and patience. In the meantime, leaders have to work with styles they know and with which they are comfortable.

Essence of participation

The Participative Style. The essence of a participatory leadership style is that leaders (managers) allow their followers (subordinates) to share in making decisions that affect their behavior. The more followers share in decision making, the more participative the style. Not all employees, however, respond favorably to a participative leadership style. In general, we can say that, like any particular leadership style, a participative style will be effective if it "fits" the specific leader-follower-situation system.

Ten participation characteristics

One researcher conducted a study on what managers think of participative leadership. From a questionnaire containing 39 leadership characteristics, 157 managers selected 10 characteristics which they rated on a scale from 1 to 7, where 1 indicated low participation and 7 indicated high participation.[42] Figure 11–5

---

[42] Larry E. Greiner, "What Managers Think of Participative Leadership," *Harvard Business Review,* vol. 51, no. 2 (March–April 1973), pp. 111–17.

gives the ten participation characteristics, their rank, and their average scale rating. These ten characteristics combine to define the prototype of a participative leader. The characteristic which ranked highest—the ultimate participative act—is "Gives subordinates a share in decision making." Of course, the extent to which subordinates share in decision making can vary along several dimensions—the degree of control the subordinates have over a decision, the issues over which that control is exercised, and the organizational level at which it is exercised.[43]

FIGURE 11–5
The Ten Highest-Rated Participation Characteristics

Rank	Characteristic	Average Scale Rating*
1	Gives subordinates a share in decision making	6.08
2	Keeps subordinates informed of the true situation, good or bad, under all circumstances	5.69
3	Stays aware of the state of the organization's morale and does everything possible to make it high	5.45
4	Is easily approachable	5.38
5	Counsels, trains, and develops subordinates	5.34
6	Communicates effectively with subordinates	5.22
7	Shows thoughtfulness and consideration of others	5.19
8	Is willing to make changes in ways of doing things	4.96
9	Is willing to support subordinates even when they make mistakes	4.92
10	Expresses appreciation when a subordinate does a good job	4.80

* 1 equals low participation and 7 equals high participation.
Source: Larry E. Greiner, "What Managers Think of Participative Leadership," *Harvard Business Review*, vol. 51, no. 2 (March–April 1973).

Is the participative leader effective?

Is the participative leader effective? Will a participatory style get good results or are certain low-participation characteristics necessary for effectiveness? Another group of 161 managers were asked to rate the 39 questionnaire items for effectiveness rather than for participation, as the 157 managers had done. The ten highest-rated effectiveness characteristics included seven of the highest-rated participation characteristics. The three additional effectiveness characteristics found were: lets the members of the organization know what is expected of them; sets high standards of performance; and knows subordinates and their capabilities.

Rensis Likert

Systems 1, 2, 3. 4. Any discussion of leadership styles has to consider the work of Rensis Likert.[44] Likert's research is supported by numerous studies conducted over a 25-year period, and it has had an important impact on management education and practice.

[43] Paul Bernstein, "Workplace Democratization: Its Internal Dynamics," *Organization and Administrative Sciences,* vol. 7, no. 3 (Fall 1976), p. 47.
[44] *The Human Organization: Its Management and Value* (New York: McGraw-Hill Book Company, 1967).

Likert identifies four basic management systems and uses descriptive terms to identify the main orientation of each system:
    System 1—Exploitative authoritative.
    System 2—Benevolent authoritative.
    System 3—Consultative.
    System 4—Participative group.

Major organizational processes

Likert suggests that each of these management systems reflects a different approach to handling several major organizational processes, such as motivation, communication, decision making, goal setting, and control. The basic thrust of Likert's work is that System 4 management makes the potentially greatest long-range contribution to organizational effectiveness. System 4 is characterized by a high degree of trust and interaction between superiors and subordinates. It involves extensive participation by subordinates in goal setting and control processes.

Principle of Supportive Relationships

Likert places great significance on the importance of genuine and trusting interpersonal and group relationships. A central idea in his view of leadership is his Principle of Supportive Relationships: "The leadership and other processes of the organization must be such as to ensure a maximum probability that in all interactions and in all relationships within the organization, each member, in the light of his background, values, desires, and expectations, will view the experience as supportive and one which builds and maintains his sense of personal worth and importance."[45]

Harwood and Weldon

An attempt to change a System 1 managed business firm into a System 4 managed firm is described in a study of the Harwood and Weldon Manufacturing Companies. The study is an account of how several management consultants introduced and implemented organizational changes that "turned around" the basic management system of a company. The study is, at one and the same time, a study of leadership, organizational development, organization change, and management consulting. From the viewpoint of leadership, the study is a case study of the beneficial effects on an organization of participatory leadership styles.[46]

Five basic styles

The Managerial Grid®. A particular approach to the idea of leadership style is provided by the "managerial grid," developed by Robert R. Blake and Jane S. Mouton.[47] The grid, shown in Figure 11–6, reflects the common theme that effective leadership requires attention to both task and people. Figure 11–6 identifies five basic

[45] Rensis Likert, *New Patterns of Management* (New York: McGraw-Hill Book Company, 1961), p. 103.

[46] A. J. Marrow, D. G. Bowers, and S. E. Seashore, *Management by Participation* (New York: Harper & Row, Publishers, 1967). The study discussed in this book took place between 1962 and 1964 and before Likert introduced the term "Systems 1, 2, 3, and 4."

[47] *The Managerial Grid* (Houston: Gulf Publishing Company, 1964).

FIGURE 11–6
The Managerial Grid®

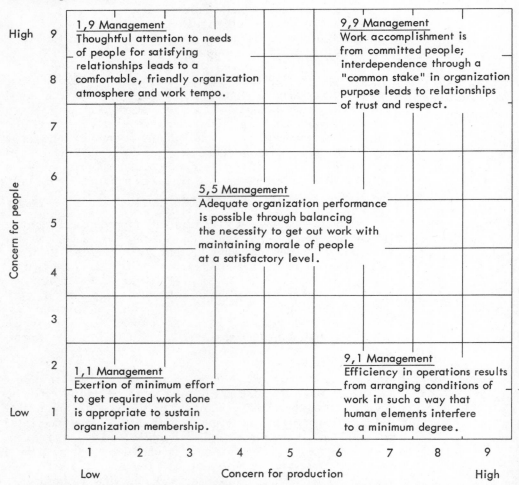

styles. The "9,9" style represents the best of both worlds—high
concern for people and high concern for production. It is not always
the best style, however, because the particular leader-followers-
situation interaction may require something less than a 9,9 style.
The managerial grid "caught on" in American business organizations as a training device. It is used along with an elaborate set of
questionnaires and training "instruments." The grid is also used as
part of a six-phase comprehensive approach to Organization Development (OD).[48] OD is discussed in Chapter 18.

[48] R. R. Blake, J. S. Mouton, L. B. Barnes, and L. E. Greiner, "Breakthrough in Organization Development," *Harvard Business Review*, vol. 42,
no. 6 (November–December 1964), pp. 133–55.

Summary box

A leader's *style* refers to a reasonably stable behavioral disposition to approach leadership situations in a particular way.

The original, classic study on leadership styles identified *three styles:* autocratic, democratic, and laissez-faire.

Leadership styles can be plotted along a continuum of varying degrees of leader authority and group freedom. This suggests *five styles:* tells, persuades, consults, joins, and delegates.

Another styles classification is based on behavior, power, and information. This classification yields *five styles:* directive, negotiative, consultative, participative, and delegative.

The *most significant point* about leadership style is that different styles lead to different *behavioral* consequences. Even if there is an ideal leadership style, specific managers and leaders have to work with styles they *know* and with which they are *comfortable.*

Although the *essence of participation* is shared decision making, a participatory leadership style involves more than shared decision making. (Ten high-ranked participation characteristics were rated; seven of the ten were judged by a group of managers to be important for effectiveness).

Rensis Likert has identified four management systems which he labels System 1, System 2, System 3, and System 4. The basic thrust of Likert's work is that System 4, a participative style, makes the greatest long-range potential contribution to organizational effectiveness. A guiding principle of System 4 is the Principle of Supportive Relationships.

The *Managerial Grid®* is based on two dimensions of leadership: concern for people and production. The grid is used to record a person's style toward these two dimensions on a scale of 1 to 9. A 9,9 position on the grid represents the highest concern for both people and production.

We cannot say that any particular leadership style is "better" than any other style. "It all depends" on the criteria used for judging styles and on the interaction of the leader, the followers, and the situation.

CHECK YOUR UNDERSTANDING

Leadership
Universalist approaches
Great man approach
Personality trait approach
Leader behavior approach
Ohio State leadership studies
  Main emphasis
  LBDQ
  Initiating structure
  Consideration
  Hi-Hi leader
Interaction influence system
Situational approaches
Contingency approach (Fiedler)
  Main emphasis
  LPC
  Task-motivated
  Relationship-motivated
  Situation favorableness
Path-goal approach (House)
  Main emphasis
  Leader behaviors

Situational variables
Propositions
Path instrumentalities
Participation in decision making
approach (Vroom and Yetton)
  Main emphasis
  Leadership methods
  Diagnostic questions
  Rules
  Feasible set
  Choice rule
Leadership styles
  Continuum of leadership styles
  Styles based on behavior, power,
  and information
  Participation characteristics
  Systems 1, 2, 3, 4 (Likert)
  Principle of Supportive Rela-
  tionships
  Managerial Grid® (Blake and
  Mouton)
  9,9 managerial style

STUDY QUESTIONS

1. In what ways are management and leadership behavior similar and in what ways are they different?

2. If an organization is well designed and well managed, why should it need leadership?

3. Be able to compare and contrast the six leadership approaches discussed in this chapter. Of what value, in your opinion, is each approach to managers? What are the limitations of each?

4. The chapter states that contemporary society is less responsive to the appeal of great man leaders. Do you agree? Explain.

5. Suppose you knew that integrity is required for leadership success. What would you do with that information if you wanted to be a successful leader?

6. Do you agree that "leaders have to work with styles they know and with which they are familiar?" Why or why not?

7. Explain the following statement: "Not all employees respond favorably to a participatory leadership style."

8. What is one overall conclusion that can be reached about leadership and leadership style from the Ohio State Leadership Studies, the work of Rensis Likert, and the Managerial Grid®?

APPLICATION: ANOTHER ARNOLD*

In the first part of this chapter, we introduced Arnold Schwarzen-egger as one type of leader. For Arnold, being a leader "all has to do with how hungry you are. I am very hungry." Since meeting Arnold, we have discussed six approaches to understanding leadership and several views of leadership styles. Perhaps this knowledge of approaches and styles will help us understand another Arnold.

Like any organization, Folsom State Prison has its leaders and its followers. As the lead-man of the tool and die shop, Arnie is one of Folsom's leaders. He is the "con boss" of 18 inmates and responsible for seeing that his operation runs smoothly. Con bosses at Folsom are chosen from a group of de facto leaders—leaders who have emerged and proven themselves among the inmates. For a man convicted of murder in the first degree and who had won a reprieve from the gas chamber only two years before, Arnie impressed everyone with his motivation, self-esteem, common sense, and sound reasoning. All of these qualities are essential to a leadership role in Folsom.

Other qualities are important to leadership at Folsom and Arnold possesses them all. Some are qualities that are useful in any organization: intelligence, fairness, mental aggressiveness. Others are qualities that are uniquely helpful in environments like Folsom. One of these is physical aggressiveness. Sometimes a fight is needed to settle an issue, and it's part of the "convict's code" that these fights are known only to the inmates. The formal supervisors and the guards are not supposed to learn about them.

Convicts at Folsom can gain respect from other convicts by the uniqueness of the crime they committed. It also helps if the crime received some newspaper and television coverage. In addition, "seniority" is a source of status: "Twenty years in Folsom earns a man the kind of respect reserved for brain surgeons and senators on the outside." The ability to hustle and manipulate money also distinguishes leaders in Folsom—as it does in many other types of organizations.

In spite of the fact that the almost 2,000 inmates in Folsom are murderers, armed robbers, and other types of "hard cons," they work together reasonably well. Work is part of the life of each con. It helps make life bearable, and "working hard and doing your own number" contribute to a long-range goal of almost every inmate—parole. Parole is the "glue that binds the mind of every man in prison."

Discuss this leadership situation from the viewpoint of the leadership styles and the approaches to understanding leadership discussed in Chapter 11.

---

* Based on Larry Victor Mann and James Roberts, "Leadership: A Case Study from Folsom Prison," *MBA*, vol. 8, no. 3 (March 1974), pp. 23–25. Reprinted with permission from the March 1974 MBA Magazine. Copyright © 1974 by MBA Communication, Inc. At the time the article was written, the authors were inmates of Folsom State Prison.

Objectives of Chapter 12

- To emphasize the pervasive role that communication plays in managing.
- To define communication and to differentiate it from information and data.
- To describe the communication process and to note sources of distortion in the process.
- To discuss formal and informal communication networks in organizations.
- To identify two barriers to personal communication effectiveness and to suggest remedies for decreasing the impact of these barriers.

Outline of Chapter 12

Communication, Information, and Data
  Role of Communication
  Definition
  Information and Data
  Restricting Communication
The Communication Process
  One-Way Communication
  Two-Way Communication
  The Arc of Distortion
  Noise
Communication Networks
  Downward Communication
  Upward Communication
  Horizontal Communication
  Informal Networks
Improving Personal Communication
  Failure to Listen
  Tendency to Evaluate

12

MANAGERIAL COMMUNICATION

Those for whom words have lost their value are likely to find that ideas have also lost their value.

Edwin Newman, in *Strictly Speaking*

Every person is a center of communication every day of his life. He communicates fear or faith, hostility or love, indifference or identification. He has the choice as to what kind of communication it shall be.

Lionel Whiston

The language man

Imagine yourself watching television some evening. The late news and the weather report are over and now it is time for the language man's nightly report of the "language-pollution index." As Neil Postman describes the scene, it might go something like this:

> Thank you, Tom. Today the language-pollution index rose to the danger point and the Governor had to request that a period of silence be imposed starting at 6 P.M. this evening. He lifted the ban at 10 P.M. this evening, and tomorrow's prospects for a healthier day seem quite good.[1]

Words with no meaning

The tongue-in-cheek proposal of a "language-pollution index" is one way of dramatizing the frustration of trying to communicate with words that have no meaning. Meaning is found only in the people who use words. That, in itself, is a useful point for managers to keep in mind. In addition, it provides a good opening for this chapter dealing with a major managerial responsibility—communication.

This chapter

In this chapter we define communication, relate it to information and data, and note the necessity for organizations to restrict communications. Next, we contrast one-way and two-way communication processes and discuss sources of distortion in communi-

---

[1] Neil Postman, "Demeaning of Meaning," in *Language in America,* edited by Neil Postman, Charles Weingartner, and Terrence P. Moran (New York: Pegasus Publishing Company, 1969), p. 20.

cation. Then, we discuss the major formal communication networks in organizations and illustrate the idea of an informal communication network. Last, we suggest remedies for reducing the impact of two important barriers to personal communication.

COMMUNICATION, INFORMATION, AND DATA

Similar to decision making

Role of Communication. Managers are interested in improving their organization's communication system and their personal communication skills because communication is one basic process through which they meet their accountability for performance. Communication is similar to decision making in that both types of behavior *pervade everything managers do.* Planning, organizing, and controlling all involve managers in specific decisions and communication acts.

Cause and symptom

Some writers consider communication so important to overall managerial performance that they write of it as "management's number one problem." In one cross-cultural study of managers, 74 percent cited communication blocks as the single greatest barrier to corporate excellence.[2] Our view is that communication failures can be: (1) both a *cause* of major managerial problems and (2) a *symptom* of more fundamental managerial failures (such as the failure to adequately plan, organize, and control) or of behavioral difficulties between individuals and groups.[3] In either case, communication is an important managerial concern.

Lifeblood of an organization

The importance of communication derives, not only from the contribution communication makes to managerial and organization performance, but also from the *basic right* of organization members to know what is going on. Communication is more than just another tool for improving organizational performance. It is the means by which individuals receive the meaning of information that influences their life in organizations. In the final analysis, it is the quality and level of communication that gives an organization its distinctively *human* characteristic. "Communication is the lifeblood of an organization."[4]

Essence of communication

Definition. What do we do when we "communicate" with another person? What is it about a frown from a supervisor or a clenched fist from another employee that communicates? Our view of the essence of communication is that it is the conveyance of the *meaning* of information. Communication may be defined as

---

[2] Robert Blake and Jane S. Mouton, *Corporate Excellence through Grid Organization Development* (Houston: Gulf Publishing Company, 1968).

[3] Raymond E. Hill and Laurie S. Baron, "Interpersonal Openness and Communication Effectiveness," in *Proceedings,* Thirty-Sixth Annual Meeting of the Academy of Management, August 11–14, 1976, p. 408.

[4] Everett M. Rogers and Rekha Agarwala-Rogers, *Communication in Organization* (New York: The Free Press, 1976), p. 7.

information flow that transfers *meaning* and *understanding* from an information source to an information receiver.

Facets of learning

Transferring meaning and understanding is not an easy task, since "meaning" is a very broad term that ultimately includes all possible reactions that people have to words and things. These reactions can be to any or all of three overlapping facets of meaning: denotation, connotation, and association.[5] That is, the same word or thing can "denote" what it is or does (for example, "managing" is a type of work); it can "connote" some implications or sentiments ("managing" is a type of work that I would like very much to do); and it can bring to mind certain "associations" ("managing" may bring to mind such associations as business, money, golf, ulcers, opportunity, pressure, and so on). Given that the meaning of a word or thing can have these several facets, it is no wonder that communication—the transfer of meaning and understanding—is so difficult.

Relevance and timing

Information and Data.   Communication is different from simple transmission of information or data; its essential ingredients are understanding and meaning. Managers rely *on* data and information *for* communication. The distinction between "data" and "information" is somewhat ambiguous. Relevance and timing are two criteria often used to distinguish data from information. Commonly, "information" is considered "data" that is, in some way, relevant to the receiver.[6] For example, certain data may be of use to a production manager but have no relevance to the work of a marketing manager. "Timing" is also important to the distinction between information and data. For example, prior to making decisions, managers may require different kinds of information; after the decisions are made, that information becomes data as far as those decisions are concerned. For managers, information is the "raw material" of communication.

Management information system—MIS

In recent years there has been a tendency to refer to the "Management Information System," (MIS). This term began to develop with advances in computer capability for the storage and processing of data. As the potentialities of computers for providing decision makers with information became apparent, an interest emerged in developing integrated, "real-time" access to information. For a short time, there was some thought that business firms could have one all-encompassing information system capable of handling all the information needs of the entire organization. The infeasibility of that idea led to a more reasonable and restricted use of the concept of a MIS. That is, MIS refers to a computer-based system for pro-

---

[5] Jum C. Nunnally, *Psychometric Theory* (New York: McGraw-Hill Book Company, 1967), p. 540.

[6] We rely here on a "common-sense" understanding of the definition of information. For 15 definitions of information, see John A. Beckett, *Management Dynamics: The New Synthesis* (New York: McGraw-Hill Book Company, 1971), pp. 96–98.

viding decision makers with information relevant to their areas of concern.

Organiza-
tional
information
systems—OIS

In terms of communication, however, computer-based management information systems account for a very limited amount of the information flow in organizations. Organizations provide information to members in a variety of ways, including computers, oral reports and instructions, memos, policy statements, the organizational reward and punishment system, sales forecasts, and production schedules. Additionally, an organization provides information by its silence or inaction, and choices of what goals *not* to pursue and what methods *not* to utilize. The main point is that an "organizational information system," or OIS must include *all* elements that contribute to information flow in organizations—not just computer-based elements.

Exception
reporting

Managers in business organizations often receive stacks of computer printouts, presumably for the purpose of providing information for facilitating job performance. However, these printouts frequently contain data that is completely irrelevant to the managers' performance. Often the printouts are never even read. In order to avoid this situation, many companies attempt to channel to managers only those printouts that contain data relevant to their area of accountability. This is sometimes called "exception reporting." However, even when the printouts contain "information" (as defined above), it does not follow that communication has occurred. It is the *meaning* of the information to the managers that is the essence of communication.

Technology

There is often no shortage of data and information in organizations. The computer, in particular, has created an information and data "explosion," and advances in duplicating and electronic equipment have accelerated data flow. The potential use of cable television, optical scanners, central data banks, and computer time-sharing causes the author of *The Information Machines* to say, "The new communications will permit the accumulation of a critical mass of human attention and impulse that up to now has been inconceivable."[7] The advancing technology of information sharing and processing that are increasingly utilized by organizations and governments are the source of the contemporary concern about the assault on individual privacy.

Limiting com-
munication

Restricting Communication. It is often advocated that communication within an organization should be "free and open" in order to recognize the right of employees to be informed about their work environment. Undoubtedly, most organizations could improve the quantity, quality, and timing of their communications. However, organizations cannot have free and open communication

---

[7] As quoted in David C. Anderson, "On Communications and Common Sense," *Wall Street Journal*, May 3, 1971. Also see Ben Bagdikian, *The Information Machines* (New York: Harper & Row, Publishers, 1971).

in a literal sense. An organization in which everyone communicates with everyone else about everything is not an organization at all. Every organization requires mechanisms that prevent "noise"— irrelevant communication.

Information overload

Too much information flow in an organization leads to "information overload." Information overload exists when a particular channel of communication cannot process the information because it is beyond the channel's capacity at a given time. A familiar example of information overload is when long-distance telephone lines are full at peak periods, such as Christmas Day. At the individual level, we experience information overload when the demands on our personal capacity to process information are beyond our capabilities within the time available.

Responding to overload

There are several possible behavioral responses to information overload: failure to process some of the information; processing some information incorrectly; letting work pile up during peak periods in the hope of catching up during a quiet period; looking for ways to cut off the information inflow; searching for people to help process some of the information; and lowering the quality of information processing.[8]

Summary box

> *Communication* gives an organization its distinctively human characteristic. It is the lifeblood of an organization.
>
> We define communication as information flow that transfers *meaning* and *understanding* from an information source to an information receiver. For managers, information is the "raw material" of communication. *Information* is *data* that is in some way relevant to the information receiver.
>
> A *management information system* (MIS) is a computer-based system for providing decision makers with information relevant to their areas of concern. An *organizational information system* (OIS) includes *all* elements that contribute to information flow in organizations.
>
> Technology has created an information and data "explosion." However, communication between people is not primarily dependent on technology. It depends on forces in people and in their environments, and it results from a communication process. We examine that process next.
>
> Every organization must attempt to strike a balance between the need for *free and open* communication and the need to *restrict* communication. Too much information leads to *information overload*.

[8] Daniel Katz and Robert L. Kahn, *The Social Psychology of Organizations* (New York: John Wiley & Sons, 1966), p. 231.

THE COMMUNICATION PROCESS

No feedback

One-Way Communication. Sometimes communication is viewed as in Figure 12–1—a simple one-way exchange that occurs between an information sender and an information receiver within a given context. You participate in one-way communication everytime you listen to and watch a television program. There is no opportunity for you to give any feedback to the information sender.

FIGURE 12–1
One-Way Communication

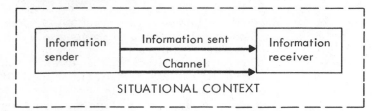

One-way assumption

One-way communication involves the assumption that the message sent is the same as the message received. There are times when this may be a perfectly reasonable assumption. Every *potential* distortion that could occur in one-way communication is not an *actual* distortion. If the relationship between senders and receivers is one of mutual confidence and trust, distortion is minimized. In any case, most organizations rely extensively on various one-way channels as means of distributing information. Managers should be sensitive to the distortion that can occur when such channels are used. Sometimes this distortion is comical, as shown in Figure 12–2.

Observations about Figure 12–1

Several observations may be made about the one-way communication exchange shown in Figure 12–1. First, the *information sender and receiver* do not have to be individuals. They may be cliques, groups, or even entire organizations. Second, the *situational context* box emphasizes that communication does not occur in isolation. All communication occurs within a system of physical, organizational, and interpersonal variables. Third, the communication *channel* includes such things as loudspeakers, written memos, closed-circuit television, bulletin boards, and face-to-face exchanges.

A process requires feedback

Two-Way Communication. A final observation about Figure 12–1 is that the absence of "feedback" that is characteristic of one-way communication implies that the receiver plays a very passive role in communication. The idea of the receiver being an integral and active part of communication is not consistent with one-way communication. Figure 12–3 shows two-way communication, in which

FIGURE 12–2
Operation Halley's Comet

A COLONEL ISSUED THE FOLLOWING DIRECTIVE TO HIS EXECU-
TIVE OFFICERS:
"Tomorrow evening at approximately 2000 hours Halley's Comet will
be visible in this area, an event which occurs only once every 75 years.
Have the men fall out in the battalion area in fatigues, and I will explain this rare phenomenon to them. In case of rain, we will not be
able to see anything, so assemble the men in the theater and I will
show them films of it."

EXECUTIVE OFFICER TO COMPANY COMMANDER:
"By order of the Colonel, tomorrow at 2000 hours, Halley's Comet
will appear above the battalion area. If it rains, fall the men out in
fatigues, then march to the theater where this rare phenomenon will
take place, something which occurs only once every 75 years."

COMPANY COMMANDER TO LIEUTENANT:
"By order of the Colonel be in fatigues at 2000 hours tomorrow
evening, the phenomenal Halley's Comet will appear in the theater.
In case of rain, in the batallion area, the Colonel will give another
order, something which occurs once every 75 years."

LIEUTENANT TO SERGEANT:
"Tomorrow at 2000 hours, the Colonel will appear in the theater with
Halley's Comet, something which happens every 75 years if it rains,
the Colonel will order the comet into the battalion area."

SERGEANT TO SQUAD:
"When it rains tomorrow at 2000 hours, the phenomenal 75-year-old
General Halley, accompanied by the Colonel, will drive his comet
through the battalion area theater in fatigues."

Source: Speech by Dan Bellus of the Santa Monica firm of Dan Bellus and Associates.
Reprinted in the *DS LETTER*, Vol. I, No. 3 (1971). Published by Didactic Systems, Inc.,
Box 457, Cranford, N.J., 07016.

the receiver is involved in a *process* of receiving information and
providing feedback to the sender. This process is dynamic and ongoing. Thus, in two-way communication, each party to the communication is both a sender and a receiver. Feedback from the
receiver allows the sender to verify whether the *meaning* of information has been transmitted.

FIGURE 12–3
Two-Way Communication Process

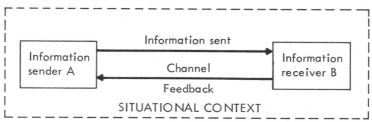

Intended and
unintended
messages

The Arc of Distortion.   An interesting way of illustrating the potential inaccuracy of one-way communication is shown in Figure 12–4. This illustration shows that the information sent often exceeds and is different from that which was intended. The result

FIGURE 12–4
The Arc of Distortion

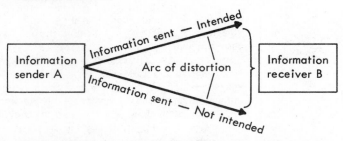

Source: Reproduced by special permission from *Handbook of Staff Development and Human Relations Training Materials Developed for Use in Africa* by Donald Nylen, J. Robert Mitchell, and Anthony Stout, p. 73, © National Training Laboratories Institute for Applied Behavioral Science.

is an "arc of distortion." Information sender A, through unintended messages, may distort the intended message sent to B. Unintended messages can result from both verbal and nonverbal causes. For example, body position can "communicate" anger, happiness, relaxation, nervousness, and defensiveness.

Words carry
different
meanings

Unintended messages can also result from the *differences* in language used in attempts to communicate. For example, General Motors Corporation discovered that the Chevrolet Nova was being poorly received by its Puerto Rican dealers. The reason was that, although Nova means "star" in Spanish, when it is spoken it sounds like "no va," which means "it doesn't go." GM resolved the problem by changing the car's name to "Caribe."[9]

General
semantics

Even people who speak the *same* language hear different meanings. A classic example of this problem is given in Figure 12–5. We all know from experience that identical words can have different meanings for different people at different times and places. These differences are a primary concern of the area of study known as "general semantics."[10] In spite of our knowledge and experience with the different meaning of words, we often act as if words have some inherent meaning. We sometimes treat words as if they are equivalent to the reality they represent.

---

[9] "More Firms Turn to Translation Experts to Avoid Costly, Embarrassing Mistakes," *Wall Street Journal*, vol. 59, no. 9, Southwest Edition (January 13, 1977), p. 32.

[10] For a well-known introduction to general semantics, see S. I. Hayakawa, *Language in Thought and Action* (New York: Harcourt Brace Jovanovich, 1949).

FIGURE 12–5
Language and Meaning

> A New York plumber wrote the Bureau [of Standards at Washington] that he had found hydrochloric acid fine for cleaning drains, and was it harmless? Washington replied: "The efficacy of hydrochloric acid is indisputable, but the chlorine residue is incompatible with metallic permanence."
>
> The plumber wrote back that he was mighty glad the Bureau agreed with him. The Bureau replied with a note of alarm: "We cannot assume responsibility for the production of toxic and noxious residues with hydrochloric acid, and suggest that you use an alternate procedure." The plumber was happy to learn that the Bureau still agreed with him.
>
> Whereupon Washington exploded: "Don't use hydrochloric acid; it eats hell out of the pipes."

Source: Stuart Chase, *Power of Words* (New York: Harcourt, Brace and Company, 1953), p. 259.

Interference

Noise. The notion of "noise" is very useful in understanding communication. Noise includes all types of interference between the transmission and the reception of messages. Noise may be viewed in the context of a "black box," because the message "goes through" or combines with the noise and both are presented to the receiver. (In general, a "black box" refers to a control system through which "inputs" pass on their way to becoming "outputs," to which there is incomplete access, and about which there is incomplete understanding.)

Effect of noise

Noise can be physical, like electrical static, or it can be variability in statistical data. Noise can be additive or negative. Static is an example of "additive" noise; a short blackout of a television program is an example of "negative" noise. Noise can be psychological, caused by the perceptual process. The effect of noise is to distort sent messages so that they are not equivalent to received messages. Noise can be intentionally introduced. A business firm may introduce "its own noise into a competitor's information system—for example, by lowering prices during a competitor's market test."[11]

---

[11] Martin K. Starr, *Management: A Modern Approach* (New York: Harcourt Brace Jovanovich, 1971), p. 506.

Summary box

> *One-way communication* occurs in a context that does not allow receiver-to-sender feedback. The absence of the opportunity for feedback increases the potential distortion between the sent and received message. One-way communication involves the assumption that the meaning of the sent message is the same as the meaning of the received message.
>
> *Two-way communication* occurs in a situational context that does allow for receiver-to-sender feedback. Provision for feedback justifies use of the term "communication process."
>
> The *arc of distortion* is one way of illustrating that the information sent often exceeds and is different from what was intended.
>
> *Noise* is any interference that occurs between transmission and reception of a message. It may be physical or psychological, additive or negative. The effect of noise is to distort sent messages.

COMMUNICATION NETWORKS

Formal and informal networks

A communication network is a set of individuals or organizational units (groups, departments, and so on) linked together by patterned communication flows. In any organization, there are several communication networks. "Formal communication networks" are established as part of the overall design of an organization in order to prescribe and limit the flow of information among organizational personnel. There are three major formal networks in most organizations: downward, upward, and horizontal. "Informal communication networks" emerge out of the formal networks and out of the experiences of people who interact at work.

Downward network

Downward Communication. "Downward communication" results from a transfer of information in which the information source is located at a higher level in the organization design than the information receiver. Downward communication is illustrated in Figure 12–6 by solid lines.

Types

The most obvious type of downward communication is when managers give instructions or other job-related information to their employees. Other types include policy statements, procedures, manuals, memos, reports, bulletin boards, and company newsletters. Employees receive information from several sources "above" them, such as their immediate superiors, planning departments, quality-control departments, personnel departments, and other staff departments.

FIGURE 12–6
Formal Communication Networks

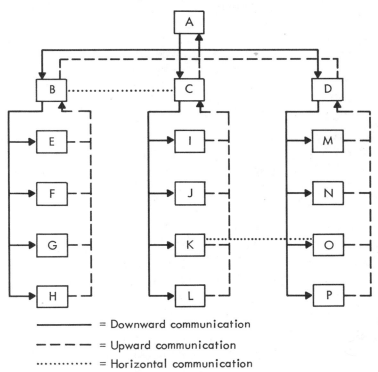

——————— = Downward communication

– – – – = Upward communication

············· = Horizontal communication

Inaccurate and inadequate

When employees complain, "We don't know what's going on around here," they are complaining primarily about the inadequacy of downward communication. Downward communication is characteristically inadequate and inaccurate. It is "inadequate" because those originating the information flow underestimate the need and desire of employees for relevant information. Downward communication processes are "inaccurate" because they seldom allow sufficient opportunity for feedback from the information receivers. Without this feedback, distortion and misinterpretation will not be discovered and evaluated. It is easy to assume that once a policy statement has been distributed in written form, it has been communicated. However, written information can be misinterpreted just like information distributed orally.

Upward network

Upward Communication. "Upward communication" results from a transfer of information in which the information source is located at a lower level in the organization design than the information receiver. This is illustrated in Figure 12–6 by dashed lines. The most obvious illustration of upward communication is when employees provide their immediate superior with information relevant to their jobs. This type of upward communication can be reduced to what the person says, "about himself . . . , about others . . . , about organizational practices and policies, and about what needs to be done and how it can be done."[12]

Steps that encourage upward communication

Managers can take some steps to encourage upward communication. They can be trusting and supporting in their own job behavior. They can set an example by engaging in upward communication to their own superiors. They can establish a program of group interviews to solicit employees' comments about their jobs.[13] They can provide various mechanisms for upward communication—grievance procedures, suggestion boxes, departmental meetings, an ombudsman, and an open-door policy.

Lessening dependency

Ultimately, however, improving upward communication depends on lessening the dependency relationship built into organization designs. Simply put, it is difficult to communicate freely with a person when that person controls your economic welfare. Employees know that information they pass upward may be used against them, and the risk of telling managers something they may not want to hear is commonly too great. Upward communication in organizations is not known for its contribution to organizational effectiveness. The nature of many manager–managed relationships is such that objective information flow is difficult to maintain.

Amount of upward communication

Sometimes it is said that there is a greater amount of upward communication in an organization than there is downward communication. One suggested reason for this is that members at the lower levels of an organization (low-status persons) will communicate with members at higher levels (high-status persons) ". . . as a 'psychological substitute' for upward movement when actual movement is not possible. . . . The amount of communication directed toward high status persons by low status persons will not be completely reciprocated."[14]

Horizontal network

Horizontal Communication. The downward and upward communication networks in an organization receive most of the attention in formal organization design. Policies and procedures support a variety of mechanisms for facilitating vertical information flow.

---

[12] Katz and Kahn, *The Social Psychology of Organizations*, p. 245.

[13] Woodruff Imberman, "Letting the Employee Speak His Mind," *Personnel*, vol. 53, no. 6 (November–December 1976), pp. 12–22.

[14] Christine Vaidya, Russell F. Lloyd, and David L. Ford, Jr., "Organizational Information Flow Characteristics: A Selected Review and Suggestions for Future Research," in *Proceedings*, Thirty-fifth Annual Meeting, Academy of Management, August 10–13, 1975, pp. 372–74.

Nevertheless, organizations need horizontal communication in order to be effective. "Horizontal communication" results from a transfer of information in which the information source and the information receiver are on the same organizational level—examples are shown by dotted lines in Figure 12–6.

Coordination

Communication between peers is necessary for organizational effectiveness to assure work coordination and to provide psychological and social support for the organization members. Horizontal communication is necessary for work coordination because it is often impossible—and undesirable—to completely specify in advance the conditions for task accomplishment. Communication between peers sometimes "fills the gap" left by inadequate organization design or by changing circumstances.

*Socio-emo-
tional support*

In addition, peer communication furnishes socio-emotional support. We like and need to communicate with those with whom we share common problems. Managers should take a positive approach to horizontal communication; that is, they should not only not discourage it, but they should positively facilitate it by providing ample opportunities for peer interaction.

*Less
structured,
less
predictable*

Informal Networks. The downward, upward, and horizontal networks are formal networks—they prescribe how and what information is supposed to flow between organizational personnel. Formal networks are structured and have a high degree of predictability. Informal networks, however, emerge spontaneously, "are less structured, and hence less predictable."[15]

*Who com-
municates
to whom*

Informal networks are determined by observing or asking "who communicates to whom." There is normally a large overlap between formal and informal networks when the communication deals with job-related information. People that interact on-the-job are likely to develop common sentiments and norms that support communication. Nevertheless, informal networks are seldom totally identical to formal networks.

Cliques

Figure 12–7 illustrates the informal network of the personnel who make up the organization chart shown in Figure 12–6. The network shows only the communication flow *within* this group of personnel. In communication network analysis, specific terms are used to identify various components of the communication network. A "clique" is a "subsystem whose elements interact with each other relatively more frequently than with other members of the communication system." Three cliques are shown in Figure 12–7.[16] The members of a clique have about half of their communication contacts with each other.

[15] Rogers and Rogers, *Communication in Organization*, p. 111.
[16] Ibid., p. 113.

FIGURE 12–7
Informal Communication Network

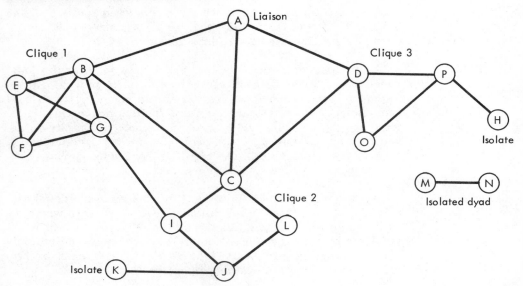

*Liaisons,
isolates,
and bridges*

A "liaison" is a person who connects two or more cliques without belonging to any of the cliques. In Figure 12–7, A is a liaison. An "isolate" is a person who does not substantially participate in the communication network.[17] K, M, and N in Figure 12–7 are isolates. A "bridge" is a person who links cliques in their communication activity, and who is also a member of a clique. D, C, I, and B are bridges.

*Use to
managers*

Drawings of informal communication networks can be useful to managers by revealing informal patterned communication flows and by highlighting differences between the formal and informal networks. These differences may provide a rational basis for altering existing formal networks to make them more in line with the informal networks. Additionally, by identifying those who fill liaison and bridge roles, it may be possible to utilize such personnel more effectively in formal communication.

---

[17] T. Harrell Allen, "Communication Networks: The Hidden Organizational Chart," *Personnel Administrator,* vol. 21, no. 6 (September 1976), p. 33.

Summary box

> A *communication network* is a set of individuals or organizational units linked together by patterned communication flows.
>
> *Formal communication networks* are established in order to prescribe and limit the flow of information among organizational personnel. There are three major formal communication networks in organizations: *downward, upward,* and *horizontal.*
>
> *Informal communication networks* emerge out of the formal networks and out of the experiences of people who interact at work.
>
> The components of an informal communication network include *cliques, liaisons, isolates,* and *bridges.*

IMPROVING PERSONAL COMMUNICATION

Communication gap

How can we improve our personal communication skills? How can we improve the prospects that the information flowing between ourselves and others will qualify as communication—the transfer of meaning? These questions are at the heart of the "communication gap" that exists in most organizations. To a large extent, the failure of personal communication in organizations is the cumulative result of individual organization members either not talking with each other, talking only at a superficial level, or not listening to each other. This section discusses two barriers that often serve to inhibit or prevent communication. The two barriers are failure to listen and the tendency to evaluate.

Managers spend time listening

Failure to Listen. The first English book wholly on listening was published in 1957.[18] Up to that time there was no shortage of books on speaking, but little emphasis was given to listening. Managers, however, spend a lot of their time listening to oral information flow. Higher-level managers, in particular, may spend the largest part of their communication time listening. Listening can be viewed as an important—and rare—managerial skill. It is estimated that almost half of our communicating time is accounted for by the process of listening.[19] Since the average rate at which people can listen (about 400 words per minute) is about twice as fast as the rate at which words can be spoken, it is understandable why people go off on mental tangents while listening. Furthermore, only about 50 percent of an orally communicated

[18] Keith Davis, *Human Behavior at Work* (New York, McGraw-Hill Book Company, 1972), p. 394.

[19] Information in this paragraph taken from R. C. Huseman, J. M. Lahiff, and J. D. Hatfield, *Interpersonal Communication in Organization: A Perceptual approach* (Boston: Holbrook Press, 1976), p. 107.

message is retained immediately after the communication occurs. These facts about listening are enough to suggest that improving listening can be an important part of efforts to improve communications.

Listening influences information flow

We are all familiar with various tricks that make us appear we are listening when, in fact, we are not. College students have discovered several imaginative ways to *not listen* to lectures. The problem is that there is no outward sign that listening is taking place. The only evidence of listening is when a person responds to another person by words or sounds, facial expression, or some form of physical activity. Without realizing it, listeners have a high degree of influence over the quality and quantity of information flow. The failure to listen tends to reduce the quantity of information the speaker shares, and it leads to the sharing of only superficial data. Successful listening, however, gives the speaker feedback that is needed in order to know that the listener wants to hear what is being said and wants to hear more.

Ten commandments for good listening

Can listening skill be developed? Undoubtedly there are techniques and rules for improving listening. For example, one author cites the "Ten Commandments for Good Listening": stop talking, put the talker at ease, show the talker you want to listen, remove distractions, empathize with the talker, be patient, hold your temper, go easy on argument and criticism, ask questions, and stop talking. Stop talking is the first and last commandment.[20]

The choice to listen

These guides to better listening are potentially useful to managers, particularly if they have nothing else to think about than improving their listening. However, managers, or anyone else, are not likely to *use* the guides unless they make the *choice* to listen. In other words, the failure to listen is not so much a function of inadequate listening skill as it is a function of the choice, conscious or unconscious, not to listen. To listen or not to listen, that is the question. Why do we choose listening or not listening as our behavior?

Listening contingencies

Listening is partly determined by the person's listening ability and skill. Perhaps training in listening could help; maybe a hearing aid is what is needed. More important, however, the environment may be such that the consequences of listening are either negative, neutral, or insufficiently positive or rewarding. If we want to improve the level of listening, we must build into the environment contingencies that reinforce good listening. In order to do that, the expected rewards of listening must be greater than the rewards of not listening.

---

[20] Davis, *Human Behavior at Work,* p. 396.

Listening must lead to reinforcing consequences

When listening is thought of as behavior, then the explanation for the pervasive failure to listen one encounters in organizations becomes apparent. There are other things—daydreaming, thinking about another problem, doodling—that the "listener" would rather do. The major reason college students do not listen to lectures is not that they do not know *how* to listen. The reason is that they do not *want* to listen. Or, put another way, the lecture does not offer sufficient reinforcing consequences to offset the consequences of doing something else. Similarly, employees in business organizations do not listen to the various "speakers" that bombard them because they calculate that listening offers an insufficient net increase in the reinforcing consequences available to them. If managers want to remedy the "failure to listen," they must make listening worthwhile.

A major barrier to communication

Tendency to Evaluate. One author suggests that "the major barrier to mutual interpersonal communication is our very natural tendency to judge, to evaluate, to approve or disapprove the statement of the other person or the other group."[21] For example, after hearing a speech we might say, "I didn't like that speech" or "That was one of the best talks I've heard in a long time." Our primary reaction, in other words, is to evaluate what we hear from our own point of view.

Communication at two levels

This tendency to evaluate heightens in situations where feelings and emotions are involved. Commonly, we communicate at two levels: The topic or *task* level, and the emotional or *feeling* level. When the communication is strictly at the task level, as in a routine job instruction, then the tendency to evaluate is not as strong. However, when the communication involves our personality, our self-image, our emotions and feelings, then we tend to listen evaluatively. All communication between people involves both levels, but the levels differ in their relative importance. Thus, when we listen we tend to evaluate, and this tendency to evaluate is strongest when feelings and emotions are involved.[22]

Listening with understanding: an experiment

One remedy for the tendency to evaluate is "listening with understanding" or "nonevaluative listening." This means simply that the listener tries to empathize with the speaker and to consider the communication from the speaker's frame of reference. As an aid in fostering listening with understanding, here is an experiment you can try in your personal communication. The next time you have an argument with another person or with a small group of friends, stop the discussion for a moment and institute this rule: Each

---

[21] Carl R. Rogers, *On Becoming a Person* (Boston: Houghton Mifflin Company, 1961), chap. 17.

[22] Leslie This, *The Leader Looks at Personal Communication* (Washington, D.C.: Leadership Resources, 1961), p. 13.

person can speak up only after first repeating the ideas and feelings of the previous speaker accurately and to that speaker's satisfaction.

Benefits and difficulty

Applying this rule can have important consequences. For one thing, the rule forces you to listen to what the other person is saying, since you have to repeat it to that person's satisfaction. Therefore, your mind has to focus on the speaker's words rather than on what you intend to say when the speaker finishes. In addition, this rule tends to reduce the emotional level of the communication and to encourage more rational discussion of differences.

Risk involved

If you try this experiment, you will find it difficult in situations where the emotional and feeling level of communication is high. It is precisely in those situations where we find it almost impossible to be empathic and to listen with understanding. Furthermore, when we listen with understanding we place ourselves in a risky position; we run the risk of being changed by the other person's point of view. If we simply listen and respond evaluatively, we confirm our own position. If we listen empathically, we risk being convinced by the other person's point of view. Change is often threatening to us because we are not sure we have flexibility to cope with it.

Summary box

> Managers can improve their personal communication skills by trying to remove two barriers: the *failure to listen* and the *tendency to evaluate*.
>
> The key to increasing the level of listening is to build into the environment *contingencies* that reinforce good listening. If managers want to remedy the failure to listen, they must make listening worthwhile.
>
> Communication between people occurs at the *task* and *feeling* levels. The tendency to evaluate heightens when feelings are involved. One remedy for the tendency to evaluate is *listening with understanding*. Such listening can have important consequences and involves the risk of being changed.

CHECK YOUR UNDERSTANDING

Communication	General semantics
Information	Noise
Data	Formal communication networks
MIS	Informal communication networks
OIS	Clique
Exception reporting	Liaison
Information overload	Isolate
One-way communication	Bridge
Two-way communication	Tendency to evaluate
Communication process	Listening with understanding
The arc of distortion	Two levels of communication

STUDY QUESTIONS

1. Explain the statement: "An organization provides information by its silence or inaction, and by its choice of what goals not to pursue."

2. It has been said that technological advances in data gathering, sharing, and processing pose a threat to individual privacy. What is your opinion about this possible threat? If it exists, how are managers affected by it, and what are their responsibilities for reducing it?

3. What are the various ways of responding behaviorally to information overload?

4. In Figures 12–1 and 12–3, one-way and two-way communications are drawn inside a "situational context" box. What are some situational factors that might influence communication?

5. What are several types of channels that organizations use in transmitting information?

6. What are some examples of noise that interfere between the transmission and the reception of messages in organizations?

7. What is your opinion of the usefulness of the "Ten Commandments for Good Listening?" What is involved in the *choice* to listen or not to listen? As a manager, how could you establish contingencies that reinforce good listening.

8. The text suggests a rule for reducing the tendency to evaluate what others are saying. What are some consequences of applying this rule? Why is this rule more difficult to apply when communications involve emotions? What risk is involved in applying the rule?

APPLICATION: COMMUNICATION EXERCISE

There is a simple way of illustrating how difficult it is to communicate using one-way communication.

1. Try the exercise shown in Figure 12–8 on someone who has not seen the particular set of boxes shown.

FIGURE 12–8
One-Way Communication Exercise

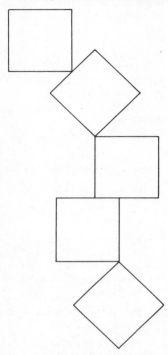

Instructions: Study the arrangement of the above boxes. With your
back to another person, instruct
the person how to draw the boxes.
Begin with the top square and describe each in succession, taking
particular note of the relationship
of each to the preceding one. No
questions are allowed. Compare
the above arrangement with that
drawn by the information receiver.
    Source: J. William Pfeifer and
John E. Jones, *A Handbook of Structured Experiences for Human Relations Training* (Iowa City. University Associates Press, 1969), pp.
13–18.

A *very common* result of this exercise is that there is a far-
from-perfect correspondence between the squares as shown in Figure 12–8 and the squares as drawn by the information receivers
in one-way communication. The lack of opportunity to ask questions of the person giving the instructions and the absence of face-
to-face contact makes it difficult for the information receiver to
draw the squares accurately.

2. Try this same exercise using a two-way communication process
which allows face-to-face contact and allows the receiver to ask questions. The results are usually much closer to the original set of boxes.

Our experience with using this exercise over a long period of time is that it brings out great individual differences in communication skills—both of senders and receivers. For example, some senders are skilled in giving directions and are familiar with drawings and angles. Such senders are able to achieve a high degree of accuracy in the one-way communication part of this exercise. This is particularly true if the receivers are skilled listeners and are familiar with drawings. The high degree of accuracy was illustrated most clearly by a group of engineering graduate students. As long as the content of the communication was familiar to them, they were able to communicate accurately using one-way communication.

3. In your opinion, what are the conditions that must be present in order for accurate one-way communication to occur?
4. Are there any precautions that communicators should keep in mind about feedback?

Objectives of Chapter 13

- To discuss conflict and stress as inevitable features of life in organizations.
- To define conflict and stress and to contrast them with related terms.
- To present a view of conflict as a process and to identify some general propositions about conflict.
- To evaluate five conflict-management styles from the viewpoint of usefulness to managers.
- To relate stress to health, to identify a few job-related stressors, and to note several approaches to coping with stress.

Outline of Chapter 13

The Nature of Conflict
  Evolution of Thinking about Conflict
  Definition
  Conflict, Competition, and Cooperation
  General Propositions about Conflict
  The Conflict Process
Conflict-Management Styles
  Competitor
  Avoider
  Accommodator
  Compromiser
  Collaborator
The Nature of Stress
  Definition
  Stressors
  Stress and Health
  Coping with Stress

13

CONFLICT AND STRESS

I can't handle it!

MBA

*Stress, like fire, can be very dangerous but
nonetheless useful if properly controlled.*

E. Kirby Warren

AMA survey

The American Management Association recently sponsored a survey of managerial interests in the area of conflict and conflict-management. The respondents in the survey were participants in one-week "update" programs sponsored by the AMA. The respondents included 116 CEOs, 76 vice presidents, and 66 middle managers. The results of the survey strongly suggests that the respondents see conflict as a topic of growing importance to them. Among others, the respondents reported that:

1. They spend about 20 percent of their time dealing with conflict;
2. Their conflict-management ability has become more important over the past ten years;
3. They rate conflict management as a topic of equal or slightly higher importance than planning, communication, motivation, and decision making;
4. Their interests in the sources of conflict emphasize psychological factors, such as misunderstanding, communication failure, personality clashes, and value differences.
5. The conflict level in their organizations is about right—not "too low" or "too high."[1]

*Increasing
importance
of conflict
management*

We agree with one of the main conclusions of the AMA survey: Conflict is a topic of increasing importance to managing. There are multiple reasons for this increasing importance, including: the growing scarcity of natural resources; the complexity and increasing interdependence of relationships between individu-

[1] Survey results reported in Kenneth W. Thomas and Warren H. Schmidt, "A Survey of Managerial Interests with Respect to Conflict," *Academy of Management Journal,* vol. 19, no. 2 (June 1976), pp. 315–18.

als, groups, organizations, and nations; the values and life style pluralism that characterizes people of all ages, sexes, and races; and the rising expectations and psychology of entitlement that are reflected in the motivation of employees, managers, owners, customers, and all others who interact in and with the organization.

Relation
to job
performance

Conflict affects job performance. Referring to the job-performance model discussed in Chapter 6, we can see that conflict can affect all components of the model. A person's *role perception* can be altered or distorted if it is the result of a perceptual process carried out in a state of conflict. Similarly, different *abilities and skills* are called into play when conflict is a key dimension of the work environment. A person's *motivation,* as reflected in expectancies, valences, and outcomes, is influenced by the psychology of a conflict situation. Finally, conflict can be the major *situational context* variable within which role perception, abilities and skills, and motivation are brought together into job performance.

This chapter

In this chapter, we trace the evolution of thinking about conflict in organizations. We define conflict as a type of overt behavior and contrast it with competition and cooperation. Next we note three general propositions about conflict and discuss the idea of conflict as a process. Five basic conflict-management styles are assessed in terms of their uses and shortcomings. The chapter ends with an introduction to the idea of stress and its relevance to managers.

THE NATURE OF CONFLICT

Three phases

Evolution of Thinking about Conflict. We can identify three phases in the development of thinking about conflict in organizations. We refer to these phases as the classical phase, the human relations phase, and the contemporary phase.

Classical
phase

The "classical" or "traditional phase" viewed conflict in organizations as dysfunctional and as a temporary imperfection in organizations that, given time and good management, can be completely removed. Early management theories (such as scientific management, administrative management, and bureaucracy—see Chapter 14) placed primary emphasis on the power of logic and rationality for solving the problems of organizations. These early theories did not consider that conflict could be rational from the viewpoint of organization members.

Predominant
until 1940s

Further, these theories tended to assume that if organizations are well managed, there would be a cooperative spirit between management and workers. A cooperative spirit is, according to the classical view, incompatible with conflict. Thus, any conflict that did arise should be temporary, and should be resolved by management and on management's terms. Although there were those who took exception to this view,[2] the classical phase predominated in management thinking from the late 19th century until around the late 1940s.

Human-relations phase

The "human-relations phase" of thinking about conflict recognized its existence but tended to view it as avoidable and as something to be "resolved." The causes of conflict were seen as lying in the personal idiosyncrasies of trouble makers, primma donnas, et cetera.[3] The human relations phase emphasized conflict as a disturbance upsetting the balance or equilibrium of an organization. This view reflected a "popular preoccupation with morals, human relations, and cooperation, and the general value that peace is good and conflict bad."[4]

Contemporary phase

The more contemporary view of conflict is that it is neither good nor bad for organizations. Conflict is simply an inevitable feature of life in organizations: "It is a fact of life that must be understood rather than fought."[5] Conflict arises between individuals, small groups, and other larger groupings within organizations. Additionally, conflict is an inevitable characteristic of the interaction between an organization and its external environments.

Conflict management

In the contemporary view, conflict is not only inevitable but it is a necessary condition for people and organizations if they are to be adaptive to change. Some degree of change is essential for organizational survival and growth, and conflict can serve as an element fostering this change. Given the potentially useful role of conflict, the contemporary view is that conflict should be "managed." "Conflict management" implies that conflict can play a role in the efficient and effective achievement of goals.

Stimulation of conflict

Thus, conflict should not simply be avoided, reduced, or resolved; it should be managed. According to one writer, managing conflict can mean "active seeking of conflict or the positive creation of the conditions that breed conflict."[6] Other authors agree: "Managing conflict may mean stimulating and creating it as well as diminishing or channeling it."[7] The idea behind this conflict-seeking notion is that, at any time, the amount of conflict in an organization may be below the perceived amount required in order to assure effective achievement of the organization's goals. Mana-

---

[2] H. C. Metcalf and L. Urwick, *Dynamic Administration: The Collected Papers of Mary Parker Follett* (New York: Harper & Row, 1942), pp. 30–49.

[3] Joe Kelly, *Organizational Behavior* (Homewood, Ill.: The Dorsey Press, 1969), pp. 499–542.

[4] James D. Thompson, "Organizational Management of Conflict," *Administrative Science Quarterly*, vol. 4, no. 4 (March 1960), p. 389.

[5] David L. Austin, "Conflict: A More Professional Approach," *Personnel Administrator*, vol. 21, no. 5 (July 1976).

[6] Stephen P. Robbins, *Managing Organizational Conflict: A Nontraditional Approach* (Englewood Cliffs, N.J.: Prentice-Hall, 1974), p. 13.

[7] Robert E. Coffey, Anthony G. Athos, and Peter F. Reynolds, *Behavior in Organizations: A Multidimensional View* (Englewood Cliffs, N.J.: Prentice-Hall, 1975), p. 172.

gerial actions may be necessary in order to bring the actual level of conflict up to the desired level. "A company void of constructive conflict is a company void of excitement, diversity, and viability."[8]

What is conflict?

Definition. "Conflict" refers to the overt behavior that results from a process in which members of organizations perceive that their goals are incompatible with goals of other members and in which they perceive the existence of some *opportunity for interfering* with the other members' achieving their goals. Conflict refers to the *deliberate behavior* of organization members that is designed to interfere with or block the attainment of goals of other organization members.[9] There are three points to emphasize about this definition of conflict:

1. *Conflict refers to overt behavior.* This behavior may be one outcome of a process in which differences and disagreements between individuals and groups have been allowed to build up. It may be important for managers to intervene in this process before conflict occurs. Nevertheless, we confine the term "conflict" to overt behavior.

2. *Conflict arises out of two perceptions:* Perceived goal incompatibility and perceived opportunity to interfere with the attainment of another's goals. Goal incompatibility is a necessary but not sufficient condition of conflict. If you perceive your goals to be incompatible with those of another person, but you have no opportunity to block the goal attainment of the other person, there is no conflict as defined here.

3. *Deliberate behavior.* Conflict requires deliberate behavior or "active striving," by one of the participants to interfere with the other participants' goal attainment.[10] If this interference is accidental or the result of something other than an intended action by one of the participants, there is no conflict as defined here.

Conflict and cooperation

Conflict, Competition, and Cooperation. Sometimes conflict is viewed as the opposite of cooperation. In one sense, this is true, because conflict implies a process where parties see their interests as mutually incompatible, whereas in a cooperative process the parties see their interests as mutually supportive.[11] However, the difficulty with this view can be seen by noting that the absence of conflict (as we have defined it) does not necessarily lead to cooperation. Similarly, the absence of cooperation does not mean that conflict will follow. Therefore, the opposite of conflict is "no conflict," and the opposite of cooperation is "no cooperation."

---

[8] Stephen P. Robbins, "Conflict Can Be Stimulating," *International Management*, vol. 28, no. 9 (September 1973), pp. 50–54.

[9] Stuart M. Schmidt and Thomas A. Kochanm "Conflict: Toward Conceptual Clarity," *Administrative Science Quarterly*, vol. 17, no. 3 (September 1972), pp. 359–70.

[10] Rensis Likert and Jane Gibson Likert, *New Ways of Managing Conflict* (New York: McGrew-Hill Book Company, 1976), p. 7.

[11] Morton Deutsch, *The Resolution of Conflict: Constructive and Destructive Processes* (New Haven: Yale University Press, 1973).

Too much cooperation

Like conflict, cooperation can have both positive and negative results. Of course, cooperative behavior is the general rule in most organizations; without cooperation, organizations would fall apart. However, if the desire for cooperation becomes so strong that genuine differences are not allowed to emerge, then an organization lacks one of the incentives to engage in essential change.

Conflict and competition

The relationship between conflict and competition is not as clear as that between conflict and cooperation. Three views are: (1) conflict and competition are overlapping but not identical forms of behavior; (2) conflict is less regulated by rules and behavioral norms than competition, and (3) conflict and competition are behaviorally different.[12]

Rationale

The rationale behind the view that conflict and competition are different goes like this: Both conflict and competition involve the perception of goal incompatibility. In competition, however, the participants do not deliberately attempt to obstruct each other's efforts to attain their goals. Competition is characerized by *parallel striving* by the competitors to achieve their goals. In conflict, one participant deliberately attempts to block the goal attainment of the other participant. Conflict is characterized by *mutual interference* by the participants in their efforts to achieve their goals. "The key behavioral difference . . . is directly analogous to the difference between participants in a race and a fight."[13]

Interdependence

General Propositions about Conflict. One proposition about conflict is that it always arises within a context of *interdependence*. If the members of an organization are in no way interdependent, it is unlikely that conflict between them will emerge. In organizations, however, almost everyone is in some way in a relationship with everyone else. The owners, managers, employees, suppliers, customers, and the general public are all interdependent in varying degrees. These interdependences are one source of conflict in organizations. However, just as interdependencies are a source of conflict, they also represent a source of cooperation in organizations.

Similarities

A second proposition about conflict is that much of it grows out of similarities in the requirements of organization members. All organizations are, in some sense, an economy in which scarce resources must be allocated. The demands on resources exceed the supply. Further, there is also in organizations a relative scarcity of power positions; the number of people seeking organizational positions of influence far exceed the supply of such positions. The typical organization can be visualized as a pyramid, and the higher up one goes in the organization the fewer the options—there is only

---

[12] Clinton F. Fink, "Some Conceptual Difficulties in the Theory of Social Conflict," *Journal of Conflict Resolution,* vol. 12, no. 4 (1968), pp. 413–58.

[13] Schmidt and Kochan, "Conflict: Toward Conceptual Clarity," p. 361.

one president. A relative scarcity of power positions gives rise to political behavior. Thus, some of the conflicts in organizations arise out of the relative scarcity of resources and rewards available for distribution to organization members with similar needs.

Differences

A third proposition about conflict in organizations is that it can emerge out of the differences in the requirements of organization members. Differences in the views of top managers about the values the organization should promote, and about the goals the organization should pursue, can be a source of conflict that permeates the entire organization. Particularly at the top levels of an organization, basic differences in the needs and values of its members can give rise, in extreme cases, to a warlike atmosphere in which the combatants are engaged in a crusade to assure the dominance of their value system. Such differences in values, needs, goals, behavioral styles, mannerisms, and motivations are causes of conflict. These differences may appear trivial and irrational to those not directly involved, but they are important causes of human conflict in organizations.

Summary box

Knowing how to manage and cope with conflict is a skill of *increasing importance* to managers. This is true because of a variety of forces, operating inside and outside of organizations, that make conflict a more probable dimension of managerial problems. Conflict can affect all components of *job performance:* role perception, abilities and skills, motivation, and the situational context.

Three phases in the development of thinking about conflict in organizations are: (1) the classical phase; (2) the human relations phase; and (3) the contemporary phase. Today, conflict is viewed as an inevitable feature of organizations that must be "managed." Managing conflict may require both the reduction and stimulation of the level of conflict.

Conflict refers to the deliberate behavior of organization members that is designed to interfere with or block the attainment of goals of other organization members. Conflict arises out of *two perceptions:* goal incompatibility and opportunity to interfere with the goal attainment of others. *Conflict, competition,* and *cooperation* are related but not synonomous types of behavior.

Three propositions about conflict are: (1) conflict arises within a context of *interdependence;* (2) conflict can grow out of the *similarities* of the requirements of organization members; and (3) conflict can emerge out of the *differences* in the requirements of organization members.

*The idea
of process*

The Conflict Process. We can gain useful insight into the nature of conflict by viewing it as a dynamic process. We have used the idea of process in discussing several topics in this book—goal setting, planning, controlling, decision making, motivation, leadership, communication, and so on. "Process" suggests a time sequence and a series of events, rather than a discrete event that occurs at one moment.

*The conflict-
episode model*

One way of viewing conflict as a process is "the conflict episode."[14] The model shown in Figure 13–1 portrays conflict as a series of stages: latent conflict; perceived conflict; felt conflict; manifest conflict; conflict resolution; and conflict aftermath. These stages, collectively, make up a conflict episode. A conflict episode is a gradual escalation of conflict through the series of stages.

FIGURE 13–1
The Conflict-Episode Model

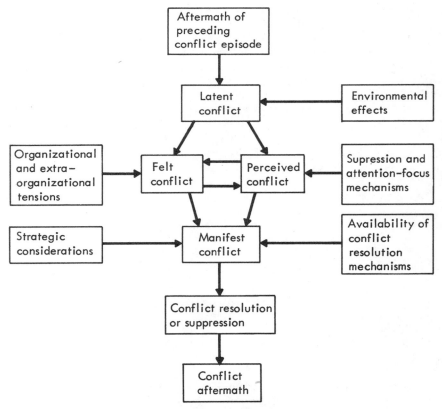

Source: Adapted from Louis R. Pondy, "Organizational Conflict: Concepts and Models," *Administrative Science Quarterly,* vol. 12, no. 3 (1967).

---

[14] Louis R. Pondy, "Organizational Conflict: Concepts and Models," *Administrative Science Quarterly,* vol. 12, no. 3 (1967), pp. 296–320.

Latent and perceived conflict

"Latent conflict" provides the necessary *antecedent conditions* for conflict in organizations. The basic types of conditions are competition for scarce resources, role conflict, competition for positions in the organization, and divergence in the goals of organization members. "Perceived conflict" is conflict about which organization members are aware. It may result from misunderstanding or lack of understanding and does not necessarily emerge out of latent conflict. Some latent conflicts are never perceived as conflicts; that is, they never reach the level of awareness.

Felt and manifest conflict

"Felt conflict" differs from perceived conflict in that "A may be aware that B and A are in serious disagreement over some policy, but it may not make A tense or anxious, and it may have no effect whatsoever on A's affection towards B."[15] "Manifest conflict" takes the form of conflictful behavior, including sabotage, open aggression, apathy, withdrawal, and minimal job performance.

Conflict resolution

"Conflict resolution" can range from approaches that essentially avoid facing up to the conflict to approaches that confront the conflict in an attempt to resolve it so that all parties achieve their goals. In the next section of this chapter, we will discuss in more detail several approaches to conflict resolution and management.

Conflict aftermath

"Conflict aftermath" represents the conditions that result from the resolution of conflict. If the conflict is genuinely resolved, it can lead to an improved relationship between organizational participants; if the conflict is inadequately resolved, it can provide the conditions for additional conflict.

Tie-in to our definition

The conflict-episode model is an aid in thinking about the antecedent conditions and the affective and cognitive states that lead up to conflictful behavior. However, as our definition of conflict suggests, we prefer to limit the usage of the word conflict to actual conflict behavior, that is, to what is referred to in the conflict episode model as "manifest conflict."

CONFLICT-MANAGEMENT STYLES

Mary Parker Follett

Almost 40 years ago, Mary Parker Follett proposed three main ways of dealing with conflict: domination; compromise; and integration. "Domination" is a style used by someone operating from a position of power. Today we refer to the domination style as a "win-lose" style, and Mary Parker Follett recognized its limitations. By "compromise," Follett means essentially what is meant by the term today. "Integration," as discussed by Follett, is very closely related to modern views of conflict management. Integration implies a creative, problem-solving approach to conflict resolution.

---

[15] Ibid., p. 302.

Follett's integration is similar to today's idea of a "win-win" conflict-management style.[16]

Conceptual foundation

Mary Parker Follett's original thinking in the area of conflict management provides a conceptual foundation for contemporary thinking on conflict management. Her three basic approaches for dealing with conflict have been elaborated upon over the past 40 years. Nevertheless, her three styles are included in the most current approaches to conflict management.

Two-dimensional thinking

Reflecting the two-dimensional thinking that is characteristic of many management models, conflict management style is often viewed in terms of a two-dimensional model. One axis on the model refers variously to the manager's concern for the goals of others, to the manager's concern for relationships (interpersonal, intergroup, et cetera), and to the manager's degree of *cooperativeness*. The other axis on the model refers variously to the manager's concern for personal goals, to the manager's concern for self, and/or to the manager's degree of *assertiveness*.

Assertiveness and cooperativeness

For purposes of our discussion we will use a two-dimensional model based on the axes of cooperativeness and assertiveness.[17] Figure 13–2 depicts five basic conflict management styles based on the degree of assertiveness and cooperativeness reflected in the manager's style. Each of these five styles is appropriate to specific types of conflict management situations.

Five styles

Descriptive labels for the five styles are shown in Figure 13–2. For purposes of our discussion we will refer to the styles as competitor, avoider, accommodator, compromiser, and collaborator. The numerical labels shown in Figure 13–2 (9,1; 1,1; 1,9; 5,5; and 9,9) relate this model to the Managerial Grid® that was discussed in Chapter 11. In discussing the five styles, the dominant theme will be that each style has both positive and negative features.

Win/lose

Competitor. A competing style is high on assertiveness and low on cooperativeness. This style is power-oriented and approaches conflict in terms of a win/lose strategy. On the negative side, a competitor may suppress, intimidate, or coerce the other parties to a conflict. It may result in others being afraid to communicate with a manager who uses this style. A competing style may prevent the real causes of a conflict from coming out into the open. The com-

---

[16] Metcalf and Urwick, *Dynamic Administration: The Collected Papers of Mary Parker Follett.*

[17] This discussion is based primarily on the view of conflict management suggested by Kenneth W. Thomas. See his "Conflict and Conflict Management," in *The Handbook of Industrial and Organizational Psychology.* Marvin D. Dunnette, ed. (Chicago: Rand McNally College Publishing Company, 1976), pp. 889–935. Also see, Kenneth W. Thomas, "Toward Multi-Dimensional Values in Teaching: The Example of Conflict Behaviors," *Academy of Management Review,* vol. 2, no. 3 (July 1977), pp. 484–90.

FIGURE 13–2
Graph of Conflict-Management Styles

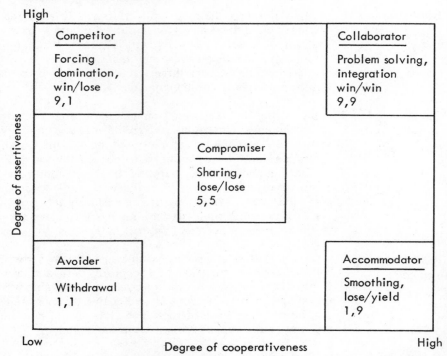

Source: Adapted from Figure 4, Five Conflict-handling Orientations, in Kenneth W. Thomas, "Conflict and Conflict Management," in *The Handbook of Industrial and Organizational Psychology*, Marvin D. Dunnette ed. (Chicago: Rand McNally College Publishing Co., 1976), p. 900.

peting, or win/lose, approach to conflict resolution ". . . generally creates forces which aggravate the struggle and does little to discover innovative, constructive solutions acceptable to all."[18]

Uses   On the positive side, a competing style may be necessary when a quick, decisive action is required, or when important but unpopular courses of action must be taken. In addition, competing may be required when "you know you're right" on an issue or as a protection against those who use a competing style against you.

Withdrawal   **Avoider.** At first glance, an avoiding style may appear to have no value as a mode of managing conflict. An avoiding style may reflect a failure to address important issues and a tendency to remain neutral when there is a need to take a position. An avoider may also exhibit detachment from conflict and a readiness to comply or conform that is based on indifference.

_____

[18] Likert and Likert, *New Ways of Managing Conflict*, p. 65.

Uses

However, an avoiding style can make sense when a conflict situation has relatively minor implications for managerial effectiveness, when there appears to be little chance for a person to "win," and when the benefits of confronting a conflict situation are overshadowed by the potential damage of confrontation. Additionally, avoiding is appropriate in order to reduce tensions, to regain perspective, and to gather additional information.

Lose/yield

Accommodator. The accommodating style is low in assertiveness and high on cooperativeness. A person who uses an accommodating style as the primary approach to conflict management may be showing too little concern for personal goals. Such a lack of concern may lead to lack of influence and recognition. It means that conflicts are resolved without each party to the conflict presenting their views in a forceful and meaningful way. An accommodator may appear to be agreeable and cooperative, but the appearance may be more apparent than real. The reality behind the appearance may be the accommodator's need for acceptance and affiliation. Further, underlying the accommodating style may be a failure to realize that interpersonal relations can be strengthened by a process of "working through" conflicts.

Uses

However, like the other conflict management styles, the accommodating style has its uses. It is useful when a conflict issue is more important to the other person; when one of the other style's disadvantages outweigh those of the accommodating style; when maintaining harmony is important; when it is advantageous to allow the other person to experience winning; and when an accommodating style on one issue may make the other person more receptive on another, more important issue.

Lose/lose

Compromiser. To some people the word "compromise" suggests weakness and lack of commitment to a position. A compromiser may be thought of as a person who puts expediency above principle or who seeks short-term solutions at the expense of long-run objectives. A compromising style results in each conflict participant sharing in some degree of winning and losing. If the compromise is based on a genuine concern for reaching a solution to a conflict, then compromising can be a variant of the win-win strategy. However, if the compromise serves to prevent an airing of the real issues in a conflict, and if it undermines trust between the conflicting parties, then the compromising style more closely approximates a lose/lose strategy.

Uses

It is important, however, to recognize the potential value of compromise. Compromise is a common and practical approach to conflict management because it often fits the realities of life in organizations. This "fit" occurs when a conflict is not important enough to either party to warrant the time and psychological investment in one of the more assertive modes of conflict management. In addition, compromise may be the only practical way of handling a conflict situation in which two equally strong and persuasive parties are attempting to work out a solution. Further, compromise may be the only approach that can yield results within the time allowed for the resolution of a conflict.

Win/win

Collaborator. Given the two dimensions of cooperativeness and assertiveness shown in Figure 13–2, the collaborating style is high on both dimensions. How is it possible to be both assertive about personal goals and cooperative about the goals of others? It is possible only if the parties to a conflict recast it as a problem-solving situation. What does this mean? A problem-solving approach requires the following conditions.

1. There is an attempt to depersonalize the conflict. That is, the parties to the conflict channel their energies to solving the problem rather than defeating each other.
2. The goals, opinions, attitudes, and feelings of all parties are seen as legitimate and acceptable concerns, and all parties are seen as playing a constructive role.
3. The parties realize that a conflict issue can make a constructive contribution to the quality of human relationships if the issue is worked through in a supportive and trusting climate in which opinions and differences are freely aired.

Not easy approach

Clearly, a problem-solving or collaborative approach is not an easy approach to conflict management. When people are engaged in conflict, there may be great emotional involvement. In such cases, it is difficult to recast a conflict situation into a problem-solving situation. In a sense, problem solving is the opposite of conflict.[19] Asking the parties to a conflict to follow a problem-solving approach is asking for a complete rethinking of all elements of the conflict situation.

Two kinds of conflict issues

Nevertheless, conflict can be converted to problem solving. It is worth doing when the issues involved are very important to both parties and cannot be compromised. These issues can be either of two basic kinds: those originating in the *task* in which the conflicting parties are involved, or those originating in the *socio-emotional* dimensions that characterize the human relationships between the parties to the conflict.

Not always best

Just because a problem-solving or collaborating style is high in both the assertiveness and cooperativeness dimensions does not mean that it is always the best approach to conflict management. Like the other four styles, the collaborating style has costs as well as benefits. Collaboration can require large investments of time and

---

[19] Alan C. Filley, *Interpersonal Conflict Resolution* (Glenview, Ill.: Scott, Foresman and Company, 1975).

energy. Managers need to make sure that this investment is directed at problems that are significant to managerial and organizational concerns. A general point worth emphasizing is that all of the conflict-management styles must be evaluated in terms of their costs as well as their benefits.

Summary box

> The *conflict-episode model* views conflict as a process consisting of a series of stages. A conflict episode is a gradual escalation of conflict through these stages: latent conflict; perceived conflict; felt conflict; manifest conflict; conflict resolution; and conflict aftermath.
>
> Over 40 years ago, *Mary Parker Follett* proposed three main ways of dealing with conflict: domination; compromise; and integration. These three approaches are included in the most current approaches to conflict management.
>
> Our discussion of conflict management styles is based on a two-dimensional model. One dimension of the model is *cooperativeness;* the other dimension is *assertiveness.* Five distinct styles representing differing degrees of cooperativeness and assertiveness are: (1) competitor; (2) avoider; (3) accommodator; (4) compromiser; and (5) collaborator.
>
> There are *two basic kinds* of conflict issues—those originating in the task and those originating in the socioemotional dimensions of human relationships. Depending upon the particular conflict issue, all five of the above-mentioned styles can be an appropriate conflict-management style.

THE NATURE OF STRESS

Stressors

This chapter opened with a report of the results of a survey indicating that conflict is an increasingly important topic to managers and to organizations. The same is true of stress! It is almost a cliché to say that jobs and job environments are stress-producing. Suicides, ulcers, and nervous breakdowns are popularly attributed to the stress created by the "stimulus overload" of long work hours, heavy workloads, decision-making responsibilities, rapidly changing environments, the pressures of time and financial constraints, career setbacks, and job loss. All of these job-related factors are supposed to be "stressors," or stress producing.

Cannot be avoided

And yet stress is not something to be, or that can be, avoided. "Even while fully relaxed and asleep, you are under some stress: your heart must continue to pump blood . . . your brain is not at complete rest while you are dreaming."[20] These examples suggest that stress is present whenever you have to provide the energy to maintain life and to adapt to a changing environment. Stress needs to be thought of in terms of levels. "Zero stress" is not a realistic goal for a living human being. Excessive stress, however, can lead to the destruction of human life. In between zero stress and excessive stress, there is a level of stress appropriate for each person.

What is stress?

Definition. Stress may be defined as "the nonspecific response of the body to any demand made upon it."[21] This definition probably is not very close to the definition you were expecting to read. It doesn't include words like "tension," "anxiety," "frustration," "nervousness," and so on. Nevertheless, the definition makes sense. Let's examine it more closely.

Stress is a response

First, stress is viewed as a "response" of a person to demands made upon the person. That means that stress is the response to stimuli rather than the stimuli themselves. This is a practical point because different individuals respond to the same stimuli in different ways. In one case, the response might be a state of anxiety or tension in excess of what is normal for that person. In the other case, the response might be well below the upper thresholds of tolerability. "With the exception of extreme and sudden life-threatening situations, it is reasonable to say that no stimulus is a stressor to all individuals exposed to it."[22] Both the objective reality of a situation and the person's unique assessment of the situation in terms of need satisfaction must be considered in appraising stress.

Indices of stress

If stress is a response of a person, what signs can be used to indicate that the response is occurring? Physiologically, stress can be inferred from changes in blood pressure, heart rate, and galvinic skin response. Behaviorally, stress may be assumed to exist when a person engages in certain types of behavior that are abnormal *for that person*. Examples of such behavior include excessive fatigue, irregularity in job performance, increased reaction time, and stuttering. In addition, the experience of stress may lead to "terrible simplifications":

> One thing we know about stress is that it is usually accompanied by feelings of arousal or agitation. . . . The problem is that when such arousal occurs, thoughts and actions become more primitive. As a person becomes more and more agitated, his thoughts become more simplistic, he notices less in his environment, he

---

[20] Hans Selye, "On Stress without Distress," *Executive Health,* vol 11, no. 11 (August 1975).

[21] Ibid.

[22] Mortimer H. Appley and Richard Trumbull, "On the Concept of Psychological Stress," in Appley and Trumbull, eds., *Psychological Stress; Issues in Research* (New York: Appleton-Century-Crofts, 1967), p. 7.

reverts to his oldest habits, and all complicated responses in his repertoire disappear.[23]

Stress is nonspecific

A second observation about our definition of stress is that it is a "nonspecific" response. What does that mean? Regardless of the demands placed upon a person by any specific stimulus (sickness, time pressures, financial responsibilities, and so on), the person must adapt and reinstate some state of normalcy or equilibrium for that person. It is the demand on the person for adaptation and equilibrium that is the essence of stress. Minor demands might be thought of as low stress, excessive demands as high stress. Whether the demands on a person are minor or excessive depends on the person and on the intensity and kind of situation in which the demands occur.

Role conflict and role ambiguity

Stressors. Almost any job-related factor is a potential stressor. In this section we note some job-related factors that research has shown are related to tension. In Chapter 6, we observed that both role conflict and role ambiguity often have been shown to be related to tension and anxiety.[24] This tension and anxiety of the job holder can adversely affect performance. Several studies support the conclusion that ". . . a clear understanding of productivity objectives and instructions indicating work objectives is associated with high performance in individuals and work units." However, this is not equivalent to saying that all role conflict and role ambiguity can be or should be removed.[25]

Need for role clarity

"Role clarity" is one way in which the effect of a stressor can be moderated by individual differences. Although role ambiguity is associated with tension and anxiety, this tends to be more true for job holders who have a high need for role clarity (high nC). "Thus, on the basis of the evidence generated so far, nC appears to moderate the relationship between degree of role clarity and job tension for persons occupying nonsupervisory, but not supervisory, roles."[26]

Boredom

Boredom also may be highly related to stress. In a study of 2,000 male workers in 23 occupations, it was found that more demanding jobs produced less anxiety, depression, and physical illness than less demanding jobs. Assembly-line workers reported the greatest dissatisfaction with their workload and the highest levels of depres-

---

[23] Karl E. Weick, "The Management of Stress," *MBA*, vol. 9, no. 9 (October 1975), p. 37. Reprinted with permission from the October 1975 MBA Magazine. Copyright © 1975 by MBA Communications, Inc.

[24] See also Robert L. Kahn, Donald M. Wolfe, Robert P. Quinn, J. Diedrick Snoek, *Organizational Stress: Studies in Role Conflict and Ambiguity* (New York: John Wiley & Sons, 1964).

[25] Alan C. Filley, Robert J. House, and Steven Kerr, *Managerial Process and Organizational Behavior*, 2d ed., (Glenview, Ill.: Scott, Foresman and Company), pp. 319, 321–24.

[26] Robert H. Miles and M. M. Petty, "Relationships between Role Clarity, Need for Clarity, and Job Tension and Satisfaction for Supervisory and Nonsupervisory Roles," *Academy of Management Journal*, vol. 18, no. 4 (December 1975), p. 881.

sion, irritation, poor appetite, and other physical problems.[27] Some jobs are too demanding for particular individuals and are a "stimulus overload" situation for those individuals. Other jobs do not demand enough of job holders and are a "stimulus underload" or a "stimulus deficit" situation.[28]

Nine stressors

One study of upper-middle level managers in Canadian organizations identified nine stressors: organization design; degree of formalization; leadership responsibilities; interpersonal demands made on the manager; communication; job expectations; work load; performance; and decision making. In this study, work load was perceived to be the highest individual stressor. The researchers found no significant relationship between the level of stress and the manager's age, education, or type of organization in which worked.[29]

Diseases

Stress and Health. Stress is related to a large number of diseases, such as peptic ulcer, migraine, hypertension, arthritis, backache, emphysema, asthma, and coronary thrombosis.[30] In addition, job-related stress is highly correlated (but not necessarily causally related) with symptoms of mental disorder.[31]

Social Readjustment Rating Scale

An interesting way of illustrating the relationship between stress-producing events and health is shown in Figure 13–3. The Social Readjustment Rating Scale (SRRS) suggests that even changes that are considered pleasant and socially desirable (marriage, gain of a new family member, for example) may be resisted by a person because they cause emotional stress and require adaptive behavior. Another researcher supports this view: "It is immaterial whether the agent or situation we face is pleasant or unpleasant. Its stressor effect depends on the *intensity* of the demand made upon the *adaptive* work of the body.[32]

Life events and health

The developers of the SRRS suggest that there is a relation between the occurrence of these 43 common life events and the health of a person. They conclude from their research:

> . . . only some of the events are negative or "stressful" in the conventional sense, i.e., are socially undesirable. Many are socially desirable and consonant with the American values of achieve-

---

[27] "Stress and Boredom," *Behavior Today*, vol. 6, no. 28 (August 11, 1975). For details of the research, see *Job Demands and Worker Health: Main Effects and Occupational Differences*, available from Institute for Social Research, Box 1248, Ann Arbor, Mich., 48106.

[28] "Looking at Stress," *Behavior Today*, vol. 6, no. 23 (June 9, 1975).

[29] Rolf E. Rogers, "Executive Stress," *Human Resource Management*, vol. 14, no. 3 (Fall 1975), pp. 21–22.

[30] Douglas Brian Gasner, "The Creation of Stress," *MBA*, vol. 9, no. 9 (October 1975), p. 42.

[31] Alan A. MacLean, "Job Stress and the Psychological Pressures of Change," *Personnel*, vol. 53, no. 1 (January–February 1976), p. 41.

[32] Seyle, "On Stress without Distress."

FIGURE 13-3
The Social Readjustment Rating Scale

Rank	Life event	Mean value
1	Death of spouse......................................	100
2	Divorce..	73
3	Marital separation...................................	65
4	Jail term..	63
5	Death of close family member......................	63
6	Personal injury or illness...........................	53
7	Marriage..	50
8	Fired at work...	47
9	Marital reconciliation................................	45
10	Retirement..	45
11	Change in health of family member.................	44
12	Pregnancy...	40
13	Sex difficulties.......................................	39
14	Gain of new family member.........................	39
15	Business readjustment...............................	39
16	Change in financial state............................	38
17	Death of close friend................................	37
18	Change to different line of work.....................	36
19	Change in number of arguments with spouse.........	35
20	Mortgage over $10,000.............................	31
21	Foreclosure of mortgage or loan.....................	30
22	Change in responsibilities at work...................	29
23	Son or daughter leaving home........................	29
24	Trouble with in-laws.................................	29
25	Outstanding personal achievement...................	28
26	Wife begin or stop work..............................	26
27	Begin or end school..................................	26
28	Change in living conditions...........................	25
29	Revision of personal habits...........................	24
30	Trouble with boss....................................	23
31	Change in work hours or conditions...................	20
32	Change in residence.................................	20
33	Change in schools....................................	20
34	Change in recreation.................................	19
35	Change in church activities...........................	19
36	Change in social activities...........................	18
37	Mortgage or loan less than $10,000...................	17
38	Change in sleeping habits............................	16
39	Change in number of family get-togethers............	15
40	Change in eating habits..............................	15
41	Vacation..	13
42	Christmas...	12
43	Minor violations of the law...........................	11

Source: Thomas H. Holmes and Richard H. Rahe, "The Social Readjustment Rating Scale," *Journal of Psychosomatic Research,* vol. 11 (1967), p. 216.

ment, success, materialism, practicality, efficiency, future orientation, conformism and self-reliance.

There was identified, however, one theme common to all these life events. The occurrence of each usually evoked or was associated with some adaptive or coping behavior on the part of the involved individual. Thus, each item has been constructed to contain life events whose advent is either indicative of or requires a significant change in the ongoing life pattern of the individual. The emphasis is on change from the existing steady state and not on psychological meaning, emotion, or social desirability.[33]

Using the SRRS

To get an idea of how the SRRS can be used, check any of the events listed that have occurred in your life in the past 12 months. Your total score is the sum of the values associated with the life events that you checked. Your score is a measure of the amount of stress you have been subjected to during the past 12 months. A high score (over 300, for example) can be used as an *indication* that you are facing high odds (about 80 percent) of becoming ill. This approach to using the SRRS is noted here only as a way of showing how stress and illness are being studied in research. We are not suggesting that the scores on the SRRS should be taken as a literal index of your chances of becoming ill.

Helping yourself

Coping with Stress. For personal reasons and to help subordinates, managers may have an interest in learning more about coping with stress. From the viewpoint of becoming more personally effective in coping with stress, several popular techniques are competing for the interests of executives. These techniques range from programs of noncompetitive physical exercises to psychotherapy. They encompass transcendental meditation (TM), Erhard Seminars Training (est), transactional analysis (TA), encounter groups, biofeedback, and behavior modification.[34]

A first step

Undoubtedly, each of the above techniques can claim some degree of success in helping people learn to live with stress. The usefulness of some of the techniques (biofeedback, behavior modification, and TM) is verified by research studies. Nevertheless, there is no panacea for stress. An important first step, however, is understanding the nature of stress and the implications of stress for personal health and satisfaction.

Helping others

From the viewpoint of helping subordinates cope with job-related stress, managers have several options available to them. Several of these options are nonevaluative listening (see Chapter 12), frequent feedback to subordinates about their job performance, eliminating unnecessary and dysfunctional role conflict and role ambiguity, and making job involvement compatible with subordinates' needs and capabilities.

Informal helping relationships

Additionally, managers can demonstrate their willingness to engage in "informal helping relationships" with peers and subordinates. One study found that these relationships are usually initiated by "helpees" (rather than helpers) who seek out those of

---

[33] Thomas H. Holmes and Richard H. Rahe, "The Social Readjustment Rating Scale," *Journal of Psychosomatic Research*, vol. 11 (1967), p. 217.

[34] For brief discussions of these techniques, see "Executive's Guide to Living with Stress," *Business Week* (August 23, 1976), pp. 75–79.

equal or greater status or position, in order to resolve job-related (as opposed to personal, emotional, or feeling-related) problems.[35] Thus, managers who are receptive and who have appropriate interpersonal skills can, through informal helping relationships, ". . . set in motion the process of dealing with stressful events as they arise and interrupt the building up of tensions."[36]

Perspective— optimal stress and conflict

Managers, of course, have other things to do besides help themselves and subordinates to cope with stress. Managers are, first and foremost, accountable for their own job performance and that of their subordinates. Zero-level stress and conflict are not feasible or desirable for effective job performance. There may be times when managers must create conflict or promote stressors. One of the manager's skills is in creating and maintaining a level of stress and conflict that is optimal over the long run. A long-run perspective would have to consider all performance, individual, and group goals for which the manager is responsible.

Summary box

> *Stress* is the nonspecific response of the body to any demand made upon it. The *essence of stress* is the demand on the person for adaptation and equilibrium. Stress cannot be avoided completely by a living human being.
>
> A *stressor* is anything that is stress-producing for an individual. With few exceptions, no stimulus is a stressor to all individuals exposed to it. For many job holders, some common stressors are role conflict, role ambiguity, boredom, organization design, work load, leadership responsibilities, interpersonal demands, and decision making.
>
> Stress is related to a large number of diseases. In addition, stress arising out of common life events, as measured by the *Social Readjustment Rating Scale,* is related to illness.
>
> Several popular *techniques to help an individual cope with stress* are transcendental meditation, biofeedback, psychotherapy, transactional analysis, behavior modification, noncompetitive physical exercise, encounter groups, and Erhard seminars training.
>
> *Managers can help subordinates* cope with stress through nonevaluative listening, providing feedback, making job involvement and subordinates' needs compatible, removing excessive role ambiguity and role conflict, and engaging in informal helping relationships.

---

[35] Ronald J. Burke, Tamara Weir, and Gordon Duncan, "Informal Helping Relationships in Work Organizations," *Academy of Management Journal,* vol. 19, no. 3 (September 1976), pp. 370–77.

[36] Ibid., p. 377.

CHECK YOUR UNDERSTANDING

Phases in thinking about conflict
Conflict
Cooperation
Competition
Conflict process
Conflict episode

Conflict-management styles
Problem-solving approach
Two kinds of conflict issues
Stress
Stressors
Social Readjustment Rating Scale

STUDY QUESTIONS

1. In what way does contemporary thinking about conflict in organizations differ from earlier thinking? What, in your opinion, accounts for this difference?

2. Explain the statement: "Organizational conflict arises within a context of interdependence and grows out of similarities and differences."

3. Give an example of how conflict in organizations could be useful? How could the absence of conflict be harmful to an organization?

4. Develop an explanation for why conflict is inevitable in organizations.

5. Are the opposing teams in a football game engaged in conflict or competition? Are you opponents in a golf match in conflict or competition?

6. Relate the conflict-episode model to a situation with which you are familiar.

7. How could you describe your personal conflict-management style? What are its advantages and disadvantages?

8. What does it mean to say that stress cannot be avoided? If it cannot be avoided, then why be concerned about it?

APPLICATION: MORE ON THE SRRS*

Figure 13–3, The Social Readjustment Rating Scale (SRRS), identifies 43 life events that are potentially stress producing. Some studies using the SRRS suggests that there may be a correlation between the occurrence of these life events and the health of a person. This application is concerned with that idea. In order to discuss the idea, it is necessary to introduce two terms, the "Schedule of Recent Experience" and the "Life Change Unit."

The Schedule of Recent Experience (SRE) is the same as the SRRS except that next to each of the 43 items a space is provided for time periods. For example, each space might represent a six-

---

* Application problem based on T. S. Holmes and T. H. Holmes, "Short-Term Intrusion into the Life Style Routine," *Journal of Psychomatic Research,* vol. 14 (1970), pp. 121–32. For additional information, see R. H. Rabe, "Life Change and Subsequent Illness Reports," in *Life, Stress and Illness,* E. K. E. Gunderson and R. H. Rabe, eds. (Springfield, Ill.: Charles C. Thomas, Publisher, 1974).

month interval. A three-year period would be six spaces. A person who is completing the SRRS is asked to check off when, if ever, each of the 43 life events occurred. If an event happened more than once in a given six-month period, the person indicates the number of times it occurred. Within each time period, the events which occurred are weighted with their appropriate value from the SRRS (for example, life event no. 22, change in responsibilities at work, has a weight of 29) and summed for a total Life Change Unit (LCU) score for that period. These LCU scores were used in the study described below.

For this study, the SRE was modified so that the person completing it could keep a daily account of events and record any day-to-day health changes such as headache, nausea, fever, eyestrain, backache, et cetera. Daily LCU scores were recorded and correlated to daily symptoms. Seventy-nine percent of all the life changes listed in the study were those of LCU magnitude less than 20; 98 percent of all the changes reported had LCU values less than 45.

In over 1,300 workdays covered by this study, there were less than a half-dozen absences from work or disruptions from daily schedules. Therefore, the health changes reported were just those which occur in everyday life, which reflect in varying degrees the life style of the individual. Statistical analyses of the data indicated a direct correlation between the magnitude of daily life changes and the occurrence of various symptoms. In other words, a person is much more likely to experience some symptoms on a day of high life change than a day of low life change. The LCU score was found to be higher on the day before and the day after symptoms are experienced, as well as on the day of occurrence.

For purposes of discussion, assume that there is validity to the idea of a correlation between life events and the health of a person and that the SRRS can be used to gather data on this correlation. How might this data be useful in an organization concerned with the management of stress?

part three

Organizations: A Macro View

Part One   In Part One of this book we defined "managing" as the work of
creating and maintaining environments in which people can accomplish goals efficiently and effectively. In addition, Part One was
concerned with four major managerial functions: *goal setting,
planning, controlling,* and *decision making.* These four functions
are crucial if managers are to fulfill their accountability for performance—the *basic theme* of this book.

Part Two   Part Two was a *micro* view of behavior in organizations. The
focus was on the *individual,* on specific *types* of individual behavior
(leadership behavior, communication behavior), and on specific
contexts of individual behavior (interpersonal, group, and conflict
contexts).

Part Three   Part Three is a *macro* view of organizations. The focus is on
the *organization* as an entity, on several *foundations* for thinking
about organizations, on *designing* of organizational structures, and
on organization *change, development, and effectiveness.*

Uses of macro   Knowledge about organizations can be useful to managers for
knowledge   several reasons. First, managing occurs in organizations. It is in
and through organizations that managers meet their accountabil-
ity for performance. Second, organizing—like goal setting, planning, controlling, and decision making—is a major function that
managers perform in carrying out their responsibilities.
                    Third, managers, like all other organization members, live in
organizations for a substantial part of their day. They are "citizens"
of organizations and live by the rules of their organization. Thus,
understanding organizations is important to managers for the same
reason it is important for all of us to understand the environment
in which we live and work.
                    Finally, managers play a key role in designing the organizations
that make up our society. They will shape our future organizations.
Managers are crucially important in determining whether our organizations will respond and adapt to changing personal and social
needs and at the same time maintain their capacity to meet those
human needs common to every age and to all people.

Chapters 14   Chapter 14 provides foundation material for understanding con-
and 15   temporary thought about organizations. It discusses *seven foundations:* Social Darwinism and the New Thought movement, scien-
tific management, administrative management, bureaucracy, the
Hawthorne studies, cooperative action, and the role of authority.
The major ideas discussed in Chapter 15 are: The organization as
a *system,* the *organization-environment* relationship, the *organi-
zation-technology* relationship, and *organizational climate.*

Chapters 16   Chapters 16 and 17 are concerned with *designing* organizations.
and 17   Chapter 16 discusses the problem of trying to visualize organization
designs—something that can never be accomplished fully. Chap-

ter 16 also discusses two major aspects of the problem of designing organizations: defining jobs and grouping jobs. Chapter 17 is concerned with additional design aspects: span of management, organizational levels, delegation, and line and staff.

Chapter 18

Chapter 18 deals with a problem that is increasingly important to managers—the problem of *change* and of how to make organizations responsive to the requirements of *both* change and stability. The chapter notes that there are several approaches to introducing change into organizations and that change is a process that requires time and planning. *Organization development* (OD), a particular approach to bringing about change is also discussed in Chapter 18. The chapter ends with a discussion of the important notion of *organization effectiveness*.

Objectives of Chapter 14

- To contrast the macro and micro views of behavior in organizations.
- To take the position that organizations are "living" only to the extent that there is life in the members of the organization.
- To define an organization as a special type of social system, and to recognize the formal and informal dimensions of an organization.
- To discuss and to identify the major propositions of several foundations of contemporary thought about organizations.

Outline of Chapter 14

14

FOUNDATIONS OF CONTEMPORARY THOUGHT ABOUT ORGANIZATIONS

> *Now said Rabbit, this is a Search, and I've Organized it—*
> *Done what to it? said Pooh,*
> *Organized it. Which means—well, its what you do to a Search, when you don't all look in the same place at once.*
>
> A. A. Milne in *The House at Pooh Corner*

> *The rules are made by the bureaucraps.*
>
> Archie Bunker

Personal experience

Most of us come in contact with organizations daily. They might be large and complex, such as universities or business organizations. They might be small, simple groupings of people, such as student, fraternal, or political organizations. In a typical day, we are likely to come into contact with grocery stores, service stations, churches, and restaurants. Our experiences with these organizations are sometimes frustrating and irritating. Organizations often waste our time and seem, at times, to deliberately harass us. Fortunately, some organizations seem responsive to our needs and try to be of service to us. Our personal experiences with these organizations contribute to our common-sense understanding of the variety of approaches to organizing. This common-sense understanding is a good foundation for examining organizations in a more systematic manner.

This chapter

Several major ideas have influenced thinking about organizations. We have chosen seven of these ideas for discussion in this chapter. We refer to them as "foundations of contemporary thought" because of their fundamental influence on thinking about organizations. The seven foundations are: Social Darwinism and the New Thought movement; scientific management; administrative management; bureaucracy; the Hawthorne studies; cooperative action; and authority. It is difficult to evaluate the precise impact of these foundations on contemporary thought about organizations. Nevertheless, there is a consensus among those who have studied organizations that they are particularly significant. Before discussing these foundations, we want to set the stage with some preliminary observations.

PRELIMINARY OBSERVATIONS

Same
objective

Macro View. Our view in these chapters on organizations is a "macro" view because the major focus is on the organization as an entity. In contrast, the view we took in Part Two, "Behavior in Organizations," was a "micro" view. The major focus there was on understanding individual behavior in organizations. Of course, it is not always possible to draw a precise line between the macro and micro views. In any case, the ultimate objective of both views is the same: To increase understanding of behavior in organizations so as to increase personal and organizational effectiveness. The objective is the same; the major focus is different.

He, she,
or it

Living Organizations. As you read these chapters you will notice that we sometimes discuss organizations as if they are alive. Some writers, in fact, refer to organizations as "living organisms." Organizations are said to be healthy or sick, and to have personality and energy. If organizations are living organisms, they have no sex. We rarely encounter a reference to an organization as a "he" or a "she" (for special reasons the Catholic Church is commonly referred to as "mother," "she," or "her"). An organization is an "it." In referring to an organization we ask, Is it effective? Is it a good place to work? Is it adaptable to changing conditions? Is it receptive to its environment? Is it socially responsible? Is it profitable?

No life of
its own

There is nothing wrong with referring to an organization as "it" so long as one important point is kept in mind. The life in an organization is in the individual people that comprise the organization. An organization has no life apart from the life that is in its employees, owners, customers, and other "real people" that interact with the organization. Underlying a statement such as "It is a socially responsible corporation," lies the socially responsible behavior of individual executives who made some key decisions about the allocation of the corporation's resources. Behind the statement, "It is a good place to work" are managers, employees, and union representatives who negotiated a set of personnel policies and practices that make it a good place to work. When you study organizations, you are studying people.

Definition
and essence

What Is an Organization? We define an organization as a social system deliberately constructed to coordinate the activities of people seeking common goals. Let's examine the elements of this definition. By referring to an organization as a "social system," we reflect our emphasis on organizations as people. Of course, the people in an organization use economic and technical resources in order to achieve goals. Thus, an organization could be viewed as a social–technical–economic system. However, our emphasis is on the organization as a social system. The "essence of an organization" is in the pattern of human relationships that exists in order to accomplish goals.

Exclusions

By referring to an organization as "deliberately constructed" we exclude such social units as families, mobs, and small, informal, *ad hoc* groups. In this connection, one well-known writer notes that organizations differ from other social groupings in their degree of conscious planning, deliberate structure, changing membership, and degree of control over their own destiny.[1]

Goal orientation

The reference to "goals" in our definition of organization reflects a consensus among writers that organizations are goal-oriented entities. For example, a prominent sociologist asserts that "The defining characteristic of an organization is its primacy of orientation to the attainment of a specific goal."[2] As we suggested in Chapter 2, we think it is useful to think of managers and organizations as pursuing a *goal system* of performance, individual, and group goals.

Practical concern

Because the defining characteristic of organization is its orientation to attaining goals, the *practical problem* becomes one of identifying the total set of relationships that enter into goal accomplishment. That set of relationships is the manager's organization. It is not always obvious what or where this organization is. It is always changing because people change, and people relating to each other are what organizations are all about. Managers need to differentiate significant from insignificant relationships, and they need to understand both the formal and informal dimensions

Two dimensions, one organization

Formal and Informal Dimensions. An organization has both formal and informal dimensions. Our definition of organization emphasizes the formal dimension. However, both dimensions are present in every real organization. Together, they make up "the organization." Even though the formal and informal dimensions of an organization can be analyzed separately, they combine, in reality, into just one organization.

---

[1] Amitai Etzioni, *Modern Organizations* (Englewood Cliffs, N.J.: Prentice-Hall, 1964), p. 4.

[2] Talcott Parsons, "Suggestions for a Sociological Approach to the Theory of Organizations," in Amitai Etzioni, *Complex Organizations: A Sociological Reader* (New York: Holt, Rinehart and Winston, 1961), p. 33.

Formal

The "formal dimension" of an organization is that pattern of relationships among organization members that is officially defined. For example, when organization designers determine that employees A, B, C, D, and E are accountable to manager F for the performance of pre-established job duties, a part of the formal organization has been determined. The organization designers may make additional efforts to clarify the exact meaning of the accountability relationship and to delineate job duties in detail. Out of this formal organization will evolve the informal dimension of organization.

Informal

The "informal dimension" of an organization is based on that set of relationships among its members that arises out of needs but which is not officially defined. For example, unofficial and informal relations between A, B, C, D, E, and F will emerge from the experience of working together in order to accomplish job duties. Additional informal relations will result from the desires that members have for affiliation, recreation, achievement, survival, and similar needs. Certain members of an organization may be liked more than others and will become involved in numerous informal relationships with other members. Other members may, through such factors as personality, seniority, or status, wield considerable influence in the organization and will become the center of important informal relations.

Summary box

An *organization* is a social system deliberately constructed to coordinate the activities of people seeking common goals. This definition emphasizes the formal dimensions of an organization. However, every real organization consists of both *formal and informal* dimensions.

Our view in Part 3, "Organizations," is a *macro* view because the major focus is on the organization as a total entity. Our view in Part 2, "Behavior in Organizations," was a *micro* view because the major focus was on individual behavior.

We sometimes discuss organizations as if they are living organisms. An organization lives, however, only in the lives of the individual people who comprise it.

The remaining parts of this chapter deal with specific ways of thinking about organizations that have been, and are, influential in shaping modern thought about behavior in organizations and about organizations, as such. The first of these ways of thinking (we refer to them as *foundations of contemporary thought about organizations*) is Social Darwinism and the New Thought Movement.

SOCIAL DARWINISM AND THE NEW THOUGHT MOVEMENT

Social climate   Thinking about management and organization is importantly influenced by prevailing social attitudes and values. It is clear that the social climate in which business organizations operate today is significantly different than it was in the late 1800s and early 1900s. Business does not enjoy the widespread and unquestioned allegiance and respect of those earlier days. Indeed, the legitimacy of business organizations, and of almost all other types of social organizations, is now subject to scrutiny.

Two themes   Although an extensive discussion of social attitudes and values is beyond the scope of this book, it is useful to highlight some of the dominant attitudes and values that affected thinking about management and organization in the early part of this century. In order to limit the scope of this discussion, two dominant themes of the post-Civil War period will be discussed: *survival* and *the power of thought*. Attitudes about survival in society—who survives and by what process—and attitudes about the power of thought in raising people from poverty to riches were important influences on thinking about organization purposes and procedures.

Social Darwinism and survival   **Survival.** Attitudes about survival in American life evolved out of the strong *individualistic tradition* that has characterized America since its beginnings. This tradition, along with the *success orientation* of the post-Civil War period, made it possible for the doctrine of Social Darwinism—an extension to the social area of the biological ideas contained in Charles Darwin's classic *Origin of the Species*—to gain favor. This doctrine argued that the total social good is enhanced by an unregulated process of struggle which will ensure the "survival of the fittest." Who succeeds in organizations and life? The fittest!

The fit and deserving   According to an organizational interpretation of Social Darwinism, those who prove themselves in the competitive struggle and, in the process, accumulate success and riches are the ones who are *most fit and deserving*. The following quotation reflects this sentiment: "In every store and factory there is a constant weeding-out process going on. No matter how good times are, this sorting continues . . . out, and forever out, the incompetent and unworthy go. It is the survival of the fittest."[3]

Natural struggle   A corollary of Social Darwinism is that those who do not survive are the *least fit and the least deserving*. This struggle for survival was seen by Social Darwinism as a *natural* struggle and,

---

[3] Quotation from Elbert Hubbard, *A Message to Garcia*, ed. R. W. G. Vail (New York: New York Public Library, 1930), p. 14; also in Reinhard Bendix, *Work and Authority in Industry* (New York: John Wiley & Sons, 1956), p. 265.

therefore, one that should not be interfered with by artificial means. If society or organizations interfere with this natural struggle by trying to help the unfit, everyone is hurt because the weak are allowed to survive. The idea that people should be left alone in their natural struggle for survival is reflected in the following:

> A human being has a life to live, a career to run. He is a center of powers to work, and of capacities to suffer. What his powers may be—whether they can carry him far or not; what his chances may be, whether wide or restricted; what his fortune may be, whether to suffer much or little—are questions of his personal destiny which he must work out and endure as he can."[4]

Sovereign man

According to Social Darwinism, the function of organizations was merely to guarantee to members the use of all their powers to enhance their own welfare: ". . . poverty does not constitute a ground for claiming assistance, and riches do not entitle men to privilege. Every man is as sovereign as every other man; each desires independence and equality with others."[5] Here is a view about organizations that says, in effect: You are on your own. If you are doing well in an organization it is because you are fit and deserving. If you are not doing well it is because you are unfit and undeserving. This type of thinking helps us understand why efforts to improve jobs and working conditions in business organizations were so minimal and unsuccessful. There is no point in helping the unfit. This view was widely held, not only by employers, but by workers as well.

Grim doctrine

The grim doctrine of Social Darwinism provided some academic respectability to the everyday practices of businessmen. Several leading industrialists of the day took an active role in promoting Social Darwinism as social and business philosophy. However, it is uncertain how many executives were familiar with or were influenced by Social Darwinism. It did not matter, however, because their actions and thoughts were "justified" by the doctrine. Nevertheless, it is easy to see that this self-fulfilling theory provides a solid base for viewing workers and employees as simply parts in a machine with no particular merit or rights except for the right to join in the struggle for survival. The "workers" were workers because they obviously lacked the character and qualities to become employers. The evidence for this was simply their low position and lack of riches. Riches, incidentally, were often considered a measure of virtue and heavenly reward. Thus, the fittest also were seen as the most virtuous.

Social Darwinism today

Social Darwinism is of more than just historical interest. It is a doctrine that guides the behavior of some organizational leaders, managers, and employees today. Social Darwinism, and the appeal to religious virtue that accompanied it, expressed important social

---

[4] Ibid., p. 258.
[5] Ibid.

values that influenced thinking about the individual in organization. These values, in turn, influence thinking today about *authority* ("If you are in a position of authority you must deserve to be there or else you wouldn't be there.") about the *superior–subordinate relationship* (You must be better than me or else you wouldn't be my superior."), and about *personnel activities* ("Let's just see who makes it to the top.").

Mental power

The Power of Thought.   Along with and complementary to Social Darwinism's emphasis on the natural struggle for survival, a social value developed that took as its central premise the power of thought. The New Thought movement had its greatest popularity in the United States from 1895 to 1915. The essential idea of this movement was that certain thoughts *in themselves* are sufficient to lead to success and wealth. Success results from mental power: "Business success is due to certain qualities of mind. Anything can be yours if you only want it hard enough. Just think of that. Anything! Try it. Try it in earnest and you will succeed. It is the operation of a mighty law."[6] This line of reasoning, which finds expression in the writings of such people as Dale Carnegie, Napoleon Hill, and W. Clement Stone, has implications for organization and management. In the final analysis, it absolves managers and organizations of any responsibility for the failure of individuals to succeed in organizations.

The right mental attitude

An extensive literature developed to reinforce Social Darwinistic ideas and to support the mental power concept of success—the fittest survive by virtue of their thoughts. If individuals are failing to succeed, they should "take thought" and develop the right character. Lack of success was accountable *only* by a failure to really try, and to think right. Here is a view about organizations that says, in effect: Success in organizations is a matter of the "right mental attitude." Only you can form the right attitude. Success is up to you. You simply have to want to succeed badly enough.

As a man thinketh

Something of the flavor of the mentality of the New Thought Movement can be picked up from this excerpt from the classic *As a Man Thinketh*:

> All that a man achieves and all that he fails to achieve is the direct result of his own thoughts. In a justly ordered universe, where loss of equipoise would mean total destruction, individual responsibility must be absolute. A man's weakness and strength, purity and impurity, are his own, and not another man's; they are brought about by himself and not by another. His condition is also his own, and not another man's. His suffering and his happiness are evolved from within. As he thinks, so he is; as he continues to think, so he remains.[7]

---

[6] Ibid., p. 260.

[7] James Allen, *As a Man Thinketh*, reprinted in *Success Unlimited*, vol. 19, no. 2 (February 1972).

The New Thought Movement is important today. Most people acknowledge the importance of the right (positive) mental attitude to job performance. At times, however, an emphasis on attitudes and mental power is used as an excuse for managers not taking specific and concrete steps to improve job performance and work environments. The right attitude helps, but training, better equipment, improved working conditions, fair benefits, and challenging jobs also help. Whatever its merits, the mentality of the New Thought Movement and of Social Darwinism is not a legitimate justification for managerial inaction in creating and maintaining productive and satisfying work environments.

Summary box

> *Social Darwinism* and the *New Thought Movement* imply this proposition: Individuals in organizations are on their own. With the right combination of character, skills, and attitudes, they will succeed. They will have only themselves to blame for their success or failure. Organizations are not and should not be an active agent in their struggle.
>
> Understanding Social Darwinism and the New Thought Movement is useful to you in studying management. First, both can be found in organizations today. They do not tell us only about organizations of the past; they enhance our understanding of the present. To paraphrase a popular expression, old social philosophies never die, they just mix in with new philosophies.
>
> Second, Social Darwinism and the New Thought Movement provide important background for understanding the impact of scientific management—perhaps the most significant development on management thought and practice in the first half of the 20th century. As we will see in the next section, scientific management, with its emphasis on rational processes and the method of science, was the antithesis of Social Darwinism, with its emphasis on natural struggle, survival of the fittest, and "right" thinking.

SCIENTIFIC MANAGEMENT

*Management
breakthrough*

Into the individualistic environment of Social Darwinism and the New Thought Movement came the first truly significant breakthrough in management ideology and practice. "Scientific management" is an approach to management and organization that places primary emphasis on the application of scientific methods to the solution of managerial and organizational problems. (We discussed some aspects of scientific management in Supplement 1B.)

Organizations as machines

Essentially, the organizations of scientific management were to be mechanisms—"machines"—for harnessing the *physical* energies of people for the efficient performance of tasks. The focus was on the physical limits of the human body in job performance. Problem solving, information processing, and other mental processes of the worker were largely ignored.

Human engineering principles

Scientific management assumed correctly that performance could be enhanced by principles of "human engineering," such as time study, motion study, and methods study. Allegedly, employees would respond to these principles, not only because the jobs would be easier and less wasteful of effort, but also because of the inducement of additional monetary benefits. The theorists of scientific management contended that these additional monetary benefits would always be desired by any truly rational, economic person. This would be particularly true if the benefits could be seen by employees as directly related to their effort and output. Thus, there was an emphasis in scientific management on "piecework wages"—systems in which wages are directly tied to quantity of production.

Mental revolution

Central Message.   Scientific management had important implications for organizations. Its central message was that it is possible for organizations to be more efficient and more rational. This possibility would materialize from the application of scientific methods and planning to the tasks of organizations. Although Taylor's emphasis was on operative-level tasks, the "mental revolution" of scientific management applied to all organizational activities. Scientific management was supposed to be a totally revolutionary way of thinking about the problems of work and organizations.

Departure from current thinking

This idea was quite a departure from the then-current thinking of employers concerning their positions. No longer was the employer's position to be justified in terms of survival (Social Darwinism) or mental power (New Thought movement). Rather, like every other job, *science* and rational problem-solving processes would determine the nature of the employer's job and the most qualified person for the job. Of course, scientific management theory did not change management practice overnight—it never fully changed it. Nevertheless, scientific management's emphasis on the application of scientific method to the problems of organization was a major change in thinking about organizations. It is a change that has continued to the present time.

People

People and Environment.   The scientific management conception of people was rather narrow. They were viewed as an essential "part" of the organization. Their needs were viewed primarily in economic terms. The employee was seen as responsive primarily to monetary incentives. It would be unfair to Taylor to say that he totally ignored the noneconomic needs of people. It is reasonable to say that his emphasis was on economic needs. There was almost no mention in scientific management of the informal relations that arise between workers on the job in order to meet their social needs. "So far as the model was concerned, the worker simply had no life outside his job or separate from his tasks."[8] The *formal* organization was seen as the necessary *and* sufficient condition for efficiency.

The emphasis on economic motives

Given the context of the times when scientific management emerged, it is understandable why its *main emphasis* was on rational-economic motives. *First,* the prevailing attitudes about workers emphasized that their condition in life was the result of their own indolence, laziness, wrong thinking, and other poor qualities. *Second,* there was no developed thinking about the multiple needs of people at work. The "economic-man" theory of human needs was the prevailing theory—in and out of organizations. Even today, the economic-man theory is considered by many to be the most accurate description of employee motivation. *Third,* the major problem facing most workers was the problem of survival—paying rent, getting enough to eat, and buying material for clothes. Thus, although it is true that scientific management was deficient (by today's standards) in its conception of people and their needs, it is possible to see why.

The lack of emphasis on environment

Scientific management had little to say about the role of the organization in its environment. The emphasis was on making the *internal operations* of the organization as efficient, rational, and predictable as possible. That scientific management ignored the relationship between the organization and its environment may be the result of two causes. *First,* forces in the environment of organizations in the early part of the 1900s did not press on organizations as they do now. The environment *was* relatively static in ways that were important to organizations. Concern for the environment was not a relevant decision parameter for executives in the early 1900s. *Second,* at the time scientific management emerged, the most pressing and pervasive problem facing managers of business organizations was that of developing efficient and effective working relationships between people inside the organizations. Thus, we can understand that scientific management concentrated on increasing the efficiency of internal operations.

---

[8] Carl M. Lichtman and Raymond G. Hunt, "Personality and Organization Theory: A Review of Some Conceptual Literature, *Psychological Bulletin,* vol. 76, no. 4 (1971), p. 273.

Summary box

> *Scientific management* implies this proposition: Beginning at the task level, a scientific (that is, objective, systematic, and logical) approach should be used to determine the best methods of work. These methods must be implemented in an organization characterized by rationality, clear lines of authority and responsibility, control mechanisms, and appropriate monetary compensation systems. The result will be twofold: greater total organization efficiency; and greater monetary rewards for the workers. However, this will be achieved only if there is cooperation between capital, management, and labor. This cooperation must be based on the scientific method rather than on arbitrary authority, tradition, or right thinking, as the ideology of Social Darwinism and the New Thought Movement had dictated.
>
> Scientific management is important to your study of managing for several reasons. *First*, the "mental revolution" of scientific management is still going on. In fact, it is stronger today than it ever was because of new developments in decision making and problem solving. Developments such as the computer and quantitative decision-making tools allow managers to be more "scientific" in their approach to problem solving. *Second*, much of today's managerial practice is directly traceable to the work of scientific-management pioneers. *Third*, since many aspects of scientific management have been severely criticized in recent years—its conception of people and its mechanistic character, for example—you should understand scientific management so that you can evaluate these criticisms and judge their importance to your own situation.

ADMINISTRATIVE MANAGEMENT

Different focus

Whereas scientific management focused its attention on management problems at the lower levels of organization, the focus of administrative management was on the upper levels of organization. This different focus is reflected in the backgrounds and writings of Frederick Taylor and Henri Fayol. Taylor was a foreman in a manufacturing plant and a consulting engineer, and his empirical work was largely with problems at the task, or "operative," level. Fayol, on the other hand, was a top executive of a large mining company. His frame of reference was the total organization, and his emphasis was on problems at the administrative level. (We discussed Taylor and Fayol in Supplement 1B.)

*Span of
control*

Main Thrust.   The main thrust of administrative management was on developing and enunciating broad generalizations—"principles"—that would be useful to managers in performing their task. Most of the principles ultimately developed were concerned with the organizing function of managers. For example, the "span of control principle" is an organizational generalization concerned with the number of employees a manager can manage effectively. This principle has evolved over the years from a statement of the precise number of subordinates a manager can manage effectively (three to five) to a statement that the actual number depends on situational factors.

*Unity of
command,
specialization*

Another principle of administrative management is the "unity of command principle." Originally, this principle prescribed that each employee should be accountable to only one superior. Now it is interpreted more generally, to mean that employees should know exactly to whom they are accountable for particular responsibilities. Another principle of administrative management is the "principle of specialization." This guide to organizational effectiveness emphasized that efficiency is increased in proportion to the amount of task specialization and, at a time when there was very little specialization of tasks, the principle made a useful contribution to organizational practices. The passing of years has shown, however, that specialization can be carried too far. Among other things, the cost of increased coordination and of low levels of job satisfaction can sometimes offset the gains of further specialization.

*Departmen-
tation*

In addition to, and as a part of its emphasis on management and organization principles, administrative management addressed itself to the problem of departmentation. "Departmentation" refers to the grouping of tasks into larger organizational units so as to minimize the total cost of carrying out activities in order to achieve a known goal. Descriptive theories of departmentation held that work in organizations should be grouped according to certain "bases."

Four bases

One early statement of these bases of departmentation included these four: purpose; process; person or things dealt with or served; and place.[9] These and other bases of departmentation are used today in designing organizations. We will discuss some of them in Chapter 16. Most organizations use several bases of departmentation because each base has specific advantages and disadvantages. Administrative management provided the first systematic analysis of these bases and of the idea of departmentation.

---

[9] Luther Gulick, "The Theory of Organization," in L. Gulick and L. Urwick, eds., *Papers on the Science of Administration* (New York: Institute of Public Administration of Columbia University, 1937), p. 15.

Criticism

Critique. The principles of administrative management theory have been criticized for their lack of empirical verification and have been scored as mere "proverbs":

> It is a fatal defect of the current principles of administration that, like proverbs, they occur in pairs. For almost every principle one can find an equally plausible and acceptable contradictory principle. Although the two principles of the pair will lead to exactly opposite organizational recommendations, there is nothing in the theory to indicate which is the proper one to apply."[10]

Defense

However, in spite of the steady flow of criticism leveled against the principles of administrative management and the bases of departmentation, they are considered by many managers and management writers as useful guides to their behavior and writing. At least, many managers *talk* as if these principles guide their behavior even though their talk is not always verified by their behavior. Commenting on the sometimes strident criticism of the administrative management principles, one writer observes:

> First, though the classical theory was derided for presenting "principles" that were really only proverbs, all the resources of organizational research and theory today [1972] have not managed to substitute better principles (or proverbs) for those ridiculed. Second, these principles, which amount to pious directives to "plan ahead," pay attention to coordination, refrain from wasting time on established routine functions, and devote managerial energies to the exceptional cases that come up, served management very well. . . . Finally, a successful and durable business of management consulting and an endless series of successful books rest upon the basic principles of the classical management school. These principles have worked and are still working, for they addressed themselves to very real problems of management, problems more pressing than those advanced by social science.[11]

---

[10] From *Administrative Behavior: A Study of Decision-Making Processes in Administrative Organizations* by Herbert A. Simon (New York: Macmillan Company, 1976), p. 20. Copyright © 1945, 1947, 1957 by Herbert A. Simon. Reprinted by permission. An example of the idea of principles occurring in pairs is the span-of-control principle (administrative efficiency is increased by limiting the span of control at any point in the hierarchy to a small number) versus the principle of organizational levels (administrative efficiency is enhanced by keeping at a minimum the number of organizational levels through which a matter must pass before it is acted upon). Ibid., pp. 20–28.

[11] From *Complex Organizations: A Critical Essay* by Charles Perrow, pp. 61–62. Copyright © 1972 by Scott, Foresman and Company. Reprinted by permission.

Summary box

> *Administrative management* implies this proposition: Given a goal, the main problem of organization is to departmentalize the activities at all levels so as to accomplish the goal at the lowest cost. The major bases of departmentation are purpose, process, customer, and geography. Departmentation leads to structural relationships which are governed by principles. The application of these principles will result in a rational, ordered, and efficient organization.
>
> Like scientific management, administrative management is still applicable. Its emphasis on the total organization is similar to modern "systems" thinking about organizations. Its major concerns—departmentation and principles—are major concerns today. Most large organizations are departmentalized according to the bases of departmentation suggested by administrative management. Many organizations are consciously designed to adhere to principles of organization even while the search for new and more valid principles continues.

BUREAUCRACY

*Popular
meaning*

The word "bureaucracy" is colloquially a synonym for inefficiency, inflexibility, and red tape. Bureaucracies are supposedly unresponsive to the demands of people and changing environments. "Bureaucratese" is a term used to describe a type of communication designed to be unclear and confusing. These popular connotations are almost the exact opposite of the meaning "bureaucracy" was supposed to have—rational, competent, and efficient organization.

*Bureaucracy
—not good,
not bad*

As the word "bureaucracy" is used by those with a special interest in organizations, it implies an organization characterized by rules, procedures, impersonal relations, and an elaborate and fairly rigid hierarchy of authority–responsibility relationships. A bureaucracy is a type of organization; the word should imply nothing derogatory. Bureaucracies are neither good nor bad. They are appropriate organizational forms in some situations, and they are inappropriate in others. A key task of managing is to determine when the drawbacks of bureaucracy are offset by more significant benefits.

*Internal
orientation*

Max Weber. The classic book on bureaucracy, Max Weber's *The Theory of Social and Economic Organization,* is a translation from the original German version of a small part of Weber's writing published before his death in 1920. The book was published in the United States in 1947.[12] Weber felt that everything about an organization should aid in the pursuit of its unique goals. His view of bureaucracy was "internally-oriented." That is, bureaucracy was, above all, a mechanism for the rational, efficient accomplishment of known goals. *External pressures* on bureaucracies were viewed by Weber as a threat to the organization's pursuit of its goals.

Main features

According to Weber the main features of bureaucratic structure are:

1. A systematic division of labor based on task specialization.
2. A stable and well-defined hierarchy of authority.
3. A consistent system of regulations and procedures concerning all positions and covering both routines and contingencies that might arise.
4. Impersonality of attitudes and interpersonal relations.
5. Written rules, decisions, and keeping of extensive files.
6. Lifetime careers based on technical competence, systematic promotions, and protection against arbitrary dismissal.

Bureaucracies exist in degrees

An organization can be considered bureaucratic depending on the extent to which the above features are present. Organizations in the real world vary in terms of bureaucratic features. Bureaucracies exist in degrees; very few conform to the "ideal type" outlined by Weber. Further, a particular organization may have some of its departments conform to the main features of bureaucracy and other departments may possess very few bureaucratic characteristics.[13]

Technical efficiency

Weber's enthusiasm for the bureaucratic model of organization is revealed by his estimate of its potential for efficiency and rationality: "Experience tends universally to show that the purely bureaucratic type of administrative organization . . . is, from a purely technical point of view, capable of attaining the highest degree of efficiency and is in this sense formally the most rational known means of carrying out imperative control over human beings."[14]

Weber's reservations

Critique. Weber, however, eventually came to fear bureaucracy and what he considered bureaucracy's potential for strangling capitalism and entrepreneurship.[15] Additionally, it is instructive to

[12] Max Weber, *The Theory of Social and Economic Organization,* ed. Talcott Parsons, trans. A. M. Henderson and Talcott Parsons (New York: Free Press of Glencoe, 1947).

[13] Richard H. Hall, *Organizations: Structure and Process* (Englewood Cliffs, N.J.: Prentice-Hall, 1972), pp. 66–72.

[14] Max Weber, "The Ideal Bureaucracy," in Gerald D. Bell, ed., *Organizations and Human Behavior* (Englewood Cliffs, N.J.: Prentice-Hall, 1967), p. 88.

[15] Robert G. Owens, *Organizational Behavior in Schools* (Englewood Cliffs, N.J.: Prentice-Hall, 1970), p. 58.

note Weber's concern about an overemphasis on the merits of bureaucracy: "It is horrible to think that the world could one day be filled with nothing but those little cogs, little men clinging to little jobs and striving toward bigger ones. . . . This passion for bureaucracy is enough to drive one to despair."[16] As the years have shown, there is ample evidence to demonstrate that Weber's concern was justified.

Practice versus theory

Needless to say, bureaucracies do not always work as well in practice as they are supposed to work in theory (not many things work as well in practice as they do in theory). Numerous writers, besides Weber, have attacked the bureaucratic model. One writer argues that impersonal relations and overreliance on rules lead to rigid behavior and other unintended consequences; another argues that rules and impersonal relations lead to minimum levels of performance—just enough to avoid punishment. This, in turn, leads to closer supervision which has the effect of further lowering the levels of performance.[17] Still another writer argues that bureaucracies tend to attract monocratic types to supervisory positions who tend to enhance feelings of helplessness and insecurity in subordinates.[18]

Defense

If bureaucracies do not always work as well as they are supposed to, neither do they work as badly as their critics allege. Weber's analysis was directed primarily at governmental institutions and the alternative forms that governmental institutions can take. Extending Weber's analysis beyond its intended scope makes it easy to criticize. Furthermore, much of the criticism of bureaucracy has been directed at a mythical "ideal type." Like most other organization models, bureaucracy is an appropriate model under certain circumstances. One gets into difficulty, however, when bureaucracy is suggested as "the" ideal form of organization.

---

[16] As quoted in Reinhard Bendix, *Max Weber: An Intellectual Portrait* (Garden City, N.Y.: Doubleday & Company, 1960), p. 455.

[17] James G. March and Herbert A. Simon, *Organizations* (New York: John Wiley & Sons, 1958), pp. 36–47.

[18] Victor Thompson, *Modern Organization* (New York: Alfred A. Knopf, 1961).

Summary box

Bureaucracy implies this proposition: In an ideal sense, the most efficient and rational organization is one in which there is a clearly defined hierarchy of offices, each office with a clearly defined area of jurisdiction, each office filled by a person tested to have the highest technical qualifications, and the entire set of offices linked together by a system of rules, procedures, and impersonal relationships.

Most work organizations are bureaucratic to some degree. As organizations become larger, they tend to take on more features of bureaucratic structure. Today's managers can benefit from knowledge of bureaucracy by understanding the need for some degree of bureaucratic structure in almost all organizations. At the same time, managers need to be sensitive to the tendency to make organizations too bureaucratic and rigid.

Scientific management, administrative management, and bureaucracy are sometimes collectively called the "classical school" of organization and management. From what has been said so far, it is evident that the major emphasis in the classical school was, and is, on *rationality* and *efficiency*. These two dimensions pervade almost everything in the classical school. Organizations are viewed as rational to the extent that they are efficient mechanisms for the accomplishment of goals.

The organizations of the classical school come across as very mechanistic or machine-like. This is true, not only because they were supposed to operate in a predictable manner like properly maintained machines, but also because they were viewed as relatively independent of their environment. Once "plugged in," they were to crank out their output that would somehow disappear into the static environment.

Obviously, this analogy can be carried too far; organizations are not machines. These theories of organizations, however, did view organizations in a mechanistic way. (In addition to being referred to as the classical school, these three theories are sometimes collectively called "machine theory"). One outcome of this viewpoint was an emphasis on the mechanics of organizations—rules, procedures, policies, position descriptions, and "principles" of organizations.

In support of the classical school, we may say that rationality and efficiency are continuing concerns of management. Although the classical school does not have all the answers about these two dimensions, it does have a significant contribution to make to understanding the de-

Summary box
(continued)

> mands of efficient and effective organizational perform-
> ance.
>   By way of criticism of the classical school, we may say
> that its propositions do not always have their intended ef-
> fect. The very rules and procedures that are proposed may
> produce inefficiency and ineffectiveness. At the risk of over-
> simplifying, we may say that the real shortcomings of the
> classical school derive from its inadequate view of human
> beings. The classical school is more incomplete than it is
> in error. Nevertheless, the propositions of the classical
> school are not universal laws applicable everywhere, and
> they provide few guides as to when they are applicable.

THE HAWTHORNE STUDIES

Evolving view
about people

The 1930s brought a major breakthrough in thinking about
people in organizations. At this time, the view of workers as a factor of production in competition with the interests of capital and
management was evolving to the view that workers' attitudes, feelings, and needs are important on the job. This did not mean the
new view replaced the old view, but only that the two views existed
side by side—as they do today. Nor did this evolving view reflect
anything more than the realization that workers' attitudes and
needs might be a contributing factor in efforts to raise productivity
and lower costs.

Management
and the
worker

The most important event of the 1930s that encouraged the
new concern for the *human dimension* in organizations was the
series of studies known as the Hawthorne studies. These studies,
which took place between 1927 and 1932, were carried out in the
Hawthorne, Illinois, plant of the Western Electric Company. The
original discussion of the studies at the Hawthorne Works is contained in *Management and the Worker*.[19] The Hawthorne studies
began a chain of research into human problems at work that is
continuing even today. They were instrumental in the early development of personnel management, industrial psychology, and
organization theory. Because of their significance to managerial
thought it is useful to you to know something of the specifics of the
Hawthorne studies.

---

[19] Fritz J. Roethlisberger and William J. Dickson, *Management and the
Worker: An Account of a Research Program Conducted by the Western
Electric Company, Hawthorne Works, Chicago* (Cambridge, Mass.: Harvard
University Press, 1939).

Routine experiment, unexpected results

Illumination Experiments. The Hawthorne plant of the Western Electric Company initiated a series of experiments on illumination. The general idea of these routine experiments, which took place between 1924 and 1927, was to determine the cause-and-effect relationship between the level or intensity of illumination at workplaces in the plant and the level of productivity. There was nothing unusual about this kind of study. The *general finding* was that changes in productivity levels could *not* be related directly to changes in levels of illumination. Regardless of whether the intensity of illumination was raised or lowered, productivity increased. Only when the level of illumination approximated ordinary moonlight did productivity drop. In 1927, these results were considered surprising because they contradicted the expectations about cause-and-effect relationships between productivity and a factor in the physical working environment.

Three phases

The illumination experiments have been called a classic example of trying to deal with a *human* situation in *nonhuman* terms. What was the explanation for the unexpected results of the experiments? No one knew for sure, so the Hawthorne studies were initiated in the hope that they would provide some answers. Three phases of the Hawthorne studies will be discussed briefly: the relay assembly test room experiments, the interviewing program, and the bank wiring observation room experiments.

Role of working conditions

Relay Assembly Test Room. The relay assembly test-room experiments consisted of a series of observations of six girls making telephone assemblies. The girls were placed in a separate room where their conditions of work were carefully controlled, where they were closely observed, and where their output was accurately measured. Every aspect of their working conditions was varied. After years of study, not a single correlation of significance was found between changes in physical working conditions and changes in output. Productivity in the relay assembly test-room continually increased, regardless of changes in working conditions. Why?

Hawthorne effect

Part of the answer may be attributed to what has come to be called the "Hawthorne effect." The six girls knew they were part of an experiment. They were being given special attention and treatment because of the experiment. They were in a novel work situation. They were consulted about work changes and were not subject to the usual restrictions imposed by management. The result of this attention and recognition caused them to have improved attitudes toward their jobs and job performance.

Unwanted effect

Over the years, the Hawthorne effect has come to be associated with the "unwanted effect" of the experimental situation itself. It is viewed as something to be "guarded against" or "controlled out of" research; it is an error to be avoided in research.[20] For example, in the relay assembly test-room experiments, the question arises, How can we isolate the effect of working conditions on productivity from the effect of the experimental situation itself? What was the experimental situation?

Alternative interpretation

From the viewpoint of the six girls being studied, the experimental situation included the experimenters saying, in varied, indirect, and subtle ways, "You're special!" The result on productivity of this special treatment is a result that traditionally has been attributed to the Hawthorne effect. However, from your knowledge of the law of effect and of behavioral consequence contingencies (see Chapter 8) you have the basis for an *alternative interpretation* of the relay assembly test-room results. That is, the six girls were altering their productivity behavior as a direct result of a different set of reinforcement contingencies.[21]

A Hawthorne discovery

In the relay room experiments, the girls became an effective and cohesive small *work group* which was uniquely supervised in a positive climate of cooperation and respect for their views. This change in the social situation at work proved a more important influence on productivity than all the changes made in their working conditions. One of the great discoveries of the Hawthorne studies was that the *meaning* of change can be as important as the change itself. But what does change mean to the workers? How do they interpret changes? Why not ask them?

Role of feelings

Interviewing Program. The revolutionary idea of asking workers "what's on your mind?" led to a three-year long interviewing study of over 21,000 employees. This study opened a new era in personnel relations and counseling. The interviewers expected to find, from these interviews, a logical relation between a person's likes or dislikes and certain items or events in the immediate work situation. Instead, they found that the behavior of workers could not be understood apart from their feelings and sentiments. Further, they found that these sentiments could be easily disguised and could be understood only in terms of the total situation of the person.

The meaning of change

For example, a person would complain about the food in the cafeteria. The food would be improved, but the complaint would remain. Or, there would be no change in the food and the complainer would remark on the improvement. The explanation for these surprising findings was that *response* to change depends on

---

[20] Robert Sommer, "Hawthorne Dogma," *Psychological Bulletin,* vol. 70, no. 6 (1968), pp. 592–95. The thesis of this article is that "Hawthorne effects, rather than being some extraneous disruptive influence in psychological research, are an important and ever-present factor in any field situation."

[21] H. M. Parsons, "What Happened at Hawthorne?" *Science,* vol. 183 (March 1974), pp. 922–32.

attitudes and feelings, which, in turn depends on personal history and the social situation at work. This idea is illustrated in the "X" Chart shown in Figure 14–1. In other words, the "meaning" of change depends on psychological and sociological variables as well as on the technical aspects of the change. The intriguing possibility that performance could be improved by changes in employees' attitudes was not missed. However, as the bank-wiring observation room experiment would show, employees' attitudes can take bizarre forms.

FIGURE 14–1
"X" Chart Showing Role of Attitudes in Determining Response to Change

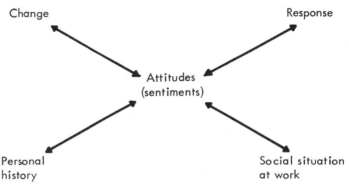

Source: *Management and Morale* by F. J. Roethlisberger, p. 21. Published by Harvard University Press. © 1941 by the President and Fellows of Harvard College. Reprinted by permission.

Four sentiments

The BWO Room Experiment. The Bank Wiring Observation (BWO) room experiment illustrates that output is a form of social behavior. The BWO room contained 24 workmen representing three occupational groups—wiremen, soldermen, and inspectors. These men were paid on a group piecework plan so the expectation would be that the men would be interested in total output. The experiment revealed, however, the existence of several sentiments:

The rate-buster sentiment:	Don't turn out too much work.
The chiseler sentiment:	Don't turn out too little work.
The squealer sentiment:	Don't say anything to a supervisor that might hurt a fellow worker.
The officious sentiment:	Don't act too officious in performing duties.

Group norms and values

The BWO room study showed the importance of work standards set by the work group and led to further study of the "informal group" and the "informal organization." In terms of the history of ideas, the "discovery" of the importance of group norms and values actually took place long before the Hawthorne studies. Nevertheless, it was a singularly important discovery for executives and business organizations.

Perspective   The Hawthorne studies qualify as a major foundation of contemporary thought about organizations. They have received a considerable amount of support and criticism over the years.[22] In 1975,
the Western Electric Company and the Harvard School of Business
sponsored a symposium celebrating the 50th anniversary of the
Hawthorne studies. In an article describing the symposium, the
following view was expressed:

> The enduring message of Hawthorne . . . has only recently
> achieved prominence . . . it takes different kinds of people and
> different kinds of organizations to perform different kinds of
> tasks.[23]

Summary box

> *The Hawthorne studies* imply this proposition: The so-
> cial situation at work can have an important influence on
> employee behavior. Although the physical conditions of
> work are important to productivity, the social situation
> must also be considered (relay assembly test-room experi-
> ments).
>
> The *response* of an employee to a change in the work
> situation depends on the "meaning" of the change to the
> employee. Meaning, in turn, depends on the employee's
> attitudes and feelings about the change. Attitudes and feel-
> ings are influenced by the social situation at work and the
> employee's personal history (interviewing program and the
> "X" Chart). Furthermore, the work group and informal
> groups can set work standards which may conflict with
> official standards (the BWO room experiments).

COOPERATIVE ACTION

Chester I.   Chester I. Barnard's *The Functions of the Executive* is consid-
Barnard   ered by many to be the most important early book presenting a
comprehensive view of organizations.[24] It was described in 1939
as ". . . a book that no senior executive, who is willing to follow
closely reasoned exposition of a vital and difficult subject, can
afford to ignore."[25]

Overriding   Barnard wrote because he felt that none of the literature on
theme   organizations discussed them in a way that corresponded to his

---

[22] See, for example, Alex Carey, "The Hawthorne Studies: A Radical
Criticism," *American Sociological Review*, vol. 32, no. 3 (June 1967) and
Jon M. Shepard, "On Alex Carey's Radical Criticism of the Hawthorne
Studies," *Academy of Management Journal*, vol. 14, no. 1 (March 1971).

[23] "Hawthorne Revisited: The Legend and the Legacy," *Organizational
Dynamics*, vol. 3, no. 3 (Winter 1975), pp. 66–80.

[24] Cambridge, Mass.: Harvard University Press, 1938.

[25] T. N. Whitehead, *Book Review Digest*, 1939 (New York: The H. W.
Wilson Company, 1940), p. 55.

personal experience as a top executive. His ideas have influenced thinking about organizational purposes, authority, decision making, and systems. In general, the overriding theme in Barnard's book is that of *cooperation* of all organization members in achieving a common purpose.

Common purpose

Purpose and Elements of Organization. The purpose of an industrial organization, Barnard argued, is the production of material goods or services; the purpose is not profit. Profit is essential to have a supply of inducements for owners. The goal of business is service. Barnard felt that the common purpose of an organization is a *moral* purpose. A key function of the executive is to inculcate this moral purpose throughout the organization—a moral purpose that arises out of the cooperative, voluntary activities of the members. The organization's goals—its common purposes—are supposed to be shared by all members. That is what gives rise to the cooperative, voluntary system.

Three main elements of an organization

Barnard viewed an organization as a *cooperative system* of consciously coordinated personal activities or "forces." Organizations, according to Barnard, had three main elements: purpose; communication; and willingness to cooperate. He defined "formal organization" as a system of consciously coordinated activities of two or more persons. He defined "informal organization" (or informal groups) as the aggregate of the personal contacts and interactions and the associated groupings of people. In general, informal groups for Barnard have a positive and necessary role to play in formal organization. He did not dwell on the potentially disruptive aspects of informal groups, as the Hawthorne studies did.

System

Barnard's early view of organizations as "systems" was a forerunner of modern systems theory of organization. We will discuss systems theory in the next chapter. Barnard argued that a system is treated as a whole because each part is related to every other part in a significant way. Further, he saw that each organization is a component of a larger system, along with physical systems, social systems, biological systems, and persons.

Essential executive functions

Executive Functions and Persons. Barnard departed from the common view that managers are supposed to plan, organize, and control the activities of a group of people. Rather, his view was that the "essential functions" of an executive are to provide a system of communication, to promote the securing of essential efforts, and to formulate and define purpose. These functions parallel Barnard's view of the three main elements in an organization.

Persons

In Barnard's view, the individual possesses certain properties which are comprehended in the word "person." Persons as participants in specific cooperative systems are regarded, in their purely functional aspects, as phases of cooperation. Persons as outside any specific organization are regarded as a unique individualization of physical, biological, and social factors, possessing a limited power of choice. Barnard's theory about the role of persons in organizations is rather impersonal or, rather, nonpersonal. Recall his view of organization as a system of "forces." These forces emanate from persons, but the persons themselves do not make up the organization. For Barnard, organizations are rational, moral, legitimate, cooperative systems of coordinated forces of two or more persons.

Summary box

> The idea of *cooperative action* is central to the writings of Chester I. Barnard. Barnard's writings imply this proposition: If organizations are cooperative, voluntary systems, then everything that goes on in organizations must be in everyone's best interest. This defining characteristic of cooperation gives rise to the essentially *moral* character of organizations. The common purpose of organization is a moral purpose. Since organizational activity is cooperative and voluntary, conflict will be minimal and groups will not engage in disruptive activities.

THE ROLE OF AUTHORITY

Importance

In any discussion of *foundations* of contemporary thought about organizations, the subject of authority must be given a prominent place. Whether authority is viewed as the "glue that holds organizations together," or as "just one source of influence within organizations," or simply as a "defining characteristic of role relationships," it is an essential and critically important dimension to life in organizations.

Authority

Authority, Power, and Influence. A distinction is commonly drawn between the terms "authority," "power," and "influence." Authority may be considered as the right of a person to issue orders and to direct the behavior of those over whom the authority is exercised. Although authority resides in a *person* (only a person can issue orders), it arises out of the demands of *position* or *role* in organizations. Thus, a person in an organization has authority by virtue of the requirements of the role held by the person. "The essence of the construct of authority is that the legitimacy of rights to prescribe behavior is part of the fabric of role relations."[26]

Expectation of compliance

When authority is exercised by a manager through the act of issuing orders, the authority is intended to guide the behavior of

---

[26] David C. Limerick, "Authority Relations in Different Organizational Systems," *Academy of Management Review*, vol. 1, no. 4 (October 1976), p. 57.

those to whom the order was issued. Authority implies the capacity to exact compliance. Supporting this capacity is the manager's control over incentives and resources.[27]

Power

"Power," on the other hand, is not necessarily associated with job position. A person can have power over another in an organization through varied means, including threats of physical violence. A person holding a gun to your back is in a position of power over you. In work organizations, many people exert power over others even though the power goes beyond the requirements of job position. Subordinates often attribute power to their manager that cannot be explained in terms of the legitimate demands of the job. Managers can and have coerced their employees by subtle threats of withholding salary increases, promotions, or desired fringe benefits. Power can be viewed as the potential capacity to exert influence over others. More precisely, "the power of a person A over a person B is the ability of A to obtain that B do something he would not have done otherwise."[28]

Influence

"Influence" is a term that covers both authority and power; it is the most general of the three terms. A manager can have influence through authority, power, or both. The sources of influence can include position, personality, seniority, persuasive abilities, competence, and expertise, among others. In contemporary thinking about organizations, there has been a relative shift away from an emphasis on authority and toward an emphasis on the multiple means of exerting influence in organizations. Nevertheless, there is a need to consider the role of all three concepts—authority, power, and influence.

Four views

Sources of Managerial Influence. Where do managers in organizations get their authority, power, and influence? Where do they get the right to issue orders and direct the behavior of others? Where do they get the right to expect obedience to their orders and to implement disciplinary procedures should their orders not be carried out in a satisfactory manner? Several answers to these questions have been given over the years, and they are not necessarily mutually exclusive. The views of the source of managerial authority that will be discussed here include the traditional, the acceptance, the contractual, and the competence views.

Traditional view

In answer to the question, "Where do managers get their authority?" the "traditional" answer has been that they get it from "up there." Just where "up there" is depends on your place in the organization. If you are a foreman, you get your authority from the general foreman who has delegated authority to you. If you are

---

[27] M. H. Berhold, "Managerial Authority in a Decision Analysis Context," *Omega,* vol. 4, no. 2 (1976), pp. 165–73.

[28] Robert Dahl, "The Concept of Power," *Behavioral Science,* vol. 2 (1957), pp. 201–15.

the general foreman, you get your authority from the plant superintendent. If you are the president of a corporation, you get your authority from the board of directors which has, by law, the authority to name the president. If this logic is extended upward, it may be said that, in the United States, the board of directors gets its authority from the laws of the state in which the corporation received its charter. These laws, in turn, are supported by the constitutional provision of the right of private property. Thus, the traditional view of authority has been that the source of authority is "up there" and that authority flows from the "top to the bottom" of organizations.

Logical and legalistic approach

Given the need in organizations for authority, the traditional view provides a logical explanation of its source. The traditional view, however, reflects a legalistic and dogmatic approach to authority. It is a necessary but insufficient explanation of the source of managerial authority. For practicing managers, the traditional view is of little help in their search for ways in which to use their authority effectively. Although there are exceptions which can sometimes be serious, the major question for the manager is not, Where do I get my authority? The major question is, What do I need to do to use my authority in an effective manner? The "acceptance view" helps the manager answer that question and also provides another view of the source of managerial authority.

Acceptance view

The acceptance view suggests that managers get their authority from their subordinates. Rather than authority coming from "up there," the acceptance view holds that managers get their authority from "down there." In the traditional view, authority flows from the top to the bottom; in the acceptance view, authority flows from the bottom to the top. The basic idea is that managers can possess an infinite amount of authority from "up there," but if they cannot get their subordinates to accept their authority, it is useless.

Emptiness of formal authority

The acceptance view is not in conflict with the traditional view; they are complementary. They deal with different aspects of the question of authority. On the one hand, if managers do not possess formal authority, they are not in a position to ask anyone to accept their orders. On the other hand, the acceptance view correctly focuses attention on the emptiness of formal authority in the absence of a consensus of those affected to accept the formal authority as legitimate. The *useful* thing about the acceptance view is that it directs the manager's attention to the conditions that must be met if acceptance of authority is to be earned.

Zone of indifference

Chester Barnard was one of the first to discuss authority in terms of acceptance. He defined authority as "the character of an order by virtue of which it is *accepted* by a contributor as governing the action he contributes" (emphasis added)."[29] Barnard sug-

[29] Chester I. Barnard, *The Functions of the Executive*, p. 167.

gested that there is a "zone of indifference" within which subordinates will accept orders from a superior as governing their behavior. Outside of this zone of indifference, however, managers must *earn* the acceptance of their subordinates. In theory, when subordinates receive orders from their superiors that are outside the subordinates' zone of indifference, the subordinates will calculate the advantages and disadvantages of accepting and of not accepting the order. This calculation results in a decision to accept or reject the order. The acceptance view encourages managers to create conditions in which authority will be accepted, rather than relying on formal job position for acceptance of authority.

Contractual view

In the "contractual view" of the source of managerial authority, the authority of the manager derives from the contract, written or implied, between the employer and the employee. This contract is essentially a *psychological contract,* although in many cases it may be complemented by a legal contract, such as those resulting from collective bargaining between management and organized labor. "The notion of a psychological contract implies that the individual has a variety of expectations of the organization and that the organization has a variety of expectations of him."[30] From the organization's viewpoint, the psychological contract is implemented through the concept of authority. From the viewpoint of individual employees, the psychological contract is implemented through their perception that they can influence their situation in the organization so that they will not be taken advantage of.

Negotiating strength

At the time of employment, the employee agrees to comply with certain requests in exchange for satisfactions that the employee seeks. The employer similarly agrees to give the employee those satisfactions in exchange for the employee's compliance with orders given by those in authority in the organization. To be most meaningful, the contractual view should imply the existence of relatively equal strength in each of the parties to the contract. The view lacks integrity when one of the parties dominates the negotiations. In practice, relative equality is seldom achieved and the negotiating parties "do the best that they can."

Interpretations of the contract

The nature of the psychological contract between the employee and the employer is a matter of considerable debate. The contract can be interpreted narrowly to mean that the employer and the employee exchange the *minimum* amount required in order to agree on a contract. On the other hand, the contract can be interpreted broadly to mean that the employer and the employee both exchange the *maximum* contribution for the mutual benefit of both parties. Unfortunately for work organizations and their members, the contracts between employers and employees often call forth minimal contributions from both parties.

---

[30] Edgar H. Schein, *Organizational Psychology,* 2d ed., (Englewood Cliffs, N.J.: Prentice-Hall, 1970), p. 12.

Competence
view

The "competence view" about the source of managerial authority holds that authority derives from the competence and expertise of those in job positions. This view is particularly relevant to understanding the authority of skilled and professional personnel. For example, research chemists in organizations in the chemical industry have a lot of influence because of their professional skills. These skills give rise to influence based on competence and expertise. The skills, in turn, are the source of the authority granted to the chemists in order to carry out their activities of research.

Staff
personnel

Many staff personnel in work organizations accumulate influence and authority as a result of their success in achieving the goals of their positions. For example, personnel managers in business organizations hold staff jobs. Their basic purpose is to assist and serve the other departments in the organization in their efforts to effectively select, train, develop, and utilize personnel. As the personnel manager builds a record of success based on competence and skill in balancing the delicate demands of the organization, the manager will begin to have more influence and authority. Conversely, failure to effectively assist other departments in meeting their personnel needs leads to a reduction in the authority, influence, and status of the personnel manager.

Summary box

> *Authority* is the right of a person to issue orders and to direct the behavior of those over whom the authority is exercised. *Power* is the potential capacity to exert influence over others. Authority is legitimate power. *Influence* is a general term that includes both authority and power.
>
> Four complementary views of the source of managerial influence are: *traditional*—authority flows from the top to the bottom of organizations; *acceptance*—authority flows from the bottom to the top; *contractual*—authority is the means through which organizations implement their psychological contracts with employees; and *competence*—authority arises out of technical and personal expertise and effectiveness in relating with people.
>
> In viewing the role of authority as a *foundation* of contemporary thought about organizations, it is reasonable to say that there is more emphasis today on the broader idea of influence. That is, granted that formal authority vested in job positions is an essential ingredient of managerial roles, relatively more attention today is devoted to alternative views of sources of managerial influence. These alternative views, particularly the acceptance and competence views, are useful in helping managers become more effective and in complementing formal authority.

CHECK YOUR UNDERSTANDING

Macro view
Micro view
Organization
Essence of organization
Formal dimension
Informal dimension
Social Darwinism
New Thought Movement
Scientific management
Administrative management
Principles of management
Bases of departmentation
Bureaucracy
Main features of bureaucratic
  structure
Classical school
Machine theory
Hawthorne studies
Illumination experiments
Relay assembly test-room
  experiment

Hawthorne effect
Interviewing program
"X" Chart
Bank wiring observation room
  experiment
Four sentiments
Chester Barnard's cooperative-
  action theme
Authority
Power
Influence
Sources of managerial influence
  Traditional
  Acceptance
  Contractual
  Competence
Zone of indifference
Psychological contract

STUDY QUESTIONS

1. You might want to remember:

Author	Book Title	Date
Frederick W. Taylor..........	Principles of Scientific Management...................	1911
L. Gulick and L. Urwick, eds....	Papers on the Science of Administration................	1937
Max Weber..................	The Theory of Social and Economic Organization, (translated)........	1947
Fritz J. Roethlisberger and William J. Dickson	Management and the Worker......	1939
Chester I. Barnard...........	The Functions of the Executive.....	1938

2. Be able to identify the propositions about organizations implied by each of the seven foundations of contemporary thought discussed in the chapter. (See Summary Boxes.)

3. Using the doctrine of Social Darwinism, be able to explain: "The workers were workers because they obviously lacked the essential character and qualities to become employers."

4. What was it about scientific management that justifies the statement that it was the first truly significant breakthrough in management ideology and practice?

5. It is said of scientific management that it ignored the relationship between the organization and its environment and that its conception of people was rather narrow. Discuss how both of these

observations can be explained, in part, by the context of the times in which scientific management emerged.

6. How does "administrative management" differ from "scientific management"?

7. What, in your opinion, does it mean to say that all organizations possess the features of bureaucratic structure in some degree? In view of this, what does it mean to refer to an entire organization as a bureaucracy?

8. What are Chester I. Barnard's three elements of organization? How does he define an organization? Be able to identify the reason Barnard argued that the purpose of organization is a "moral purpose." What essential executive functions did Barnard identify?

APPLICATION: A DIFFERENT PERSPECTIVE

Chapter 14 is titled "Foundations of Contemporary Thought about Organizations." The chapter takes a historical approach, that is, the chapter views "foundations" as specific things, such as a social philosophy (Social Darwinism), a set of studies (Hawthorne Studies), or a particular theory (Bureaucracy).

This application asks you to draw on the material presented in Chapter 14 and to look at it from a different perspective. This different perspective views "foundations" as a set of ideas or "basic handles" for analyzing organizations. The manner with which various organization theories have dealt with these ideas is one way of differentiating the theories and is one way of differentiating real organizations.

Figure 14–2 can be used to facilitate the development of the perspective suggested above. The column on the left represents the basic handles that will be used for analyzing organization theories or related notions. These theories are identified at the top of the remaining columns in Figure 14–2.

The task then, is to relate a basic handle to a theory. For example, consider "people" as a basic handle. Organization theories differ in the way they view people, in the emphasis they give to people, in their view of their obligation to people, and in what people they consider as "in" the organization. In a similar manner, theories can differ in their conceptualization of the other basic handles shown in Figure 14–2.

On the basis of your reading of Chapter 14 and other reading that you have done, fill in the cells in Figure 14–2 that represent the intersection of a basic handle with an organization theory.

FIGURE 14–2
Basic Handles and Theories Relevant to Organizations

"Basic Handles," or Ideas for Thinking about Organizations	Theories Relevant to Organizations			
	Social Darwinism	Classical School Theories	Hawthorne Studies	Theory of Chester Barnard
People				
Internal and external environment				
Authority				
Conflict and cooperation				
Purpose of the organization				

Objectives of Chapter 15

- To view the organization as a system and to discuss several key components of that idea, such as system elements, characteristics, boundaries, and synergism.

- To introduce the external environment as a critical variable affecting organizational performance and effectiveness.

- To introduce technology as another critical variable that can influence organizations and that has received major attention over the past 20 years.

- To discuss briefly a relatively new variable, organizational climate, that may prove useful in furthering understanding of organizations and of behavior in organizations.

Outline of Chapter 15

15

CONTEMPORARY THOUGHT ABOUT ORGANIZATIONS

The social structure in organizations of the future will take on some unique characteristics. . . . organizations will become . . . temporary systems . . . organized around problems-to-be-solved . . . by relative groups of strangers . . . linking pin personnel will be necessary . . . groups will be conducted on organic rather than on mechanical lines. . . .

Warren G. Bennis

Last chapter

Let's begin this chapter by recalling the seven "foundations" discussed in Chapter 14. *Social Darwinism* and the *New Thought Movement* reflected attitudes and values of society that influenced thinking about organizations. *Scientific management, administrative management,* and *bureaucracy* were presented as foundations that emphasized rationality and efficiency—two themes that pervade the "classical school" of organization and management. The *Hawthorne studies* were important because of their insights into employees' attitudes, informal groups, change, and the social situation at work. Finally, we discussed *cooperative* action as the central theme in the writings of Chester I. Barnard and the *role of authority* as a crucial dimension to life in organizations.

This chapter

In this chapter we will be discussing organizations in a very different way than we did in the previous chapter. A key word in this chapter is "relationships." Contemporary thought about organizations is dominated by several critical types of relationships. Three of these that this chapter discuss are: the organization as a system of elements that are related to each other; the organization–environment relationship; and the organization–technology relationship. In addition, the idea of "organizational climate" is introduced, and its various roles discussed.

THE ORGANIZATION AS A SYSTEM

Popular idea

No idea has so captured the imagination of contemporary management writers and practitioners as the system idea. The management process itself is considered a system. Organizations are viewed as systems. The systems approach is used in problem analysis, and systems design is a respected field of study and professional practice. Degree programs in systems analysis are offered by many universities. General Systems Theory (GST) is heralded as a developing set of general principles that applies to all types of systems. The systems idea is everywhere. And with some justification.

GST

General Systems Theory. The idea of an organization as a system evolved out of what is called "General Systems Theory." This term was first used in 1920:

> There exist models, principles, and laws that apply to generalized systems or their subclasses irrespective of their particular kind, the nature of the component elements, and the relations or "forces" between them. We postulate a new discipline called General Systems Theory. General Systems Theory is a logico-mathematical field whose task is the formulation and derivation of these general principles that are applicable to "systems" in general.[1]

Three main aspects

In broad terms, there are three main aspects of GST. The *first* is "system science"—the scientific exploration of wholes and wholeness. The goal is to develop GST in mathematical terms. The *second* is "system technology"—techniques, models, and mathematical approaches of systems engineering. There is a spectrum ranging from highly sophisticated mathematical theory to computer simulation to more or less informal discussion of system problems. The *third* is "system philosophy"—the reorientation of thought and world view following the introduction of "system" as a new scientific paradigm (in contrast to the analytic, mechanistic, linear-causal paradigm of classical science).

A new paradigm

GST, then, is an all-encompassing way of looking at "wholes" wherever they are found, and they are found everywhere. Systems thinking is important in psychology, sociology, economics, cybernetics, as well as in many of the physical sciences. The following quotation suggests that systems theory will play a major role in the study of organizations:

> Systems theory does provide a new paradigm for the study of social organizations and their management. At this state it is obviously crude and lacking in precision. In some ways it may not be much better than older paradigms which have been accepted and used for a long time (such as the management process ap-

---

[1] Ludwig von Bertalanffy, "The History and Status of General Systems Theory," *Academy of Management Journal*, vol. 15, no. 4 (December 1972), p. 411.

proach). As in other fields of scientific endeavor, the new paradigm must be applied, clarified, elaborated, and made more precise. But it does provide a fundamentally different view of the reality of social organizations and can serve as the basis for major advancements in our field.[2]

*Examples
of systems*

What Is a System?   Almost anything can be viewed as a system. An automobile is a mechanical system of hundreds of parts. A flower is a botanical system. A horse is a zoological system. A human being is a physiological and psychological system consisting of cells, a heart, lungs, attitudes, expectations, and many other elements. A business firm is a socio-technical system because it combines human organization and a technology of machines, materials, production and marketing processes, and so forth.

Definition

The common feature in all of the above examples is that of interacting elements. A "system" may be defined as a set of interacting elements. When something, such as an organization, is examined from a systems perspective or viewpoint it means that particular attention is directed to both elements *and* interaction. In this holistic view of organizations, "The component on which one may temporarily focus is understandable only in relation to other components and the total system's functions or operations."[3]

Parts

Analysis and Synthesis.   When an organization is examined primarily from the viewpoint of its elements, components, or parts, we can say that the viewpoint of *analysis* is being applied. "Analysis" is the process of separating a whole into its parts for the purpose of learning more about their nature and function. For example, the viewpoint of analysis was characteristic of Frederick Taylor's scientific-management approach (see Chapter 14). There is no question that scientific management did and still does contribute to greater efficiency in business firms. The viewpoint of analysis is an essential one in any effort to fully understand organizations and their parts. A whole cannot be understood without an understanding of the parts that make up the whole.

Wholes

The viewpoint of *synthesis* is also essential to understanding organizations. The parts of an organization cannot be understood apart from their relationships to each other. "Synthesis" is the opposite of analysis. It is the process of putting together parts or elements so as to form a whole. Synthesis focuses on interactions and relationships of parts. Trying to understand an organization without adequate attention to synthesis is equivalent to trying to under-

---

[2] Fremont E. Kast and James E. Rosenzweig, "General Systems Theory: Applications for Organization and Management," *Academy of Management Review*, vol. 15, no. 4 (December 1972), p. 457.

[3] F. Kenneth Berrien, "A General Systems Approach to Organizations," in *Handbook of Industrial and Organizational Psychology*, Marvin D. Dunnette, ed. (Chicago: Rand McNally College Publishing Company, 1976), p. 61.

stand a human being by separately examining the heart, lung, liver, brain, and so on.

Systems thinking

The systems idea that we are discussing in this chapter is noted for its focus on synthesis. The systems idea, as applied to organizations, has shifted attention somewhat away from analysis and toward synthesis. Systems thinking does not, of course, discard the analytical perspective. To do so would be to discard an essential source of understanding about organizations. True systems thinking attempts to capture the benefits of both analysis and synthesis.

Example

How does this discussion of analysis and synthesis relate to a business firm? In order to understand a business firm, which is one type of organization, we must understand its elements (analysis) and the nature and requirements of the relations between the elements (synthesis). For example, two elements or functions in most business firms are production and marketing. Full understanding of these two functions requires an understanding of their subfunctions and of the relationships between them. Subfunctions of production include engineering, quality control, maintenance, inventory control, production control, and the set of jobs that directly produce the product. Subfunctions of marketing include sales promotion, advertising, sales forecasting, marketing research, pricing, customer relations, and the system of jobs that directly sell and distribute the product.

Synergistic effect

Synergism. "Synergism" means that the simultaneous action of the various parts of an organization together produce a greater total effect than would the individual parts acting independently. In short, "the whole is greater than the sum of its parts"—an idea that can be traced at least to Aristotle. Thus, contemporary thought about organizations as systems emphasizes the synergistic effect that results from increasing the effectiveness of the interaction and integration of system parts.

A potential effect

The synergistic effect is not an inevitable result of system behavior. Rather, it is a potential effect. For example, if a small group is viewed as a system, it does not necessarily follow that the "whole" (the output of the group) will be "greater than the sum of its parts" (the output that could have resulted from the group members working individually). It is a common experience of group members that group activity is often less efficient and effective than individual activity. Thus, the synergistic effect should be looked upon by managers as a potential effect of the functioning of a system. Or, we can say that synergism is a result of *effective* systems.

Environmental independence

Closed and Open Systems. Systems are sometimes referred to as "closed" or "open." A closed system is a set of interacting elements that functions independently of its environment. That is, in order to function properly, the system requires no intervention from people, things, or forces outside of itself. Perhaps the notion of a perpetual-motion machine comes closest to capturing the essence of the closed-system idea.

Organizations are not closed systems

There are, of course, no organizations that literally function independently of their environment. However, there are organizations, or subparts of organizations, that, through the behavior of their leaders, act *as if* they are closed systems. They act as if external forces, if ignored or denied, will go away. They do not view the demands of these external forces as an integral part of the organization's functioning.

Environmental interdependence

An open system is "a set of elements standing in interrelation among themselves and with the environment."[4] When we refer to an organization as a "system," we are referring to an open system. Clearly, all organizations—hospitals, schools, business firms, and so on—must interact with and are dependent on their environment. An organization that is not adaptive and responsive to its environment could not survive or grow over any extended period of time.

Practical value

The practical value of the closed system–open system distinction is captured by the term "relative." That is, no organization can be either completely closed or open to its environment. An organization must seek the relative degree of openness and closedness that is appropriate to it. Total closedness would lead to lack of support from important environmental groups, such as customers, general public, suppliers, and government. Total openness would lead to insufficient attention to internal structure and operations. Every organization has to be responsive to demands placed on it by both its internal and external environments.

What is in and out?

System Boundaries. Every system has boundaries that separate it from other systems and from its environment. A system must be ". . . delineated by identifiable boundaries from its environmental suprasystem."[5] For example, if we are to think of a business firm as a system, then we must be able to identify those elements that are "in the system" and those elements that are "out of the system." The elements out of the system represent the system's *external environment* and those in the system represent the system's *internal environment*.

Identifying system boundaries

The problem of identifying system boundaries can be a difficult one for managers. Ultimately, the problem is resolved by drawing an essentially, but not totally, arbitrary distinction between those

[4] Bertalanffy, "The History and Status of General Systems Theory," p. 417.

[5] Fremont E. Kast and James E. Rosenzweig, *Organization and Management: A Systems Approach*, 2d ed. (New York: McGraw-Hill Book Company, 1974), p. 101.

elements that will be considered inside and outside of the system. The distinction is arbitrary because ". . . the boundaries of a system are always set by the observer, not by the nature of the thing observed," but the distinction is not totally arbitrary because the nature of the thing observed ". . . will make certain boundaries more workable than others."[6] One writer has compared the problem of finding the boundary of an organization or system to that of finding the boundary of a cloud.[7] Presumably the boundary of a cloud can be determined by selecting a specific density of moisture that will be used to determine what belongs to the cloud and what belongs to the cloud's environment. But what is the equivalence to density of moisture in an organization?

Example

Suppose you are the manager of the personnel function in a large business firm. Where is your system? What elements will be included in it? How will you define its boundaries? What boundary-spanning roles will be necessary for linking elements within the system with those outside of it?[8] You will not be able to answer these questions in a manner that is completely satisfactory. Your practical solution will have to be to select those elements that you "feel" are relevant to your particular domain of accountability. This, in turn, requires you to have some criteria for determining relevance. Since your criteria may differ from those of another manager, your system boundaries may also differ from those set by another manager. Thus, boundaries are somewhat arbitrary. Identifying appropriate system boundaries is a skill that can differentiate effective from ineffective managers.

Different views

System Elements. If an organization is a system, and a system is a set of interacting elements, precisely what are the interacting elements in an organization? One nice feature of the systems idea is that different views of elements are possible. For example, an organization can be viewed as a system of interacting:

Individuals or groups of individuals.
Roles (such as chief executive officer, marketing manager, accountant, machine operator).
Functions (such as marketing, production, finance, personnel, accounting).
Key decision-making points.
Communication and information flow points.

[6] Alfred Kuhn, "Boundaries, Kinds of Systems, and Kinds of Interactions," in *General Systems and Organization Theory: Methodological Aspects*, Arlyn J. Melcher, ed. (Kent, Ohio: Kent State University Press, 1975), p. 45.

[7] William H. Starbuck, "Organizations and their Environments," in Marvin D. Dunnette, ed., *Handbook of Industrial and Organizational Psychology* (Chicago: Rand McNally College Publishing Company, 1976), p. 1,071.

[8] Howard Aldrich and Diane Herker, "Boundary Spanning Roles and Organization Structure," *Academy of Management Review*, vol. 2, no. 2 (April 1977), pp. 217–30.

*Generic
subsystems*

Each of the above views of system elements can provide a useful perspective for managers. Figure 15–1 presents a view of system elements that has been influential during the past several years. The five "generic subsystems" shown in Figure 15–1 are system elements that are essential to *any* organization. The basic idea is that all five of these elements or generic subsystems must be functioning at a satisfactory level in order for the organization to survive and grow.

FIGURE 15–1
Generic Subsystems of an Open System

1. The "productive subsystem" is the total system of activities concerned with the production of the product. In a public-accounting firm, the productive subsystem is the total system of activities concerned with the provision of audits, tax returns, and client services.
2. The "supportive subsystem" acquires needed inputs for the productive system and disposes of the systems output. In addition, the supportive subsystem has the function of maintaining a favorable external environment for the system. For example, in a business firm, hiring, purchasing, marketing, and public relations could be considered part of the supportive subsystem. Many business firms have established separate organizational units to deal with organization–environment relations.
3. The "maintenance subsystem" is concerned with preserving the basic character of the system. For example, training activities and compensation plans could be considered part of the maintenance subsystem.
4. The "adaptive subsystem" is concerned with organizational survival in a changing environment. It is supposed to sense relevant changes in the external environment and translate their meaning to the organization. Research and development activities could be considered part of the adaptive subsystem.
5. The "managerial subsystem" is concerned with controlling, coordinating, and directing the other subsystems.

Source: Daniel Katz and Robert L. Kahn, *The Social Psychology of Organizations* (New York: John Wiley & Sons, 1966).

*Cycle of
events*

System Characteristics.[9]   Several common characteristics of organizations as open systems can be identified. *First,* every organization engages in a "cycle of events" that involves importing, transforming, and exporting energy. The use of the term "energy" here reflects the influence of General Systems Theory. GST had its origin in the biological sciences and is concerned with the organization of living things. For a business firm, energy takes the form of human inputs, financial resources, materials and equipment, products, and services produced.

---

[9] This section is based on Daniel Katz and Robert L. Kahn, *The Social Psychology of Organizations* (New York: John Wiley & Sons, 1966).

Negative entropy

A second characteristic of organizations as open systems is that they import more energy than they export. This characteristic is sometimes called "negative entropy." It simply means that if an open system is to survive and grow it must take in more energy than it puts out. For a business firm, an obvious illustration of negative entropy is long-run profitability. However, negative entropy refers to all forms of energy, not just to financial resources.

Information processing

A third characteristic of an open system is that it "processes information." That is, it has to have processes for deciding what information it will allow into the system, for storing and interpreting the information, and for deciding on responses to the information. Since the information-processing capability of any system is limited, systems must have coding processes that screen incoming information. This is one of the reasons for saying that organizations cannot be "totally open" to their environment. That is, they cannot process all the information that is available in the environment.

Growth and maintenance

A fourth characteristic of open systems is that they have both "growth" and "maintenance" tendencies. That is, there are forces in them that favor stability and resist change. There are also forces in open systems that favor change and seek out opportunities for innovation, renewal, and growth. The balancing over time of growth and maintenance tendencies serves to maintain the basic character of the system.

Equifinality

A final characteristic of an open system is "equifinality." "The general principle, which characterizes all open systems, is that there does not have to be a single method for achieving an objective."[10] Equifinality emphasizes flexibility in selecting *means* that will be used to achieve *ends*. It creates a concern for goals over methods. The recognition of equifinality as a characteristic of all open systems is, in part, a reaction to earlier ways of thinking. The Classical School (see Chapter 14) often reflected a "one best way" mentality. For example, the prescriptions of administrative management and bureaucracy were not communicated as flexible guides to be adapted to specific circumstances. Rather, they came across and were picked up as relatively inflexible guides to behavior, regardless of the conditions to which they were to be applied.

---

[10] Ibid., p. 27.

Summary box

> Viewing organizations as systems is an approach that evolved out of *General Systems Theory* (GST). GST's three main aspects are system science, system technology, and system philosophy.
>
> A *system* is a set of interacting elements. The *systems viewpoint* focuses on elements (analysis) and on element interaction (synthesis). It focuses on the organization as a total entity. An idea that is fundamental to the systems viewpoint is *synergism*—the whole is greater than the sum of its parts. The synergistic effect is a result of *effective systems.*
>
> A *closed system* is independent of its environment; an *open system* engages in interaction with people, things, and forces in its environment. All organizations are open systems. However, organizations differ in their degree of openness to the environment.
>
> *System boundaries* separate elements in a system from those outside of it. Elements that are outside of the system are in the system's *external environment.* System boundaries rarely can be precisely identified.
>
> There are a variety of ways of viewing *system elements.* One influential approach has been to view an organization as a system of five *generic subsystems*—productive, supportive, maintenance, adaptive, and managerial.
>
> Five *characteristics* that open systems have in common are: a cycle of importing, transforming, and exporting events; negative entropy; information processing; growth and maintenance tendencies; and equifinality.
>
> To round out this chapter's discussion of contemporary thought about organizations, we will examine three additional topics:
>
> 1. The organization–environment relationship.
> 2. The organization–technology relationship.
> 3. Organizational climate.

THE ORGANIZATION–ENVIRONMENT RELATIONSHIP

Internal dynamics

Introduction.　Most of the "foundations" discussed in Chapter 14 concentrated on problems of "internal dynamics"—problems arising out of an organization's structure, operations, and demands for efficiency. The organization's external environment was largely ignored or considered as relatively constant. It was not viewed as a major causal variable influencing the organization's structure, operations, or the behavior of organization members.

*External
dynamics*

Problems of "external dynamics"—problems arising out of the organization's relationship with its external environment—began to receive attention with the development of the open systems idea. When an organization is viewed as an open, rather than as a closed, system, the importance of the system–environment interaction becomes apparent. One prominent system theorist suggested in 1950 that the importance of open and closed connections to the environment is the means whereby living organisms could be distinguished from inanimate objects.[11]

*Task
environment*

By the 1950s, one writer was asserting that ". . . the impact of environmental factors on behavior in organizations is one of the most important tasks for organizational theorists."[12] This writer then coined the phrase "task environment" to refer to the information inputs from external sources that are potentially relevant to the organization. The "information inputs" are stimuli to which an organization is exposed (through the perceptions of the organization's leaders) and to which it must respond. The "external sources" are customers, suppliers, competitors, pressure groups, government agencies, bankers, and others that are directly related to the tasks of an organization. The different parts of an organization can have different task environments. That is, any one organization can face multiple task environments.

Essential idea

Over the years, different terms have been introduced to mean more or less the same thing as task environment. Some of these terms are "transactional environment," "organizational set," and "organizational domain."[13] The essential idea that these terms intend to convey is that of a set of conditions, influences, or forces external to an organization that has relevance to the goals and tasks of the organization. We will refer to this set of conditions, influences, or forces simply as the "environment," recognizing, as we use the term, that there is no precise agreement among writers or management practitioners about its meaning.[14]

---

[11] Ludwig von Bertalanffy, "The Theory of Open Systems in Physics and Biology," *Science,* vol. 3 (January 1950), pp. 23–29. This reference to von Bertalanffy is noted in Dennis S. Mileti and David F. Gillespie, "An Integrated Formalization of Organization-Environment Interdependencies," *Human Relations,* vol. 29, no. 1 (1976), pp. 85–86.

[12] William R. Dill, "Environment as an Influence on Managerial Autonomy," *Administrative Science Quarterly,* vol. 2 (March 1958), p. 442.

[13] Fred E. Emery and Eric L. Trist, "The Causal Texture of Organizational Environments," *Human Relations,* vol. 18 (February 1965), pp. 21–32; William M. Evan, "The Organizational Set: Toward a Theory of Interorganizational Relations," in Merlin B. Brinkerhoff and Philip R. Kunz, eds., *Complex Organizations and their Environments* (Dubuque, Iowa: W. C. Brown Company, 1972), pp. 326–40; James D. Thompson, *Organizations in Action* (New York: McGraw-Hill Book Company, 1967).

[14] An example of this point is the way in which technology is viewed. A firm's technology can be viewed as an aspect of the firm's internal environment, as a variable dependent upon the firm's product markets, or as both. See Bernard C. Reimann and Arant R. Negandhi, "Organization Structure and Effectiveness: A Canonical Analysis," in *The Management of Organization Design,* R. H. Kilmann, L. R. Pondy, and D. P. Slevin, eds. (New York: North-Holland, 1976), vol. 2, pp. 192–93.

Two studies

During the 1960s, some studies of organizations were beginning to make the point that different types of environments have an influence on the effectiveness of organizations. Two studies that have had an important impact on thinking about the organization-environment relationship are the Burns and Stalker studies and the Lawrence and Lorsch studies.[15]

Stable and dynamic environments

The Burns and Stalker Studies. These studies examined 20 industrial firms in the United Kingdom. These 20 firms, representing a variety of industries, were operating in both stable and dynamic environments. A "stable environment" is characterized by slow rates of technological and market changes; a "dynamic environment" is characterized by faster rates of change and by greater uncertainty.

Organic and mechanistic

The general finding of the Burns and Stalker studies is that successful firms in stable environments were mechanistic in structure, whereas successful firms in dynamic environments tended to more organic or flexible structures and operational processes. The words "mechanistic" and "organic" have become common adjectives for describing organizations. A mechanistic organization is highly centralized and bureaucratized. It places major emphasis on formalized authority and communication. An organic organization is highly decentralized and flexible. It places major emphasis on influence processes based on competence and expertise.

Central message

The central message of the Burns and Stalker studies is this: Different types of organizational structures and processes can be effective depending upon the nature (stable versus dynamic) of the external environment in which the organization functions. In the words of Burns and Stalker:

> When novelty and unfamiliarity in both market situation and technical information become the accepted order of things, a fundamentally different kind of management system becomes appropriate from that which applies to a relatively stable commercial and technical environment.[16]

Main question, main answer

The Lawrence and Lorsch Studies. These studies raised this question: What kinds of organizations are most effective under different environmental conditions of certainty and uncertainty? The studies concluded with this answer: The most effective organizations are those that approach their environmentally required states of differentiation and integration. This notion of a contingent relationship between an organization's environment and the or-

---

[15] Tom Burns and G. M. Stalker, *The Management of Innovation* (London: Tavistock Publications, 1961); Paul R. Lawrence and Jay W. Lorsch, *Organization and Environment: Managing Differentiation and Integration* (Boston: Harvard University, Graduate School of Business Administration, Division of Research, 1967).

[16] Burns and Stalker, *The Management of Innovation*, p. vii.

ganization's internal functioning is a major source of the phrase "contingency theory of organizations."

Differentiation and integration

"Differentiation" and "integration" have become household words in discussions of the organization-environment relationship. What do they mean? Integration refers to the quality of the state of collaboration that exists among departments or subunits in an organization. Differentiation refers to the functional specialization within an organization and to the attitudinal and behavioral differences resulting from this specialization. Differentiation is the extent to which organization units are different in terms of members' behavior and orientations and the unit's formal practices.

Example

For example, the separation, in a business firm, of marketing and production represents one type of functional specialization. The attitudes and behavior of personnel in each of these two functional specialties will tend to differ by virtue of the demands of the specialty. The Lawrence and Lorsch studies suggest that the most successful firms are those that have the degree of differentiation that is dictated by the degree of certainty-uncertainty and change in the firm's environment. In general, a high degree of uncertainty and change in the environment dictates a high degree of differentiation and integration.

Predispositions

In addition to the contingent relationship between an organization's environment and its internal functioning, more recent work in the Lawrence and Lorsch tradition suggests another contingent variable—predispositions of the members of organizational units.[17] For example, the professionals who make up the research and development unit within an organization may prefer to work under conditions of autonomy, self-control, and ambiguity. Such professionals may be more productive and obtain more satisfaction in an organization design characterized by few rules, loose supervision, and infrequent evaluations by superiors. Conversely, the personnel who work in a production unit within the same organization may prefer more direction and job clarity and may desire closer working relationships with peers. Such personnel may be more productive and satisfied in an organization design characterized by greater formality, closer supervision, and more frequent performance appraisals. Thus, the most appropriate design for these two organizational units—research and development, and production—may be different because of the different predispositions of the members of the units. The most appropriate organization design, therefore, is contingently related to predispositions of members *and* to environmental factors.[18]

---

[17] Jay W. Lorsch and John J. Morse, *Organizations and Their Members: A Contingency Approach* (New York: Harper & Row, Publishers, 1974).

[18] Jay W. Lorsch, "Contingency Theory and Organization Design: A Personal Odyssey," in *Management of Organization Design*, vol. I, R. H. Kilmann, L. R. Pondy, and D. P. Slevin, eds. (New York: North-Holland, 1976), p. 143.

Major contribution

The Lawrence and Lorsch studies have generated a significant amount of interest, support, and criticism.[19] In describing their original study, Lawrence and Lorsch had this to say:

> The major contribution of this study is not the identification of any "type" of organization that seems to be effective under a particular set of conditions. Rather, it is the increased understanding of a complex set of interrelationships among internal organizational states and processes and external environmental demands.[20]

Summary box

> The organization–environment relationship was generally ignored by most of the *foundations of contemporary thought* about organizations that were discussed in Chapter 14. The idea of an organization as an *open system* forces attention on the organization–environment relationship.
>
> In the 1950s, the term *task environment* was coined to refer to the perceived information inputs to an organization that came from external sources. Other terms for the task environment are "organizational set" or "domain" and "transactional environment." All these terms contain the essential idea of environment: a set of conditions, influences, or forces external to an organization that has relevance to the organization's goals and tasks.
>
> In the 1960s, the Burns and Stalker studies concluded that *mechanistic* organizations are most appropriate in stable environments, and *organic* organizations are most appropriate in dynamic environments.
>
> Also in the 1960s, the Lawrence and Lorsch studies concluded that the degree of environmental uncertainty dictates the most appropriate degrees of *differentiation* and *integration* for successful firms.
>
> In the 1970s, the importance of the organization–environment relationship to thinking about organizations is well established. We will discuss three additional aspects of this relationship: the enacted environment; characteristics of environment; and negotiating strategies.

---

[19] For example, see the following four references: Henry Tosi, Ramon Aldag, and Ronald Storey, "On the Measurement of the Environment: An Assessment of the Lawrence and Lorsch Environmental Uncertainty Scale," *Administrative Science Quarterly*, vol. 18, no. 1 (March 1973), pp. 27–36; Richard N. Osborn and James G. Hunt, "Environment and Organizational Effectiveness," *Administrative Science Quarterly*, vol. 19, no. 2 (June 1974), pp. 231–46; H. Kirk Downey and John W. Slocum, "Uncertainty: Measures, Research, and Sources of Variation," *Academy of Management Journal*, vol. 18, no. 3 (September 1975), pp. 562–78; and Thomas H. Dulz, "The Concept of Environmental Uncertainty: Lawrence and Lorsch Revisited," *Proceedings* of the Eastern Academy of Management, 1977, pp. 72–75.

[20] Lawrence and Lorsch, *Organization and Environment: Managing Differentiation and Integration,* p. 133.

Role of .
perception

The Enacted Environment. The task environment of an organization becomes known to organization leaders through their perceptual and attention-focusing processes. "The organization responds only to what it perceives; those things that are not noticed do not affect the organization's decisions and actions." In other words, the *objective reality* of an organization's environment influences the organization's decision makers only to the extent that it is *perceived reality*. In the short run, there may be crucial differences between an organization's objective and perceived environments. These differences ". . . may be tolerable for lengthy periods in many real circumstances."[21]

Reacting
versus
enacting

The term "enacted environment" is sometimes used to refer to the external environment that is perceived by organizational leaders. The term conveys the idea that "the human actor does not *react* to an environment, he enacts it. It is this enacted environment, and nothing else, that is worked upon by the processes of organizing."[22]

Role of
structure and
processes

The idea of enacted environment suggests the important role of the perceptual skills and processes of an organization's leaders. It suggests, for example, that "The same environment one organization perceives as unpredictable, complex, and evanescent, another organization might see as static and easily understood."[23] Additionally, the organization's information acquisition and processing procedures play a critical role in determining what aspects of the environment will be brought to the attention of the organization's leaders. It is reasonable to argue that organic and highly differentiated and integrated organizations (which are more likely to have diverse types of information acquisition and processing procedures) ". . . will be more likely to produce complex, differentiated managerial perceptions of the environment."[24] Thus, the structure and processes of an organization are not only *influenced by* the environment but are also an *influence on* the environment through their impact on the organization's perceptual and attention processes.

Types of
enactment

In order to make the idea of enacted environment more specific, it is useful to identify different types of enactment. One classification includes four types: domain defenders, reluctant reactors,

---

[21] Raymond E. Miles, Charles C. Snow, and Jeffrey Pfeffer, "Organization-Environment: Concepts and Issues," *Industrial Relations,* vol. 13, no. 3 (October 1974), p. 249.

[22] Karl E. Weick, "The Enacted Environment," *The Social Psychology of Organizing* (Reading, Mass.: Addison-Wesley Publishing Company, 1969).

[23] William H. Starbuck, "Organization and Their Environments," in *Handbook of Industrial and Organizational Psychology,* Marvin D. Dunnette, ed. (Chicago: Rand McNally College Publishing Company, 1976), p. 1,080.

[24] Miles, Snow, and Pfeffer, "Organization-Environment: Concepts and Issues," p. 250.

anxious analyzers, and enthusiastic prospectors.[25] "Domain defenders" are organizations whose leaders perceive little change or uncertainty in the environment and who are inclined to make only minor adjustments in organizational structure and processes. "Reluctant reactors" perceive slightly more change and uncertainty and adjust structure and processes when forced to do so by environmental pressures. "Anxious analyzers" perceive still more change and uncertainty and readily adopt structure and process changes previously adopted by competing organizations. "Enthusiastic prospectors" are organizations whose leaders continually perceive change and uncertainty and who initiate responses to environmental trends.

Complexity

Characteristics of Environment. Several characteristics of the environment are examined in discussions of the organization–environment relationship. Three of these characteristics are complexity, change, and uncertainty. "Complexity" refers to the "degree to which an individual or group in an organizational unit must deal with few or many factors that are similar or dissimilar to one another."[26] Complexity is influenced by both the number and similarity of factors and by the environmental location of the factors. In other words, an organization's environment is not monolithic. It is made up of many subenvironments or groups, each of which "presses on" an organization and demands a response.

Change

"Change" refers to the extent to which the major factors that must be considered by an organization or one of its units are perceived to be stable or dynamic. A key element to consider about change is the extent to which it is predictable. Change can be occurring at a very rapid rate but, if it is predictable, it is much easier for an organization to cope with it. Further, an organization may perceive stability in one of its subenvironments (for example, among its customers) and rapid change in another subenvironment (for example, in production technology).

Uncertainty

The characteristic of environmental "uncertainty" has received substantial attention ever since the Burns and Stalker and the Lawrence and Lorsch studies. Uncertainty has been referred to as the "central concept" in the examination of the organization–environment relationship. Although some objective measures of uncertainty are available, it is *perceived* environmental uncertainty that receives most attention. Attempts to measure perceived environmental uncertainty have focused on such dimensions as: lack of clarity of information; uncertainty of causal relationships; time span of environmental feedback about results; lack of knowledge of the consequences of an incorrect decision; and the lack of suffi-

[25] Ibid., p. 257.

[26] Don Hellriegel and John W. Slocum, Jr., *Organizational Behavior: Contingency Views* (St. Paul, Minn.: West Publishing Company, 1976), p. 63.

cient knowledge to estimate the impact of environmental forces on organizational effectiveness.[27]

Competition and coalitions

Negotiating Strategies. Leaders of organizations use a variety of strategies in dealing with their enacted task environment. These strategies range from competition to coalition.[28] "Competition" is a strategy that is least costly to the organization in terms of the organization's control over decisions. When a business firm competes with another firm, it does not give up any of its control over decision making in the firm. On the other hand, "coalitions" such as mergers and consolidations, are very costly ways for an organization to adapt to an environmental force. When a business firm merges with another firm, the decision-making processes in both firms are fundamentally altered.[29]

Contracting

Between competition and coalition, organizations can choose negotiating strategies that vary in cost as measured by control over decision making. For example, if suppliers are a major source of environmental uncertainty, "contracting" can be a useful strategy. A long-term contract with a supplier reduces uncertainty for both parties. As a result of the contract, the supplier is better able to predict sales demand and the customer organization is assured of an adequate supply of the contracted item. In terms of decision making autonomy, "Contracts represent relatively small reductions in the autonomy of the organizations involved."[30]

Co-optation

Another negotiating strategy that lies between competition and coalition is "co-optation."[31] In co-optation, representatives of relevant groups in the task environment are placed on boards of directors or given some other role in the decision-making processes of an organization. A good example of co-optation is when a banker is placed on the board of directors of a business firm so as to reduce the uncertainty of the firm's access to funds. A similar example is when a member of a minority group is placed on the

[27] Lawrence and Lorsch, *Organization and Environment: Managing Differentiation and Integration,* and Robert Duncan, "Characteristics of Organizational Environments and Perceived Environmental Uncertainty." *Administrative Science Quarterly,* vol. 17 (September 1972), pp. 313–27.

[28] For a more complete discussion of several of these strategies, see Jay R. Galbraith, *Organization Design* (Reading, Mass.: Addison-Wesley Publishing Company, 1977), pp. 204–19; also see James D. Thompson and William J. McEwen, "Organizational Goals and Environment: Goal-Setting as an Interaction Process," *American Sociological Review,* vol. 23 (February 1958), pp. 23–31.

[29] Jeffrey Pfeffer, "Merger as a Response to Organizational Interdependence," *Administrative Science Quarterly,* vol. 17, no. 3 (September 1972), pp. 382–94. Also see Jeffrey Pfeffer and Phillip Nowak, "Joint Ventures and Interorganizational Interdependence," *Administrative Science Quarterly,* vol. 21, no. 3 (September 1976), pp. 398–418.

[30] Orlando Behling and Chester Schiesheim, *Organizational Behavior: Theory, Research, and Application* (Boston: Allyn & Bacon, 1976), p. 359.

[31] Philip Selznick, *TVA and the Grass Roots: A Study in the Sociology of Organization* (Berkeley and Los Angeles: University of California Press, 1949).

board of directors of a business firm. This would allow the minority group member (the co-opted individual) to play a role in a variety of decisions (not just minority-related decisions) made by the business firm's board of directors. Presumably, an organization's managers would use co-optation as a negotiating strategy only after carefully considering the probable benefits resulting from the loss of decision-making autonomy.

Third parties, changing task environment

In addition to competition, coalition, contracting, and co-optation, there are other negotiating strategies available to an organization. For example, an organization can attempt to influence its task environment through the use of ". . . third parties such as trade associations, coordinating groups, or government agencies."[32] Additionally, if an organization finds that it cannot cope with some element of its task environment, the organization can change its task environment. For example, if there is a problem with a supplier of a needed material, the organization can choose to become its own supplier. Thus, the organization would diversify (vertically integrate) its operations and become less dependent on outside sources. Another example of changing the task environment is when a business firm drops a particular product line that is not making a sufficient contribution to the firm's profitability.

Summary box

> The *enacted environment* refers to the external environment of an organization that is perceived through the perceptual and attention-focusing processes of organizational leaders. One classification of types of enactment includes: domain defenders; reluctant reactors; anxious analyzers; and enthusiastic prospectors.
>
> Three *characteristics* of the environment that are important to the organization–environment relationship are complexity, change, and uncertainty. Uncertainty has been referred to as the *central concept* in the examination of the organization–environment relationship.
>
> Several *negotiating strategies* that an organization can use in dealing with its environment are: competition; coalition; contracting; co-optation; third parties; and changing the task environment.

THE ORGANIZATION–TECHNOLOGY RELATIONSHIP

McDonald's and Cadillac

Introduction. There is no reason to be turned off by the word "technology." Whenever there are people at work there is a tech-

---

[32] Miles, Snow, and Pfeffer, "Organization-Environment: Concepts and Issues," p. 251.

nology supporting their job performance. When you walk into a McDonald's, you see people working with a technology. Part of this technology includes hamburger grills, french-frying pans, cash registers, freezers, warmers, and coffee pots. Less visible but still part of McDonald's technology, are the organizational policies and work procedures that guide job behavior, the state of knowledge guiding the operations of the firm, and the decision-making processes that are utilized. When you walk into a Cadillac automobile assembly plant, you see people working with a different technology—conveyor belts, automated equipment, pulleys, and so on. Complementing these physical aspects of technology is an elaborate technology of goals, policies, procedures, job methods, information, and information-communication processes.[33]

Definition

At both McDonald's and the Cadillac plant, you see part of a socio-technical system—people and technology interacting and influencing each other. "Technology" may be defined as "the types and patterns of activity, equipment and material, and knowledge or experience used to perform tasks."[34] A key idea to pick up here is that technology is more than the physical dimensions of a work environment.

Technology and behavior

There are two reasons why technology is of particular interest to managers and students of managing. One reason is that technology directly influences the attitudes and behavior of *individuals* at work. The classic case of this type of influence is the assembly line—"the classic symbol of the subjection of man to machine in our industrial age."[35] The assembly line—with its mechanically set conveyor belt; its work methods and motions predetermined by individuals other than the worker; and its highly restricted opportunities for workers to engage in social interaction—is the prime example of a technology that contributes to feelings of alienation, frustration, and boredom for many (but not all) workers.[36]

Technology and organization

In addition to the influence of technology on individual behavior, there is a second reason for managerial interest in technology. Technology can be a variable influencing the formal structure of an organization. One view is that technology is the preeminent, independent variable that causes an organization to be structured and operated in a certain way. This view is sometimes referred to

---

[33] Although there are clear differences in the technology supporting a McDonald's and a Cadillac assembly plant, there are also similarities. Both operations produce a large volume of a standardized product. Both are examples of mass-production technology.

[34] David F. Gillespie and Dennis S. Mileti, "Technology and the Study of Organizations: An Overview and Appraisal," *Academy of Management Review*, vol. 2, no. 1 (January 1977), p. 8.

[35] Charles R. Walker and Robert H. Guest, *The Man on the Assembly Line* (Cambridge, Mass.: Harvard University Press, 1952).

[36] Jerome Abarbanel, *Redefining the Environment: Behavior and the Physical Setting* (Ithaca, N.Y.: Cornell University, New York State School of Industrial and Labor Relations, 1972), pp. 3–5.

as "technological determinism." A less extreme view is that technology can both influence the organization and be influenced by the organization. That is what we mean by the phrase "organization–technology relationship." This relationship was first brought into focus by the Woodward studies.

Three types of production technology

The Woodward Studies.[37]   Joan Woodward and her colleagues studied 100 small manufacturing and processing firms in southeast England. They classified the production technologies of most of the firms into three categories: (A) small batch and unit production; (B) large batch and mass production; and (C) process production. (See Figure 15–2.) Within each category, different de-

FIGURE 15–2
Woodward's Classification of Production Systems

Classification Category	Degree of Technical Complexity	Description
A. Small batch and unit production	I	Production of simple units to customers' requirements
	II	Production of technically complex units
	III	Fabrication of large equipment in stages
	IV	Production of small batches
B. Large batch and mass production	V	Production of large batches
	VI	Production of large batches on assembly lines
	VII	Mass production
C. Process production	VIII	Intermittent production of chemicals in batches
	IX	Continuous-flow production of liquids, gases, and crystalline substances

Source: Joan Woodward, *Industrial Organization: Theory and Practice* (London: Oxford University Press, 1965).

grees of technical complexity were identified. "Technical complexity" is "the extent to which the production process is controllable and its results predictable."[38] The least technically complex production system was included in Category A. It is a system for the production of simple units to the customers' requirements. The most technically complex system was included in Category C. It is a continuous-flow production process for liquids, gases, and crystalline substances.

Relation of technology to structure

Woodward gathered information about the organization of the 100 firms and then related the information to the type of production system. In general, Woodward found that there were definite

[37] Joan Woodward, *Industrial Organization: Theory and Practice* (London: Oxford University Press, 1965).

[38] Joan Woodward, *Management and Technology* (London: H.M. Stationary Office, 1958), p. 12.

relationships between structure and technical demands. More specifically, Woodward found that those firms employing large batch and mass production technologies (category B—midrange technical complexity) were characterized by *mechanistic* organization structure and processes. Conversely, firms employing small batch and unit production technologies (category A—low technical complexity), and firms employing process production technologies (category C—high technical complexity) were characterized by *organic* organization structures and processes. (Recall our use of the terms "mechanistic" and "organic" in discussion of the Burns and Stalker studies.)

Relation of structure to success

In addition, the Woodward studies found that the successful firms included in the "large batch and mass production category" tended to have *mechanistic* structures and processes. In the other two categories, the successful firms tended to have *organic* structure and processes. Thus, Woodward found a relation not only between technology and organization structure and processes, but also a relation between structure and success.

Significance

What is the broader significance of the Woodward studies for the study of organizations? It is that they were the first major studies to focus on the organization–technology relationship. As such, they have been influential in directing attention to the role of technology. They have led to other studies which have increased understanding of how technology affects organization. For example, one study concludes that the effect of technology on an organization is influenced by the *size* of the organization—the smaller the organization, the more crucial technology will be to organization structure.[39]

Practical value

From the viewpoint of individual managers or potential managers (like yourself), what is the practical value of studies of the organization–technology relationship? What contribution can knowledge gained from these studies make to improving managerial and organizational effectiveness? In our opinion, these studies say several things to managers: The technology used in your area of accountability can be having an effect on job performance. Technology can directly influence job performance by its effect on the form and processes of an organization. In short, technology can be a major causal variable influencing the behavior of people at work. These people, in turn, can influence technology. It is the interactive relationship between people and technology that is captured by the term *socio-technical system*.

39 D. J. Hickson, D. S. Pugh, and D. C. Pheysey, "Operations Technology and Organizational Structure: An Empirical Reappraisal," *Administrative Science Quarterly*, vol. 14, no. 3 (September 1969), pp. 378–97.

Summary box

> *Technology* refers to the types and patterns of activity, equipment and materials, and knowledge or experience used to perform tasks. Technology can directly influence *individual* behavior, and it can influence the formal structure and processes of an *organization*. The latter type of influence is discussed in this chapter.
>
> The *Woodward studies* demonstrated that there can be a relationship between the type of production technology used in a small manufacturing firm and the type of organizational system (mechanistic versus organic) used in the firm. Additionally, the Woodward studies found a relation between type of organizational system and business success.

ORGANIZATIONAL CLIMATE

A new term

During the past 10 to 15 years, a new term, "organizational climate," has been used with increasing frequency to identify a variable that may be related to organizational effectiveness. It has been referred to as "One of the most important but least understood concepts in management."[40] The importance to management of the concept of organizational climate derives from its power to ". . . pull together a lot of experiences that make up the overall 'feel' of a place. Climate is only *one* way of looking at a system and its effects on its members and itself."[41]

Contingent variable

We can place organizational climate within the context of this chapter by noting that climate can be a *contingent variable*. That is, just as external environment and technology can be contingent variables affecting the most appropriate form and processes of an organization, so to can climate be a contingent variable. Further, all three of these variables can be interrelated. Presumably, the concept of organizational climate plays some role in furthering our understanding of the need to match organizations and their members with the demands of the organization's tasks.

Definition

What Is Organizational Climate? Organizational climate refers to a descriptive perception of a set of attributes of a work environment. Let's examine three key words in this definition of organizational climate: "descriptive," "perception," and "attributes."

---

[40] Don Hellriegel and John W. Slocum, Jr., "Organizational Climate: Measures, Research and Contingencies," *Academy of Management Journal*, vol. 17, no. 2 (June 1974), p. 255.

[41] Fritz Steele and Stephen Jenks, *The Feel of the Work Place: Understanding and Improving Organization Climate* (Reading, Mass.: Addison-Wesley Publishing Company, 1977), p. vi.

Descriptive

First, organizational climate is a descriptive perception of attributes of a work environment. That is, the perception is not evaluative of the work environment, but simply describes what a member of the work environment perceives the environment to be. For example, a statement that might be used to measure climate is, "I have a high degree of autonomy in my job." An evaluative statement dealing with the same topic is, "I do not like the degree of autonomy I have on my job." The former statement attempts to describe reality as perceived by the member of the organization. The latter statement evaluates perceived reality against the member's internal needs, values, attributes, and motivations. The former statement is a measure of organizational climate; the latter statement is a measure of job satisfaction.[42]

Perception

Second, organizational climate is a descriptive perception. This means that climate is subject to all the complexities of perceptual processes. It means that the same set of objective attributes can be perceived by different organization members as reflecting different climates. Thus, climate is dependent not only on objective attributes of a work environment, but also on the interacting effects of those attributes with the perceptions and personalities of individual organization members.[43] This does not mean that it is impossible to get some consensus about the climate within an organization. It does mean, however, that care must be taken in generalizing a particular view of climate to all organization members. A given organization or work environment can have multiple climates, and these climates can change as fast as the perceptions of organization members can change.

Attributes

Third, organizational climate is a descriptive perception of a set of attributes. What attributes, or characteristics, of a work environment are included within organizational climate? What exactly is being perceived in the process of formulating a view of organizational climate? There have been several answers given to those questions over the past few years.[44] However, there is some agreement that the various measures of climate have four factors in common:[45]

---

[42] Benjamin Schneider and Robert A. Snyder, "Some Relationships Between Job Satisfaction and Organizational Climate," *Journal of Applied Psychology,* vol. 60, no. 3 (1975), pp. 318–28.

[43] For further information see H. Russell Johnston, "A New Conceptualization of Source of Organizational Climate," *Administrative Science Quarterly,* vol. 21 (March 1976), pp. 95–103.

[44] For example, see G. H. Litwin and R. A. Stringer, Jr., *Motivation and Organizational Climate* (Boston: Harvard University, Graduate School of Business Administration, Division of Research, 1968), and B. Schneider and C. J. Bartlett, "Individual Differences and Organizational Climate II: Measurement of Organizational Climate by the Multitrait-Multirater Matrix," *Personnel Psychology,* vol. 23 (1970), pp. 493–512.

[45] J. P. Campbell, M. D. Dunnette, E. E. Lawler III, and K. E. Weick, Jr., *Managerial Behavior, Performance, and Effectiveness* (New York: McGraw-Hill Book Company, 1970), pp. 387–403. More recently, these four factors, especially the first two, have been shown to be consistent with other re-

1. Individual autonomy—the degree of freedom individuals have to be their own boss and to exercise considerable decision-making discretion.
2. Consideration, warmth, and support—the degree to which these dimensions describe the superior-subordinate relationship.
3. The degree of structure imposed upon the position—the degree to which the objectives of, and methods for, the job are established and communicated to individuals by superiors.
4. Reward orientation—the overall reward system in the organization.

Varying importance

The above four factors may be considered as dimensions of a work environment that are commonly included within the concept of organizational climate. Undoubtedly there are other dimensions that could be included. These dimensions can vary in importance in their relative contribution to individual perceptions of organizational climate. For some, individual autonomy may be the most important dimension; for others, reward orientation may be more important. Furthermore, for a particular individual, there is no reason to think that these dimensions are constant in importance: ". . . a climate that is good for a person at one stage of his or her development may not be appropriate for a later one—there is not necessarily a continuing good match between people and climates."[46]

Independent variable

Roles of Climate.[47]   There are several ways that the organizational climate can contribute to understanding of organizations and behavior in organizations. It can be viewed as an independent variable having a potential impact on other variables, such as job performance, job satisfaction, and overall organizational effectiveness. There is, at present, very little evidence that climate is an independent variable in job performance. Climate and job satisfaction are often found to be related to each other but the cause-effect nature of this relationship is not clear.

Dependent variable

Organizational climate can be viewed as a dependent variable. For example, perceptions of climate have been found to vary among employees at different levels in an organization. Thus, climate is dependent upon position level in the organization. Climate perceptions also have been found to depend on perceptions of the presence of rules and regulations governing behavior. For exam-

search. See H. P. Sims, Jr. and W. LaFollette, "An Assessment of the Litwin and Stringer Organizational Climate Questionnaire," *Personnel Psychology*, vol. 28, pp. 19–38.

[46] Steele and Jenks, *The Feel of the Work Place: Understanding and Improving Organization Climate*, p. 3.

[47] This section is based on Hellriegel and Slocum, "Organizational Climate: Measures, Research, and Contingencies," pp. 263–76. Also see Gary Dessler, *Organization and Management: A Contingency Approach* (Englewood Cliffs, N.J.: Prentice-Hall, 1976), pp. 187–95.

ple, the presence of large numbers of rules and regulations has been shown to contribute to a perception of climate as "closed."

Intervening variable

Organizational climate has been viewed as an intervening variable that moderates the impact of independent variables (such as the leadership style of a key executive) on dependent variables (such as job performance and job satisfaction. For example, one study experimentally controlled three leadership styles—authoritarian, democratic-friendly, and achievement-oriented.[48] Each of these styles had the effect of creating different organizational climates which, in turn, had different impacts on performance and satisfaction. The "achieving climate" was associated with higher productivity. The "democratic-friendly climate" was associated with higher job satisfaction.

Summary box

> *Organizational climate* is one way of looking at an organization and its effect on its members and itself. It may be viewed as a contingent variable—a descriptive perception of a set of *attributes* of a work environment. Four attributes or factors that are commonly included within organizational climate are: individual autonomy; consideration, warmth, and support; the degree of structure imposed upon job positions; and reward orientation.
>
> In its role of contributing to understanding of organizations and of behavior in organizations, organizational climate can be viewed as an independent, dependent, or intervening variable.

CHECK YOUR UNDERSTANDING

The Organization as a System
  General Systems Theory
  System
  Analysis and synthesis
  Synergism
  Closed and open systems
  System boundaries
  System elements
  Generic subsystems
  System characteristics
  Negative entropy
  Equifinality
The Organization–Environment
  Relationship
  Internal and external dynamics

Lawrence and Lorsch studies
Differentiation
Integration
Enacted environment
Domain defenders
Reluctant reactors
Anxious analyzers
Enthusiastic prospectors
Characteristics of environment
Negotiating strategies
The Organization–Technology Relationship
  Technology
  Technological determinism
  The Woodward studies

[48] Litwin and Stringer, *Motivation and Organizational Climate.*

Task environment
Transactional environment
Organizational set
Organizational domain
Burns and Stalker studies
Mechanistic organization
Organic organization

Types of production tech-
    nologies
Organizational climate
    Attributes of organizational
    climate
    Roles of climate

STUDY QUESTIONS

1. What are some criteria that managers might use in identifying boundaries of systems for which they are accountable?

2. Explain: The problem of identifying system boundaries is resolved by drawing an essentially, but not totally, arbitrary distinction between those elements that will be considered inside and outside of the system.

3. What are some alternative views of the interacting elements that make up an organizational system?

4. Identify some specific activities within a business firm that are illustrative of each of the five generic subsystems of an open system.

5. Discuss: It is reasonable to argue that organic and highly differentiated and integrated organizations will be more likely to produce complex, differentiated managerial perceptions of the environment.

6. What is the external environment of the accounting department within a large manufacturing firm? How could the manager of that department utilize the ideas of differentiation and integration?

7. Identify examples of each of the negotiating strategies noted in the text and distinguish them in terms of their decision-making control cost.

8. What is the difference, in your opinion, between measures of organizational climate and measures of job satisfaction? What is the difference between measures of climate and measures of the "structure" of an organization?

APPLICATION: ORGANIZATIONAL CLIMATE*

Sullair Corporation is a small (under 700 employees) business firm located in Michigan City, Indiana. Sullair manufactures rotary-screw air compressors for the construction industry. It appears to be performing that basic function in a very profitable manner. Between 1972 and 1975, Sullair's sales tripled to $49 million and its net income more than doubled during the same period. Although Sullair's economic performance may have its ups and downs (the construction industry is not known for its pre-

---

* Information for this application was acquired from several sources, but primarily from Morris S. Thompson, "Sullair's Chief Stresses Fringe Benefits with Apparent Success," *The Wall Street Journal*, July 7, 1976.

dictability and certainty), the company has already made a name for itself because of its unusual management practices and organizational climate.

Chapter 15 identified four attributes that are commonly associated with the notion of organizational climate: individual autonomy; reward orientations; structure; and consideration, warmth, and support. Evidence of individual autonomy at Sullair is easy to find. Workers at the plant are given a high degree of flexibility in choosing their own work schedules and job duties. For example, most workers are on a four-day–10-hour per day work week but others are on a traditional schedule or a three-day–13-hr per day schedule. In addition, with the agreement of one of the two plant supervisors, workers can, within limits, rotate from one job to another. Workers are also personally responsible for the inspection of their own work.

Sullair minimizes organizational and other forms of structure. The president of Sullair, Donald C. Hoodes, feels that "most plants are overorganized, overmanaged, and too grim." Consequently, Sullair has no foremen, no timeclocks, no formal inspection process, and no personnel department.

Rewards at Sullair are diverse and generous. Production workers earn average wages, but fringe benefits for all workers are equal to about 27 percent of base pay, or about $2,600 per employee. These benefits include, among other things, fully paid insurance (life, health, dental, and hospitalization) and stock-ownership and profit-sharing plans. There is no formal pension plan. Only one employee has retired, and the company informally pays him a pension and continues his benefits.

An indication of a climate characterized by consideration, warmth, and support can be found in the remark of an employee who quit and came back to Sullair: "I went to work at a steel mill, but I was just a number there." At Sullair, employees must be more than a number. In addition to the autonomy and responsibility that characterize their jobs, employees have a variety of amenities available to them: an olympic-size swimming pool, tennis courts, free swimming and tennis lessons, a basketball court, sauna, squash courts, three-course meals at the company's Cafe' La Bastille for 80 cents, gasoline at reduced rates, 10 percent supermarket discounts, school tuition grants, and a company pub "with free booze at 4 P.M."

Absenteeism at Sullair is near zero. Turnover is way below industry standards. Commenting on Sullair's approach, Mr. Hoodes says, "Eat, drink, and make money. . . . You can't ask men who are graduated from high school or college to follow arbitrary rules. You can't run an overorganized or overdisciplined company in this, or maybe any other country."

What do you think the odds are that the organizational climate of Sullair Corporation might be possible in larger business organizations? Discuss.

Objectives of Chapter 16

- To identify the meaning and basic problem of organization design.
- To emphasize the point that an organization design cannot be completely visualized.
- To illustrate several types of organization charts.
- To introduce and discuss several aspects of the design and grouping of jobs in an organization.

Outline of Chapter 16

16

DESIGNING AND GROUPING OF JOBS

The right structure does not guarantee results. But the wrong structure aborts results and smothers even the best-directed efforts.

Peter F. Drucker

If you have a Mickey Mouse job and you put a good man in it, the odds are that you will wind up with a Mickey Mouse man.

Business Week

INTRODUCTION

Working relationships

What Is Organization Design? The *design* or *structure* of an organization is the relatively stable set of formally defined working relationships among the members of the organization. The way in which these relationships are defined answers questions such as: Who reports to whom? How will work be divided? How will it be grouped? How tightly will job specifications be defined? How many subordinates will report to a single manager? How will organization members communicate with each other? The way in which these questions are answered can have an important influence on overall managerial and organizational effectiveness.

All organizations have a design

At the beginning of a discussion of organization design, it is useful to point out that all organizations have a design. This is true, regardless of the size and complexity of the organization. Organizations ranging from giant corporations doing business throughout the world to "Mom and Pop" convenience stores have an organization design. The design problem is one that must be resolved by all organizations. It may be resolved in a very informal, unplanned, almost unconscious way, as in most small organizations. Or, it may be resolved by means of an ongoing, deliberate, knowledge and experience-supported process, as in many large and medium-size firms.

507

From the
chief executive
officer (CEO)
to supervisors

Keep in mind that when we use the term "organization design," we are not referring only to the design of total organizations such as American Telephone and Telegraph, General Motors, or International Business Machines. True, these are organizations on a grand scale, and they each have a design. In each of these business firms, however, there may be hundreds of organization designs—one for each area of managerial accountability. In short, all managers have organization design problems. When you are the CEO, your design problem encompasses the total organization; when you are a supervisor, your design problem encompasses that part of the total organization for which you have performance accountability. In both cases, and in all cases inbetween, organization design problems are present.

Goal
achievement

The Basic Problem.   The basic problem of organization design is to find that set of patterned, interacting relationships among organization members that will assure the achievement of goals efficiently and effectively. This emphasis on goal achievement is implied by Peter F. Drucker when he says that organization design should be results-oriented: "Above all, the structure has to be such that it highlights the results that are truly meaningful; that is, the results that are relevant to the idea of the business, its excellence, its priorities, and its opportunities."[1]

Continuing
problem

Designing organizations is a continuing problem for managers. It is unrealistic to think of an organization's design as permanent. Rather, managers need to continually appraise the relevance of an organization design to the organization's goals and to its environment. For example, in Chapter 15 we discussed the Lawrence and Lorsch studies. In those studies, the most successful business firms were those with organization designs most appropriate (as measured by degree of differentiation and integration) to their environment. When environments are characterized by change, complexity, and uncertainty, there is a continual need for reappraising and revising organization designs.

Emphasis on
formal
dimension

This chapter concentrates on the "formal" dimension of organization design. In Chapter 14, we observed that every real organization is made up of both a formal and an informal dimension (or organization). The formal and informal organizations can be analyzed separately, but they combine in reality to make up "the organization." Managers do not "design" the *informal* organization. They may wish they could design it. They do, in fact, have some influence on the informal organization because it evolves out of the formal organization—another reason why the formal organization design is so important.

---

[1] Peter F. Drucker, *Managing by Results* (New York: Harper & Row, Publishers, 1964), p. 216.

This chapter

This is the first of two chapters on designing organizations. In this chapter we will consider two major aspects of the basic problem of designing organizations: designing jobs, and grouping jobs. But first we emphasize that an organization design cannot be completely visualized.

Organization charts

Visualizing Organization Designs. Organization designs exist, but they cannot be completely visualized. You do not actually *see* an organization design. Some possible *shapes* of organization designs are shown in organization charts such as those in Figure 16–1. The "pyramid with positions" and the "matrix" shapes will be further illustrated later in this chapter. The "linking pin" shape is supposed to reflect the idea that managers at one level serve as the link between effective work groups at that level and the next higher level. The "wheel" shape of organization design places the top managers in the middle of the wheel, and the "pyramid" shape places the top managers at the peak of the pyramid. The symbolism here is that in the wheel, organization members move "out" from the center. In the pyramid, organization members move "down" from the top; they are subordinates and lower-level managers.

Eisenhower, Nixon, and Carter

Recently the organization of the White House staffs of Presidents Eisenhower, Nixon, and Carter were compared. Whereas the Eisenhower and Nixon staffs reportedly were pyramidal in their organization, Carter's staff was described in terms of a wheel in which "The President is the hub and his top assistants are the spokes—equally positioned, in theory, to feed the boss with information and advice from many quarters."[2]

Reality of designs

Organization charts are simply attempts to show in a visual way the reality of organization design. The reality, however, is in the actual relationships among people in the organization, and it cannot be shown fully through any visual aid. The actual design of an organization can be understood only through the *behavior* that defines and characterizes the relationships between organization members. These relationships cannot be fully comprehended by drawing a line between two boxes on an organization chart. Even the organizational chart shown in Figure 16–2 does not tell the whole organization design story.

---

[2] "How Jimmy's Staff Operates," *Time,* April 25, 1977, pp. 21–22.

FIGURE 16–1
Selected Shapes of Organization Designs as Shown by Organization Charts

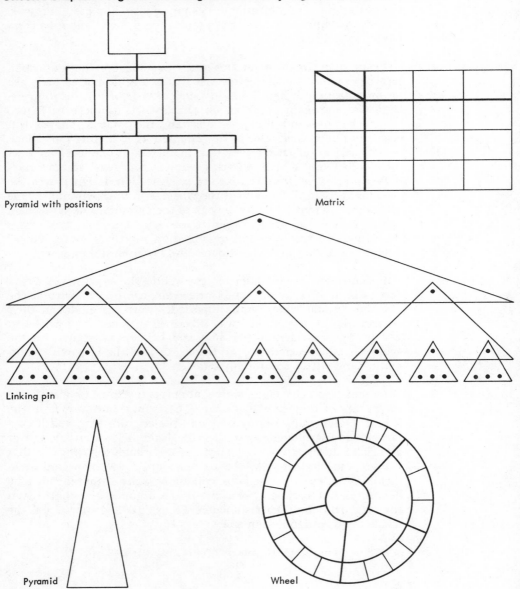

Pyramid with positions

Matrix

Linking pin

Pyramid

Wheel

FIGURE 16–2
Organizational Chart

Summary box

> The *design* or *structure* of an organization is the rela-
> tively stable set of formally defined working relationships
> among the members of the organization. Every real organi-
> zation is made up of both a formal and an informal dimen-
> sion (or organization). This chapter concentrates on the
> formal dimension.
>
> The *basic problem* of organization design is to find that
> set of patterned, interacting relationships between and
> among organization members that will assure the achieve-
> ment of goals efficiently and effectively. Designing organi-
> zations is a *continuing problem* for managers.
>
> Organization designs cannot be completely visualized.
> Organization *charts* are attempts to show schematically
> the reality of organization design. However, the reality
> itself is in the behavior that defines and characterizes the
> relationships between organization members.

DESIGNING JOBS

*First logical
step*

Introduction.   Given a system of performance, group, and individual goals to accomplish, the first logical step in designing an
organization is to define tasks and jobs that are essential to accomplishing the goals. Every organization design requires that work
be divided into specific jobs—otherwise there is no organization
problem. The total work to be done needs to be divided into jobs
because of physical and mental limitations of human beings and
because of the demands for efficiency and effectiveness.

*Division
of labor*

On the one hand, efficiency results from division of labor because it allows for specialization of effort and the easier acquisition of job skills because less learning is required. On the other
hand, dividing work into units that are too small can lead to inefficiency and ineffectiveness for a variety of reasons, including
lack of challenge and interest in jobs, increased problems of coordination between jobs, idle time when volume of work is insufficient for specialized jobs, and inflexibility of employees' work skills.

*Trial-and-
error
methods*

There are several processes used in organizations to divide the
total work to be done into separate jobs. Often these processes are
very loose and unsystematic. A manager might decide that a jobholder has too much work to do. Another person is hired in order
to "help" the overworked jobholder. Gradually, through a process
of trial-and-error, a new full-time job is created for the recently
hired employee. The new job may consist of parts of other jobs
plus additional duties.

Job analysis

Sometimes a more systematic process is used in order to identify a set of duties known as a job. "Job analysis" is such a process. Job analysis identifies required tasks and responsibilities, determines necessary qualifications of the jobholder, and identifies authority-accountability relationships relevant to the job. Methods that might be used in performing a job analysis include: (1) examining previous job analyses of the position; (2) observing the behavior of the present incumbent; (3) interviewing the job incumbent, the supervisor, and others who have some contact with the position; (4) having the incumbent fill out a questionnaire or keep a diary of critical incidents that occur on the job; and (5) using job analysis specialists to systematically determine job duties.[3]

Job descriptions and specifications

Very often in large government, educational, and business organizations, the duties of jobholders are put in writing. Forms called "job descriptions" and "job specifications" may be used for communicating to jobholders what their duties are. In addition, these forms may be useful in the "job evaluation" process (the process of determining a compensation plan for employees of an organization), in training, in performance appraisal, and in personnel selection and recruitment.[4]

Use of job descriptions

Although job descriptions are sometimes prepared for top managerial positions, they most often are used for supervisory, clerical or operative jobs. Job descriptions can be worthless if they are not kept current, are based on inappropriate job-analysis methods, or written in general and meaningless phrases.[5] However, if they are prepared in a professional manner, are one part of an integrated personnel system, and are kept current, they can be a useful managerial tool. Furthermore, carefully prepared job descriptions may be necessary in order to satisfy federal equal employment opportunity guidelines for valid personnel selection tests.[6]

Job scope

Two Job Dimensions. The division of work into a specific job requires the identification of two job dimensions: job scope and depth.[7] "Job scope" refers to the number of different operations performed by the worker and to the frequency of repetition of the job cycle. A "wide job scope" means that the person holding the job performs a large number of different operations and repeats

---

[3] William F. Glueck, *Personnel: A Diagnostic Approach* (Dallas: Business Publications, 1974), p. 113.

[4] Job analysis and job evaluation are usually discussed in books about personnel management. They are outside of the scope of this book.

[5] Donald E. Britton, "Are Job Descriptions Really Necessary?" *Personnel Administrator*, vol. 20, no. 1 (January 1975), pp. 47–49.

[6] Craig Eric Schneier, "Content Validity: The Necessity of a Behavioral Job Description," *Personnel Administrator*, vol. 21, no. 2 (February 1976), pp. 38–44.

[7] Alan C. Filley, Robert J. House, and Steven Kerr, *Managerial Process and Organizational Behavior*, 2d ed. (Glenview, Ill.: Scott, Foresman and Company, 1976), pp. 339–40.

the job cycle infrequently. Conversely, a "narrow job scope" means that fewer different operations are performed and the job cycle is repeated frequently.

Job depth

"Job depth" refers to the relative influence workers have over their work environment and the degree to which they can plan and carry out their work under conditions of self control. "Both the same type of job and different jobs can vary in depth. One foreman may have greater job depth than another foreman, and we would expect a foreman's job to have greater depth than an assembly-line worker under his direction."[8]

*The best
job design*

The most appropriate degree of job scope and depth depends on the total set of factors unique to the management and organization. This statement does not provide you with a neat answer to the problems of job design, but it does highlight the importance of avoiding preconceptions about particular job designs being "best." The best job design is one that matches the performance and productivity requirements of a job with the unique needs and values of the jobholder.

*Assembly-line
jobs*

Perhaps the most dramatic illustration of jobs having limited job scope and depth can be found on the assembly line of a mechanized manufacturing operation. One such job that often comes to mind is the assembler of automobiles in a Detroit assembly plant. Such jobs commonly entail few different operations, very frequent repetition of the job cycle, almost no worker influence over the work environment, and literally constant supervision of workers by foremen. Although this type of job is not the typical job of the American worker, it is often used as the example that best exemplifies the frustrations of jobs with narrow scope and depth.

*Costs of
narrow scope
and depth*

In recent years, there has been an increased concern expressed by workers, management writers, executives, and the general public about the "costs" of jobs with extremely narrow depth and scope. Some of these costs include higher production costs, lower quantity and quality of production, alienation of workers, and friction between management and workers. There is also the general cost to society of jobs that are unchallenging, repetitive, and boring —jobs that have had most of their potential for creativity and personal development engineered out of them. The contemporary concern for the costs of jobs with narrow scope and depth has led to interest in job redesign. The thrust of most discussions of job redesign is that jobs should be "enriched."

*What is job
enrichment?*

Job Enrichment.   Job enrichment refers to the process of upgrading, enlarging, or enriching a job by increasing its depth and scope. Sometimes the term "job enlargement" is used as a syno-

---

[8] Ibid., p. 340.

nym for job enrichment.[9] However, when a distinction between the two terms is made, job enlargement refers to an increase in job scope, but "job enrichment" implies at least some increase in job depth.

Horizontal and vertical job loading

Another way of noting the distinction between job enlargement and enrichment is to use terms suggested by Frederick Herzberg. Herzberg refers to an increase in job scope as "horizontal job loading" and to an increase in job depth as "vertical job loading."[10] Job enrichment, or vertical job loading, provides for the jobholder's psychological growth by designing "motivators" (see Supplement 6A) into jobs.

Job enrich-ment logic

The logic behind many attempts to implement job enrichment appears to be based on the following line of reasoning:

1. The design of a job is a major variable influencing the job-holder's satisfaction and performance.

2. There needs to be a match between the kinds of satisfactions and outcomes provided by a job and the satisfactions and outcomes desired or needed by the jobholder. This match is essential in order to sustain high levels of job productivity—the ultimate objective of job design.

3. Most jobholders desire or need from their jobs such things as: a sense of achievement; recognition; increased responsibility; the opportunity to be involved in decision making; and the opportunity for personal and professional growth and development.

4. Therefore, to the extent practical, jobs should be designed and redesigned so as to provide the above job outcomes. Presumably, these job outcomes will lead to improved employee attitudes—particularly higher levels of job satisfaction, to greater motivation, and ultimately to improved job performance behavior.

A problem with the logic

Under many circumstances, the above line of reasoning may be valid. However, one problem is that it does not take into account the role of *individual differences*—differences in job knowledge and skills and in needs and goals. The problem is in generalizing about what outcomes employees want from their jobs.[11] Not all employees

---

[9] William E. Reif and Fred Luthans, "Does Job Enrichment Really Pay Off?" *California Management Review*, vol. 15, no. 1 (Fall 1972), p. 30.

[10] Frederick Herzberg, "One More Time: How Do You Motivate Employees," *Harvard Business Review*, vol. 46, no. 1 (January–February 1968), pp. 53–62.

[11] Charles L. Hulin, "Individual Differences and Job Enrichment: The Case against General Treatments," in J. R. Maher, ed., *New Perspectives in Job Enrichment* (New York: Van Nostrand Reinhold Company, 1971).

want their jobs enriched.[12] Not all want a high degree of involvement with their job.[13] Job enrichment can place demands on workers to change their behavior, to alter their social relationships, to work harder, and to become more involved in their jobs. Perhaps for the majority of workers these demands are too much to ask, and the rewards of meeting the demands too marginal *from their viewpoint.*

> The introduction of a job enrichment program may have a negative impact on some workers and result in feelings of inadequacy, fear of failure, and a concern for dependency. For these employees, low level competency, security, and relative independence are more important than the opportunity for greater responsibility and personal growth in enriched jobs.[14]

Example of role of individual differences

One dimension on which employees differ is their degree of acceptance and internalization of the work norms and values of the middle class. Such norms and values include ". . . positive affect for occupational achievement, a belief in the intrinsic value of hard work, a striving for the attainment of responsible positions, and a belief in the work-related aspects of Calvinism and the Protestant ethic."[15] The suggestion here is that many blue-collar workers will respond negatively to job enrichment because they are alienated from the specific norms and values implicit in job enrichment.

Beyond individual differences

In addition to the individual differences that characterize employees, there are other factors that will influence the results of job-enrichment efforts. Some of these factors or contingencies may include: (1) the employee's degree of satisfaction with work context variables such as pay, job security, relations with co-workers, relationship with supervisor, and general working conditions;[16] (2) the overall organizational climate, particularly the extent to which it is characterized by trust, support, and consideration; (3) the management philosophy, including attitudes toward change and leadership styles;[17] (4) the nature of the organization–environment relationship, (5) the nature of the organization–technology rela-

[12] Howard R. Smith, "The Half-Loaf of Job Enrichment," *Personnel,* vol. 53, no. 2 (March–April 1976), pp. 24–31.

[13] Job involvement "is the degree to which the person identifies with his job, actively participates in it, and considers his performance important to his self-worth." See S. D. Saleh and James Hosek, "Job Involvement: Concepts and Measurements," *Academy of Management Journal,* vol. 19, no. 2 (June 1976), p. 223.

[14] Reif and Luthans, "Does Job Enrichment Really Pay Off?" p. 36.

[15] Charles L. Hulin and Milton R. Blood, "Job Enlargement, Individual Differences, and Worker Responses," in W. E. Scott, Jr. and L. L. Cummings, eds., *Readings in Organizational Behavior and Human Performance* (Homewood, Ill.: Richard D. Irwin, 1973).

[16] Greg R. Oldham, J. Richard Hackman, and Jone L. Pearce, "Conditions under which Employees Respond Positively to Enriched Work," *Journal of Applied Psychology,* vol. 61, no. 4 (1976), pp. 395–403.

[17] Mitchell Fein, "Job Enrichment: A Reevaluation," *Sloan Management Review,* vol. 15, no. 2 (Winter 1974), p. 85.

tionship;[18] (6) the nature and duties of the job itself;[19] and (7) the particular part of the organization in which the job is located.[20]

Summary box

> Given a system of performance, group, and individual goals, a *logical first step* in organization design is to define tasks and jobs that are essential to accomplishing the goals.
>
> Processes used in organizations to divide the total work to be done range from trial-and-error methods to more systematic approaches such as *job analysis*. Organizations often utilize written *job descriptions* and *job specifications* as part of their efforts to define jobs.
>
> Two basic dimensions of a job are scope and depth. *Job scope* refers to the number of different operations performed by the jobholder and to the frequency of repetition of the job cycle. *Job depth* refers to the relative influence the jobholder has over the work environment and to the degree of self-control in planning and performing the job.
>
> *Job enrichment* refers to the process of upgrading, enlarging, or enriching a job by increasing its depth and scope. Another term for job enrichment is vertical job loading.
>
> A key idea to keep in mind in job-enrichment efforts is *individual differences*. The essence of this idea is that there must be a congruence between job design (scope and depth) and the unique needs and values of the jobholder.
>
> In addition to the role of individual differences, job-enrichment efforts are influenced by other factors or *contingencies* in the work environment.

Need for growth satisfaction

The Job Characteristics Model.[21]   Figure 16–3 summarizes a descriptive job enrichment model. We view the model as a useful way of thinking about several elements of job design. The model is intended as a guide to job design and to job redesign. The first point to make about the model is that it recognizes the role of

[18] Ibid., pp. 75–76.

[19] Eugene F. Stone and Lyman W. Porter, "Job Characteristics and Job Attitudes: A Multivariate Study," *Journal of Applied Psychology,* vol. 60, no. 1 (1975), pp. 57–64.

[20] Randall B. Dunham, "Reactions to Job Characteristics: Moderating Effects of the Organization," *Academy of Management Journal,* vol. 20, no. 1 (March 1977), pp. 42–65.

[21] This section is based on J. Richard Hackman and Greg R. Oldham, "Development of the Job Diagnostic Survey," *Journal of Applied Psychology,* vol. 60, no. 2 (1975), pp. 159–70. For further discussion of this model, see J. Richard Hackman, "Work Design," in *Improving Life at Work: Behavioral Science Approaches to Organizational Change,* J. Richard Hackman and J. Lloyd Suttle, eds. (Santa Monica, Calif.: Goodyear Publishing Company, 1977).

FIGURE 16–3
The Job Characteristics Model

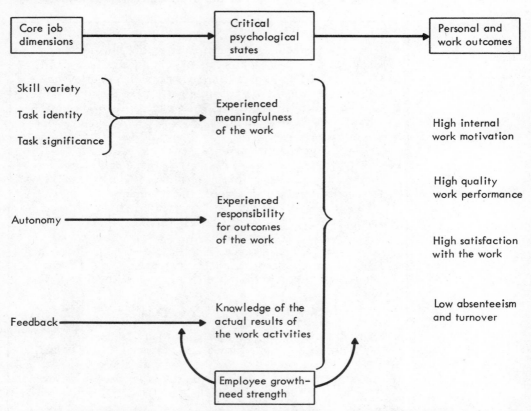

Source: J. Richard Hackman and Greg R. Oldham, "Development of the Job Diagnostic Survey," *Journal of Applied Psychology*, vol. 60, no. 2 (1975), p. 161. Copyright 1975 by the American Psychological Association. Reprinted by permission.

individual differences. Specifically, the model takes into account the moderating role of an individual's desire to obtain *growth satisfaction* from work. In other words, the higher an individual's desire for growth satisfaction, the more positively the individual is assumed to respond to the motivating potential of the job. This is assumed "apparently because high growth need individuals more strongly value the internal rewards that can be obtained from good performance on a challenging task."[22]

Core job dimensions

The motivating potential of the job is seen as depending on five core job dimensions. The "core job dimensions" are: skill variety; task identity; task significance; autonomy; and feedback. An in-

_____
[22] Oldham, Hackman, and Pearce, "Conditions under which Employees Respond Positively to Enriched Work," p. 396.

strument known as the Job Diagnostic Survey (JDS) is used to obtain measures of a jobholder's perception of the degree to which the five core job dimensions characterize the job.[23] These measures are then used to obtain a "motivating potential score."[24] Note that the JDS obtains measures of core job dimensions, and therefore provides a psychological, as opposed to an objective, definition of a job.[25]

Three psychological states, personal outcomes

The JDS also provides measures of three psychological states that the model suggests must be present for a given employee in order for the positive personal outcomes to result.[26] The three psychological states are experienced meaningfulness of the work, experienced responsibility for outcomes of the work, and knowledge of the actual results of the work activities. To the extent the jobholder experiences the three psychological states, the model suggests that personal and work outcomes will be influenced.

The idea

Perspective on Job Enrichment. The idea of enriching jobs is certainly appealing. It is not an idea that one would readily want to argue against. Job enrichment is also an idea that is "in." Hundreds of magazine articles extol the virtues of job enrichment. A few articles even report on job enrichment applications in such business firms as General Foods, General Motors, American Telephone and Telegraph, various firms in Sweden, and others.[27] Recently, some articles have focused on the problems of maintaining job-enrichment programs once they have been initiated.[28]

---

[23] Parallel with the development of the JDS has been the development of the JCI, the Job Characteristic Inventory. The JCI obtains perceptual measures on six core job dimensions—variety, autonomy, task identity, feedback, dealing with others, and friendship opportunities. See Henry P. Sims, Jr., Andrew D. Szilagyi, and Robert T. Keller, "The Measurement of Job Characteristics," *Academy of Management Journal*, vol. 19, no. 2 (June 1976), pp. 195–212.

[24] Motivating Potential Score (MPS) $= \left[\dfrac{\text{Skill Variety} + \text{Task Identity} + \text{Task Significance}}{3} \right] \times \text{Autonomy} \times \text{Feedback}.$

[25] Donald P. Schwab and L. L. Cummings, "A Theoretical Analysis of the Impact of Task Scope on Employee Performance," *Academy of Management Review*, vol. 1, no. 2 (April 1976), pp. 23–35.

[26] The JDS does not measure "work outcomes" such as productivity, turnover, or absenteeism.

[27] Richard E. Walton, "How to Counter Alienation in the Plant," *Harvard Business Review*, vol. 50 no. 6 (November–December 1972), pp. 70–81; "GM Zeroes in on Employee Discontent," *Business Week*, May 12, 1973, p. 142; Robert Janson, "Job Enrichment: Challenge of the 1970s, in Fred Luthans, ed., *Contemporary Readings in Organizational Behavior* (New York: McGraw-Hill Book Company, 1972), pp. 379–85; Richard B. Peterson, "Swedish Experiments in Job Reform," *Business Horizons*, vol. 19, no. 3 (June 1976), pp. 13–22; Ted Mills, "Human Resources: Why the New Concern?" *Harvard Business Review*, vol. 53, no. 2 (March–April 1975), pp. 120–34.

[28] "Stonewalling Plant Democracy," *Business Week*, March 28, 1977, pp. 78–82; and "Battling Boredom," *Wall Street Journal*, Vol. 59, no. 41 (March 1, 1977), pp. 1, 20.

*Job
performance
model*

The contemporary discussion of and experimentation with job enrichment is based on the premise that the design of a job is a major variable influencing the jobholder's satisfaction and performance. How shall we think about this premise? In Chapter 6, a model for understanding an individuals' job performance was discussed. Recall that this model suggests that job performance takes place within a *situational context* and depends on an individual's *abilities and skills, role perceptions,* and *motivation.* Therefore, any discussion of the role of job design on job performance must take into account these four factors.

*Expectancy
theory*

Implicit in most discussions of job enrichment is that the enrichment of a job will alter the motivation of the jobholder. Our discussion (in Chapter 6) of motivation was developed around expectancy theory of motivation and its two basic concepts, expectancy and valence. Therefore, if job enrichment is to affect the motivation of a jobholder, it must do so by influencing valence and expectancy.[29]

Conclusion

In conclusion, our perspective on job enrichment places job enrichment within the context of an overall job performance model, including a particular view of motivation–expectancy theory. This perspective helps one avoid the simplistic assumption that job enrichment necessarily leads to higher levels of job satisfaction and job performance. In addition, this perspective allows one to focus on the ultimate purpose of a job's design. That purpose is to contribute to improved *job performance.*

Summary box

> *The job characteristics model* was outlined. The model takes into account the role of individual differences in the need to obtain growth satisfaction from job performance. The model considers that these differences moderate the relationship between five core job dimensions, three critical psychological states, and various personal and work outcomes.
>
> A useful *perspective* is gained by placing job enrichment within the context of the job-performance model discussed in Chapter 6. This model views job performance in terms of situational context, abilities and skills, role perceptions, and motivation (expectancy and valence). Thus, in evaluating the actual or potential impact of job enrichment, these four factors must be considered.
>
> This chapter has looked on *designing jobs* as the first logical step in designing an organization. Next, we turn to the second logical step, *grouping jobs.*

[29] Schwab and Cummings, "A Theorical Analysis of the Impact of Task Scope on Employee Performance."

GROUPING JOBS

Grouping jobs—de-partmentation

A second step to take in designing organizations, is to group jobs in organizations into larger organizational units called divisions, sections, units, or departments. We will refer to this step as "departmentation" because that is the term widely used in management education. The term applies generally to the process of grouping jobs into some type of organizational unit. It is not limited to those job groupings that lead only to what are commonly thought of as formal departments.

Bases: function, geography

Bases of Departmentation.   The various approaches to departmentation are called "bases of departmentation." The common bases of departmentation are function, geographic area, product (or project or brand), customer, equipment, and process. For example, if a manufacturing plant is organized around the activities of production, marketing, finance, and engineering, it is departmentalized by function. If the marketing activities of a national firm are divided into northern, southern, eastern, and western sales regions, it is departmentalized by geographic area.

Bases: product, customer, equipment, process

The Lincoln-Mercury Division of the Ford Motor Company is an example of departmentation by product. The men's clothing department in a large retail store is departmentation by type of customer. The data-processing department in a business organization is an example of departmentation by equipment and function. An assembly operation in a manufacturing plant is usually organized according to the assembly process. Because of their basic importance in business organizations, we will consider functional and product departmentation in more detail.

Function vs. product

Fundamental Choice.   For many business firms, a fundamental choice in the various bases of departmentation is between the functional and the product bases.[30] The reason this is a fundamental choice is because each of the two bases provides an organization design with a distinct advantage. The choice of one of the bases often means foregoing the advantages of the other. The major advantage of functional departmentation is specialization; the major advantage of product departmentation is coordination: ". . . the real issue managers face is a question of when, as organizations grow, to add a product level of organization to coordinate the functional organization around various products."[31]

[30] Jay R. Galbraith, "Matrix Organization Designs," *Business Horizons,* vol. 14, no. 1 (February 1971), and Arthur H. Walker and Jay W. Lorsch, "Organizational Choice: Product vs. Function," *Harvard Business Review,* vol. 46, no. 6 (November–December 1968), pp. 129–38.

[31] Jay Lorsch, "Contingency Theory and Organization Design: A Personal Odyssey," in Ralph H. Kilman, Louis R. Pondy, and Dennis P. Slevin, eds., *The Management of Organization Design: Strategies and Implementation,* vol. 1 (New York: North-Holland, 1976), p. 149.

Functional de-
partmentation

"Functional departmentation" is the grouping of work based on the nature of the work involved. Those jobs that are similar in nature and purpose tend to be grouped together. Thus, the marketing department in a manufacturing firm may be subdivided and grouped into the marketing-oriented subfunctions of advertising, sales promotion, marketing research, forecasting, and direct sales. The production department may be departmentalized into engineering, maintenance, quality control, production control, inventory control, and direct production work.

Illustration

A simplified functional form of organization design is shown in Figure 16–4. It is *simplified* because it does not show all the functions commonly found in a manufacturing organization—for example, finance and personnel (this incompleteness is shown in Figure 16–4 by the arrows on each end of the horizontal line

FIGURE 16–4
Simplified, Functional Organization Design

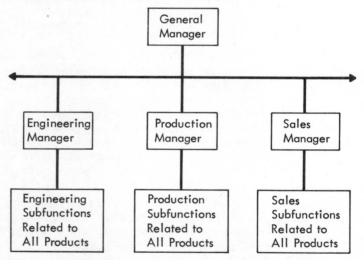

under the general manager). It is *functional* because the basic organization design is developed around the activities of engineering, production, and sales. Each manager is responsible for the performance of the people who work in those subfunctions related to the manager's functional area—engineering, production, or sales. This responsibility relationship is indicated by the solid lines connecting the boxes on the organization chart. The lines tell only that a formal relationship exists. They do not tell anything about the exact nature of that relationship.

Advantages
and
disadvantages

Functional departmentation has some potential advantages. It allows for specialization of skills within functions. Further, it avoids some of the duplication of effort found in other bases of departmentation. For example, establishing a personnel department allows for specialization of skills in the personnel area and also means that those skills do not have to be duplicated elsewhere in the organization. Functional departmentation has some potential disadvantages, including problems of coordination between functions, the development of functional loyalties that may generate conflicts between functions, and the problem of developing executives with cross-functional perspectives.

*Product de-
partmentation*

"Product departmentation" is the grouping of work based on the nature of the product or service to be provided. In general, a business firm will utilize product departmentation when its earlier design, based on functional departmentation, no longer provides the necessary degree of coordination between functions. A simplified product organization design is shown in Figure 16–5.

FIGURE 16–5
Simplified Product Organization Design

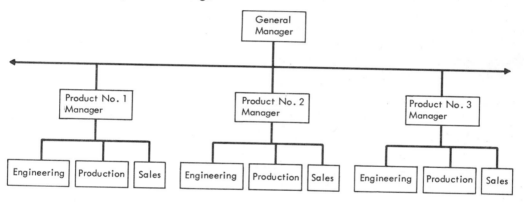

*Advantages
and
disadvantages*

In contrast to functional departmentation, product departmentation facilitates the coordination of effort required to produce the particular product. Further, it assures that most of the work required for the production and distribution of a particular product will be under the supervision of a single manager. This assures clear accountability for all aspects of the product's management. Product departmentation also allows employees to identify with a particular product. On the other hand, product departmentation does not allow for the specialization of skills that is possible under functional departmentation.

*Four factors
to consider
in product–
functional
choice*

Four factors that should be considered in choosing the appropriate degree of product and functional departmentation are:[32]

1. *Diversity of the Product Line.* The more diverse and changing the product line, the more the advantage of product departmentation. When product lines are diverse and products are

[32] Galbraith, "Matrix Organization Designs."

changing frequently, it becomes more difficult for specialized functional managers to keep abreast of the changes and the demands of a multiple product line.

2. *Interdependencies.* The greater the need for coordination between engineering, production, and sales, the more product departmentation suggests itself.

3. *Level of Technology.* The greater the need for expertise and specialized skills, the more likely that a higher degree of functional departmentation is desirable.

4. *Economies of Scale.* Expensive equipment may dictate departmentation around the particular function served by the equipment. The cost of purchasing several pieces of the equipment in order to implement product departmentation may be excessive in comparison to the benefits gained. Organization size is an influence on the choice between product and functional departmentation in the sense that larger organizations are in a better position to absorb some of the costs associated with product departmentation.

Consumer packaged-goods companies

An Illustration—Brands and Markets. An illustration of the organizational choice between product and functional departmentation can be found in organizations that sell a large, diversified line of consumer packaged goods. Examples of such companies include Procter & Gamble (P&G), PepsiCo, Eastman Kodak, Levi Strauss, Lever Brothers, and H. J. Heinz Company. For many years these types of companies have relied on product (or brand) departmentation as the main means of marketing their product line. Procter & Gamble, for example, pioneered the "brand manager" approach to organization design. P&G divides its marketing effort into more than 50 product or brand groups and, according to *Business Week:*

> Each group usually handles one brand and includes a brand manager, assistant brand manager, and one or two brand assistants. The brand manager assigns his two or three assistants broad areas of responsibility, and within a tight framework of checks and balances, they work closely with corporate specialists. . . .
>
> The Tide group, for instance, might want to change its package design. The group would work with the art and package design department on the new design. The sales department would help evaluate how the change might affect shelf space, stacking special displays, and trade reaction. The market research department would probably run some tests. And the manufacturing department would advise on costs and timetables.[33]

Profit accountability

Organization design according to product or brands has worked very well for firms marketing consumer packaged goods. Furthermore, it can effectively pinpoint profit accountability; that is, when competent product or brand managers know they are responsible

---

[33] "The Brand Manager: No Longer King," (June 9, 1973), pp. 59–60.

for all phases of a product, accountability is pinpointed. Functional departmentation, however, would spread this profit accountability among sales, advertising, production, and so forth.

Shift away from brand manager

On the other hand, *Business Week* reports some shifting away from the brand manager approach to organization design in companies where it has been traditional—PepsiCo, Purex, Eastman Kodak, and Levi Strauss. Reasons given for this shift include shorter product life cycles, the introduction of many new products, the need for product decisions to be made at the top levels of the organization in order to take into account broad social and consumer concerns, and the segmentation of markets. Market segmentation is the differentiation of a product's market according to such factors as customers' age, type of customer, income level, customer life-style, and geographic location.[34]

Shift to market departmentation

The shift in organization design away from product or brand management has brought a corresponding shift toward a modern version of functional departmentation. The emphasis is on specialization of skills in planning, finance, distribution, market planning, and economic analysis. Some companies are switching from an emphasis on brands to an emphasis on "markets." For example, Eastman Kodak now has separate profit centers that represent markets such as business systems, consumer products, international operations, motion pictures and education, professional customers, and commercial and industrial markets.

Combining functional and product departmentation

Matrix Organization Designs.   An approach to organization design that attempts to combine the advantages of both functional and product departmentation is the "matrix design." The matrix design is not applicable to routine types of organizational problems; for example, organizing for the high-volume production of a standardized product. "It is when work performed is for specific project contracts that a matrix organization can be used effectively."[35]

Matrix organization charts

Two examples of simplified matrix organization designs are shown in Figures 16–6 and 16–7. Both Figures 16–6 and 16–7 show that the dominant base of departmentation is the functional base—engineering, production, and sales. In theory, this allows for specialization of effort and results in the availability of essential specialized skills. The coordination advantages of product departmentation are achieved in the matrix design through the use of product or service managers. Although the term "product manager" is in common usage in business organizations, the matrix design idea applies as well to managers of services. The concept of a product does not have to be limited to something

---

[34] Ibid.

[35] John F. Mee, "Matrix Organization," *Business Horizons,* vol. 7, no. 2 (Summer 1964), p. 71.

FIGURE 16–6
Simplified Matrix Organization Design

	Functions	Engineering Manager	Production Manager	Sales Manager
Product, Project, or Service				
Product No. 1 Manager		Engineering Personnel	Production Personnel	Sales Personnel
Product No. 2 Manager		Engineering Personnel	Production Personnel	Sales Personnel
Product No. 3 Manager		Engineering Personnel	Production Personnel	Sales Personnel

General Manager

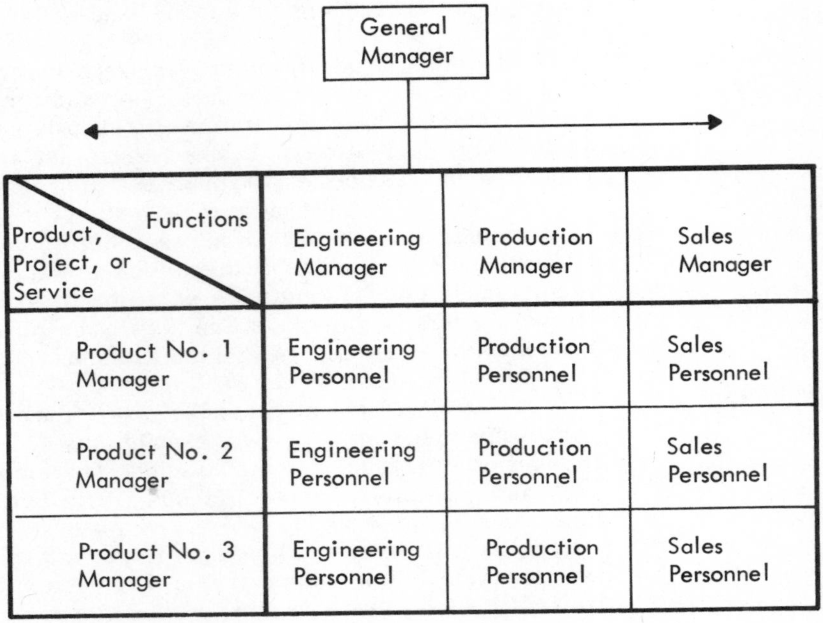

with tangible characteristics. Many organizations that produce and distribute services, especially public organizations, could benefit from a matrix design.

Product managers

These product managers are, in essence, product coordinators with varying degrees of authority over the functional department personnel. Although actual practice varies, the influence of product managers is largely a function of their ability to elicit the active cooperation of functional managers and functional personnel. Of course, the product manager's position is supported by the fact that it is an officially designated part of the formal organization design. Furthermore, the product manager has direct access to the general manager who, in turn, is in a position of authority over the functional departments. Nevertheless, product managers must rely primarily on their personal skills in achieving the necessary coordination to engineer, produce, and sell the products for which they are accountable.

Applying a matrix design

In actual applications of matrix organization designs, it is not unusual for specific personnel in each of the functional departments to be assigned to a particular product manager. In such a case, the functional personnel remain under the authority of the functional manager, but they "receive directly or indirectly from the [product] manager information about what has to be done and

FIGURE 16–7
Simplified Matrix Organization Design

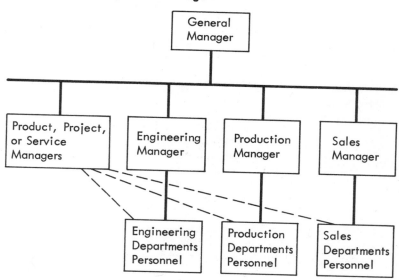

when."[36] This type of arrangement can present a problem for managers unless authority and responsibility relationships are clearly understood.[37] Otherwise, both the functional personnel and the managers may be confused as to who has the legitimate authority —the functional manager or the product manager.[38]

Product managers with line authority

In other cases, the functional personnel are placed under the line authority of the product or project manager for a limited period of time. The length of this period will vary with several factors. For example, in cases where the "product" involved is a large-scale project, such as those associated with the space program or with large contracts with the Department of Defense, functional personnel may be "on assignment" to product (or project) managers for several years. More commonly, however, the temporary assignment of functional personnel to product managers will cover

---

[36] Joseph A. Litterer, *The Analysis of Organizations* (2nd ed.; New York: John Wiley & Sons, 1973), p. 647.

[37] For a discussion of authority and responsibility ambiguities that may arise in matrix designs, see Jay R. Galbraith, *Organization Design*, (Reading, Mass.: Addison-Wesley Publishing Company, 1977), pp. 167–73, and Charles C. Martin, *Project Management: How to Make It Work* (New York: AMACOM, 1976), chap. 3.

[38] The potential problem of conflict of authority between functional and product managers has been compared to the potential problem of conflict in a family. Being raised by both a mother and a father, many of us have experienced conflicts between "these two powerful forces in our lives." Presumably there are offsetting advantages to being raised under two sources of authority. See Donald Ralph Kingdon, *Matrix Organization: Managing Information Technologies* (London: Tavistock Publications, 1973), p. 104.

a shorter period of time. As you would expect, the increased mobility of personnel in the fluid, project-oriented, matrix organization design may create behavioral problems not found in the more stable functional and product designs. These problems must be evaluated in terms of the contribution the matrix design makes to overall organizational effectiveness.

When is a matrix design appropriate?

Matrix organization design originated in business firms that had large contracts with various agencies of the federal government. Such contracts require extensive use of highly specialized skills—an advantage of the functional base of departmentation, and coordination and integration of thousands of diverse activities—an advantage of product departmentation. Thus, matrix organization design provides an approach to the organization of large-scale projects that is responsive to both the need for specialization and for integration.

General use

The use of matrix designs, however, is not limited to large-scale projects. Many firms have found it a useful approach for handling the introduction of new products. In general, any time there is a special project requiring specialized skills and coordination of multiple activities, the matrix design is a legitimate one to consider. Furthermore, since the ongoing operations of today's complex organizations require tradeoffs between specialization and coordination, the use of matrix designs is undoubtedly widespread. The label may be missing, but the essence of the matrix design may be there. "You can have the game without the name."[39]

Former base of departmentation

An Illustration—Matrix Design. An illustration of a modified matrix design is provided by Auerbach Associates, Inc., a firm founded to do system design, programming, and consulting work in the field of information systems.[40] Formerly, Auerbach's primary base of departmentation was *geography*. Each geographic region was a profit center under the accountability of a manager. Each profit center served the commercial, industrial, governmental, and educational markets in its region. This geographic departmentation had the advantage of providing a broad range of services to customers within a locality.

Disadvantages

However, the geographic departmentation had several disadvantages. It caused duplication of skills between regions and created regional loyalties that sometimes hampered interregion information and personnel exchange. Furthermore, the profit-center manager had to be a highly skilled generalist, whereas regional personnel were specialists. This created problems of developing executives

---

[39] Leonard R. Sayles, "Matrix Management: The Structure with a Future," *Organizational Dynamics,* vol. 5, no. 2 (Autumn 1976), pp. 2–17.

[40] Isaac L. Auerbach, "Remodel the Pyramid before It Crumbles," *Innovation,* no. 29 (March 1972), pp. 22–29.

with the generalist skills required to manage a regional profit center.

New base of departmenta- tion

Auerbach decided to completely redesign its organization. It adopted a modified matrix design. Essentially, the new design developed around *markets* rather than around geographic regions. The company identified important markets and made the functional specialists accountable to market-oriented project managers rather than to regional administrators. Figure 16–8 illustrates the before-and-after of the Auerbach Associates, Inc., organization design (the firm's entire set of organizational relationships is not shown in Figure 16–8).

General point

Matrix design provides an excellent illustration of a useful general point: *Organization design must take whatever form required to facilitate the achievement of organization goals in an efficient and effective manner.* Design is a means to an end. There are no organization designs that *must* be used or that are always right. There will always be a need for managers to come up with imaginative and unique solutions to the basic problem of organization design—finding that set of patterned relationships among organization members that will best contribute to the efficient and effective achievement of goals.

Summary box

> The process of grouping activities and jobs into larger organizational units is called *departmentation.* Common *bases of departmentation* include: function, geographic area, product (or project or brand), customer or market, equipment, and process.
>
> You often will find several bases of departmentation in one organization. Each base has its advantages and disadvantages in terms of the demands of specific situations. Functional departmentation, however, is found to some extent in almost every organization.
>
> One of the basic departmentation choices managers make is between *product* departmentation and *functional* departmentation. Factors to consider in making this choice include diversity of product line, interdependencies, level of technology, and economies of scale.
>
> The discussion of *changing bases* of departmentation in some organizations that market consumer packaged goods, and of *matrix organization designs*, suggests that designing organizations is a continuing concern of managers. They need to be sure that their organization designs are responsive to changing technical, environmental, market, and human conditions.

FIGURE 16–8
Auerbach Associates Matrix Design

BEFORE

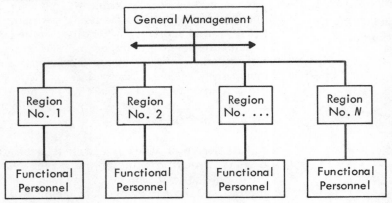

Geographic/Functional
Departmentation

AFTER

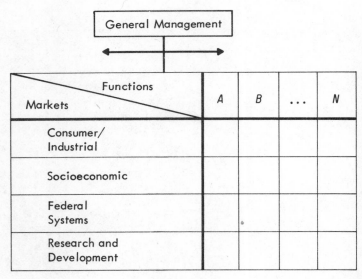

Market/Functional
Matrix Departmentation

Source: Isaac L. Auerbach, "Remodel the Pyramid before it Crumbles," *Innovation,* no. 29 (March 1972).

CHECK YOUR UNDERSTANDING

Organization design
Basic problem of organization design
Organization charts
Job analysis
Job analysis methods
Job description
Job evaluation
Job scope
Job depth
Job enrichment
Job enlargement
Horizontal job loading
Vertical job loading

Job involvement
Job characteristics model
  Growth satisfaction
  Core job demensions
  Motivating potential
  Job Diagnostic Survey (JDS)
  Critical psychological states
  Personal outcomes
Bases of departmentation
Functional departmentation
Brand manager
Market departmentation
Matrix organization design

STUDY QUESTIONS

1. Distinguish between informal and formal organization. What is meant by the statement, "Managers do not design the informal organization"?

2. Explain the following statement: "No one has ever seen an organization design."

3. What exactly does an "organization chart" chart? What important aspects of an organization design are not shown on an organization chart?

4. This chapter contains an extended discussion of job design. What, in your opinion, would a discussion of job design written in the early part of this century have emphasized?

5. Critique the statement: "Job enrichment improves job satisfaction and job performance."

6. Outline a series of statements that could serve as a logic or line of reasoning for thinking about the role of job enrichment on job performance.

7. Know the common bases of departmentation and be able to give examples of each. Identify the advantages of the functional and the product bases of departmentation. What factors determine a choice between the two?

8. Under what conditions would a matrix organization design be appropriate?

APPLICATION: CHANGE IN BASE OF DEPARTMENTATION

Figures 16–9 and 16–10 represent the "before-and-after" of the organization design of the marketing department of a very large industrial organization in an energy-related field. The "after" design is in effect at the time of this writing. Each box on the chart represents a high-level executive position. The chart of the "after" design does not show the set of managerial positions reporting to the wholesale-fuels business manager or the industrial and consumer business manager. The charts reflect a basic change in the primary base of departmentation used in the marketing department.

1. What do you think are the distinct advantages and disadvantages of the organization designs reflected in the two charts?

2. What are the major business lines identified in the "after" chart, and what are the major support functions for these business lines?

FIGURE 16–9
The Marketing Department: Before

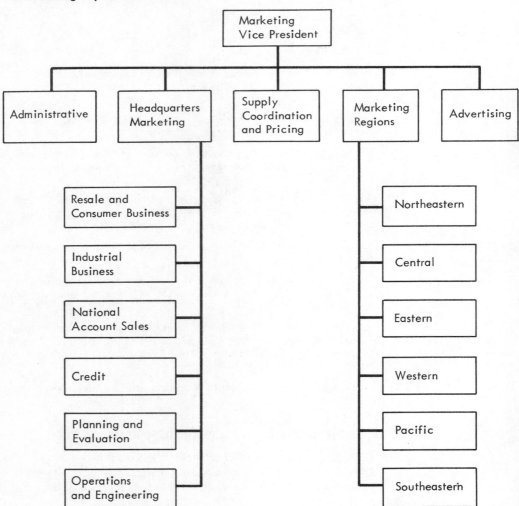

FIGURE 16–10
The Marketing Department: After

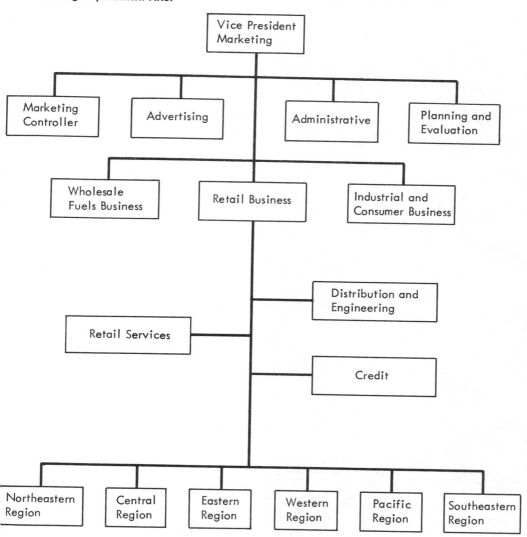

Objectives of Chapter 17

- To discuss four additional aspects of the basic problem of designing organizations:

  Span of Management
  Organizational Levels
  Delegation
  Line and Staff

Outline of Chapter 17

17

FURTHER ASPECTS OF THE DESIGN PROBLEM

Structure is not just a concern of perverse people who compulsively need to have things spelled out and formalized. It is a requirement for stability, survival, and success in even the most informal of organizations.

Harold J. Leavitt, William R. Dill, and
Henry B. Eyring

This chapter

Chapter 16 discussed two major aspects of the basic problem of designing organizations: defining jobs and grouping jobs. This chapter continues the discussion of organization design by examining span of management, organizational levels, delegation, and line and staff. The chapter ends with an overall recap of our two-chapter discussion of *designing organizations*.

SPAN OF MANAGEMENT

Basic question

Once jobs are defined and bases of departmentation selected, a question that must be answered is, How many subordinates will report directly to each manager? This is the span-of-management question. Obviously there are limits to the number of subordinates that a manager can manage effectively. But what determines the limits? There is quite a history to the answer to that question.

Two stages

Brief Historical Note. Span of management has been one of the most widely discussed ideas in management and organization theory. In general the idea has had a *two-stage evolution.*[1] The first stage was to specify absolute spans; the more contemporary stage tends to specify spans in more general terms.

---

[1] For the definitive discussion of and bibliography on span of management, see David D. Van Fleet and Arthur G. Bedeian, "A History of the Span of Management." *Academy of Management Review*, vol. 2, no. 3 (July 1977), pp. 356–72.

First stage

For years it was customary to state a fixed number in response to the question of managerial span. For example, top executives, it was said, should not have a span of more than three to six subordinates. Foremen or supervisors, on the other hand, could have a span of 10 to 15. The difference in these two spans arises from the nature of the relationship between top executives and their subordinates and between foremen and their subordinates. In the first instance, three to six subordinates was considered maximum because of the complexity of the problems discussed by top executives and their subordinates.[2] In the latter case, where problems encountered tend to be more routine, a span of 10 to 15 was considered "optimum."[3]

V. A. Graicunas

You may wonder why earlier discussions of span of management focused on the idea of a specific number of subordinates that is optimum for lower-level managers and for top executives. This line of reasoning received theoretical support from Vytautas A. Graicunas who, in 1933, suggested the idea that as the number of subordinates increases *arithmetically*, the number of potential relationships between the manager and subordinates increases *geometrically*. Graicunas offered a set of equations that demonstrated that, for example, with three subordinates there were 18 possible relationships but with nine subordinates there are 2,376 possible relationships.[4]

Graicunas' essential point

There is nothing useful for you to gain from a detailed discussion of Graicunas' equations. His essential point, however, is still valid. It comes down to the idea that when one additional person enters the set of relationships existing in a manager-subordinates situation, the one person increases the potential number of relationships by more than one. Following Graicunas, most writers tended to discuss span of management (more commonly referred

---

[2] One study of the spans of Chief Executive Officers (CEOs) in 100 large companies found that the median span was 9, with a range of 1 to 24. Ernest Dale, *Planning and Developing the Company Organization Structure* (New York: American Management Association, 1952).

[3] In Chapter 15, the Woodward studies were discussed. Concerning spans, these studies found that supervisors' spans (range = 15 to 48) were larger than executives' spans (range = 4 to 10). In both cases, the spans varied with the type of production process. The smallest spans were in unit production firms and the largest were in mass production firms. Joan Woodward, *Industrial Organization: Theory and Practice* (London: Oxford University Press, 1965), p. 69.

[4] V. A. Graicunas, "Relationship in Organizations," in Luther Gulick and L. Urwick, eds., *Papers on the Science of Administration* (New York: Institute of Public Administration, 1937), pp. 181–87.

Graicunas' basic equation is $C = N(2^N/2 + N - 1)$ where C represents the potential relationships and N represents the number of subordinates reporting directly to the manager. Thus, if $N = 3$, $C = 18$; if $N = 9$, $C = 2,376$; and if $N = 18$, $C = 2,359,602$!

If A represents the manager and B, C, and D represent three subordinates, then the 18 possible relationships are: AB, AC, AD, AB with C, AB with D, AC with B, AC with D, AD with B, AD with C, AB with CD, AC with BD, AD with CB, BC, BD, CB, CD, DB, and DC. The implication is that each of these 18 combinations potentially requires different behavior.

to in earlier writings as "span of control") in terms that prescribed optimum, absolute spans.

Second stage

Contemporary View. In contrast to an emphasis on absolute spans, the contemporary view of span is more flexible. Spans are not stated in absolute terms. Three points about the contemporary view are worth noting:

Span is important

1. Span of management is important to overall organization and managerial effectiveness. The basic idea, suggested by Graicunas, is a valid one to consider in designing organizations. An increase in the number of subordinates reporting to a manager does increase the *complexity* of the manager's job.

> Clearly . . . there is a limit beyond which the size of a work group and the complexity of a manager's job cannot be extended without resulting in undesirable consequences for the organization, for the manager, and for the members of the work group.[5]

No absolute span

2. There is no absolute span that applies in all situations. To the extent that earlier writings specified such a span they were too dogmatic. However, the spans often specified in earlier writings do find some support in actual organization practice. For example, when subordinates require personal, face-to-face supervision and where subordinates' jobs interlock, the limit on span does appear to be in the range of four to six.[6] Nevertheless, it is pointless to search for a span that applies, *in general*. The practical question about span is, What span is best for a particular manager in terms of getting the job done?[7]

Factors affecting span

3. The appropriate span for a manager depends on three factors: First, *the manager* (knowledge, ability, influence, personality, energy, and health, to name some of the factors); second, *the subordinates* (their training, understanding and acceptance of policies and rules, skills, knowledge, motivations, relationship with the manager, and so on); and third, *situational variables*.

Situational variables

Potentially relevant situational variables include: the nature and size of the work group; the availability of assistants to the

---

[5] Alan C. Filley, Robert J. House, and Steven Kerr, *Managerial Process and Organizational Behavior*, 2d ed., Glenview, Ill.: Scott, Foresman and Company, 1976), p. 422.

[6] Ibid.

[7] A relatively new dimension to the debate over span of management is that of measurement. Span usually is considered to be the quotient resulting from dividing the total number of subordinates by the total number of superiors. Recently, some writers have suggested that this "raw span" is less meaningful than an "adjusted span" that takes into account time spent by supervisors in managing subordinates and the number of helpers available to the superiors. See William G. Ouchi and James B. Dowling, "Defining the Span of Control," *Administrative Science Quarterly*, vol. 19, no. 3 (September 1974), pp. 357–65.

manager; the nature of the job; the frequency of reporting relationships; the geographic dispersion of the superior and the subordinates; and the desire of managers as the same organizational level to have the same span. An "Application" at the end of this chapter discusses how one company used several situational variables in determining supervisory spans.

ORGANIZATIONAL LEVELS

Levels and span

Relation of Levels to Span. Decisions about span of management have an influence on organizational levels. The number of levels in an organization is the number of different rankings between operative employees and top managers. The number of levels tends to vary inversely with the size of the span of management. In general, the wider the span, the fewer the levels.

Example of relation of levels and spans

For example, suppose that an organization has 64 operative employees to be supervised and that it uses a span of eight. Each of eight supervisors will have eight subordinates and the supervisors will report to one manager. An organization chart reflecting a span of eight is shown in Figure 17–1(A). If the organization decides to change the span it uses to four, then 16 supervisors are needed to supervise the 64 employees. The 16 supervisors will report to four general supervisors and these, in turn, will report to one manager. Figure 17–1(B) reflects the span of four.[8]

Tall and flat organizations

Relation of Levels to Size. Organizations with many levels are called "tall," while those with fewer levels are called "flat." Tallness and flatness of organization design are relative to the total size of the organization. For example, in Figure 17–1, given the 64 operative employees, the design of B is taller than that reflected in A.

Organization size

Organization size usually refers to the number of people employed by an organization. Size can be an important variable influencing organization design, in general, and the relative advantages of tall or flat designs, in particular.[9] Since coordination and communication problems tend to be complex in large organizations, a tall structure may be best. Tall design allows for closer managerial control and, since each manager's span is small, makes coordination of subordinate work easier. On the other hand, the more levels there are in an organization, the more opportunity there is for distortion in communication both upward and downward.

---

[8] Example based on Gary Dessler, *Organization and Management: A Contingency Approach* (Englewood Cliffs, N.J.: Prentice-Hall, Inc., 1976), p. 115. © 1976. Reprinted by permission of Prentice-Hall, Inc., Englewood Cliffs, N.J.

[9] Larry E. Pate and John B. Cullen, "The Influence of Organization Size on Organization Structure," in *Proceedings,* Southwest Division Academy of Management, 1977, pp. 282–86; Lyman W. Porter and Edward E. Lawler III, "Properties of Organization Structure in Relation to Job Attitudes and Job Behavior," *Psychological Bulletin,* vol. 64, no. 1 (1965), pp. 23–51.

FIGURE 17–1
Relation of Levels and Spans

A. Span of 8, 3 levels

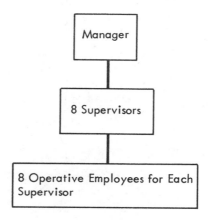

B. Span of 4, 4 levels

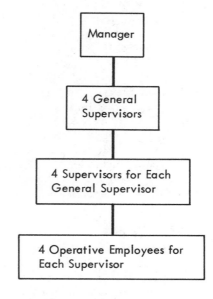

Levels,
attitudes,
and behavior

Other Implications of Levels. There are several consistent find-ings from research on organizational levels that suggest a rela-tionship between levels and employees' attitudes and behavior. One of these findings is that people holding jobs at higher levels in an organization tend to have higher job satisfaction than those holding jobs at lower levels.[10] This finding is consistent both for nonman-

---

[10] Porter and Lawler, "Properties of Organization Structure."

agement and management personnel. Further, employees tend to perceive that jobs at higher levels of the organization place additional requirements on them. Finally, the level at which you are in an organization may influence the amount of information you receive, the types of interpersonal relationships you have on the job, and the types of decisions you make.

General
implication

The general implication of these findings is that organization level can be a variable influencing behavior in organizations. As such, it, like span of management, needs to be considered when organizations are being designed. Also, like span, there is no precise guide to the "right number" of levels for an organization to have.

Summary box

> The *two major ideas* discussed so far in this chapter are span of management and organizational levels.
>
> *Span of management* refers to the number of subordinates that report directly to a manager. There is no one correct span for all situations. The number that is most appropriate for a particular manager depends on three factors: the manager; the subordinates; and the situational variables.
>
> Span of management and *organizational levels* are related. The number of levels in an organization tends to vary inversely with the size of the span. Depending on the size of an organization, and the number of levels, organizations are tall or flat. Size is usually measured in terms of number of employees.
>
> A consistent finding from research on organizational levels is that personnel at the higher levels in an organization tend to have relatively more job satisfaction than personnel at lower levels.

DELEGATION

What is
delegation?

Introduction. Delegation is the basic process used to create an organization. The essence of an organization is the patterned network of authority and responsibility relationships that is established to achieve goals. Delegation is the process of creating this network of relationships.

Example

When a manager delegates, a new *accountability relationship* is created. Specifically, when manager A, who is responsible for and has authority to carry out activities 1, 2, 3, 4, 5, 6, 7, and 8, gives B responsibility for 1, 4, and 6 and makes B accountable for the efficient and effective performance of those activities, the process of delegation has occurred.

Need

The need for delegation derives from the relationship between a manager's set of responsibilities and the manager's personal capacity to meet those responsibilities. Some managers underdelegate and others overdelegate (see Figure 17–2) or delegate the wrong things, but all managers are involved to some extent with the process of delegation. "It's a safe general rule that [managers] simply can't handle all . . . responsibilities and still do a good job on the important ones."[11]

FIGURE 17–2
Delegation

" . . . it became a successful business. Then on the advice of my consultant, I began to delegate more authority to my junior executives . . . even took an occasional day off . . ."

The Wall Street Journal

Reasons why managers underdelegate

Some managers can delegate effectively, whereas others cannot or are hesitant to even try. Reasons sometimes suggested for why managers do not delegate include: lack of confidence in subordinates; fear of competition; fear of losing credit and recognition; fear of exposing weaknesses; an "I can do it better myself" attitude; a need to "know everything that is going on"; and lack of time to explain the delegation and to train subordinates for their

---

[11] Auren Uris, *The Executive Deskbook* (New York: Van Nostrand Reinhold Company, 1970), p. 64.

newly assigned responsibilities.[12] These concerns are very real to managers and cannot be ignored. Whatever their basis in fact, they can effectively hinder and/or prevent the process of delegation.

Six guides

Delegation Guides.   Six guides that serve as aids—not inflexible laws or principles—to managers in carrying out the process of delegation are the scalar principle, unity of command, parity of authority and responsibility, fixation of responsibility, residual authority and responsibility, and exception principle.[13] These guides are discussed briefly below.

The scalar principle: vertical design

1. "The scalar principle guide" states that authority and responsibility should flow vertically from the highest level of the organization to the lowest. The scalar principle establishes the vertical structure or design of the organization. It establishes the "hierarchy of authority and responsibility relationships."

Overlaps, splits, floats

This guide has often been interpreted to mean that all responsibilities in an organization should be clearly defined and assigned to particular positions. In this view, overlaps and splits in responsibilities should be avoided. An "overlap" occurs when responsibilities fall under the accountability of two or more executives. A responsibility is "split" when it is carried out by more than one organizational unit. As a practical matter, however, in the design of an organization it is impossible to anticipate all responsibilities. It may be desirable to have overlaps and splits; and it may be valuable to leave some responsibilities unassigned, or "floating" in order to see who will take the initiative. Also, in the design of organizations it may be undesirable to define precisely the nature of job responsibilities. It is possible to *overdefine* job positions, and thus lose the value of individual initiative in defining the scope and depth of jobs.

Unity of command: one activity, one superior

2. "The unity of command guide" states that for any given activity an employee should be made accountable to only one superior. Traditionally, this idea was interpreted narrowly to mean that each employee should have only one superior. However, a more useful interpretation of this idea is that there should be a one-subordinate—one superior combination for each particular activity engaged in by the subordinate.

Example

For example, an engineer often works on several projects during a day, and each of the projects may be under the supervision of a different supervisor. This need create no problems as long as it is clearly understood that the engineer is accountable to each

---

[12] R. Alec MacKenzie, *The Time Trap* (New York: AMACOM, 1972), p. 133.

[13] These and other guides to organization and management are discussed at length in Ralph C. Davis, *The Fundamentals of Top Management* (New York: Harper & Bros., 1951).

supervisor of each project. Violation of the idea of unity of command would mean, in this case, that while working on a particular project the subordinate would be accountable to more than one project supervisor.

Parity of authority and responsibility

3. "The parity of authority and responsibility guide" states that delegation of responsibility should be accompanied by an equal delegation of authority. This simply means that if a person is going to be responsible for an activity, the person should be given the necessary authority to carry out that activity. Operationally, there is a difficulty with this guide because it is impossible to know when authority is "equal to" responsibility. How is this measured? Another difficulty with this guide is that sometimes authority is delegated in degrees. Thus, a subordinate may be given responsibility for an area of work but will not be given full authority to carry out that responsibility until the subordinate shows the capacity to handle it effectively. As a training technique, some managers will assign their subordinates responsibilities but will give them authority in increments based on evidence of their competence.

Fixation of responsibility

4. "The fixation of responsibility guide" states that the process of delegation does not relieve the executives of any of their authority, responsibility, and accountability. Although as a manager you may delegate some of your responsibilities to your subordinates, you cannot abdicate your accountability for the way in which those responsibilities are carried out. The fixation of responsibility guide to delegation is sometimes given as the rationale for saying that a manager can delegate authority but not responsibility. What the process of delegation does, in effect, is to create additional authority and responsibility. That is, when you delegate, you do not lose any of your authority and responsibility, but your subordinate receives authority and responsibility for which he or she will be held accountable.

Residual authority and responsibility

5. "The residual authority and responsibility guide" states that there are certain responsibilities that cannot be delegated. These responsibilities represent those aspects of the manager's job that make up its unique character. Commonly, these essential activities involve relationships *between* areas of managerial jurisdiction. For example, a manager cannot delegate some of the tasks that involve the manager with other departments and with other sets of objectives. Further, a manager cannot delegate tasks that are primarily concerned with the coordination of activities within the manager's area of responsibility. If all of the manager's tasks could be delegated, there would be no need for that managerial job.

The exception principle

6. One problem that many managers have with the process of delegation is that they retain their desire to know everything about anything that is going on. They may skillfully apply the five guides

discussed above, but they also may insist on being kept informed of all details that could possibly affect their area of responsibility. The "exception principle guide" can be useful in helping managers overcome this tendency. The exception principle guide states that managers need to be kept informed primarily of significant *deviations* from goals and plans. They do not need to be informed that actions *are* conforming to plans or that actions *are* within allowable tolerance limits. A preoccupation with details and routine matters detracts from a manager's capacity to handle more important problems—problems that require the manager's unique contribution and problems that cannot be delegated.

General rule

Centralization and Decentralization. As a general rule, decision-making authority should be delegated to the lowest organizational level having the required competence and knowledge and consistent with organizational needs for coordination and control. The rationale behind this normative statement is that overall organizational effectiveness is enhanced when decision-making authority is so dispersed.

Practice

As a practical matter, the *lowest* organizational level that meets the requirements of the above general rule may be very *high* in the organization. For example, the required competence and knowledge to make major capital outlay decisions may exist only at the top levels of an organization. Similarly, decisions involving new products, research directions, and dividend policies may have to be made by top-level executives. However, lower-level managers may be most competent and knowledgeable about major decision problems involving particular operating areas. For example, managers of individual plants of large manufacturing corporations often have wide-ranging authority to make decisions affecting the plant. These same plant managers, however, play a very minor role in corporate-wide decision making.[14]

Relative terms

Organizations in which decision-making authority is widely delegated are said to be "decentralized." Organizations in which most decision-making authority is retained by executives at the top levels are said to be "centralized." Obviously, these are relative terms. That is, every organization is decentralized to some extent or there could be no real organization. There is no organization in which *all* decision-making power is retained by top-level executives.

---

[14] "The Managers," *The Wall Street Journal*, vol. 59, no. 78, Southwest Edition (April 21, 1977), pp. 1, 37.

Summary box

> *Delegation* is the basic process used to create an organization. The process of delegation creates a new accountability relationship. The need for delegation derives from the relationship between a manager's responsibilities and capabilities.
>
> *Six guides* that are useful as aids to managers in carrying out the process of delegation are: the scalar principle; unity of command; parity of authority and responsibility; fixation of responsibility; residual authority and responsibility; and the exception principle.
>
> The result of the process of delegation is that an organization has some degree of *decentralization and centralization.* An organization in which authority is widely delegated is commonly characterized as a "decentralized" organization.
>
> As a general rule, authority should be delegated to the lowest organizational level having the requisite competence and knowledge, consistent with requirements for coordination and control.

LINE AND STAFF

*Common
terms*

The terms "line" and "staff" are widely used in almost all types of organizations. In spite of efforts to dismiss the terms as "obsolete,"[15] their usage continues—probably because real organizations find the terms helpful. We will discuss line and staff as types of *authority* and as types of *functions.*

*Line
authority*

Types of Authority. The term "line authority" is commonly used to mean the right of a manager to demand accountability from subordinates for their performance of assigned responsibilities. It includes the right to give job instructions and other commands to subordinates as well as the expectation that the instructions and commands will be carried out. The idea of line authority encompasses that set of rights and expectations that is generally associated with the superior–subordinate relationship.

*Staff
authority*

The term "staff authority," on the other hand, is commonly used to refer to a relationship between organizational participants that is "advisory." For example, the staff authority of a personnel department may include the right to offer advice to other departments on such matters as hiring, training, compensation, collective bargaining, labor law, and safety. In addition, there is generally an

---

[15] Gerald G. Fisch, "Line-Staff Is Obsolete," *Harvard Business Review,* vol. 39, no. 5 (September–October, 1961).

understanding in organizations that, when such advice is offered or sought, it will be listened to and given fair consideration. However, the decision to accept or reject the advice remains with the departments to which the advice was offered.

Principle of compulsory staff advice

A traditional management guide is that an executive should not make an important decision until staff groups which can contribute sound advice or assistance have had a chance to do so. The right of final decision, however, rests with the line executive. This guide has been referred to as the "principle of compulsory staff advice."[16] The "authority" or influence of a staff department or person arises from competence, status, and experience in assisting other people in the organization.

Special case

Functional Authority.   Under certain circumstances, it is necessary or desirable to reinforce the authority of a staff department or person. In such cases, the idea of functional authority is relevant. "Functional authority" refers to a situation in which the normal staff authority of a staff department or person is extended to include line authority over certain matters *outside* of the staff department or outside the staff person's normal sphere of operations. Examples of functional authority that are commonly used in American business organizations follow:

Quality control department example

1. Quality control department personnel (normally a staff department) will be given line authority to go into production departments (line departments), make inspections and, if quality is below desired levels, order the production department to stop production. In the absence of functional authority, the quality control inspector would simply advise the production department foreman that quality is below desired levels. The production department foreman would then make the decision about stopping the production.

Personnel department example

2. A personnel department (normally considered a staff department) is sometimes given line authority to hire new personnel. College recruiters are given authority to hire new college graduates for admission into a company's executive training program. Personnel departments often hire unskilled workers without directly getting the approval of the departments in which the workers will be employed. In the absence of this functional authority, the personnel department would simply refer prospective employees to the departments. The actual hiring would be done by the operating manager of the department. In companies that operate under a collective bargaining agreement, the personnel department may be given functional authority over terminations—that is, only the labor-relations specialists can fire an employee. The reason for this is to minimize the grievances filed because of misinterpretations of the collective bargaining agreement.

---

[16] Davis, *The Fundamentals of Top Management*, p. 453.

Using functional authority

    Functional authority relationships can be useful and essential to effective organizational performance. They can expedite work and facilitate coordination. They need cause no particular problems in organization design *as long as they are clearly understood* by those organizational participants affected by them. It is important to make sure that the scope of the functional authority relationship is clearly defined and limited only to those relationships where the violation of unity of command and the interference with normal line-and-staff relationships can be justified in terms of organizational effectiveness.

Combining line, staff, and functional authority

    In order to function effectively, most organizations require both line and staff authority relationships. Only very small organizations can get by with an organization design of only line authority relationships. Furthermore, functional authority relationships are very common as a means of coordinating and integrating the working relationship between organization members with line authority and members with staff authority. The *most common* type of organization design combines line, staff, and functional authority relationships.

Line functions

    Types of Functions. Sometimes you will encounter the terms "line" and "staff" used differently than they are used above. They are often used to identify types of jobs. Traditionally, line jobs or "line functions" have been considered as those that contribute directly toward the "primary objective" of the organizational unit.

Staff functions

    For example, in a manufacturing plant, the line functions are commonly considered to be sales, production, and finance, since these three (and only these three) functions contribute *directly* to the primary objective of the manufacturing firm—the production and distribution of customer goods and services. All other jobs in the manufacturing firm would be considered as "staff functions" because, in one way or another, they assist or advise the line functions. That is, they contribute *indirectly* to the primary objective.

Line and staff organization

    The essence of the traditional notion of line and staff is that these are certain functions—line functions—that are absolutely essential to carrying out the primary objective of the organizational unit. Other functions, although important, are facilitative to the line functions. The total set of line functions in an organization is the "line organization"; the set of staff functions represents the "staff organization." Most actual organizations represent a combination "line-and-staff organization."

Primary versus system

    Two Problems. There are two major problems associated with the traditional view of line and staff as types of functions. *First,* it has already been argued (in Chapter 2) that most significant management situations should not be characterized as having a "primary" objective. The argument made was that managers are accountable for a *system* of goals and the entire system must be satisfied. Given this view, a concept of line and staff based on the notion of a primary objective is untenable.

*Direct
versus
indirect*

Second, even if a primary objective could be identified, it is still arbitrary to say that some functions contribute "directly" to that objective and others only "indirectly." Management writers have argued back and forth about which functions are line and which are staff. The argument serves little purpose because any classification of functions into line and staff will be somewhat arbitrary. There is a "gray area" into which several functions fall. Most writers agree that production, sales, and finance contribute directly to the ultimate purpose of a business organization. However, what about engineering, research, and purchasing?

*Practical
value*

Although there are the above problems with the traditional view of line and staff, you can still use it in practical situations. Essentially the line and staff idea says: Identify those responsibility areas that represent the major source of your accountabilities. These responsibilities are your line duties, and the organization that you design for directly carrying them out is your line organization. It is in your line organization that the major goals for which you will be held accountable will be achieved. Those activities that do not directly contribute to the major source of your accountabilities are your staff duties, and the organization that you design for directly carrying them out is your staff organization. Your staff organization exists to facilitate the performance of your line organization.

*Personnel
manager*

Illustration. It may be useful to illustrate the use of some of the terms discussed in this section. Suppose that you are the manager of a personnel department in a manufacturing plant.

1. Personnel is a *staff function* relative to the entire organization because, most would agree, it does not contribute directly to the ultimate purposes of the entire organization. Thus, the personnel department is almost always considered a staff department. The personnel manager is a *staff manager* with respect to the entire organization.
2. As a staff manager, the personnel manager has *staff authority* with respect to those parts of the organization the manager is responsible for advising. Of course, the advice can be rejected by those who receive it.
3. In selected areas, the personnel manager may be assigned *functional authority*. That means the manager's "advice" carries the weight of line authority. The manager has the authority to issue direct commands and to expect they will be carried out.
4. Within the personnel department, the personnel manager has *line authority* over those employees who work in the depart-

ment. Also, within the personnel department, there are *line and staff functions*. The line functions are those that contribute directly to the personnel department's major purposes; the staff functions facilitate accomplishment of the line jobs.

Summary box

> The terms *line* and *staff* are sometimes used to identify a particular type of influence relationship between organization members. *Line authority* refers to the right of a manager to demand accountability from subordinates for their performance of assigned responsibilities. *Staff authority* refers to an advisory relationship between organizational participants.
>
> When managers have staff authority they essentially have the right to try to be an influence over those whom they advise. Although their effort to be influential can receive support from devices such as the *principle of compulsory staff advice*, it is ultimately supported by their record of competent and timely advice.
>
> *Functional authority* refers to the right of a person with staff authority to exercise line authority over a designated task that is outside the person's normal sphere of operations.
>
> The terms line and staff are also used to refer to types of jobs or functions. *Line functions* contribute directly to the primary or major goals of the organizational unit. The total set of line functions is the *line organization*. *Staff functions* represent all other jobs that are necessary to facilitate the accomplishment of line functions. The total set of staff functions is the *staff organization*.

DESIGNING ORGANIZATIONS: A RECAP

Organization design

1. The formal "organization design," or structure, is the relatively stable set of officially defined working relationships among the members of the organization.

Basic problem

2. The basic problem of organization design is to identify the patterned set of working relationships that will best contribute to the total system of performance, group, and individual goals.

Reality

3. The reality of an organization design is in the working relationships that characterize organization members. This reality cannot be visualized completely through organization charts, pictures, or manuals.

Job design

4. Assuming the existence of goals, the first step in designing organizations is to design jobs. Several ideas relevant to job design

are job: analysis; description; scope; depth; enlargement; and enrichment.

Grouping jobs

5. Another step in designing an organization is that of "grouping jobs." Several ways of grouping jobs are by: product; function; process; customer; equipment; and geography. The matrix design attempts to combine the advantage of product and function bases of departmentation.

Span

6. "Span of management" refers to the number of subordinates reporting directly to a manager. The most appropriate span for a particular manager depends on the manager, the subordinates, and situational variables.

Levels

7. "The number of levels" in an organization refers to the number of different rankings between operative employees and top managers. Levels are related to span of management, organization size, and the attitudes and behavior or organization members.

Delegation

8. "Delegation" is the process of distributing authority throughout an organization. An organization with widely dispersed decision-making authority is said to be a decentralized organization. Six guides for helping managers carry out the process of delegation were discussed.

Line and staff

9. "Line" and "staff" are still important organizational concepts. Several ideas related to these terms are: line authority; staff authority; functional authority; line function; staff function; line organization; staff organization; line manager; staff manager; and principle of compulsory staff advice.

Conclusion

10. The way in which organizations are designed can have an important impact on the organization's effectiveness. The impact derives largely from the way the design facilitates effective working relationships between the people and facilities that enter into achieving goals. As we indicated at the beginning of Chapter 16, "The right structure does not guarantee results. But the wrong structure aborts results and smothers even the best-directed efforts."[17]

CHECK YOUR UNDERSTANDING

Span of management
   V. A. Graicunas
   Absolute span
   Factors affecting span
Organizational levels
   Tall and flat organization
   Organization size

Delegation
   Scalar principle
   Overlaps
   Splits
   Floats
   Unity of command

---

[17] Peter F. Drucker, *Managing by Results* (New York: Harper & Row, Publishers, 1964), p. 216.

Parity of authority and respon-
sibility
Fixation of responsibility
Residual authority and respon-
sibility
Exception principle
Centralization
Decentralization
Line and staff
Line authority

Staff authority
Principle of compulsory staff
advice
Functional authority
Line function
Staff function
Line organization
Staff organization
Line manager
Staff manager

STUDY QUESTIONS

1. How is current thinking about span of management different from that of years ago? What is the relationship between span of management and the number of organizational levels?

2. What are some of the relationships that have been shown from research to exist between organizational levels and employees' attitudes and behavior?

3. What are several reasons why managers might underdelegate?

4. Why, in your opinion, might it be useful to have "floating" responsibilities in an organization? How might "overlaps" and "splits" contribute to organizational effectiveness?

5. What are some of the difficulties that might be encountered in an attempt to apply the parity of authority and responsibility delegation guide?

6. What, in your opinion, are specific responsibilities that cannot be delegated by:
    a. The president of the United States.
    b. A college teacher.
    c. A high-level business executive.
    d. The pope of the Roman Catholic Church.
    e. A foreman in an automobile plant.

7. What are some of the factors that should be considered in determining the most appropriate degree of decentralization for an organization?

8. What are some precautions that should be taken when creating functional authority relationships?

APPLICATION: SPANS AND LEVELS*

During the early 1960s one of the major divisions (hereafter referred to as "the company") of a large business firm in the aircraft industry experimented with a unique approach to making decisions about the span of management. A brief discussion of this experience will serve two purposes. First, it will communicate how one

---

* Information for this Application comes from C. W. Barkdull, "Span of Control: A Method of Evaluation," *Michigan Business Review*, vol. 15 (1963), pp. 25–32, telephone conversations with Frank Belasco, May 1977, and written correspondence, October, 1977.

firm attempted to utilize a systematic approach to solving an organization design problem. Second, by looking at this experience almost two decades later, we can better appreciate some of the variables influencing the success of the systematic approach.

The primary factor that is relevant to this discussion is that, in the late 1950s and early 1960s, the company was experiencing a very rapid growth rate. New contracts with the federal government necessitated hiring large numbers of new personnel. Between 1956 and 1961, the number of employees increased from about 4,000 to 30,000. Clearly, such a situation called for some definite guidelines (not dogmatic rules) for use by those responsible for organization design decisions. One of these decision areas is span of management because, in some cases, span is a major consideration in determining the most appropriate organization design.

The company had some criteria concerning supervisory ratios —that is, the number of nonsupervisory personnel divided by the number of supervisors in a particular organizational unit. However, these criteria did not prevent a situation from developing in which new organizational levels were being created in order to maintain narrow spans between the top and lower levels of the company. Spans at the level just below the general manager ranged from 5 to 10, and spans at the lowest level ranged from 15 to 18. However, between the top and lowest levels, spans averaged three—too narrow in the view of company personnel who were concerned with organization design. The company decided to begin a program of increasing spans and decreasing levels.

The major steps in the program were:

1. Identification of major factors affecting span decisions. The seven factors identified are shown below:

	Supervisory Index Scale Range
Factors relating to the type of work supervised	
a. Similarity of the functions supervised	1–5
b. Geographic contiguity of functions supervised	1–5
c. Complexity of functions supervised	2–10
Factors relating to the personnel supervised	
d. Direction and control required by the personnel supervised	3–15
Factors relating to the supervisory position	
e. Coordination required of the supervisor	2–10
f. Planning required of the supervisor	2–10
g. Organizational assistance received by the supervisor	None

2. Development of a "supervisory index"—an index of the relative difficulty of a particular supervisory job. The determination of this index involved assigning each supervisory job a numerical value on each of the first six factors in the table above. The seventh factor, "organizational assistance received by the supervisor," was taken account of by means of fractional multiplier values which reduced the total supervisory index. In general, a high supervisory

index (the theoretically highest index $= 55$ before adjustment for organizational assistance) suggested the desirability of narrow spans, and vice versa. The company found that, in practice, there was little relationships between actual spans and those suggested by the supervisory index.

3. Determination of standard spans. Using the supervisory index, actual spans, and statistical analysis (linear regression), the company developed standard "span ranges" applicable to supervisory jobs with specific supervisory index values.

4. Implementation of the program. Steps were taken by the company to assure that the program would be introduced and implemented in a reasonable and systematic manner.

What were the results of this program for the company? Some components of the company were able to increase the average spans and, as a result, decrease the number of organizational levels. These changes, in turn, reduced some costs and presumably had favorable impacts on communication and supervisory effectiveness.

What is the status of this program in the late 1970s? In order to arrive at an answer to that question, we called an organization-planning specialist at the company, Frank Belasco. Mr. Belasco was extremely helpful in providing the following perspectives.

1. From the beginning, the real benefit of the program derived from the systematic analysis of the span problem. That is, the seven factors were useful in appraising supervisory positions from the viewpoint of span. They provided a conceptual tool for span analysis. The numerical support (supervisory index, et cetera) for this tool was only mildly useful. The numbers were difficult to communicate as a creditable, useful approach to making span decisions.

2. At the time the program was implemented, the company had one major product, a flying test bed vehicle used for testing air-breathing engines. Other programs were in the development phase but not yet progressed to manufacturing hardware. The company utilized a functional type of organization design—one in which span decisions are particularly relevant. However, after the program was introduced, two other factors became important. First, the growth rate of the company began to level off. Second, the company became a two-product company, spacecraft and missiles. For purposes of producing these products, the company utilized a project-matrix type of organization design—one in which span decisions are less important than in a functional design.

3. Span is "A handy management tool. We look at it everyday from a companywide perspective." Mr. Belasco commented that, in general, a company goal is "to increase the span so as to get it broad enough so that managers will stay out of the nitty gritty and pay more attention to their essentially managerial duties."

How might this illustration be used to support the idea of a "contingency theory of organizational design"?

Objectives of Chapter 18

- To emphasize the importance to managers of change and the demands of both change and stability.
- To present a framework for thinking about change in organizations.
- To introduce the idea of approaches to introducing change.
- To discuss types of human response to change, giving special attention to resistance to change.
- To define organization development (OD) and to discuss its evolution and future.
- To introduce the idea of organizational effectiveness—the "bottom line" of the managerial job.

Outline of Chapter 18

Organizational Change
Change and Stability
A Change Framework
Approaches to Introducing Changes
Response to Change
Organizational Development
What Is OD?
Characteristics, Values, and Objectives
Evolution of OD
Organizational Effectiveness
Criteria of Organizational Effectiveness
Frame of Reference
Macro and Micro
Organizational Effectiveness and Goals

ORGANIZATIONAL CHANGE AND EFFECTIVENESS

The structures of society need to be looked at. . . .
Are there structures that could be reformed and
transformed through man's intentional activity so that
human responsiveness might be nurtured and personal
life fulfilled?

Perry LeFevre

Forever and ever the moon will follow the sun.

Anonymous

This chapter
This chapter examines two important aspects of organizations
—their need to be responsive to change and their effectiveness. In
our discussion of *organizational change* we will note the importance of both change and stability, present a framework for thinking about the forces for change and the status quo that "press on"
an organization, identify approaches to introducing change, and
discuss various types of response to change. In addition, organization development (OD), a particular approach to changing organizations, is introduced. The chapter ends with a discussion of the
important notion of *organizational effectiveness*. Several criteria
that can be used in measuring effectiveness are identified, the role
of different frames of references is noted, and the relation between
effectiveness and goals is emphasized.

ORGANIZATIONAL CHANGE

Change is
a fact
The fact of change needs no proof because it is immediately
and continuously evident to our senses. We may not like change.
We may not know exactly what is changing. The meaning of the
changes may not be clear. We may not know how to respond to
the changes. However, one thing is clear. Change is a fact. Response to change is an essential requirement of organizational ef-

fectiveness. "Change or die" is the way one business firm conveys this idea in a full-page advertisement in *The Wall Street Journal*.[1]

Future shock

With some hyperbole, it often is said that no period in history can match the present in the magnitude and rapidity of the changes bombarding individuals, groups, organizations, and nations. Alvin Toffler has coined the phrase "future shock" to identify our new condition of being overwhelmed by change.[2]

Learning to cope

It really doesn't matter whether there is more change today than in the past. What matters for managers is that the forces of change are significant and pervasive. They affect human behavior at work and the efficiency and effectiveness of work performance. "Learning how to cope with change" may be one of the most important types of learning for managers and all other organization members: "Managers . . . must learn to build and manage a human group that is capable of anticipating the new, capable of converting its vision into technology, products, processes and services—and willing and able to accept the new."[3]

Need for change

Change and Stability. Managers are confronted with a somewhat paradoxical situation. On the one hand, they must be responsive to the demands for change in work environments. They must anticipate changes and, viewing their accountability broadly, they must exercise leadership in bringing changes to the organizations they manage. Managers must be "change seekers" and "change agents."

Need for stability

On the other hand, managers must respond to the demands for stability in work environments. To some extent, managers are supposed to impose order. They want work to "flow," they want to respond only to "exceptions" to plans, and they want to minimize the frequency of "disruptions." The more fluid and changing a situation, the more difficult it is to manage efficiently and effectively. Thus, managers must also be "stability seekers" and "stability agents."

Need for balance

The paradox is that managers must create and maintain work environments that balance the demands of *both* stability and change. Both these demands affect the manager's accountability for performance. At the present time, when the demands of change are so obvious and pervasive, there may be a tendency to minimize the importance of stability to organizational effectiveness. Everything is not changing; everything does not need changing. "Everything nailed down is *not* coming loose."

---

[1] Vol. 53, no. 54, Southwest Edition, March 19, 1974, p. 13.

[2] *Future Shock* (New York: Random House, 1970).

[3] Quotation attributed to Peter F. Drucker in William Maass, "Making Organizations Adaptive to Change," *Innovation*, no. 30 (April 1972), p. 51.

*Two types
of forces*

A Change Framework.[4]   Figure 18–1 is a framework for thinking about change in organizations. The framework shows that there are two types of forces that press on an organization. "Driving forces" are those that encourage change, growth, and development. "Restraining forces" are those that encourage stability, the status quo, and that resist change. Examples are shown in Figure 18–2. Neither driving nor restraining forces should be viewed as inherently good or bad. They are simply forces that require organizational response.

FIGURE 18–1
A Framework for Thinking about Organizational Change

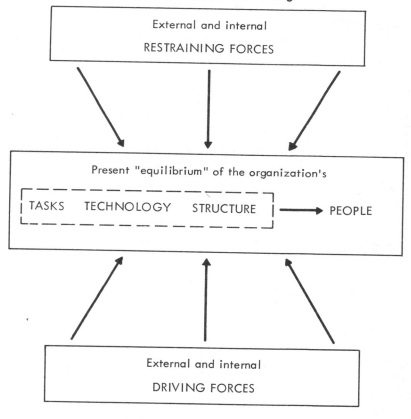

Two sources

Both driving and restraining forces can be external or internal. *Internal forces* have their immediate source inside the organization. *External forces* have their immediate source outside the or-

---

[4] Based, in part, on Kurt Lewin, "Quasi-Stationary Social Equilibria and the Problems of Permanent Change," in Newton Margulies and Anthony P. Raia, *Organizational Development: Values, Process, and Technology* (New York: McGraw-Hill Book Company, 1972), pp. 65–70.

FIGURE 18–2
Examples of Forces Pressing on Organizations

| Type of Force | Immediate Source of Driving or Restraining Force | |
	External	Internal
Driving	Shorter product-life cycles Need for different channels of distribution Shortages of raw materials Changing capital markets Changing status of world powers Consumerism Environmentalism Increased government regulation Changing cultural and social values	Increased demand by employees for greater job satisfaction Desire by employees to have more say in decision making Increased knowledge of new ways to organize Demands for more effective appeal systems Higher expectations by employees concerning their work environment Need to improve firm's rate of return on investment
Restraining	Continuing demands of customers for traditional products and services Existence of strong pressure groups (trade associations, unions) who have vested interests Inability of groups promoting change to mobilize into effective forces for change Need to maintain continuity with traditional customs, values, and norms Failure of external groups to perceive need for change	Existing power and social relationships and traditions Vested interests and coalitions Security and certainty of the existing situation and fear of the unknown Lack of effective strategies for introducing and implementing change Inability to perceive actual need for change Lack of confidence in managers that they can cope with change Any internal force that is reinforced by the status quo

ganization. Examples of these types of forces are also shown in Figure 18–2.[5]

Tasks and structure

Figure 18–1 shows that the driving and restraining forces can press on an organization's tasks, structure, technology, and people.[6] This is one way of thinking about the major interdependent variables in an organization at which change efforts can be directed. "Tasks" refer, of course, to the actual jobs that are performed in an organization. As we noted in Chapter 16, jobs vary in scope and depth, and change efforts directed at the task, or job, are variable attempts to alter scope or depth. The job-characteristics model dis-

---

[5] In practice, it may be difficult to clearly distinguish internal and external forces because the forces that press on an organization are often interrelated. Furthermore, as noted in Chapter 15, in our discussion of open systems, it is not always clear what is "inside" an organization and what is "outside."

[6] See Harold J. Leavitt, "Applied Organizational Change in Industry: Structural, Technological and Humanistic Approaches, in James G. March, ed., *Handbook of Organizations* (Chicago: Rand McNally & Company, 1965), pp. 1,144–70.

cussed in Chapter 16 is an example of a model that might be used to guide a task-focused change effort. "Structure," or design, refers to the relatively stable set of formally defined working relationships among the members of an organization. Examples of structure-focused change efforts are: altering the spans of management of executives; changing the number of organizational levels; changing from one base of departmentation (for example, a functional base) to another base of departmentation (for example, a product base); and altering line-and-staff functional authority relationships.

Technology and people

"Technology" refers to the types and patterns of activity, equipment and materials, and knowledge or experience used to perform tasks. Examples of technology-focused change efforts include: changing problem-solving and decision-making processes; introducing a computer to facilitate managerial planning and controlling; and converting from a unit production to a mass production technology. "People" refers, of course, to the individuals in an organization. Examples of people-focused approaches to change include: MBO; leadership and supervisory training; team-building workshops; sensitivity training; transactional analysis; assertiveness training; and traditional job-training programs.

Change focus

Change efforts in organizations can be initially directed at one or all the four variables mentioned above. Furthermore, specific approaches to organizational change vary in their impact on each of these variables.[7] For example, management by objectives (MBO) is one approach that can be used to change the way managers set goals and plans. As an approach to change, MBO is likely to have more direct impact on people and tasks than on technology and structure.[8] A change in the structure of an organization has a direct effect on people but may not affect tasks and technology at all.

Impact on people

"In the final analysis, however, most organizational change efforts, regardless of initial focus, must take account of the fact that *people are being called upon to do things differently.*"[9] Even though the initial focus of an organizational change may be to change some aspect of the organization's tasks, technology, or structure, the ultimate impact of the change will be on people. Thus, when we speak of changing organizations, we are speaking primarily of changing the behavior of people. In Figure 18–1, this idea is shown by placing tasks, technology, and structure in a dotted-line box arrowing into people.

---

[7] For a discussion of this idea, see Don Hellriegel and John W. Slocum, Jr., *Organizational Behavior: Contingency Views* (St. Paul, Minn.: West Publishing Company, 1976), chap. 13.

[8] Ibid., p. 406.

[9] Newton Margulies and John Wallace, *Organizational Change: Techniques and Applications* (Glenview, Ill.: Scott, Foresman and Company, 1973), p. 2.

*Three
possibilities
for change*

If an organization's tasks, technology, structure, or personnel are to change from their state of equilibrium, one or more of the following must occur: (1) There must be a net change in the *magnitude* of the driving or restraining forces; (2) there must be a change in the *direction* of one or more of the driving or restraining forces; and (3) a new driving or restraining force must be *added* or an old one must be *eliminated.*

*Three-phase
change
process*

Insofar as an organizational change requires a change in the *behavior of people,* it is useful to think in terms of a three-phase change process. The three phases are unfreezing, moving, and refreezing.[10] These three phases recognize that behavioral change is a process that takes time. People usually do not make significant behavioral changes overnight.

Unfreezing

"Unfreezing" refers to the idea that before a person will be willing to change present behavior, that person has to recognize his or her behavior as inappropriate, irrelevant, or in some way inadequate to the demands of a particular situation.

Moving

"Moving" is the phase of learning new behavior. Unfreezing creates a vacuum unless alternative behavior is available. It is one thing to know that your present job behavior is not adequate; it is something else to know what behavior is adequate. Thus, behavioral change requires that alternative behavior exists, that it is known; and it is a realistic alternative for the persons involved.

Refreezing

"Refreezing" of new, learned behavior means that the person accepts the new behavior as a permanent part of his or her behavioral repertoire. The person has to experiment with the behavior, see that it is effective, and assimilate it with other behavior and attitudes.

Difficulties

In concluding our discussion of the change framework shown in Figure 18–1, the following quotation serves to highlight some of the difficulties inherent in major organizational changes:

> Anyone who has planned major organizational change knows (a) how difficult it is to foresee accurately all the major problems involved, (b) the enormous amount of time needed to iron out the kinks and get people to accept the change, (c) the apparent lack of internal commitment on the part of many to help make the plan work, manifested partly, (d) by people at all levels resisting taking the initiative to make modifications that they see are necessary so that the new plan can work.[11]

---

[10] Lewin, "Quasi-Stationary Social Equilibria and the Problems of Permanent Change."

[11] Attributed to Chris Argyris in John M. Thomas and Warren G. Bennis, eds., *Management of Change and Conflict* (Harmondsworth, Eng.: Penguin Books, 1972), p. 205.

Summary box

> Managers are confronted with the task of balancing the demands for *both* change and stability.
>
> Our discussion of the change framework shown in Figure 18–1 has included the following major points:
>
> 1. There are both *driving* and *restraining forces* that press on an organization.
>
> 2. These forces originate from both *inside* and *outside* of the organization.
>
> 3. Change efforts in organizations can be directed at *four interdependent variables:* tasks; structure; technology; and people.
>
> 4. In the final analysis, most organizational change efforts have an impact on *people*.
>
> 5. In order for change to occur there must be a change in (*a*) the *magnitude*, (*b*) the *direction*, or (*c*) the *number* of the driving and restraining forces.
>
> 6. With respect to changing the behavior of people, a *three-phase process* is unfreezing, moving, and refreezing.

Approach affects response

Approaches to Introducing Changes. One factor that affects the response to changes is the manner in which the changes are introduced into the organization. Sometimes changes are introduced without consulting any of those affected by the changes. Additionally, too much change in too brief a time may create resistance and, ultimately, prevent any change from occurring.

Power distribution continuum

Approaches to introducing organization change may be discussed in terms of a "power distribution" continuum.[12] At one end of the continuum are approaches which rely on unilateral authority and little or no participation by subordinates. The middle of the continuum represents approaches that share authority between managers and subordinates. At the other end of the continuum are delegated approaches. This idea of different approaches to introducing change is shown in Figure 18–3.

FIGURE 18–3
Continuum Showing Approaches to Introducing Organization Change

Unilateral action approaches	Sharing of power approaches	Delegated authority approaches

---

[12] Larry E. Greiner, "Patterns of Organization Change," *Harvard Business Review*, vol. 45, no. 3 (May–June 1967), pp. 119–30.

Unilateral
action

"Unilateral action" approaches rely on formal position power and one-way communication. Examples include orders issued unilaterally by managers at one level in the organization to personnel at a lower level, replacement of key personnel, and top-management initiated changes in organization design. Although unilateral action approaches are common in practice, they are not necessarily the most effective.[13]

Sharing
of power

"Sharing of power" approaches utilize varying degrees of participation by subordinates in the change process. The emphasis is on sharing, not abdicating, power. For example, a manager might identify a need for change and develop alternative ways of meeting the need. Subordinates might then be allowed to choose from the alternatives the one they feel is best. Sharing of power approaches have been found to be associated with successful change efforts.[14] Among other things, such approaches help to lower the levels of conflict, stress, and tension which accompany change.[15]

Delegated
authority

"Delegated authority" approaches to introducing change actually turn over to subordinates the task of defining and deciding on the change problem. In delegated approaches, managers minimize their authority role. An example of a delegated approach is when managers provide subordinates with information describing a problem situation and then allow the group to define the problem, develop alternatives, and select a solution. Use of delegated approaches are rare in practice and have been associated with unsuccessful change efforts in organizations.[16]

No best
approach

There is no "best" approach to introducing change. There are cases when the time and cost requirements of shared power approaches cannot be justified in terms of benefits to the organization. Some changes must be implemented immediately and require the quickness of unilateral action. Not all managers have the knowledge or skill to utilize shared power or delegated power approaches. Furthermore, a particular manager will utilize several approaches to introducing change, depending on the nature of the change and the specific context within which it will occur. Although it is probably true that most changes in organizations are introduced using some variation of unilateral action, there is an

---

[13] L. E. Greiner and L. B. Barnes, "Organization Change and Development," in *Organizational Change and Development*, G. W. Dalton, P. R. Lawrence, and L. E. Greiner, eds. (Homewood, Ill.: Richard D. Irwin, 1970).

[14] Ibid.

[15] E. A. Johns, *The Sociology of Organizational Change* (Oxford: Pergamon Press, 1973), p. 155.

[16] Michael Beer and James W. Driscoll, "Strategies for Change," in *Improving Life at Work: Behavioral Science Approaches to Organizational Change*, J. Richard Hackman and J. Lloyd Suttle, eds., (Santa Monica, Calif.: Goodyear Publishing Company, 1976), p. 368.

increasing recognition of the value and appropriateness of shared power approaches.[17]

Managers play key role

Although approaches to introducing and implementing change in organizations may become relatively more participative or democratic, there also will continue to be a heavy reliance on unilaterally imposed change. Managers, and top managers in particular, by virtue of their accountability for efficient and effective work performance, are going to insist on playing a key role in defining and deciding on the need for change.

People are adaptive

Response to Change. Human beings are very adaptive. Their capacity to adapt to changing circumstances is limited, but enormous. The adaptive characteristic of "modern man" has been described in these words: "He is a creature who adapts reality to his own ends, who transforms reality into a congenial form . . . he is extremely good at adaptive behavior—at doing or learning to do things that increase his chances for survival or for satisfaction."[18]

Neutral response

From the manager's viewpoint of accountability for achieving goals, human response to change can be neutral, positive, or negative. A "neutral response" may be the most common type of behavioral response to change in organizations. Although changes are taking place constantly in organizations, they do not affect every individual equally, nor is any one individual affected by all changes. In fact, the first reaction of most employees to the claim of widespread and pervasive change could well be, "What change?" As a practical matter, many of the changes "swirling around us" never directly touch us and our response to them is neutral—from a behavioral viewpoint, we are indifferent to the changes.

Positive response

A "positive response" to change means that, from the perspective of managers, the response contributes to the efficient and effective accomplishment of goals for which they are accountable. Subordinates who respond positively to change are referred to as cooperative, adaptive, progressive and "able to cope with change." Changes that are perceived by employees to be in their best interest are welcomed by employees—pay increases, more benefits, and promotions. Even changes that require major modifications in their behavior are not always resisted by employees. Their response depends on such factors as how the change was introduced, what capacity the employees have for coping with the change, and what changes in human interactions are involved.

---

[17] T. Lupton, "Organizational Change: Top-Down or Bottom-Up Management?" *Personnel Review*, vol. 1, no. 1 (Autumn 1971), pp. 22–28.

[18] Bernard Berelson and Gary Steiner, *Human Behavior: An Inventory of Scientific Findings* (New York: Harcourt, Brace, and World, 1964), p. 662.

Negative response

A "negative response" to change by employees is commonly viewed by managers as dysfunctional to goal achievement. Employees who respond negatively to change may be viewed as stubborn, uncooperative, set in their ways, and "unable to cope." However, from the viewpoint of employees, response to change is neither positive nor negative; it is simply behavior that makes sense from *their* viewpoint. Their viewpoint may not be the same as that of the firm in which they work. Employees may see the consequences of change, not so much at the level of the firm as at the level of their own social existence as a whole, including their family and community life.

Resistance to change

Resistance to change may be sensible to employees because they "perceive the change as a threat to their existing or anticipated level of need-satisfaction."[19] The threat may be perceived or actual, but it is "real" to the employee, nevertheless. The change may create a situation of uncertainty, fear, insecurity, and loss of self-esteem. In short, the expected consequences of the change may be viewed as negative by employees. In such a case, resistance by employees to changes instituted by managers should be expected.

Red flag

Resistance to change should not be viewed by managers as necessarily bad. This point was expressed 25 years ago in a classic discussion of resistance to change: "I think that . . . management will do better to look at it this way: when resistance does appear, it should not be thought of as something to be *overcome*. Instead, it can best be thought of as a useful red flag—a signal that something is going wrong."[20]

Resistance can be beneficial

Resistance can signal to managers the need for improved communication about the meaning and purposes of a change. It can reveal the need for more effective approaches to introducing and implementing the change. Resistance can suggest the need for more realistic timing. It can reveal the inadequacy of current procedures for anticipating changes. Further, resistance to change may be indicative of an organizational climate in which organizational members feel free to express their legitimate concerns. In light of these possible benefits of resistance to change, it may be said that the *absence* of resistance to change may be harmful to organizations.

Management not always right

In discussions by managers about employees' resistance to change there is often the implied assumption that resistance is irrational and beyond the comprehension of reasonable men—the managers are assumed to be reasonable men. One writer expresses this idea in these words: "There is a general assumption that management is always rational in changing its direction or modifying

---

[19] Johns, *The Sociology of Organizational Change*, p. 61.

[20] Paul R. Lawrence, "How to Deal with Resistance to Change," *Harvard Business Review*, vol. 32, no. 3 (May–June 1954), p. 56.

its objectives to achieve its goals better and that operators are stupid, emotional or irrational in not responding in the way they should."[21]

Manager's problem

It is relatively easy to get employees to accept changes that are clearly in their best interests. Furthermore, the problem of getting employees to accept changes that they *inaccurately perceive* to be contrary to their best interests is, at least, manageable. However, many changes that occur are simply not in the best interests of particular employees, and it is unreasonable to think that managers can prevent resistance to such changes. Although intelligent and sensitive managers can often prevent many of the causes of employees' resistance to change from arising, there are some situations that, in the final analysis, are best described as "win–lose" situations. When the employees are the losers, their resistance is very understandable.

Summary box

> *Approaches to introducing change* in an organization may be classified along a power-distribution continuum. *Unilateral action* approaches rely on formal position power and one-way communication. *Sharing of power* approaches utilize varying degrees of subordinate participation but managers play an authoritative role in the change process. In *delegated* approaches, managers may participate in the change process but their authority role is minimized.
>
> Human beings are very *adaptive to change.* Nevertheless, from the viewpoint of managers, subordinates' *response to change* may be neutral, positive, or negative. Negative response to change commonly is viewed by managers as something to be avoided.
>
> Employees' *resistance to change* can be thought of as a red flag—a signal that something could be wrong. Resistance to change can be beneficial. The *absence* of resistance to change could be harmful to an organization.

ORGANIZATION DEVELOPMENT

OD

Organization development, commonly referred to as "OD," is both a discipline in which academic degrees can be earned and a type of work in which livelihoods can be earned. At the present time, it is no doubt easier to do the former than the latter. OD, as a discipline and as a practice, is interested in the skills, techniques, theories and models, and processes that can be useful in bringing about orderly change in organizations.

---

[21] Joan Woodward, "Resistance to Change," *Journal of Management Studies* (1968), p. 138.

Humanistic values

Earlier in this chapter, we noted that change efforts in organizations can be directed at four interdependent variables: tasks; structure; technology; and people. OD change efforts can focus on any of these variables. However, regardless of its specific focus, OD places a high priority on humanistic values and goals consistent with those values. OD is "a way of looking at the whole human side of organizational life."[22]

Definition

What Is OD? OD is a management-supported, systems approach to planned organization change that utilizes behavioral science knowledge as a major means of achieving the goal of greater organization effectiveness. The word "organization" in this definition refers to any system of patterned, working relationships between organization members. Thus, OD can be directed at the total organization (such as General Motors Company) or at any organizational unit within it.

In practice

The above definition of OD is not always recognizable in the "real-world" activities that are labeled OD. In some business firms OD is just a new label put on some old activities—organization planning, personnel, or management development. In other firms, OD is used to refer to a "comprehensive strategy for organization improvement,"[23] and is, in fact, implemented in that way.[24] In most business firms and other types of organizations, the term "OD" is not used at all, and among some businessmen it has negative connotations.

Character-istics

Characteristics, Values, and Objectives. Additional insight into OD is gained by noting several of its characteristics. OD change efforts often use the services of a third-party change agent or OD consultant. OD implies a relatively long-term and ongoing process. It emphasizes the importance of goal-setting and planning activities. OD is associated with skills and techniques aimed at developing more effective work groups or teams.[25]

Values

The OD emphasis on the human dimensions of organizations is reflected in the following list of humanistic values:

1. Providing opportunities for people to function as human beings rather than as resources in the productive process.
2. Providing opportunities for each organization member, as well as for the organization itself, to develop to his full potential.

[22] W. Warner Burke, Jack Fordyce, and Stanley Jacobson, "What is OD?" *News and Reports* from NTL Institute for Applied Behavioral Science, vol. 2, no. 3 (June 1968), p. 1.

[23] Harold M. F. Rush, *Organization Development: A Reconnaissance* (New York: The Conference Board, 1973), p. 2.

[24] William F. Dowling, "The Corning Approach to Organization Development," *Organizational Dynamics*, vol. 3, no. 4 (Spring 1975), pp. 16–34.

[25] Kenneth N. Wexley and Gary A. Yukl, *Organizational Behavior and Personnel Psychology* (Homewood, Ill.: Richard D. Irwin, 1972), pp. 335–37.

3. Seeking to increase the effectiveness of the organization in terms of *all* of its goals.

4. Attempting to create an environment in which it is possible to find exciting and challenging work.

5. Providing opportunities for people in organizations to influence the way in which they relate to work, the organization, and the environment.

6. Treating each human being as a person with a complex set of needs, all of which are important in his work and in his life.[26]

Objectives

The objectives or goals of OD change efforts are consistent with OD's humanistic values. Included in OD's objectives are:

1. To develop a self-renewing, *viable* system that can organize in a variety of ways depending on tasks. . . .

2. To optimize the effectiveness of both the stable (the basic organization chart) and the temporary systems (the many projects, committees, etc.), through which much of the organization's work is accomplished. . . .

3. To move toward *high collaboration* and *low competition* between interdependent units. . . .

4. To create conditions where conflict is brought out and managed. . . . The goal is to move the organization towards seeing conflict as an inevitable condition and as problems that need to be *worked* before adequate decisions can be made.

5. To reach the point where decisions are made on the basis of information source rather than organization role. This means to move toward a *norm* of the *authority of knowledge* as well as the authority of role.

6. To create an open, problem-solving climate throughout the organization.

7. To build trust among individuals and groups throughout the organization.

8. To increase the sense of "ownership" of organization objectives throughout the work force.

9. To increase self-control and self-direction for people within the organization.[27]

Unstructured groups

Evolution of OD. The beginnings of what is now known as OD go back to the mid-1940s. At that time, Kurt Lewin and his colleagues at the Research Center for Group Dynamics at the Massachusetts Institute of Technology were working on the use of small discussion groups as a vehicle for achieving change in behavior. This work led to discovery of the potential benefits of unstructured, leaderless small groups for acquiring behavioral knowledge and bringing about behavioral change. That is, when several people are placed in a small group situation where the main item on the

[26] Newton Margulies and Anthony P. Raia, *Organization Development: Values, Process, and Technology* (New York: McGraw-Hill Book Company, 1972), p. 3.

[27] Richard Beckhard, *Organization Development: Strategies and Models* (Reading, Mass.: Addison-Wesley Publishing Company, 1969), p. 13–14, and Burke, Fordyce, and Jacobson, "What Is OD?" p. 1.

agenda is to learn *from and about each other* through group inter-action, significant learning can take place.

*T-Groups,
laboratory
training*

These unstructured, small group situations can become "labora-tories" in which the group participants, through *processes of open and authentic communication with each other* in an atmosphere of *mutual trust and respect,* can become more self-aware and more interpersonally competent. These types of groups are commonly called "T-Groups" ("T" stands for Training) and the group process often is called "sensitivity training." This type of training, when accompanied by related readings, lectures, theory discussions, group exercises, intergroup exercises, personal skills training, and feedback sessions, is called "laboratory training."[28]

*Bridging
the gap*

In the late 1950s, attempts were made to try to bridge the gap between the type of *individual*-oriented learning that results from "T-grouping" and the type of learning required to bring about change in behavior in ongoing work *organizations.* In other words, more effective individuals do not necessarily lead to more effective organizations. These individuals must have their personal skills and motivations complemented by effective work environments. Effective individuals are a necessary but not sufficient condition for organizational effectiveness.

*OD and
laboratory
training*

Even though laboratory training is, even today, an important part of many OD efforts it should not be thought of as synonymous with OD. Laboratory training is one of the approaches used by OD practitioners in their attempts to achieve objectives of OD efforts. However, much of the total effort in an OD project involves such activities as gathering data, analyzing data, and sharing informa-tion obtained in data gathering and analysis with those affected by it. These three activities sometimes are referred to as "action re-search" or "survey feedback."[29]

*Specific
approaches*

In addition to laboratory training and survey feedback, many other specific approaches to change are common to OD as it is practiced today. Many of these approaches have been discussed earlier in the book—MBO, job enrichment, the Managerial Grid®, the nominal group technique, and problem-solving and conflict-management training. Additional OD approaches include attitude surveys, role analysis, transactional analysis (TA), team building, interviewing, and communication improvement. In a recent analy-

---

[28] Leland P. Bradford, Jack R. Gibb, and Kenneth D. Benne, *T-Group Theory and Laboratory Method* (New York: John Wiley & Sons, 1964). See also Paul C. Buchanan, "Laboratory Training and Organization Develop-ment," *Administrative Science Quarterly,* vol. 14 (September 1969), pp. 466–80.

[29] Frank Friedlander and L. Dave Brown, "Organization Development," in Karl O. Magnusen, ed., *Organizational Design, Development, and Behavior: A Situational Approach* (Glenview, Ill.: Scott, Foresman and Company, 1977), p. 321.

sis of 37 OD-related research studies (conducted from 1957 to 1975), it was found that the most common approaches to change were team building, sensitivity and laboratory training, and approaches related to survey feedback.[30]

From the sixties to the seventies

Thus, throughout the 1960s and 1970s, OD evolved from its origin in the individual-oriented methodology of T-Groups and laboratory training to its present status. OD now utilizes a great variety of approaches that contribute to organizational effectiveness. One OD expert's view of some of the changes that have occurred in OD from about the mid-sixties to the mid-seventies is summarized in Figure 18–4.

FIGURE 18–4
A View of Changes in OD: From Mid-1960s to Mid-1970s *

From	To
A field limited almost exclusively to business and industrial organizations	A field affecting many different organizational types
Advocating a specific managerial style [a participative style]	Emphasizing the situation or contingency approach
Democracy as the primary value advocated	Authenticity as the primary value
A field based largely on the social technology of laboratory training and survey feedback	A field based on a broader range of social technology
Using consultants who are non-directive, purely process-oriented practitioners	Using consultants who are authoritative specialists
Considering the OD practitioner as the change agent	Considering the line manager and administrator as the change agents
OD practitioners working almost exclusively with management	Working with both managers and persons at all organizational levels
Being merely a glamorous name for training	Being a function that has organizational legitimacy in and of itself, with attendant power and official status

* Source: W. Warner Burke, "Changing Trends in Organization Development," in W. Warner Burke, ed., *Current Issues and Strategies in Organization Development* (New York: Human Sciences Press, 1977), pp. 22–35.

Future

It is difficult to project accurately the future of what is now called OD. However, it is reasonable to project that changing organizations will increasingly require a planned approach that actively involves top management and key personnel and that is supported by behavioral science knowledge and skills. OD is such

[30] See Larry E. Pate, Warren R. Nielsen, and Paula C. Brown, "Advances in Research on Organization Development: Toward a Beginning," *Proceedings* of the Annual Meeting of the Academy of Management, 1976, pp. 390–91.

an approach. It is not tied to any particular technique for bringing about change. Rather, it recognizes the value of a diverse set of change techniques and strategies. One of OD's greatest needs is for a theory or model that can make sense of OD's techniques.[31]

Summary box

> OD stands for organization development. It is an academic discipline and a type of work. In general, OD places high priority on humanistic values and goals.
>
> OD may be *defined* as a management-supported, systems approach to planned organization change that utilizes behavioral science knowledge as a major means of achieving the goal of greater organizational effectiveness. Several *characteristics*, *values*, and *objectives* of OD were itemized in the chapter.
>
> Two major OD techniques are *laboratory training* and *survey feedback*. Today, OD utilizes a wide variety of approaches to changing an organization's tasks, structure, technology, and people.

ORGANIZATIONAL EFFECTIVENESS

The bottom line

Presumably the reason for *changing* or *developing* organizations is to make them more effective. Organizational effectiveness is the "bottom line"; it is the reason for managerial work. But how do we know when an organization is "more effective"? What is organizational effectiveness? How can it be measured?

Multiple criteria

Criteria of Organizational Effectiveness. Several criteria that have been used in studies of organizational effectiveness are shown in Figure 18–5.[32] Although there is some overlap in these criteria, they do suggest that effectiveness must be evaluated using multiple criteria: "Single prescriptions for effectiveness are like mirages: desirable but distant, receding, unreal."[33] It follows from the multiple criteria idea that an organization can be highly effective by some criteria and highly ineffective by other criteria.

Time dimension

Some criteria of effectiveness may be more important than others to the survival of an organization. Survival is considered by

[31] W. Warner Burke, "Changing Trends in Organization Development," in W. Warner Burke, ed., *Current Issues and Strategies in Organization Development* (New York: Human Sciences Press, 1977), p. 38–39.

[32] For descriptions of these 30 indicators of organizational effectiveness, see John P. Campbell, "Contributions Research Can Make in Understanding Organizational Effectiveness," *Organization and Administrative Sciences*, vol. 7, nos. 1–2 (Spring–Summer 1976), pp. 36–38.

[33] Paul E. Mott, *The Characteristics of Effective Organizations*, (New York: Harper & Row, Publishers, 1972), p. 184.

FIGURE 18–5
Measures of Organizational Effectiveness

Absenteeism	Motivation
Accidents	Overall effectiveness
Achievement emphasis	Participation and shared
Conflict–cohesion	influence
Control	Planning and goal setting
Efficiency	Productivity
Evaluations by external	Profit
entities	Quality
Flexibility–adaptation	Readiness
Goal consensus	Role and norm
Growth	congruence
Information management and	Satisfaction
communication	Stability
Internalization of organiza-	Training and development
tional goals	emphasis
Managerial interpersonal skills	Turnover
Managerial task skills	Utilization of environment
Morale	Value of human resources

Source: John P. Campbell, "Contributions Research Can Make in Understanding Organizational Effectiveness," *Organization and Administrative Sciences*, vol. 7, nos. 1–2 (Spring–Summer 1976), pp. 36–38.

some writers as "the ultimate, or long-run, measure of organizational effectiveness."[34] In this view, criteria such as productivity, efficiency, absenteeism, turnover, satisfaction, and accidents are short-run measures of effectiveness. Thus, time is a dimension that can be used in differentiating criteria of organizational effectiveness.

Examples of frames of reference

Frame of Reference. "All definitions of effectiveness involve some assumptions with respect to frame of reference."[35] For example, in the view of the individual member of the organization, satisfaction, motivation, and morale criteria may be of foremost importance. From the view of stockholders, profitability may be the most important criterion. From the view of top executives, growth, productivity, profit, and achievement emphasis may be crucial.

Inside perspective

All the examples in the above paragraph represent the frames of reference of particular organization members who are "inside" the organization. This suggests that organizational effectiveness

[34] James L. Gibson, John M. Ivancevich, and James H. Donnelly, Jr., "Organizational Effectiveness," in *Organizations: Behavior, Structure, and Processes* (Dallas: Business Publications, 1976), p. 65.

[35] Daniel Katz and Robert L. Kahn, "The Concept of Organizational Effectiveness," in *The Social Psychology of Organizations* (New York: John Wiley & Sons, 1966), p. 170.

can be viewed from both an inside and outside perspective.[36] The "inside perspective" is more likely to evaluate effectiveness in terms of the efficient use of resources and in terms of the efficient functioning of the organization. In a business firm, the inside perspective might utilize such effectiveness measures as return on investment, labor productivity, accident rates, percent of plant capacity utilized, absenteeism and labor turnover rates, percent of increase in market share, and so on.

Outside perspective

When organizational effectiveness is evaluated by people who are outside the organization, there is likely to be more emphasis on the role the organization plays in the larger system of which it is a part. The "outside perspective" tends to evaluate the effectiveness of an organization in terms of the various outputs of the organization, not in terms of its internal efficiency. Thus, the outside perspective might consider effectiveness measures such as the extent to which an organization hires members of minority groups as employees, the record of the organization in environmental concerns, and the extent to which the organization promotes a high quality of work life for its employees. Further, the outside perspective is fundamentally interested in whether the organization is performing its basic social function. For example, producing economic goods and services with appropriate quantity–quality–cost trade-offs is the basic social function of business firms and is a fundamental concern of the outside perspective of organizational effectiveness.

Possible conflict— example

There are two implications of these two perspectives of organizational effectiveness. First, the two are not always compatible. For example, in order to increase internal efficiency and labor productivity, a decision may be made to increase the level of job specialization in a business firm. This decision may have the effect of reducing employees' job scope and depth. Assuming that this decision has the consequence of increasing internal efficiency, it may also have the consequence of lowering the quality of work life for the employees involved. This may reduce organizational effectiveness for the employees. Further, this lowering of the quality of work life may ultimately become a matter of concern in the larger society and be viewed as an indication of organizational *ineffectiveness* in meeting the legitimate needs of employees. The way in which organizations utilize human resources is a matter of increasing social concern.

Another example

Another example of the possible conflict between the inside and outside perspectives has to do with various illegal or questionable business practices. Practices such as administered pricing, payoffs to influential government personnel, and industrial espionage are

---

[36] Robert Dubin, "Organizational Effectiveness: Some Dilemmas of Perspective," *Organization and Administrative Sciences,* vol. 7, nos. 1–2 (Spring–Summer 1976), pp. 7–13.

sometimes justified by the need to be efficient and to do "what everybody else does." Whatever the contribution of such practices to internal efficiency and to the satisfaction of the needs of particular employees, they are probably not in the long-run interests of society.

Taking both perspectives into account

A second implication of the inside and outside perspectives of organizational effectiveness has to do with the need to take both views into account. Organizational roles need to be identified that span the two perspectives. Such roles will increase the probability that both internal efficiency and social utility criteria will be taken into account. Additionally, such roles will direct explicit attention to tradeoffs involved in decisions in which there is conflict between the two perspectives. For example, in decisions involving pollution, energy-conservation, and affirmative action, there are clear tradeoffs between internal efficiency and external effectiveness.[37]

Effectiveness of the total organization

Macro and Micro. There is another point that also is important to understanding organizational effectiveness. That point has to do with the tendency to think of organizational effectiveness in global, macro terms. For example, regardless of how many effectiveness measures are used by a business firm, the tendency is to refer to the *firm's* effectiveness. Effectiveness is viewed as a characteristic of the total, global firm. How profitable was *General Motors* last year? How many patients did *Good Samaritan Hospital* care for last year? How many academic degrees were awarded last year by the *University of Chicago*? How effective was *Pizza Hut*? These types of questions are common and useful, up to a point.

Effectiveness of subunits of the organization

The problem with a global or macro concept of effectiveness is that it can hide micro ineffectiveness. For example, overall profitability of a business firm can be excellent, but profitability of specific products may be poor. A firm's profitability is a kind of arithmetic mean and, like such averages, can be influenced by extreme values at either end of an array of figures. The general point here is that both macro and micro measures of effectiveness must be considered. Further, not all effectiveness measures are equally relevant to all organizational subunits.

Centrality of goals

Organizational Effectiveness and Goals. In Chapter 2, we referred to goals as the strategic managing variable. This label is intended to convey the central role that goals play in managing. Since organizational effectiveness is the "bottom line" of managerial work, it is not surprising that goals are central to the notion of organizational effectiveness. Organizations are often viewed as goal-seeking entities: "In fact, on a general level, it has been suggested that effectiveness itself could best be understood in terms

---

[37] Ibid.

of the extent to which an organization is successful . . . in the pursuit of . . . goals."[38] Goal achievement may not be the only way to look at organizational effectiveness, but goals do play a central role.

Goal system   In Chapter 2, we presented a view of the manager's goal system. For convenience, this view is illustrated again in Figure 18–6. Relating this goal-system idea to organizational effectiveness, we may say that effectiveness ultimately must be evaluated in terms of a *satisfactory degree of attainment* of individual, performance, and group goals. Note that group goals take into account the interests and concerns of groups "outside" the organization. In addition, evaluations of effectiveness must take into account, not only actual goal attainment, but also the organization's capacity to continue to satisfy individual, performance, and group goals.

FIGURE 18–6
A Manager's Goal System

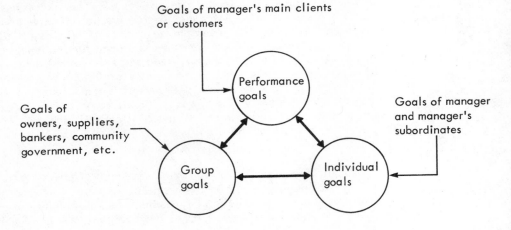

Accountability   The basic theme of this book is that managers are accountable
for   for job performance—their own and that of their subordinates.
performance   This job performance takes place within an organizational context. It is the collective job performance of all the organization's members that determines the effectiveness of an organization and its parts.

---

[38] Richard M. Steers, *Organizational Effectiveness: A Behavioral View* (Santa Monica, Calif.: Goodyear Publishing Company, 1977).

Summary box

> There is no single criterion that can be used to evaluate the effectiveness of an organization. Effectiveness must be evaluated using *multiple criteria,* although some criteria may be more important than others to the survival of an organization. Both macro and micro measures of effectiveness must be considered.
>
> Organizational effectiveness can be viewed from both an *inside and outside perspective.* An inside perspective tends to emphasize internal efficiency, and an outside perspective emphasizes social utility. These two perspectives can conflict with each other and suggest the need for organizational roles that span both perspectives.
>
> *Goal attainment* and the capacity for future goal attainment are centrally important to the notion of organizational effectiveness. Effectiveness in satisfying group, individual, and performance goals is an integral part of the manager's accountability for performance.

CHECK YOUR UNDERSTANDING

Organizational change
  Driving forces
  Restraining forces
  Major change variables
  Three possibilities for change
  Three-phase change process
  Power distribution continuum
  Three approaches to introducing change
  Types of response to change
Organization development

Values and objectives of OD
T-group
Sensitivity training
Laboratory training
Survey feedback
Organizational effectiveness
  Criteria of effectiveness
  Role of frame of reference
  Macro and micro views
  Relation of goals to effectiveness

STUDY QUESTIONS

1. How, in your opinion, does change affect the capacity of managers to meet their accountability for performance?

2. What, in your opinion, are some important factors that affect managerial performance that are not changing?

3. How can managers learn how to better cope with change that affects their area of accountability?

4. Argue pro and con: Managers, by nature of their work, resist change.

5. Identify a major type of change that has occurred in an organization with which you are familiar. Analyze the change using the change framework shown in Figure 18–1.

6. Explain how employee resistance to management-initiated changes might prove beneficial to the long-run effectiveness of the changes.

7. The chapter states that OD emphasizes humanistic values. Most people would probably express themselves as being in favor of making organizations more "human." What, in your opinion, are some problems that might be encountered in attempts to give human values a higher priority in organizations.

8. Identify some of the changes that have occurred in OD since the mid-1960s.

APPLICATION: UNSUCCESSFUL CHANGE EFFORTS

Chapter 18 states that organizational change efforts can be directed at four major variables: tasks, technology, structure, and people. Some approaches to change place primary focus on one of these variables, although the other variables might also be affected. This application describes two actual change efforts. The first is primarily a task-focused approach. The second is primarily a people-focused approach.

Task-Focused Change Effort. MMC is a division of a large industrial firm and is located in a metropolitan area of the Southwest. MMC decided to initiate a "job enrichment" program on a limited basis in the machine shop. The "trial run" was intended to provide information useful in deciding whether to extend job enrichment to other MMC operations.

One of the major elements in the job-enrichment program was an emphasis on "work teams." Members of these teams were given opportunities to schedule their own work, to determine output standards, and to engage in coordination activities with personnel in other operations of the machine shop.

The job enrichment program lasted (on paper) for about three years. Some of the reasons given for scrapping the program were: (1) those who were not part of the program resented the special treatment of the "enriched employees"; (2) the supervisors of the enriched employees were viewed by higher-level managers as too tolerant of the employees when they were absent or late for work (although productivity had not been adversely affected by this perceived excessive tolerance, management was concerned about the trend); and (3) the work-team supervisors thought that there was a high degree of ambiguity in management's communication to them of the program's objectives and operational procedures.

People-Focused Change Effort. In the mid-1970s, PipeCo, a manufacturer of equipment used in the physical distribution of oil and gas, decided to institute an MBO program. MBO's impact is primarily on people, but can (and probably will if it is successful) affect tasks, technology, and structure. In this MBO application, the program was initiated, implemented, and supported primarily by staff personnel having responsibility for employee development. On paper, the MBO program was well conceived and the mechanics of its implementation were intelligently "worked through." PipeCo's MBO program was an immediate failure.

According to key personnel within PipeCo, the company is now "operating without goals." When they were asked how it is possible for a large business firm to operate without goals, their response was; "Any bureaucracy can operate without goals. For particular products, there is often a guaranteed market and the firm can operate quite profitably without goals—in the MBO sense."

The major reason given for the failure of PipeCo's MBO program was that "top management was involved in the program, but not committed to it." The crucial difference to the program between involvement and commitment was clarified in this way. "Suppose a chicken and a pig are observing a human being eating ham and eggs for breakfast. For the chicken, the breakfast requires involvement; for the pig it requires commitment."

What do these two examples suggest about the *process* of introducing and implementing change in organizations?

part four

Managing: Recap and Epilogue

Chapter 19   We have covered a lot of territory in this book. Our discussion
has ranged from techniques (MBO, Zero-Based Budgeting, Delphi
Forecasting) to broad ideas (leadership, organization, behavioral
consequences). It has ranged from topics that lend themselves to
very precise analysis (linear programming, PERT, decision matrices, Pareto's curve) to those that still are characterized by im-
precision and mystery (motivation, behavior). In any case, we
have "touched base" with a very broad and diverse set of ideas,
all of which have some relevance to the task of managing. In Chapter 19, we attempt to bring some of these ideas together. It is a
recap chapter that should help you recall specific ideas and help
you see them as part of an overall way of looking at the manager's
task.

Chapter 20   Chapter 20 is a personal epilogue. In a sense, it is a partial statement of our philosophy about organizations and about managing.
It is an attempt to suggest an ultimate reason why managing can
be and should be viewed as a type of work having great potentialities for helping people lead more fully human lives.

Objective of Chapter 19

- To present a concise summary of the major ideas included in *Managing: Toward Accountability for Performance*

Outline of Chapter 19

19

MANAGING: A RECAP

This chapter

The purpose of this chapter is to put before you in a few pages an overview of the major ideas that we have discussed throughout the book. This overview can help you recall and integrate specific ideas that we included in the three major parts of the book—general management, behavior in organizations, and organizations. A word of caution: This overview will not make much sense unless you have read the preceding 18 chapters. The overview is a *recap* for purposes of *recall.* It is intended as an aid in integrating the broad and diverse body of knowledge that makes up the body of this textbook.

MANAGING

Definition

"Managing," or "management," is the work of creating and maintaining environments in which people can accomplish goals efficiently and effectively. These environments involve the integrated use of human, financial, and natural resources for the purpose of achieving goals. The test of whether a job is a managerial or a nonmanagerial job is whether the person occupying the job position is accountable for the job performance of those over whom the person has authority.

Universal activity

Managing is a universal activity—it occurs in all types, sizes, and functions of organizations and at all levels of organizations. A fundamental assumption of this book is that there is some knowledge about managing that, if learned and applied appropriately, can increase the odds that you will be effective as a manager. There are, of course, many aspects of managing that cannot be learned from this or any other book. Nevertheless, this book provides a foundation that should prove useful to *thinking* like a manager.

Approaches to study

There are several approaches that can be taken to the study of managing. Some of these are the traditional, case-method, behavioral, decision-making, quantitative, and contingency approaches. In this book we draw on all of these approaches but the major emphasis is on the behavioral approach. The diversity of approaches suggests that there is no "one best way" to study managing, just as there is no one best way to manage.

583

ACCOUNTABILITY FOR PERFORMANCE

Basic theme,
narrow view

The basic theme of this book is that managers are accountable for their own job performance and for the job performance of others. Accountability for efficient and effective performance is the essence of the manager's job. In one sense, the idea of accountability can be viewed in a very narrow, but nevertheless important, way. It can mean simply that managers are accountable to their immediate superiors for performance results in their area of responsibility. This is the most fundamental type of managerial accountability.

Broad view

The notion of accountability for performance can, however, be viewed more broadly. Managers are accountable to their subordinates and peers. They are accountable to their profession. They are accountable to various groups—consumers, the general public, community and government organizations—outside the organization in which they work. In the future, it is likely that managers will increasingly be attempting to find practical ways of meeting the demands of an increasingly broad and complex definition of their accountability for performance. It is also likely that one of the skills that will become more characteristic of effective managers is the skill to comprehend the full scope of their accountability for performance.

GOALS

Strategic role

Goals or objectives are viewed in the book as the strategic managing variable. From the viewpoint of logic, goals are the starting point of managerial thought and action. They provide the basis for planning, organizing, decision making, controlling, and almost every other type of managerial activity. From the viewpoint of behavior, goals often do not play as strategic a role in managing as would be suggested by logic. Goals that are meaningful in guiding the behavior of managers are the exception rather than the rule in organizations.

Definition,
uses, criteria

We define goals as desired results toward which behavior is directed. Simply saying something is a goal does not make it a goal. The test of a goal is its actual effect on the behavior of people. This takes the form of providing targets and standards for behavior, of serving as a basis for evaluating change, and of providing the rationale for plans, controls, and decisions. Goals are more likely to have effect on the behavior of people if they meet these criteria: measurable; attainable; acceptable; congruent; and compared with alternatives.

Goal system

All managers must be concerned with achieving multiple and interacting goals. We use the term "goal system" to refer to this idea. The manager's goal system includes performance, group, and individual goals. One of the major concerns of managers and employees is how to constructively integrate individual goals with the performance goals of organizations.

Goal-setting process

How are goals established in an organization? The goal-setting process is often a complex, human behavioral process. Three ideas that help to convey something of the nature of the goal-setting process are: imperfect rationality; ends-means chain; and coalition formation. One widely used approach to the goal-setting process is management by objectives, MBO. There are three ideas that are basic to most applications of MBO: interactive goal setting; implementation; and performance appraisal.

MANAGERIAL PLANNING

Definition, primacy of planning

"Managerial planning" is the process of determining in advance specifically what should be done in order to achieve particular goals, how it should be done, when and where it should be done, and who should do it. Sometimes the phrase "primacy of planning" is used to convey the importance of planning to managerial effectiveness. This is a particularly appropriate phrase when goal setting is included, as it is by some writers, as part of planning. In this book we separated our discussions of goal setting and planning in order to give emphasis to goals as the strategic managing variable. In addition, we noted that planning, budgeting, and forecasting have different meanings.

Characteristics, premises

The practice of managerial planning can be aided by giving conscious consideration to characteristics of plans and to planning premises. "Characteristics of plans" include scope, repetitiveness, flexibility, and time span. "Planning premises" are assumptions about the environment in which plans are to be implemented. In this connection, premises need to be made for both the external and internal environment of the organization or of organizational subunits. The need to establish premises for the external environment suggests that managers must be able to assess their environments and obtain information from it. A four-mode scanning process is one view of how managers obtain information about the external environment.

Planning process

Some managerial planning is nothing more sophisticated than making snap, "seat-of-the-pants" judgments about what action to take tomorrow. However, most organizations utilize, in varying degrees, some sort of formal planning process. The particular form varies from organization to organization. Nevertheless, the notion of a general or conceptual planning process that can be adapted to particular needs is a useful notion. One view of a conceptual planning process and an illustration of a formal planning process were presented.

MANAGERIAL CONTROLLING

Definition,
control
process

"Managerial controlling" is the process of assuring that actions are in line with desired results (goals). There are four fundamental elements involved in the control process: a predetermined goal, standard, or plan; measurement of actual performance against the goal (sensor); comparison of actual performance with the goal (comparator); and corrective action when required (activator). The extent to which these four elements operate automatically as part of a control system is the basis for distinguishing open and closed-loop control systems.

Four
controllable
aspects

What exactly do managers control when they are engaged in managerial controlling? In general, there are four aspects of people and things that can be controlled: quantity; quality; time; and cost. In controlling these four aspects of people and things it is useful to recall that overcontrol creates problems for managers just as undercontrol does. As in any managerial activity, a guiding principle in controlling is that the costs incurred should be justified by the benefits received. Control is not an end in itself but is one means of assuring goal accomplishment.

Planning and
controlling
techniques

Several techniques useful to managers in planning and controlling are: Pareto's law and curve, control tolerances, zero-base budgeting, Delphi forecasting, cost points, and PERT.

MANAGERIAL DECISION MAKING

Definition,
elements,
process

A decision is a choice from among a set of alternatives. Every decision involves three elements: choice, alternatives, and a goal or goals. Generally, a decision is one step or phase in a decision process that begins with problem recognition and ends with implementation and follow-up.

Types

Managerial decision making is a type of behavior that enters into almost everything else that managers do. The decisions that managers make can be roughly grouped into two types—programmed (decisions made in response to repetitive and routine problems) and unprogrammed (decisions that are unique and involve creative solutions).

Decision
matrix

Sometimes decision problems can be thought of in terms of a decision-matrix framework. This framework involves three components: strategies; states of nature (having varying degrees of certainty, risk, and uncertainty); and outcomes or pay-offs. There are several techniques that can be used as aids to managers when using the decision-matrix framework.

When is a decision right? Good-enough decisions	There are two ways to evaluate the correctness of a decision. One way is to appraise the results or consequences of the decision after it has been implemented. The other way is to appraise the process that was used at the time the decision was made. In either case, decision makers almost always must be satisfied with decisions that are good enough rather than optimal. The conditions essential for making an optimal decision rarely exist, and boundaries to rationality or "givens" are always present in any significant managerial decision-making problem.
Styles	Decision makers and problem solvers use differing styles of behavior. One way of getting at this idea is through the psychological functions of sensing (S), intuiting (N), thinking (T), and feeling (F). These functions can be used to identify four styles (ST, SF, NT, NF), each of which is appropriate to certain types of decision problems and at various stages in problem solving.

JOB PERFORMANCE

Four variables, situational factors	Our general framework for understanding individual job performance behavior includes four interdependent variables: situational factors; role perceptions; abilities and skills; and motivation. "Situational factors" make up the "doing" context within which the job performance of an individual takes place. Situational factors can be part of the immediate work environment (for example, working conditions, materials, supervisory style, co-workers), part of the intermediate work environment (such as organization policies, leadership philosophy, organization structure), or part of the external environment (type of industry, political pressures, cultural norms, et cetera).
Role perceptions, role episode, abilities and skills	"Role perceptions" refer to the way in which employees define their job. They are concerned with the employees' perception of "what to do" in order to perform their job in an effective manner. We used the role episode as a framework for thinking about the process of role taking and the process of forming role perceptions. "Abilities and skills" are the "can do" component of job performance. Abilities are characteristics of individuals; skills refer to their level of proficiency in specific tasks.
Pay-off	When thinking about the problem of improving job performance, a useful question to ask is, Which of the four variables we have mentioned will yield the greatest pay-off in improving job performance? Our discussion in this book focused heavily on the motivation variable. Nevertheless, altering situational factors, role perceptions, and abilities and skills may be a more direct and useful approach to improving job performance.

MOTIVATION

Will do

Situational factors, role perceptions, and abilities and skills interact with a person's motivation to determine job performance. Motivation is the "will do" component of performance. We used expectancy theory as our basic approach to understanding the motivation process. "Expectancy theory" is a cognitive approach to understanding behavior that assumes behavior is voluntary and that it results from a highly rational choice process.

Expectancy theory

Expectancy theory has two basic concepts: valence and expectancy. Valence refers to the intensity of a person's desire for some expected need-related behavioral consequence or outcome. There are two types of expectancies. Expectancy 1 refers to a person's perception of the relationship between effort and performance. Expectancy 2 refers to a person's perception of the relationship between performance and desired outcomes. In effect, expectancy theory suggests that the level of motivation of an employee—the "will do" component of job performance—depends on how intensely the employee wants certain outcomes and the employee's expectancy estimates. Expectancy theory is complex, and difficult to apply in a work situation. We viewed it primarily as a way of thinking about the motivation process.

COGNITIVE VARIABLES

Motives

Four specific cognitive variables that influence a person's motivation are: motives; perceptions; attitudes; and values. A "motive" is an inner state that activates, directs, sustains, and stops behavior toward goals. Two views of motives (or needs) that have had a major influence on managerial education and practice are Maslow's needs-hierarchy theory and Herzberg's two-factor theory. Three specific motives that have received substantial attention in the management literature are affiliation, power, and achievement.

Perception

"Perception" is the process by which individuals attach meaning to their experience. Our perceptions involve perceptual selectivity —the process of letting some perceptions into our cognitive map and keeping out others. Perceptual selectivity depends on both stimulus and personal factors. Our perceptions also involve perceptual organization—the process concerned with the way we gather information and categorize it into our cognitive systems. The process of perceptual organization is influenced by perceptual tendencies such as category accessibility, frame of reference, adaptation level, stereotyping, halo effect, implicit personality, first impressions, and projection.

Attitudes

An "attitude" is an internal state of a person that is focused on objects, events, or people that exist in the person's psychological world. Sometimes attitudes are viewed as consisting of affective, cognitive, and conative components. At other times attitudes are viewed simply as a person's affect, or feeling, toward an attitude object. Several important attitude characteristics are: valence; multiplexity; relation to needs; and centrality, or salience. In general, managers should avoid the tendency to infer a causal link between a person's attitudes and that person's behavior. We examined this idea as it applies to the relationship between job satisfaction and performance.

Values

"Values" are beliefs about what is good and bad. They provide a general guidance system for a person's behavior. A "personal value system" is a relatively permanent perceptual framework which shapes and influences the general nature of an individual's behavior. The personal value systems of managers have been measured for research and training purposes by a 66-concept instrument known as the Personal Values Questionnaire, PVQ. Another instrument for measuring values is the Study of Values.

BEHAVIORAL CONSEQUENCES

Internal, external

In trying to understand the "will do" component of job performance behavior, two approaches may be used. The "cognitive approach" focuses primarily on variables that are internal to a person. Expectancy theory is an example of a cognitive approach; motives, perceptions, attitudes, and values are types of cognitive variables. A different approach to understanding the "will do" component of job performance is to focus primarily on the consequences of behavior. In "the consequences, or reinforcement, approach" the major source of behavioral understanding is seen as being external to the person. It is in the person's environment and in the contingencies that link behavior and consequences.

Controversy

The consequences approach utilizes an elaborate set of terms (reinforcers, punishers, contingencies, schedules, shaping) in order to communicate its main ideas. Taken together, these ideas represent a technology or technique for changing or "modifying" behavior. There is considerable controversy about the use of this technology on human beings. The controversy centers on practical, ethical, and legal issues. Our view is that the consequences approach has considerable potentiality for managerial practice. Of course, any approach to managing can be abused. Nevertheless, the consequences approach—to the extent that it can be applied —can be applied in a way consistent with the needs of individual employees and with the need for greater managerial and organizational effectiveness. Managers can draw on both the cognitive and consequences approaches to understanding the "will do" component of job performance.

THE INTERPERSONAL AND GROUP CONTEXTS

Interpersonal

Included in the "doing context" of individual job performance behavior are interpersonal and group relationships. That is, the way an individual employee behaves is, in part, influenced by the nature of his or her interpersonal and group relationships. In connection with the interpersonal context, the major ideas we examined were: interpersonal response traits; the needs and exchange approaches to interpersonal attraction; interpersonal congruence and self-disclosure; and the Johari window.

Group

It is well known that groups at work—formal or informal—can have a powerful impact on their members. This impact derives from the control that groups have over ambient and discretionary stimuli. In addition, the size, composition, cohesiveness, and norms of groups influence the behavior of group members. This behavior can be classified as task-related, maintenance-related, and individual-related; occurs at both the content and process levels; and can be described by using the A-I-S model. An additional insight into the behavior of individual group members is gained by examining the relationship between the individual interest of a group member and the collective interest of the group. Such an examination suggests the distinction between public and private goods and the phenomenon of the free-rider tendency.

MANAGERIAL LEADERSHIP

Definition, approaches

"Leadership" is behavior that elicits voluntary follower behavior beyond that associated with required performance on a job. It is the influential increment over and above mechanical compliance with the routine directives of the organization. Our analysis of managerial leadership examined universalist and situational approaches. In general, the study of leadership has moved away from attempting to isolate personality traits or behaviors that are necessary for effective leadership. The emphasis today is on viewing leadership as an interaction–influence system consisting of the leader, the followers, and the unique situation. Three approaches that are consistent with this newer emphasis are the contingency, path-goal, and participation-in-decision-making approaches.

Style

"Leadership style" refers to a reasonably stable mode of behavior that the leader uses in his or her efforts to exert the influential increment that is the essence of leadership. Managers may use several styles, depending on the needs of the situation, but may have a tendency to favor one style over another. Some labels that might be used to refer to specific styles are: directive; negotiative; consultative; participative; and delegative. The Managerial Grid® and Systems 1–2–3–4 are two specific approaches to identifying leadership styles. From the manager's viewpoint, the major issue with respect to leadership styles is that different styles lead to different behavioral consequences. There is no one style that is best in all situations.

MANAGERIAL COMMUNICATION

Definition, overload, feedback barriers

"Communication" is information flow that transfers meaning and understanding from an information source to an information receiver. In organizations, this information flow occurs within formal and informal communication networks. It is essential that this information flow be restricted, or else the effectiveness of the organization will be hampered by information overload and by the "noise" of nonessential information. A key idea for improving communication is to build into the information flow the opportunity for the receiver to provide the source with feedback. Feedback is essential to the idea of a communication process because it makes the receiver an integral and active part of communication. Managers might improve their personal communication by attempting to reduce the impact of two barriers to successful communication —the tendency to evaluate and the failure to listen.

CONFLICT AND STRESS

New interest

There is a growing emphasis in management education and practice on conflict. This emphasis derives from the recognition that conflict is an inevitable and pervasive feature of life in organizations. No one expects conflict to become less important. There is also a new awareness that conflict can be managed and that conflict can have positive, as well as negative, consequences for an organization.

Conflict episode, definition, styles

The conflict-episode model is a useful way of thinking about conflict as a process consisting of stages that both precede and follow "conflictful behavior." Such behavior is overt behavior that results from a process in which members of organizations perceive that their goals are incompatible with goals of other members and in which they perceive the existence of some opportunity for interfering with the other members achieving their goals. One approach to thinking about conflict-management styles is in terms of different combinations of assertiveness and cooperativeness.

Stress

"Stress" is the nonspecific response of the body to any demand made upon it. Almost any job-related factor is a potential stressor for someone. There is an emerging interest in the subject of stress because of its potential impact on job performance, because of evidence that stress and health are related, because of new knowledge and techniques useful to the task of coping with stress, and because of a growing interest in the quality of work life. Many organizations sponsor activities designed to reduce stress of organization members.

ORGANIZATIONS: THEORY

Definition, theorizing trends

An organization is a social system deliberately constructed to coordinate the activities of people seeking common goals. Every organization has both a formal and an informal dimension that combine to make up "the organization." Over the last 100 years there have been several major ideas or events that have influenced thinking about organizations, including Social Darwinism, scientific management, administrative management, bureaucracy, the Hawthorne studies, the writing of Chester I. Barnard, and evolving ideas about the role of authority in organizations. Recently, systematic theorizing about organizations has borrowed heavily from General Systems Theory. Organizations are viewed as systems of interacting elements or subsystems that interact with their external environment. Thus, contemporary organization theory is occupied—perhaps preoccupied—with the nature and implications of the organization–environment relationship. This theorizing carries a practical message for managers: Forces in the external environment can play a major role in determining the ultimate effectiveness of organizations and the appropriateness of particular organization designs.

ORGANIZATIONS: DESIGN

Definition, basic problem

The design or structure of an organization is the relatively stable set of formally defined working relationships among the members of an organization. All organizations, large and small, have a design. The basic problem of organization design is to find that set of patterned, interacting relationships between and among members that will assure the achievement of goals efficiently and effectively. Several major concerns that are part of the organization design problem are: the design of jobs; the grouping of jobs; span of management; organizational levels; delegation; and line and staff. A substantial body of knowledge exists that can be helpful to managers in their efforts to deal with each of these concerns.

ORGANIZATIONS: CHANGE AND EFFECTIVENESS

Change and stability, framework

Managers must be responsive to the demands for both change and stability in work environments. Both these demands must be balanced in order to create and maintain effective work environments. One framework for thinking about the demands on organizations for change and stability includes driving and restraining forces pressing on the equilibrium of the organization's tasks, technology, structure, and people. In order for organizational change to occur, there must be a change in the number, magnitude, or direction of the driving and restraining forces.

Response
to change,
introducing
change

The response of organization members to change may be neutral, positive, or negative. A negative response can make sense from the viewpoint of individual employees and can be useful to the organization as a "red-flag"—a signal that something is going wrong. The manner in which change is introduced into an organization can have an influence on the type of response the change elicits from organization members. OD is one approach to introducing and implementing major change in organizations that places high priority on humanistic values and goals.

Effectiveness

There are multiple criteria that can be used in evaluating the effectiveness of an organization. Which criteria are most appropriate to a specific organization depends on which frame of reference or perspective (outside or inside) is given the most weight. In either case, organizational effectiveness must be evaluated in terms of the achievement of the organization's system of performance, group, and individual goals.

A FINAL CHECK

In Chapter 1 we asked, What can you expect to learn about managing from this book? We answered the question by making the six points below. Read them again and assess for yourself to what extent the expectations have been realized. You can expect:

1. To be exposed to a comprehensive and contemporary discussion of the academic discipline of managing,
2. To learn some managerial language, concepts, and theories that can serve as a foundation for your further study of managing,
3. To become acquainted with a few managerial techniques that can be applied to the solution of specific managerial problems,
4. To learn material that will serve as a background for developing your own personal philosophy and theory of managing,
5. To be exposed to information applicable to personal and managerial problems you will encounter in the "real world,"
6. To learn something about what it's like to *think like a manager!*

EPILOGUE: ORGANIZATIONS AS HUMAN COMMUNITIES

20

*Why should there not be a patient confidence in the
ultimate justice of the people? Is there any better
or equal hope in the world?*

Abraham Lincoln

*The basic, underlying, never-varying tradition of
our Republic is insistence upon the worth of
the individual.*

Dean Acheson

This chapter   This chapter discusses an idea that is particularly important to organizations, now and in the future. That idea is community. The main theme of this chapter is that managers should strive to make human communities of the organizations they manage.

When organizations fail to provide a life-in-community for their members, there is a loss of human potential and human experience that is unmeasurable by any common yardstick. Surely the loss must be considered enormous. In our view, it is the most glaring weakness of contemporary organizations.

However, when organizations are human communities, or when they try to achieve their appropriate degree of community, they benefit from the quality of human experience that is characteristic of community. The extent of this benefit is also unmeasurable. Acquiring it may represent the most difficult challenge facing organization leaders.

In the paragraphs that follow, we explore the meaning of community, suggest that organizations should seek their appropriate degree of community, identify several bases of community, and note some problems that managers might encounter in their efforts to make human communities of organizations.

THE MEANING OF COMMUNITY

*Place and
social
organization*

The word community is used in diverse ways. It is used figuratively, as in "community of interest," the "business community," or the "Jewish community" to represent an intangible bond or common interest. "Community" is sometimes used simply to mean a physical concentration of people in one place or geographic location. Beyond this place-oriented conception, community can imply social organization among the individuals. When thinking of the community one lives in, one has in mind a place characterized by some form of social organization and interaction.

*Beyond place
and social
organization*

Many definitions of "community," however, suggest something more than just place and social organization. "Community" has been defined as "any process of social interaction which gives rise to a more intensive or more extensive attitude and practice of interdependence, cooperation, collaboration, and unification."[1] Another definition says "community" is characterized by a "high degree of personal intimacy, emotional depth, moral commitment, social cohesion, and continuity in time . . . founded on man conceived in his wholeness."[2]

*Chester I.
Barnard*

The concept of community suggested by the latter definitions is important for all social organizations, including business firms. Almost 40 years ago. Chester Barnard described its essential importance in formal organizations, as follows:

> It [the condition of communion] is the feeling of personal comfort in social relations that is sometimes called solidarity, social integration, the gregarious instinct, or social security (in the original, not in its present debased economic, sense). It is the opportunity for comradeship, for mutual support in personal attitudes. The need for communion is a basis of informal organization that is essential to the operation of every formal organization.[3]

SEEKING THE APPROPRIATE DEGREE OF COMMUNITY

*Community
as an ideal*

In one sense there are no social organizations that have realized their full potential as community. Just as complete personal self-development is an unrealizable goal, so community is an ideal realized only to a limited degree by groups and organizations. The kind of organization influences the degree of community. Communities based on kinship (the family), for example, will normally realize greater potential as community than will organizations based on proprietary or contractual relationships (business organizations).

---

[1] E. C. Lindeman, "Community," *Encyclopedia of Social Science* (New York: The Macmillan Company, 1930), p. 103.

[2] E. Digby Baltzell, ed., *The Search for Community in Modern America* (New York: Harper & Row, Publishers, 1968), p. 2.

[3] Chester Barnard, *The Functions of the Executive* (Cambridge, Mass.: Harvard University Press, 1968), p. 148.

<table>
<tr><td>Practical
point</td><td>The practical point is that there is a degree of community appropriate to particular types of organizations. The appropriate degree depends, in part, on what people in the organization decide the degree will be. Although external factors such as type of industry, market conditions, and cultural patterns have an influence, to a great extent the members of an organization decide what degree of community they will have. A legitimate goal for every business firm is to attain its appropriate degree of community. Why?</td></tr>
</table>

*Practical
point*

The practical point is that there is a degree of community appropriate to particular types of organizations. The appropriate degree depends, in part, on what people in the organization decide the degree will be. Although external factors such as type of industry, market conditions, and cultural patterns have an influence, to a great extent the members of an organization decide what degree of community they will have. A legitimate goal for every business firm is to attain its appropriate degree of community. Why?

*Macro
view*

In the first place, and from the macro viewpoint of society, business firms are social organizations. As social organizations they are obligated to perform their primary economic function effectively. Beyond that, however, business firms must "behave" in ways consistent with society's values. Insofar as honesty, integrity, and mutual trust are values of society then these also must be values implicit in business behavior. These values are paramount in the concept of community.

Micro view

In the second place, and from the micro view of the individual, personal fulfillment occurs, for most people, in community and in interaction with other people. "The institutions and conventions of society . . . are the positive means through which a man can achieve a true life in community and can fully develop and express the sociality which is an essential characteristic of his nature."[4] Insofar as personal fulfillment of individuals is a reason for the existence of social organizations, they should attempt to attain their appropriate degree of community.

*Worth of the
individual*

In our view, the personal fulfillment of individuals is the foundation and the reason for the existence of all social organizations. In the final analysis, the progressive development of individual human beings is the measure against which social organizations and their managers must be evaluated. The idea of community places a high value on the worth of the individual and on the individual's personal development. Indeed, that is community's primary value. Individuals are valued not because they possess a specialized skill or because they produce or consume a lot, but because they are human beings. Community is an organizational value that is in tune with the nature of *human* beings.

BASES OF COMMUNITY

*Traditional
bases*

The traditional bases of community have been kinship, sovereignty, and common dedication to an ideal. Of these three, the latter has most significance for business organizations. Its motivating force as a source of community should not be discounted. Some business organizations are pursuing goals to which em-

---

[4] E. L. Mascall, *The Importance of Being Human* (New York: Columbia University Press, 1958), p. 38.

ployees can be committed. More frequently, the goals and values of particular parts of business organizations can elicit a deep commitment from its participants. It may be difficult to feel an involvement with the goals of General Electric, for example, but it may be easy to become committed to the goals of one of its divisions.

Business fills human needs

The idea of community based on a common dedication to an ideal should be given more attention by business managers. There is nothing intrinsic to business activity that disqualifies it as an activity to which people can feel commitment. The needs business activity fills are human needs. It is humanitarian to participate in activities that have as their purpose the fulfillment of peoples' needs for economic goods and services. Cannot such participation elicit more commitment than now seems to be the case?

Psychological contract

Another base for community in business is the implied contract between individuals and the organization. In spite of real and well-publicized labor-management friction, this contract can be a source of goodwill between employees and employers. It can be something that binds people to organizations—most employees want their organization to succeed. Unfortunately, the opposite desire—employees not caring about the organization succeeding—is also prevalent. Do managers understand the nature of contracts between the organization and its various constituents? Are managers sensitive to the organization's reliance on these contracts as positive forces operating within the organization?

Mutual service

The contract between an employer and an employee is inadequately conceived as simply hiring the services of a functional agent. If the norm of community is to guide business organizations, the contract must imply personal development—a much broader notion than that of a person hired merely to perform a work function. The organization must serve the employee just as the employee must serve the organization.

Work

A third base for community is work itself. Work is the foundation on which business organizations can build community. This is, at once, a strength and a weakness for business. It is a weakness because of the many jobs that simply offer no opportunity for personal fulfillment. It is a strength because so much can be done, and is being done, to make work a source of personal development.

Meaningless work

Meaningless and degrading work—work that contributes nothing to the enlargement of one's sense of competence—not only denies individuals' esteem and fulfillment but also prevents the development of the community in which self-development is realized. It may be true that not everyone seeks fulfillment through their work; some seek it and find it off the job. One wonders, however. "If there is little honor or manliness in the working part of a man's life can much hope be placed in the leisure part?"[5]

Central value

Community must be seen as a central organizational value—not as an organizational luxury. Any change in an organization's central values is likely to have significance for its structure, communication, operating procedures, job design, wage and salary plans, authority and responsibility relationships, to name a few. The form of change may not be evident. The presence of community, for example, does not necessarily imply broader participation in decision making. Community and centralized decision making are not intrinsically opposed. For example, community has a rich tradition in the Catholic Church and yet it was experienced within a highly autocratic set of structural relationships. Universities, on the other hand, have broad participation in the decision-making process but are often characterized by a minimal degree of life-in-community. Community implies no single type of organizational structure or managerial style and is not a matter of particular strategies or tactics.

Size, complexity, trust

Problems. Even if serious efforts are made to further implement the value of community in organizations, serious problems will be encountered. To mention one, the size and complexity of business operations makes the achievement of community more difficult. Almost any business organization, however, is a set of interrelated communities, and it is not necessary to think of a business firm as "a" community. Another problem is the absence of trust essential to a community. It is not customary in American culture to perceive work and the working environment as an opportunity for self-development and enlarging one's sense of solidarity with other human beings. Just where this is supposed to be accomplished is not always clear.

Community and effectiveness

Perhaps most important operationally are the conflicts that arise between community and economic effectiveness, both of which are central to business operations. It is possible that an overemphasis on the value of community, which tends to emphasize the organization's internal environment, may cause an adverse effect on the capacity of the organization to adapt to the requirements of the external environment. The demands of the internal environment are for integration and solidarity, whereas adapting to the demands of the external environment may require increased differentiation and fragmentation of roles.

Future shock

"Future shock" will complicate the goal of community. As Alvin Toffler suggests, the transience, diversity, and novelty that sur-

---

[5] Paul Goodman, "The Missing Community," quoted in David W. Menar and Scott Greer, *The Concept of Community* (Chicago: Aldine Publishing Company, 1969), p. 361.

rounds us today will accelerate in the future.[6] This may require radical changes in the conception of organizations. They may have to be *ad hoc* in character, ready to adapt to rapidly changing environments. There will be more "temporary systems" in which people do not have time to develop close personal relationships. Such systems make community more difficult to achieve. These developments, already influencing most business operations, will require imaginative leadership if the goal of community is to be further realized.

A worthy goal   But with enlightened leadership and management, it is possible to achieve significantly higher levels of life-in-community in organizations. It will not be easy because there are always forces—real or imagined—that make it difficult to place highest priority on individuals and their personal development. Nevertheless, if people in organizations will take their own personal fulfillment seriously, organizations will move slowly and with great effort, toward becoming human communities. That is a worthy goal toward which professional managers can direct their knowledge, skill, and experience.

---

[6] Alvin Toffler, *Future Shock* (New York: Bantam Books, 1971).

cases

CASES

1. Bob Kelly

Bob Kelly is one of the fewer than 2 percent of American workers who work on an assembly line. Despite a certain amount of monotony in his job he is relatively happy with it—at least he was until recently. Although not very challenging to Bob's abilities, his job of installing four bolts on the bumper of every car that comes down the line—one car every minute—gives Bob security and time to think about other things. However, Bob is disturbed about a recent change in his job.

One month ago, management decided to double the amount of his work because an efficiency study had shown that his job was "light." His new job requirement calls for installing eight bolts on each bumper, and Bob feels this amount is in excess of what is reasonable. He simply cannot keep up with the faster pace and already has received two weeks in disciplinary layoffs because of the higher job standard. Increased tension is developing between Bob and his foreman. Bob knows he cannot afford more disciplinary layoffs, and he is developing very negative attitudes toward his job, his foreman, and the company.

Bob's foreman has plenty of problems of his own. He knows the recent job changes are causing difficulty for Bob and numerous other workers. However, as one of the approximately 8,000 assembly-line foremen in the U.S. automobile industry, he is under constant pressure to increase production and to improve quality. This pressure comes from several sources including his general foreman, his superintendent, and other foremen, and from inspectors who oversee his zone of accountability. At the same time, Bob's foreman has to deal with his workers and the union. His problem is compounded because of his weakened authority position. He has no authority to hire, fire, or transfer workers, and the union committeeman has the authority to appeal disciplinary decisions. "I'm a punching bag. I get my ears beat off from both sides of the fence."

The top management of Bob's company also has problems. For one thing, there has been a shift in the type of problem that occupies management. In the past, management concerned itself primarily with problems internal to the company operations. These were the problems management knew how to handle best.

Now, however, management must address itself to problems about which it has very little experience. Consumer groups are pushing for safer and better cars. Federal emission standards are causing enormous problems. Environmental groups are pushing for cleaner engines, and strong local environmental laws are pressing on some operations to "clean up or close up." Foreign competition is increasingly intensive in the expanding market for smaller and more fuel efficient cars. Additionally, foreign car manufacturers appear to have a competitive advantage due to lower labor costs and lower steel prices. Amid growing public sentiment that the company become more "socially responsible," management finds that the old-fashioned problems of higher costs, lower productivity, increased absenteeism, poor quality, and consumer resistance to higher prices are getting more acute.

In the middle of all of these big problems and controversies is Bob Kelly, and thousands of others like him. He wonders what is in store for him. Job security is foremost on his mind. Although not an overly cautious man, Bob realizes that he needs stable employment at good wages in order to make ends meet. Prospects of moving to another type of work or place of work are not good. Besides, he really doesn't want to change jobs. "I feel more and more helpless to do anything about what's happening to me. I'm boxed into a worsening situation and I don't know what to do about it. I'm unhappy on the job and I worry while I'm off the job."

The change in Bob's job resulted from a very broad reorganization of the company. The reorganization brought about the merger of previously independent operations. One result of the merger was that job duplications became apparent and action by management was taken to eliminate them where possible. The company felt that these moves to improve efficiency were essential to the company's operations because of increasing labor costs, lower profit margins, and intense competitive pressures. As one company spokesman commented, "We just won't be able to 'cut it' in this market unless we shape up our costs." Eliminating duplicate assembly-line operations and making "light" jobs more "heavy" was a reasonable way, the company felt, to cut costs.

Whatever the merits of the cost cuts from the company's viewpoint, the workers are not taking kindly to them. Already layoffs are common. Workers feel the recent job changes are another example of a "speed up." In addition, the merger of operations has forced changes in the union structure. Some local union jobs have been eliminated because of the consolidation of local unions. Several local contracts have had to be renegotiated, and the process was everything but cordial. Power struggles with some local unions are creating friction among union members.

The consensus of the workers is that the company is clearly engaging in pressure tactics to produce more efficiency, lower unit costs, and lower personnel requirements. Particularly irksome to the workers is the company practice of using computers to develop time standards for jobs. One employee was heard to comment,

"The machine is telling me how long to take to do my job." The computer "told" Bob he should be able to put eight (rather than four) bolts on a bumper every 60 seconds.

Every day seems to bring additional friction between the company and the workers. The workers are becoming more militant in their demands. Some sabotage on the assembly line has already occurred. On one occasion the plant was forced to close down when a group of workers cut off the power to a key conveyor belt system in protest against a superintendent they claimed was being "abusive." Another major problem is the steady stream of short-term strikes or "mini-strikes." These mini-strikes generally cover a weekend, but that is long enough to disrupt production. Although the mini-strikes have stopped, a climate of tension, suspicion, and distrust appears to be a long-run prospect.

Another problem causing concern is overtime. The company insists that overtime work is necessary periodically in order to meet production goals. The mini-strikes have created an increased need for overtime. The workers, however, do not always want to work overtime when the need arises. Further, they want overtime work to be on a voluntary basis. In a reference to approaching collective bargaining sessions, one management official said, "If they [United Auto Workers] are serious about voluntary overtime, we are on a collision course."

Meanwhile, the company is going ahead with its merger plans. A company spokesman noted, "We expected some troubles with our reorganization but we feel we are progressing on schedule toward our projected target date." The target date is the expected completion date for the companywide merger operations. By that time literally thousands of job changes will have occurred with serious implications for workers, unions, and, ultimately, the car buyer.

The situation is not all bad. The company has maintained a relatively good earnings position and has instituted several internal changes that are well received by workers. There are signs that some progress is being made in efforts to "enrich" jobs. For example, one huge operation involving hundreds of workers is now divided into several smaller operations. This change has resulted in better communications, more positive worker attitudes, constructive suggestions for work methods, lower absenteeism, and lower labor turnover. Another well-received change is the experiment with the "team approach" to assembly operations in which teams of three to six workers are assembling entire trucks. The team approach seems to increase worker satisfaction with jobs, but it is too early to tell whether the approach is efficient and there are some indications that the approach creates some accountability problems.

Most of the changes described above have occurred over a long period of time and with great difficulty. Management is not completely sold on these new ideas. However, the perseverance of a few top executives makes it possible for the company to try out some newer approaches. It remains true, however, that experimenting with new approaches is not characteristic of the company as a whole. Furthermore, the union leaders are not always favorable to the idea of experimenting with new approaches to old problems. Some workers view the experiments as just another way for the company to "get more out of the worker." Others simply are not that interested in the experiments. "We're just not all that excited about enriching this job" expresses the sentiments of many workers. What workers do seem most interested in is such things as longer vacations, earlier retirement, more holidays, and shorter workweeks. In other words, these interests reflect a desire to "escape" from the job rather than a desire to "enrich" it.

2. Alpha and Beta

Five years ago Alpha Company and Beta Company became separate corporate subsidiaries of their parent company, a large multinational corporation. Until that time both companies had operated as product-line divisions of the parent. Alpha had sales of over $40 million, while Beta's sales equaled about $25 million.

Both companies operated in an external environment characterized by extensive government regulation of their production and marketing activities. Alpha's sales growth over the past several years had been due primarily to price increases and there was some evidence (discovered during the planning process) of growing customer resistance to further increases. Unlike Beta Company, which benefited from a high-quality and unique product line, Alpha's sales depended primarily on a single product line in a maturing market.

The two companies had strong sales organizations, heavy research expenditures, and rapid sales growth. However, the board chairman that Alpha and Beta shared recognized that it was going to be difficult for the two subsidiaries to sustain their sales growth unless greater attention was focused on strategic considerations. Therefore, he recommended to the Alpha and Beta presidents that they initiate long-range planning.

Both companies appointed a planning officer. In both companies the person appointed was new to planning. Alpha's planning officer had a marketing research background and was pleased by the new assignment. Beta's planning officer was a top-notch accountant who was very active in the accounting profession.

After several none-too-productive meetings between the planning officers and key personnel in each of the two companies, consultants were called in to assist in preparing an approach to the introduction of formal planning.

The consultants recommended to each company that it form a planning committee and prepare a "plan for planning." The consultants provided each company with guidelines and other types of assistance in preparing its plan for planning. Among other things, the consultants suggested a two-phase approach to planning.

The first phase, a six-month assessment, would entail identification of the company's present position, strengths, weaknesses, planning premises, opportunities, and constraints. The basic process used in the assessment phase would be to assign individual managers project responsibility for the examination of specific problem areas. These managers would then interact with the planning officer and the planning committee through meetings.

The second phase of the approach to planning, a six-month strategic planning phase, would use the data from the assessment phase as a basis for establishing long-range goals in key-result areas, selecting growth opportunities, developing product/market strategies, determining resource requirements, and projecting expected results.

The managements of Alpha and Beta carefully considered the various recommendations of the planning consultants. The recommendations, if followed, would entail working closely with the consultants, particularly in the assessment phase, and, perhaps of more concern to management, devoting a substantial amount of time and effort to planning—a fuzzy type of activity with which neither management felt particularly comfortable.

Alpha's management group was, in general, receptive to the consultants' recommendations. Alpha began its formal planning program in early 1977. Alpha's president, a sales- and marketing-type executive, had been appointed only recently, and most of Alpha's senior managers were new to their positions and to the company.

Beta's management group was less receptive to the consultants' recommendations. It felt that some of the recommendations were not useful and were a "planning overkill"—a formalization and documentation of the obvious. Beta's lack of enthusiasm for the planning recommendation led to behaviors that, in effect, short-cut the assessment phase. Beta's president had been with the company for most of his career and had been the senior marketing executive for over ten years. Most of the Beta management group had held their jobs for two or more years.

Alpha's experience with formal planning had its ups and downs. Planning can be frustrating because it deals in intangibles and offers no immediate feedback to the planners about their behavior. The first months of planning at Alpha were characterized by false starts, defensive behavior, and angry exchanges between senior managers. Enormous amounts of time were devoted to formal planning meetings. These meetings, some of which were held away from the company facilities, not only dealt with topics related to planning, but also with topics related to the effectiveness of the managers as a "team." Many of the managers got to know each other much better at a personal level during these meetings.

Gradually, Alpha's planning efforts began to pay off. Meetings were more issue-oriented and were dealt with in a nondefensive manner. An open and trusting climate prevailed. The managers became more confident of their ability to formulate plans based on an informed understanding of the environment in which the plans would be put into operation. In early 1978 Alpha's management presented its strategic plan to the chairman and board members of the parent company. It was obvious to the chairman and board members that Alpha was well on the way to integrating a formal planning program into its total approach to managing. Although Alpha still had much to learn and had not yet obtained a balance between long- and short-range planning, it was fair to say that planning was a reality at Alpha.

Beta's experience, on the other hand, was not as favorable as Alpha's. Superficial, unorganized, lacking preparation, and suffering from sloppy staff work were all descriptive of Beta's planning. The climate in the company was not conducive to open discussion of issues. Meetings were irregular and nonproductive. When Beta made its presentation to the parent chairman and board members the result was predictable and disappointing. It took Beta three months longer than Alpha to prepare its presentation. The final strategic plan contained little of substance.

3. Phil Coffman

Phil Coffman was about two hours late in arriving home from work when he walked in the door with a worried expression on his face. Debra, Phil's wife, was quick to observe that something was on Phil's mind, and she guessed that the "something" had to do with the job promotion Phil had been expecting.

Phil: I just can't see the logic of the argument. It isn't reasonable to ask a person to make a basic change in his behavior; I'm not even sure that I can change the way the company wants me to. I never have been an outgoing type of individual. If the company wants a glad-handing, public-relations type man for a department head then it shouldn't have made me acting department head in the first place.

Debra: Are they on you again about not talking enough at meetings, Phil?

Phil: Yes, it's that again. When it comes right down to it, a person at Alco is evaluated in terms of how much he talks. It doesn't really matter what you say, just so you say something. Those committee meetings drive me up a wall! You wouldn't believe the crap that some of those guys come up with just to be saying something. Well, I'm not going to talk just to hear myself talk. When I've got something to say, I'll say it; when I don't, I'll keep my mouth shut.

Debra: You're right! That's just the way you are. I don't see why you should have to change. Alco isn't the only company in the world, and it seems that lately Alco is putting so much pressure on its scientists to come up with "practical" ideas. As you've told me before, a certain amount of those pressures are OK, but too many of them stifle your initiative.

Phil: That's part of the problem at Alco. The entire research function has become so overorganized that the individual researcher is lost in the shuffle. The R&D department under Drew Phillips has become a bureaucracy. That's why so much emphasis is put on meetings and talking. I don't mind them when they're productive and deal with something I know about. Believe me, Debra, when we're discussing physical chemistry, I'm right in there carrying the ball. But when we're away from scientific facts and in to talk about whether some new idea will "sell" or whether it's "practical," I just don't have anything to contribute. Frankly, some of the other guys can outtalk me in those areas, and I just don't feel comfortable. Why should I make myself look foolish?

Debra: Well, Phil, what are we going to do about it? Has something special happened that has made you so upset?

Phil: It's that promotion to department head of physical chemistry. I had a talk today with Forrest (Forrest Milberger, manager of research labs) about the promotion. He brought it up at the end of a conversation we were having about some technical problems. It was a good conversation. You know how well Forrest and I get along; we're really good friends. Even though he's my boss, he and I respect and trust each other and can have an honest conversation. Anyhow, he told me that he has been very satisfied with my work—he's told me that several times—and that he had turned in his recommendation for my promotion to department head. He went over again our discussion of six months ago about how, if I did a good job as acting department head of physical chemistry, he would recommend me for the permanent department head position. Well, he kept his word! But, there's one catch. More talk or no promotion.

Debra: Did Forrest really put it like that?

Phil: Not exactly, but that's the message that comes through loud and clear. Forrest is great. He knows what kind of a person I am. He really doesn't want me to change. After all, he's a scientist too. I think he'd still like to be working in the lab rather than supervising what everyone else does. He never has caved in to being an administrator and thinking of everything in dollars and cents. Forrest knows that I'm a good scientist and that I'm doing a good job for Alco. He feels a good department head of physical chemistry should, first and foremost, be a good scientist. Nevertheless, Forrest has his job to do. He's responsible for other departments in the research laboratory besides physical chemistry, and he's got to worry about Phillips (Drew Phillips) and Kahanek (Vernon Kahanek, Alco's president). They're always on his back to come up with something that will sell.

Debra: Did he make any suggestions to you or give you any advice?

Phil: He tried to look at it from both sides. Although he understands my position, he tried to make a case for the views of Phillips and Kahanek. He talked about how these meetings serve the purpose of reinforcing what Phillips wants to hear. The way people talk at meetings can have a lot to do with their status and influence in the company. Forrest also said, and I agree, that sometimes casual talking and rambling during one of the meetings will tick off an idea in someone's mind that he otherwise wouldn't have had. Sometimes all that useless talk does, in fact, lead to something. But for every time it does, there must be 50 times that it's just a waste of time.

Debra: If Forrest is so lukewarm about this talking problem why does your promotion depend on it?

Phil: All Forrest does is recommend my promotion to Phillips. Forrest told me that he had a long talk with Drew and, by the end of the conversation, it was clear that my promotion depended on some change in my behavior during those blasted meetings. Forrest said Drew interprets my silence to mean that I don't know anything. Not only that, but sometimes Kahanek sits in on our weekly meetings of the research lab department heads, and, I guess, he gets the impression that I'm not a very strong representative for the physical chemistry department.

Debra: You've never talked much about Drew or Vernon. What are they like?

Phil: Drew is in charge of the entire R&D function at Alco; It's a big job and he gets paid plenty for it. Years ago, he was a pretty good scientist, at least that's what I've been told. But, he decided to go up the administrative ladder because he saw real limits to his career progress unless he moved into management. He's a full-fledged administrator now—body and soul. Now, I think he looks on scientists as half nuts. I've heard him refer to scientists as "problems." He has frequent contact with Vernon; he's really Vernon's line of communication to the research lab. Drew is big on committee meetings and he likes to think everyone is participating. With Drew it's "participate or else. . . !"

Debra: What about Vernon?

Phil: Vernon's got his job to do. He's got to keep this company going and he's done a good job of it over the years. Early in his career he came up with some new product ideas that turned out to be real winners for the company. He's a practical guy; he wants to see our research efforts lead to something that will make a difference on the profit and loss statement. One of his favorite questions is, "Will this sell?" If the answer to that question isn't a clear yes, you can just see his face sink. In other words, why bother with it if it won't sell? But that's the way this entire industry is. The R is going out of R&D. What everyone wants now is low-risk, fast-payback, product development. So Vernon isn't any different than others who hold the same position as he does.

For a while Vernon attended our research lab meetings on a regular basis, and he drove some of us crazy. I'll admit he's sharp, particularly in the area of new product development, but he just doesn't understand research or scientists. He keeps bugging us to come up with some high-profit, high-volume new products.

Debra: From what you say, Phil, it looks to me like you—I should say, we—have a serious problem. I know you, and I'm not sure I want you to try to change yourself. Who knows what that kind of change will lead to? Besides, if being an extrovert doesn't come natural to you, everyone will know you're faking it. But, I'd hate to see you leave Alco. You've been doing so good there and you get along so well with Forrest. The money and security are good and we need both of those now that we have this new home and the children are in school.

Phil: I know you're right, Debra, we do have a problem. I'm not sure I'm cut out for this department head job. If it means changing my behavior so much, is it worth it? The way things are now, I get a lot of respect from the other scientists, and that means something. Also, I respect myself; I feel I have professional integrity the way I am now. How long could I keep that if I were a department head? Still, I do like the challenge of the department head job. It provides an opportunity to help get the other guys to work together. And, let's face it, there is a substantial salary increase tied-in with the promotion, and, who knows, I might keep going up that "ladder of success." Maybe I could change a little. There is a grain of truth in what the company says about the value of these meetings and all the talking. But how can I go about changing? Where can I learn to be an extrovert?

4. The Captain's Table*

Note: Do not read this case until directed to do so by your instructor. It has been set up as a Prediction Case so that you can test your analysis by answering questions before reading the entire case.

PART I

The Captain's Table is located on a well-traveled highway near two small cities in the eastern part of the country. Employing a total of about 40 people as waitresses, cooks, kitchen help, bartenders, and hostesses, the Captain's Table caters to businessmen entertaining customers and "dress-up dining" by residents of the area. It also has rooms available for wedding parties and other social functions. Overall, it is considered to be one of the best restaurants in the area.

The owner of the Captain's Table, Mr. Rogers, had bought the restaurant in 1945, and working closely with his manager, Bill Hayes, changed what was once a rather ordinary restaurant into a well-known and highly profitable enterprise. Over the years the business relationship between Mr. Rogers and his manager has developed into a social relationship. Both men belonged to the same yacht club, where they frequently entertained one another for dinner, as well as to the same church. On the job, Bill was given absolute authority to make decisions in Mr. Rogers' name.

Working closely with the manager was the head chef, Henry Plante, who often attended the informal meetings between Bill and Mr. Rogers where problems concerning the restaurant were

* Reprinted from Allen R. Cohen, Stephen L. Fink, Herman Gadon, and Robin D. Willits, *Effective Behavior in Organizations* (Homewood, Ill.: Richard D. Irwin, Inc., 1976). Used with permission.

discussed. With Mr. Rogers' approval, Bill and Henry had a business policy of allowing their employees the most freedom possible in the belief that this would produce a high degree of satisfaction and conscientiousness on the part of employees. As one of the waitresses exclaimed, "Working here is really a joy, everyone knows one another and gets along well. . . ."

In the kitchen, Henry exerted just enough authority to maintain discipline, but allowed the frequent blowoffs that come from the long hours and hot working conditions. His only real rule was to "treat the customer to the meal you would like to eat." His success was demonstrated by the many compliments he received from the customers. His standard reply to such compliments was to thank the customer, but explain that it was due to the contributions of his employees.

On several occasions when a well-known customer complimented him, Henry relayed the compliment to the rest of the kitchen help. This was well received and gave them great pride in their work. Said one employee about Henry, "I've worked in restaurants all my life, but here it's more than a job." It was the belief of many of the customers that it was Henry who made the restaurant a success.

In the dining room and lounge, Bill also allowed his employees considerable freedom, and encouraged them to make immediate decisions on their own without prior consultations. Said Bill, "My people are good, intelligent people, and I have complete faith in them." Under this policy the dining room personnel were allowed to fraternize with the kitchen help during the slow hours and even allowed to order drinks from the bar without fear of reprimand. When the monthly bar costs were tabulated Bill never questioned any of the employees' signed slips. He had said many times that as long as they did a good job, he didn't care how much they drank. High morale and customer satisfaction attested to the job they did and Bill saw no reason to change it. Interaction was high among all employees and nearly everyone was on a first name basis. Picnics and social events were arranged whenever possible to promote what was considered to be "one big happy family."

On several occasions when the work was slow and the day tedious, the kitchen help would play a game called "Air Raid." This would always produce lots of banter and joking as the help would bang on pots and pans and hide under the preparation table, in anticipation of flying meatballs and other food left over from the day. It was not unusual to see Henry as bombardier leading the battle and it usually ended by sending the waitresses to the bar with an order for beers for the "survivors." On Henry's day off, the dishwashers would help the cooks prepare the meals and someone else was designated as "honorary bombardier" during the "Air Raid" game.

A few months ago Bill retired and left the restaurant to live in Florida. Before he left Mr. Rogers ordered the restaurant closed for a day and gave a party for him with only employees and personal friends invited. Contributions of over $1,000 from the employees and a gold watch from Mr. Rogers with the inscription "To Bill, in appreciation for the many years of loyal service, 1945–1973" were given to him.

Discussion Questions

1. What kind of person should Mr. Rogers look for as a replacement for Bill? What criteria should he use in selecting a replacement? Why?
2. If you were Mr. Rogers, what are some of the questions you would ask applicants, interviewing for the manager's job, to help you judge their suitability?
3. What information would you be sure to give qualified applicants about the restaurant so that they too could make á judgment about whether they would fit in? Why?

PART II

Faced with the problem of replacing Bill, Mr. Rogers hired Mr. Robert Nielson. Nielson was a former maitre d' with extensive restaurant experience. He came highly recommended by the owner of another local restaurant. In an hour-long meeting with Henry and Mr. Roberts, Bob was told of the working relationship between employees and the former manager. In addition, the excellence of the restaurant was heavily emphasized and his new and expanded duties explained. As maitre d' he was in charge of front of the house operations, but now he would be in charge of the entire restaurant. To this he replied, "I'm sure I can do a good job for you" and the meeting ended.

Although greeted with enthusiasm by everyone, only two weeks passed before Mr. Nielson began having problems with the help. As he constantly reminded people, "My name is Mr. Nielson, not Bill Hayes!"

As the new manager, one of Bob's first actions was to keep a careful record of all bar expenditures. When his first monthly tabulation showed over $500 in free drinks, he was overheard to say, "This place is unbelievably sloppy. It may have made money, but there is enormous waste. Five hundred dollars for drinks per month is $6,000 per year directly off of profits, not to mention the inefficiency of people who are not completely sober." He brought the matter to Henry's attention and blamed the kitchen for excessive drinking. "How can anyone do his work when he's half drunk?" he fumed in a fit of anger. Henry's only reply was that no one was going to tell him and his help how much they could or could not drink, and that he saw no reason to stop. The matter was dropped, but another problem arose on Henry's next day off.

As was the custom whenever Henry had a day off, several of the dishwashers pitched in to help prepare the meals in the kitchen. Due to an unpredicted noon-time crowd, the kitchen ran short of clean dishes and service slowed, although not considerably. "As a matter of fact," one waitress mentioned somewhat sarcastically to another, "no one but an old fussbudget like him would have ever noticed it." Bob, however, saw matters differently. Storming into the kitchen, he demanded to know what was going on. When he saw the dishwashers working on the preparations, he became quite angry and yelled at them to get back to their own jobs because they were not getting paid to do the cooking. "No-good lazy cooks" he muttered as he left the kitchen. With the dish-washers no longer helping out, the cooks staged a mini-slowdown in protest. For the rest of the day, there was constant friction with Bob barking orders like a marine drill sergeant, and the cooks ignoring them. The end of the night saw Bob extend the dining room hours from 9:00 until 10:00 P.M., with the cooks and kitchen help vowing to throw him out bodily if he came back into the kitchen again.

The next day, Henry had just entered the restaurant when Bob accosted him. In an emotional tirade, Bob blamed the whole mess on Henry, exclaiming that his lack of responsible leadership would no longer be tolerated. Henry sat quietly until Bob left, and then proceeded into the kitchen. When the dishwashers and cooks began talking all at once, Henry meekly threw up his hands and said "I've had it with him" and was gone for the rest of the day. Although business was conducted as usual, morale was at an all time low. When Henry failed to show up the following day, Bob became quite irritated and went in and out of the kitchen yelling at everyone in sight. Even the waitresses, to whom Bob had gen-erally remained good-natured, came under his verbal abuses. Finally, with everyone's patience wearing thin, the day came to an end.

During the next few months, the situation deteriorated even further. Henry was in and out of the kitchen, morale was low, the cooks were preparing sloppy meals, and no one any longer took much pride in his job. As one of the waitresses remarked, "I used to like working here, but now I'm looking for another job." Several of the other employees began to express similar feelings. Bob, blaming the deterioration of morale and the gradual loss of busi-ness on Henry and the rest of the kitchen help, hired a new cook to speedup and improve the quality of the meals. Henry, feeling that he was being replaced went to Mr. Rogers and explained that although he had enjoyed working for him, he could no longer work under existing conditions, and was going to quit. Solemnly, Mr. Rogers sat back and listened to Henry, wondering what he should do.

Discussion Questions

1. What factors led to the problems that have now developed?
2. What assumptions did Bill, Henry, Bob, and Mr. Rogers have (*a*) about human motivation and (*b*) about leadership?
3. What options did Henry have when Bob Nielson began to push him? Why did Henry respond as he did?

4. What problems, if any, would have occurred if Mr. Nielson had been "another Bill Hayes" in his manner of fulfilling his role?
5. What should Mr. Rogers do now? Why?

5. Dick Spencer*

After the usual banter when old friends meet for cocktails, the conversation between a couple of university professors and Dick Spencer, a former student who was now a successful businessman, turned to Dick's life as a vice president of a large manufacturing firm.

"I've made a lot of mistakes, most of which I could live with, but this one series of incidents was so frustrating that I could have cried at the time," Dick said in response to a question. "I really have to laugh at how ridiculous it is now, but at the time I blew my cork."

Spencer was plant manager of Modrow Company, a Canadian branch of the Tri-American Corporation. Tri-American was a major producer of primary aluminum with integrated operations ranging from the mining of bauxite through the processing to fabrication of aluminum into a variety of products. The company also made and sold refractories and industrial chemicals. The parent company had wholly-owned subsidiaries in five separate United States locations and had foreign affiliates in 15 different countries.

Tri-American mined bauxite in the Jamaican West Indies and shipped the raw material by commercial vessels to two plants in Louisiana where it was processed into alumina. The alumina was then shipped to reduction plants in one of three locations for conversion into primary aluminum. Most of the primary aluminum was then moved to the company's fabricating plants for further processing. Fabricated aluminum items included sheet, flat, coil, and corrugated products; siding; and roofing.

Tri-American employed approximately 22,000 people in the total organization. The company was governed by a board of directors which included the chairman, vice chairman, president, and 12 vice presidents. However, each of the subsidiaries and branches functioned as independent units. The board set general policy, which was then interpreted and applied by the various plant managers. In a sense, the various plants competed with one another as though they were independent companies. This decentralization in organizational structure increased the freedom and authority of the plant managers, but increased the pressure for profitability.

The Modrow branch was located in a border town in Canada. The total work force in Modrow was 1,000. This Canadian sub-

---

* Used with permission of Prof. Margaret Fenn, Graduate School of Business Administration, University of Washington, Seattle.

sidiary was primarily a fabricating unit. Its main products were foil and building products such as roofing and siding. Aluminum products were gaining in importance in architectural plans, and increased sales were predicted for this branch. Its location and its stable work force were the most important advantages it possessed.

In anticipation of estimated increases in building product sales, Modrow had recently completed a modernization and expansion project. At the same time, their research and art departments combined talents in developing a series of 12 new patterns of siding which were being introduced to the market. Modernization and pattern development had been costly undertakings, but the expected return on investment made the project feasible. However, the plant manager, who was a Tri-American vice president, had instituted a campaign to cut expenses wherever possible. In his introductory notice of the campaign, he emphasized that cost reduction would be the personal aim of every employee at Modrow.

Salesman.   The plant manager of Modrow, Dick Spencer, was an American who had been transferred to this Canadian branch two years previously, after the start of the modernization plan. Dick had been with the Tri-American Company for 14 years, and his progress within the organization was considered spectacular by those who knew him well. Dick had received a master's degree in business administration from a well-known university at the age of 22. Upon graduation he had accepted a job as salesman for Tri-American. During his first year as a salesman, he succeeded in landing a single, large contract which put him near the top of the sales-volume leaders. In discussing his phenomenal rise in the sales volume, several of his fellow salesmen concluded that his looks, charm, and ability on the golf course contributed as much to his success as his knowledge of the business or his ability to sell the products.

The second year of his sales career, he continued to set a fast pace. Although his record set difficult goals for the other salesmen, he was considered a "regular guy" by them, and both he and they seemed to enjoy the few occasions when they socialized. However, by the end of the second year of constant travelling and selling, Dick began to experience some doubt about his future.

His constant involvement in business affairs disrupted his marital life, and his wife divorced him during the second year with Tri-American. Dick resented her action at first, but gradually seemed to recognize that his career at present depended on his freedom to travel unencumbered. During that second year, he ranged far and wide in his sales territory, and successfully closed several large contracts. None of them was as large as his first year's major sale, but in total volume he again was well up near the top of salesmen for the year. Dick's name became well known in the corporate headquarters, and he was spoken of as "the boy to watch."

Dick had met the president of Tri-American during his first

year as a salesman at a company conference. After three days of golfing and socializing they developed a relaxed camaraderie considered unusual by those who observed the developing friendship. Although their contacts were infrequent after the conference, their easy relationship seemed to blossom the few times they did meet. Dick's friends kidded him about his ability to make use of his new friendship to promote himself in the company, but Dick brushed aside their jibes and insisted that he'd make it on his own abilities, not someone's coattail.

By the time he was 25, Dick began to suspect that he did not look forward to a life as a salesman for the rest of his career. He talked about his unrest with his friends, and they suggested that he groom himself for sales manager. "You won't make the kind of money you're making from commissions," he was told, "but you will have a foot in the door from an administrative standpoint, and you won't have to travel quite as much as you do now." Dick took their suggestions lightly, and continued to sell the product, but was aware that he felt dissatisfied and did not seem to get the satisfaction out of his job that he had once enjoyed.

By the end of his third year with the company Dick was convinced that he wanted a change in direction. As usual, he and the president spent quite a bit of time on the golf course during the annual company sales conference. After their match one day, the president kidded Dick about his game. The conversation drifted back to business, and the president, who seemed to be in a jovial mood, started to kid Dick about his sales ability. In a joking way, he implied that anyone could sell a product as good as Tri-American's, but that it took real "guts and know-how" to make the products. The conversation drifted to other things, but this remark stuck with Dick.

Sometime later, Dick approached the president formally with a request for a transfer out of the sales division. The president was surprised and hesitant about this change in career direction for Dick. He recognized the superior sales ability that Dick seemed to possess, but was unsure that Dick was willing or able to assume responsibilities in any other division of the organization. Dick sensed the hesitancy, but continued to push his request. He later remarked that it seemed that the initial hesitancy of the president convinced Dick that he needed an opportunity to prove himself in a field other than sales.

Trouble Shooter. Dick was finally transferred back to the home office of the organization and indoctrinated into productive and administrative roles in the company as a special assistant to the senior vice president of production. As a special assistant, Dick was assigned several trouble-shooting jobs. He acquitted himself well in this role, but in the process succeeded in gaining a reputation as a ruthless headhunter among the branches where he had performed a series of amputations. His reputation as an amiable, genial, easy-going guy from the sales department was the antithesis of the reputation of a cold, calculating headhunter which he earned in his trouble-shooting role. The vice president, who was Dick's boss, was aware of the reputation which Dick had earned but was pleased with the results that were obtained. The faltering departments that Dick had worked in seemed to bloom with new life and energy after Dick's recommended amputations. As a result, the vice president began to sing Dick's praises, and the president began to accept Dick in his new role in the company.

Management Responsibility. About three years afer Dick's switch from sales, he was given an assignment as assistant plant manager of an English branch of the company. Dick, who had remarried, moved his wife and family to London, and they attempted to adapt to their new routine. The plant manager was English, as were most of the other employees. Dick and his family were accepted with reservations into the community life as well as into the plant life. The difference between British and American philosophy and performance within the plant was marked for Dick who was imbued with modern managerial concepts and methods. Dick's directives from headquarters were to update and upgrade performance in this branch. However, his power and authority were less than those of his superior, so he constantly found himself in the position of having to soft pedal or withhold suggestions that he would have liked to make, or innovations that he would have liked to introduce. After a frustrating year and a half, Dick was suddenly made plant manager of an old British company which had just been purchased by Tri-American. He left his first English assignment with mixed feelings and moved from London to Birmingham.

As the new plant manager, Dick operated much as he had in his trouble-shooting job for the first couple of years of his change from sales to administration. Training and reeducation programs were instituted for all supervisors and managers who survived the initial purge. Methods were studied and simplified or redesigned whenever possible, and new attention was directed toward production which better met the needs of the sales organization. A strong controller helped to straighten out the profit picture through stringent cost control; and, by the end of the third year, the company showed a small profit for the first time in many years. Because he felt that this battle was won, Dick requested transfer back to the United States. This request was partially granted when nine months later he was awarded a junior vice president title, and was made manager of a subsidiary Canadian plant, Modrow.

Modrow Manager. Prior to Dick's appointment as plant manager at Modrow, extensive plans for plant expansion and improvement had been approved and started. Although he had not been in on the original discussions and plans, he inherited all the problems that accompany large-scale changes in any organization. Construction was slower in completion than originally planned, equipment arrived before the building was finished, employees were upset about the extent of change expected in their work routines with the installation of additional machinery and, in general, morale was at a low ebb.

Various versions of Dick's former activities had preceded him, and on his arrival he was viewed with dubious eyes. The first few months after his arrival were spent in a frenzy of catching up. This entailed constant conferences and meetings, volumes of reading of past reports, becoming acquainted with the civic leaders of the area, and a plethora of dispatches to and from the home office. Costs continued to climb unabated.

By the end of his first year at Modrow, the building program had been completed, although behind schedule, the new equipment had been installed, and some revamping of cost procedures had been incorporated. The financial picture at this time showed a substantial loss, but since it had been budgeted as a loss, this was not surprising. All managers of the various divisions had worked closely with their supervisors and accountants in planning the budget for the following year, and Dick began to emphasize his personal interest in cost reduction.

As he worked through his first year as plant manager, Dick developed the habit of strolling around the organization. He was apt to leave his office and appear anywhere on the plant floor, in the design offices, at the desk of a purchasing agent or accountant, in the plant cafeteria rather than the executive dining room, or wherever there was activity concerned with Modrow. During his strolls he looked, listened, and became acquainted. If he observed activities which he wanted to talk about, or heard remarks that gave him clues to future action, he did not reveal these at the time. Rather he had a nod, a wave, a smile, for the people near him, but a mental note to talk to his supervisors, managers, and foremen in the future. At first his presence disturbed those who noted him coming and going, but after several exposures to him without any noticeable effect, the workers came to accept his presence and continue their usual activities. Supervisors, managers, and foremen, however, did not feel as comfortable when they saw him in the area.

Their feelings were aptly expressed by the manager of the siding department one day when he was talking to one of his foremen: "I wish to hell he'd stay up in the front office where he belongs. Whoever heard of a plant manager who had time to wander around the plant all the time. Why doesn't he tend to his paper work and let us tend to our business?"

"Don't let him get you down," joked the foreman. "Nothing ever comes of his visits. Maybe he's just lonesome and looking for a friend. You know how these Americans are."

"Well, you may feel that nothing ever comes of his visits, but I don't. I've been called into his office three separate times within the last two months. The heat must really be on from the head office. You know these conferences we have every month where he reviews our financial progress, our building progress, our design progress, and so on? Well, we're not really progressing as fast as we should be. If you ask me we're in for continuing trouble."

In recalling his first year at Modrow, Dick had felt constantly pressured and badgered. He always sensed that the Canadians he worked with resented his presence since he was brought in over the heads of the operating staff. At the same time he felt this subtle resistance from his Canadian work force, he believed that the president and his friends in the home office were constantly on the alert, waiting for Dick to prove himself or fall flat on his face. Because of the constant pressures and demands of the work, he had literally dumped his family into a new community and had withdrawn into the plant. In the process, he built up a wall of resistance toward the demands of his wife and children who, in turn, felt as though he was abandoning them.

During the course of the conversation with his university friends, he began to recall a series of incidents that probably had resulted from the conflicting pressures. When describing some of these incidents, he continued to emphasize the fact that his attempt to be relaxed and casual had backfired. Laughingly, Dick said, "As you know, both human relations and accounting were my weakest subjects during the master's program, and yet they are two fields I felt I needed the most at Modrow at this time." He described some of the cost procedures that he would have liked to incorporate. However, without the support and knowledge furnished by his former controller, he busied himself with details that were unnecessary. One day, as he describes it, he overheard a conversation between two of the accounting staff members with whom he had been working very closely. One of them commented to the other, "For a guy who's a vice president, he sure spends a lot of time breathing down our necks. Why doesn't he simply tell us the kind of systems he would like to try, and let us do the experimenting and work out the budget?" Without commenting on the conversation he overheard, Dick then described himself as attempting to spend less time and be less directive in the accounting department.

Another incident he described which apparently had real meaning for him was one in which he had called a staff conference with his top-level managers. They had been going "hammer and tongs" for better than a hour in his private office, and in the process of heated conversation had loosened ties, taken off coats, and really rolled up their sleeves. Dick himself had slipped out of his shoes. In the midst of this, his secretary reminded him of an appointment with public officials. Dick had rapidly finished up his conference with his managers, straightened his tie, donned his coat, and had wandered out into the main office in his stocking feet.

Dick fully described several incidents when he had disappointed, frustrated, or confused his wife and family by forgetting birthdays, appointments, dinner engagements, etc. He seemed to be describing a pattern of behavior which resulted from continuing pressure and frustration. He was setting the scene to describe his baffling and humiliating position in the siding department. In looking back and recalling his activities during this first year, Dick commented on the fact that his frequent wanderings throughout the plant had resulted in a nodding acquaintance with the workers, but probably had also resulted in foremen and supervisors spending more time getting ready for his visits and reading meaning into them afterwards than attending to their specific duties. His attempts to know in detail the accounting procedures being used required long hours of concentration and detailed conversations with the accounting staff, which were time-consuming and very frustrating for him, as well as for them. His lack of attention to his family life resulted in continued pressure from both wife and family.

The Siding Department Incident. Siding was the product which had been budgeted as a large profit item of Modrow. Aluminum siding was gaining in popularity among both architects and builders, because of its possibilities in both decorative and practical uses. Panel sheets of siding were shipped in standard sizes on order; large sheets of the coated siding were cut to specifications in the trim department, packed, and shipped. The trim shop was located near the loading platforms, and Dick often cut through the trim shop on his wanderings through the plant. On one of his frequent trips through the area, he suddenly became aware of the fact that several workers responsible for the disposal function were spending countless hours at high-speed saws cutting scraps into specified lengths to fit into scrap barrels. The narrow bands of scrap which resulted from the trim process varied in length from 7 to 27 feet and had to be reduced in size to fit into the disposal barrels. Dick, in his concentration on cost reduction, picked up one of the thin strips, bent it several times and filled it into the barrel. He tried this with another piece, and it bent very easily. After assuring himself that bending was possible, he walked over to a worker at the saw and asked why he was using the saw when material could easily be bent and fitted into the barrels, resulting in saving time and equipment. The worker's response was, "We've never done it that way, sir. We've always cut it."

Following his plan of not commenting or discussing matters on the floor, but distressed by the reply, Dick returned to his office and asked the manager of the siding department if he could speak to the foreman of the scrap division. The manager said, "Of course. I'll send him up to you in just a minute."

After a short time, the foreman, very agitated at being called to the plant manager's office, appeared. Dick began questioning him about the scrap disposal process and received the standard answer: "We've always done it that way." Dick then proceeded to review cost-cutting objectives. He talked about the pliability of the strips of scrap. He called for a few pieces of scrap to demonstrate the ease with which it could be bent, and ended what he thought was a satisfactory conversation by requesting the foreman to order heavy-duty gloves for his workers and use the bending process for a trial period of two weeks to check the cost saving possible.

The foreman listened throughout most of this hour's conference, offered several reasons why it wouldn't work, raised some questions about the record-keeping process for cost purposes, and finally left the office with the forced agreement to try the suggested new method of bending, rather than cutting, for disposal. Although Dick was immersed in many other problems, his request was forcibly brought home one day as he cut through the scrap area. The workers were using power saws to cut scraps. He called the manager of the siding department and questioned him about the process. The manager explained that each foreman was responsible for his own processes, and since Dick had already talked to the foreman, perhaps he had better talk to him again. When the foreman arrived, Dick began to question him. He received a series of excuses, and some explanations of the kinds of problems they were meeting by attempting to bend the scrap material. "I don't care what the problems are," Dick nearly shouted, "when I request a cost-reduction program instituted, I want to see it carried through."

Dick was furious. When the foreman left, he phoned the maintenance department and ordered the removal of the power saws from the scrap area immediately. A short time later the foreman of the scrap department knocked on Dick's door reporting his astonishment at having maintenance men step into his area and physically remove the saws. Dick reminded the foreman of his request for a trial at cost reduction to no avail, and ended the conversation by saying that the power saws were gone and would not be returned, and the foreman had damned well better learn to get along without them. After a stormy exit by the foreman, Dick congratulated himself on having solved a problem and turned his attention to other matters.

A few days later Dick cut through the trim department and literally stopped to stare. As he described it, he was completely nonplussed to discover gloved workmen using hand shears to cut each piece of scrap.

6. Savemore Food Store 5116*

The Savemore Corporation is a chain of 400 retail supermarkets located primarily in the northeastern section of the United States. Store 5116 employs over 50 persons, all of whom

* This case was written under the supervision of Professor J. W. Hennessey, Jr., The Amos Tuck School, Dartmouth College, and it is reprinted with his permission. The case originally appeared in Austin Grimshaw and John W. Hennessey, Jr., *Organizational Behavior: Cases and Readings* (New York: McGraw-Hill Book Company, 1960).

live within suburban Portage, New York, where the store is located.[1]

Wally Shultz served as general manager of store 5116 for six
years. Last April he was transferred to another store in the chain.
At that time the employees were told by the district manager,
Mr. Finnie, that Wally Shultz was being promoted to manage a
larger store in another township.

Most of the employees seemed unhappy to lose their old manager. Nearly everyone agreed with the opinion that Shultz was a
"good guy to work for." As examples of his desirability as a boss
the employees told how Wally had frequently helped the arthritic
black porter with his floor mopping, how he had shut the store
five minutes early each night so that certain employees might
catch their busses, of a Christmas party held each year for employees at his own expense, and his general willingness to pitch
in. All employees had been on a first-name basis with the manager. About half of them had begun work with the Savemore
Corporation when the Portage store was opened.

Wally Shultz was replaced by Clark Raymond. Raymond, about
25 years old, was a graduate of an Ivy League college and had
been with Savemore a little over one year. After completion of his
six-month training program, he served as manager of one of the
chain's smaller stores before being advanced to store 5116. In
introducing Raymond to the employees, Mr. Finnie stressed his
rapid advancement and the profit increase that occurred while
Raymond had charge of his last store.

I began my employment in store 5116 early in June. Mr. Raymond was the first person I met in the store, and he impressed
me as being more intelligent and efficient than the managers I had
worked for in previous summers at other stores. After a brief
conversation concerning our respective colleges, he assigned me to
a cash register, and I began my duties as a checker and bagger.

In the course of the next month I began to sense that relationships between Raymond and his employees were somewhat
strained. This attitude was particularly evident among the older
employees of the store, who had worked in store 5116 since its
opening. As we all ate our sandwiches together in the cage (an
area about 20 feet square in the cellar fenced in by chicken
wire, to be used during coffee breaks and lunch hours), I began
to question some of the older employees as to why they disliked
Mr. Raymond. Laura Morgan, a fellow checker about 40 years of
age and the mother of two grade-school boys, gave the most specific answers. Her complaints were:

1. Raymond had fired the arthritic black porter on the grounds
   that a porter who "can't mop is no good to the company."
2. Raymond had not employed new help to make up for normal

---

[1] At the time of this case, the author, a college student, was employed for
the summer as a checker and stockboy in store 5116.

attrition. Because of this, everybody's work load was much heavier than it ever had been before.

3. The new manager made everyone call him "mister . . . he's unfriendly."

4. Raymond didn't pitch in. Wally Shultz had, according to Laura, helped people when they were behind in their work. She said that Shultz had helped her bag on rushed Friday nights when a long line waited at her checkout booth, but "Raymond wouldn't lift a finger if you were dying."

5. Employees were no longer let out early to catch busses. Because of the relative infrequency of this means of transportation, some employees now arrived home up to an hour later.

6. "Young Mr. Know-it-all with his fancy degree . . . takes all the fun out of this place."

Other employees had similar complaints. Gloria, another checker, claimed that, ". . . he sends the company nurse to your home every time you call in sick." Margo, a meat wrapper, remarked "everyone knows how he's having an affair with that new bookkeeper he hired to replace Carol when she quit." Pops Devery, head checker who had been with the chain for over ten years, was perhaps the most vehement of the group. He expressed his views in the following manner: "That new guy's a real louse . . . got a mean streak a mile long. Always trying to cut corners. First it's not enough help, then no overtime, and now, come Saturday mornings, we have to use boxes for the orders 'til the truck arrives.[2] If it wasn't just a year 'til retirement, I'd leave. Things just aren't what they used to be when Wally was around." The last statement was repeated in different forms by many of the other employees. Hearing all this praise of Wally, I was rather surprised when Mr. Finnie dropped the comment to me one morning that Wally had been demoted for inefficiency, and that no one at store 5116 had been told this. It was important that Mr. Shultz save face, Mr. Finnie told me.

A few days later, on Saturday of the busy weekend preceding the July 4 holiday, store 5116 again ran out of paper bags. However, the delivery truck did not arrive at ten o'clock, and by 10:30 the supply of cardboard cartons was also low. Mr. Raymond put in a hurried call to the warehouse. The men there did not know the whereabouts of the truck but promised to get an emergency supply of bags to us around noon. By 11 o'clock, there were no more containers of any type available, and Mr. Raymond reluctantly locked the doors to all further customers. The 20 checkers and packers remained in their respective booths, chatting among themselves. After a few minutes, Mr. Raymond requested that they all retire to the cellar cage because he had a few words

---

[2] The truck from the company warehouse bringing merchandise for sale and store supplies normally arrived at ten o'clock Saturday mornings. Frequently, the stock of large paper bags would be temporarily depleted. It was then necessary to pack orders in cardboard cartons until the truck was unloaded.

for them. As soon as the group was seated on the wooden benches in the chicken-wire enclosed area, Mr. Raymond began to speak, his back to the cellar stairs. In what appeared to be an angered tone, he began, "I'm out for myself first, Savemore second, the customer third, and you last. The inefficiency in this store has amazed me from the moment I arrived here. . . ."

At about this time I noticed Mr. Finnie, the district manager, standing at the head of the cellar stairs. It was not surprising to see him at this time because he usually made three or four unannounced visits to the store each week as part of his regular supervisory procedure. Mr. Raymond, his back turned, had not observed Finnie's entrance.

Mr. Raymond continued, "Contrary to what seems to be the opinion of many of you, the Savemore Corporation is not running a social club here. We're in business for just one thing . . . to make money. One way that we lose money is by closing the store on Saturday morning at 11 o'clock. Another way that we lose money is by using a 60-pound paper bag to do the job of a 20-pound bag. A 60-pound bag costs us over two cents apiece; a 20-pound bag costs less than a penny. So when you sell a couple of quarts of milk or a loaf of bread, don't use the big bags. Why do you think we have four different sizes anyway? There's no great intelligence or effort required to pick the right size. So do it. This store wouldn't be closed right now if you'd used your common sense. We started out this week with enough bags to last 'til Monday . . . and they would have lasted 'til Monday if you'd only used your brains. This kind of thing doesn't look good for the store, and it doesn't look good for me. Some of you have been bagging for over five years . . . and you ought'a be able to do it right by now . . ." Mr. Raymond paused and then said, "I trust I've made myself clear on this point."

The cage was silent for a moment, and then Pops Devery spoke up: "Just one thing, Mis-tuh Raymond. Things were running pretty well before you came around. When Wally was here we never ran out'a bags. The customers never complained about overloaded bags or the bottoms falling out before you got here. What're you gonna tell somebody when they ask for a couple of extra bags to use in garbage cans? What're you gonna tell somebody when they want their groceries in a bag, and not a box? You gonna tell them the manager's too damn cheap to give 'em bags? Is that what you're gonna tell 'em? No sir, things were never like this when Wally Shultz was around. We never had to apologize for a cheap manager who didn't order enough then. What'ta you got to say to that, Mis-tuh Raymond?"

Mr. Raymond, his tone more emphatic, began again. "I've got just one thing to say to that, Mr. Devery, and that's this: store 5116 never did much better than break even when Shultz was in charge here. I've shown a profit better than the best he ever hit in six years every week since I've been here. You can check that fact in the book upstairs any time you want. If you don't like the

way I'm running things around here, there's nobody begging you
to stay . . ."

At this point, Pops Devery interrupted and, looking up the
stairs at the district manager, asked, "What about that, Mr. Finnie? You've been around here as long as I have. You told us how
Wally got promoted 'cause he was such a good boss. Supposin' you
tell this young fellar here what a good manager is really like? How
about that, Mr. Finnie?"

A rather surprised Mr. Raymond turned around to look up the
stairs at Mr. Finnie. The manager of store 5116 and his checkers
and baggers waited for Mr. Finnie's answer.

7. The Slade Company*

Ralph Porter, production manager of The Slade Company, was
concerned by reports of dishonesty among some employees in the
Plating Department. From reliable sources, he had learned that a
few men were punching the time cards of a number of their work-
mates who had left early. Mr. Porter had only recently joined the
Slade organization. He judged from conversations with the previous production manager and other fellow managers that they
were, in general, pleased with the over-all performance of the
Plating Department.

The Slade Company was a prosperous manufacturer of metal
products designed for industrial application. Its manufacturing
plant, located in central Michigan, employed nearly 500 workers,
who were engaged in producing a large variety of clamps, inserts,
knobs, and similar items. Orders for these products were usually
large and on a recurrent basis. The volume of orders fluctuated in
response to business conditions in the primary industries which
the company served. At the time of this case, sales volume had
been high for over a year. The basis upon which The Slade Company secured orders, in rank of importance, were quality, delivery,
and reasonable price.

The organization of manufacturing operations at the Slade
plant is shown in Exhibit 1. The departments listed there are,
from left to right, approximately in the order in which material
flowed through the plant. The diemaking and setup operations required the greatest degree of skill, supplied by highly paid, long-
service craftsmen. The finishing departments, divided operationally and geographically between plating and painting, attracted
less highly trained but relatively skilled workers, some of whom
had been employed by the company for many years. The remaining operations were largely unskilled in nature and were characterized by relatively low pay and high rate of turnover of personnel.

The plating room was the sole occupant of the top floor of the

EXHIBIT 1
Manufacturing Organization

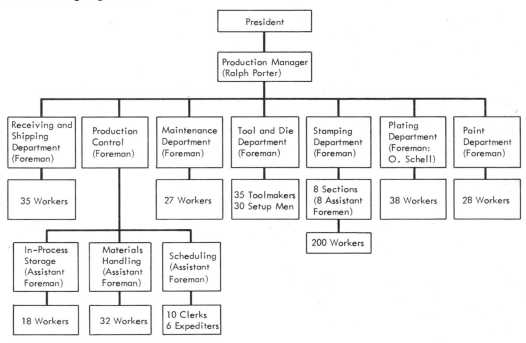

plant. Exhibit 2 shows the floorplan, the disposition of workers, and the flow of work throughout the department. Thirty-eight men and women worked in the department, plating or oxidizing the metal parts or preparing parts for the application of paint at another location in the plant. The department's work occurred in response to orders communicated by production schedules, which were revised daily. Schedule revisions, caused by last-minute order increases or rush requests from customers, resulted in short-term volume fluctuations, particularly in the plating, painting, and shipping departments. Table 1 outlines the activities of the various jobs, their interrelationships, and the type of work in which each specialized. Table 2 rates the various types of jobs in terms of the technical skill, physical effort, discomfort, and training time asso ciated with their performance.

The activities which took place in the plating room were of three main types:

1. Acid dipping, in which parts were etched by being placed in baskets which were manually immersed and agitated in an acid solution.
2. Barrel tumbling, in which parts were roughened or smoothed by being loaded into machine-powered revolving drums containing abrasive, caustic, or corrosive solutions.

EXHIBIT 2
Plating Room Layout

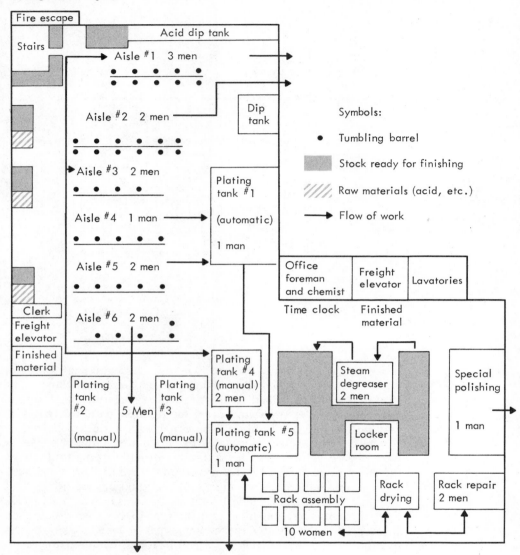

3. Plating—either manual, in which parts were loaded on racks and were immersed by hand through the plating sequence; or automatic, in which racks or baskets were manually loaded with parts which were then carried by a conveyor system through the plating sequence.

Within these main divisions, there were a number of variables, such as cycle times, chemical formulas, abrasive mixtures, and so forth, which distinguished particular jobs as they have been categorized in Table 1.

The work of the plating room was received in batch lots whose size averaged 1,000 pieces. The clerk moved each batch, which was accompanied by a routing slip, to its first operation. This routing slip indicated the operations to be performed and when each major operation on the batch was scheduled to be completed, so that the finished product could be shipped on time. From the accumulation of orders before him, each man was to organize his own work schedule so as to make optimal use of equipment, materials, and time. Upon completion of an order, each man moved the lot to its next work position or to the finished material location near the freight elevator.

The plating room was under the direct supervision of the foreman, Otto Schell, who worked a regular 8:00 to 5:00 day, five days a week. The foreman spent a good deal of his working time attending to maintenance and repair of equipment, procuring

TABLE 1
Outline of Work Flow, Plating Room

Aisle 1: Worked closely with Aisle 3 in preparation of parts by barrel tumbling and acid dipping for high-quality* plating in Tanks 4 and 5. Also did a considerable quantity of highly specialized, high-quality acid-etching work not requiring further processing.

Aisle 2: Tumbled items of regular quality* and design in preparation for painting. Less frequently, did oxidation dipping work of regular quality, but sometimes of special design, not requiring further processing.

Aisle 3: Worked closely with Aisle 1 on high-quality tumbling work for Tanks 4 and 5.

Aisles 4 and 5: Produced regular tumbling work for Tank 1.

Aisle 6: Did high-quality tumbling work for special products plated in Tanks 2 and 3.

Tank 1: Worked on standard, automated plating of regular quality not further processed in plating room, and regular work further processed in Tank 5.

Tanks 2 and 3: Produced special, high-quality plating work not requiring further processing.

Tank 4: Did special, high-quality plating work further plated in Tank 5.

Tank 5: Automated production of high- and regular-quality, special- and regular-design plated parts sent directly to shipping.

Rack assembly: Placed parts to be plated in Tank 5 on racks.

Rack repair: Performed routine replacement and repair of racks used in Tank 5.

Special polishing: Processed, by manual or semimanual methods, odd-lot special orders which were sent directly to shipping. Also, sorted and reclaimed parts rejected by inspectors in the shipping department.

Steam degreaser: Took incoming raw stock, processed it through caustic solution, and placed clean stock in storage ready for processing elsewhere in the plating room.

---

* Definition of terms: *High or regular quality:* The quality of finishes could broadly be distinguished by the thickness of plate and/or care in preparation. *Regular or special work:* The complexity of work depended on the routine or special character of design and finish specifications.

TABLE 2
Skill Indices by Job Group*

Jobs	Technical Skill Required	Physical Effort Required	Degree of Discomfort Involved	Degree of Training Required†
Aisle 1...........................	1	1	1	1
Tanks 2–4.......................	3	2	1	2
Aisles 2–6.......................	5	1	1	5
Tank 5...........................	1	5	7	2
Tank 1...........................	8	5	5	7
Degreasing......................	9	3	7	10
Polishing........................	6	9	9	7
Rack assembly and repair.......	10	10	10	10

* Rated on scales of 1 (the greatest) to 10 (the least) in each category.
† Amount of experience required to assume complete responsibility for the job.

supplies, handling late schedule changes, and seeing that his people were at their proper work locations.

Working conditions in the plating room varied considerably. That part of the department containing the tumbling barrels and the plating machines was constantly awash, alternately with cold water, steaming acid, or caustic soda. Men working in this part of the room wore knee boots, long rubber aprons, and high-gauntlet rubber gloves. This uniform, consistent with the general atmosphere of the "wet" part of the room, was hot in the summer, cold in winter. In contrast, the remainder of the room was dry, relatively odor-free, and provided reasonable stable temperature and humidity conditions for those who worked there.

The men and women employed in the plating room are listed in Table 3. This table provides certain personal data on each department member, including a productivity-skill rating (based on subjective and objective appraisals of potential performance), as reported by the members of the department.

The pay scale implied by Table 3 was low for the central Michigan area. The average starting wage for factory work in the community was about $1.25. However, working hours for the plating room were long (from 60 hours to a possible and frequently available 76 hours per week). The first 60 hours (the normal five-day week) were paid for on straight-time rates. Saturday work was paid for at time and one half. Sunday pay was calculated on a double-time basis.

As Table 3 indicates, Philip Kirk, a worker in Aisle 2, provided the data for this case. After he had been a member of the department for several months, Kirk noted that certain members of the department tended to seek each other out during free time on and off the job. He then observed that these informal associations were enduring, built upon common activities and shared ideas about what was and what was not legitimate behavior in the department. His estimate of the pattern of these associations is diagrammed in Exhibit 3.

TABLE 3
Plating Room Personnel

Location	Name	Age	Marital Status	Company Seniority (in years)	Department Seniority (in years)	Pay per Hour	Education*	Familial Relationships	Productivity Skill Rating†
Aisle 1	Tony Sarto	30	M	13	13	$1.50	HS	Louis Patrici, uncle / Pete Facelli, cousin	1
	Pete Facelli	26	M	8	8	1.30	HS	Louis Patrici, uncle / Tony Sarto, cousin	2
Aisle 2	Joe Iambi	31	M	5	5	1.20	2 yrs. HS		2
	Herman Schell	48	S	26	26	1.45	GS	Otto Schell, brother	8
Aisle 3	Philip Kirk	23	M	1	1	.90	College		‡
	Dom Pantaleoni	31	M	10	10	1.30	1 yr. HS		2
	Sal Maletta	32	M	12	12	1.30	3 yrs. HS		3
Aisle 4	Bob Pearson	22	S	4	4	1.15	HS	Father in tool and die dept.	1
Aisle 5	Charlie Malone	44	M	22	8	1.25	GS		7
	John Lacey	41	S	9	5	1.20	1 yr. HS	Brother in paint dept.	7
Aisle 6	Jim Martin	30	S	7	7	1.25	HS		7
	Bill Mensch	41	M	6	2	1.10	GS		4
Tank 1	Henry LaForte	38	M	14	6	1.25	HS		6
Tanks 2 and 3	Ralph Parker	25	S	7	7	1.20	HS		4
	Ed Harding	27	S	8	8	1.20	HS		4
	George Flood	22	S	5	5	1.15	HS		5
	Harry Clark	29	M	8	8	1.20	HS		3
	Tom Bond	25	S	6	6	1.20	HS		4
Tank 4	Frank Bonzani	27	M	9	9	1.25	HS		2
	Al Bartolo	24	M	6	6	1.25	HS		3
Tank 5	Louis Patrici	47	S	14	14	1.45	2 yrs. college		1
Rack assembly	Ten women	30–40	9M, 1S	10 (av.)	10 (av.)	1.05	GS (av.)	Six with husbands in company	4 (av.)
Rack maintenance	Will Partridge	57	M	14	2	1.20	GS	Tony Sarto, nephew	7
	Lloyd Swan	62	M	3	3	1.10	GS	Pete Facelli, nephew	7
Degreasing	Dave Susi	45	S	1	1	1.05	HS		5
	Mike Maher	41	M	4	4	1.05	GS		6
Polishing	Russ Perkins	49	M	12	2	1.20	HS		4
Foreman	Otto Schell	56	M	35	35	n.a.	HS	Herman Schell, brother	3
Clerk	Bill Pierce	32	M	10	4	1.15	HS		4
Chemist	Frank Rutlage	24	S	2	2	n.a.	2 yrs. college		6

* HS = high school; GS = grade school.
† On a potential scale of 1 (top) to 10 (bottom), as evaluated by the men in the department.
‡ Kirk was the source of data for this case and therefore in a biased position to report accurately perceptions about himself.

EXHIBIT 3
Informal Grouping in the Plating Room

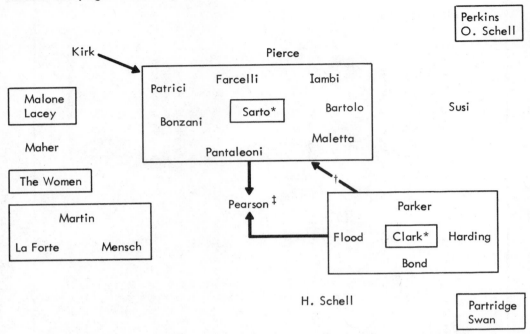

* These boxes indicate those men who clearly demonstrated leadership behavior (most closely personified the values shared by their groups, were most often sought for help and arbitration, and so forth).

† While the two- and three-man groupings had little informal contact outside their own boundaries, the five-man group did seek to join the largest group in extraplant social affairs. These were relatively infrequent.

‡ Though not an active member of any group; Bob Pearson was regarded with affection by the two large groups.

The Sarto group, so named because Tony Sarto was its most respected member and the one who acted as arbiter between the other members, was the largest in the department. The group, except for Louis Patrici, Al Bartolo, and Frank Bonzani (who spelled each other during break periods), invariably ate lunch together on the fire escape near Aisle 1. On those Saturdays and Sundays when overtime work was required, the Sarto group operated as a team, regardless of weekday work assignments, to get overtime work completed as quickly as possible. (Few department members not affiliated with either the Sarto or the Clark groups worked on week ends.) Off the job, Sarto group members often joined in parties or weekend trips. Sarto's summer camp was a frequent rendezvous.

Sarto's group was also the most cohesive one in the department in terms of its organized punch-in and punch-out system. Since the men were regularly scheduled to work from 7:00 A.M. to 7:00 P.M. weekdays, and since all supervision was removed at 5:00 P.M., it was possible almost every day to finish a "day's work" by 5:30 and leave the plant. What is more, if one man were to stay until 7:00 P.M., he could punch the time cards of a number of men and help them gain free time without pay loss. (This system operated on week ends also; at which times members of supervision were present, if at all, only for short periods.) In Sarto's group the duty of staying late rotated, so that no man did so more than once a week. In addition, the group members would punch a man in in the morning if he were unavoidably delayed. However, such a practice never occurred without prior notice from the man who expected to be late and never if the tardiness was expected to last beyond 8:00 A.M., the start of the day for the foreman.

Sarto explained the logic behind the system to Kirk:

> You know that our hourly pay rate is quite low, compared to other companies. What makes this the best place to work is the feeling of security you get. No one ever gets laid off in this department. With all the hours in the week, all the company ever has to do is shorten the work week when orders fall off. We have to tighten our belts, but we can all get along. When things are going well, as they are now, the company is only interested in getting out the work. It doesn't help to get it out faster than it's really needed—so we go home a little early whenever we can. Of course, some guys abuse this sort of thing—like Herman—but others work even harder, and it averages out.
>
> Whenever an extra order has to be pushed through, naturally I work until 7:00. So do a lot of the others. I believe that if I stay until my work is caught up and my equipment is in good shape, that's all the company wants of me. They leave us alone and expect us to produce—and we do.

When Kirk asked Sarto if he would not rather work shorter hours at higher pay in a union shop (Slade employees were not organized), he just laughed and said: "It wouldn't come close to an even trade."

The members of Sarto's group were explicit about what constituted a fair day's work. Customarily, they cited Herman Schell, Kirk's work partner and the foreman's brother, as a man who consistently produced below that level. Kirk received an informal orientation from Herman during his first days on the job. As Herman put it:

> I've worked at this job for a good many years, and I expect to stay here a good many more. You're just starting out, and you don't know which end is up yet. We spend a lot of time in here; and no matter how hard we work, the pile of work never goes down. There's always more to take its place. And I think you've found out by now that this isn't light work. You can wear yourself out fast if you're not smart. Look at Pearson up in Aisle 4. There's a kid who's just going to burn himself out. He won't last long. If he thinks he's going to get somewhere working like that, he's nuts. They'll give him all the work he can take. He makes it tough on everybody else and on himself, too.

Kirk reported further on his observations of the department:

As nearly as I could tell, two things seemed to determine whether or not Sarto's group or any others came in for weekend work on Saturday or Sunday. It seemed usually to be caused by rush orders that were received late in the week, although I suspect it was sometimes caused by the men having spent insufficient time on the job during the previous week.

Tony and his group couldn't understand Herman. While Herman arrived late, Tony was always half an hour early. If there was a push to get out an extra amount of work, almost everyone but Herman would work that much harder. Herman never worked overtime on weekends, while Tony's group and the men on the manual tanks almost always did. When the first exploratory time study of the department was made, no one in the aisles slowed down, except Herman, with the possible exception, to a lesser degree, of Charlie Malone. I did hear that the men in the dry end of the room slowed down so much you could hardly see them move; but we had little to do with them, anyway. While the men I knew best seemed to find a rather full life in their work, Herman never really got involved. No wonder they couldn't understand each other.

There was quite a different feeling about Bobby Pearson. Without the slightest doubt, Bob worked harder than anyone else in the room. Because of the tremendous variety of work produced, it was hard to make output comparisons, but I'm sure I wouldn't be far wrong in saying that Bob put out twice as much as Herman and 50 percent more than almost anyone else in the aisles. No one but Herman and a few old-timers at the dry end ever criticized Bobby for his efforts. Tony and his group seemed to feel a distant affection for Bob, but the only contact they or anyone else had with him consisted of brief greetings.

To the men in Tony's group the most severe penalty that could be inflicted on a man was exclusion. This they did to both Pearson and Herman. Pearson, however, was tolerated; Herman was not. Evidently, Herman felt his exclusion keenly, though he answered it with derision and aggression. Herman kept up a steady stream of stories concerning his attempts to gain acceptance outside the company. He wrote popular music which was always rejected by publishers. He attempted to join several social and athletic clubs, mostly without success. His favorite pastime was fishing. He told me that fishermen were friendly, and he enjoyed meeting new people whenever he went fishing. But he was particularly quick to explain that he preferred to keep his distance from the men in the department.

Tony's group emphasized more than just quantity in judging a man's work. Among them had grown a confidence that they could master and even improve upon any known finishing technique. Tony himself symbolized this skill. Before him, Tony's father had operated Aisle 1 and had trained Tony to take his place. Tony in his turn was training his cousin Pete. When a new finishing problem arose from a change in customer specifications, the foreman, the department chemist, or any of the men directly involved would come to Tony for help, and Tony would give it willingly. For example, when a part with a special plastic embossing was designed, Tony was the only one who could discover how to treat the metal without damaging the plastic. To a lesser degree, the other members of the group were also inventive about the problems which arose in their own sections.

Herman, for his part, talked incessantly about his feats in design and finish creations. As far as I could tell during the year I worked in the department, the objects of these stories were obsolete or of minor importance. What's more, I never saw any department member seek Herman's help.

Willingness to be of help was a trait Sarto's group prized. The most valued help of all was of a personal kind, though work help was also important. The members of Sarto's group were constantly lending and borrowing money, cars, clothing, and tools among themselves and, less frequently, with other members of the department. Their daily lunch bag procedure typified the common property feeling among them. Everyone's lunch was opened and added to a common pile, from which each member of the group chose his meal.

On the other hand, Herman refused to help others in any way. He never left his aisle to aid those near him who were in the midst of a rush of work or a machine failure, though this was customary throughout most of the department. I can distinctly recall the picture of Herman leaning on the hot and cold water faucets which were located directly above each tumbling barrel. He would stand gazing into the tumbling pieces for hours. To the passing, casual visitor, he looked busy; and as he told me, that's just what he wanted. He, of course, expected me to act this same way, and it was this enforced boredom that I found virtually intolerable.

More than this, Herman took no responsibility for breaking-in his assigned helpers as they first entered the department, or thereafter. He had had four helpers in the space of little more than a year. Each had asked for a transfer to another department, publicly citing the work as cause, privately blaming Herman. Tony was the one who taught me the ropes when I first entered the department.

The men who congregated around Harry Clark tended to talk like and copy the behavior of the Sarto group, though they never approached the degree of inventive skill or the amount of helping activities that Tony's group did. They sought outside social contact with the Sarto group; and several times a year, the two groups went "on the town" together. Clark's group did maintain a high level of performance in the volume of work they turned out.

The remainder of the people in the department stayed pretty much to themselves or associated in pairs or triplets. None of these people were as inventive, as helpful, or as productive as Sarto's or Clark's groups, but most of them gave verbal support to the same values as those groups held.

The distinction between the two organized groups and the rest of the department was clearest in the punching-out routine. The women could not work past 3:00 P.M., so they were not involved. Malone and Lacey, Partridge and Swan, and Martin, La Forte, and Mensch arranged within their small groups for punch-outs, or they remained beyond 5:00 and slept or read when they finished their work. Perkins and Pierce went home when the foreman did. Herman Schell, Susi, and Maher had no punch-out organization to rely upon. Susi and Maher invariably stayed in the department until 7:00 P.M. Herman was reported to have established an arrangement with Partridge whereby the latter punched Herman out for a fee. Such a practice was unthinkable from the point of view of Sarto's group. It evidently did not occur often because Herman usually went to sleep behind piles of work when his brother left, or, particularly during the fishing season, punched himself out early. He constantly railed against the dishonesty of other men in the department, yet urged me to punch him out on several emergency occasions.

Just before I left The Slade Company to return to school after 14 months on the job, I had a casual conversation with Mr. Porter, the production manager, in which he asked me how I had enjoyed my experience with the organization. During the conversation, I learned that he knew of the punchout system in the Plating Department. What's more, he told me, he was wondering if he ought to "blow the lid off the whole mess."

indexes

NAME INDEX

SUBJECT INDEX

A

Abilities, and job performance and satisfaction, 210, 219, 221–22, 226, 267, 287, 292, 520, 587–88

Accommodating style and conflict management, 431, 433

Accountability, as basic theme of book, 12–15, 444, 574, 584; *see also* Management, accountability of, for performance *and* Manager(s), accountability of, for performance

Achievement, as a motive, 245–46, 245 n

Activator (control process), 125, 132–33, 586

Administering, 8–9

Administrative management, and organization theory, 444, 448, 457–60, 479, 592

Affective component (attitude), 260, 268, 287, 587

Affiliation motive, 244, 246

Aggression, as a motive, 244

A-I-S (activities, interactions, sentiments) model, and group behavior, 360–62, 590

Alcoholics Anonymous (AA) and reinforcement theory, 324

Allport-Vernon-Lindzey Study of Values, 271, 273

Altruism, as a motive, 244

American Federation of Labor, 36

American Management Association, and survey on conflict and conflict-management, 421–22

American Motors Corporation (AMC), 64

American Telephone and Telegraph (AT&T), 70, 75, 508, 519

Apollo program, 139

Applications, 19–21, 28, 38–39, 66–68, 143–44, 157–58, 182–85, 196–97, 207–8, 233–35, 247–48, 275, 284–85, 298, 397, 417–19, 440–41, 476, 531–33, 551–53, 576–77

Arc of distortion, and one-way communication, 406

As a Man Thinketh (Allen), 453

Assertiveness training, 559

Assumptions about people, as cognitive variables, 210, 257–58, 276–85, 302

Attitude(s)

and behavior, 266–67

changing, 265–66, 268

characteristics of, 262–63, 268

as cognitive variable, 210, 252, 259–68, 302, 588–89

components of, 260–62, 268

definition of, 259–60, 268

effect of, on behavior, 260–62

and Hawthorne effect, 465–67, 479

and management, 266–68

measurement of, 264–65

process of forming, 263–64, 268

role of groups in forming, 263, 268

Attraction, interpersonal, 211, 334–37, 590

Auerbach Associates, Inc., 526–30

Authority

and decision making, 544

delegated, 561–62

functional, 546–49, 559

line, 545, 549

and power and influence, 470–71

role of, and organization theory, 444, 448, 470–74, 479, 592

sources of managerial, 471–74

staff, 545, 548–49

Avoidance, as a contingency, 307–8, 312

Avoiding style, and conflict management, 430–31, 433

B

Bank Wiring Observation room experiment, 467–68

Behavior; *see also* Group(s), behavior in; Individual behavior; *and* Interpersonal behavior

affecting change in organizations, 16, 555–70, 576–77, 584, 589

and attitudes, 266–67

modification of, 317, 438, 563

role of profits in understanding, 72–73

Behavioral approach, and study of management, 24, 27, 583; *see also* Management, our approach to studying

Behavioral consequences, 301–26, 589

and contingencies, 295, 306–12

This book has been set in 9 and 8 point Primer, leaded 2 points. Part numbers are 30 point Venus Bold Extended and chapter numbers are 72 point Caslon. Part and chapter titles are 24 point Venus Bold Extended. The maximum size of the type area is 32 by 48½ picas.